James R. Green

English Linguistics

Edited by
Harold Hungerford
Jay Robinson
James Sledd

ENGLISH LINGUISTICS

An Introductory Reader

Scott, Foresman and Company

Contents

Preface

To anthologize is arrogant—especially in linguistics, now. Of his remarkably unsettled subject, with its long history, the anthologist should know the best that has been thought and said; and to knowledge and good judgment he should add the ability to mediate between the professional and the layman, in excellent English prose. So nobody should anthologize.

Why have we? Because so far as we know, better scholars, who might have made a better book of this same kind, haven't made it. There are a dozen or more linguistic readers, but we have not found one yet that is quite right for our quite typical courses.

We are English teachers, not linguists; but it is part of our job to introduce students of English, at various levels, to the study of the English language. Our students range from sophomores to graduates; many of them are going to be teachers too. Sometimes in just one term, and rarely in more than three, we have to help most of them find out whatever they are likely to about English grammar, English dialectology, and the history of English.

Of course we know the argument that our students should get their introduction to English linguistics from professed linguists; we also know that in the present state of the academic world, they can't. Most colleges and many of the smaller universities have no departments of linguistics, and in those that do, the available courses are often unsuitable for students like ours, who are not linguists and don't want to be. If they are to learn anything about the mother tongue (and they ought to), they will have to learn it in English departments from teachers of English, who know and largely share their students' needs, their backgrounds, their weaknesses, and their strengths.

The hundreds of teachers who each year do such work as ours are not supremely fortunate in their textbooks. There are almost no suitable books about dialects and dictionaries; the available histories, though some of them are excellent, are rather old-fashioned and say little or nothing about principles or methods; and the superabundant grammars pose a problem by their superabundance. If the teacher chooses an older grammar, like Jespersen's *Essentials*, he fears that his students will not be up to date. If he chooses a newer grammar, he fears that it will be tendentious and that even its author will disown it soon. Besides, the teacher of teachers knows that his students, when they begin to teach, may be required to teach grammars of more kinds than one.

For several years, to meet these difficulties, we did what many English teachers are compelled to do: either we supplemented our main texts, our grammars and histories, with linguistic anthologies, or we made up long supplementary reading lists and sent our students off to vex the librarians and one another as they competed for volumes of *Language*. But the mechanical arrangements for using a long reading list were never satisfactory.

As for the anthologies, they seemed to us to meet some needs quite well —but not *our* needs. Either they were too elementary, and stuffed with things which good students found condescending or even mildly offensive; or they were too advanced, too specialized, too much the work of professionals writing only for other professionals. We wanted professional writing too; but we wanted a broader range of interests, and we wanted our professionals to be writing for a wider audience of intelligent readers, not just their fellow members of the Executive Committee of the LSA.

And so we undertook our task.

The quality of what we selected was our first concern, and of *that* we are confident—Jespersen, for example, Bloomfield, Chomsky, three pieces by Sapir. With one or two exceptions, the essays we have chosen are either quintessentially representative or truly excellent, or both. We have tried to be fair in choosing, neither dogmatic nor indecisive; and without denying the present, we have tried to keep some continuity with the past. Schoolroom grammar still lives, at least in the schoolroom; and it is useless for a teacher to berate it if his students have never read it. Hence Goold Brown, not just for shock effect. No explanation is needed for the representation of a good many scholars whose prime commitment has been to learning, not schools among the learned; and if intrinsic merit will not do it (as we think it often will), then the same argument that we made for Brown will justify the presence of eminent American structuralists. As for the generative grammarians, the likely criticism is that we have not given them space enough. We would agree, except that their work (and vulgarizations of it) is now the most easily available of all. When we ourselves teach this anthology, we will teach it in conjunction with a generative grammar; and we think both books will be made more valuable by the combination.

But other teachers, faced with our same problems, will decide for themselves how these readings may best be used. We hope the introductions are sensible, and especially the questions, which are meant to take students as far as we can along the road of our own bewilderments and understandings. We have tried not to make them too hard for the best freshmen and good sophomores, nor too easy for graduates in English. In a field where revolution follows revolution and the most settled doctrines are highly tentative, students do need some help in following such continuities as there are.

The three editors are not all equally deserving of praise or blame for all parts of the book. Mr. Sledd wrote this preface. Mr. Hungerford wrote first versions of the introduction, the headnotes, and the questions for Part One; Mr. Sledd, who wrote the final drafts, takes final responsibility. Part Two is mainly Mr. Robinson's, though Mr. Sledd summarized Atwood's account of dialect features and provided most of the apparatus for Weinreich's essay and his own. Part Three again is mainly Mr. Robinson's, except that final responsibility for the introduction belongs once more to Mr. Sledd. As usual in a collaboration, each of the editors freely criticized his colleagues, sometimes to their profit.

But the scissors and paste don't matter. The essays do.

H. H.

J. R.

J. S.

English Linguistics

Part 1
Theories of Language and Languages: Some Grammars

Only human beings possess language, and it is at the same time the most valuable and the most embarrassing possession man has—the most valuable because it enables men to realize most fully their other human potentialities, the most embarrassing because it has been so difficult to understand. Human beings without language would not *be* human beings; but just what *is* it that they would lack?

To say that such answers as there are must be sought in grammars will disenchant many readers. To most adult Americans, *grammar* is a word of fear—a subject of which the little that is worth knowing has long been known, especially by the furious aged maidens who presided over the seventh grade until pot and Project English drove them out. But the excommunication of *ain't*-sayers and the elaboration of the mysteries of *who* and *whom* are not the chief activities of serious grammarians. Grammar and grammars, universal and particular, are the theory of language and of languages, and today as at no other time in recent years the study of grammar is attracting young minds of the highest quality. As students of English or French or Mohawk or Swahili, they are concerned, of course, with the words of those languages and the way they are put together and pronounced in meaningful sentences; but they are also concerned to discover those things which are common to all languages because, presumably, they reflect the qualities of the human mind. An introductory volume of readings in English linguistics may appropriately begin, then, with Sapir's great essay on language in general and with selections representing a variety of approaches to linguistic description, from the schoolmasterly pronouncements of Goold Brown to the psychological and philosophical speculations of Noam Chomsky. The conflicting views may be understood, tested, judged according to their different purposes—but by no means fully reconciled. Like literary criticism and literary history, grammar is a continuing enterprise, not a fixed body of authoritative doctrine.

Crabbed quaint Goold Brown represents the schoolroom tradition in its better days—a tradition which every grammarian should know because it would not have survived so long if there had not been truth in it and because a man understands his subject best if he knows its history. The truly reprehensible modern pedagogue is not the learned traditionalist, who should be valued and protected, like whooping cranes, but the ignorant progressive who rejects tradition without studying it and reads nothing earlier than last year. Though the greater blunder is ignorance of the present, ignorance of the past has its dangers too.

It is ignorance of both past and present which allows the use of *tradition* and *traditional* as terms of unqualified reproach for such very different grammarians as Brown and Jespersen. Brown, the older man, the provincial schoolmaster, knew little of the developing linguistics of his day. Jespersen, a great individualist but never provincial, knew the best that was thought and said among the English linguists of his changing time, who in turn valued his work for the learning and insight which make it relevant still. When generative grammarians call him traditional, they mean that he was one in the long series of Western linguists which began in pre-Christian Greece, that he did not share the ideas and methods of American structuralism (in the generative view, a rather aberrant movement), but that as a man of his time he also lacked the concepts and techniques which might have allowed him to approach the generative goal of fully explicit statement. The judgment is not tempered by self-doubt, yet it is not condemnatory: Chomsky thinks of his own work as in many ways a return to scholarly traditional inquiries after the structuralist interlude.

Those, then, are the four broadly different kinds of grammar represented by the four selections which Sapir's more general essay introduces—the grammar of the schools before its final corruption, traditional scholarly grammar (or scholarly nonstructural grammar, or prestructural grammar), American structural grammar, and transformational generative grammar. Zealous readers will easily add more polysyllables to that incomplete catalogue, like the tagmemics of Kenneth Pike or the stratificational grammar of Sydney Lamb; and every reader will share the editors' regret that lack of space and knowledge forbade real representation of European work, either British or Continental.

SCHOOLROOM GRAMMAR

Schoolroom grammar is like female virtue: for centuries everyone taught it and considerable numbers practiced it; now everyone has given it up, though it still has something to recommend it. One may safely guess that for the older authors in this anthology, the first introduction to the formal study of language came by way of the schoolroom tradition, whose patrons would include such great men as Plato and Aristotle, Cicero and Quintilian, Ben Jonson and Samuel Johnson. Schoolroom grammar for centuries made part of a coherent educational system, and it contributed to quite respectable philosophies. For the purposes for which it was developed, the students and teachers for whom it was intended, and the times in which it was formed, it was a workable system of grammatical analysis. But it grew old, and suffered the common fate of the over-thirties.

The rudiments of the schoolroom method of analysis—often called parsing—were first developed as instruments for the study of formal logic. Formal logic, until the nineteenth century, was syllogistic logic, and syllogizing was often taken as the type of human reasoning:

All A's are B's (*e.g.*, All men are mortals).
X is an A (Socrates is a man).
Ergo, X is a B (Therefore, Socrates is a mortal).

A little juggling with "the operations of the mind" could match the parts of syllogisms with grammatical entities too—propositions and their terms with judgment and conception; and since one step in validating a syllogism is to make sure that all its terms are what they ought to be, grammarians and philosophers alike had an interest in subjects and predicates, nouns and verbs. A tradition of "logical" definitions of the parts of speech was thus established early and was sanctioned by philosophical authority.

Understandably, the language of daily life, whose colloquies are not conducted in syllogisms, could be looked upon as negligible at best and at worst as barbarous: only the rational discourse of the deeply learned, the highly civilized, was amenable to grammatical study. Such an attitude was strongly supported by the importance of rhetoric in ancient and medieval education. It was the rhetorician who defended just causes in the courts of law, or inspired the young by his praise of famous men, or moved decision makers to virtuous choice and action for the common good; and grammar was looked upon as prerequisite to the study of oratory. The consequence was that grammar remained limited to the more formal varieties of language, and firmly linked to its companions in the trivium. It was adapted to still another extraneous purpose because of the continuing dominance of Latin long after the fall of Rome and the rise of the vernaculars. To enter the world of learning, the student had first to master Latin, and grammar was the means to its mastery. The grammatical study of the mother tongue became the child's first step toward the study of foreign languages, principally the study of the perfect language of the noble Romans.

The first important modern English grammars were therefore heavily influenced by Latin models. Lyly's grammar, the work of humanist scholars in the early sixteenth century, remained the dominant Latin grammar throughout England for over two hundred years. It was intended, like sixteenth-century Latin dictionaries, to cleanse the language of medieval impurities and to restore the genuine diction of the golden age; and though the cyclic theory of linguistic growth, perfection, and decay may at times encourage reverence for a golden present, most Englishmen, when the theory was applied to their native speech, followed the Latinists in looking backward. Thus the influence of Latin models on English grammars was twofold. It encouraged a retrospective purism, and it encouraged a description of English which made it look as much like Latin as possible, so that the child who went on to scholarship would already be familiar with paradigms and ablative absolutes. *"O mensa,"* he recited; "O thou table!"

The instance is not imaginary; within living memory, the Irish potato, native of Peru, could not be eaten in an English college without first thanking God for it in excellent Latin. This combination of snobbism and respect for the less relevant portions of the past appears in English grammars of the eighteenth century, when the nation of shopkeepers were only beginning to change the face of the earth and the form of human life, and to build the shopkeepers' empire, by the force of their industrial revolution. As the defilement of the planet and the degradation of the subject peoples turned more and more have-nots into haves, the risen middle class grew anxious to appear both urban and urbane, and painfully conscious that its language often betrayed a rural or plebeian origin. Books would have to provide what a genuine but rejected cultural inheritance had not, and the printing presses vomited books of etiquette, guides to letter writing, dictionaries, and still-Latinate grammars in a world where English was long since dominant. Grammarians once more assumed a new function. They would teach the "Purity and Politeness of Expression" which had become "the only external Distinction . . . between a Gentleman and a Valet, a Lady and a Mantua-maker"—or, in the United States, where ladies and gentlemen were scarce, they would raise farmers and tradesmen to the level of respectable dignity which was fitting for the citizens of the new republic, and would preserve the language of the frontier from relapsing into barbarism. The grammar which had served logic, rhetoric, and pure Latinity now had to provide badges of status for the upwardly mobile.

The absurdity of English usage as a status symbol in a society where all men are equal is too close to middle-class Americans to be savored like the social pretensions of the brewer's son in eighteenth-century England: not enough of us have laughed at "functional grammar," the "grammar of errors," with its emphasis on socially disapproved "mistakes"; and if we consider the student strange who comes away from such teaching with the conviction that in this world it is just not possible for him to be good, we count it perversity and flat rebellion when the child of the inner city refuses to bother about *ain't* or the proper Yankee diphthongs in *wide* and *out*. We cannot accept the death of the world where proper speech set classes above masses and opened the doors to power.

Goold Brown, of course, had never heard the catch phrase *inner city*. Before we faced it, however, he and his contemporaries had faced the great problem of the grammarian as arbiter of standards: *What* standards? A multitude were available, and not all of them had to do with status, since it is much too easy to give the schoolboy's ready answer, "the rise of the middle class," to *every* question about the less ancient history of schoolroom grammar. In theory, at least three principal sets of standards could be invoked. The first was the norms of universal grammar—the belief, to put it crudely, that because all languages are constructed on the same principles, in dubious cases the speakers of one may profitably consult the usage of another. For Englishmen, this meant in practice the appeal to Latin. The second set of standards were analogies within the native language, regularities which could be extended to instances of irregularity or doubt: since *about* is English but *abouts* is not, *thereabouts* should be avoided. The third set involved appeals to "custom," the actual usage of those having prestige; but the conviction that grammatical sin was universal set limits on the appeal to use. "Present, national, and reputable" was a popular formula, but grammarians found it easy to discover the disreputable everywhere.

In practice, too many grammarians simply indulged their personal prejudice, or copied the prejudice of their rivals, almost as if the object of the game were to blacken the reputations of as many innocent phrases as one could. One of Goold Brown's lists of "Improprieties for Correction," taken at random, includes Bunyan, Swift, Addison, Hume, Steele, Scott, Dryden, Shakespeare, six rival grammarians, a couple of rhetoricians, and a pride of clerics. The absurdity of such judgments was irrelevant for persons whose only linguistic concern was to prove that their class was lower middle, not upper lower: anything will do for a status symbol if it allows one to scorn one's neighbor. For serious grammarians, however, the schoolroom tradition, by the early twentieth century, had come to look very much like a long road to a dead end. Logic was no longer the syllogism, rhetoric was dead, Latin was dying a second death, and historical lexicography had exposed the absurdity of schoolmasterly shibboleths. A good old-fashioned grammar, like the famous Kittredge and Farley, could still say a great many true and useful things about English in a vocabulary that most literate people could understand; its authors were learned and discriminating men. But the typical schoolroom grammarian of the twentieth century was not a Kittredge, nor even a Goold Brown. In fact, he was not likely to be a he at all, but a spinster of stronger character than intellect. The abuses of schoolroom grammar were a continuing invitation to forget its virtues and magnify its vices, and English education in the United States still suffers from the resultant failure to maintain a balanced view.

TRADITIONAL SCHOLARLY GRAMMAR

In the sixteenth century Erasmus, and in the seventeenth, Milton, concerned himself with the education of children. By the nineteenth century, schoolmasters and scholars were more often different breeds, and schoolroom grammar and scholarly linguistics were rather distantly related. A similar development may be seen in English lexicography, where the commercial market—the term is significant—came to be dominated by the

Americans Webster and Worcester, neither of whom worked centrally in the great tradition of European dictionary making. Webster talked about Babel and the dispersion while the great Continentals were developing the hypothesis of Indo-European linguistic unity.

The discovery of linguistic history, and the rediscovery of phonetics, meant that nineteenth-century linguists meticulously compared the shapes of thousands of words in dozens of languages; and to their writing of descriptive grammars they applied the same zeal for ascertaining the details of actual use, whether or not it conformed to the prescriptions of the schoolroom. Since many of these historically minded scholars lived and worked on the Continent, they made no claim to the native speaker's authority in disputed matters, but carefully gathered innumerable citations on which to base their statements. Their concern is with the actual, the tangible, the concrete—with what *is* instead of what ought to be. To some modern students, that is at once their greatest strength and their greatest weakness—their strength because their multi-volumed grammars are so solidly documented that it is hard to quarrel with their factual observations, their weakness because examples usurp the place of analysis and obscure the generalizations which they are meant to illustrate. But to neglect the exceptional in language, the unique fact, is to neglect the lexicon—which scholars were unlikely to do in the century of the Grimms, Littré, and Sir James Murray.

Another form of condescension to men like Jespersen is to praise them only as predecessors, to cite bits and pieces from their work, individual insights, which structural or generative grammarians have built into the fabric of new grammars. The game is easy enough to play. To begin with, Jespersen anticipated many of the criticisms which American structuralists would later aim at the schoolroom tradition; thus many traditional grammarians and rhetoricians, like the famous Sir Arthur Quiller-Couch, instructed their charges to avoid the passive and "worship the active voice," but Jespersen more helpfully catalogued the situations where competent writers have found the passive useful. Again, the distinguished structuralist Charles Fries taught hundreds of American schoolteachers to list the grammatical devices of English as inflections, word order, and function words; if Fries's students had known Fries's predecessors as Fries did, they would have recognized the diminished echo of the last chapter of *Essentials of English Grammar*. As for the generative grammarians, they quote Jespersen more often than any other of the grammarians whom they call traditional; yet probably some popularizers do not realize that the use of *do* in affirmation, negation, and questions was a commonplace before *Syntactic Structures*, that *extraposition* is Jespersen's term, or that Jespersen related sentences like "The path is easy to find" and "What is easy is to find the path" long before it became fashionable to relate them in our classrooms. Readers of

The Sound Pattern of English might even ponder whimsically over the following paragraph, in which Jespersen described the phonetic chapters in *Essentials:*

> Throughout much emphasis has been laid on alternations—differences in sound that have arisen historically and have more or less torn asunder forms which were originally alike and are still to some extent felt as belonging together. Nothing can better than these make a student realize vividly what is the meaning of phonetic change.

Yet it is unfair to both Jespersen and the generativists to think of him only as a kind of linguistic John the Baptist, a learned and insightful man who would have been a generative grammarian if he had not been so untimely born. For Jespersen was no a-theoretical gatherer of facts. In *The Philosophy of Grammar, Analytic Syntax,* and a number of other books, he developed his own distinctive theories—his own notions of the parts of speech, of junction, nexus, and the three ranks, of syntax and morphology; and repeatedly, in the selection which follows, he speaks of himself in terms which set him quite apart from the generative school. In particular, his ideas of syntax and morphology would have made it permanently impossible for him to talk about deep structure and surface structure as many generativists have done. In morphology, as Jespersen saw it, the grammarian looked at language from without, from the hearer's point of view, and moved from form (externally conceived) through function in to meaning. Syntax, starting from within, reversed that movement, so that in Jespersenian syntax "meaning is everything." For Jespersen, therefore, deep structure was not grammatical structure at all, but semantic structure. To be sure, in "The path is easy to find," *the path* "is formally the subject of the sentence" yet "at the same time as it were the object of *find:* what is easy is to find the path." The point was, that a notional object and a grammatical object were not the same thing. "Synonyms are not grammatically identical"; "what is distinctly notional and what is purely grammatical should be kept apart"; and it was a mistake to say that *"He is unkind to all opposing him* contains an abridged dative clause." Jespersen would have considered meaning-preserving transformations no more than paraphrases.

Does one arrive at certainty in such matters, at a single unequivocal Truth? or are some questions of linguistics abiding questions, to which there will always be a plurality of answers, none of them whole and final? For the scholar, the extreme of allowable dogmatism is that he chooses the best answer that he can and bets his scholarly life on it—knowing perfectly well that he may lose his gamble.

AMERICAN STRUCTURAL GRAMMAR

The spectacular losses of gambling popularizers of American structuralism are now gruesomely familiar: in 1959 James Sledd published an English grammar (drafted between '52 and '54) which was accurately described as out of date at the meeting where its publication was announced; and the thrusts and counterthrusts by more distinguished combatants like Hockett and Chomsky have been immortalized by *Time* magazine itself. An introductory textbook is no place for an extended account of the intellectual antecedents of American structuralism, its development, its temporary triumph, and its sudden decline. The name *structuralism* itself would demand a long disquisition on *structure* as a twentieth-century conjuring word in many disciplines, from psychology to literary criticism; and having described the revolt against atomistic fact gathering, one would have to show how structure was conceived by linguists in Prague, Geneva, Copenhagen, and how these new currents blended with a thorough knowledge of Indo-European linguistic history in the work of great men like Leonard Bloomfield. The less unrealistic purpose here is to make possible the understanding reading of a single essay by a well-known American structuralist, Henry Lee Smith, Jr.

Smith's confidence, and his confident disapproval of the schoolroom tradition, were endemic among structuralists in the early 50's. Often they thought of themselves as building a new linguistics in a new world, to which much (perhaps most) earlier work was simply irrelevant. And Smith's frequent repetition of the word *culture* points to one determinant of this attitude—the fact that many American linguists were anthropologists, who had rightly set themselves the task of recording the rapidly dying languages of the American Indians. The niceties of reference grammars of English seemed remarkably unhelpful to men who had to work out the grammar of an unwritten non-Indo-European language from a few hours of recorded speech.

The peculiar demands of a unique and uniquely absorbing task could easily be mistaken for necessary conditions on all linguistic analysis. The languages which anthropological linguists typically studied were not only unwritten; they were very different from English, and hard to learn by English-speaking investigators, who commonly achieved only "a casual practical facility" in them. When there were so many languages and so few linguists to record them, learning to speak them with a native's skill was either an impossibly high ideal or an impossible waste of time, and worrying about meanings seemed less important than puzzling out enough of the sound system to devise a usable spelling. Once written records were available, a language had at least been saved from oblivion. Though many of the finer points of structure might have been overlooked, further analysis of the records could very well lead to a tolerable brief description or structural sketch.

The conditions here grossly oversimplified were not alone, however, in shaping the character of popular American structural grammars. Ideas about science and psychology had their influence too. In the 1930's—and later—it was possible to put great faith in direct and relatively undirected observation, particularly of things that one could count or measure; and in linguistics it was possible to talk with scientific conviction about stimuli and responses and habit formation, to define meaning as hearer's response and speaker's situation, and to put a firm taboo on words like *mind*. When the observable speech behavior had been fully and accurately described, explanation had also been accomplished; statements about mind and meaning were merely inaccurate and misleading paraphrases of what had already been scientifically said.

Various restrictive theories combined, then, with the necessities of a practical situation to make *rigor* a favorite word among American structuralists, who were justly proud of their wide experience with exotic languages and of the resultant technical virtuosity. Manuals of investigative and descriptive procedure were an important product of their work. One widespread vulgarization of a favorite doctrine had it that the chief levels of a grammatical description are phonology, morphology, syntax, and semantics. The levels had to be described in that order, with no reference to the morphology in the phonology, none to the syntax in the morphology; and the entire process of segmentation and classification of elements of the formal structure had to be completed before meanings could be described. So, for example, in the phonology one stated the phonetic character and distribution of the allophones of the vowel and two consonants which are the phonemes that distinguish the morpheme *cat* from other forms; in the morphology one talked about the structure of words, like *cats, cat's, catty,* and *catlike;* in the syntax one talked about *the big cat* as an endocentric construction of head and modifier, and about *The cat eats fish* as a specimen of the favorite subject-predicate sentence type, to which one might then assign the meaning "actor-action-goal." The phonology was the indispensable foundation of the entire structure. In particular, phonology was often held to provide the clues to segmentation at higher levels—to tell us, for instance, that *after dinner* in *After dinner, the three older boys left the house* is a sentence modifier of the whole remaining combination of a subject with a predicate. Such analysis by successive dichotomy was called immediate constituent analysis. It was applied (or its application was attempted) not just to baby sentences but to sentences of all degrees of complexity. The distinction between surface structure and deep structure was not drawn.

So long as the analytical procedures of American structuralism were used on hitherto unanalyzed languages, their success seemed brilliant and undeniable. The younger structuralists had the great advantage that their teachers, Bloomfield and Sapir, were founders not followers, linguists of the first rank who were above discipular limitations; and to real talents of their own, the younger members of the guild added considerable skill and vigor as propagandists. When the second world war gave them a highly publicized opportunity to apply their methods in the practical teaching of foreign languages for the military, an effective means of public argument was put into their hands; and when the war ended they expanded their activity in the description of the familiar languages of Europe, especially English, and consequently in the language classrooms, in the teaching of reading, and even in literary criticism. A decade of bustling optimism followed. It was even believed that if the techniques of analysis could be stated with a little more precision, they could be made mechanical. One would only have to follow the program, like a machine, to discover the grammar of any language.

A theory is never so severely tested as when men follow it boldly to its consequences. The American structuralist, after thirty years of widening knowledge and growing power, had the courage of the convictions which still found expression in 1960 in Smith's essay. In the view of many observers, however, the structuralist and his popularizers had overreached themselves. His mechanical procedure of discovery had never materialized; the popularizing structural grammars of English leaked as badly as any others, and worse than many; and though the teachers' associations were evangelizing the schools, the structural phoneme and linguistically based criticism had not rejuvenated the humanities. The more restrained and prudent scholars in the United States, like the European scholars with whom war's end restored communication, had never gone all the way with the propagandists, and as the inherent limitations of structural description became clearer, attempts to patch the system were paralleled by direct attacks on its foundations. Smith's highly representative essay, when it appeared, was representative of a rapidly closing era.

TRANSFORMATIONAL GENERATIVE GRAMMAR

Noam Chomsky, who was under thirty when his small blue paperback *Syntactic Structures* set a new direction for American linguistics, explains himself better than editors are likely to explain him. He is both traditionalist and innovator—a traditionalist in returning to older conceptions of the function of a grammarian, an innovator in bringing to grammar, techniques and theories from modern logic and mathematics. Though he came to linguistics through structuralism, he has rejected many of the most essential structural doctrines—for example, the notion that the structure of a language is basically rather simple and that all the signals of structure are physical, overt. On the contrary, for Chomsky and his followers a language is like an iceberg in lying mostly below the surface—hence the careful distinction of deep and surface structure. Chomsky has also rejected the behaviorism of the structuralists for the older psychological assumption that men are hereditarily predisposed to the acquisition of certain kinds of knowledge, and that in particular they have an innate *faculté de langage*, a "language acquisition device," which accounts for the fact that all normal children acquire language in substantially the same manner. The study of universal grammar, Chomsky believes—of the principles that underlie the processes of sentence-formation in all languages—may lead to deep knowledge of the human mind.

Grammars of Chomsky's kind are popularly called transformational because one kind of rule which they employ is called a transformation; they are also called generative because their aim is to describe the sentences of a language by a system of rules which in principle could produce them all. The theory of such grammars has changed so fast that most of its early statements are now obsolete—particularly *Syntactic Structures* (1957). Though the obsolescence has been more in techniques and strategies than in basic aims, it has confused many linguists for whom the techniques and strategies *were* the grammar. One of the commonest popular misconceptions is that structural and transformational grammars are compatible, so that an eclectic system could be devised which would have the elements and distinctive merits of them both, with structural grammar, say, providing the phonology, and with transformations relating sets of sentences one to the other. An equally misguided criticism is that generative grammarians, in postulating abstract hypothetical entities like deep structures, are somehow untrue to the observable facts, where the reality of language lies.

As Chomsky frequently insists, final answers in linguistics are few, and hard to come by. No one, after reading him, would say either that nothing has been or remains to be accomplished. Such freedom from dogmatism, without indecisiveness, is as welcome as the breaking down of the barriers which had separated American linguistics from a wider intellectual world.

SUGGESTED READINGS

The best place to start is with Edward Sapir's *Language: An Introduction to the Study of Speech* (1921) and his posthumously published *Selected Writings* (1958). Either will show the range of Sapir's interests and the depth of his knowledge. Another good starter would be Otto Jespersen's *Selected*

Writings (also posthumous, 1962) or his *Language: Its Nature, Development, and Origin* (1922). Most of the material in these four books is nontechnical and intended for the general reader. Somewhat more difficult but still accessible is Leonard Bloomfield, *Language* (1933), the bible of American structuralists.

The grammars called traditional may be seen at their best in Jespersen's *Essentials of English Grammar* (1933) and (with a somewhat different emphasis) in George Lyman Kittredge and Frank Edgar Farley, *Advanced English Grammar* (1913). Happily, such grammars continue to be published. A favorable recent specimen by an American is Ralph B. Long, *The Sentence and Its Parts* (1961). For more detailed information there are Jespersen's *Modern English Grammar* (7 vols., 1909–1949) and the similarly expansive works of Etsko Kruisinga (*A Handbook of Present-Day English*) and Henrik Poutsma (*A Grammar of Late Modern English*).

American structural grammars include Charles Carpenter Fries, *The Structure of English* (1952), W. Nelson Francis, *The Structure of American English* (1958), and Archibald A. Hill, *Introduction to Linguistic Structures* (1958). Fries' book was of seminal importance; Francis' has been a popular college text; Hill's is the most ambitious specimen of "phonological syntax."

New discussions of transformational grammar, at all levels of competence and difficulty, appear almost weekly: much research is based on unpublished papers which are duplicated for circulation among insiders. The beginner may want to turn to Roderick Jacobs and Peter Rosenbaum, *Grammar 1* and *Grammar 2* (1967), for the most elementary introduction, or to their *English Transformational Grammar* (1968), for a more advanced treatment. Serious readers will certainly want to follow Chomsky's thought, at least from *Syntactic Structures* (1957) through *Aspects of the Theory of Syntax* (1965); *The Sound Pattern of English* (1968), by Chomsky and Morris Halle, is hard going. An enlightening anthology, now somewhat dated, is Jerry Fodor and Jerrold Katz, *The Structure of Language* (1964). The bibliography to Chomsky's essay in the present collection is fairly thorough.

LANGUAGE

Edward Sapir (1884–1939) brought to his work in linguistics both an enormous knowledge of languages and their structures and a constant concern with the interplay between these languages and the social and cultural milieus in which they existed. Essays by Sapir open each of the three sections of this reader because, quite simply, they remain among the best general discussions that can be found; they reflect at every word his originality and his insistence that linguistic knowledge and method must also serve some larger end. Throughout his life Sapir held that grammatical analysis is one way of getting at some of the humanness of mankind. And in his later years he became particularly interested in the way language can be seen as shaping culture—shaping, in fact, the world view of the speakers of each individual language.

Sapir left behind him no rigorously formulated body of grammatical doctrine; from his published writings it is clear that his theories and analytical methods were in development all his life, and that he was never doctrinaire about either. Much of his work was on American Indian languages, whose study, in the early years of the twentieth century, promised exciting discoveries which more conventional linguistic scholarship seemed not to offer so abundantly. And Sapir moved more and more from brilliant close analyses of particular languages to broad hypotheses—many of them still warmly debated—about patterns of relationship among dozens or hundreds of languages.

The article which follows was originally written as the entry "Language" for the *Encyclopaedia of the Social Sciences*. In it, Sapir's characteristic preoccupation with the relation between the form of a language and the functions it serves can be seen clearly. He first defines language in terms of its form and functions, and then goes on to summarize the major systems of classifying and relating languages (which entails a summary of the patterns of linguistic change). He concludes with a discussion of the ties between language and culture.

The gift of speech and a well ordered language are characteristic of every known group of human beings. No tribe has ever been found which is without language and all statements to the contrary may be dismissed as mere folklore. There seems to be no warrant whatever for the statement which is sometimes made that there are certain peoples whose vocabulary is so limited that they cannot get on without the supplementary use of gesture, so that intelligible communication between members of such a group becomes impossible in the dark. The truth of the matter is that language is an essentially perfect means of expression and communication among every known people. Of all aspects of culture it is a fair guess that language was the first to receive a highly developed form and that its essential perfection is a prerequisite to the development of culture as a whole.

There are some general characteristics which apply to all languages, living or extinct, written or unwritten. In the first place language is primarily a system of phonetic symbols for the expression of communicable thought and feeling. In other words, the symbols of language are differentiated products of the vocal behavior which is associated with the larynx of the higher mammals. As a mere matter of theory it is conceivable that something like a linguistic structure could have been evolved out of gesture or other forms of bodily behavior. The fact that at an advanced stage in the history of the human race writing emerged in close imitation of the patterns of spoken language proves that language as a purely instrumental and logical device is not dependent on the use of articulate sounds. Nevertheless, the actual history of man and a wealth of anthropological evidence indicate with overwhelming certainty that phonetic language takes precedence over all other kinds of communicative symbolism, which are by comparison either substitutive, like writing, or merely supplementary, like the gesture accompanying speech. The speech apparatus which is used in the articulation of language is the same for all known peoples. It consists of the larynx, with its delicately adjustable glottal chords, the nose, the tongue, the hard and soft palate, the teeth and the lips. While the original impulses leading to speech may be thought of as localized in the larynx, the finer phonetic articulations are chiefly due to the muscular activity of the tongue, an organ whose primary function has of course nothing whatever to do with sound production but which in actual speech behavior is indispensable for the development of emotionally expressive sound into what we call language. It is so indispensable in fact that one of the most common terms for language or speech is "tongue." Language is thus not a simple biological function even as regards the simple matter of sound production, for primary laryngeal patterns of behavior have had to be completely overhauled by the interference of lingual, labial and nasal modifications before a "speech organ" was ready for work. Perhaps it is because this speech organ is a diffused and secondary network of physiological activities which do not correspond to the primary functions of the organs involved that language has been enabled to free itself from direct bodily expressiveness.

Not only are all languages phonetic in character; they are also "phonemic." Between the articulation of the voice into the phonetic sequence, which is immediately audible as a mere sensation, and the complicated patterning of phonetic sequences into such symbolically significant entities as words, phrases and sentences there is a very interesting process of phonetic selection and generalization which is easily overlooked but which is crucial for the development of the specifically symbolic aspect of language. Language is not merely articulated sound; its significant structure is dependent upon the unconscious selection of a fixed number of "phonetic stations," or sound units. These are in actual behavior individually modifiable; but the essential point is that through the unconscious selection of sounds as phonemes definite psychological barriers are erected between various phonetic stations, so that speech ceases to be an expressive flow of sound and becomes a symbolic composition with limited materials or units. The analogy with musical theory seems quite fair. Even the most resplendent and dynamic symphony is built up of tangibly distinct musical entities or notes which in the physical world flow into each other in an indefinite continuum but which in the world of aesthetic composition and appreciation are definitely bounded off against each other, so that they may enter into an intricate mathematics of significant relationships. The phonemes of a language are in principle a distinct system peculiar to the given language, and its words must be made up, in unconscious theory if not always in actualized behavior, of these phonemes. Languages differ very widely in their phonemic structure. But whatever the details of these structures may be, the important fact remains that there is no known language which has not a perfectly definite phonemic system. The difference between a sound and a phoneme can be illustrated by a simple example in English. If the word matter is pronounced in a slovenly fashion, as in the phrase "What's the matter?" the t sound, not being pronounced with the full energy required to bring out its proper physical characteristics, tends to slip into a d. Nevertheless, this phonetic d will not be felt as a functional d but as a variety of t of a particular type of expressiveness. Obviously the functional relation between the proper t sound of such a word as matter and its d variant is quite other than the relation of the t of such a word as town and the d of down. In every known language it is possible to distinguish merely phonetic variations, whether expressive or not, from symbolically functional ones of a phonemic order.

In all known languages phonemes are built up into distinct and arbitrary sequences which are at once recognized by the speakers as meaningful symbols of reference. In English, for instance, the sequence g plus o in the word go is an unanalyzable unit and the meaning attaching to the symbol cannot be derived by relating to each other values which might be imputed to the g and to the o independently. In other words, while the mechanical functional units of language are phonemes, the true units of language as symbolism are conventional groupings of such phonemes. The size of these units and the laws of their mechanical structure vary widely in the different

languages and their limiting conditions may be said to constitute the phonemic mechanics, or phonology, of a particular language. But the fundamental theory of sound symbolism remains the same everywhere. The
formal behavior of the irreducible symbol also varies within wide limits in
the languages of the world. Such a unit may be either a complete word, as
in the English example already given, or a significant element, like the
suffix *ness* of goodness. Between the meaningful and unanalyzable word or
word element and the integrated meaning of continuous discourse lies the
whole complicated field of the formal procedures which are intuitively
employed by the speakers of a language in order to build up aesthetically
and functionally satisfying symbol sequences out of the theoretically
isolable units. These procedures constitute grammar, which may be defined
as the sum total of formal economies intuitively recognized by the speakers
of a language. There seem to be no types of cultural patterns which vary
more surprisingly and with a greater exuberance of detail than the morphologies of the known languages. In spite of endless differences of detail,
however, it may justly be said that all grammars have the same degree of
fixity. One language may be more complex or difficult grammatically than
another, but there is no meaning whatever in the statement which is sometimes made that one language is more grammatical, or form bound, than
another. Our rationalizations of the structure of our own language lead to
a self-consciousness of speech and of academic discipline which are of course
interesting psychological and social phenomena in themselves but have
very little to do with the question of form in language.

Besides these general formal characteristics language has certain psychological qualities which make it peculiarly important for the student of social
science. In the first place, language is felt to be a perfect symbolic system,
in a perfectly homogeneous medium, for the handling of all references and
meanings that a given culture is capable of, whether these be in the form of
actual communications or in that of such ideal substitutes of communication as thinking. The content of every culture is expressible in its language
and there are no linguistic materials whether as to content or form which
are not felt to symbolize actual meanings, whatever may be the attitude of
those who belong to other cultures. New cultural experiences frequently
make it necessary to enlarge the resources of a language, but such enlargement is never an arbitrary addition to the materials and forms already
present; it is merely a further application of principles already in use and in
many cases little more than a metaphorical extension of old terms and
meanings. It is highly important to realize that once the form of a language
is established it can discover meanings for its speakers which are not simply
traceable to the given quality of experience itself but must be explained to
a large extent as the projection of potential meanings into the raw material

of experience. If a man who has never seen more than a single elephant in the course of his life nevertheless speaks without the slightest hesitation of ten elephants or a million elephants or a herd of elephants or of elephants walking two by two or three by three or of generations of elephants, it is obvious that language has the power to analyze experience into theoretically dissociable elements and to create that world of the potential intergrading with the actual which enables human beings to transcend the immediately given in their individual experiences and to join in a larger common understanding. This common understanding constitutes culture, which cannot be adequately defined by a description of those more colorful patterns of behavior in society which lie open to observation. Language is heuristic, not merely in the simple sense which this example suggests but in the much more far reaching sense that its forms predetermine for us certain modes of observation and interpretation. This means of course that as our scientific experience grows we must learn to fight the implications of language. "The grass waves in the wind" is shown by its linguistic form to be a member of the same relational class of experiences as "The man works in the house." As an interim solution of the problem of expressing the experience referred to in this sentence it is clear that the language has proved useful, for it has made significant use of certain symbols of conceptual relation, such as agency and location. If we feel the sentence to be poetic or metaphorical, it is largely because other more complex types of experience with their appropriate symbolisms of reference enable us to reinterpret the situation and to say, for instance, "The grass is waved by the wind" or "The wind causes the grass to wave." The point is that no matter how sophisticated our modes of interpretation become, we never really get beyond the projection and continuous transfer of relations suggested by the forms of our speech. After all, to say that "Friction causes such and such a result" is not very different from saying "The grass waves in the wind." Language is at one and the same time helping and retarding us in our exploration of experience, and the details of these processes of help and hindrance are deposited in the subtler meanings of different cultures.

A further psychological characteristic of language is the fact that while it may be looked upon as a symbolic system which reports or refers to or otherwise substitutes for direct experience, it does not as a matter of actual behavior stand apart from or run parallel to direct experience but completely interpenetrates with it. This is indicated by the widespread feeling, particularly among primitive people, of that virtual identity or close correspondence of word and thing which leads to the magic of spells. On our own level it is generally difficult to make a complete divorce between objective reality and our linguistic symbols of reference to it; and things, qualities and events are on the whole felt to be what they are called. For the normal person every experience, real or potential, is saturated with verbalism. This explains why so many lovers of nature, for instance, do not feel that they are truly in touch with it until they have mastered the names of a great many flowers and trees, as though the primary world of reality were a verbal one and as though one could not get close to nature unless one first mastered the terminology which somehow magically expresses it. It is this constant interplay between language and experience which removes language from the cold status of such purely and simply symbolic systems as mathematical symbolism or flag signaling. This interpenetration is not only an intimate associative fact; it is also a contextual one. It is important to realize that language may not only refer to experience or even mold, interpret and discover experience but that it also substitutes for it in the sense that in those sequences of interpersonal behavior which form the greater part of our daily lives speech and action supplement each other and do each other's work in a web of unbroken pattern. If one says to me "Lend me a dollar," I may hand over the money without a word or I may give it with an accompanying "Here it is" or I may say "I haven't got it. I'll give it to you tomorrow." Each of these responses is structurally equivalent, if one thinks of the larger behavior pattern. It is clear that if language is in its analyzed form a symbolic system of reference it is far from being merely that if we consider the psychological part that it plays in continuous behavior. The reason for this almost unique position of intimacy which language holds among all known symbolisms is probably the fact that it is learned in the earliest years of childhood.

It is because it is learned early and piecemeal, in constant association with the color and the requirements of actual contexts, that language in spite of its quasi-mathematical form is rarely a purely referential organization. It tends to be so only in scientific discourse, and even there it may be seriously doubted whether the ideal of pure reference is ever attained by language. Ordinary speech is directly expressive and the purely formal pattern of sounds, words, grammatical forms, phrases and sentences are always to be thought of as compounded with intended or unintended symbolisms of expression, if they are to be understood fully from the standpoint of behavior. The choice of words in a particular context may convey the opposite of what they mean on the surface. The same external message is differently interpreted according to whether the speaker has this or that psychological status in his personal relations, or whether such primary expressions as those of affection or anger or fear may inform the spoken words with a significance which completely transcends their normal value. On the whole, however, there is no danger that the expressive character of language will be overlooked. It is too obvious a fact to call for much emphasis. What is often overlooked and is, as a matter of fact, not altogether easy to understand is that the quasi-mathematical patterns, as we have called them, of the grammarian's language, unreal as these are in a contextual sense, have nevertheless a tremendous intuitional vitality; and that these patterns, never divorced in experience from the expressive ones, are nevertheless easily separated from them by the normal individual. The fact that almost any word or phrase can be made to take on an infinite variety of meanings seems to indicate that in all language behavior there are intertwined in enormously complex patterns isolable patterns of two distinct orders. These may be roughly defined as patterns of reference and patterns of expression.

That language is a perfect symbolism of experience, that in the actual contexts of behavior it cannot be divorced from action and that it is the carrier of an infinitely nuanced expressiveness are universally valid psychological facts. There is a fourth general psychological peculiarity which applies more particularly to the languages of sophisticated peoples. This is the fact that the referential form systems which are actualized in language behavior do not need speech in its literal sense in order to preserve their substantial integrity. The history of writing is in essence the long attempt to develop an independent symbolism on the basis of graphic representation, followed by the slow and begrudging realization that spoken language is a more powerful symbolism than any graphic one can possibly be and that true progress in the art of writing lay in the virtual abandonment of the principle with which it originally started. Effective systems of writing, whether alphabetic or not, are more or less exact transfers of speech. The original language system may maintain itself in other and remoter transfers, one of the best examples of these being the Morse telegraph code. It is a very interesting fact that the principle of linguistic transfer is not entirely absent even among the unlettered peoples of the world. Some at least of the drum signal and horn signal systems of the west African natives are in principle transfers of the organizations of speech, often in minute phonetic detail.

Many attempts have been made to unravel the origin of language but most of these are hardly more than exercises of the speculative imagination. Linguists as a whole have lost interest in the problem and this for two reasons. In the first place, it has come to be realized that there exist no truly primitive languages in a psychological sense, that modern researches in archaeology have indefinitely extended the time of man's cultural past and that it is therefore vain to go much beyond the perspective opened up by the study of actual languages. In the second place, our knowledge of psychology, particularly of the symbolic processes in general, is not felt to be sound enough or far reaching enough to help materially with the problem of the emergence of speech. It is probable that the origin of language is not a problem that can be solved out of the resources of linguistics alone but that it is essentially a particular case of a much wider problem of the genesis of symbolic behavior and of the specialization of such behavior in the laryngeal region, which may be presumed to have had only expressive functions to begin with. Perhaps a close study of the behavior of very young children under controlled conditions may provide some valuable hints, but it seems dangerous to reason from such experiments to the behavior of precultural man. It is more likely that the kinds of studies which are now in progress of the behavior of the higher apes will help supply some idea of the genesis of speech.

The most popular earlier theories were the interjectional and onomatopoetic theories. The former derived speech from involuntary cries of an expressive nature, while the latter maintained that the words of actual language are conventionalized forms of imitation of the sounds of nature. Both of these theories suffer from two fatal defects. While it is true that both interjectional and onomatopoetic elements are found in most languages, they are always relatively unimportant and tend to contrast somewhat with the more normal materials of language. The very fact that they are constantly being formed anew seems to indicate that they belong rather to the directly expressive layer of speech which intercrosses with the main level of referential symbolism. The second difficulty is even more serious. The essential problem of the origin of speech is not to attempt to discover the kinds of vocal elements which constitute the historical nucleus of language. It is rather to point out how vocal articulations of any sort could become dissociated from their original expressive value. About all that can be said at present is that while speech as a finished organization is a distinctly human achievement, its roots probably lie in the power of the higher apes to solve specific problems by abstracting general forms of schemata from the details of given situations; that the habit of interpreting certain selected elements in a situation as signs of a desired total one gradually led in early man to a dim feeling for symbolism; and that in the long run and for reasons which can hardly be guessed at the elements of experience which were most often interpreted in a symbolic sense came to be the largely useless or supplementary vocal behavior that must have often attended significant action. According to this point of view language is not so much directly developed out of vocal expression as it is an actualization in terms of vocal expression of the tendency to master reality, not by direct and ad hoc handling of its elements but by the reduction of experience to familiar forms. Vocal expression is only superficially the same as language. The tendency to derive speech from emotional expression has not led to anything tangible in the way of scientific theory and the attempt must now be made to see in language the slowly evolved product of a peculiar technique or tendency which may be called the symbolic one, and to see the relatively meaningless or incomplete part as a sign of the whole. Language then is what it is essentially not because of its admirable expressive power but in spite of it. Speech as behavior is a wonderfully complex blend of two pattern systems, the symbolic and the expressive, neither of which could have developed to its present perfection without the interference of the other.

It is difficult to see adequately the functions of language, because it is so deeply rooted in the whole of human behavior that it may be suspected that there is little in the functional side of our conscious behavior in which language does not play its part. The primary function of language is generally said to be communication. There can be no quarrel with this so long as it is distinctly understood that there may be effective communication without overt speech and that language is highly relevant to situations which are not obviously of a communicative sort. To say that thought, which is hardly possible in any sustained sense without the symbolic organization brought by language, is that form of communication in which the speaker and the person addressed are identified in one person is not far from begging the question. The autistic speech of children seems to show that the purely communicative aspect of language has been exaggerated. It is best to admit that language is primarily a vocal actualization of the tendency to see reality symbolically, that it is precisely this quality which renders it a fit instrument for communication and that it is in the actual give and take of social intercourse that it has been complicated and refined into the form in which it is known today. Besides the very general function which language fulfils in the spheres of thought, communication and expression which are implicit in its very nature there may be pointed out a number of special derivatives of these which are of particular interest to students of society.

Language is a great force of socialization, probably the greatest that exists. By this is meant not merely the obvious fact that significant social intercourse is hardly possible without language but that the mere fact of a common speech serves as a peculiarly potent symbol of the social solidarity of those who speak the language. The psychological significance of this goes far beyond the association of particular languages with nationalities, political entities or smaller local groups. In between the recognized dialect or language as a whole and the individualized speech of a given individual lies a kind of linguistic unit which is not often discussed by the linguist but which is of the greatest importance to social psychology. This is the subform of a language which is current among a group of people who are held together by ties of common interest. Such a group may be a family, the undergraduates of a college, a labor union, the underworld in a large city, the members of a club, a group of four or five friends who hold together through life in spite of differences of professional interest, and untold thousands of other kinds of groups. Each of these tends to develop peculiarities of speech which have the symbolic function of somehow distinguishing the group from the larger group into which its members might be too completely absorbed. The complete absence of linguistic indices of such small groups is obscurely felt as a defect or sign of emotional poverty. Within the confines of a particular family, for instance, the name Georgy, having once been mispronounced Doody in childhood, may take on the latter form forever after; and this unofficial pronunciation of a familiar name as applied to a particular person becomes a very important symbol indeed of the solidarity of a particular family and of the continuance of the sentiment that keeps its members together. A stranger cannot lightly take on the privilege of saying Doody if the members of the family feel that he is not entitled to go beyond the degree of familiarity symbolized by the use of Georgy or George. Again, no one is entitled to say "trig" or "math" who has not gone through certain familiar and painful experiences as a high school or undergraduate student. The use of such words at once declares the speaker a member of an unorganized but psychologically real group. A self-made mathematician has hardly the right to use the word "math" in referring to his own interests because the student overtones of the word do not properly apply to him. The extraordinary importance of minute linguistic differences for the symbolization of psychologically real as contrasted with politically or sociologically official groups is intuitively felt by most people. "He talks like us" is equivalent to saying "He is one of us."

There is another important sense in which language is a socializer beyond its literal use as a means of communication. This is in the establishment of rapport between the members of a physical group, such as a house party. It is not what is said that matters so much as that something is said. Particularly where cultural understandings of an intimate sort are somewhat lacking among the members of a physical group it is felt to be important that the lack be made good by a constant supply of small talk. This caressing or reassuring quality of speech in general, even where no one has anything of moment to communicate, reminds us how much more language is than a mere technique of communication. Nothing better shows how completely the life of man as an animal made over by culture is dominated by the verbal substitutes for the physical world.

The use of language in cultural accumulation and historical transmission is obvious and important. This applies not only to sophisticated levels but to primitive ones as well. A great deal of the cultural stock in trade of a primitive society is presented in a more or less well defined linguistic form. Proverbs, medicine formulae, standardized prayers, folk tales, standardized speeches, song texts, genealogies, are some of the more overt forms which language takes as a culture preserving instrument. The pragmatic ideal of education, which aims to reduce the influence of standardized lore to a minimum and to get the individual to educate himself through as direct a contact as possible with the facts of his environment, is certainly not realized among the primitives, who are often as word bound as the humanistic tradition itself. Few cultures perhaps have gone to the length of the classical Chinese culture or of rabbinical Jewish culture in making the word do duty for the thing or the personal experience as the ultimate unit of reality. Modern civilization as a whole, with its schools, its libraries and its endless stores of knowledge, opinion and sentiment stored up in verbalized form, would be unthinkable without language made eternal as document. On the whole, we probably tend to exaggerate the differences between "high" and "low" cultures or saturated and emergent cultures in the matter of traditionally conserved verbal authority. The enormous differences that seem to exist are rather differences in the outward form and content of the cultures themselves than in the psychological relation which obtains between the individual and his culture.

In spite of the fact that language acts as a socializing and uniformizing force it is at the same time the most potent single known factor for the growth of individuality. The fundamental quality of one's voice, the phonetic patterns of speech, the speed and relative smoothness of articulation, the length and build of the sentences, the character and range of the vocabulary, the stylistic consistency of the words used, the readiness with which words respond to the requirements of the social environment, in particular the suitability of one's language to the language habits of the person addressed—all these are so many complex indicators of the personality. "Actions speak louder than words" may be an excellent maxim from the pragmatic point of view but betrays little insight into the nature of speech. The language habits of people are by no means irrelevant as unconscious indicators of the more important traits of their personalities, and the folk is psychologically wiser than the adage in paying a great deal of attention willingly or not to the psychological significance of a man's language. The normal person is never convinced by the mere content of speech but is very sensitive to many of the implications of language behavior, however feebly (if at all) these may have been consciously analyzed. All in all, it is not too much to say that one of the really important functions of language is to be constantly declaring to society the psychological place held by all of its members. Besides this more general type of personality expression or fulfilment there is to be kept in mind the important role which language plays as a substitutive means of expression for those individuals who have a greater than normal difficulty in adjusting themselves to the environment in terms of primary action patterns. Even in the most primitive cultures the strategic word is likely to be more powerful than the direct blow. It is unwise to speak too blithely of "mere" words, for to do so may be to imperil the value and perhaps the very existence of civilization and personality.

The languages of the world may be classified either structurally or genetically. An adequate structural analysis is an intricate matter and no classification seems to have been suggested which does justice to the bewildering variety of known forms. It is useful to recognize three distinct criteria of classification: the relative degree of synthesis or elaboration of the words of the language; the degree to which the various parts of a word are welded together; and the extent to which the fundamental relational concepts of the language are directly expressed as such. As regards synthesis languages range all the way from the isolating type, in which the single word is essentially unanalyzable, to the type represented by many American Indian languages, in which the single word is functionally often the equivalent of a sentence with many concrete references that would in most languages require the use of a number of words. Four stages of synthesis may be conveniently recognized: the isolating type, the weakly synthetic type, the fully synthetic type and the polysynthetic type. The classical example of the first type is Chinese, which does not allow the words of the language to be modified by internal changes or the addition of prefixed or suffixed elements to express such concepts as those of number, tense, mode, case relation and the like. This seems to be one of the more uncommon types of language and is best represented by a number of languages in eastern Asia. Besides Chinese itself Siamese, Burmese, modern Tibetan, Annamite and Khmer, or Cambodian, may be given as examples. The older view, which regarded such languages as representing a peculiarly primitive stage in the evolution of language, may now be dismissed as antiquated. All evidence points to the contrary hypothesis that such languages are the logically extreme analytic developments of more synthetic languages which because of processes of phonetic disintegration have had to reëxpress by analytical means combinations of ideas originally expressed within the framework of the single word. The weakly synthetic type of language is best represented by the most familiar modern languages of Europe, such as English, French, Spanish, Italian, German, Dutch and Danish. Such languages modify words to some extent but have only a moderate formal elaboration of the word. The plural formations of English and French, for instance, are relatively simple and the tense and modal systems of all the languages of this type tend to use analytic methods as supplementary to the older synthetic one. The third group of languages is represented by such languages as Arabic and earlier Indo-European languages, like Sanskrit, Latin and Greek. These are all languages of great formal complexity, in which classificatory ideas, such as sex gender, number, case relations, tense and mood, are expressed with considerable nicety and in a great variety of ways. Because of the rich formal implications of the single word the sentence tends not to be so highly energized and ordered as in the first mentioned types. Lastly, the polysynthetic languages add to the formal complexity of the treatment of fundamental relational ideas the power to arrange a number of logically distinct, concrete ideas into an ordered whole within the confines of a single word. Eskimo and Algonquin are classical examples of this type.

From the standpoint of the mechanical cohesiveness with which the elements of words are united, languages may be conveniently grouped into four types. The first of these, in which there is no such process of combination, is the isolating type already referred to. To the second group of languages belong all those in which the word can be adequately analyzed into a mechanical sum of elements, each of which has its more or less clearly established meaning and each of which is regularly used in all other words into which the associated notion enters. These are the so-called agglutinative languages. The majority of languages seem to use the agglutinative technique, which has the great advantage of combining logical analysis with economy of means. The Altaic languages, of which Turkish is a good example, and the Bantu languages of Africa are agglutinative in form. In the third type, the so-called inflective languages, the degree of union between the radical element or stem of the word and the modifying prefixes or suffixes is greater than in the agglutinative languages, so that it becomes difficult in many cases to isolate the stem and set it off against the accreted elements. More important than this, however, is the fact that there is less of a one to one correspondence between the linguistic element and the notion referred to than in the agglutinative languages. In Latin, for instance, the notion of plurality is expressed in a great variety of ways which seem to have little phonetic connection with each other. For example, the final vowel or diphthong of *equi* (horses), *dona* (gifts), *mensae* (tables) and the final vowel and consonant of *hostes* (enemies) are functionally equivalent elements the distribution of which is dependent on purely formal and historical factors which have no logical relevance. Furthermore in the verb the notion of plurality is quite differently expressed, as in the last two consonants of *amant* (they love). It used to be fashionable to contrast in a favorable sense the "chemical" qualities of such inflective languages as Latin and Greek with the soberly mechanical quality of such languages as Turkish. But these evaluations may now be dismissed as antiquated and subjective. They were obviously due to the fact that scholars who wrote in English, French, and German were not above rationalizing the linguistic structures with which they were most familiar into a position of ideal advantage. As an offshoot of the inflective languages may be considered a fourth group, those in which the processes of welding, due to the operation of complex phonetic laws, have gone so far as to result in the creation of patterns of internal change of the nuclear elements of speech. Such familiar English examples as the words sing, sang, sung, song will serve to give some idea of the nature of these structures, which may be termed symbolistic. The kinds of internal change which may be recognized are changes in vocalic quality, changes in consonants, changes in quantity, various types of reduplication or repetition, changes in stress accent and, as in Chinese and many African languages, changes in pitch. The classical example of this type of language is Arabic, in which as in the other Semitic languages nuclear meanings are expressed by sequences of consonants, which have, however, to be connected by significant vowels whose sequence patterns establish fixed functions independent of the meanings conveyed by the consonantal framework.

Elaboration and technique of word analysis are perhaps of less logical and psychological significance than the selection and treatment of fundamental relational concepts for grammatical treatment. It would be very difficult, however, to devise a satisfactory conceptual classification of languages because of the extraordinary diversity of the concepts and classifications of ideas which are illustrated in linguistic form. In the Indo-European and Semitic languages, for instance, noun classification on the basis of gender is a vital principle of structure; but in most of the other languages of the world this principle is absent, although other methods of noun classification are found. Again, tense or case relations may be formally important in one language, for example, Latin, but of relatively little grammatical importance in another, although the logical references implied by such forms must naturally be taken care of in the economy of the language as, for instance, by the use of specific words within the framework of the sentence. Perhaps the most fundamental conceptual basis of classification is that of the expression of fundamental syntactic relations as such versus their expression in necessary combination with notions of a concrete order. In Latin, for example, the notion of the subject of a predicate is never purely expressed in a formal sense, because there is no distinctive symbol for this relation. It is impossible to render it without at the same time defining the number and gender of the subject of the sentence. There are languages, however, in which syntactic relations are expressed purely, without admixture of implications of a nonrelational sort. We may speak therefore of pure relational languages as contrasted with mixed relational languages. Most of the languages with which we are familar belong to the latter category. It goes without saying that such a conceptual classification has no direct relation to the other two types of classification which we have mentioned.

The genetic classification of languages is one which attempts to arrange the languages of the world in groups and subgroups in accordance with the main lines of historical connection, which can be worked out on the basis either of documentary evidence or of a careful comparison of the languages studied. Because of the far reaching effect of slow phonetic changes and of other causes languages which were originally nothing but dialects of the same form of speech have diverged so widely that it is not apparent that they are but specialized developments of a single prototype. An enormous amount of work has been done in the genetic classification and subclassification of the languages of the world, but very many problems still await research and solution. At the present time it is known definitely that there are certain very large linguistic groups, or families, as they are often called, the members of which may, roughly speaking, be looked upon as lineally descended from languages which can be theoretically reconstructed in their main phonetic and structural outlines. It is obvious, however, that languages may so diverge as to leave little trace of the original relationship. It is therefore very dangerous to assume that languages are not at last analysis divergent members of a single genetic group merely because the evidence is negative. The only contrast that is legitimate is between languages known to be historically related and languages not known to be so related. Languages known to be related cannot be legitimately contrasted with languages known not to be related.

Because of the fact that languages have differentiated at different rates and because of the important effects of cultural diffusion, which have brought it about that strategically placed languages, such as Arabic, Latin and English, have spread over large parts of the earth at the expense of others, very varied conditions are found to prevail in regard to the distribution of linguistic families. In Europe, for instance, there are only two linguistic families of importance represented today, the Indo-European languages and the Ugro-Finnic languages, of which Finnish and Hungarian are examples. The Basque dialects of southern France and northern Spain are the survivors of another and apparently isolated group. On the other hand, in aboriginal America the linguistic differentiation is extreme and a surprisingly large number of essentially unrelated linguistic families must be recognized. Some of the families occupy very small areas, while others, such as the Algonquin and the Athabaskan languages of North America, are spread over a large territory. The technique of establishing linguistic families and of working out the precise relationship of the languages included in these families is too difficult to be gone into here. It suffices to say that random word comparisons are of little importance. Experience shows that very precise phonetic relations can be worked out between the languages of a group and that on the whole fundamental morphological features tend to preserve themselves over exceedingly long periods of time. Thus modern Lithuanian is in structure, vocabulary and, to a large extent, even phonemic pattern very much the kind of a language which must be assumed as the prototype for the Indo-European languages as a whole. In spite of the fact that structural classifications are in theory unrelated to genetic ones and in spite of the fact that languages can be shown to have influenced each other, not only in phonetics and vocabulary but also to an appreciable extent in structure, it is not often found that the languages of a genetic group exhibit utterly irreconcilable structures. Thus even English, which is one of the least conservative of Indo-European languages, has many far reaching points of structure in common with as remote a language as Sanskrit in contrast, say, to Basque or Finnish. Again, different as are Assyrian, modern Arabic and the Semitic languages of Abyssinia they exhibit numerous points of resemblance in phonetics, vocabulary and structure which set them off at once from, say, Turkish or the Negro languages of the Nile headwaters.

The complete rationale of linguistic change, involving as it does many of the most complex processes of psychology and sociology, has not yet been satisfactorily worked out, but there are a number of general processes that emerge with sufficient clarity. For practical purposes inherent changes may be distinguished from changes due to contact with other linguistic communities. There can be no hard line of division between these two groups of changes because every individual's language is a distinct psychological entity in itself, so that all inherent changes are likely at last analysis to be peculiarly remote or subtle forms of change due to contact. The distinction, however, has great practical value, all the more so as there is a tendency among anthropologists and sociologists to operate far too hastily with wholesale linguistic changes due to external ethnic and cultural influences. The enormous amount of study that has been lavished on the history of particular languages and groups of languages shows very clearly that the most powerful differentiating factors are not outside influences, as ordinarily understood, but rather the very slow but powerful unconscious changes in certain directions which seem to be implicit in the phonemic systems and morphologies of the languages themselves. These "drifts" are powerfully conditioned by unconscious formal feelings and are made necessary by the inability of human beings to actualize ideal patterns in a permanently set fashion.

Linguistic changes may be analyzed into phonetic changes, changes in form and changes in vocabulary. Of these the phonetic changes seem to be the most important and the most removed from direct observation. The factors which lead to these phonetic changes are probably exceedingly complex and no doubt include the operation of obscure symbolisms which define the relation of various age groups to one another. Not all phonetic changes, however, can be explained in terms of social symbolism. It seems that many of them are due to the operation of unconscious economies in actualizing sounds or combinations of sounds. The most impressive thing about internal phonetic change is its high degree of regularity. It is this regularity, whatever its ultimate cause, that is more responsible than any other single factor for the enviable degree of exactness which linguistics has attained as a historical discipline. Changes in grammatical form often follow in the wake of destructive phonetic changes. In many cases it can be seen how irregularities produced by the disintegrating effect of phonetic change are ironed out by the analogical spread of more regular forms. The cumulative effect of these corrective changes is quite sensibly to modify the structure of the language in many details and sometimes even in its fundamental features. Changes in vocabulary are due to a great variety of causes, most of which are of a cultural rather than of a strictly linguistic nature. The too frequent use of a word, for instance, may reduce it to a commonplace term, so that it needs to be replaced by a new word. On the other hand, changes of attitude may make certain words with their traditional overtones of meaning unacceptable to the younger generation, so that they tend to become obsolete. Probably the most important single source of changes in vocabulary is the creation of new words on analogies which have spread from a few specific words.

Of the linguistic changes due to the more obvious types of contact the one which seems to have played the most important part in the history of language is the "borrowing" of words across linguistic frontiers. This borrowing naturally goes hand in hand with cultural diffusion. An analysis of the provenience of the words of a given language is frequently an important index of the direction of cultural influence. Our English vocabulary, for instance, is very richly stratified in a cultural sense. The various layers of early Latin, mediaeval French, humanistic Latin and Greek and modern French borrowings constitute a fairly accurate gauge of the time, extent and nature of the various foreign cultural influences which have helped to mold English civilization. The notable lack of German loan words in English until a very recent period, as contrasted with the large number of Italian words which were adopted at the time of the Renaissance and later, is again a historically significant fact. By the diffusion of culturally important words, such as those referring to art, literature, the church, military affairs, sport and business, there have grown up important trans-national vocabularies which do something to combat the isolating effect of the large number of languages which are still spoken in the modern world. Such borrowings have taken place in all directions, but the number of truly important source languages is surprisingly small. Among the more important of them are Chinese, which has saturated the vocabularies of Korean, Japanese and Annamite; Sanskrit, whose influence on the cultural vocabulary of central Asia, India and Indo-China has been enormous; Arabic, Greek, Latin and French. English, Spanish and Italian have also been of great importance as agencies of cultural transmission, but their influence seems less far reaching than that of the languages mentioned above. The cultural influence of a language is not always in direct propor-tion to its intrinsic literary interest or to the cultural place which its speakers have held in the history of the world. For example, while Hebrew is the carrier of a peculiarly significant culture, actually it has not had as important an influence on other languages of Asia as Aramaic, a sister language of the Semitic stock.

The phonetic influence exerted by a foreign language may be very con-siderable, and there is a great deal of evidence to show that dialectic peculiarities have often originated as a result of the unconscious transfer of phonetic habits from the language in which one was brought up to that which has been adopted later in life. Apart, however, from such complete changes in speech is the remarkable fact that distinctive phonetic features tend to be distributed over wide areas regardless of the vocabularies and structures of the languages involved. One of the most striking examples of this type of distribution is found among the Indian languages of the Pacific coast of California, Oregon, Washington, British Columbia and southern Alaska. Here are a large number of absolutely distinct languages, belonging to a number of genetically unrelated stocks, so far as we are able to tell, which nevertheless have many important and distinctive phonetic features in common. An analogous fact is the distribution of certain peculiar phonetic features in both the Slavic languages and the Ugro-Finnic lan-guages, which are unrelated to them. Such processes of phonetic diffusion must be due to the influence exerted by bilingual speakers, who act as unconscious agents for the spread of phonetic habits over wide areas. Primitive man is not isolated, and bilingualism is probably as important a factor in the contact of primitive groups as it is on more sophisticated levels.

Opinions differ as to the importance of the purely morphological influence exerted by one language on another in contrast with the more external types of phonetic and lexical influence. Undoubtedly such influences must be taken into account, but so far they have not been shown to operate on any great scale. In spite of the centuries of contact, for instance, between Semitic and Indo-European languages we know of no language which is definitely a blend of the structures of these two stocks. Similarly, while Japanese is flooded with Chinese loan words, there seems to be no structural influence of the latter on the former. A type of influence which is neither one of vocabulary nor of linguistic form, in the ordinary sense of the word, and to which insufficient attention has so far been called, is that of meaning pattern. It is a remarkable fact of modern European culture, for instance, that while the actual terms used for certain ideas vary enormously from language to language, the range of significance of these equivalent terms tends to be very similar, so that to a large extent the vocabulary of one language tends to be a psychological and cultural translation of the vocabulary of another. A simple example of this sort would be the translation of such terms as Your Excellency to equivalent but etymologically unrelated terms in Russian. Another instance of this kind would be the interesting parallelism in nomenclature between the kinship terms of affinity in English, French and German. Such terms as *mother-in-law, belle-mère* and *Schwiegermutter* are not, strictly speaking, equivalent either as to etymology or literal meaning but they are patterned in exactly the same manner. Thus *mother-in-law* and *father-in-law* are parallel in nomenclature to *belle-mère* and *beau-père* and to *Schwiegermutter* and *Schwiegervater.* These terms clearly illustrate the diffusion of a lexical pattern which in turn probably expresses a growing feeling of the sentimental equivalent of blood relatives and relatives by marriage.

The importance of language as a whole for the definition, expression and transmission of culture is undoubted. The relevance of linguistic details, in both content and form, for the profounder understanding of culture is also clear. It does not follow, however, that there is a simple correspondence between the form of a language and the form of the culture of those who speak it. The tendency to see linguistic categories as directly expressive of overt cultural outlines, which seems to have come into fashion among certain sociologists and anthropologists, should be resisted as in no way warranted by the actual facts. There is no general correlation between cultural type and linguistic structure. So far as can be seen, isolating or agglutinative or inflective types of speech are possible on any level of civilization. Nor does the presence or absence of grammatical gender, for example, seem to have any relevance for the understanding of the social organization or religion or folklore of the associated peoples. If there were any such parallelism as has sometimes been maintained, it would be quite impossible to understand the rapidity with which culture diffuses in spite of profound linguistic differences between the borrowing and giving communities. The cultural significance of linguistic form, in other words, lies on a much more submerged level than on the overt one of definite cultural pattern. It is only very rarely, as a matter of fact, that it can be pointed out how a cultural trait has had some influence on the fundamental structure of a language. To a certain extent this lack of correspondence may be due to the fact that linguistic changes do not proceed at the same rate as most cultural changes, which are on the whole far more rapid. Short of yielding to another language which takes its place, linguistic organization, largely because it is unconscious, tends to maintain itself indefinitely and does not allow its fundamental formal categories to be seriously influenced by changing cultural needs. If the forms of culture and language were then in complete correspondence with one another, the nature of the processes making for linguistic and cultural changes respectively would soon bring about a lack of necessary correspondence. This is exactly what is found to be the case. Logically it is indefensible that the masculine, feminine and neuter genders of German and Russian should be allowed to continue their sway in the modern world; but any intellectualist attempt to weed out these unnecessary genders would obviously be fruitless, for the normal speaker does not actually feel the clash which the logician requires.

It is another matter when we pass from general form to the detailed content of a language. Vocabulary is a very sensitive index of the culture of a people and changes of meaning, loss of old words, the creation and borrowing of new ones are all dependent on the history of culture itself. Languages differ widely in the nature of their vocabularies. Distinctions which seem inevitable to us may be utterly ignored in languages which reflect an entirely different type of culture, while these in turn insist on distinctions which are all but unintelligible to us. Such differences of vocabulary go far beyond the names of cultural objects, such as arrow point, coat of armor or gunboat. They apply just as well to the mental world. It would be difficult in some languages, for instance, to express the distinction which we feel between "to kill" and "to murder" for the simple reason that the underlying legal philosophy which determines our use of these words does not seem natural to all societies. Abstract terms, which are so necessary to our thinking, may be infrequent in a language whose speakers formulate their behavior on more pragmatic lines. On the other hand, the question of the presence or absence of abstract nouns may be bound up with the fundamental form of the language; and there exist a large number of primitive languages whose structure allows of the very ready creation and use of abstract nouns of quality or action.

There are many language patterns of a special sort which are of interest to the social scientist. One of these is the tendency to create tabus for certain words or names. A very widespread custom among primitive peoples, for instance, is the tabu which is placed not only on the use of the name of a person recently deceased but of any word that is etymologically connected in the feeling of the speakers with such a name. This means that ideas have often to be expressed by circumlocutions or that terms must be borrowed from neighboring dialects. Sometimes certain names or words are too holy to be pronounced except under very special conditions, and curious patterns of behavior develop which are designed to prevent one from making use of such interdicted terms. An example of this is the Jewish custom of pronouncing the Hebrew name for God, not as Yahwe or Jehovah but as Adonai, My Lord. Such customs seem strange to us but equally strange to many primitive communities would be our extraordinary reluctance to pronounce obscene words under normal social conditions. Another class of special linguistic phenomena is the use of esoteric language devices, such as passwords or technical terminologies for ceremonial attitudes or practices. Among the Eskimo, for example, the medicine man has a peculiar vocabulary which is not understood by those who are not members of his guild. Special dialectic forms or otherwise peculiar linguistic patterns are common among primitive peoples for the texts of songs. Sometimes, as in Melanesia, such song texts are due to the influence of neighboring dialects. This is strangely analogous to the practice among ourselves of singing songs in Italian, French or German rather than in English, and it is likely that the historical processes which have led to the parallel custom are of a similar nature. Thieves' jargon and secret languages of children may also be mentioned. These lead over into special sign and gesture languages, many of which are based directly on spoken or written speech; they seem to exist on many levels of culture. The sign language of the Plains Indians of North America arose in response to the need for some medium of communication between tribes speaking mutually unintelligible languages. Within the Christian church may be noted the elaboration of gesture languages by orders of monks vowed to silence. Not only a language or a terminology but the mere external form in which it is written may become important as a symbol of sentimental or social distinction. Thus Croatian and Serbian are essentially the same language but they are presented in very different outward forms, the former being written in Latin characters, the latter in the Cyrillic character of the Greek Orthodox church. This external difference, associated with a difference of religion, has of course the important function of preventing people who speak closely related languages or dialects but who wish for reasons of sentiment not to confound themselves in a larger unity from becoming too keenly aware of how much they actually resemble each other.

The relation of language to nationalism and internationalism presents a number of interesting sociological problems. Anthropology makes a rigid distinction between ethnic units based on race, on culture and on language.

It points out that these do not need to coincide in the least—that they do not, as a matter of fact, often coincide in reality. But with the increased emphasis on nationalism in modern times the question of the symbolic meaning of race and language has taken on a new significance and, whatever the scientist may say, the layman is ever inclined to see culture, language and race as but different facets of a single social unity, which he tends in turn to identify with such a political entity as England or France or Germany. To point out, as the anthropologist easily can, that cultural distributions and nationalities override language and race groups does not end the matter for the sociologist, because he feels that the concept of nation or nationality must be integrally imaged by the non-analytical person as carrying with it the connotation, real or supposed, of both race and language. From this standpoint it really makes little difference whether history and anthropology support the popular identification of nationality, language and race. The important thing to hold on to is that a particular language tends to become the fitting expression of a self-conscious nationality and that such a group will construct for itself in spite of all that the physical anthropologist can do a race to which is to be attributed the mystic power of creating a language and a culture as twin expressions of its psychic peculiarities.

So far as language and race are concerned, it is true that the major races of man have tended in the past to be set off against each other by important differences of language. There is less point to this, however, than might be imagined, because the linguistic differentiations within any given race are just as far reaching as those which can be pointed out across racial lines, yet they do not at all correspond to subracial units. Even the major races are not always clearly sundered by language. This is notably the case with the Malayo-Polynesian languages, which are spoken by peoples as racially distinct as the Malays, the Polynesians and the Negroes of Melanesia. Not one of the great languages of modern man follows racial lines. French, for example, is spoken by a highly mixed population which is largely Nordic in the north, Alpine in the center and Mediterranean in the south, each of these subraces being liberally represented in the rest of Europe.

While language differences have always been important symbols of cultural difference, it is only in comparatively recent times, with the exaggerated development of the ideal of the sovereign nation and with the resulting eagerness to discover linguistic symbols for this ideal of sovereignty, that language differences have taken on an implication of antagonism. In ancient Rome and all through mediaeval Europe there were plenty of cultural differences running side by side with linguistic ones, and the political status of Roman citizen or the fact of adherence to the Roman Catholic church was of vastly greater significance as a symbol of the individual's place in the world than the language or dialect which he happened to speak. It is probably altogether incorrect to maintain that language differences are responsible for national antagonisms. It would seem to be much more reasonable to suppose that a political and national unit, once definitely formed, uses a prevailing language as a symbol of its identity, whence gradually emerges the peculiarly modern feeling that every language should properly be the expression of a distinctive nationality. In earlier times there seems to have been little systematic attempt to impose the language of a conquering people on the subject people, although it happened frequently as a result of the processes implicit in the spread of culture that such a conqueror's language was gradually taken over by the dispossessed population. Witness the spread of the Romance languages and of the modern Arabic dialects. On the other hand, it seems to have happened about as frequently that the conquering group was culturally and linguistically absorbed and that their own language disappeared without necessary danger to their privileged status. Thus foreign dynasties in China have always submitted to the superior culture of the Chinese and have taken on their language. In the same way the Moslem Moguls of India, while true to their religion, which was adopted by millions in northern India, made one of the Hindu vernaculars the basis of the great literary language of Moslem India, Hindustani. Definitely repressive attitudes toward the languages and dialects of subject peoples seem to be distinctive only of European political policy in comparatively recent times. The attempt of czarist Russia to stamp out Polish by forbidding its teaching in the schools and the similarly repressive policy of contemporary Italy in its attempt to wipe out German from the territory recently acquired from Austria are illuminating examples of the heightened emphasis on language as a symbol of political allegiance in the modern world.

To match these repressive measures there is the oft repeated attempt of minority groups to erect their language into the status of a fully accredited medium of cultural and literary expression. Many of these restored or semimanufactured languages have come in on the wave of resistance to exterior political or cultural hostility. Such are the Gaelic of Ireland, the Lithuanian of a recently created republic and the Hebrew of the Zionists. In other cases such languages have come in more peacefully because of a sentimental interest in local culture. Such are the modern Provençal of southern France, the Plattdeutsch of northern Germany, Frisian and the Norwegian *landsmaal*. It is doubtful whether these persistent attempts to make true culture languages of local dialects that have long ceased to be of primary literary importance can succeed in the long run. The failure of modern Provençal to hold its own and the very dubious success of Gaelic make it seem probable that following the recent tendency to resurrect minor languages will come a renewed leveling of speech more suitably expressing the internationalism which is slowly emerging.

The logical necessity of an international language in modern times is in strange contrast to the indifference and even opposition with which most people consider its possibility. The attempts so far made to solve this problem, of which Esperanto has probably had the greatest measure of practical success, have not affected more than a very small proportion of the people whose international interests and needs might have led to a desire for a simple and uniform means of international expression, at least for certain purposes. It is in the less important countries of Europe, such as Czechoslovakia, that Esperanto has been moderately successful, and for obvious reasons. The opposition to an international language has little logic or psychology in its favor. The supposed artificiality of such a language as Esperanto or of any of the equivalent languages that have been proposed has been absurdly exaggerated, for in sober truth there is practically nothing in these languages that is not taken from the common stock of words and forms which have gradually developed in Europe. Such an international language could of course have only the status of a secondary form of speech for distinctly limited purposes. Thus considered the learning of a constructed international language offers no further psychological problem than the learning of any other language which is acquired after childhood through the medium of books and with the conscious application of grammatical rules. The lack of interest in the international language problem in spite of the manifest need for one is an excellent example of how little logic or intellectual necessity has to do with the acquirement of language habits. Even the acquiring of the barest smattering of a foreign national language is imaginatively equivalent to some measure of identification with a people or a culture. The purely instrumental value of such knowledge is frequently nil. Any consciously constructed international language has to deal with the great difficulty of not being felt to represent a distinctive people or culture. Hence the learning of it is of very little symbolic significance for the average person, who remains blind to the fact that such a language, easy and regular as it inevitably must be, would solve many of his educational and practical difficulties at a single blow. The future alone will tell whether the logical advantages and theoretical necessity of an international language can overcome the largely symbolic opposition which it has to meet. In any event it is at least conceivable that one of the great national languages of modern times, such as English or Spanish or Russian, may in due course find itself in the position of a de facto international language without any conscious attempt having been made to put it there.

Study Questions

1. "Language," says Sapir, "is an essentially perfect means of expression and communication among every known people" (p. 16). Speakers of Sinhalese, an Indo-European language of Ceylon, have had difficulty in translating scientific writings: for that purpose, they have had to adopt and adapt words from Sanskrit and from the international scientific vocabulary. Poets sometimes complain that English poetry is hard to write now because the English language is changing so fast that its words no longer carry shared and stable connotations. Some Frenchman say their language has been corrupted by words borrowed from English, like *bifteck* "beefsteak" and *match de football* "football game."

    Do facts and ideas like these disprove Sapir's statement on p. 16? What, precisely, do you think the statement means?

2. Sapir (p. 16) calls language "primarily a system of phonetic symbols," yet he also says (p. 21) that linguistic systems "do not need speech in its literal sense in order to preserve their substantial integrity." How does he conceive the relationship between speech and writing? Does he treat writing too lightly?

3. According to Sapir, grammar is "the sum total of formal economies intuitively recognized by the speakers of a language" (p. 18). "The quasi-mathematical patterns" which the grammarian describes have "tremendous intuitional vitality," Sapir goes on (p. 21), so that (for example) the "psychological barriers" between phonemes may make a speaker of American English hear a physical *d* as if it were a *t*. Are concrete acts of speech, particular utterances, real bits of language or merely *signs* of language, indirect physical evidence from which one may draw conclusions about language as a psychological entity? Is language directly observable?

4. Though people are just as dead in a "garden of memory" as in a graveyard, words like *graveyard* and *cemetery* often become taboo and are replaced by gentler terms; why? If the language of a religious ritual or a sacred text is changed, is the change "merely external," or is the real world of the devotee somehow changed as well? How does the expression "the real world" beg the question which Sapir raises when he says (p. 19) that language "interpenetrates" experience and allows us to create a "world of the potential intergrading with the actual" (p. 19)?

5. Why, according to Sapir (p. 24), do small social groups develop and maintain distinctive forms of speech? Why does it seem ridiculous— if it does—for a middle-aged professor to use his students' slang? Do Sapir's remarks on language as a symbol of social unity have any bearing on the problem of teaching middle-class English to children from the slums? Will the expressive value of language grow smaller if the speech of different groups and regions becomes more uniform?

6. "Modern civilization," Sapir tells us, "would be unthinkable without language made eternal as document" (p. 25). What forms, besides that of books, might the documents take? In the "electronic world" of the latter twentieth century, has the importance of language been reduced "as a means of communication," socialization, "cultural accumulation and historical transmission"?

7. What three criteria does Sapir suggest (p. 26) for the structural classification of languages? What four stages of synthesis does he recognize? How does he distinguish isolating, agglutinative, and inflective languages (p. 27)? What is the difference between "pure relational languages" and "mixed relational languages" (p. 29)? What is meant by a "family" of languages (p. 29)? Can inherent linguistic changes be distinguished from changes due to contact (p. 30)? Can you explain the suggestion that some phonetic changes are due to "the operation of obscure symbolisms which define the relation of various age groups to one another" (p. 31)? What does Sapir say about changes in syntax (sentence structure)? How does the rate of linguistic change prevent "complete correspondence" between the "structure of a language" and "the forms of culture" (p. 34)?

8. Is there any serious idea in the old saying that England and America are divided by a common language? What direct experience have you had of the relations between differences in language and national and racial differences? What effects would you foresee from the worldwide adoption of a single language, natural or artificial, as a means of international communication?

Goold Brown

OF THE SCIENCE OF GRAMMAR

The New England Quaker schoolmaster, Goold Brown (1791–1857), learned Latin and Greek from his schoolmaster father while he was still a child; but dutiful intelligence did less than money would have done to get him a fresher, wider education. College was not for him, and years of devoted self-instruction left him still provincial: he had the imprudence to look backward, and though one of his textbooks kept a place in the schools for over a century, probably no living man has got through the Chinese wall of his monstrous *Grammar of English Grammars* (1851). The book is remembered, when it is, mainly because so many of its "improprieties for correction" are from the volumes of competing pedagogues.

It was typical of Brown that he should expect schoolboys to profit from parsing sentences mechanically and from correcting errors which writing books about parsing had not kept their elders from making. Brown's failure as a grammarian was not that he was traditional but that he buried tradition under a trash-heap of reprobated blunders and pedantic annotations. He was learned enough. The tradition he had inherited gave him a clear view of what one now calls the humanities, and the traditional system of his grammar allowed him to say much that was true and useful about English and encouraged him to think seriously about the good use of language and about the wider relevance of his studies. He remained a pedant. Though time, place, and poverty unite to excuse him, he did nothing to deepen or enrich his heritage. *The Grammar of English Grammars* was "first printed in Boston in 1850 and 1851": one would never guess, from reading in it, that one of the great centuries of linguistics was half over.

By the twentieth century the life had gone out of schoolroom grammar, though scholars had both preserved the grammatical tradition and enriched it with new historical knowledge. Wider acquaintance with non-Indo-European languages, and new ways of describing them, would soon make the grammatical world of Goold Brown look intolerably cramped and quaint. Yet his ideals (or some of them) remain tenable, for all of his failure to realize them. "Some acquaintance with the history of grammar as a science, as well as some knowledge of the structure of other languages than our own, is necessary to him who professes to write for the advancement of this branch of learning."

1. Language, in the proper sense of the term, is peculiar to man; so that, without a miraculous assumption of human powers, none but human beings can make words the vehicle of thought. An imitation of some of the articulate sounds employed in speech, may be exhibited by parrots, and some-

Goold Brown, "Of the Science of Grammar," from *The Grammar of English Grammars*. 10th ed. (New York, 1878), pp. 21–30.

times by domesticated ravens, and we know that almost all brute animals have their peculiar natural voices, by which they indicate their feelings, whether pleasing or painful. But *language* is an attribute of reason, and differs essentially not only from all brute voices, but even from all the chattering, jabbering, and babbling of our own species, in which there is not an intelligible meaning, with division of thought, and distinction of words.

2. Speech results from the joint exercise of the best and noblest faculties of human nature, from our rational understanding and our social affection; and is, in the proper use of it, the peculiar ornament and distinction of man, whether we compare him with other orders in the creation, or view him as an individual preëminent among his fellows. Hence that science which makes known the nature and structure of speech, and immediately concerns the correct and elegant use of language, while it surpasses all the conceptions of the stupid or unlearned, and presents nothing that can seem desirable to the sensual and grovelling, has an intrinsic dignity which highly commends it to all persons of sense and taste, and makes it most a favourite with the most gifted minds. That science is Grammar. And though there be some geniuses who affect to despise the trammels of grammar rules, to whom it must be conceded that many things which have been unskillfully taught as such, deserve to be despised; yet it is true, as Dr. Adam remarks, that, "The study of Grammar has been considered an object of great importance by the wisest men in all ages." [1]

3. Grammar bears to language several different relations, and acquires from each a nature leading to a different definition. *First*, It is to language, as knowledge is to the thing known; and as doctrine, to the truths it inculcates. In these relations, grammar is a science. It is the first of what have been called the seven sciences, or liberal branches of knowledge; namely, grammar, logic, rhetoric, arithmetic, geometry, astronomy, and music. *Secondly*, It is as skill, to the thing to be done; and as power, to the instruments it employs. In these relations, grammar is an art; and as such, has long been defined, *"ars rectè scribendi, rectèque loquendi,"* the art of writing and speaking correctly. *Thirdly*, It is as navigation, to the ocean, which nautic skill alone enables men to traverse. In this relation, theory and practice combine, and grammar becomes, like navigation, a practical science. *Fourthly*, It is as a chart, to a coast which we would visit. In this relation, our grammar is a textbook, which we take as a guide, or use as a help to our own observation. *Fifthly*, It is as a single voyage, to the open sea, the highway of nations. Such is our meaning, when we speak of the grammar of a particular text or passage.

[1] Alexander Adam, *Latin and English Grammar* (Edinburgh, 1772; Boston, 1803), p. iii. (We have replaced Brown's brief references with fuller notes, based as far as possible on his own bibliography.—*Eds.*)

4. Again: Grammar is to language a sort of self-examination. It turns the faculty of speech or writing upon itself for its own elucidation; and makes the tongue or the pen explain the uses and abuses to which both are liable, as well as the nature and excellency of that power, of which these are the two grand instruments. From this account, some may begin to think that in treating of grammar we are dealing with something too various and changeable for the understanding to grasp; a dodging Proteus of the imagination, who is ever ready to assume some new shape, and elude the vigilance of the inquirer. But let the reader or student do his part; and, if he please, follow us with attention. We will endeavour, with welded links, to bind this Proteus, in such a manner that he shall neither escape from our hold, nor fail to give to the consulter an intelligible and satisfactory response. . . .

5. If for a moment we consider the good and the evil that are done in the world through the medium of speech, we shall with one voice acknowledge, that not only the faculty itself, but also the manner in which it is used, is of incalculable importance to the welfare of man. But this reflection does not directly enhance our respect for grammar, because it is not to language as the vehicle of moral or of immoral sentiment, of good or of evil to mankind, that the attention of the grammarian is particularly directed. A consideration of the subject in these relations, pertains rather to the moral philosopher. Nor are the arts of logic and rhetoric now considered to be properly within the grammarian's province. Modern science assigns to these their separate places, and restricts grammar, which at one period embraced all learning, to the knowledge of language, as respects its fitness to be the vehicle of any particular thought or sentiment which the speaker or writer may wish to convey by it. Accordingly grammar is commonly defined, by writers upon the subject, in the special sense of an art—"the *art* of speaking or writing a language with propriety or correctness." [2]

6. Lily says, "Grammatica est rectè scribendi atque loquendi ars;" [3] that is, "Grammar is the art of writing and speaking correctly." Despauter,[4] too, in his definition, which is quoted in a preceding paragraph, not improperly placed writing first, as being that with which grammar is primarily concerned. For it ought to be remembered, that over any fugitive colloquial dialect, which has never been fixed by visible signs, grammar has no control; and that the speaking which the art or science of grammar teaches, is exclusively that which has reference to a knowledge of letters. It is the certain tendency of writing, to improve speech. And in proportion as books are

---

[2] Noah Webster, *An American Dictionary of the English Language.*
[3] William Lyly, *Brevissima Institutio*, the famous old Latin grammar which Brown apparently used in a London edition of 1793.
[4] Brown used a 1517–18 edition of the Latin grammar of John Despauter, "a Flemish grammarian."

multiplied, and the knowledge of written language is diffused, local dialects, which are beneath the dignity of grammar, will always be found to grow fewer, and their differences less. There are, in the various parts of the world, many languages to which the art of grammar has never yet been applied; and to which, therefore, the definition or true idea of grammar, however general, does not properly extend. And even where it has been applied, and is now honoured as a popular branch of study, there is yet great room for improvement: barbarisms and solecisms have not been rebuked away as they deserve to be.

7. Melancthon says "Grammatica est certa loquendi ac scribendi ratio, Latinis Latinè." [5] Vossius, "Ars benè loquendi eóque et scribendi, atque id Latinis Latinè." [6] Dr. Prat, *"Grammatica est rectè loquendi atque scribendi ars."* [7] Ruddiman also, in his Institutes of Latin Grammar, reversed the terms *writing* and *speaking*, and defined grammar *"ars rectè loquendi scribendique"*;[8] and, either from mere imitation, or from the general observation that speech precedes writing, this arrangement of the words has been followed by most modern grammarians. Dr. Lowth embraces both terms in a more general one, and says, "Grammar is the art of *rightly expressing* our thoughts by words." [9] It is, however, the province of grammar, to guide us not merely in the expression of our own thoughts, but also in our apprehension of the thoughts, and our interpretation of the words, of others. Hence, Perizonius,[10] in commenting upon Sanctius's imperfect definition, *"Grammatica est ars rectè loquendi,"* not improperly asks, *"et quindi intelligendi et explicandi?"* "and why not also of understanding and explaining?" Hence, too, the art of *reading* is virtually a part of grammar; for it is but the art of understanding and speaking correctly that which we have before us on paper. And Nugent has accordingly given us the following definition: "Grammar is the art of reading, speaking, and writing a language by rules."[11]

8. The word *rectè*, rightly, truly, correctly, which occurs in most of the foregoing Latin definitions, is censured by the learned Richard Johnson, in his Grammatical Commentaries, on account of the vagueness of its meaning. He says, it is not only ambiguous by reason of its different uses in the Latin classics, but destitute of any signification proper to grammar. But

---

[5] Philipp Melancthon (1497-1560), German Protestant scholar. "Grammar is the established art of speaking and writing, by the Latins in Latin," etc.

[6] Presumably from Gerhard Voss (1577-1649), another German Protestant classicist: "Grammar is the art of speaking well and therefore of writing well too, and that in Latin by the Latins."

[7] Possibly the Samuel Prat (d. 1723) who wrote a two-volume Latin grammar. "Grammar is the art of speaking and writing correctly."

[8] Thomas Ruddiman (1674-1757), Scottish philologist.

[9] Robert Lowth (1710-1787), bishop of London and author of *A Short Introduction to English Grammar* (1762 and many later editions).

[10] Perizonius was the fancy name of the Dutch classicist Jakob Voorbroek (1651-1715).

[11] Probably Thomas Nugent (d. 1772), *Dictionary of the French and English Languages* (London, 1767). Nugent translated the Greek and Latin grammars of Port Royal.

even if this be true as regards its earlier application, it may well be questioned, whether by frequency of use it has not acquired a signification which makes it proper at the present time. The English word *correctly* seems to be less liable to such an objection; and either this brief term, or some other of like import, (as, "with correctness"—"with propriety,") is still usually employed to tell what grammar is. But can a boy learn by such means what it is, *to speak and write grammatically?* In one sense, he can; and in another, he cannot. He may derive, from any of these terms, some idea of grammar as distinguished from other arts; but no simple definition of this, or of any other art, can communicate to him that learns it, the skill of an artist.

9. R. Johnson speaks at large of *the relation of words* to each other in sentences, as constituting in his view the most essential part of grammar; and as being a point very much overlooked, or very badly explained, by grammarians in general. His censure is just. And it seems to be as applicable to nearly all the grammars now in use, as to those which he criticised a hundred and thirty years ago. But perhaps he gives to the relation of words, (which is merely their dependence on other words according to the sense,) an earlier introduction and a more prominent place, than it ought to have in a general system of grammar. To the right use of language, he makes four things to be necessary. In citing these, I vary the language, but not the substance or the order of his positions. *First*, That we should speak and write words according to the significations which belong to them: the teaching of which now pertains to lexicography, and not to grammar, except incidentally. "*Secondly*, That we should observe *the relations* that words have one to another in sentences, and represent those relations by such variations, and particles, as are usual with authors in that language." *Thirdly*, That we should acquire a knowledge of the proper sounds of the letters, and pay a due regard to accent in pronunciation. *Fourthly*, That we should learn to write words with their proper letters, spelling them as literary men generally do.

10. From these positions, (though he sets aside the first, as pertaining to lexicography, and not now to grammar, as it formerly did,) the learned critic deduces first his four parts of the subject, and then his definition of grammar. "Hence," says he, "there arise Four Parts of Grammar; *Analogy*, which treats of the several parts of speech, their definitions, accidents, and formations; *Syntax*, which treats of the use of those things in construction, according to their relations; *Orthography*, which treats of spelling; and *Prosody*, which treats of accenting in pronunciation. So, then, the true definition of Grammar is this: Grammar is the art of *expressing the relations* of things in construction, with due accent in speaking, and orthography in writing, according to the custom of those whose language we learn." Again he adds: "The word *relation* has other senses, taken by itself; but yet the

relation of words one to another in a sentence, has no other signification than what I intend by it, namely, of cause, effect, means, end, manner, instrument, object, adjunct, and the like; which are names given by logicians to those relations under which the mind comprehends things, and therefore the most proper words to explain them to others. And if such things are too hard for children, then grammar is too hard; for there neither is, nor can be, any grammar without them. And a little experience will satisfy any man, that the young will as easily apprehend them, as *gender, number, declension,* and other grammar-terms." [12]

11. It is true, that *the relation of words*—by which I mean that connexion between them, which the train of thought forms and suggests—or that dependence which one word has on an other according to the sense—lies at the foundation of all syntax. No rule or principle of construction can ever have any applicability beyond the limits, or contrary to the order, of this relation. To see what it is in any given case, is but to understand the meaning of the phrase or sentence. And it is plain, that no word ever necessarily agrees with an other, with which it is not thus connected in the mind of him who uses it. No word ever governs an other, to which the sense does not direct it. No word is ever required to stand immediately before or after an other, to which it has not some relation according to the meaning of the passage. Here then are the relation, agreement, government, and arrangement, of words in sentences; and these make up the whole of syntax—but not the whole of grammar. To this one part of grammar, therefore, the relation of words is central and fundamental; and in the other parts also, there are some things to which the consideration of it is incidental; but there are many more, like spelling, pronunciation, derivation, and whatsoever belongs merely to letters, syllables, and the forms of words, with which it has, in fact, no connexion. The relation of words, therefore, should be clearly and fully explained in its proper place, under the head of syntax; but the general idea of grammar will not be brought nearer to truth, by making it to be "the art of *expressing the relations* of things in construction," &c., according to the foregoing definition.

12. The term *grammar* is derived from the Greek word *gramma,* a letter. The art or science to which this term is applied, had its origin, not in cursory speech, but in the practice of writing; and speech, which is first in the order of nature, is last with reference to grammar. The matter or common subject of grammar, is language in general; which, being of two kinds, *spoken* and *written,* consists of certain combinations either of sounds or of visible signs, employed for the expression of thought. Letters and sounds, though often heedlessly confounded in the definitions given of vowels, consonants,

---

[2] Richard Johnson, *Grammatical Commentaries* (chiefly on Lyly's Latin grammar; London, 1706), p. 4.

&c., are, in their own nature, very different things. They address themselves to different senses; the former, to the sight; the latter, to the hearing. Yet, by a peculiar relation arbitrarily established between them, and in consequence of an almost endless variety in the combinations of either, they coincide in a most admirable manner, to effect the great object for which language was bestowed or invented; namely, to furnish a sure medium for the communication of thought, and the preservation of knowledge.

13. All languages, however different, have many things in common. There are points of a philosophical character, which result alike from the analysis of any language, and are founded on the very nature of human thought, and that of the sounds or other signs which are used to express it. When such principles alone are taken as the subject of inquiry, and are treated, as they sometimes have been, without regard to any of the idioms of particular languages, they constitute what is called General, Philosophical, or Universal Grammar. But to teach, with Lindley Murray and some others, that "Grammar may be considered as *consisting of two species*, Universal and Particular," and that the latter merely "applies those general principles to a particular language," is to adopt a twofold absurdity at the outset.[13] For every cultivated language has its particular grammar, in which whatsoever is universal, is necessarily included; but of which, universal or general principles form only a part, and that comparatively small. We find therefore in grammar no "two species" of the same genus; nor is the science or art, as commonly defined and understood, susceptible of division into any proper and distinct sorts, except with reference to different languages— as when we speak of Greek, Latin, French, or English grammar.

14. There is, however, as I have suggested, a certain science or philosophy of language, which has been denominated Universal Grammar; being made up of those points only, in which many or all of the different languages preserved in books, are found to coincide. All speculative minds are fond of generalization; and, in the vastness of the views which may thus be taken of grammar, such may find an entertainment which they never felt in merely learning to speak and write grammatically. But the pleasure of such contemplations is not the earliest or the most important fruit of the study. The first thing is, to know and understand the grammatical construction of our own language. Many may profit by this acquisition, who extend not their inquiries to the analogies or the idioms of other tongues. It is true, that every item of grammatical doctrine is the more worthy to be known and regarded, in proportion as it approaches to universality. But the principles of all practical grammar, whether universal or particular, com-

---

[13] "Murray the Grammarian" (1745–1826), compiler of the *Grammar of the English Language* (1795), the most famous of eighteenth-century English grammars.

mon or peculiar, must first be learned in their application to some one language, before they can be distinguished into such classes; and it is manifest, both from reason and from experience, that the youth of any nation not destitute of a good book for the purpose, may best acquire a knowledge of those principles, from the grammatical study of their native tongue.

15. Universal or Philosophical Grammar is a large field for speculation and inquiry, and embraces many things which, though true enough in themselves, are unfit to be incorporated with any system of practical grammar, however comprehensive its plan. Many authors have erred here. With what is merely theoretical, such a system should have little to do. Philosophy, dealing in generalities, resolves speech not only as a whole into its constituent parts and separable elements, as anatomy shows the use and adaptation of the parts and joints of the human body; but also as a composite into its matter and form, as one may contemplate that same body in its entireness, yet as consisting of materials, some solid and some fluid, and those curiously modelled to a particular figure. Grammar, properly so called, requires only the former of these analyses; and in conducting the same, it descends to the thousand minute particulars which are necessary to be known in practice. Nor are such things to be despised as trivial and low: ignorance of what is common and elementary, is but the more disgraceful for being ignorance of mere rudiments. "Wherefore," says Quintilian, "they are little to be respected, who represent this art as mean and barren; in which, unless you faithfully lay the foundation for the future orator, whatever superstructure you raise will tumble into ruins. It is an art, necessary to the young, pleasant to the old, the sweet companion of the retired, and one which in reference to every kind of study has in itself more of utility than of show. Let no one therefore despise as inconsiderable the elements of grammar. Not because it is a great thing, to distinguish consonants from vowels, and afterwards divide them into semivowels and mutes; but because, to those who enter the interior parts of this temple of science, there will appear in many things a great subtilty, which is fit not only to sharpen the wits of youth, but also to exercise the loftiest erudition and science." [14]

16. Again, of the arts which spring from the composition of language. Here the art of logic, aiming solely at conviction, addresses the understanding with cool deductions of unvarnished truth; rhetoric, designing to move, in some particular direction, both the judgement and the sympathies of men, applies itself to the affections in order to persuade; and poetry, various in its character and tendency, solicits the imagination, with a view to delight, and in general also to instruct. But grammar, though intimately connected with all these, and essential to them in practice, is still too distinct

---

[14] The "most celebrated book" by the first-century Roman rhetorician Quintilian (see para. 23–25 below) was *De Institutione Oratoria*, of which Brown here quotes Book i, Chapter 4.

from each to be identified with any of them. In regard to dignity and interest, these higher studies seem to have greatly the advantage over particular grammar; but who is willing to be an ungrammatical poet, orator, or logician? For him I do not write. But I would persuade my readers, that an acquaintance with that grammar which respects the genius of their vernacular tongue, is of primary importance to all who would cultivate a literary taste, and is a necessary introduction to the study of other languages. And it may here be observed, for the encouragement of the student, that as grammar is essentially the same thing in all languages, he who has well mastered that of his own, has overcome more than half the difficulty of learning another; and he whose knowledge of words is the most extensive, has the fewest obstacles to encounter in proceeding further.

17. It was the "original design" of grammar, says Dr. Adam, to facilitate "the acquisition of languages;" and, of all practical treatises on the subject, this is still the main purpose. In those books which are to prepare the learner to translate from one tongue into another, seldom is any thing else attempted. In those also which profess to explain the right use of vernacular speech, must the same purpose be ever paramount, and the "original design" be kept in view. But the grammarian may teach many things incidentally. One cannot learn a language, without learning at the same time a great many opinions, facts, and principles, of some kind or other, which are necessarily embodied in it. For all language proceeds from, and is addressed to, the understanding; and he that perceives not the meaning of what he reads, makes no acquisition even of the language itself. To the science of grammar, the *nature of the ideas* conveyed by casual examples, is not very essential: to the learner, it is highly important. The best thoughts in the best diction should furnish the models for youthful study and imitation; because such language is not only the most worthy to be remembered, but the most easy to be understood. A distinction is also to be made between use and abuse. In nonsense, absurdity, or falsehood, there can never be any grammatical authority; because, however language may be abused, the usage which gives law to speech, is still that usage which is founded upon the *common sense* of mankind.

18. Grammar appeals to reason, as well as to authority, but to what extent it should do so, has been matter of dispute. "The knowledge of useful arts," says Sanctius, "is not an invention of human ingenuity, but an emanation from the Deity, descending from above for the use of man, as Minerva sprung from the brain of Jupiter. Wherefore, unless thou give thyself wholly to laborious research into the nature of things, and diligently examine the *causes* and *reasons* of the art thou teachest, believe me, thou shalt but see with other men's eyes, and hear with other men's ears. But the minds of many are preoccupied with a certain perverse opinion, or rather ignorant conceit, that in grammar, or the art of speaking, there are no causes, and

that reason is scarcely to be appealed to for any thing;—than which idle notion, I know of nothing more foolish;—nothing can be thought of which is more offensive. Shall man, endowed with reason, do, say, or contrive any thing, without design, and without understanding? Hear the philosophers; who positively declare that nothing comes to pass without a cause. Hear Plato himself; who affirms that names and words subsist by nature, and contends that language is derived from nature, and not from art."

19. "I know," says he, "that the Aristotelians think otherwise; but no one will doubt that names are the signs, and as it were the instruments, of things. But the instrument of any art is so adapted to that art, that for any other purpose it must seem unfit; thus with an auger we bore, and with a saw we cut wood; but we split stones with wedges, and wedges are driven with heavy mauls. We cannot therefore but believe that those who first gave names to things, did it with design; and this, I imagine, Aristotle himself understood when he said, *ad placitum nomina significare*.[15] For those who contend that names were made by chance, are no less audacious than if they would endeavour to persuade us, that the whole order of the universe was framed together fortuitously."

20. "You will see," continues he, "that in the first language, whatever it was, the names of things were taken from Nature herself; but, though I cannot affirm this to have been the case in other tongues, yet I can easily persuade myself that in every tongue a reason can be rendered for the application of every name; and that this reason, though it is in many cases obscure, is nevertheless worthy of investigation. Many things which were not known to the earlier philosophers, were brought to light by Plato; after the death of Plato, many were discovered by Aristotle; and Aristotle was ignorant of many which are now everywhere known. For truth lies hid, but nothing is more precious than truth. But you will say, 'How can there be any certain origin to names, when one and the same thing is called by different names, in the several parts of the world?' I answer, of the same thing there may be different causes, of which some people may regard one, and others, an other. . . . There is therefore no doubt, that of all things, even of words, a reason is to be rendered: and if we know not what that reason is, when we are asked; we ought rather to confess that we do not know, than to affirm that none can be given. I know that Scaliger thinks otherwise; but this is the true account of the matter."

21. "These several observations," he remarks further, "I have unwillingly brought together against those stubborn critics who, while they explode reason from grammar, insist so much on the testimonies of the learned. But have they never read Quintilian, who says, (Lib. i, Cap. 6,) that,

---

[15] "Words have meaning by convention." The argument was whether words are naturally suited to the things they mean, or whether their meanings are conventional.

'Language is established by reason, antiquity, authority, and custom?' He therefore does not exclude reason, but makes it the principal thing. Nay, in a manner, Laurentius, and other grammatists, even of their fooleries, are forward to offer *reasons,* such as they are. Moreover, use does not take place without reason; otherwise, it ought to be called abuse, and not use. But from use authority derives all its force; for when it recedes from use, authority becomes nothing: whence Cicero reproves Cœlius and Marcus Antonius for speaking according to their own fancy, and not according to use. But, 'Nothing can be lasting,' says Curtius, (Lib. iv,) 'which is not based upon reason.' It remains, therefore, that of all things the reason be first assigned; and then, if it can be done, we may bring forward testimonies; that the thing, having every advantage, may be made the more clear.'' [16]

22. Julius Caesar Scaliger, from whose opinion Sanctius dissents above, seems to limit the science of grammar to bounds considerably too narrow, though he found within them room for the exercise of much ingenuity and learning. He says, "Grammatica est scientia loquendi ex usu; neque enim constituit regulas scientibus usus modum, sed ex eorum statis frequentibusque usurpationibus colligit communem rationem loquendi, quam discentibus traderet.''[17] "Grammar is the science of speaking according to use; for it does not establish rules for those who know the manner of use, but from the settled and frequent usages of these, gathers the common fashion of speaking, which it should deliver to learners." This limited view seems not only to exclude from the science the use of the pen, but to exempt the learned from any obligation to respect the rules prescribed for the initiation of the young. But I have said, and with abundant authority, that the acquisition of a good style of writing is the main purpose of the study; and, surely, the proficients and adepts in the art can desire for themselves no such exemption. Men of genius, indeed, sometimes affect to despise the pettiness of all grammatical instructions; but this can be nothing else than affectation, since the usage of the learned is confessedly the basis of all such instructions, and several of the loftiest of their own rank appear on the list of grammarians.

23. Quintilian, whose authority is appealed to above, belonged to that age in which the exegesis of histories, poems, and other writings, was considered an essential part of grammar. He therefore, as well as Diomedes, and other ancient writers, divided the grammarian's duties into two parts; the one including what is now called grammar, and the other the explanation of authors, and the stigmatizing of the unworthy. Of the opinion referred to by Sanctius, it seems proper to make here an ampler citation.

[16] Francisco Sanchez, or Sanctius, *Minerva,* Book i, Chapter 2. *Minerva* (1587) was "long the standard work on Latin grammar."
[17] J. C. Scaliger (1484–1558), *De Causis Linguae Latinae,* Book iv, Chapter 76.

It shall be attempted in English, though the paragraph is not an easy one to translate. I understand the author to say, "Speakers, too, have their rules to observe; and writers, theirs. Language is established by reason, antiquity, authority, and custom. Of reason the chief ground is analogy, but sometimes etymology. Ancient things have a certain majesty, and, as I might say, religion, to commend them. Authority is wont to be sought from orators and historians; the necessity of metre mostly excuses the poets. When the judgment of the chief masters of eloquence passes for reason, even error seems right to those who follow great leaders. But, of the art of speaking, custom is the surest mistress; for speech is evidently to be used as money, which has upon it a public stamp. Yet all these things require a penetrating judgement, especially analogy; the force of which is, that one may refer what is doubtful, to something similar that is clearly established, and thus prove uncertain things by those which are sure." [18]

24. The science of grammar, whatever we may suppose to be its just limits, does not appear to have been better cultivated in proportion as its scope was narrowed. Nor has its application to our tongue, in particular, ever been made in such a manner, as to do *great* honour to the learning or the talents of him that attempted it. What is new to a nation, may be old to the world. The development of the intellectual powers of youth by instruction in the classics, as well as the improvement of their taste by the exhibition of what is elegant in literature, is continually engaging the attention of new masters, some of whom may seem to effect great improvements; but we must remember that the concern itself is of no recent origin. Plato and Aristotle, who were great masters both of grammar and of philosophy, taught these things ably at Athens, in the fourth century *before* Christ. Varro, the grammarian, usually styled the most learned of the Romans, was *contemporary* with the Saviour and his apostles. Quintilian lived in the *first* century of our era, and before he wrote his most celebrated book, taught a school twenty years in Rome, and received from the state a salary which made him rich. This "consummate guide of wayward youth," as the poet Martial called him, being neither ignorant of what had been done by others, nor disposed to think it a light task to prescribe the right use of his own language, was at first slow to undertake the work upon which his fame now reposes; and, after it was begun, diligent to execute it worthily, that it might turn both to his own honour, and to the real advancement of learning.

25. He says, at the commencement of his book: "After I had obtained a quiet release from those labours which for twenty years had devolved upon me as an instructor of youth, certain persons familiarly demanded of me,

---

[18] *De Institutione Oratoria*, Book i, Chapter 6. Brown refers to p. 48 of an unspecified edition.

that I should compose something concerning the proper manner of speaking; but for a long time I withstood their solicitations, because I knew there were already illustrious authors in each language, by whom many things which might pertain to such a work, had been very diligently written, and left to posterity. But the reason which I thought would obtain for me an easier excuse, did but excite more earnest entreaty; because, amidst the various opinions of earlier writers, some of whom were not even consistent with themselves, the choice had become difficult; so that my friends seemed to have a right to enjoin upon me, if not the labour of producing new instructions, at least that of judging concerning the old. But although I was persuaded not so much by the hope of supplying what was required, as by the shame of refusing, yet, as the matter opened itself before me, I undertook of my own accord a much greater task than had been imposed; that while I should thus oblige my very good friends by a fuller compliance, I might not enter a common path and tread only in the footsteps of others. For most other writers who have treated of the art of speaking, have proceeded in such a manner as if upon adepts in every other kind of doctrine they would lay the last touch in eloquence; either despising as little things the studies which we first learn, or thinking them not to fall to their share in the division which should be made of the professions; or, what indeed is next to this, hoping no praise or thanks for their ingenuity about things which, although necessary, lie far from ostentation: the tops of buildings make a show, their foundations are unseen." [19]

26. But the reader may ask, "What have all these things to do with English Grammar?" I answer, they help to show us whence and what it is. Some acquaintance with the history of grammar as a science, as well as some knowledge of the structure of other languages than our own, is necessary to him who professes to write for the advancement of this branch of learning—and for him also who would be a competent judge of what is thus professed. Grammar must not forget her origin. Criticism must not resign the protection of letters. The national literature of a country is in the keeping, not of the people at large, but of authors and teachers. But a grammarian presumes to be a judge of authorship, and a teacher of teachers; and is it to the honour of England or America, that in both countries so many are countenanced in this assumption of place, who can read no language but their mother tongue? English Grammar is not properly an indigenous production, either of this country or of Britain; because it is but a branch of the general science of philology—a new variety, or species, sprung up from the old stock long ago transplanted from the soil of Greece and Rome.

---

[19] *Ibid.*, Prooemium.

27. It is true, indeed, that neither any ancient system of grammatical instruction nor any grammar of an other language, however contrived, can be entirely applicable to the present state of our tongue; for languages must needs differ greatly one from an other, and even that which is called the same, may come in time to differ greatly from what it once was. But the general analogies of speech, which are the central principles of grammar, are but imperfectly seen by the man of one language. On the other hand, it is possible to know much of those general principles, and yet be very deficient in what is peculiar to our own tongue. Real improvement in the grammar of our language, must result from a view that is neither partial nor superficial. "Time, sorry artist," as was said of old, "makes all he handles worse." And Lord Bacon, seeming to have this adage in view, suggests: "If Time of course alter all things to the worse, and Wisdom and Counsel shall not alter them to the better, what shall be the end?"[20]

28. Hence the need that an able and discreet grammarian should now and then appear, who with skillful hand can effect those corrections which a change of fashion or the ignorance of authors may have made necessary; but if he is properly qualified for his task, he will do all this without a departure from any of the great principles of Universal Grammar. He will surely be very far from thinking, with a certain modern author, whom I shall notice in an other chapter, that, "He is bound to take words and explain them as he finds them in his day, *without any regard to their ancient construction and application.*"[21] The whole history of every word, so far as he can ascertain it, will be the view under which he will judge of what is right or wrong in the language which he teaches. Etymology is neither the whole of this view, nor yet to be excluded from it. I concur not therefore with Dr. Campbell, who, to make out a strong case, extravagantly says, "It is *never from an attention to etymology*, which would frequently mislead us, but from custom, the only infallible guide in this matter, that the meanings of words in present use must be learnt."[22] Jamieson too, with an implicitness little to be commended, takes this passage from Campbell; and, with no other change than that of *"learnt"* to *"learned,"* publishes it as a corollary of his own.[23] It is folly to state for truth what is so obviously wrong. Etymology and custom are seldom at odds; and where they are so, the latter can hardly be deemed infallible.

[20] Francis Bacon (1561-1626), *Essays*, "Of Innovations."
[21] Samuel Kirkham, *English Grammar in Familiar Lectures* (2d ed., Harrisburg, Pa., 1825; 12th ed., New York, 1829), p. 28.
[22] George Campbell, *The Philosophy of Rhetoric* (London, 1776; Philadelphia, 1818), p. 188.
[23] Alexander Jamieson, *A Grammar of Rhetoric* (1st American ed., New Haven, 1820), p. 42.

Study Questions

1.   Why, according to Brown (para. 1, 2), can't animals talk? What relevance of grammar to psychology does Brown suggest (para. 4)? What guarantees that all languages, in Brown's view, must have many things in common (para. 13)? How does he contrast practical and speculative grammar (para. 15)? What does he consider the best approach to the speculative variety?

2.   What organization does Brown accept for the field of liberal knowledge generally (para. 3)? How does he contrast grammar as an art to the arts of logic, rhetoric, and poetic (para. 16)? What practical values does he see in studying the grammar of one's native language?

3.   A number of twentieth-century structural grammars have had three parts: phonology, the description of the sound system; morphology, the description of the structure of words; syntax, the description of structures into which words enter as units. Sometimes a description of the writing system has been added (graphemics or graphology). Can you relate that organization to the scheme which Brown takes from Richard Johnson's *Grammatical Commentaries* on Lyly's Latin grammar?

4.   Brown's own grammar includes a prosody as well as an orthography (though much of the prosody is devoted to punctuation). Does he think of a language as "primarily a system of phonetic symbols"? How does he believe that speech and writing are related? With which does he think the grammarian is concerned?

5.   What is the connection between Brown's notion of language as "an attribute of reason" and his notion of "the relation of words" (para. 11)? What opposition between different standards of correctness is he developing when he opposes Sanctius to Scaliger, reason to authority? What distinction does Brown intend between "use and abuse" (para. 17)? Try to explain the standard quoted from Quintilian (para. 23). How might one either attack or defend a modern statement that "essentially, in the usage of native speakers, whatever is, is right"?

THE SYSTEM OF GRAMMAR

Schoolmasters like Goold Brown and scholars like Otto Jespersen have alike been dismissed as "traditional" by devotees of newer grammars. The adjective might do for Brown (though "schoolroom grammarian" would be more accurate), but it is right for Jespersen only if it is understood as praise: his insight, learning, versatility, and independence established his place between the great men who preceded him and the great men who have followed. Among his many distinguished books, *The Essentials of English Grammar* is only one; but there is hardly a better brief grammar of English, and its value is increased by the long essay which explains and justifies it. Both "The System of Grammar" and *The Essentials* are full of ideas which later scholars have made their own: neither the book nor the essay has been made irrelevant by the intellectual advances (some linguists would say the scientific revolution) which they have helped to stimulate.

Jens Otto Harry Jespersen (1860–1943) was professor of English at the University of Copenhagen from 1893 until his retirement from teaching in 1925—a retirement he refused to postpone because he wanted younger men to have their chance to flourish unhindered by the dominance of the old. The act was characteristic of Jespersen's enduring liberalism—liberalism in the etymological sense of concern for the freedom of the human spirit. But his last work had to be done under the shadow of Nazi Germany.

By temperament and by calling, Jespersen was concerned with the concrete actuality of languages, with linguistic systems in their use. He did not attempt mathematically precise descriptions, and prescriptive rigor was his aversion. He filled his books with examples of "sentences as these are actually spoken and understood in practical life," and to their analysis he brought his distinctive concepts of morphology and syntax, of word classes, of nexus, junction, and the three ranks. "In syntax," he said, "meaning is everything."

The Essentials of English Grammar has thirty-six chapters, which "The System of Grammar" discusses in order. After a short introduction, the next five chapters of *Essentials* are devoted to the sound system and its history and to spelling. Chapters vii through ix present Jespersen's tools of analysis. The tenth chapter is entitled "Sentence-structure." There, and in the following chapters through xxvii, Jespersen discusses "both forms and their use," dividing his subject according to grammatical categories and relations like subject, object, the passive, case, and person. Chapter xxviii deals with affirmation, negation, and questions, Chapters xxix through xxxv with dependent nexus; and the retrospective final chapter—morphological in Jespersen's sense of moving from forms toward meanings—surveys the formal devices of English expression.

From *Selected Writings of Otto Jespersen*. Abridged from pages 487–528 by permission of Munksgaard, Copenhagen, Denmark.

The following pages have been occasioned by the elaboration of *The Essentials of English Grammar* (abbreviated EEG), as I found that I owed the reader some explanations and justifications of various things in that book, which could not very well find their place in the preface or in the introductory chapter. . . .[1]

In EEG I have tried to give as clear and concise an exposition as possible of the whole subject, including various observations on details which I do not remember ever meeting with in similar works. I have laid especial stress on the choice of good illustrative examples, and have, as a matter of course, drawn largely on those quotations which I had collected for my MEG. . . .[2] It is not possible in a grammar to do without some examples which are somewhat dull and seem to say nothing apart from the grammatical rule they are selected to illustrate, but it is possible to reduce the number of such examples to a minimum, and fortunately a great many rules can be illustrated by means of sentences which are in themselves interesting and valuable. . . .

I have also avoided the drawing up of paradigms like those still found in some grammars, e.g. "I love. Thou lovest. He loves. We love. You love. They love", or "I shall go. You will go. He will go. We shall go. You will go. They will go." Such things justify utterances like Herbert Spencer's about "that intensely stupid custom, the teaching of grammar to children", or J. Runciman's "The textbooks mostly used for grammar are sixpennyworths of horror calculated to make a lad loathe his own language" (*Contemporary Review*, 1888, p. 43).

With regard to the question what is to be considered correct or not correct in grammar I must repeat what I have said elsewhere that it is not, of course, my business to decide such questions for Englishmen: the only thing I have had to do is to observe English usage as objectively as I could. But psychological and historical studies often make one realize that much of what is generally considered "bad grammar" is due neither to sheer perversity nor ignorance on the part of the speaker or writer, but is ultimately due to the imperfections of the language as such, i.e. as it has been handed down traditionally from generation to generation (or rather from older to younger children), or else to general tendencies common to all

[1] ["The System of Grammar" should be read complete, either in *Linguistica* or in *Selected Writings of Otto Jespersen;* but it runs to over forty pages. We have tried to reduce it to feasible size without obscuring its principal ideas. Our chief omissions (all of which are marked) include the following: most of the first paragraph and about half of the second; the brief discussion of EEG 2-6; slightly more than a paragraph from the discussion of EEG 7; the argumentative part of the discussion of case (EEG 14); two short paragraphs from the discussion of person (EEG 15); the paragraph on EEG 19 (gender); most of the discussion of EEG 20-21, on number, and all of EEG 22-27, on degree, tense, and mood; and most of the discussion of EEG 32 (the infinitive).—*Eds.*]

[2] [MEG is Jespersen's masterpiece, his seven-volume *Modern English Grammar*. A thorough acquaintance with it is very helpful to an understanding reading of contemporary transformational generative grammarians.—*Eds.*]

mankind—tendencies which in other cases have led to forms or usages which are recognized by everybody as perfectly normal and unobjectionable. This is why the profoundest students of languages are often more tolerant than those who judge everything according to rule-of-thumb logic or to the textbooks of grammar that were the fashion in their own schooldays.

The arrangement of the whole matter in EEG is different from that in MEG. The reason is chiefly to be sought in the fact that the bigger work has gradually, under the pressure of various circumstances, developed into a series of monographs which do not, or do not yet, form a connected systematic whole. In the smaller book I had therefore to take up the question of the best way of presenting such a complicated matter as the grammatical structure of the English language. An important point was not to dismember the subject too much, not to break it up into many isolated details, but everywhere to treat together such facts as formed naturally connected wholes. In the phonological part, therefore, instead of taking each sound and its history separately, I have divided the matter according to the great comprehensive changes that have affected the sound-system as a whole. In this way—though I have not used the word phoneme and the new technical terms introduced by the recent "phonological" school developed especially in Prague—I think that I have done justice to the valuable theories advanced by that school, even more than in MEG and *Lehrbuch der Phonetik*,[3] in which some of its points of view may be found *in nuce*.

In what may be called the central part of the grammar the principle adduced above has led to the discarding of the usual division of grammar into the theory of forms (accidence, morphology), the theory of word-formation, and the theory of sentence and of the use of forms (syntax). Within each of these divisions the common practice is to subdivide according to the parts of speech (word-classes), having one chapter for substantives, another for adjectives, etc. In most grammars such things of prime importance, at any rate for the structure of English, as the use of the unchanged word and of word-order are treated very inadequately, while those things that are common to more than one word-class are torn asunder. Instead of this more or less traditional arrangement I have *divided the subject according to the principal categories* of a really grammatical order, dealing, within each of the chapters thus originated, with both forms and their use, comprising under "forms" both word-formation and word-order. My impression is that this arrangement serves better than any other to bring out what is really characteristic of the grammatical structure of the language

---

[3] [Jespersen was among the eminent phoneticians of his day. His textbook on phonetics had its second edition at Leipzig in 1913.—*Eds.*]

dealt with, but on the other hand it must be admitted that a similar arrangement would not have been possible to the same extent in any of the cognate languages. In Latin, Old English and German, to take only some of the best-known examples, the forms for case and number are so inextricably mixed up in substantives that it would be impossible or impracticable to deal with case and number separately. In the verbs we should be still less able to isolate the forms for person, number, and tense. The extent to which it is possible to treat each of these fundamental categories separately, thus enables us to measure how far the language concerned has advanced towards the ideal state in which the same grammatical sign has always the same meaning or function, and the same notion is always expressed by the same means.

I shall now follow the order of the chapters of EEG: on some of them I have only a few remarks, while on others there is more to say. . . .

7. Word-classes. In EEG no attempt is made to define logically what is understood by a substantive, an adjective, etc.[4] The traditional classification—with some small variations, it is true—has shown a persistent vitality through the ages, and in practice there is general agreement between grammarians, whether practical schoolmasters or historical students, as to the class to which each word in any given context should be assigned. But as soon as we begin to ask what is the underlying logical basis of the classification and to define each of the classes, difficulties arise into which it is not necessary to enter in a work of the character of EEG. Some would say that substantives denote things and what are conceived as things, and they would maintain that the difference between say *pride* and *proud*, *admiration* and *admire* is that the former word in each pair is thought of as a thing. But surely an ordinary mind has no such feeling when speaking of a woman's pride or of our admiration for the great poets—the definition really amounts to saying that pride and admiration are treated *grammatically* in the same way as names of things like pearls and trees, and the definition thus is nothing but a *circulus vitiosus*.

It may not be amiss to call attention to the fact that in ordinary parlance we extend the use of the word 'thing' so as to include what could not properly be called a 'thing', as in:

I shall speak to him the first thing in the morning. | The only thing left for us was to run away | Auth. Version Gen. 34.7 hee had wrought folly in Israel, in lying with Iacobs daughter; which thing ought not to be done | Carlyle, French Revolution 119. He finds no special notice taken of him at Versailles,—a thing the man of true worth is used to.

---

[4][By "logically" Jespersen means semantically: "a noun is the name of a person, place, or thing," etc.—*Eds.*]

When Wells's "First men in the moon" found traces of the activity of the lunar beings they said "they can make things and do things"—meaning in the first instance substantial things in the ordinary sense of the word, but by the second term nothing but "they act in various ways". In these sentences the reader may find some justification of the definition of "action substantives" as comprised under the term of 'things', but what about the following quotations?

Hart, Bellamy Trial 301 I wasn't beautiful or peaceful or gentle or gracious or gay or strong, but I made myself all those things for him | Benson, David Blaize 166 Why didn't you sit on it or something, when he came in? | Walpole, Silver Thorn 161 He simply felt that she had been badly treated—the very last thing she had been.

Here *thing* stands not for any substantive, but for an adjective, a verb or a participle. Cf. also Iago's "For I am nothing, if not criticall".

An adjective does not, as is often said . . . , denote a quality (for that is what a substantive like *beauty* or *pride* or *cleverness* does) but means "having a quality"—and that definition does not even fit all adjectives, but only "qualifiers" and alongside of these we have "quantifiers" like *many, numerous, few,* etc.[5]

A variant of the usual definitions is found in Alan H. Gardiner's recent important work *The Theory of Speech and Language* (Oxford 1932): "The so-called parts of speech are distinctions among words based not upon the nature of the objects to which they refer, but upon the mode of their presentation. Thus the name of anything presented *as* a thing is a 'noun', and the name of anything presented *as* an action or . . . *as* a process, is a 'verb'. In the verb *to cage*, reference is made to the thing called a *cage*, but it is not presented as a thing but as an action. In the noun *assassination* reference is made to an action, but it is not presented as an action but as a thing" (p. 10). "An adjective, on this view, is the name of a thing presented to the listener, not as a thing, but as an attribute" (p. 39).

Here I should first take exception to the example *cage*, for the relation between the substantive *cage* and the verb *I cage* = 'I shut up in a cage' is not the same as in other instances of grammatical homophones, like *fight, sleep, air, plant,* etc. When I use the verb *cage* I do not "present" a cage (which is a real thing) as an action, but speak of an action that has some relation to that thing. And if I say that a face is beautiful, I do not present a thing called *beauty* as an attribute to the face. I can see no other meaning in the verb *present* as here used than 'treat grammatically', and then we have the same *petitio principii* as above. But Dr. Gardiner promises further explanations of his view in his second volume.

---

[5] [Jespersen's note on the term *quantifier:* "I am glad to see that the latter expression, which I think I have coined myself, has been adopted by others, Mr. Ogden among them." Jespersen is the source for a good many other currently fashionable terms, such as *extraposition.—Eds.*]

It seems to me much more correct to say, as I virtually did in PG,[6] that what is denoted by most substantives is characterized by several qualities, not always easy to define, and that an adjective singles out some one quality, which is applicable to a variety of objects. The chief difficulty is with nexus-substantives, which are dealt with adequately in none of the current definitions, and which really form a class apart: *a dependent nexus concentrated into one word*, cf. below under 30.

Curme defines the verb as "that part of speech by means of which we make an assertion or ask a question".[7] Accordingly "Nonsense!" and "Where?" are verbs!

Verbs are generally in grammatical treatises as well as in dictionaries named in the infinitive, Lat. *amare*, Fr. *aimer*, G. *lieben*, etc., and correspondingly E. *love* or *to love*. I have preferred to give them in the finite form (*I*) *love*, because the finite forms are more characteristic of the real essence of verbs than the infinitive, which in many ways still retains some syntactical features of its substantival origin. With one class of English verbs it is also impossible to give the infinitive because it has no existence: *can, may, must*, etc. The usual practice is especially faulty when many grammarians, chiefly foreigners, speak of the rules for the use of *to be to*, for this infinitive with *to: to be to* (*write*) is practically non-existent. One might just as well give rules for the use of *to shall*. But it is of course perfectly natural and correct to speak of *I am to* (*write*) and give rules for that just as for *I shall* (*write*).

The last class, 'particles', contains adverbs, prepositions, coordinating and subordinating conjunctions. I have elsewhere (PG 88) given my reasons for treating these together: the difference between the various functions of one and the same word, e.g., *before* in "I have been here many times before", "many times before my marriage", and "many times before I was married" is not important enough to cause it to be placed in different categories; in one employment it is like an intransitive verb (has no object), in the others it is 'transitive' and has in one case a substantive, in another a clause as its object. . . .

As a matter of fact, I think it possible to gain a really valuable insight into the essential structure of the English language without any abstruse logical analysis of what a "word" or what a "substantive", etc., is. The important thing is that the student should recognize a substantive when he finds it, and that can be achieved through showing him a sufficient number

---

[6] [Jespersen's *Philosophy of Grammar*, now available in paperback (Norton Library, 1965), is solid evidence against the odd belief that his generation of scholarly grammarians were somehow averse to theory.—*Eds.*]

[7] [George O. Curme, *English Grammar* (Barnes & Noble paperback, 1947 *et seq.*), p. 22. This book is partly based on Curme's *College English Grammar* of 1925, which Jespersen is quoting. Curme is better remembered for his larger volumes, *Syntax* (1931) and *Parts of Speech and Accidence* (1935).—*Eds.*]

of specimens, just as a child learns to know a cat and a dog not through
any definition but by seeing a certain number of individuals and hearing
the appropriate word applied to them.

In a very short preliminary survey of the most important flexions of
these word-classes the term *base* is introduced for that form of the verb
which has no 'ending' and which according to circumstances can be used as
an infinitive, an imperative, a present indicative and a present subjunctive.
Next we go on to the "Derivation" of one word-class from another. The
examples given of the various classes comprise in a number of cases the
same form given under two or even three different headings. The form
taken by itself thus gives no clue to the class under which the word is to be
included, but if we see how the word 'behaves' towards other words and
how other words behave towards it in various circumstances, we obtain
tests by which we can tell whether such a form is a substantive, an adjective, an adverb or a verb: *fight* is a substantive if it can take *a* or *the* before
it, and if it adds *s* in the plural, but a verb if it is changed into *fought* when a
fight in the past time is thought of, if it adds *s* in the third person, etc. By
such tests we see that *love* is a substantive in *his former love for her*, but a
verb in *he did love her once*, and the two words are seen to be parallel to
admiration and *admire* respectively. *American* is sometimes a substantive
('two Americans arrive'), sometimes an adjective ('two American guests'),
cp. 'two Spaniards arrive' and 'two Spanish guests'. *Long* belongs to one
word-class in 'a long stay', to another in 'he stayed long', and to a third in
'I long to see her', etc., etc.

We have here one of the most characteristic features of the structure of
English, the number of 'grammatical homophones', but it would be entirely
wrong to describe this as the capacity in English of "using substantives as
verbs", etc., a substantive is always used as a substantive, a verb as a
verb, etc.

Some German linguistic thinkers see a trait of national psychology in the
frequency in English of phrases like *have a look, a shave, a smoke, take care,
give a glance, a kick*, etc.: they are taken as "gegenständliches denken" or
"objective thinking" with its preference for things or objects as more
concrete than the more abstract verbs. As the substantives used in these
phrases are not names of 'things', it seems more natural to see in the pre-
dilection of English for expressions of this kind the same purely grammatical
trait as in the numerous cases in which English has a small auxiliary in the
beginning of the sentence, which embodies the marks of tense, person, and
number, and reserves the really significant word (verb) for a later place:
he does (not) write, does he write, will he write, he has written, is he writing,
etc., etc.

In innumerable cases we derive verbs from substantives, substantives
from verbs, etc., without any distinctive ending, but this is not the only

way, and we are thus naturally led to those cases in which endings and similar means are used (*belief believe, strong strength strengthen, admire admiration, child childish, clever cleverness cleverly*, etc.). It will be seen that I have thus managed to squeeze in a bit—and a most important bit—of the theory of word-formation into this chapter. Other bits follow in other chapters.

8. Ranks. *Poor* in "the poor are always with us" is often said to be an adjective used substantively; other grammarians even say that it has become a substantive. *Stone* in *stone wall* is termed a substantive used adjectively or a substantive turned into an adjective. *Above* in *the above remark* is termed an adverb used adjectively or turned into an adjective; *my way* in *he would not look my way* is called an adverbial use of the substantive (with its pronoun). Clauses are divided into substantival clauses (or noun clauses), adjectival clauses (or adjective clauses) and adverbial clauses (or adverb clauses).

All these expressions are misleading because they use terms relating to the classification of words ('parts of speech') in speaking of a classification which has some points of similarities with this one but is really based on something fundamentally distinct—moves, as it were, in a different plane—namely the classification according to the 'rank' of a member of a grammatical combination. While the former classification concerns words only, so that it is possible in a dictionary to say what class a word belongs to, the distinction we are now going to deal with, concerns not only single words, but word groups, including clauses, and has no existence except in combinations actually found in connected purposive speech.

We have three grammatical ranks, here designated with Roman numerals:

I　Primary (this term is better than 'principal' which I used at first)

II　Secondary

III　Tertiary.

In "The French are a great nation" *the French* is an adjective primary, in "The Americans are a great nation" *the Americans* is a substantive primary; both *the French* and *the Americans* are thus primaries, but belong to different word-classes as shown by the fact that only *the Americans* has the flexional ending *s*. In the same way these groups can be the object of a verb, as in "I admire the French", "I admire the Americans", or the object of a preposition, as in "with the French", "with the Americans".

Examples of secondaries are: "a *French* actor", "a *Saturday-to-Monday* visit", "a *long* stay".

In some languages, e.g. German and Danish, it is not always easy to distinguish between adjectives that have become substantives and adjectives used as primaries. In English there may be a few doubtful cases, but in general we have indubitable criteria: *a black* and *the black* = 'negro' can stand by itself in the singular (with the definite and indefinite article), which an adjective like *poor* can not; it can form a plural *blacks* and a genitive: *the black's skin*. Curme thinks that I am wrong in denying the name of substantive to *the poor* because it has no *s* in the plural: he calls attention to the fact that some substantives have an unchanged plural. This is true, but all words from other word-classes that are turned into substantives, form their plurals regularly in *s*. And, as remarked, the plural is not the only thing which makes *black* into a substantive, different from adjectives. If language itself keeps two things distinctly apart as in Shakespeare's "Sweets to the sweet" he would be a bad grammarian who would persist in lumping them together as "adjectives that have become substantives".

Examples of tertiaries are: "he stayed *long*", "he stayed *a week*", "he stayed *from Saturday to Monday*", "he stood there *hat in hand*". (The term 'subjunct', which I used in former publications, is superfluous).

While a finite verb is always a secondary (to the subject, which is primary), participles and infinitives may according to circumstances be any of the three ranks.

The rank division is very important with regard to pronouns: some pronouns are always primaries (e.g. *I*, *mine*, *somebody*, *anything*), others are always secondaries (e.g. *every*, *my*), others again are used sometimes in one, sometimes in another rank, e.g. *that:* "that is true" (I), "that time" (II), "he was that angry" (III; vulgar). *None:* "none of his brothers" (I), "of none effect" (II; half archaic), "none the less" (III).

Clause primaries, secondaries and tertiaries are treated below.

From a logical point of view it is true that we have more ranks than the three, as a tertiary may be further determined, as in "an unusually well written article", where the tertiary *well* is determined by *unusually*, which thus might be called a logical quaternary, but as we nowhere find any *grammatical* criteria for such subordination, the three ranks are all that a grammarian needs distinguish.

The distribution into three ranks is found not only in sentences, where the subject and object are always primaries, but also within elements that constitute themselves one of the three ranks: the whole group "a very long time" is a primary in "a very long time passed", a tertiary in "he stayed there a very long time", but in both cases the group consists of the primary *time*, the secondary *long* and the tertiary *very* (*a* is also a secondary).

The theory of ranks as here outlined affords us means of expressing in a precise and natural way what with the usual grammatical terminology presents considerable difficulty, as when *what* is often called a substantival pronoun, which in *what branch* is made into an adjectival pronoun; in *what one* this adjectival pronoun is substantivized by *one*. Or: *top* is a substantive; in *top branch* it has become an adjective or an adjective-equivalent, but in *the top one* it is again substantivized. Instead it is better to say: *what* is always a pronoun, and *top* is always a substantive: in *what happened?* and *the top fell down* they are primaries, but in *what branch, what one, the top branch, the top one* they are secondaries to the primaries *branch* and *one*.

It is perhaps worth noticing that when we speak in grammar of a word 'governing' another, it is as a rule one belonging to a lower rank that governs one of a higher rank; a verb (II) governs an object (I), a preposition (III) governs an object (I), a conjunction (III) governs a clause (I): the conjunction + the clause may be either I, II or III.

9. Junction and nexus are terms introduced to designate two fundamentally different ways of combining primaries and secondaries. Typical examples are *the running dog*, junction: *running* (II) is adjunct to *dog* (I), and on the other hand *the dog runs*, nexus: *runs* (II) is adnex to *dog*. Other examples of nexus are: I saw (made) *the dog run*, I caused *the dog to run, the running of the dog*. In "he painted *the red door*" we have a junction, in "he painted *the door red*" a nexus.

There is more life, more dramatic movement in a nexus than in a junction which is like a picture.

In a junction we have one idea which is linguistically broken in two, as when instead of *a giant* we say *a tall man*, instead of *a stench, a disagreeable smell*. In a nexus, on the other hand, two distinct ideas are combined to represent a process—the ways in which this combining is effected are described in chapter 10 (independent nexus) and 29–35 (dependent nexus).

The relation between a primary and an adjunct is in some cases quite simple and logical (a red door, the Pacific Ocean, a criminal action), in others more complicated and subject to idiomatic restrictions (a Pacific Islander, a criminal lawyer).

Combinations akin to, but not exactly identical with, junctions are found in *Mr. Smith, Miss Smith, Lydia Smith, Miss Lydia Smith*, etc. This leads to various kinds of apposition, as in *Sven Hedin, the celebrated explorer* or *they were all of them drunk, they neither of them looked up*, and this again to 'loose' or 'unattached participles', which are condemned in most cases, but are considered perfectly legitimate e.g. in "Strictly speaking, he ought to have been punished". A new term is wanted for elements which stand outside the sentence while in it they are represented by a pronoun: "He was a great novelist, that Charles Dickens", "Inferiority complex—what exactly does that mean". In such cases I speak of *extraposition;* thus I say that the infinitive or the clause is in extraposition in "it is difficult to account for this" or "it struck me that he was decidedly paler than usual". Extraposition is extremely frequent in French, e.g. *moi* je dis ça; je dis ça, *moi; le capitaine* où est-il?

In this chapter as in the preceding one a few new terms have been introduced, but it will be found on closer inspection that they, too, are very useful in describing accurately various grammatical phenomena which otherwise would have to be designated by long and necessarily vague circumlocutions.

10. Under *sentence-structure* we naturally deal first with that type of sentence which is by many scholars considered the normal type, by others even the only one deserving the name of sentence, namely the combination of a subject and a predicate, the latter having as its chief constituent part a finite verb. In our terminology this is an independent nexus: the subject is a primary, and the verb a secondary. But there may be two primaries: a subject and an object, or even three, as there may be two objects.

In some words (pronouns) a case-form serves to distinguish the subject from the object, but an even more important way of distinguishing them is word-order, and thus we are naturally led to a consideration of the most important rules for word-order. The usual order is S (subject)—V (verb)— O (object), but in some cases (questions, exclamations, parenthetical insertions, sentences with a preposed negative) there is an opposite tendency to have V before S; the consequence is the compromise with a small auxiliary verb before S and the important verb after S: v—S—V—O: Could John see Henry | Did John see H? | Never did I see the like, etc. Other exceptions to the general rule (when, e.g., the object is an interrogative or relative pronoun) have also to be considered here: parts of the important, but too often neglected theory of word-order thus find a natural place here at the very beginning of the syntactical chapters.

Sometimes the subject is not expressed: Thank you! | Confound it! etc., and even more than the subject may be left out (by "prosiopesis", an expression which however is not used in "Essentials"): (Have you) got a match? (I shall) see you again tomorrow. Very often a sentence consists only of a predicative: Splendid! How annoying! In these cases it is legitimate (though I have preferred not to use these expressions in EEG) to speak of "ellipsis" or "omission", because it is easy to see what is left out ("understood"), but it is not legitimate to speak of such sentences as imperfect or incomplete: the meaning is expressed just as completely and intelligibly as in the most perfectly balanced sentence containing a subject and a finite verb. Nor is the ellipsis-explanation legitimate in a great many cases in which grammarians of the old school are fond of using it: it is a dangerous weapon, which should be used very sparingly indeed.

It can never be applied to *amorphous* sentences, which are frequently called forth by strong emotion and in which it would be perfectly futile to look for something that is left out or understood, or to say what 'part' of a sentence they are: they range from 'inarticulate' sounds like clicks (*Tck! Tut!* and others for which our alphabet is totally inadequate) through *Hm! Hurrah! Yes!* to words and word-groups that can be used as parts of sentences of the first type: Thanks! What? Nonsense! An aeroplane! This way, ladies! Oh, those women! There is surely no reason why such exclamations should not be recognized as complete and perfectly normal sentences.

The terms 'main sentence' and 'main clause' are superfluous. They are often used of what remains when 'dependent clauses' are removed, but that would mean that in a sentence like "What I cannot understand is that John got angry when he heard the way in which they spoke of his father" the 'main sentence' or 'main clause' consists only of the small word *is!* It is much better to use the term *sentence* of the whole and *clause* (not 'dependent clause') of any part of a sentence which contains a dependent nexus and resembles a sentence in its structure (ch. 33 ff.).

11. Relation of verb to subject and object. Here again some of the usual definitions do not hold water. The subject cannot be defined by means of such words as active and agent, for they do not cover such cases as "He lost his father in the war" or "he was surprised" or "the garden swarms with bees" (otherwise expressed "bees swarm in the garden"). Nor can the object be defined as the person or thing directly affected by the action, for in "John loves Ann", "John sees the moon" John is more directly affected than Ann or the moon. All this is a direct consequence of the many-sidedness of the relations that are found in human life and have to be expressed in human language.

A logical analysis will in each case bring out one or more things ('things' or 'persons') having relation to the action or state implied in the verb; if there is only one it is the subject, if there are two, the one that stands in the closest relation to the verb is its subject, the other the object; if three, the more or less close relation determines them as being subject, direct and indirect object. An indirect object can better be dispensed with than a direct object, and that than the subject, but the difference is one of degree only. Many ideas expressed by means of a verb are such that they have relation to one primary only, they are permanently intransitive; but most verbs may at any rate occasionally have relation to two (or three) primaries; if the more remote of these is not expressed they are used intransitively (I shall pay; he plays well), otherwise they are used transitively (I shall pay the bill, pay the driver, pay the driver two shillings; he plays golf, or the violin, etc.). Tertiaries stand in a looser relation to the verb than either subject or object (I shall pay the bill the day after tomorrow), but sometimes it is difficult to draw a sharp line between object and tertiary (it costs two shillings).

In "he happened to fall" the notional subject is a nexus "he . . . to fall": that is what happened. In such cases I use the term "split subject". In "the path is easy to find" it is not completely satisfactory to say that "the path" is the subject and that the infinitive is used as a subordinate (supine-like) supplement or complement to *easy:* the curious thing is that *the path,* which is formally the subject of the sentence is at the same time as it were the object of *find:* what is easy is to find the path. Several phenomena of a related character have to be examined though it is not important to invent special terms for them.

Various types of objects have always been more or less recognized by grammarians (result: he built a house; he dreamt a curious dream; instrument: she nodded her head). Though these and the constructions of many verbs with both direct and indirect object are, of course, treated fully in the grammar, they require no remarks in this paper. I shall only mention here that the chapter dealing with objects has been chosen as the best place in which to deal with reflexive and reciprocal pronouns as the linguistic expression of the fact that subject and object are, completely or partially, identical. Under direct and indirect object some new sections are added to the theory of word-order: he showed the strangers the way; he gave it me, etc. This chapter also deals with transitivity and intransitivity, among other things the curious use in "His plays won't act, and his poems won't sell", as well as the transitivity of some adjectives which can take an object: "he is not worth his salt".

12. Passive. By means of a passive instead of an active turn the relation between the two primaries connected with a verb is reversed. The chief reasons why a passive turn is used are (1) the active subject is unknown, (2) it is self-evident, (3) considerations of tact or delicacy, (4) greater interest in the passive than in the active subject, (5) ease of connexion with another sentence. In the recent development by which that which in the active is the indirect object may be made the subject of the passive, the greater interest generally felt for persons than for things has played a role no less than the loss of the distinctive case-forms. In "everybody laughed at Jim" *Jim* may be considered the object of the whole combination verb + preposition, and consequently may be made the subject of the passive: "Jim was laughed at by everybody"; in set phrases modern English goes even further: "She will be taken good care of". In this sentence as well as in "He was offered a reward" we see that a passive verb can have an object.

13. Predicatives. A distinction should be made between the two terms predicate and predicative. The former is the more comprehensive term: in "He was angry with me for speaking ill of his brother" everything except *he* is the predicate, but only *angry* is the predicative. Many logicians, and even some grammarians, are in the habit of analysing every sentence as containing a copula (link-verb) and a predicative, thus forcing all sentences into the same Procrustean bed without much regard to common sense or

to idiom, for in English at any rate "he talks French" and "he is talking French" are not the same thing.

The best way of dealing grammatically with predicatives is not the usual one of starting with sentences containing the colourless verb *is*, but to take these as the final or nearly final links in a long series of descriptions, in which we pass from instances of extraposition ("There he sat, a giant among dwarfs") through gradual transitions ("We parted the best of friends", "he married young") to constructions in which the verb loses more of its full concrete force ("The natives go naked all the year", "she stood godmother to his child", "he stood about six feet high") and finally to constructions with verbs like *seem, prove, sound, look, be, remain, become,* etc. After these we may treat the numerous sentences in which not even a colourless link-verb is used; an interesting class contains those ironic exclamations in which a negative meaning is imparted: "He a gentleman!"; cf. also "Pretty mess we shall be in by then!" Such sentences present many interesting features which are inadequately treated in ordinary grammars.

In connexion with the question what can be a predicative it will be natural to treat the rules for the use or non-use of the definite and indefinite article in predicatives, as well as the idiomatic English use of abstract words as predicatives (as in "when I was your age" and "she turned lead-colour").

In EEG I have not thought it necessary to speak of the logical meaning of *is* with a predicative, though I have treated it at some length elsewhere, but as my view has been criticized, I may say a little more on this matter here. In rare cases only *is* means perfect identity, what logisticians denote by the sign ≡: everyday language has little use for such judgments of identity ("So that's that!"). *Is* generally means 'belongs to (is one part, or one member of) the class denoted by the predicative'. The subject thus is more special than the predicative. Therefore we understand that when one of the two is a proper name, this is nearly always the subject, and we see the reason why the predicative is so often provided with the indefinite article ("He is a liar"). Adjectives are as a rule less special than substantives, hence their frequent use in the predicative position ("The flower was white").

Now it has recently been objected to my view (by Brøndal, *Morfologi og syntax* (1932), p. 96) that it is easy to find examples in which the subject is less special than the predicative. Three examples are given; let me take the last one first: "All is vanity". But surely the meaning of this is that vanity is so comprehensive a category that whatever you may mention falls within it. The sentence thus confirms instead of refuting my contention. The same is really true of the negative sentence "nothing is more foolish" because its actual meaning is "everything [else] is less foolish"—in other words "this [what you say] is more foolish than anything else, this belongs to the class comprising the most foolish things".

Finally we have the sentence "This is to be medieval Paris by night" ("Dette skal være Paris ved nat i middelalderen", better translated: "This is meant to be, or This represents . . ."). But surely *this* is as special, as concrete as possible, and the actual meaning is "What you see here is [part of] medieval Paris by night".

Brøndal says "The more or less abstract pronouns which stand at the beginning of the sentence as subjects are undoubtedly in themselves much more general [langt almenere] than the final elements which are to be taken as predicatives [attribut]". As already remarked *this* at any rate is not abstract, and *all* and *nothing* are difficult to class as either abstract or concrete. Brøndal also does justice to my view when he goes on to say that I seem to aim not at the meaning of words as such, but rather at the actual nuance in which the word is used in the given situation and context. Yes, exactly: I always like to move in the concrete everyday world and try to find out rules for sentences as these are actually spoken and understood in practical life.

14. Case. In many pronouns we have distinct case-forms: *I me, he him, who whom*, etc. What names are we to use for these? It seems best to call them nominative and objective: historically the latter case corresponds in form to the Old English dative, but has taken over the functions of the OE accusative as well: it would be misleading to use either of these terms to the exclusion of the other and even more misleading to use both, calling *me* an accusative in "she sees me" and a dative in "she gives me a penny".

With regard to the use of these forms English is at present in a stage of transition, in which the old way of distinguishing is giving way to a new system. The psychological causes of this change, as well as of the exclusive use of *you* in colloquial English, where the old language distinguished four forms *thou thee ye you*, were examined in *Progress in Language* 1894 (this chapter reprinted in *Chapters on English*). Some parts of this disquisition have found their way into EEG. Here I shall only call attention to the interesting fact not fully explained in my previous book that one and the same formula may be applied to the personal and to the interrogative-relative pronouns though seemingly the development has gone in two directions, towards the use of the objective instead of the nominative in the personal pronouns, and the use of the nominative *who* instead of the objective *whom:* In both cases the tendency is to use the old nominative exclusively in immediate conjunction with a verb: I go | do I go | who goes | Who did you see? | Who is that letter from?—but to use the old objective in all other positions: Not me! | What would you do if you were me? | he is bigger than me | is she as tall as me? In the case of *who* curiously enough the only two combinations in which *whom* is still naturally used are after *than* (Mr. N. than whom no one is more competent to form a judgment), where *whom* was thought incorrect a few centuries ago but is now recognized by everybody—and concatenated clauses like "children whom we think are hungry", where nearly all grammarians agree in considering *whom* a gross error. It is well worth observing that these are really the only instances in which the pronoun is not followed immediately by a finite verb—this is what the popular feeling has seized on so as to arrive at a rule similar to that obtaining with regard to *me*, etc.

In the substantives we have no case-distinction corresponding to that between *I* and *me*, but on the other hand a genitive: this case is found only with some of the pronouns (its, his, whose, and then nobody's etc.); while in others we have the so-called possessive pronouns: *my mine, your yours*, etc.

The man thus has the same functions as *I* and *me*. Now what term are we to use for this case? Obviously neither nominative, accusative, dative nor objective would be adequate, and I see no better way than to use Sweet's name 'common case' (though Sonnenschein with some right asks: Common to what?).

It will be seen that I recognize only a small number of cases in modern English—smaller than in OE or Latin—and not the same number for substantives as for pronouns. . . . The number of cases to be recognized in a language (at one particular stage of its development) must be decided by the forms found in that language: case-distinctions are not notional or logical, but exclusively grammatical categories. No purely logical analysis can lead to a distinction between nominative, accusative, dative, etc. Nor can a comparison with other languages and their case-distinctions be regarded as decisive, for that would lead to consequences which no grammarian would accept. Some languages, even among those akin to English, have an instrumental case: shall we therefore recognize an instrumental in "throw stones"? Some languages have a special case, or even two special cases in which predicatives are put: shall we say that 'a teacher' is in the "predicative" case in "he is a teacher" and in the "illative" in "he became a teacher"? Thus we might continue—there is no end to the number of cases we might in this way be led to admit. . . .

15. Person. It is perhaps to be regretted that the word person should have been used in grammar from very old times of the distinction between (1) speaker, (2) spoken to, (3) neither speaker nor spoken to. This is the correct definition of 'the third person', for 'what is spoken of' applies to the subject, no matter what 'person' it is. *It* and *what* and *the sun* are all of them 'third persons' though, of course, not 'persons' in the ordinary non-grammatical sense. *We* is not a typical 'first person' in the same way

as *I*, of which it is said to be the plural, for it comprises either the second person or one or more belonging to the third person: hence the distinction made in some languages between an inclusive and an exclusive 'we'. Of this we have a feeble reverberation in English, in so far as *let us* is pronounced *let's* only when it is = myself + the person or persons addressed, so that it means an exhortation to common action (*let's go* = 'allons-nous-en, gehen wir'), but otherwise keeps the vowel of *us* (*let us go* = 'set us free', 'permettez-nous d'aller'). The dubious 'personal' character of *we* is also reflected in the hesitation between "most of us lost our heads" and "lost their heads". . . .

16–18. Pronouns. Many things concerning pronouns are dealt with in other chapters, namely those things that they have in common with other words (ranks, number, case, also person). In these chapters they are dealt with individually, and distributed into three sub-classes. Pronouns are indicators, and the indication may be either definite or indefinite or finally one of totality.

Among the pronouns of definite indication we have first those generally termed personal, which may be defined pronouns of contextual identification, because what they import in each case is nearly always made clear by the context or situation. The same is true to some extent of the pronouns of pointing (demonstrative in the true sense) which may be said to be parallel to the three persons, at any rate if there is a tripartition: *this* (with the pronominal adverbs *here* and *now*) referring to *I*, *that* (with *there* and *then*) to *you*, and *yon* (with *yonder*) to *he*, etc. But the distinction between the second and third person is not carried through in English, as *that* (with *there, then*) to a great extent has taken over the part of *yon* (*yonder*) which is nearly obsolete.

When such pronouns are called definite, it should be borne in mind that this is true of nearly all cases in which they are used, but that they are sometimes used idiomatically in such a way that it is at any rate difficult to see exactly what they refer to. Thus we have unspecified *it* in "it rains"; "we must have it out some day"; "you will catch it"; unspecified *they* in "they say he was murdered", unspecified *those* in "there are those who believe it", etc. Such uses can only be accounted for from the essential vagueness of the human mind, whose expressions cannot always be forced into strict logical compartments.

The, "the definite article", is *that* with a weakening of the demonstrative force. *The* in a great many cases also refers to the context or situation: this is "the article of complete determination". In other cases it has to be supplemented by some other determining word or words, e.g. "the man we are talking about", "the man in the moon", "the plays of Shakespeare": this is "the article of incomplete determination". The use of the definite article in any of the languages in which it is found presents so many idiomatic features that it is no wonder that most grammarians are apt to give either too strict or too loosely worded rules and often fail to see the logical reasons underlying the various usages.

Among pronouns of definite indication we have also *same*, the pronoun of identity, and *such*, the pronoun of similarity, and then a group which most people will be surprised to see included in this class, namely the relatives. But it seems clear that *who* in "the man who said that" is just as definite as "the man . . . he said that"—very often in colloquial speech *he* is used where literary language uses the relative—and that the only difference is that the relative pronoun serves to underline the connexion with what precedes by subordinating the nexus in which it occurs instead of coordinating it with the main nexus.

In the sub-class of pronouns of indefinite indication we meet first *one* and its weaker counterpart the indefinite article, the treatment of which presents difficulties similar to those encountered with *the;* then the 'pronoun of difference' *other* (the exact opposite of *same*) and a word which is not always considered a pronoun, viz. *a certain*, which may be termed the 'pronoun of discretion', because it serves in a curious way the purpose of indicating that the man or thing spoken of is definite enough in the mind of the speaker, but is purposely left indefinite in a communication to the hearer. Its pronominal character is shown by the use in the plural in a way other adjectives do not admit: 'certain of his friends pretend . . . '.

Further this class comprises *some*, the 'pronoun of unspecified quantity', and the two 'pronouns of indifference', *any* and *either*, the latter referring to two only, while *any* is used of indifferent choice among a greater number. And finally we reckon among pronouns of indefinite indication all interrogative pronouns. Their inclusion in this sub-class is analogous to that of the relative pronouns (chiefly the same forms) in the previous sub-class: an interrogative *who, which, what* besides being indefinite imparts an exhortation to the hearer to solve the uncertainty of the speaker by a definite answer.

The third sub-class 'pronouns of totality' are partly positive: *all, both, each, every*, partly negative: *no (none)* and *neither*. It is easy to see that these are really neither definite nor indefinite and therefore must form a class of their own. . . .

20–21. Number. Here . . . the notional (natural) categories are simple enough, but the grammatical expressions are more complicated. Naturally we distinguish between 1, 2, 3, 4 . . . in a series extending as far as we care to go (when we don't care to go further we speak of 'infinite' numbers), and it is also natural to single out *one* and lump together what is more than one as 'plural' and to give linguistic expression to that idea. Further, it is natural to have expressions for indefinite numbers: *some sixty, sixty odd, many, few,* etc. *Some* with a singular substantive is also indefinite: perhaps one, perhaps a little more or less: "he stayed here some week."

It is a great advantage of the English language that secondary words are so often indifferent with regard to number: the *red* rose, the *red* roses; I *can* sing, we *can* sing; he *went,* they *went.* Still some secondary words make a distinction between singular and plural: *this* rose, *these* roses; he *goes,* they *go.* Where such distinctions exist, they are apt to create difficulties, but the number of these is smaller in English than in most related languages.

Though many grammarians use the word *collective* in a very loose way, it is possible—and important—to give a logically consistent meaning to this term if we understand that it is logically the opposite of *mass-word,* with which idea it is often confused: a *collective* is logically at the same time one and more than one, it means a higher unit, but still a unit though consisting of more than one, and as it is a unit it is possible to form a new plural from it. Examples are *family, nation, party;* (a cricket) *eleven;* a *dozen,* etc. Some words may be used metaphorically of a body of persons: the *Bench* (= judges), the *town.* This double-sidedness of collectives gives rise to various interesting grammatical phenomena.

Mass-words are totally different, logically they are neither singular nor plural because what they stand for is not countable. But as a natural consequence of the grammatical structure of our languages any substantive has to be formally either a singular or a plural, so we have singular mass-words such as *gold, tea,* and plural mass-words like *embers, dregs.* The same applies to immaterial mass-words: singular *leisure, knowledge,* plural *mathematics, measles* (but these are often treated grammatically as singulars). It is not possible linguistically to keep the category of mass-words clearly distinct from countables because many words are used in both capacities: *much cake, many cakes; his hair is sprinkled with grey = he has some grey hairs,* etc.

We speak of *generic number* when an assertion is made equally applicable to each member of a whole class. Linguistically there is no fixed rule for such cases: sometimes the singular, sometimes the plural is used, sometimes there is no article, sometimes the definite and sometimes the indefinite article, so that the italicized words in the following sentences are really on the same footing logically speaking: *Man* is mortal; *a cat* has nine lives; *the dog* is vigilant; *dogs* are vigilant; *the English* are fond of out-door sports. We must specially mention the use of mass-words without the article: *Lead* is heavier than *iron; art* is long, etc.

The uncertainty in all such cases shows that we have here to do with a notional, not a grammatical category. . . .

28. Affirmation, Negation, Question. A question implies a request to the hearer(s) to answer. (Other requests, asking the hearer to act in a specified

way, are expressed by means of imperatives, of amorphous sentences like "Two third returns Brighton" or "Hands up!", or of other sentences pronounced in a commanding tone, e.g. "You will pack at once and leave this house", etc.).

Among affirmative sentences we must specially mention emphatic statements; and common to all the three categories here treated is the extensive use of *do*, . . . by which an auxiliary attracting the marks for person, number and tense is placed first and the real significant word comes later without any flexional marks. In this chapter again we have occasion to speak of the important role played in English by word-order.

Next come seven chapters dealing with dependent nexuses.

29. The simplest form consists of a mere collocation of a primary and an adnex. The nexus itself may be an object or a tertiary, but the essential one-ness of these two constructions is overlooked in ordinary grammars, in which the first is termed variously "accusative of the direct object and an objective predicate", "accusative with the predicative", "predicative of object" or "double object" and the second "absolute construction" ("absolute nominative" or "absolute accusative", "absolute participle"). Examples of the first are "we found *the cage empty, the bird gone;* she thought him *a great scholar;* she made *him happy;* he painted *the door red;* this drove *him mad;* he had *a tooth out;* he slept *himself sober;* you cannot explain *this away;* after a preposition: don't speak with *your mouth full;* she sat with *the colour quite gone from her face";* etc. etc. Examples of the second kind (nexus tertiaries) are: "*All things considered* the offer seems reasonable; *that being so*, he wasted no words on the matter; he tumbled down *head foremost;* he stood there, *hat in hand* and *pipe in mouth*". [8] It will be seen that the name "absolute participle" is not felicitous, for no participle is required—and "absolute" is not to the point.

It is easy to see that in each of these combinations we have not a junction, but as clear a nexus as in clauses like "we found that the cage was empty", "when all things are considered", etc. But of course this is not the same thing as saying that we have here "abridged" clauses: synonyms are not grammatically identical, and clauses cannot be considered the "real thing", of which the other constructions are only substitutes. Besides, it is not easy everywhere to find a clause expressing exactly the same idea as that found in the nexus-constructions.

30. Nexus-substantives. These are generally denoted by the unmeaning name of "abstracts", and their real essence as implying a nexus is over-

---

[8] [The editors have italicized the dependent nexuses.—*Eds.*]

looked. There are two kinds, one containing the idea of a predicative (*pride* = being proud; *kindness* = being kind, etc.) and the other containing the idea of a verb (*sleep, fight, conquest, examination:* nomina actionis—but can sleep be termed an action?).

The most interesting thing in connexion with these words is the way in which that element which in a sentence (with a finite verb) would be the subject or an object is expressed in connexion with a nexus-substantive. As to the predicative nexus-words there is little difficulty, as there can be only one member combined with them, which then is put in the genitive (the woman's pride, her pride, kindness, etc.) or expressed by an *of*-phrase (the pride, kindness of the woman). With the verbal nexus-substantives there are two possibilities, and if we have a genitive, we therefore distinguish between a subjective and an objective genitive, as in *the Doctor's arrival* and *the Doctor's defeat*, respectively. We may say that in the first case the substantive is taken in an active, in the second in a passive sense. In both instances an *of*-phrase may be substituted for the genitive.

In some cases both what would be the subject and what would be the object are expressed, as in "his avoidance of my brother", and as with full verbs in the passive there is now a tendency to use the preposition *by:* "The reception of the guests by Lady Miller" (= Lady Miller's reception of the guests). Those who use case-terms for prepositional phrases are here confronted with a difficulty: can *by Lady Miller* be termed a subjective genitive? If so, would the term be extended to the parallel use in "The guests were received by Lady Miller?" And is *over matter* in "the control of mind over matter" an objective genitive? Is it not better to avoid all such case-terms?

31. The gerund. In English this is always formed with the ending *-ing* which is also used for the first participle, and this coincidence involves some questions of great historical and theoretical interest which will not, however, be dealt with in this place. The gerund is a nexus-substantive, which differs from other nexus-substantives, in so far as it has acquired some of the syntactical peculiarities of finite verbs: it can have an adverb (tertiary) joined to it, it has a perfect and a passive; this verbal character is also manifested when it can take an object without *of* and when it can have a subject preposed in the common case. . . .

32. The Infinitive. Nothing is really gained by defining the infinitive as "the most general form of the verb", or "the verb-form that expresses the verbal notion without predicating it of any subject" or "that form of the verb which denotes action or existence without limitation of person, number or tense". This last definition is obviously wrong as far as many languages are concerned, for in Portuguese, for instance, we have infini-

tives inflected as to person and number, and numerous languages have tense-forms in the infinitive (Greek, Latin; cf. also the English perfect infinitive). And what does it mean to say that the infinitive does not predicate the verbal notion of any subject? The same can be said of such a form as *can* or *may* or any Danish present like *skriver:* only when a subject is mentioned, such forms predicate the verbal notion of the subject, but then they do it effectively,—and the same is true of the infinitive in connexions like "he made the horse run". Further it should be remembered that many languages have a so-called historical infinitive, which predicates just as well as any finite form. Nor is anything gained by ranging the infinitive as one of the "moods" of the verb.

Comparative grammar long ago discovered that the infinitive in our (Aryan) family of languages was originally a verbal substantive (nomen actionis) i.e. what is here called a nexus-substantive. And though the infinitive has in many ways lost much of its substantival character and has adopted many syntactical constructions originally reserved for finite verb-forms, it has never lost its capacity of expressing a nexus. Hence its place in my system after nexus-substantives and gerunds and before (dependent) clauses, which generally contain a finite verb. . . .

33–35. Clauses are distributed according to their rank into primary, secondary and tertiary clauses. Among the first a special name is needed for those that are commonly called 'noun-clauses' or 'substantive clauses' as in "I believe that he is ill". Curme (in his review of my vol. III) thinks that my reason for objecting to the name of noun clause is that these clauses have not the formal characteristics of a noun; but, as I have said expressly (III.2.1), I have three reasons, (1) these clauses are not really nouns or substantives, but have only one quality in common with substantives, namely that of being able to stand as primaries, (2) the same quality is found also in many interrogative and relative clauses, (3) I prefer using the word 'noun' in the original and wider sense in which it comprises both substantives and adjectives. I am glad to find that Collinson speaks of my words *content-clause* and *contact-clause* as "neat word-coinages designed to embody his [my] classifications with sharper relief".

Examples of interrogative clauses that are subjects or objects, thus primaries, are "How he got there was the problem", "I don't know how he got there", "All depends on how he got there". There is some tendency to do without a preposition before such a clause . . . .

Examples of relative clauses as primaries are "Who steals my purse steals trash", "Whoever says so is a liar", "What money I have is at your disposal", "You may marry whom you like", "You may dance with whom you like". Unfortunately it is not quite superfluous to state expressly that it is the whole relative clause that is the subject, the object of the verb, or the object of the preposition, in such cases, and not an imaginary *he*, etc., to which the relative clause is an adjunct. . . .

36. Retrospect. This gives a morphological survey of the various grammatical means employed in English: the unchanged word, stress and tone, other phonetic modifications, endings, separate roots (what German scholars call *suppletivwesen*), form-words (empty words like auxiliaries, prepositions, etc.) and word-order. This synopsis might have been supplemented with a similar review of the notions expressed grammatically; but this has been deemed superfluous, seeing that such a survey is really already contained in the headings of most of the chapters, together with remarks in the chapters themselves. The fullest conspectus of that kind is the one found in the "Notional survey of time-expressions", 26.9.

In connexion with this retrospect there is a small collection of grammatical synonyms, like "Shakespeare's plays—the plays of Shakespeare", "I beg your pardon—What did you say?", etc. They serve to illustrate what ought to be an axiom in all linguistic disquisitions, namely that the mere fact that two constructions or expressions mean the same thing is not sufficient to class them together grammatically or to use the same grammatical term in speaking of them. But grammarians often sin against this fundamental principle, as has already been pointed out in some of the preceding pages. It is the same fallacy that is at the bottom of such expressions in recent books as the following: . . . "*To trifle with* in *He is not a man to trifle with* is an abridged relative clause". "*He is unkind to all opposing him* contains an abridged dative clause". "*Happened* is adverbial in *he happened to fall*". "The ing in *missed being, kept recurring*, is only an apparent object, the governing verb being in reality a modifier only". "The *to* of the infinitive has become a conjunction, so that we speak of a *to*-clause just as we speak of a *that*-clause: I am not eager to go". In all such cases— and they might be multiplied—we are according to my view justified in speaking of squinting-grammar—grammar squinting at translations in other languages or at other constructions in the same language—instead of looking straight before one, as one should always try to do.

The man who wants to write "Essentials of English Grammar" is confronted with a great many difficulties. Often he will hesitate what to include and what to leave out: for what is essential and what not? Then there is the elusive character of much of the matter itself. Usage wavers on many points. English Grammar forms a system—but is not everywhere systematic. What is distinctly notional and what is purely grammatical should be kept apart—but to make the distinction is not always an easy matter. Grammatical phenomena can, and should, be looked at from two angles: from without and from within. The former is the morphological, the latter the syntactic point of view—but sometimes one and sometimes the other presses forward as the more important. Perfect lucidity and precision is impossible without a good terminology—but the usual grammatical terms are often unsatisfactory and insufficient. Hence the necessity of coining a few new terms. There are thus many pitfalls for the grammarian—not to mention those occasioned by the fact that English is not the writer's mother-tongue. Let me hope I have not fallen into too many of them.

Study Questions

1. Is Jespersen, like Brown, primarily concerned with correctness? In his discussion of EEG 10, does Jespersen condemn "amorphous sentences"? What explanations, other than perversity or ignorance, does he suggest for what is called bad grammar? Why does he say, in his discussion of EEG 11, that the old simple definitions of grammatical relations cannot stand? Would Jespersen agree with Brown that language is "an attribute of reason," or does he derive the traits of language (EEG 16–18) from other qualities of the human mind?

2. In the discussion of EEG 32, does Jespersen treat the infinitive as a substantive (noun) or as a verb? Where does he place the infinitive in his system of analysis? How would you characterize the description (EEG 9) of "the relation between a primary and an adjunct"? What does Jespersen consider "the best way of dealing grammatically with predicatives" (EEG 13)? Elsewhere Jespersen spoke of English grammar as "not always consistent or perfect" but "living and developing under continual fluctuations and undulations"; could you relate his use of "scalar" description (where everything is clear at A and B, but there are indistinct stages in between) to this conception of the English language? Can syntactic irregularity be precisely described?

3. Jespersen rejects "the usual division of grammar into the theory of forms . . . , the theory of word-formation, and the theory of [the] sentence," and gives instead his own definitions of morphology and syntax (EEG 36): what are they? Does the greater part of his book move from forms through functions to meanings, or from meanings through functions to forms? What does Jespersen mean by "generic number" (EEG 20–21), and with which article is it expressed in

English? Is the category notional or grammatical? Can grammar be distinguished from semantics?

4. What word-classes or parts of speech (EEG 7) does Jespersen recognize? Why does he not try to define them? Does he think that brief definitions would be necessary for less advanced students? When he says that "a substantive is always used as a substantive, a verb as a verb," does he mean (for example) that nouns cannot be used as adjectives (*a stone wall*) or adjectives as nouns (*sick people, a room for the sick, a sick room*)?

5. In Jespersen's system of ranks, is a noun always a primary, or an adjective always a secondary? To what ranks does he assign adverbs, finite verbs, prepositions, conjunctions, pronouns, articles, participles, infinitives, clauses? How could the phrase *the furiously barking dog* justify the decision that *barks* in *The dog barks furiously* is a secondary?

6. Consider the following diagram:

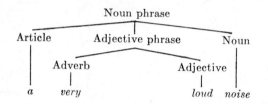

To what ranks would Jespersen assign the noun phrase as a whole the adjective phrase, each of the individual words? What do *a, very* and the adjective phrase each modify?

7. Jespersen's system allows for just three ranks, though in a sentence like the following there might seem to be six:

He gave a not quite absolutely indecently absolute refusal.

i ii   ii vi v   iv   iii   ii   i

What is the rank of *refused*, and what is the rank of *absolutely*, in *He refused absolutely?* Is the change of rank from *absolutely* (iii) to *absolute* (ii), or from *refused* (ii) to *refusal* (i), accompanied by a change in form? Do *absolute* and *absolutely* belong to the same part of speech, or do *refused* and *refusal?* Does *absolutely* change either its form or its part of speech when its rank shifts from iii to iv? To what one part of speech do all three words belong in the phrase *not quite absolutely?* Why, then, did Jespersen limit his ranks to three?

8. Of the two expressions *Deans seem mean* and *mean deans*, which contains both a predicate and a predicative (EEG 13)? Which shows only the adjective-noun relation, not the subject-verb relation? Which contains a single word that belongs to the same rank and class as the whole expression? Which expression is a junction, and which a nexus (EEG 9)? From the sentence *He found happiness in temperance and industry*, can one conclude that he (whoever he was) was industrious, that he was temperate, and that he was happy? Can a nexus consist of only one word? Can a junction? Between junction and nexus, what differences can you state?

9. To what single sentences can you relate the two sentences *It happened* and *He fell* (EEG 11)? How many nexuses are there in *The path is easy to find?* If *he* is a definite pronoun, and if the two sentences *The man looked drunk* and *He was driving* can be related to *The man who was driving looked drunk*, is relative *who* a definite pronoun or an indefinite? How does Jespersen classify it (EEG 16–18)? How does he classify interrogative pronouns? Could his classification be supported by relating the question *Who stole my watch?* to the statement *Someone stole my watch?* To what sentences (independent nexuses) can you relate the nexus-substantive *the reception of the guests by Lady Miller* (EEG 30)? Could the concept of nexus be used to show how one sentence is related to another, or how complicated sentences can be analyzed as combinations of simple ones?

10. According to Jespersen (EEG 11), *Bees swarm in the garden* is another way of saying *The garden swarms with bees;* do the two sentences therefore have the same structure at some deep level? Since an object of result, like *house* in *He built a house*, and an instrumental object, like *head* in *She nodded her head* ("with her head"), bear different semantic relations to their verbs, do they belong to different grammatical structures? In *We found the cage empty* (EEG 29), Jespersen calls *the cage empty* a nexus, just like *that the cage was empty;* but he refuses to say that *the cage empty* is an "abridged" clause: why? What does he mean by "squinting grammar" (EEG 36)?

Henry Lee Smith, Jr.

LINGUISTICS: A MODERN VIEW OF LANGUAGE

Henry Lee Smith, Jr. (1913–) became professor of linguistics and English and chairman of the department of anthropology and linguistics at the University of Buffalo in 1956. During World War II he worked with the army's foreign language program and after the war in the Foreign Service Institute of the State Department, developing techniques and materials for the rapid teaching of foreign languages.

In 1951 Smith and George L. Trager published *An Outline of English Structure*, a ninety-page pamphlet which influenced nearly all subsequent structural grammars of English, both by the phonological system it presented and by its assumptions about the nature of language. Substantially the same conclusions, in a less technical form, appear in the following selection, in which Smith covers nearly as much ground as many full-length structural grammars. (We have omitted several pages on applied linguistics.)

Smith's strongly anthropological orientation, his almost missionary enthusiasm, and his vigorous, aggressive style had much to do with the success of American structuralism among English teachers in the 1950's. Subsequent research has suggested that many of the generalizations about English in Smith's paper need to be modified and narrowed, that they are too sweeping; but many teachers have been reluctant to abandon them. Generative grammarians have not shared that reluctance, and Smith has not been unaware of their criticisms as he has continued the development of his thought—for example, in "The Concept of the Morphophone," in *Language* for March of 1967.

* * *

I

Language is man's first and greatest invention. It is, indeed, the very mark of humanity, for man is human only by virtue of *human* communication systems, of which language is the hub and center. To understand language and the communication processes clustered about it is, then, in a very real sense to understand the essence of our humanity.

But a clear understanding of the importance of language in human society is not easily come by. It is unfortunate that most of us, unless we have made a rather diligent effort to understand the implications of modern linguistics, have an almost totally irrelevant, not to say erroneous, conception of the role that language plays. Not only that; because of an equally unfortunate tendency to cling tenaciously to the common misconceptions—for reasons we will discuss later—many of us find it difficult to revise our "natural" way of thinking about language sufficiently to comprehend the significant facts of the modern science of linguistics.

To understand what language *is*, we first might try to eliminate some prevalent misconceptions; to determine, in the interests of clarity, what language is not. Most people think of language as *words*—generally words on the printed page. But language is *not* words. It is far more than that. It is a system, a pattern, a structure of communication. Writing is for the most part no more than an incomplete and inconsistent *symbolization* of the communication process associated with language. But for the group that speaks it, language symbolizes the common experience, the culture, of the group. Writing, then, actually *is a symbolization of a symbolization.*

This is not, of course, to underestimate the importance of writing, which is certainly one of the two or three greatest of all of man's inventions. But language precedes writing. We must constantly remind ourselves that language is as old as man. Writing, on the other hand, has a history of only a few thousand years. The distinction is a critical one. Speech is prior to writing in every sense, but the unhappy confusion between language and writing continues to be universal among all literate people.

This universal confusion between speech and writing is today the principal obstacle to a clear understanding of the nature and function of language. Furthermore, it is compounded by the fact that *words*, spoken words and written words as well, seem to almost all of us to be the smallest significant unit in communication. And well they might. Words do appear to have meaning in themselves and do seem to be the smallest units that do. What we commonly fail to realize is that language is enormously complicated, that it is the most minutely patterned and structured of any of man's cultural systems. What we do not perceive is that the word, which seems so obviously to be a totality in itself, is actually already a part of a still smaller pattern, which is much more difficult to identify.

And yet, strangely enough, all of us *have* learned to differentiate and reproduce these minute units and the patterns into which they fit. We have learned how they are woven into words, how words enter into still larger patterns and, finally, how the whole of language intermeshes with other systems of communication. All of us have learned these things, and we learned them before we were six years old. This remarkable achievement —quite possibly it is the greatest intellectual feat any of us ever performs —is accomplished early, thoroughly, and almost entirely *outside of our awareness.*

Paradoxically, it is actually the ease and thoroughness with which we assimilate our native tongue that makes it so difficult for us to examine language objectively. Precisely because we have, as it were, absorbed the basic systems of communication without ever being consciously aware of their intricate relationship, we are usually entirely unable as adults to become systematically aware of the fundamental structure of the several systems involved in communication or of their close and harmonious interrelationship. Because the whole complicated process is "second nature to us now," and because the true structuring is obscured and only partially represented in writing, we are commonly unable to observe the process with anything that approaches scientific objectivity. This failure to understand structure and function is the basic reason for our inability to comprehend how meaning really is conveyed. But more of words and meaning later. For the moment it is enough to have established three fundamental concepts:

Language is not writing.
Speech is prior to writing.
Communication requires more than language.

What we are saying then is that because of our inability to remember the actual learning of the complexities of language and the other communication systems associated with it, and because of our preoccupation as educated people with the printed page, we are confused and largely mistaken concerning the structure of language itself. We are blissfully unaware that there is system, order, and pattern in communication systems other than language. In recent years, however, scientific investigators have more and more clearly revealed the importance of the communication systems that parallel and supplement speech. As we study language, it becomes increasingly obvious that speech doesn't take place in a vacuum. It is surrounded, as it were, by patterned bodily motions, technically the kinesic system, and by systematically analyzable vocalizations, called paralanguage but more simply described as tone of voice.

It may be hard to believe that we perceive the minutest rise of an eyebrow or half-nod of a head or flick of a finger while we talk; but we do detect them because as children we *learned* to recognize the patterns of a communication system based on bodily motion as well as on sound. It may seem even more surprising that among the many other phenomena associated with language, such events as levels of overloudness and oversoftness, degrees of drawl and clipping of portions of utterance, and increased or decreased height of pitch, can now be accurately measured and evaluated in the communication process. These paralinguistic events, like the bodily motions that accompany speech, were learned by all of us as part of the total system. It may seem hardest of all to realize that all of these associated activities actually contribute large portions of the meaning of what we say—meaning which we habitually and unhesitatingly ascribe only to words. But communication is actually the sum of all of these interacting events, and the act of speech differs from culture to culture as the component parts are varied.

In other words, in no culture does a person simply "talk." Communication goes on only when human beings interact through the interplay of each of the separate systems with all of the others. Each individual system provides an effective means of modifying or *commenting* on the portions of the message that are being carried by the others. Indeed, for considerable stretches of conversation we may not use language at all but carry on our end of the interaction entirely by the appropriate use of the other systems. How important these associated systems are to language and meaning is clearly revealed in such familiar remarks as, "It's not what he said but how he said it that I didn't [or did] like," and "It wasn't his words so much as his tone of voice that got me."

But kinesics and paralanguage are not merely modifiers of language, though when we talk we are constantly reinforcing, emphasizing, and sometimes even negating, what we are saying by how we are saying it. Because man is a social animal and because communication is a social process, our tone of voice and "tone of body" simultaneously and throughout the entire process of interaction clearly and emphatically send additional messages as to how we feel, who we think we are, and how we evaluate the person or persons with whom we are interacting in relation to ourselves.

No single part or segment of the total system we have been describing has any fixed, self-contained meaning. Instead, the significance of any communicative event—word, phrase, construction, pitch rise or fall, gesture, or what you will—is entirely a function of its relation to the whole shape and pattern of the situation. Language and communication are basically interpersonal processes taking place in a structured social situation. Only when the society in which they live has a definite and commonly accepted pattern can human beings interact effectively. They must have something steady under their feet in the form of a myriad of common experiences and similar expectancies. Obviously, language itself and the other communication systems associated with it are among the most important of the basic cultural patterns. They are the structured *modes* of interaction.

It is evident, then, that we distort the picture if we think of communication as going on only through language alone, and if we think of language as a train of little vehicles of differing but constant shapes into which we pour pure meaning—distilled thought and idea. We distort the picture still further if we think that "thoughts" and "ideas" exist prior to our "putting them into words." We don't "think" and then talk. We think *because* we can and do talk and because we are thus able to interact with others.

Communication is interaction. The ability to communicate effectively depends upon how well the individuals concerned know and accept a common, many-leveled, complex, integrated package of cultural norms and values. The more they share a common culture, the closer their views and evaluations, the more effective will be the interaction.

If one accepts this concept, it is evident that communication is more than language and that language is far more than words or letters on a printed page. The creator of literature and the writer of a business letter are alike in that both have only the letters of the alphabet and a sprinkling of punctuation conventions with which to represent this wonderfully complex symphony we have been describing. No writer has more than the written language through which to transmit his understanding, his experience, his emotions, his reactions, his ideas. What is equally important is that no reader who is not a speaker of the same language with experience in the same culture can be moved by the written page to re-create, even in part, the writer's world, his beliefs, and his interactions.

Though incomplete and inconsistent, though a derived and secondary system, writing is a marvelous invention. In the hands of a skillful artificer it can be made to carry much more than a mere recording of linguistic events, but writing remains primarily a sort of shorthand reminder to the native speaker of something that has been said or could be said in the language. From many points of view, written language is a separate dialect from the standard colloquial. It has, as we know, individual characteristics and advantages. It is more immediately accessible than the spoken language. Written language has a permanence in contrast to the ephemeral character of speech. By the very virtue of the fact that it must stand alone, the written language is always more rigidly structured and more insistent on precision and clarity. For these reasons, if for no others, it should be studied, understood, and mastered. But we should not assume that we can or should talk the way we write, any more than that we can write "just the way we talk."

The student of language and culture is aware of the differences between the spoken and the written language. He realizes that one form cannot be translated directly into the other, that what may be effective in one may actually bring about disruption of communication in the other. He knows that "correctness" as laid down in a set of prescriptive rules for effective writing may well lead to awkwardness and incongruities of speech that draw attention from *what* is being said and direct it rather to *how* it is said. He is aware that the most effective speech or writing is that which draws the least attention to itself, which strikes the receiver as the most appropriate for the situation as defined by the culture.

If one follows this line of reasoning, he must accept the fact that there can be no one "best" form of speech or writing. Any usage that is inappropriate on any level is a "bad" usage for that particular situation. By the same token, usage that is consistent with the other elements of the culture and accurately reflects them is "good" and appropriate.

It is true that in every culture certain usages are condemned, avoided, or tabooed. Because he is necessarily interested in the culture which language reflects, the modern student is just as interested in the occurrences of "them things" as he is in the occurrences of "those things." Since he is well aware of the correlations between the *status* of individuals and their use of language, he is able to learn much about status systems by analyzing linguistic usage and vice versa. He studies all levels of language, but he must accept the language of those with the status of "educated"—however the culture may understand this term—as a trustworthy guide to what the culture considers acceptable and effective usage.

In the development of the modern science of linguistics, it has been necessary to revise drastically or discard totally many theories which once were generally accepted. For example, we are no longer held in thrall by the myth that languages are "just like" plants or other living organisms. We now know that languages change in time because all culture is in a constant process of change, realignment, and readjustment. Changes in one area of culture sometimes seem to take place very rapidly. Other areas seem to resist change almost completely. Moreover, languages don't "get born," "grow old," and "die." Any language, and hence every language, has an equal amount of history behind it. This is true because every culture has an equal amount of history behind it.

To us who have been taught an "evolutionistic" approach to history, these statements are likely to seem strange. We are used to thinking that the Australian Aborigines or the Tasmanians or the Tierra del Fuegans are at an earlier stage of "evolution" than we, since their technology, by our standards, is so little developed. It is easy, of course, to take the next "logical" step, to think of them as having only relatively recently started the climb toward "civilization" and hence only recently having developed languages. It is all the easier for us to make this common error because by our standards their languages are obviously poor, impoverished, rude, illogical, and imprecise.

But all the evidence we now have at hand indicates that such an ethnocentric view has no foundation in fact. As all men on the surface of the earth are members of *Homo sapiens*, so all men speak fully developed languages of the kind the species must have been speaking ever since it was differentiated as a species. Wherever we find historical evidence of the existence of man, we find remains of his material culture, his tools and implements. Though an ape may solve a problem that immediately confronts him by improvising a tool, to conceive the idea of shaping a piece of wood or stone to meet a problem imagined and projected into the future is beyond the capacity of any apes we know about today. To make tools requires conceptual thinking; to pass on to others the techniques of tool making requires communication and interaction of the true human sort—in short, it requires language.

Culture is only as old as language, and *Homo sapiens* and other species of true men have from the beginning been symbol-making and tool-making animals. But man has never answered the universal problems of human existence in exactly the same way at all times and in all circumstances. Consequently, human cultures differ in content, emphasis, and arrangement. Language, being part of culture, is, by necessity, similarly selective, because languages and cultures "fit" one another. Thus, the rest of culture is not only *transmitted* through language but language *reflects* aspects, facets, attitudes, and assumptions in the culture as well. Languages are different in large part because cultures are different, and cultures are different to a considerable extent because languages are different. Language and culture are inextricably interwoven into a seamless fabric. All languages function in relation to the culture of which they are a part in essentially the same way.

It follows from what we have been discussing, then, that there can be no "better" or "worse" language, no more highly developed language, no more "primitive" language. It is obvious that one would be hard put to find a vocabulary for inside plumbing in a culture that had no inside plumbing. But once the blessings of modern technology are diffused to a people and integrated into the culture, we find no language that cannot perfectly adequately talk about the new cultural acquisitions. What is important to a culture will be reflected in the vocabulary of the language. It must be remembered, however, that what is important to one group is often considered laughably trivial in another. In our culture, for example, we are greatly preoccupied with time, its use and apportionment. Consequently, our vocabulary abounds in items that allow us to interact in accordance with the value we place on scheduling. The Australian Aborigines are obsessed, from our point of view, by the importance of kinship. Who a man is, what he does, and when he does it depends on his position in the kinship system. Our culture, on the other hand, plays down kinships. We value a man not because of his family relationships but because of what he does on his own. Naturally, the Australian language abounds in kinship terms, and we manage with a relative handful of imprecise and cumbersome terms like "cousin," "uncle," "brother-in-law." It's not surprising that when European missionaries began working with the Australians, they were soon asked by the Aborigines how they managed with such a miserably developed language. Vocabularies, then, are different because cultures are concerned with different things. As we shall see, the over-all structuring and patterning of a language not only reflects the culture but also in no inconsiderable way affects the very outlook on life of the people who speak it.

It may appear that we have avoided the question as to how language originated. If we have, it is because we can never know. Even if we could, the question, interesting as it is, is essentially unimportant. What *is* important is that man is human because he can talk and that structurally languages are essentially the same kinds of systems wherever we find them. It is essential for us to realize that *every* language carries out the functions that *all* languages must perform and that each does the job just about as well or badly, as efficiently or inefficiently, as logically or illogically as any other language. If we consider our way of life as obviously the best and most advanced, we are obviously going to consider our kind of languages the most advanced and civilized. If we are going to believe that our concepts, coupled with our technology, represent the very acme of human development, we cannot help but be struck by the fact that languages of other cultures seem ill-equipped to handle those things we have developed, named, and put high on our list of values.

And now, one final word in this vein. Languages don't die, but people do. Latin did not *die;* Cicero did. When there are no more speakers of a language, it ceases to change; and when it no longer changes, it becomes what we call a "dead" language. Various natural or man-induced catastrophes may obliterate the speakers and their society. Or the speakers of a language may find it expedient for a variety of reasons simply to adopt the language of another group. Even today, many of us rail at the "decay" our language is undergoing. We might feel a little better, though perhaps a little less sure of our convictions, if we realized that this feeling is as old as humanity. The old ways are always the best ways. The young never have a real understanding of the proprieties. The son disrespects his father. All these lamentations can be heard in all languages, at all times and in all climes. Despite this, man has come a long way and will go a long way farther. Change is inevitable, and there are always enough conservatives to put on the brakes when they need to be applied.

What is perhaps an even more hopeful sign is that there are always the divinely discontented who want to tinker and experiment, to look into and behind the things that everybody knows and accepts as unalterable and unchanging. Language will be altered, as all things are altered, through time. It is, perhaps, the slowest of all cultural systems to change. But the flexibility and the potentiality for change that are inherent in all languages remain. It is, indeed, a measure of the flexibility and capacity for change in human beings.

II

The student of language and culture understands and accepts the necessity for change. But by no means does he adopt a throwing-of-the-hat-over-the-windmill point of view. He knows that each society has the responsibility of socializing the unfinished, uncivilized individuals that are born into it. He realizes that each society must devise means to assure that each member handles the language in a way that permits him to interact successfully with the other members of his group in a way appropriate to his age, sex, and status. If the culture is literate, every effort must be made to give at least a certain segment of the population control of the literary language both as readers and writers. But knowing all this, the student of language and culture is at times greatly concerned about how little actually is known about languages and communication. He is even more concerned when he sees the extent to which much that is taught about language, its nature and function, is confusing, irrelevant, or downright mistaken.

We have already noted that man, by virtue of his ability to conceptualize, has alone developed the power to make symbols and to make tools. The two are inextricably joined. As his symbol systems are among his most valuable tools, so often do his tools serve as symbols. Thus man's ability to create and manipulate symbols is certainly at the base of his development of culture. But culture with its systems of interrelated symbols must be *learned*. We are born only with the *ability to learn* to become human beings. It is true that any human being can learn any language and, hence, the content of any culture. But marvelous as the human brain is, this learning process is possible only because culture is a series of structured systems with basic components and compositions related to one another, not random agglomerations. The student of language and culture must be, then, a student of structure and pattern. Cultures make sense to those who learn them because they have or strive for internal related consistency. But in any given culture, this consistency itself may seem extremely arbitrary and even nonsensical to the carriers of a different culture. Language, being culture, in the absolute sense is always arbitrary in the relationship between its symbols and the rest of culture. Thus the hand in which I hold my pencil as I write this is still the same thing whether I call it hand or whether, as the Frenchman does, I call it *la main*. Even the onomatopoeic words, which we customarily assume resemble the sounds they represent, are purely arbitrary. A sheep that has been raised in an English-speaking country says *baa,* and a stone thrown into an English pond goes *splash*—but sheep and stones in Arabic or Chinese surroundings make very different noises indeed. Language, we must keep reminding ourselves, is a system of arbitrary, patterned vocal symbols, which must be learned so that human beings can interact and communicate in terms of the total culture in which and through which the language is interwoven.

Language in a very real sense, then, is culture. But like all cultural systems, language is composed of unique units which pattern together in unique ways. Language is language; the kinship system is the kinship system; the technological system is the technological system. Each system can be analyzed in and of itself—in terms of its own components, in terms of its own structure. Though it is true that language uniquely reflects and transmits the other systems embedded in the culture, to try to analyze the structure of language by studying the other cultural systems reflected in it merely obscures the structure of all the systems. To put it another way: if we really want to understand how language relates to the other systems of culture—and this is what *meaning* really means—we first must understand the structure of language. We can get at meaning *only through structure*, and we cannot get at structure through meaning.

The act of speech is a highly complex series of events. They can be studied from many points of view. For example, obviously speech has a physiological basis. The noises we produce are made by parts of our bodies: lips, tongue, teeth, nasal cavity, velum or soft palate, the pharynx, the larynx with its vocal cords or lips, the pulmonary cavity, the diaphragm. Usually we call these the organs of speech, but more properly they are primarily organs of eating and breathing, the function of speech having been overlaid. Another field related to speech, the relation of certain areas of the brain and the neurological connections between these and the articulators, is fascinating and really as yet little understood. The sounds of speech can be studied on the same basis as the other sounds in the physical world by the acoustic physicist. The psychologist may consider the events of speech as the sending and receiving of certain kinds of stimuli. The specialist in communication theory would look at speech as a means of conveying information and would be concerned with the amount of redundancy present in the messages sent and received.

But the student of language and culture, particularly the linguistic scientist, is concerned with *language as a structured system*. Most of us define language as a vehicle for communicating thoughts and ideas, but the linguist is primarily concerned with the structure of the vehicle itself. It is his view that the structure itself may be one of the principal shapers of what we have always called thoughts and ideas. From physicists and physiologists, he has learned that no human being ever utters the same speech sound exactly the same way twice in his lifetime, and he has been told that the number of noises that can be uttered by the so-called speech organs are infinite. Yet he knows from his own experience that people do make noises that are reacted to as *the same* by members of the speaker's group, that the way these noises pattern and arrange themselves is predictable and analyzable, and that they must be learned by all speakers of a given language. He has discovered that, in any linguistic system, the noises selected differ from every other system and that the way they are hierarchically patterned differs from language to language. But he has also discovered that although languages differ, all languages perform the same functions in relation to the rest of the cultures of which they are a part.

Languages are similar in function though different in structure, but all languages present human beings with the same problem: they must be learned. As we have seen, there are no languages which can objectively be called primitive and none which can with any validity be termed highly developed. But are there any languages that in absolute terms can be called "harder" or "easier" for the individual in the society to learn? Hardly, since throughout the world all physiologically normal human beings are in full control of the structures of their languages by the time they are five and a half or six years of age. This does not mean children have as extensive vocabularies as they will when they are adults. Nor does it mean that they know the meaning of all the words they use in the patterned arrangements they can control. For instance, a child of four who is unable to tell time can ask the question, "Is twenty-seven and a half minutes past five before or after half-past five?" and receive a meaningful answer from an adult.

Children seem to learn all languages with equal facility. What is even more amazing, a child from three to six can learn several different languages at the same time without apparent difficulty and can keep them all straight as long as individuals with whom he has significant relationships consistently speak the same language or languages to him. Conceivably, for example, a child's father might speak to him an equal amount of time in both English and German, his mother might use only French to him and his nurse only Chinese. If he were, say, in a Spanish-speaking country, he would soon speak Spanish with the children with whom he played and have no trouble keeping all the languages apart or in switching from one to the other as he spoke with the proper person. Difficulty would arise only if the father should unexpectedly switch to French, or the mother and the child's playmates try English or the nurse German. How people talk and what language they use seems to be very early associated by human beings with the relationships which "significant others" bear to them. Any disturbance between linguistic and other communicative behavior and the child's growing awareness of his relationships with those with whom he interacts seems to confuse him in both the areas of communication and in the relationship. Here we seem to have another substantiation of the interdependence of language and other aspects of culture.

But even though we have some inkling of the way the child responds to disturbances, we still know almost nothing about how the child actually learns language. About all that we do know is that language is not learned in a vacuum but only within the complex social matrix that surrounds it. The child is learning about culture as he learns language, and as he learns language he is able to extend his control over other parts of culture. Within the area of communication, language is perceived and reacted to only in conjunction with associated systems, with the whole complex of events surrounded, so to speak, by a continuous series of stimuli and responses involving many senses—the tactile, the olfactory, and the gustatory.

As the child begins to sense his own individuality, he seems to react noticeably—at about six weeks—to kinesic and paralinguistic events and very soon thereafter to the intonation features of language itself. Soon he babbles, obviously with a purpose, and before he is a year old, he is often able to imitate whole stretches of phenomena which make a certain amount of sense to eager adults. Recognizable words or groups of words are uttered and occur in what appear to be meaningful contexts. The child is rewarded for his success by positive communicative behavior in all of the associated systems—tactile, kinesic, paralinguistic, and linguistic—and corrected in the same way for his blunders. And before we know it, we can't stop his constant prattle.

Even though we know very little more than this about how the process actually takes place, we do know that if anything occurs to disrupt it, there seems to be an adverse effect on the developing personality of the child. He must be properly stimulated by other human beings to interact. Inappropriate stimulation, overstimulation, or understimulation can contribute to marked personality maladjustment. But more of these implications later.

III

We must now see how the linguist actually lays bare the structure of the language that the child must learn in order to function as a member of his social group. As we have said, no part of culture, least of all language, could be learned by anyone unless it was highly patterned, structured, and predictable. No language could be learned unless the speakers were, so to speak, partners to an agreement to use in their interaction only certain sounds and only in certain kinds of arrangements. This fact is of the greatest importance to the linguist, because it means that any individual who is able successfully to interact with others of his linguistic group is a fit source of information as to the language that every other member of the same group, by necessity, has had to learn. In other words, a really complete description of the structure of the language of only one individual is, in theory at least, actually a description of the structure of the language of the whole group.

Each individual serves as a "window into his culture" since he has been obliged, in order to survive at all, to learn the set and accepted ways in which his group interacts. True enough, the student of language and culture is well aware that in every group certain persons are considered to be more skillful, artistic, and successful in their use of the language, and he knows that there are always correlations between linguistic usage and the status of the individual. He has also learned that there will be patterned differences that can be correlated with different geographic regions. But these differences can be easily analyzed, recorded, and related to each other once the linguist has arrived at the *over-all pattern* of the language, the *norm* from which each seemingly idiosyncratic deviation can be measured.

In establishing the over-all pattern, level by level, step by step, the linguist is doing what all scientists do. He is observing phenomena or events and endeavoring to set up hypothetical statements to account for them and their systematic interrelationship. Most linguists agree that language has sound, form, and meaning and that each level must be analyzed as separate, though interdependent, *systems*. That is, language is ultimately a selection of patterned noises "we make with our faces." But obviously it is much more. Each language selects certain sounds, and *only* certain sounds, as its building blocks. These sounds go into making the forms—words, endings, constructions, sentences. Then selection operates again, for not all the possible combinations of sounds are utilized and not all the possible combinations of forms ever appear. The forms that *do* occur, as against those that don't, form the basis for the way that the language ties up with the real world of experience, the culture of the speakers.

Let us look at a few examples of this patterning at various levels. English has no sounds in its inventory like the ones represented in German by "ch" or in French by "u." But then neither French nor German has a sound like the ones represented by "th" in English. Then, too, English does not permit the sound written "ng" to appear at the beginnings of words and does not permit a combination of sounds like "kn" or "spk" anywhere. Going to the next level, words like "boy" and "girl" can be followed by "-ish" to give boyish and girlish, but "fish" must be followed by "-y" to give a corresponding kind of word, "fishy." And finally, "The tall man smoked the black cigar" is an acceptable occurrence as a sentence, whereas "The green horse smoked the blue orange" would strike us as ridiculous, *not* because the sentence is at odds with the grammatical structure of English but because we know through our experience that horses aren't green, they don't smoke, oranges aren't blue, and nobody can smoke an orange. However, such sentences as, "Tall the man cigar the smoked black" would be palpably impossible as an occurrence *and* as a sentence, since it violates grammatical patterns of the language.

But the linguist's first job is to determine the classes of related but contrasting sounds that the language has *selected* to do its work. The organs of speech are capable of producing an infinite number of sounds, but each language settles, so to speak, for a relatively small number of sound types. Even though no person utters any sound exactly the same way twice and though each speaker varies in his utterances from every other speaker, still the marvelous computer we call the brain is able, with hardly any hesitation, to segment a continuous flow of speech sounds into discrete elements and to differentiate "same" and "different," "significant" and "nonsignificant."

The study of the sounds of speech, technically called *phonology*, is usually divided between *phonetics*, the analysis of the similarities and differences in recurring speech sounds, and *phonemics*, the grouping of phonetically similar speech sounds into contrasting classes. What does this mean? Well, first, the linguist knows that each speech sound, or *phone*, we actually perceive— like the first sounds in "pin," "tin," "kin," and "bin"—are themselves composed of bundles of smaller units, the articulations. The initial phones we are examining share the articulation of "stopness" in common. That is, each of these initial sounds is characterized by a momentary stopping of the air passage followed by a release. But the stoppage for *p* and *b* is made by the two lips, that for the *t*, by the tip of the tongue against the ridge behind the teeth, and that for the *k* by the back of the tongue against the soft palate. The principal articulation that distinguishes *p* from *b* is the use of a concommitant vibration of the vocal cords—*voice*—for the *b* as against its absence for the *p*. Every time any one of these sounds occurs we have learned to hear them as *contrasting* with each other; they are members of separate phonemes —*p*, *t*, *k*, *b*. Moreover, initial occurrences of the phonemes *p*, *t*, *k* are all characterized by *stronger* over-all articulation than the voiced initial *b*, a phenomenon noticed also when we compare initial *t*'s and *k*'s with their voiced counterparts, *d* and *g*. Also all the voiceless stops are released by a noticeable puff of breath—aspiration—while this articulation feature is absent with the voiced stops. But what does the linguist do, for example, with the stops he hears in words like "spin," "spun," "sport"? Here we have a voiceless bilabial stopping like that with the members of the *p*-phoneme but an unaspirated and weak release as in the case of members of the *b*-phoneme. Our conclusion is to assign it to the *p*-phoneme since nowhere in English do we get an *s* followed by a voiced stop. To put it another way, we decide that the voiceless-voiced articulation contrast carries more "weight" in the phonological system than the other articulations. Arbitrary? Maybe, but most languages seem to rely more heavily on the voiceless-voiced distinction than other articulation features. Thus any phone can be a member of only one phoneme; there can be no dual membership or overlapping. Our conclusion is, of course, further borne out when we find that members—allophones—of the *t* and *k* phonemes are similarly weak and unaspirated when following *s*.

By this process of classification, the linguist determines the phonemes and their membership and also the permitted and nonpermitted occurrences of phonemes in groupings and sequences. English has forty-five phonemes according to most linguists today—about average for the languages of the world. Some languages may have as few as eighteen or twenty phonemes, and some have been reported to have as many as sixty-five.

It is important to realize that phonemes are not limited to vowels and consonants. Other classes of sounds like pitch and stress are of the utmost importance. English, for example, has thirty-three vowel and consonant—segmental—phonemes and twelve "accentual" or suprasegmental phonemes. The twenty-one consonants are: *p, t, k; b, d, g; č* ("ch" as in "*church*"), *ǰ* ("j" and "dge" as in "*judge*"); *f, θ* ("th" as in "*thin*"), *s, š* ("sh"); *v, ð* ("th" as "*then*"), *z, ž* ("s" as in "*measure*"); *m, n, ŋ* ("ng" as in "*sing*"); *l; r*.

In the list above, where some unfamiliar symbols have had to be introduced in order to get one symbol for each consonant phoneme, some of the many vagaries of the English spelling system immediately appear. A single phoneme may have many representations, as in the writing of both "j" and "dge" for *ǰ*, or in writing *ž* by "z" or "s" as in "azure" and "measure." Then, too, we may have only *one* spelling for two different phonemes, as in the case of "th" for both *θ* and *ð*. Sometimes, as well, one spelling device may represent either a single phoneme or two phonemes following each other, as in the use of "ng" to represent both the *ŋ* in "singer" and the *ŋg* of "finger."

But if we think our spelling system is incomplete and inconsistent in representing the consonants, we are in for a much greater shock when we realize how inadequately our inherited Latin alphabet serves us in representing our vowel and semivowel sounds. We all learned in school that we had five vowels—"a," "e," "i," "o," "u," and sometimes "y" and "w." Actually, one would think that a little listening would have made it quite clear that we have many more vowel phonemes than this. No speaker of English fails to contrast the vowel sounds in *pit, pet, pat, put, putt, pot*. Here are *six* contrasting short vowel phonemes, and it will be noted that the letter "u" is doing double duty in representing the *u* of *put* and the vowel sound in "cut," "but," "shut." (The symbol *ə* is commonly used by linguists to represent this phoneme; it is called *schwa.*)

But six short vowels are not the whole story in the over-all pattern of English. In rapid speech most speakers contrast the vowel in "just," the adverb—"I *just* got here"—with "just," the adjective—"The *just* man." This sound is also heard in the pronunciation of many speakers for the first vowel in the word "children." It can always be heard in contrast with *i, e, ə,* so that "gist," "jest" and "just" (adjective) are all distinct from "just" (adverb). So, too, Coastal New England speakers will quite regularly use a short *o*-vowel in "home," "whole," "road," "coat," which makes the words sound to the ears of a speaker from, say, Philadelphia quite like "hum," "hull," "rud" and "cut." But still this "New England 'short *o*' " is in contrast with the Philadelphian's and the New Englander's vowels in "hum," where both would use the vowel we write *ə*. To speakers from most other parts of the country, the Coastal New Englander's vowel in "pot" is also noticeably different. Where most Americans use a vowel with no lip-rounding in this word and others like it, the New Englander rounds his lips slightly, as does the speaker of British English, though the latter's vowel is usually said with more tenseness of articulation.

For English as a whole, then, there is a stockpile of at least nine contrasting *short* vowel phonemes, though not all dialects will necessarily select the same phonemes in words which we have come to spell the same way. We can arrange and represent these nine short vowels as follows, using special symbols where our writing system is deficient:

i as in "pit"	*ɨ* as in "just" (adverb), "children"	*u* as in "put"
e as in "pet"	*ə* as in "cut"	*o* as in "home," "whole," in New England
æ as in "pat"	*a* as in "pot"	*ɔ* as in "pot," "lot," in New England

And still we haven't finished with the vowel sounds. So far, we have said nothing about the so-called "long vowels" and "diphthongs." Structurally, there are no "long" vowels in English, but only diphthongal *complex nuclei,* composed of two segments, the first of which may be any one of the nine short vowels, the second segment, one of three following, "gliding" *semivowel* phonemes—*y, w, h*. The *y* following a short vowel is heard as a glide to a higher and "fronter" tongue position. The following *w* indicates a higher and "backer" tongue position with increasing lip-rounding. And the *h* after vowels is experienced as a glide to a more central and "relaxed" tongue position. You can *feel* and hear these in pronouncing slowly the words "pie," "pow," and "pa" which the linguist would analyze as *pay, paw,* and *pah,* respectively. Though you may not feel the gliding so noticeably in pronouncing the syllables "ee" and "oo"—where the tongue already starts quite high in articulating the first segment—these syllables, too, are structural diphthongs, *iy* and *uw* respectively. An analysis of this kind may come as a bit of a shock, but the similarity between the *y*'s, *w*'s, and *h*'s that *precede* vowels and those that follow is readily apparent if we just listen and feel what goes on inside our mouths. Thus "ye," "woo," and "hah" are analyzed *yiy, wuw, hah*. Notice also such words as "you" = *yuw*, "we" = *wiy*, "he" = *hiy*, "woe" = *wow*, "high" = *hay*.

So when we add to the list of the nine short vowels, the twenty-seven possible combinations of short vowel with following semivowel, we reach the rather staggering total of thirty-six possible vowel nuclei for all the dialects of English to draw from! This is a rather far cry from "a," "e," "i," "o," "u" and sometimes "y" and "w." Thus, the inadequacy of our writing system is reflected not only in the insufficient number of symbols, but also in the inconsistent use of the symbols that do exist. Nevertheless, the spelling of English words has become standardized, so that speakers of various dialects all learn one correct spelling of each word. This leads all too often to the mistaken conclusion that words have one and only one correct pronunciation. Confused as we are between language and writing, we feel that letters "have sounds" and that we "pronounce letters." Nothing, of course, could be further from the truth. Variations in pronunciation always have occurred and always will occur, particularly in a language that covers as much territory as English. Letters don't "have sounds" and aren't "pronounced." Our uniform spelling merely serves as a triggering device to the speakers of the various standard dialects. We all look at the same arrangement of letters, but to each of us the letters call up different acceptable pronunciations of the same words. These different pronunciations are principally the result of the different vowel nuclei, simple and complex, which each dialect selects.

For example, in my speech (and in the speech of all Americans who learned their English east of the Allegheny Mountains), the words "merry," "marry," "Mary" have three contrasting vowel nuclei—*e, æ*, and *eh*, respectively. But in Buffalo, where I write this, all three of the words rhyme, as they do in all dialects of "Western New England" origin. Moreover, the Buffalonian pronounces all of the words with the complex nucleus *eh*, so that all three rhyme with my pronunciation of "Mary." On the other hand, a speaker from the Middle West, say Wisconsin, will pronounce all three with the short vowel, *e*, so that each would rhyme with my pronunciation of *merry*. Still other speakers will pronounce *marry* as I do, with the short vowel as in "pat," but will not distinguish between "merry" and "Mary," pronouncing each with either *e* or *eh*.

Again each dialect area shows a different selection from the over-all pattern. It is wrong to assume that one is correct and another incorrect; they are all standard variations. Nor are the selections haphazard. They are *patterned*. Without being at all aware of what he is doing, each speaker will follow the selection patterns of his particular geographical region, his dialect area. Thus, if we simply determine the vowel patterning for the various dialect areas, we can often tell quite accurately where a speaker learned his English. And if we hear certain vowels characteristic of Coastal New England or Coastal Southern speech appearing in a pattern that is predominantly Northern Middle Western, we can be quite sure this speaker has moved from his original dialect area.

So the spelling system must be all things to all men. Consequently it is incomplete and inconsistent in its relation to each dialect and in its relation to the sounds of the language as a whole. Poor as it may be in representing the vowel and consonant sounds, it is in the representation of the accentual or suprasegmental sounds where it really fails us. These features are handled by just a sprinkling of spelling and punctuation conventions which make the representation of vowels and consonants look quite accurate and full by comparison. Yet it is just these accentual features in the spoken language that we rely on most to tell us "what goes with what, and how." For example, we have all been forced to do a double take when confronted with a newspaper headline like the one I saw in a local paper not long ago:

REPORT NUMBER OF SAFE JOBS HERE

Since the headline was written at a time when industry in the area was laying off employees in many plants *and* when the local police were trying to round up the perpetrators of a number of robberies, I had to read the story to find out which situation was being reported on. The ambiguity, of course, is due to the fact that different degrees of *stress*, or "loudness," can fall on the words "safe" and "jobs." Even the best dictionaries to the contrary notwithstanding, there are *four*—not two or three—relative degrees of stress, or loudness, which we have all learned to distinguish as *significant* in our language.

To put it in the language of the linguist, English has four *stress phonemes*. We can designate these *primary* ('), *the loudest; secondary* (ˆ); *tertiary* ('); and *weak* (ˇ). Thus if I read the headline with secondary stress on "safe" and primary on "jobs" the meaning had to do with security of employment. But if I read "safe" with primary and "jobs" with tertiary, a series of crimes was being reported. In the first instance, the stress pattern signaled that "safe" *modified* "jobs," to use traditional grammatical terminology, whereas in the second case, the stress pattern signaled a "compound" noun.

We are all aware, of course, of the change of use and meaning signaled by a change in stress. Here are a few familiar examples (weak stress is not marked):

Modifiers   whîte + hóuse, nêw + Yórker, lông + ísland, (as in sáfe + jobs).
Compounds   líght + hòuse, Whíte + Hòuse, hóuse + kèeper, wíne + bàrrel, sét + ùp, úp + sèt (as in sáfe + jòb). Note also *compounds* with the reverse stress pattern, tertiary and primary: Nèw + Yórker, Lòng + Ísland, sèt + úp (v.), ùp + sét.

The + in the above examples symbolizes a *transition* or juncture phoneme, generally termed *plus juncture*. Plus juncture is in contrast to *normal transition*, which, however, is not a phoneme. Note the following:

Normal Transition	nítràte	grá' mòther	grá' frùit
Plus Juncture	níght + ràte	grán + mòther	grápe + frùit
	Nýe + trâit	gránd + mòther	

These patterns may be combined, so that a compound can be modified by a preceding word—rêd + (wíne + bàrrel), "a wine-barrel red in color" or *lîght* + (hóuse + kèeper), "a housekeeper who doesn't weigh much." Also, compounds can be extended a word at a time, as in (*lìght* + *hòuse*) + *kêeper*, "keeper of a lighthouse," and *lìght* + (*hóuse* + *kèeper*), "a person who does light housekeeping." In each case, the pattern of stresses tells us how the words are bound together and what grammatical relationship each has to each.

Of equal, if not greater, importance as a basis for determining the various grammatical patterns of the language are the four significant levels of relative pitch—the four *pitch* phonemes—and the three *terminal juncture* phonemes. The four pitch phonemes can be symbolized by the numerals 1, 2, 3, 4, with *one* representing the lowest significant pitch level and *four*, the highest. Pitch phonemes differ from stress phonemes by having *scope*, that is, a significant pitch level continues over several syllables, each with its own stress, until another significant occurrence of pitch takes place.

At the end of each sequence of pitches, we have learned to make our voice "behave" in certain regular ways. For instance, the voice might "trail off" into silence, quite rapidly, but still perceptibly. Or the voice might rise slightly in pitch and intensity. Finally, in contrast to both of these junctures, we might hear the pitches "squeezed," so to speak, on either side of what we might describe as a "slight break or pause." These three contrasting ways of ending sequences of pitches constitute the terminal juncture phonemes, and a sequence of pitches bounded by one of these is called an *intonation pattern*. The terminal juncture that "trails off" is referred to as *double-cross juncture* (⌗), the one that rises, *double-bar juncture* (‖), and the one where the pitch neither fades off nor rises, but is "squeezed," *single-bar juncture* (│).

The pitches and terminal junctures can be quite easily distinguished if we listen closely to ourselves as we read the following examples aloud in a normal, conversational tempo. Notice that within any intonation pattern only one syllable bears a primary stress.

(1) Hè's + gôǐng + tǒ + Lóndǒn ⚡ (simple statement)

(2) Hè's + gôǐng + tǒ + Lóndǒn ‖ (echo question)

(3) Hè's + gôǐng + tǒ + Lóndǒn ‖ (surprised echo question)

(4) Whŷ's + hè + gôǐng + tǒ + Lóndǒn ⚡ (and not some other place)

(5) Whât'rě + wè + hávǐng | fǒr + dínněr | Móthěr ‖ (polite question)

(6) Whât'rě + wè + hávǐng | fǒr + dínněr | Móthěr ⚡ (not so respectful or polite to Mother; literally "talking down")

(7) Whât'rě + wè + hávǐng | fǒr + dínněr | Móthěr ⚡ (signals little respect for Mother as a person and less for her abilities as a cook)

(8) Hè + hâs + ǎ + vérў + plêasǎnt | pèrsǒnálǐtў ⚡ (that's all he has, and it's sort of specious pleasantness at that)

(9) Hè + hâs + ǎ + vérў + plêasǎnt | pèrsǒnálǐtў ‖ (tentative approval, but almost demands a qualifying statement beginning with "but")

(10) Hè + hâs + ǎ + vérў + plêasǎnt | pèrsǒnálǐtў ⚡ (a real compliment, in this culture)

These sentences not only exemplify the pitches and terminal junctures and remind us of the inadequacy of the writing system, but they also serve to re-emphasize that meaning is more than just the sum of the "meaning of the words." Sentences (8) through (10), for example, would appear identically on the printed page, each punctuated by a period. But in the spoken language, the different intonation patterns combined with the words give vastly different meanings to the three sentences.

The grammatical significance of different intonation patterns can be similarly demonstrated. For instance

(1) Hè + pássed | thě + câr + òn + thě + ríght ⚡

means that the driver passed a car that was on the right of something else, perhaps another car. But

(2) Hè + pâssed + thě + cár ‖ òn + thě + ríght ⚡

means the driver passed the car on his or the car's right-hand side. Intona-

tion signals to us that the words in the sentences form different *constituents*
and also that the *relationships* between the constituents are quite different.
We have seen before how important phonology can be as a foundation for
the study of grammar through such examples as those in which stress
differences signaled different relationships between the words "safe" and
"jobs" in *sáfe + jòbs* and *sáfe + jòbs*. But phonology not only helps us by
furnishing an unequivocal and formal basis for deciding "what goes with
what" *within* the sentence; it also allows us once and for all to decide what
a sentence *is* and when it ends. We are no longer forced to "define" a
sentence as "expressing a complete thought" or even as something bounded
by silence or a "pause." A sentence can now be seen as one of several
easily statable sequences of words, phrases, or clauses bounded by certain
kinds of intonation patterns.

The study of the relationship of word to word in phrases, of phrase to
phrase and of clause to clause, we will call *syntax*. Though the term syntax
has generally been used to cover the study of *every* relationship and construction in language above the composition of single words, we will limit the use
of the term to cover only the composition of the syntactic *sentence*. But it is
to the study of the word itself that we must now return.

The basic unit in the formation of words is the *morpheme*, and hence we
will call this level of linguistic analysis *morphemics*, though *morphology* is the
more usual term. Like "phoneme," the term "morpheme" designates a *class*
of related, recurring events. For instance, the various ways we form the
plural—"-s," "-es," "-en," etc.—can be grouped together into one class,
which we will call the *plural morpheme*. This is quite analogous to the
way in which we classified different kinds of "p"-sounds into one *p*-phoneme.
To oversimplify, we can say that each constituent of each morpheme is
ultimately a phoneme, but that the word is composed of various, patterned
combinations of *morphemes*. Morphemes, themselves, can be variously
classified, depending upon their position and function in the word. Examine
the following passage:

The ungrateful tiger, unseen and unheard by the sheep, moved
quickly in the direction of his former friends. The monkeys and the
horses saw him coming, faster, and faster. They ran, but the bats,
though they couldn't see, sensed his approach. They swooped down
on the defenseless sheep, and the entire flock stampeded through the
clearing.

Our passage exemplifies both the recurrence of morphemes and some of
the basic types of morphemes in the language. Morphemes in the position of

the "un-" in "ungrateful," "unseen" and "unheard," the "de-" of "defenseless" and the "di-" of "direction" are called *prebases*. The "-ful," "-ly," "-er," "-tion," "-less" are termed *postbases*. The unmarked morphemes are called *bases*, and those with double underlinings are designated *grammatical* or *inflectional suffixes*. Such occurrences as "ône + bóy," "twô + bóy§"; "ône + hórse," "twô + hórse§"; "Jôhn + móve§," "Jôhn + móved"; "hḛ + hít," "hít + hìm" furnish the basis for setting up the suffix morphemes, which are functionally quite different from the prebases and postbases. Three sets of grammatical suffixes can be arrived at, and through them we can classify the words to which they may be attached as *nouns*—inflected for plural and possessive, *pronouns*—inflected for number, case, and gender, and, finally, *verbs*—inflected for third person singular, past tense, past participle, present participle, and having an uninflected "name form."

Parenthetically, it is important to realize here the difference between an *uninflected* form and a "zero form." Even though "sheep" has no phoneme following it in the plural, this zero occurrence is *not* nothing, but a real piece of structure, because of the overwhelming number of examples of inflected plurals. But *bóy* in English, like all nouns, is *uninflected* in the singular. Not so for Latin, where nouns in the singular *are* inflected— "amicu§," "servu§," etc., and where a form like "puer" shows a zero form of the nominative singular morpheme of the second declension.

Nouns, pronouns, and verbs, the three classes of words or "parts of speech," if you will, which we have pointed out above, are the only three inflected word classes in English. All other words are uninflectable, and their classification depends upon other modes of analysis. Though some other word classifications are possible at the level of morphemics, "adverbs" cannot be distinguished from "adjectives," nor can "prepositions" from "conjunctions." Differentiations of this kind must be left until we can study two or more words in relationship to each other. This, as we have said is the province of syntax, the next higher level of analysis.

But it is time to define "word." But remember, we are defining it *only for English*. Though everybody is quite sure that he "knows" what a word is, the linguist is aware that much more rigor is necessary, since his experience has shown him that "word" must be defined quite differently for different languages. Since the linguist is basing his definition on *form* and not on *meaning*, his definition will both "prove the obvious" and seem to go against the "canons of common sense."

For English, then, a word must have one base morpheme and *only* one. In addition, it must have a stress morpheme, or *word superfix*, which must contain one primary stress and *only* one, though stresses other than primary may also be present. Thus the minimal case of a word in English would be a base like *boy-* combined with a word superfix consisting of a single primary stress, resulting in the word *bóy*. But words may have pre- and postbases and, of course, grammatical suffixes. Word superfixes may thus become quite complicated as the number of prebases, postbases and suffixes increases. The maximum extent of a single word would seem to contain three prebases, six, or possibly seven, postbases and two suffixes:

àntĭ-dĭs-ĕ-stàb-l-ìsh-mĕnt-árĭ-ăn-ĭsm̆-s'—if you can imagine such a noun in the plural possessive.

The pre- and postbases are underlined once, the grammatical suffixes, twice, and the base, three times. Notice also that the second suffix—the possessive—which *follows* the plural, is actually a zero form, though represented in the writing system by an apostrophe. The word superfix would be:

$$` \smile + \smile + \smile + `\ ` + \smile + \ ' \smile \smile + \smile \smile$$

Again, this extended grouping of morphemes is *by definition* only one word, since it contains only one base and is combined with a word superfix containing only one primary stress. Conversely, even though we "feel" that *Whíte + Hòuse, Lòng + Ísland* and such compounds ought to be one word because they refer to only one thing in the culture, they are by definition, *phrases*, because they contain *two* bases and hence two words. Also the process by which two words are combined to form a phrase is on the level of syntax. For combinations consisting of two words, or a word and a phrase, or two phrases are combined under a *phrase superfix*, which is not a morpheme but a unit of syntax. Phrase superfixes always contain a primary stress, a transition, and a stress less than primary. When two words, each with word superfixes consisting of a primary stress, enter into combination, *one* of the primary stresses of *one* of the word superfixes must be reduced under the operation of the phrase superfix, while the other remains. Thus the word *sáfe* when combined with the word *jóbs* under the phrase superfix ^ + ′ results in the phrase *sâfe + jóbs*, but when the same two words are combined with the phrase superfix ′ + `, the result is the phrase *sáfe + jòbs*. As we have seen, intonation patterns, too, are syntactic units and furnish indications as to the more complex relationships within the sentences.

Linguists have learned a great deal more about the fascinating complexities of syntax and are now reaching into an area beyond syntax which we will call *semology*. Obviously, linguist and traditional grammarian alike are concerned with the analysis of the *permitted distribution* patterns within the sentence and within stretches of more than one sentence—*discourse*. For example, in such a sentence as "John made Bill money" in contrast with

"John made Bill captain," we "know" that the relationship between *made*, *Bill*, and *money* is different from that between *made*, *Bill*, and *captain*. *Syntactically*, however, both sentences are identical—they are examples of the *double-object* relationship. Semologically, however, we can set up two different relationships, as tested by such sentences as "John gave Bill money" versus a non-occurring "John gave Bill captain" and "John named Bill captain" as against the non-occurring "John named Bill money." Verbs like *give*, *tell*, etc., will be found distributed with only certain nouns in the *second* object position. These verbs, we can say, govern the semological *indirect object* relationship, whereas verbs like *call*, *name*, etc., are distributed with *another* group of nouns which we can designate as semological *object complements*. The permitted verb-noun distributions are systematically different, even though a verb like "make" has a unique distribution in that it occurs in both semological relationships.

Though semology is at present pretty much *terra incognita*, it is becoming increasingly evident that much that makes both traditional grammar and the more modern "positional" or "pattern" grammar unsatisfactory is the result of failing to draw a clear line between what we have called syntax and what we are calling *semology*. Such familiar "syntactic" concepts as "modification," "question sentences," "declarative sentences," or "vocatives," as well as the study of what has been called the "grammatical meaning" of morphemes, are now seen to be semological rather than strictly syntactic. Also the study of the structuring of discourse itself—the structure of multiple, systematically patterned semological occurrences—is in the realm of semology. Syntax stops with the analysis of the single sentence or sentence fraction, a phonologically marked occurrence taken from semology; semology studies the patterning of distributions within the occurrence, and the patterned distribution of occurrences within discourse. . . .

Study Questions

1. "Language," says Smith (p. 91), "is a system of arbitrary, patterned vocal symbols." Of what "levels" (Part Three) does he say that the system consists? What does he mean by *phonology, morphology, syntax, semology?* Is there any order in which the investigating linguist must approach these levels? Why is Smith's analysis of sentences sometimes called "phonological syntax"? What might be meant by calling Smith's linguistics "taxonomic"? Do you find an answer in Smith's statement (omitted here) that "sentence

patterns . . . break down, segment, and categorize the flow of experience"? What do you think he means by "over-all pattern"?

2.   In Smith's view, no phone can be a member of more than one phoneme: "there can be no dual membership or overlapping" (p. 96). A single contrast, he also suggests, is enough to establish a phonemic distinction. With these ideas in mind, consider a dialect where the medial consonants of *writer* and *rider* are phonetically identical but the stressed diphthongs are phonetically different. Would the consonants be phonemically the same? Would the diphthongs? If the long diphthong in *rider* is phonemically distinct from the shorter diphthong in *writer*, is the vowel of *pot* phonemically distinct from the vowel of *pod?* Does Smith give any *argument* for not allowing overlapping? Why should just one contrast be allowed to establish a phonemic distinction?

3.   Do you agree with Smith that language which calls attention to itself is ineffective (p. 86)? Can you think of lines of verse which you particularly remember for their language? If culturally defined "appropriateness" is the standard for good usage, does room remain for *criticism* of the culture, or for linguistic innovation? In the search for good usage, should one consider only the actual linguistic practice of the educated, or should one consult their opinions about usage too? Would you accept a statement that linguistics is "the true foundation of a meaningful literary criticism"? Why, or why not?

Noam Chomsky

THE FORMAL NATURE OF LANGUAGE

Noam Chomsky (1928–) is Ward professor of linguistics at Massachusetts Institute of Technology, and perhaps the best-known and most-discussed figure
in American linguistics today. Himself a vigorous controversialist, he directly
attacked American structuralism in his book *Syntactic Structures* (1957) and
opened an often-acrimonious debate which is still bothering linguistic peacemakers and delighting many less genteel observers.

Generative grammar has developed with startling rapidity since 1957. *Syntactic Structures* has been obsolete for some time, and work at MIT and elsewhere ranges very widely over linguistic theory and language families. Chomsky himself reviewed some changes and pointed the way to others in *Aspects
of the Theory of Syntax* (1965); *The Sound Pattern of English*, which he published in 1968 with his colleague Morris Halle, has already been called the
twentieth century's most important book on English phonology. In these
circumstances, it is quite unsafe to predict what generative theory and practice
will be in another ten years—except that they will be different. The selection
which follows should, therefore, be read as a statement of the situation in the
middle distance of the receding past (*i.e.*, early 1967).

Though new ideas of the nature of language entail new techniques of description and history, the revolution of the generativists is not just a matter of
refined manipulations. It would be an admirable thing to build a grammar
which could in principle enumerate all the possible sentences of a language,
with their syntactic structures, their meanings, and directions for their pronunciation; but the generative grammarian would not be content with making
better grammars. He aims beyond possibility—to explore the human mind,
to discover what it is in men that lets them talk, that makes them competent
to say and understand, in endlessly new sentences, whatever men can know.
If that ambition is anything more than an empty dream, it reopens whole vistas of knowledge and inquiry which the linguist as technician had been content
to close. Linguists no longer feel a compulsion to apologize, as some of them
once did, when they talk about meaning or about universal grammar; and
their subject is once again a near neighbor of psychology and philosophy.

New breadth and depth bring new difficulty. The essay here reprinted was
originally published as an appendix to Eric Lenneberg's *Biological Foundations
of Language* and was intended as a brief, nontechnical summary. Chomsky
begins by distinguishing competence from performance—the native speaker's
mastery of the rules that determine the sound and the intrinsic meaning of
sentences, on the one hand, from his "actual observed use of language" on the
other. Linguistic analysis, for Chomsky, is the study of competence. Its aim,
for particular languages, is to discover the rules which match the meanings of
sentences to their phonetic shapes; its broader aim is to discover the principles

of universal grammar, the "limiting conditions" to which all "human languages are subject" because the human mind is what it is. These conditions are of three kinds—syntactic, semantic, and phonological—which determine the three components of a generative grammar; and after establishing that "framework for the study of linguistic structure," Chomsky considers the three components one by one, with simple examples drawn from English. It should be remembered that his emphasis is where it has always been, not on the writing of one more English grammar, but on the general principles to which the study of individual languages may lead. To discover the presumably narrow limits "on the structure of human language," he concludes, would be "a highly suggestive contribution to theoretical psychology."

GENERAL PROPERTIES OF LANGUAGE

Many generations of productive scholarship notwithstanding, the questions to which this Appendix is addressed can receive only quite tentative answers. There are few languages for which descriptions in depth are available, and only selected aspects of language have been studied with sufficient care and success to provide support for conclusions of a general nature. Still, it is possible, with some degree of confidence, to outline certain properties and conditions that distinguish human languages among arbitrary systems of symbol manipulation, communication, and self-expression.

COMPETENCE AND PERFORMANCE

At the crudest level of description, we may say that a language associates sound and meaning in a particular way; to have command of a language is to be able, in principle, to understand what is said and to produce a signal with an intended semantic interpretation. But aside from much unclarity, there is also a serious ambiguity in this crude characterization of command of language. It is quite obvious that sentences have an intrinsic meaning determined by linguistic rule and that a person with command of a language has in some way internalized the system of rules that determine both the phonetic shape of the sentence and its intrinsic semantic content—that he has developed what we will refer to as a specific *linguistic competence*. However, it is equally clear that the actual observed use of language—actual *performance*—does not simply reflect the intrinsic sound-meaning connections established by the system of linguistic rules. Performance involves many other factors as well. We do not interpret what is said in our presence simply by application of the *linguistic* principles that determine the phonetic and semantic properties of an utterance. Extralinguistic beliefs concerning the speaker and the situation play a fundamental role in determining how speech is produced, identified, and understood. Linguistic performance is, furthermore, governed by principles of cognitive structure—(for example, by memory restrictions) that are not, properly speaking, aspects of language.

To study a language, then, we must attempt to disassociate a variety of factors that interact with underlying competence to determine actual performance; the technical term "competence" refers to the ability of the idealized speaker-hearer to associate sounds and meanings strictly in accordance with the rules of his language. The grammar of a language, as a model for idealized competence,[1] establishes a certain relation between sound and meaning—between phonetic and semantic representations. We may say that the grammar of the language L generates a set of pairs (s, I), where s is the phonetic representation of a certain signal[2] and I is the semantic interpretation assigned to this signal by the rules of the language. To discover this grammar is the primary goal of the linguistic investigation of a particular language.

The general theory of linguistic structure is concerned with discovering the conditions that any such grammar must meet. This general theory will be concerned with conditions of three kinds: conditions on the class of admissible phonetic representations, the class of admissible semantic representations, and the systems of rules that generate paired phonetic and semantic representations. In all three respects, human languages are subject to stringent limiting conditions. There is no difficulty in constructing systems that do not meet these conditions, and that do not, therefore, qualify as potential human languages despite the fact that they associate sound and meaning in some definite way. Human languages are systems of a highly specific kind. There is no *a priori* necessity for a system relating sound and meaning to be of this kind. As this chapter proceeds, we shall mention some of the highly restrictive conditions that appear to be essential properties of human language.

A grammar generates a certain set of pairs (s, I), where s is a phonetic representation and I its associated semantic interpretation. Similarly, we might think of a performance model as relating sound and meaning in a specific way. A perceptual model, PM, for example, might be described, as in (1), as a device that accepts a signal as input (along with much else) and assigns various grammatical representations as "output."

---

[1] The term "grammar" is often used ambiguously to refer both to the internalized system of rules and to the linguist's description of it.

[2] To be more precise, a certain class of signals that are repetitions of one another, in a sense to which we return subsequently.

(1)

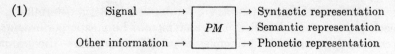

Signal ⟶ [PM] → Syntactic representation
→ Semantic representation
Other information → → Phonetic representation

A central problem for psychology is to discover the characteristics of a system PM of this sort. Clearly, in understanding a signal, a hearer brings to bear information about the structure of his language. In other words, the model PM incorporates the grammar G of a language. The study of how sentences are understood—the general problem of speech perception—must, obviously, remain within narrow limits unless it makes use of this basic property of a perceptual model. But it is important to distinguish clearly between the function and properties of the perceptual model PM and the competence model G that it incorporates. Both G and PM relate sound and meaning; but PM makes use of much information beyond the intrinsic sound-meaning association determined by the grammar G, and it operates under constraints of memory, time, and organization of perceptual strategies that are not matters of grammar. Correspondingly, although we may describe the grammar G as a system of processes and rules that apply in a certain order to relate sound and meaning, we are not entitled to take this as a description of the successive acts of a performance model such as PM—in fact, it would be quite absurd to do so. What we have said regarding perceptual models is equally applicable to production models. The grammatical rules that generate phonetic representations of signals with their semantic interpretations do not constitute a model for the production of sentences, although any such model must incorporate the system of grammatical rules. If these simple distinctions are overlooked, great confusion must result.

In this chapter, attention is focused on competence and the grammars that characterize it; when speaking of semantic and phonetic interpretation of sentences, we refer exclusively to the idealized representations determined by this underlying system. Performance provides data for the study of linguistic competence. Competence, in the sense just described, is one of many factors that interact to determine performance. In general, we would expect that in studying the behavior of a complex organism, it will be necessary to isolate such essentially independent underlying systems as the system of linguistic competence, each with its intrinsic structure, for separate attention.

INITIAL STEPS TOWARD A STUDY OF COMPETENCE

Turning to the study of underlying competence, let us first take note of a few very obvious properties of the grammar of a human language. It is, first of all, quite clear that the set of paired phonetic and semantic representations generated by the grammar will be infinite. There is no human language in which it is possible, in fact or in principle, to specify a certain sentence as the longest sentence meaningful in this language. The grammar of any language contains devices that make it possible to form sentences of arbitrary complexity, each with its intrinsic semantic interpretation. It is important to realize that this is no mere logical nicety. The normal use of language relies in an essential way on this unboundedness, on the fact that language contains devices for generating sentences of arbitrary complexity. Repetition of sentences is a rarity; innovation, in accordance with the grammar of the language, is the rule in ordinary day-by-day performance. The idea that a person has a "verbal repertoire"—a stock of utterances that he produces by "habit" on an appropriate occasion—is a myth, totally at variance with the observed use of language. Nor is it possible to attach any substance to the view that the speaker has a stock of "patterns" in which he inserts words or morphemes. Such conceptions may apply to greetings, a few clichés, and so on, but they completely misrepresent the normal use of language, as the reader can easily convince himself by unprejudiced observation.[3]

To discover the grammar of some language user, we must begin by obtaining information that bears on his interpretation of sentences, on the semantic, grammatical and phonetic structure that he assigns to them. For example, for the study of English, it would be important to discover such facts as the following. Consider the sentence frames (2) and the words "persuaded," "expected," and "happened":

(2) (a) John____Bill that he should leave
　　 (b) John____Bill to leave
　　 (c) John____to leave
　　 (d) It is____that Bill will leave

The word "persuaded" can be inserted in (a) and (b), but not (c) or (d); "expected" can be inserted in (b), (c), (d), but not (a); "happened" can be inserted only in (c). Inserting "persuaded" in (a), we derive an ambiguous sentence, the interpretation of which depends on the reference of "he"; under one interpretation, the sentence is a near paraphrase of (b), with "persuaded" inserted. When "expected" appears in (b) and (c), the subject-verb relation holds between "Bill" and "leave" in (b), but between "John"

---

[3] Or by some simple calculations of the number of sentences and "patterns" that might be needed, for empirical adequacy, in such repertoires. For some relevant comments, see G. A. Miller, E. Galanter, and K. H. Pribram, *Plans and the Structure of Behavior*, Holt, Rinehart and Winston (1960), pp. 145f.; G. A. Miller and N. Chomsky, "Finitary models of language users," in R. D. Luce, R. Bush, and E. Galanter (eds.), *Handbook of Mathematical Psychology*, Vol. II, John Wiley, New York, 1963, p. 430.

and "leave" in (*c*). The sentence "John happened to leave" has roughly the same meaning as "it happened that John left," but "John expected to leave" is not even a remote paraphrase of "it expected that John left." Such facts as these can be stated in many ways, and we might use one or another technique to make sure of their accuracy. These are facts about the competence of the speaker of English. They can be used as a basis for discovering his internalized grammar.

Let us consider the status of such observations with slightly greater care. These observations actually bear directly on the output of a perceptual model such as (1); they relate to the structures assigned to signals by the hearer. Our characterization of the output of (1) is a construct based on evidence of this sort. Then, the perceptual model *PM* itself is a second-order construct. Abstracting further, we can study the grammar that constitutes one fundamental component of (1) as a third-order construct. Thus the evidence cited in the preceding paragraph actually has a bearing on grammar only indirectly. We must, in other words, presuppose the legitimacy of each abstraction. There seems little question of the legitimacy of abstraction in such cases as these, and there is an overwhelming mass of evidence of the sort cited. Once again, we note that idealization of the kind just described is inescapable if a complex organism is to be studied in a serious way.

This process of abstraction can be carried one step further. Consider an acquisition model *AM* that uses linguistic data to discover the grammar of the language to which this data pertains.

(3)

$$\text{Linguistic data } \rightarrow \boxed{\ AM\ } \rightarrow \text{Grammar}$$

Just how the device *AM* selects a grammar will be determined by its internal structure, by the methods of analysis available to it, and the initial constraints that it imposes on any possible grammar. If we are given information about the pairing of linguistic data and grammars, we may try to determine the nature of the device *AM*. Although these are not the terms that have been used, linguistics has always been concerned with this question. Thus modern structural linguistics has attempted to develop methods of analysis of a general nature, independent of any particular language, and an older and now largely forgotten tradition attempted to develop a system of universal constraints that any grammar must meet. We might describe both these attempts as concerned with the internal structure of the device *AM*, with the innate conception of "human language" that makes language acquisition possible.[4]

---

[4] The existence of innate mental structure is, obviously, not a matter of controversy. What we may question is just what it is and to what extent it is specific to language.

UNIVERSAL GRAMMAR

Let us now turn to the study of underlying competence, and consider the general problem of how a sound-meaning pairing might be established. As a preliminary to this investigation of universal grammar, we must ask how sounds and meanings are to be represented. Since we are interested in human languages in general, such systems of representation must be independent of any particular language. We must, in other words, develop a universal phonetics and a universal semantics that delimit, respectively, the set of possible signals and the set of possible semantic representations for any human language. It will then be possible to speak of a language as a particular pairing of signals with semantic interpretations, and to investigate the rules that establish this pairing. Our review of the general properties of language thus falls naturally into three parts: a discussion of universal phonetics, of universal semantics, and of the overarching system of universal grammar. The first two topics involve the representation of idealized form and semantic content; the theory of universal grammar deals with the mechanisms used in natural languages to determine the form of a sentence and its semantic content.

The importance of developing a universal semantics and universal phonetics, in the sense of the last paragraph, was clearly recognized long before the development of modern linguistics. For example, Bishop Wilkins in his *Essay Towards a Real Character and a Philosophical Language* (1668) attempted to develop a universal phonetic alphabet and a universal catalogue of concepts in terms of which, respectively, the signals and semantic interpretations for any language can be represented. The phonetic alphabet is based on a system of phonetic properties developed in terms of point and manner of articulation. Each phonetic symbol is analyzable as a set of such properties; in modern terms, it is analyzable as a set of *distinctive features*. It is furthermore tacitly assumed that the physical signal is determined, by language-independent principles, from its representation in terms of phonetic symbols. The concepts that are proposed as units of semantic interpretation are also analyzable into fixed properties (semantic features) of some sort, for example, animate-inanimate, relational-absolute, agent-instrument, etc. It is tacitly assumed that the semantic interpretation of a sentence is determined by universal, language-independent principles from the concepts comprised in the utterance and the manner in which they are grammatically related (for example, as subject-predicate).[5] Although the defects in execution in such pioneering studies as that of Wilkins are obvious, the general approach is sound. The theory of universal phonetics has

---

[5] This assumption is not explicit in Wilkins, but is developed in other seventeenth and eighteenth century work. See Chomsky, *Cartesian Linguistics*, Harper and Row, New York, 1966, for references and discussion.

been intensively pursued along the lines just indicated with considerable success; the parallel theory of universal semantics has, in contrast, been very little studied.

UNIVERSAL GRAMMAR: UNIVERSAL PHONETICS

The theory of universal phonetics attempts to establish a universal phonetic alphabet and a system of laws. The alphabet defines the set of possible signals from which the signals of a particular language are drawn. If the theory is correct, each signal of a language can be represented as a sequence of symbols of the phonetic alphabet. Suppose that two physical events are represented as the same sequence. Then in any language they must be repetitions of one another.[6] On the other hand, two physical events might be regarded by speakers of one language as repetitions and by speakers of another language as nonrepetitions. In this case, the universal alphabet must provide the means for distinguishing them. Representation in terms of the universal alphabet should provide whatever information is necessary to determine how the signal may be produced, and it should, at the same time, correspond to a refined level of perceptual representation. We stress once again, however, that actual performance involves other factors beyond ideal phonetic representation.

The symbols of the universal phonetic alphabet are not the "primitive elements" of universal phonetic theory. These primitive elements include rather, what have been called (*phonetic*) *distinctive features*, properties such as voicing, frontness-backness, stress, etc.[7] Each of these features can be thought of as a scale in terms of which two or more values can be distinguished (how many values need be distinguished is an open question, but the number is apparently quite small for each feature). A symbol of the phonetic alphabet is properly to be regarded as a set of features, each with a specified value. A signal, then, is represented as a sequence of such sets.

Three obvious properties of language are reflected in a phonetic theory of this sort. The first is its discreteness—the fact that only a determinable finite number of signals of any given length can be nonrepetitions. The second property is the unboundedness of language—the fact that a signal can be of arbitrary length, so that a language will contain infinitely many semantically interpreted signals. In addition to these formal properties, a

---

[6] In an appropriate sense of repetition. Thus any two physical signals are in some way distinct, but some of the differences are irrelevant in a particular language, and others are irrelevant in any language.

[7] A theory of phonetic distinctive features is developed in R. Jakobson, G. Fant, and M. Halle, *Preliminaries to Speech Analysis*, Cambridge, Mass., 1951 (2nd ed., M.I.T. Press, Cambridge, Mass., 1963). A revised and, we think, improved version will appear in N. Chomsky and M. Halle, *Sound Pattern of English*, Harper and Row, New York (forthcoming). [The *Sound Pattern* appeared in 1968.—*Eds.*]

phonetic theory of this sort reflects the fact that two segments of a signal, represented by two symbols of the universal alphabet, may be alike in certain respects and distinct in others; and that there are, furthermore, a fixed number of such dimensions of sameness and difference and a fixed number of potentially significant points along these dimensions. Thus, the initial segments of *pin* and *bin*[8] differ with respect to voicing and aspiration but not (significantly) with respect to point of articulation; the two consonants of *cocoa* differ with respect to neither point of articulation nor voicing, but only with respect to aspiration; etc.

It is important to note that the distinctive features postulated in universal phonetic theory are absolute in several senses but relative in others. They are absolute in the sense that they are fixed for all languages. If phonetic representation is to provide sufficient information for identification of a physical signal, then specification of feature values must also be absolute. On the other hand, the features are relative when considered in terms of the notion of repetition-nonrepetition. For example, given three absolute values designated 1, 2, 3 in terms of the feature front-back, we might find that in language L_1 two utterances that differ only in the values 1, 2 of frontness-backness are distinguished as nonrepetitions but utterances differing only in the values 2, 3 are not; whereas in language L_2 the opposite might be the case. Each language would use the feature front-back to distinguish nonrepetitions, but the absolute value 2 that is "front" in one language would be "back" in the other.

In addition to a system of distinctive features, a universal phonetic theory will also attempt to formulate certain laws that govern the permitted sequences and permitted variety of selection in a particular language. For example, Jakobson has observed that no language uses both the feature labialization and the feature velarization for distinguishing nonrepetitions, and he has suggested a more general formulation in terms of which these two features can be regarded as variants of a single, more abstract feature. Generalizations of this sort—particularly when they can be supported by rational argument—can be proposed as laws of universal phonetics.

UNIVERSAL GRAMMAR: UNIVERSAL SEMANTICS

Although universal phonetics is a fairly well-developed subject, the same cannot be said of universal semantics. Here, too, we might hope to establish a universal system of semantic features and laws regarding their interrela-

---

[8] Observe that although the order of phonetic segments is a significant fact, there is no reason to assume that the physical event represented by a particular sequence of phonetic symbols can be analyzed into successive parts, each associated with a particular symbol.

tions and permitted variety. In fact, the problem of determining such features and such laws has once again become a topic of serious investigation in the past few years,[9] and there is some promise of fruitful development. It can be seen at once that an analysis of concepts in terms of such features as animateness, action, etc. (see p. 113) will hardly be adequate, and that certain features must be still more abstract. It is, for example, a fact of English that the phrase "a good knife" means "a knife which cuts well." Consequently the concept "knife" must be specified in part in terms of features having to do with characteristic functions (not just physical properties), and in terms of an abstract "evaluation feature"[10] that is determined by such modifiers as "good," "terrible," etc. Only by such an analysis can the semantic relationship between "this is a good knife" and "this knife cuts well" be established. In contrast, the irrelevance of "this is a good knife for digging with" to "this knife cuts well" shows that the semantic interpretation of a sentence is determined by grammatical relations of a sort that are by no means transparent.

As in the case of universal phonetics, we might hope to establish general principles regarding the possible systems of concepts that can be represented in a human language and the intrinsic connections that may exist among them. With the discovery of such principles, universal semantics would become a substantive discipline.

UNIVERSAL GRAMMAR: UNIVERSAL SYNTAX

Suppose that a satisfactory theory of universal phonetics and of universal semantics were at hand. We could then define a language as a set of sentences, where a sentence is a particular kind of sound-meaning pair, and go on to study the systems of rules that define human languages. But in fact only the theory of universal phonetics is sufficiently well-established to support this enterprise. Consequently, we must approach the study of language structure in a slightly more indirect way.

Notice that although the notion "semantic representation" is itself far from clear, we can, nevertheless, find innumerable empirical conditions that

---

[9] See J. Katz, *The Philosophy of Language*, Harper and Row, 1965, for a review of some recent work. For another view, see U. Weinreich, Explorations in semantic theory, in T. A. Sebeok (ed.), *Current Trends in Linguistics*, Vol. 3 of *Linguistic Theory*, Mouton and Co., The Hague (1966); and for comments on this and further developments, see J. Katz, *Recent Issues in Semantic Theory* (in preparation). There has also been quite a bit of recent work in descriptive semantics, some of which is suggestive with respect to the problems discussed here. [Katz's reply to Weinreich appeared in *Foundations of Language*, III (May, 1967), 124–194; Weinreich's further remarks are in the same volume of the same journal, pp. 296–299.—*Eds.*]

[10] For discussion of this notion, see J. Katz, Semantic theory and the meaning of "good," *J. Philos.*, LXI, No. 23 (1964).

an explication of this notion must meet. Consider, for example, the following sentence:

(4)   What disturbed John was being disregarded by everyone.

It is clear, first of all, that this expression has two distinct interpretations. Under one interpretation, it means that John was disturbed by the fact that everyone disregarded him; under the second, it means that everyone was disregarding the things that disturb John. Under the first of these interpretations, a certain grammatical relation holds between "disregard" and "John," namely, the same relation that holds between these items in "Everyone disregards John" (the "verb-object" relation). Under the second interpretation neither this nor any other grammatically significant relation holds between "disregard" and "John." On the other hand, if we insert the word "our" between "was" and "being," the sentence is unambiguous, and no grammatical relation holds between "disregard" and "John," although the verb-object relation now holds between "disregard" and "we" (an underlying element of "our").

Examples of this sort can be elaborated indefinitely. They provide conditions of adequacy that the notion "semantic interpretation" must meet (for example, relations of paraphrase and implication and the property of ambiguity must be correctly reflected), and they illustrate clearly some of the ways in which the semantic interpretations of linguistic expressions must be determined from those of their grammatically related parts.

From such considerations, we are led to formulate a more restricted but quite significant immediate goal for the study of linguistic structure. Still taking a language to be a set of sentences, let us consider each abstract "sentence" to be a specific pairing of a phonetic representation with an abstract structure of some sort (let us call it a *deep structure*) that incorporates information relevant to semantic interpretation. We can then study the system of rules that determines this pairing, in a particular language, and the general characteristics of such rules. This enterprise will be significant to the extent that these underlying deep structures do actually provide a way to meet the empirical conditions on semantic interpretation. Semantic theory, as it progresses, will then provide means for enriching deep structures and associating semantic interpretations with them. The empirical significance of a full theory of grammar, comprising a universal phonetics, semantics, and syntax, will depend in part on the extent to which conditions on semantic interpretation can be satisfied by systematic use of the devices and principles that this theory supplies.

Summarizing these remarks, let us establish the following framework for the study of linguistic structure. The *grammar* of a language is a system of rules that determine a certain pairing of sound and meaning. It consists of a *syntactic component*, a *semantic component*, and a *phonological component*. The syntactic component defines a certain (infinite) class of abstract objects (D, S), where D is a *deep structure* and S a *surface structure*. The deep structure contains all information relevant to semantic interpretation; the surface structure, all information relevant to phonetic interpretation. The semantic and phonological components are purely interpretive. The former assigns semantic interpretations to deep structures; the latter assigns phonetic interpretations to surface structures. Thus the grammar as a whole relates semantic and phonetic interpretations, the association being mediated by the rules of the syntactic component that define paired deep and surface structures. The study of the three components will, of course, be highly integrated; each can be investigated to the extent that it is clear what conditions the others impose upon it.

This formulation should be regarded as an informal first approximation. When we develop a precise theory of grammatical structure—for example, the particular version of the theory of transformational grammar sketched below—we will provide a technical meaning for the terms "deep structure" and "surface structure," and in terms of these technical meanings, we can then raise the empirical (not conceptual) question of how deep and surface structures contribute to and determine semantic and phonetic interpretations. In the technical sense that is given to the concepts of deep and surface structure in the theory outlined below, it seems to me that present information suggests that surface structure completely determines phonetic interpretation and that deep structure completely determines certain highly significant aspects of semantic interpretation. But the looseness of the latter term makes a more definite statement impossible. In fact, I think that a reasonable explication of the term "semantic interpretation" would lead to the conclusion that surface structure also contributes in a restricted but important way to semantic interpretation, but I will say no more about this matter here.

Universal grammar might be defined as the study of the conditions that must be met by the grammars of all human languages. Universal semantics and phonetics, in the sense described earlier, will then be a part of universal grammar. So defined, universal grammar is nothing other than the theory of language structure. This seems in accord with traditional usage. However, only certain aspects of universal grammar were studied until quite recently. In particular, the problem of formulating the conditions that must be met by the rules of syntax, phonology, and semantics was not raised in any explicit way in traditional linguistics, although suggestive and nontrivial steps toward the study of this problem are implicit in much traditional work.[11]

A grammar of the sort described previously, which attempts to characterize in an explicit way the intrinsic association of phonetic form and semantic content in a particular language, might be called a *generative grammar*[12] to distinguish it from descriptions that have some different goal (for example, pedagogic grammars). In intention, at least, traditional scholarly grammars are generative grammars, although they fall far short of achieving the goal of determining how sentences are formed or interpreted. A good traditional grammar gives a full exposition of exceptions to rules, but it provides only hints and examples to illustrate regular structures (except for trivial cases—for example, inflectional paradigms). It is tacitly presumed that the intelligent reader will use his "linguistic intuition"—his latent, unconscious knowledge of universal grammar—to determine the regular structures from the presented examples and remarks. The grammar itself does not express the deep-seated regularities of the language. For the purpose of the study of linguistic structure, particular or universal, such grammars are, therefore, of limited value. It is necessary to extend them to full generative grammars if the study of linguistic structure is to be advanced to the point where it deals significantly with regularities and general principles. It is, however, important to be aware of the fact that the concept "generative grammar" itself is no very great innovation. The fact that every language "makes infinite use of finite means" (Wilhelm von Humboldt) has long been understood. Modern work in generative grammar is simply an attempt to give an explicit account of how these finite means are put to infinite use in particular languages and to discover the deeper properties that define "human language," in general (that is, the properties that constitute universal grammar).

We have been concerned thus far only with clarification of concepts and setting of goals. Let us now turn to the problem of formulating hypotheses of universal grammar.

STRUCTURE OF THE PHONOLOGICAL COMPONENT

The syntactic component of a generative grammar defines (generates) an infinite set of pairs (D, S), where D is a deep structure and S is a surface

---

[11] See Chomsky, *op. cit.*, for discussion.

[12] See p. 109. In general, a set of rules that recursively define an infinite set of objects may be said to *generate* this set. Thus a set of axioms and rules of inference for arithmetic may be said to generate a set of proofs and a set of theorems of arithmetic (last lines of proofs). Similarly, a (generative) grammar may be said to generate a set of structural descriptions, each of which, ideally, incorporates a deep structure, a surface structure, a semantic interpretation (of the deep structure) and a phonetic interpretation (of the surface structure).

structure; the interpretive components of the grammar assign a semantic representation to D and a phonetic representation to S.

Let us first consider the problem of assigning phonetic representations to surface structures. As in the previous discussion of universal phonetics, we take a phonetic representation to be a sequence of symbols of the universal phonetic alphabet, each symbol being analyzed into distinctive features with specific values. Stating the same idea slightly differently, we may think of a phonetic representation as a matrix in which rows correspond to features of the universal system, columns correspond to successive segments (symbols of the phonetic alphabet), and each entry is an integer that specifies the value of a particular segment with respect to the feature in question. Our problem, then, is to determine what information must be contained in the surface structure, and how the rules of the phonological component of the grammar use this information to specify a phonetic matrix of the sort just described.

Consider once again the example (4) which we repeat in (5) for ease of reference:

(5)   What ⚹ disturb-ed ⚹ John ⚹ was ⚹ be-ing ⚹ dis-regard-ed ⚹ by ⚹ every-one.

To first approximation,[13] we may think of (5) as a sequence of the *formatives* "what," "disturb," "ed," "John," "was," "be," "ing," "dis," "regard," "ed," "by," "every," "one," with the *junctures* represented by the symbols ⚹ and - in the positions indicated in (5). These junctures specify the manner in which formatives are combined; they provide information which is required by the interpretive rules of the phonological component. A juncture must, in fact, be analyzed as a set of features, that is, as a single-column matrix in which the rows correspond to certain features of the junctural system and each entry is one of two values which we may represent as + or −. Similarly, each formative will be analyzed as a matrix in which columns stand for successive segments, rows correspond to certain *categorial features*, and each entry is either + or −. Therefore, the entire sentence (5) can be regarded as a single matrix with the entries + and −.[14]

The categorial features include the universal features of the phonetic system, along with *diacritic* features which essentially indicate exceptions to rules. Thus the matrix corresponding to "what" in the dialect in which the corresponding phonetic representation is [wat], will contain three seg-

---

[13] The analysis that is presented here for purposes of exposition would have to be refined for empirical adequacy.

[14] Notice that every two successive formatives are separated by a juncture, as is necessary if the representation of (5) as a single matrix is to preserve the formative structure. For present purposes, we may think of each segment of a formative as unmarked for all junctural features and each juncture as unmarked for each formative feature.

ments, the first specified as a labial glide, the second as a low back unrounded vowel, the third as an unvoiced dental stop consonant (these
specifications given completely in terms of the + and − values of features
supplied by the universal phonetic system). The rules of the phonological
component, in this case, will convert this specification in terms of + and −
values into a more detailed specification in terms of integers, in which the
value of each segment with respect to the phonetic features (for example,
tongue height, degree of aspiration, etc.) is indicated to whatever degree of
accuracy is required by the presupposed theory of universal phonetics, and
with whatever range of variation is allowed by the language. In this example, the assigned values will simply refine the bifurcation into + and −
values given in the underlying matrix for "what" in (5).

The example just cited is unusually simple, however. In general, the rules
of the phonological component will not only give a finer specification of the
underlying division into + and − values, but will also change values significantly and, perhaps, insert, delete, or rearrange segments. For example, the
formative "by" will be represented with an underlying matrix consisting of
two columns, the second of which is specified as a high front-vowel (specification given in terms of values of features). The corresponding phonetic
matrix, however, will consist of three columns, the second of which is specified as a low back-vowel and the third as a palatal glide (the specification
here being in terms of integral valued entries in a phonetic matrix).[15]

The surface structure of (5), then, is represented as a matrix in which one
of two values appears in each entry. The fact that only two values may appear indicates that this underlying matrix really serves a purely classificatory function. Each sentence is classified in such a way as to distinguish it
from all other sentences, and in such a way as to determine just how the
rules of the phonological component assign specific positional phonetic
values. We see, then, that the distinctive features of the universal phonetic
system have a *classificatory function* in the underlying matrix constituting a
part of the surface structure, and a *phonetic function* in the matrix constituting the phonetic representation of the sentence in question. Only in the
former function are the distinctive features uniformly binary; only in the
latter do they receive a direct physical interpretation.

The underlying classificatory matrix just described does not exhaust the
information required by the interpretive phonological rules. Beyond this,
it is necessary to know how the sentence in question is subdivided into
phrases of varying size, and what types of phrase these are. In the case of
(5), for example, phonological interpretation requires the information that
"disturb" and "disregard" are verbs, that "what disturbed John" is a noun

---

[15] The reasons for this analysis go beyond the scope of this discussion. For details see Chomsky and Halle,
op. cit.

phrase, that "John was being" is not a phrase at all, and so on. The relevant information can be indicated by a proper bracketing of the sentence with labeled brackets.[16] The unit contained within paired brackets [$_A$ and]$_A$ will be referred to as a phrase of the category A. For example, the sequence "what ⚹ disturb-ed ⚹ John" in (5) will be enclosed within the brackets [$_{NP}$,]$_{NP}$, indicating that it is a noun phrase; the formative "disturb" will be enclosed within the brackets [$_V$,]$_V$, indicating that it is a verb; the whole expression (5) will be enclosed within the brackets [$_S$,]$_S$, indicating that it is a sentence. The sequence "John was being" will not be enclosed within paired brackets, since it is no phrase at all. To take an extremely simple example, the sentence, "John saw Bill," might be represented in the following way as a surface structure, where each orthographically represented item is to be regarded as a classificatory matrix:

(6)   [$_S$ [$_{NP}$ [$_N$ John]$_N$]$_{NP}$ [$_{VP}$ [$_V$ saw]$_V$ [$_{NP}$ [$_N$ Bill]$_N$]$_{NP}$]$_{VP}$]$_S$

This representation indicates that "John" and "Bill" are nouns (N's) and "saw" a verb (V); that "John" and "Bill" are, furthermore, noun phrases (NP's); that "saw Bill" is a verb phrase (VP); and that "John saw Bill" is a sentence (S). It seems that interpretation of a sentence by the phonological component of the grammar invariably requires information which can be represented in the way just described. We therefore postulate that the surface structure of a sentence is a properly labeled bracketing of a classificatory matrix of formatives and junctures.

The phonological component of a grammar converts a surface structure into a phonetic representation. We have now given a rough specification of the notions "surface structure" and "phonetic representations." It remains to describe the rules of the phonological component and the manner in which they are organized.

The evidence presently available suggests that the rules of the phonological component are linearly ordered in a sequence $R_1, \ldots R_n$, and that this sequence of rules applies in a cyclic fashion to a surface structure in the following way. In the first cycle of application, the rules $R_1, \ldots, R_n$ apply in this order to a maximal continuous part of the surface structure containing no internal brackets. After the last of these rules has applied, innermost brackets are erased and the second cycle of application is initiated. In this cycle, the rules again apply in the given order to a maximal continuous part of the surface structure containing no internal brackets. Innermost brackets are then erased, and the third cycle is initiated. The process continues until

---

[16] In the obvious sense. Thus [$_A$...[$_B$...]$_B$...[$_C$...]$_C$...]$_A$ would, for example, be a proper bracketing of the string ... in terms of the labeled brackets [$_A$,]$_A$,[$_B$,]$_B$,[$_C$,]$_C$, but neither of the following would be proper bracketings:

$$[_A \cdots [_B \cdots]_A; \qquad [_A \cdots [_B \cdots]_A \cdots]_B$$

the maximal domain of phonological processes (in simple cases, the entire sentence) is reached. Certain of the rules are restricted in application to the level of word-boundary—they apply in the cycle only when the domain of application is a full word. Others are free to iterate at every stage of application. Notice that the principle of cyclic application is highly intuitive. It states, in effect, that there is a fixed system of rules that determines the form of large units from the (ideal) form of their constituent parts.

We can illustrate the principle of cyclic application with some rules of stress assignment in English. It seems to be a fact that although phonetic representations for English must allow five or six different values along the distinctive feature of stress, nevertheless, all segments can be unmarked with respect to stress in surface structures—that is, stress has no categorial function (except highly marginally) as a distinctive feature for English. The complex stress contours of the phonetic representation are determined by such rules as (7) and (8).[17]

(7)   Assign primary stress to the left-most of two primary stressed vowels, in nouns.

(8)   Assign primary stress to the right-most stress-peak, where a vowel V is a stress-peak in a certain domain if this domain contains no vowel more heavily stressed than V.

Rule (7) applies to nouns with two primary stresses; rule (8) applies to a unit of any other kind. The rules apply in the order (7), (8), in the cyclic manner described above. By convention, when primary stress is assigned in a certain position, all other stresses are weakened by one. Notice that if a domain contains no stressed vowel, then rule (8) will assign primary stress to its right-most vowel.

To illustrate these rules, consider first the surface structure (6). In accordance with the general principle of cyclic application, the rules (7) and (8) first apply to the innermost units $[_N$ John $]_N$, $[_V$ saw $]_V$, and $[_N$ Bill $]_N$. Rule (7) is inapplicable; rule (8) applies, assigning primary stress to the single vowel in each case. Innermost brackets are then erased. The next cycle deals with the units $[_{NP}$ John $]_{NP}$ and $[_{NP}$ Bill $]_{NP}$ and simply reassigns primary stress to the single vowel, by rule (8). Innermost brackets are then erased, and we have the unit $[_{VP}$ saw Bill $]_{VP}$ as the domain of application of the rules. Rule (7) is again inapplicable, since this is not a noun; rule (8)

---

[17] These are simplified, for expository purposes. See Chomsky and Halle, *op. cit.*, for a more accurate account. In particular, we must assume that if rule (7) is applicable at a particular stage in the cycle, then rule (8) is not applied to the phrase to which rule (7) has applied, at this stage of the cycle. Notice that in this exposition we are using the term "applies" ambiguously, in the sense of "available for application" and also in the sense of "actually modifies the sequence under consideration."

assigns primary stress to the vowel of "Bill," weakening the stress on "saw"
to secondary. Innermost brackets are erased, and we have the unit [$_S$ John
saw Bill]$_S$ as the domain of application. Rule (7) is again inapplicable, and
rule (8) assigns primary stress to "Bill," weakening the other stresses and
giving "John saw Bill," which can be accepted as an ideal representation of
the stress contour.

Consider now the slightly more complex example, "John's blackboard
eraser." In the first application of the cycle, rules (7) and (8) apply to the
innermost bracketed units "John," "black," "board," "erase"; rule (7) is
inapplicable, and rule (8) assigns primary stress in each case to the right-
most vowel (the only vowel, in the first three). The next cycle involves the
units "John's" and "eraser," and is vacuous.[18] The domain of application
for the next cycle is [$_N$ black board]$_N$. Being a noun, this unit is subject to
rule (7), which assigns primary stress to "black," weakening the stress on
"board" to secondary. Innermost brackets are erased, and the domain of
application for the next cycle is [$_N$ black board eraser]$_N$. Again rule (7)
applies, assigning primary stress to "black" and weakening all other stresses
by one. In the final cycle, the domain of application of the rules is [$_{NP}$ John's
black board eraser]$_{NP}$. Rule (7) is inapplicable, since this is a full noun-
phrase. Rule (8) assigns primary stress to the right-most primary stressed
vowel, weakening all the others and giving "John's blackboard eraser." In
this way, a complex phonetic representation is determined by independently
motivated and very simple rules, applying in accordance with the general
principle of the cycle.

This example is characteristic and illustrates several important points.
The grammar of English must contain the rule (7) so as to account for the
fact that the stress contour is falling in the case of the noun "blackboard,"
and it must contain rule (8), to account for the rising contour of the phrase
"black board" ("board which is black"). The principle of the cycle is not,
strictly speaking, part of the grammar of English but is rather a principle of
universal grammar that determines the application of the particular rules of
English or any other language, whatever these rules may be. In the case
illustrated, the general principle of cyclic application assigns a complex
stress contour, as indicated. Equipped with the principle of the cycle and
the two rules (7) and (8), a person will know[19] the proper stress contour for

---

[18] The word "eraser" is, at this stage, bisyllabic.
[19] As earlier, we refer here to "tacit" or "latent knowledge," which can, perhaps, be brought to consciousness with proper attention but is surely not presented to "unguided intuition."

"John's blackboard eraser" and innumerable other expressions which he may never have heard previously. This is a simple example of a general property of language; *certain universal principles must interrelate with specific rules to determine the form (and meaning) of entirely new linguistic expressions.*

This example also lends support to a somewhat more subtle and far-reaching hypothesis. There is little doubt that such phenomena as stress contours in English are a perceptual reality; trained observers will, for example, reach a high degree of unanimity in recording new utterances in their native language. There is, however, little reason to suppose that these contours represent a *physical* reality. It may very well be the case that stress contours are not represented in the physical signal in anything like the perceived detail. There is no paradox in this. If just two levels of stress are distinguished in the physical signal, then the person who is learning English will have sufficient evidence to construct the rules (7) and (8) (given the contrast "blackboard," "black board," for example). Assuming then that he knows the principle of the cycle, he will be able to perceive the stress contour of "John's blackboard eraser" even if it is not a physical property of the signal. The evidence now available strongly suggests that this is an accurate description of how stress is perceived in English.

It is important to see that there is nothing mysterious in this description. There would be no problem in principle in designing an automaton that uses the rules (7) and (8), the rules of English syntax, and the principle of the transformational cycle to assign a multi-leveled stress contour even to an utterance in which stress is not represented at all (for example, a sentence spelled in conventional orthography). The automaton would use the rules of syntax to determine the surface structure of the utterance, and would then apply the rules (7) and (8), in accordance with the principle of the cycle, to determine the multi-leveled contour. Taking such an automaton as a first approximation to a model for speech perception [see (1), p. 110], we might propose that the hearer uses certain selected properties of the physical signal to determine which sentence of the language was produced and to assign to it a deep and surface structure. With careful attention, he will then be able to "hear" the stress contour assigned by the phonological component of his grammar, whether or not it corresponds to any physical property of the presented signal. Such an account of speech perception assumes, putting it loosely, that syntactic interpretation of an utterance may be a prerequisite to "hearing" its phonetic representation in detail; it rejects the assumption that speech perception requires a full analysis of phonetic form followed by a full analysis of syntactic structure followed by semantic interpretation, as well as the assumption that perceived phonetic form is an accurate point-by-point representation of the signal. But it must be kept in mind that there is nothing to suggest that either of the rejected assumptions is correct, nor is there anything at all mysterious in the view just outlined that rejects these assumptions. In fact, the view just outlined is highly plausible, since it can dispense with the claim that some presently undetectable physical properties of utterances are identified with an accuracy that goes beyond anything experimentally demonstrable even under ideal conditions, and it can account for the perception of stress contours of novel utterances[20] on the very simple assumption that rules (7) and (8) and the general principle of cyclic application are available to the perceptual system.

There is a great deal more to be said about the relative merits of various kinds of perceptual model. Instead of pursuing this topic, let us consider further the hypothesis that rules (7) and (8), and the principle of cyclic application, are available to the perceptual system and are used in the manner suggested. It is clear how rules (7) and (8) might be learned from simple examples of rising and falling contour (for example, "black board" contrasted with "blackboard"). But the question then arises: how does a person learn the principle of cyclic application? Before facing this question, it is necessary to settle one that is logically prior to it: why assume that the principle is learned at all? There is much evidence that the principle is used, but from this it does not follow that it has been learned. In fact, it is difficult to imagine how such a principle might be learned, uniformly by all speakers, and it is by no means clear that sufficient evidence is available in the physical signal to justify this principle. Consequently, the most reasonable conclusion seems to be that the principle is not learned at all, but rather that it is simply part of the conceptual equipment that the learner brings to the task of language acquisition. A rather similar argument can be given with respect to other principles of universal grammar.

Notice again that there should be nothing surprising in such a conclusion. There would be no difficulty, in principle, in designing an automaton which incorporates the principles of universal grammar and puts them to use to determine which of the possible languages is the one to which it is exposed. *A priori*, there is no more reason to suppose that these principles are themselves learned than there is to suppose that a person learns to interpret visual stimuli in terms of line, angle, contour, distance, or, for that matter, that he learns to have two arms. It is completely a question of empirical fact; there is no information of any general extralinguistic sort that can

---

[20] And other aspects. The argument is, in fact, much more general. It must be kept in mind that speech perception is often impaired minimally, or not at all, even by significant distortion of the signal, a fact difficult to reconcile with the view that phonetic analysis in detail is a prerequisite for analysis of the syntactic and semantic structure.

be used, at present, to support the assumption that some principle of universal grammar is learned, or that it is innate, or (in some manner) both. If linguistic evidence seems to suggest that some principles are unlearned, there is no reason to find this conclusion paradoxical or surprising.

Returning to the elaboration of principles of universal grammar, it seems that the phonological component of a grammar consists of a sequence of rules that apply in a cyclic manner, as just described, to assign a phonetic representation to a surface structure. The phonetic representation is a matrix of phonetic feature specifications and the surface structure is a properly labeled bracketing of formatives which are, themselves, represented in terms of marking of categorial distinctive features. What evidence is now available supports these assumptions; they provide the basis for explaining many curious features of phonetic fact.

It is important to notice that there is no *a priori* necessity for the phonological component of a grammar to have just these properties. These assumptions about universal grammar restrict the class of possible human languages to a very special subset of the set of imaginable "languages." The evidence available to us suggests that these assumptions pertain to the language acquisition device AM of (3), p. 112; that is, that they form one part of the schematism that the child brings to the problem of language learning. That this schematism must be quite elaborate and highly restrictive seems fairly obvious. If it were not, language acquisition, within the empirically known limits of time, access and variability, would be an impenetrable mystery. Considerations of the sort mentioned in the foregoing discussion are directly relevant to the problem of determining the nature of these innate mechanisms, and, therefore, deserve extremely careful study and attention.

STRUCTURE OF THE SEMANTIC COMPONENT

Let us now consider the second interpretive component of a generative grammar, the system of rules that converts a deep structure into a semantic representation that expresses the intrinsic meaning of the sentence in question. Although many aspects of semantic interpretation remain quite obscure, it is still quite possible to undertake a direct investigation of the theory of deep structures and their interpretation, and certain properties of the semantic component seem fairly clear. In particular, as we have noted earlier, many empirical conditions on semantic interpretation can be clearly formulated. For example, we know that sentence (4) on p. 117 must be assigned at least two semantic representations, and that one of these must be essentially the same as the interpretation assigned to both (9) and (10).

(9)   Being disregarded by everyone disturbed John.

(10)   The fact that everyone disregarded John disturbed him.[21]

Furthermore, it is clear that the semantic representation of a sentence depends on the representation of its parts, as in the parallel case of phonetic interpretation. For example, in the case of (10), it is obvious that the semantic interpretation depends, in part, on the semantic interpretation of "everyone disregarded John"; if the latter were replaced in (10) by "life seemed to pass John by," the interpretation of the whole would be changed in a fixed way. This much is transparent, and it suggests that a principle like the principle of cyclic application in phonology should hold in the semantic component.

A slightly more careful look at the problem shows that semantic interpretation must be significantly more abstract than phonological interpretation with respect to the notion of "constituent part." Thus the interpretation of "everyone disregarded John" underlies not only (10), but also (9) and (4), and in exactly the same way. But neither (4) nor (9) contains "everyone disregarded John" as a constituent part, as does (10). In other words, the deep structures underlying (9) and (10) should both be identical (or very similar) to one of two deep structures underlying (4), despite the wide divergence in surface structure and phonetic form. It follows that we cannot expect deep structure to be very close to surface structure in general.

In the case of a sentence like (6) ("John saw Bill"), there is little difference between deep and surface structure. Semantic interpretation would not be far from the mark, in this case, if it were quite parallel to phonetic interpretation. Thus the interpretation of "saw Bill" can be derived from that of "saw"[22] and that of "Bill," and the interpretation of (6) can be determined from that of "John" and that of "saw Bill." To carry out such interpretation we must know not only the bracketing of (6) into constituents, but also the grammatical relations that are represented; that is, we must know that "Bill" is the *direct-object* of "saw" and that the subject-predicate relation holds between "John" and "saw Bill" in "John saw Bill." Similarly, in the slightly more complex case of "John saw Bill leave," we must know that the subject-predicate relation holds between "John" and "saw Bill leave" and also between "Bill" and "leave."

Notice that at least in such simple cases as (6), we already have a mechanism for representing grammatical relations of just the sort that are required for semantic interpretation. Suppose that we define the relation

---

[21] The latter is again ambiguous in an entirely different way from (4), depending on the reference of "him." We will assume, throughout, that it refers to *John*.

[22] But the interpretation of this depends on that of "see" and that of "past tense"; hence, these separate items must be represented in the deep structure, though not, in this case, in the surface structure.

subject-of as the relation holding between a noun phrase and a sentence of which it is an immediate constituent[23] and the relation predicate-of as holding between a verb phrase and a sentence of which it is an immediate constituent. The subject-predicate relation can then be defined as the relation holding between the subject of a sentence and the predicate of this sentence. Thus, in these terms, "John" is the subject and "saw Bill (leave)" the predicate of "John saw Bill (leave)," and the subject-predicate relation holds between the two. In the same way, we can define the relation *direct-object* (in terms of the immediate constituency of verb and noun phrase in verb phrase) and others in a perfectly appropriate and satisfactory way. But returning now to (6), this observation implies that a *labeled bracketing* will serve as the deep structure (just as a labeled bracketing will serve as the surface structure); it contains just the information about constituency and about grammatical relations that is required for semantic interpretation.

We noted that in "John saw Bill leave" the subject-predicate relation holds between "Bill" and "leave," as well as between "John" and "saw Bill leave." If (6) or something very much like it—see, for example, note 22—is to be taken as the deep structure, with grammatical relations defined as previously, then the deep structure of "John saw Bill leave" will have to be something like (11) (many details omitted):

(11) $[_S [_{NP} \text{John}]_{NP} [_{VP} [_V \text{saw}]_V [_S [_{NP} \text{Bill}]$

$_{NP} [_{VP} [_V \text{leave}]_V]_{VP}]_S]_{VP}]_S$

The labeled bracketing (11) expresses the subject-predicate relation between "John" and "saw Bill leave" and between "Bill" and "leave," as required.

Moving to a somewhat more complex example, the sentences (9) and (10) (as well as (4) under one interpretation) will each have to contain something like (12) in the deep structure:

(12) $[_S [_{NP} \text{everyone}]_{NP} [_{VP} [_V \text{disregards}]_V [_{NP} \text{John}]_{NP}]_{VP}]_S .$

If this requirement is met, then we will be able to account for the fact that, obviously, the meaning of (4) (= "what disturbed John was being disregarded by everyone") in one interpretation and of (9) (= "being disregarded by everyone disturbed John") is determined in part by the fact

---

[23] A phrase X is an immediate constituent of the phrase Y containing X if there is no phrase Z which contains X and is contained in Y. Thus, the noun phrase "John" is an immediate constituent of the sentence "John saw Bill," [analyzed as in (6)], but the noun phrase "Bill" is not, being contained in the intervening phrase "saw Bill." "John saw" is not an immediate constituent of the sentence, since it is not a phrase; "John" is not an immediate constituent of "John saw," since the latter is not a phrase.

Notice that the definitions proposed here for grammatical functions and relations make sense only when restricted to deep structures, in general.

that the direct-object relation holds between "disregard" and "John" and the subject-predicate relation between "everyone" and "disregards John," despite the fact that these relations are in no way indicated in the surface structure in (4) or (9).

From many such examples, we are led to the following conception of how the semantic component functions. This interpretive component of the full generative grammar applies to a deep structure and assigns to it a semantic representation, formulated in terms of the still quite obscure notions of universal semantics. The deep structure is a labeled bracketing of minimal "meaning-bearing" elements. The interpretive rules apply cyclically, determining the semantic interpretation of a phrase X of the deep structure from the semantic interpretations of the immediate constituents of X and the grammatical relation represented in this configuration of X and its parts.

Superficially, at least, the two interpretive components of the grammar are rather similar in the way in which they operate, and they apply to objects of essentially the same sort (labeled bracketings). But the deep structure of a sentence will, in nontrivial cases, be quite different from its surface structure.

Notice that if the notions "noun phrase," "verb phrase," "sentence," "verb," can receive a language-independent characterization within universal grammar, then the grammatical relations defined above (similarly, others that we might define in the same way) will also receive a universal characterization. It seems that this may be possible, and certain general lines of approach to such a characterization seem clear (see p. 147). We might then raise the question of whether the semantic component of a grammar contains such particular rules as the rules (7) and (8) of the phonological component of English or whether, alternatively, the principles of semantic interpretation belong essentially to universal grammar. However, we will put aside these and other questions relating to the semantic component, and turn next to the discussion of the one noninterpretive component of the grammar—which we have called its "syntactic component." Notice that as in the case of the phonological component, insofar as principles of interpretation can be assigned to universal rather than particular grammar, there is little reason to suppose that they are learned or that they could in principle be learned.

STRUCTURE OF THE SYNTACTIC COMPONENT

The syntactic component of a grammar must generate (see note 12) pairs (D, S), where D is a deep structure and S an associated surface structure. The surface structure S is a labeled bracketing of a sequence of formatives and junctures. The deep structure D is a labeled bracketing that determines a certain network of grammatical functions and grammatical relations among the elements and groups of elements of which it is composed. Obviously, the syntactic component must have a finite number of rules (or rule schemata), but these must be so organized that an infinite number of pairs (D, S) of deep and surface structures can be generated, one corresponding to each interpreted sentence (phonetically and semantically interpreted, that is,) of the language.[24] In principle, there are various ways in which such a system might be organized. It might, for example, consist of independent rules generating deep and surface structures and certain conditions of compatibility relating them, or of rules generating surface structures combined with rules mapping these into the associated deep structure, or of rules generating deep structures combined with rules mapping these into surface structures.[25] Choice among these alternatives is a matter of fact, not decision. We must ask which of the alternatives makes possible the deepest generalizations and the most far-reaching explanation of linguistic phenomena of various sorts. As with other aspects of universal grammar, we are dealing here with a set of empirical questions; crucial evidence may be difficult to obtain, but we cannot conclude from this that there is, in principle, no right and wrong in the matter.

Of the many alternatives that might be suggested, the linguistic evidence now available seems to point consistently to the conclusion that the syntactic component consists of rules that generate deep structures combined with rules mapping these into associated surface structures. Let us call these two systems of rules the *base* and the *transformational* components of the syntax, respectively. The base system is further subdivided into two parts: the *categorial* system and the *lexicon*. Each of these three subparts of the syntax has a specific function to perform, and there seem to be heavy universal constraints that determine their form and interrelation. The general structure of a grammar would, then, be as depicted in diagram (13):

(13)

$$\begin{array}{c} & & \text{Semantic representation} \\ & \nearrow^{S} & \\ \xrightarrow{B} \text{Deep structure} & & \\ & \searrow_{T} & \\ & \text{Surface structure} \xrightarrow{P} \text{Phonetic representation} \end{array}$$

[24] In fact, we might think of a grammar as assigning a semantic interpretation to all possible sentences (this being a clear notion, given theories of universal phonetics and semantics), including those that deviate from rules of the language. But this is a matter that we will not go into any further here.

[25] The question of how the syntactic component is organized should not be confused, as it all too often is, with the problem of developing a model of performance (production or perception). In fact, any of the kinds of organization just described (and others) could be used as the basis for a theory of performance of either kind.

The mapping $\underset{\rightarrow}{S}$ is carried out by the semantic component; $\underset{\rightarrow}{T}$ by the transformational component; and $\underset{\rightarrow}{P}$ by the phonological component. Generation of deep structures by the base system (by the operation $\underset{\rightarrow}{B}$) is determined by the categorial system and the lexicon.

The lexicon is a set of lexical entries; each lexical entry, in turn, can be regarded as a set of features of various sorts. Among these are the phonological features and the semantic features that we have already mentioned briefly. The phonological features can be thought of as indexed as to position (that is, first, second, etc.); aside from this, each is simply an indication of marking with respect to one of the universal distinctive features (regarded here in their categorial function) or with respect to some diacritic feature (see p. 120), in the case of irregularity. Thus the positionally indexed phonological features constitute a distinctive feature matrix with the entries given as $+$ or $-$ values, as described earlier. The semantic features constitute a "dictionary definition." As noted previously, some of these at least must be quite abstract; there may, furthermore, be intrinsic connections of various sorts among them that are sometimes referred to as "field structure." In addition, the lexical entry contains syntactic features that determine the positions in which the entry in question may appear, and the rules that may apply to structures containing it as these are converted into surface structures. In general, the lexical entry contains all information about the item in question that cannot be accounted for by general rule.

Aside from lexical entries, the lexicon will contain redundancy rules that modify the feature content of a lexical entry in terms of general regularities. For example, the fact that vowels are voiced or that humans are animate requires no specific mention in particular lexical entries. Much of the redundant lexical information can, no doubt, be provided by general conventions (that is, rules of universal grammar) rather than by redundancy rules of the language.

The lexicon is concerned with all properties, idiosyncratic or redundant, of individual lexical items. The categorial component of the base determines all other aspects of deep structure. It seems that the categorial component is what is called a *simple* or *context-free phrase structure grammar*. Just what such a system is can be understood quite easily from a simple example. Suppose that we have the *rules* (14):

(14) S   → NP VP
      VP → V NP
      NP → N
      N   → Δ
      V   → Δ

With these rules we construct the derivation (15) in the following way. First write down the symbol S as the first line of the derivation. We interpret the first rule of (14) as permitting S to be replaced by NP VP, giving the second line of (15). Interpreting the second rule of (14) in a similar way, we form the third line of the derivation (15) with VP replaced by V NP. We form the fourth line of (15) by applying the rule NP $\rightarrow$ N of (14), interpreted the same way, to both of the occurrences of NP in the third line. Finally, we form the final two lines of (15) by applying the rules N $\rightarrow$ Δ and V $\rightarrow$ Δ.

(15) S
     NP VP
     NP V NP
     N V N
     Δ V Δ
     Δ Δ Δ

Clearly, we can represent what is essential to the derivation (15) by the tree-diagram (16).

(16)

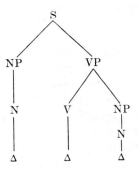

In the diagram (16), each symbol dominates the symbols by which it was replaced in forming (15). In fact, we may think of the rules of (14) as simply describing the way in which a tree diagram such as (16) can be constructed. Evidently, (16) is just another notation for the labeled bracketing (17):

(17) $[_\text{S} \ [_\text{NP} \ [_\text{N} \ \Delta \ ]_\text{N} \ ]_\text{NP} \ [_\text{VP} \ [_\text{V} \ \Delta \ ]_\text{V} \ [_\text{NP} \ [_\text{N} \ \Delta \ ]_\text{N} \ ]_\text{NP} \ ]_\text{VP} \ ]_\text{S}$.

Domination of some element by a symbol A in (16) (as, for example, V NP is dominated by VP) is indicated in (17) by enclosing this element by the labeled brackets $[_\text{A}, \ ]_\text{A}$. If we have a lexicon which tells us that "John" and "Bill" can replace the symbol Δ when this symbol is dominated by N (that is, is enclosed by $[_\text{N}, \ ]_\text{N}$), and that "saw" can replace Δ when it is dominated by V, then we can extend the derivation (15) to derive "John saw Bill," with the associated structure that we have given as (6). In fact, (6) derives from (17) by replacing the first occurrence of Δ by "John," the second by "saw," and the third by "Bill."

Notice that the rules (14) in effect define grammatical relations, where the definitions are given as on p. 129. Thus, the first rule of (14) defines the subject-predicate relation and the second, the verb-object relation. Similarly, other semantically significant grammatical functions and relations can be defined by rules of this form, interpreted in the manner indicated.

Restating these notions in a more formal and general way, the categorial component of the base is a system of rules of the form $A \rightarrow Z$, where A is a category symbol such as S (for "sentence"), NP (for "noun phrase"), N (for "noun"), etc., and Z is a string of one or more symbols which may again be category symbols or which may be *terminal* symbols (that is, symbols which do not appear on the left-hand side of the arrow in any base rule). Given such a system, we can form *derivations*, a derivation being a sequence of lines that meets the following conditions: the first line is simply the symbol S (standing for sentence); the last line contains only terminal symbols; if X, Y are two successive lines, then X must be of the form $\ldots A \ldots$ and Y of the form $\ldots Z \ldots$, where $A \rightarrow Z$ is one of the rules. A derivation imposes a labeled bracketing on its terminal string in the obvious way. Thus given the successive lines $X = \ldots A \ldots$, $Y = \ldots Z \ldots$, where Y was derived from X by the rule $A \rightarrow Z$, we will say that the string derived from Z (or Z itself, if it is terminal) is bracketed by $[_A,]_A$. Equivalently, we can represent the labeled bracketing by a tree diagram in which a node labeled A (in this example) dominates the successive nodes labeled by the successive symbols of Z.

We assume that one of the terminal symbols of the categorial component is the dummy symbol Δ. Among the nonterminal symbols are several that stand for *lexical categories*, in particular N for ("noun"), V (for "verb") ADJ (for "adjective"). A lexical category A can appear on the left-hand side of a rule $A \rightarrow Z$ only if Z is Δ. Lexical entries will then be inserted in derivations in place of Δ by rules of a different sort, extending the derivations provided by the categorial component. Aside from Δ, indicating the position in which an item from the lexicon may appear, the terminal symbols of the categorial component are grammatical elements such as *be*, *of*, etc. Some of the terminal symbols introduced by categorial rules will have an intrinsic semantic content.

A labeled bracketing generated by base rules (that is, by the phrase structure rules of the categorial component and by the rule of lexical insertion mentioned in the preceding paragraph), will be called a *base phrase-marker*. More generally, we will use the term "phrase-marker" here to refer to any string of elements properly bracketed with labeled brackets.[26] The

---

[26] It may be that a slightly more general notion of "phrase-marker" is needed, but we will put this question aside here.

rules of the transformational component modify phrase-markers in certain fixed ways. These rules are arranged in a sequence $T_1, \ldots, T_m$. This sequence of rules applies to a base phrase-marker in a cyclic fashion. First, it applies to a configuration dominated by S (that is, a configuration $[_S \ldots]_S$) and containing no other occurrence of S. When the transformational rules have applied to all such configurations, then they next apply to a configuration dominated by S and containing only S-dominated configurations to which the rules have already applied. This process continues until the rules apply to the full phrase-marker dominated by the initial occurrence of S in the base phrase-marker. At this point, we have a surface structure. It may be that the ordering conditions on transformations are looser—that there are certain ordering conditions on the set $\{T_1, \ldots, T_m\}$, and that at a given stage in the cycle, a sequence of transformations can apply if it does not violate these conditions—but I will not go into this matter here.

The properties of the syntactic component can be made quite clear by an example (which, naturally, must be much oversimplified). Consider a subpart of English with the lexicon (18) and the categorial component (19).

(18) *Lexicon: it, fact, John, Bill, boy, future* (Noun)
                dream, see, persuade, annoy (Verb)
                sad (Adjective)
                will (Modal)
                the (Determiner)

(19) S → (Q) NP AUX VP
      VP → be ADJ
      VP → V (NP) (of NP)
      NP → (DET) N (that S)
      AUX → past
      AUX → M
      N, V, ADJ, DET, M → Δ

In (19), parentheses are used to indicate an element that may or may not be present in the rule. Thus the first line of (19) is an abbreviation for two rules, one in which S is rewritten $Q\ NP\ AUX\ VP$, the other in which S is rewritten $NP\ AUX\ VP$. Similarly, the third line of (19) is actually an abbreviation for four rules, etc. The last line of (19) stands for five rules, each of which rewrites one of the categorial symbols on the left as the dummy terminal symbol Δ.

This categorial component provides such derivations as the following:

(20) (a) S
        NP AUX VP
        NP AUX be ADJ
        N AUX be ADJ

```
        N past be ADJ
        Δ past be Δ

(b)  S
     NP AUX VP
     NP AUX V NP of NP
     DET N AUX V N of DET N that S
     DET N M V N of DET N that S
      Δ    Δ  Δ  Δ  Δ  of  Δ    Δ   that S
      Δ    Δ  Δ  Δ  Δ  of  Δ    Δ   that NP AUX VP
      Δ    Δ  Δ  Δ  Δ  of  Δ    Δ   that NP AUX V
      Δ    Δ  Δ  Δ  Δ  of  Δ    Δ   that N AUX V
      Δ    Δ  Δ  Δ  Δ  of  Δ    Δ   that N past V
      Δ    Δ  Δ  Δ  Δ  of  Δ    Δ   that Δ past Δ
```

These derivations are constructed in the manner just described. They impose labeled bracketings which, for clarity, we will give in the equivalent tree representation:

(21)   **(a)** and **(b)**

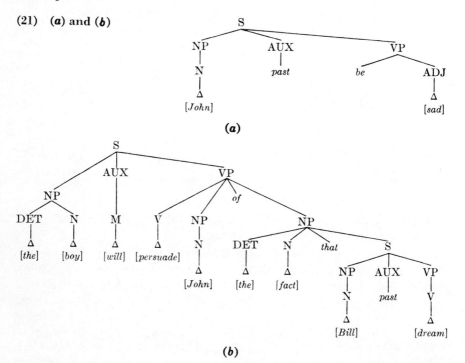

(a)

(b)

We now use the lexicon to complete the base derivations (20a), (20b). Each entry in the lexicon contains syntactic features which identify the occurrences of Δ that it can replace in a derivation. For example, the items of the five rows of (18) can replace occurrences of Δ that are dominated, in the tree representations of (21), by the categorial symbols N, V, ADJ, M, DET, respectively.

But the restrictions are much narrower than this. Thus of the verbs in (18) (line 2), only *persuade* can replace an occurrence of Δ dominated by V when this occurrence of V is followed in the VP by: NP of NP. We can form "... *persuade John of the fact*," but not "... *dream (see, annoy) John of the fact.*" Similarly, of the nouns in (18) (first line) only *fact* can appear in the context DET—*that* S (that is, "the fact that John left"); only *it* in a NP of the form—*that* S;[27] only *fact, boy,* and *future* in a NP of the form DET— ("the fact," "the boy," "the future"), etc. Details aside, the general character of such restrictions is quite clear. Assuming, then, that the lexical entries contain the appropriate lexical features, we can extend the base derivations of (20) to give the terminal strings (22), inserting the items enclosed in brackets in (21).

(22) (*a*) *John past be sad*
      (*b*) *the boy will persuade John of the fact that Bill past dream*

We can also form such terminal strings as (23), with other choices in derivations.

(23) *Q the boy will dream of the future*
      it that John past see Bill past annoy the boy
      John will be sad
      John past see the future

In this way, we form full base derivations, using the rules of the categorial component and then substituting lexical entries for particular occurrences of the dummy symbol Δ in accordance with the syntactic features of these lexical entries. Correspondingly, we have the labeled brackets represented as (21), with lexical entries substituted for occurrences of Δ in the permitted ways. These are the base phrase-markers.

Notice that the rules that introduce lexical entries into base phrase-markers are entirely different in character from the rules of the categorial component. The rules of (19) that were used to form (20) are of a very elementary sort. Each such rule allows a certain symbol A in the string ... A ... to be rewritten as a certain string Z, *independently of the context of A and the source of A in the derivation.* But in introducing lexical entries in place of Δ, we must consider selected aspects of the phrase-marker in which Δ appears. For example, an occurrence of Δ can be replaced by "John" if it

---

[27] This may not seem obvious. We return to the example directly.

is dominated in the phrase-marker by N, but not by V. Thus the rules of lexical insertion really apply not to strings of categorial and terminal symbols, as do the rules of the categorial component, but to phrase-markers such as (21). Rules which apply to phrase-markers, modifying them in some specific way, are referred to in current terminology as (*grammatical*) *transformations*. Thus the rules of lexical insertion are transformational rules, whereas the rules of the categorial component are simply rewriting rules.

Let us now return to the examples (22*a*), (22*b*). Consider first (22*a*), with the base phrase-marker (21*a*).[28] We see at once that (21) contains just the information required in the deep structure of the sentence "John was sad." Clearly, the string *past be* is simply a representation of the formative "was," just as *past see* represents "saw," *past persuade* represents "persuaded," etc. With a rule that converts *past be* to the formative "was," we form the surface structure of the sentence, "John was sad." Furthermore, if we define grammatical functions and relations in the manner described earlier (see p. 128), then (21) expresses the fact that the subject-predicate relation holds between *John* and *past be sad*, and it also contains semantic information about the meaning-bearing items *John, past, sad;* we may assume, in fact, that *past* is itself a symbol of a universal terminal alphabet with a fixed semantic interpretation, and the semantic features of the lexical entries of *John* and *sad* can also be assumed to be selected, like the phonological features of these entries, from some universal system of representation of the sort discussed above. In short, (21*a*) contains all information required for semantic interpretation, and we can, therefore, take it to be the deep structure underlying the sentence "John was sad."

What is true of this example is true quite generally. That is, the base phrase-markers generated by the categorial component and the lexicon are the deep structures that determine semantic interpretation. In this simple case, only one rule is needed to convert the deep structure to a surface structure, namely, the rule converting *past be* to the formative *was*. Since this rule is clearly a special case of a rule that applies as well to any string of the form *past* V, it is really a very simple transformational rule (in the terminology above) rather than an elementary rule of the type that we find in the categorial component. This observation can be generalized. The rules that convert deep structures to surface structures are transformational rules.

Suppose now that instead of the derivation (20*a*) we had formed the very similar derivation (24):

(24)   S

     Q NP AUX VP

---

[28] We henceforth suppose (21*a*) and (21*b*) to be extended to full phrase-markers by insertion of appropriate lexical entries, as indicated.

Q NP AUX be ADJ
Q N AUX be ADJ
Q N M be ADJ
Q Δ Δ be Δ
Q John will be sad

with its associated phrase-marker. We intend the symbol Q to be a symbol of the universal terminal alphabet with a fixed semantic interpretation, namely, that the associated sentence is a question. Suppose that the transformational component of the syntax contains rules that convert phrasemarkers of the form Q NP AUX ... to corresponding phrase-markers of the form AUX NP ... (that is, the transformation replaces Q by AUX, leaving the phrase-marker otherwise unchanged). Applied to the phrasemarker corresponding to (24), this rule gives the labeled bracketing of the sentence, "Will John be sad?"; that is, it forms the surface structure for this sentence.

Suppose that in place of (24) we had used the rule rewriting AUX as *past*. The question transformation of the preceding paragraph would give a phrase-marker with the terminal string "past John be sad," just as it gives, "Will John be sad?" in the case of (24). Evidently, we must modify the question transformation so that it inverts not just *past*, in this case, but the string *past be*, so that we derive finally, "Was John sad?" This modification is, in fact, straightforward, when the rules are appropriately formulated.

Whether we select M or *past* in (24), the generated base phrase-marker once again qualifies as a deep structure. The grammatical relation of *John* to *will (past) be sad* is exactly the same in (24) as in (20a), with the definitions proposed previously, as required for empirical adequacy. Of course, the surface forms do not express these grammatical relations, directly; as we have seen earlier, significant grammatical relations are rarely expressed directly in the surface structure.

Let us now turn to the more complex example (20b)—(21b)—(22b). Once again, the base phrase-marker (21b) of (22b) expresses the information required for the semantic interpretation of the sentence "The boy will persuade John of the fact that Bill dreamt," which derives from (22b) by a transformational rule that forms "dreamt" from *past dream*. Therefore, (21b) can serve as the deep structure underlying this sentence, exactly as (21a) can serve for "John was sad," and the phrase-marker corresponding to (24) for "Will John be sad?"

Suppose that in rewriting NP in the third line of (20b), we had selected not DET N *that* S but N *that* S [see the fourth line of (19)]. The only lexical item of (18) that can appear in the position of this occurrence of N is *it*. Therefore, instead of (22b), we would have derived

(25)   *the boy will persuade John of it that Bill past dream,*

with grammatical relations and lexical content otherwise unmodified. Suppose now that the transformational component of the syntax contains rules with the following effect:

(26)   (*a*) *it* is deleted before *that* S
       (*b*) *of* is deleted before *that* S

Applying (26*a*) and (26*b*) to (25) in that order, with the rule that converts *past dream* to "dreamt," we derive the surface structure of "The boy will persuade John that Bill dreamt." The base phrase-marker corresponding to (25) serves as the deep structure underlying this sentence.

Notice that the rule (26*a*) is much more general. Thus suppose we select the NP *it that Bill past dream* as the subject of *past annoy John*, as is permitted by the rules of (18), (19). This gives

(27)   *it that Bill past dream past annoy John*

Applying the rule (26*a*) (and the rules for forming past tense of verbs), we derive, "That Bill dreamt annoyed John." Alternatively, we might have applied the transformational rule with the effect of (28):

(28)   A phrase-marker of the form *it that S X* is restructured as the corresponding phrase-marker of the form *it X that S.*

Applying (28) to (27), we derive, "It annoyed John that Bill dreamt." In this case, (26*a*) is inapplicable. Thus (27) underlies two surface structures, one determined by (28) and the other by (26*a*); having the same deep structure, these are synonymous. In the case of (25), (28) is inapplicable and, therefore, we have only one corresponding surface structure.

We can carry the example (25) further by considering additional transformational rules. Suppose that instead of selecting *Bill* in the embedded sentence of (25), we had selected *John* a second time. There is a very general transformational rule in English and other languages providing for the deletion of repeated items. Applying this rule along with other minor ones of an obvious sort, we derive

(29)   *The boy will persuade John to dream.*

from a deep structure that contains, as it must, a subphrase-marker that expresses the fact that *John* is the subject of *dream*. Actually, in this case the deep phrase-marker would be slightly different, in ways that need not concern us here, in this rough expository sketch.

Suppose now that we were to add a transformation that converts a phrase-marker of the form NP AUX V NP into the corresponding passive, in the obvious way.[29] Applying to phrase-markers very much like (21*b*), this rule would provide surface structures for the sentences "John will be

---

[29] Notice that this transformation would modify the phrase-marker to which it applies in a more radical way than those discussed above. The principles remain the same, however.

persuaded that Bill dreamt (by the boy)" [from (25)] and "John will be persuaded to dream (by the boy)" [from (29)]. In each case, the semantic interpretation will be that of the underlying deep phrase-marker. In certain cases, the significant grammatical relations are entirely obscured in the surface structure. Thus in the case of the sentence "John will be persuaded to dream," the fact that "John" is actually the subject of "dream" is not indicated in the surface structure, although the underlying deep structure, as we have noted, expresses this fact directly.

From these examples we can see how a sequence of transformations can form quite complicated sentences in which significant relations among the parts are not represented in any direct way. In fact, it is only in artificially simple examples that deep and surface structure correspond closely. In the normal sentences of everyday life, the relation is much more complex; long sequences of transformations apply to convert underlying deep structures into the surface form.

The examples that we have been using are stilted and unnatural. With a less rudimentary grammar, quite natural ones can be provided. For example, in place of the sentences formed from (27) by (26) or (28) we could use more acceptable sentences such as "that you should believe this is not surprising," "it is not surprising that you should believe this," etc. Actually, the unnaturalness of the examples we have used illustrates a simple but often neglected point, namely, that the intrinsic meaning of a sentence and its other grammatical properties are determined by rule, not by conditions of use, linguistic context, frequency of parts, etc.[30] Thus the examples of the last few paragraphs may never have been produced in the experience of some speaker (or, for that matter, in the history of the language), but their status as English sentences and their ideal phonetic and semantic interpretations are unaffected by this fact.

Since a sequence of transformations can effect drastic modifications in a phrase-marker, we should not be surprised to discover that a single surface structure[31] may result from two very different deep structures, that is, that certain sentences are ambiguous (for example, sentence (4) on p. 117). Ambiguous sentences provide a particularly clear indication of the inadequacy of surface structure as a representation of deeper relations.[32]

---

[30] These factors may affect performance, however. Thus they may affect the physical signal and play a role in determining how a person will interpret sentences. In both producing and understanding sentences, the speaker-hearer makes use of the ideal phonetic and semantic interpretations, but other factors also play a role. The speaker may be simply interested in making himself understood—the hearer, in determining what the speaker intended (which may not be identical with the literal semantic interpretation of the sentence or sentence fragment that he produced). Once again, we must insist on the necessity for distinguishing performance from competence if either is to be studied in a serious way.

[31] More accurately, surface structures that are sufficiently close so as to determine the same phonetic representation.

[32] Modern linguistics has made occasional use of this property of language as a research tool. The first general discussion of how ambiguity can be used to illustrate the inadequacy of certain conceptions of syntactic structure is in C. F. Hockett's, Two models for grammatical description, *Word* 10:210–231 (1954), reprinted in M. Joos (ed.), *Readings in Linguistics*, Washington (1957).

More generally, we can easily find paired sentences with essentially the same surface structure but entirely different grammatical relations. To mention just one such example, compare the sentences of (30):

(30)   (*a*) I persuaded the doctor to examine John.
          (*b*) I expected the doctor to examine John.

The surface structures are essentially the same. The sentence (30*a*) is of the same form as (29). It derives from a deep structure which is roughly of the form (31):

(31)

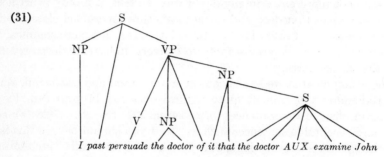

I past persuade the doctor of it that the doctor AUX examine John

This deep structure is essentially the same as (21*b*), and by the transformational process described in connection with (29), we derive from it the sentence (30*a*). But in the case of (30*b*), there are no such related structures as "I expected the doctor of the fact that he examined John," ". . . of the necessity (for him) to examine John," etc., as there are in the case of (30*a*). Correspondingly, there is no justification for an analysis of (30*b*) as derived from a structure like (31). Rather, the deep structure underlying (30*b*) will be something like (32) (again omitting details):

(32)

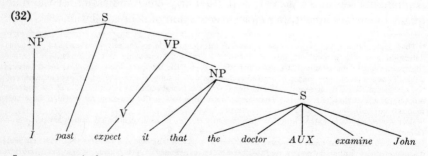

I past expect it that the doctor AUX examine John

There are many other facts that support this analysis of (30*a*) and (30*b*). For example, from a structure like (32) we can form, "What I expected was that the doctor (will, should, etc.) examine John," by the same rule that forms, "What I saw was the book," from the underlying NP-V-NP structure, "I saw the book." But we cannot form "What I persuaded was that the doctor should examine John," corresponding to (30*a*), because the underlying structure (31) is not of the form NP-V-NP as required by this transformation. Applying rule (26*a*) to (32), we derive "I expected that the doctor (will, should, etc.) examine John." We derive (30*b*), instead, by use of the same rule that gives (29), with "to" rather than "that" appearing with the embedded sentence, which, in this case, contains no other representative of the category AUX.

Details aside, we see that (30*a*) is derived from (31) and (30*b*) from (32), so that despite near identity of surface structure, the deep structures underlying (30*a*) and (30*b*) are very different. That there must be such a divergence in deep structure is not at all obvious.[33] It becomes clear, however, if we consider the effect of replacing "the doctor to examine John" by its passive, "John to be examined by the doctor" in (30*a*) and (30*b*). Thus we have under examination the sentences (33) and (34):

(33)   (*a*) I persuaded the doctor to examine John [= (30*a*)].
       (*b*) I persuaded John to be examined by the doctor.
(34)   (*a*) I expected the doctor to examine John [= (30*b*)].
       (*b*) I expected John to be examined by the doctor.

The semantic relation between the paired sentences of (34) is entirely different from the relation between the sentences of (33). We can see this by considering the relation in truth value. Thus (34*a*) and (34*b*) are necessarily the same in truth value; if I expected the doctor to examine John then I expected John to be examined by the doctor, and conversely. But there is no necessary relation in truth value between (33*a*) and (33*b*). If I persuaded the doctor to examine John, it does not follow that I persuaded John to be examined by the doctor, or conversely.

In fact, exchange of active and passive in the embedded sentence preserves meaning, in a rather clear sense, in the case of (30*b*) but not (30*a*). The explanation is immediate from consideration of the deep structures underlying these sentences. Replacing active by passive in (32), we then go on to derive (34*b*) in just the way that (30*b*) is derived from (32). But to derive (33*b*), we must not only passivize the embedded sentence in (31), but we must also select "John" instead of "the doctor" as the object of the verb "persuade"; otherwise, the conditions for deletion of the repeated noun

---

[33] It seems, in fact, that this phenomenon has escaped the attention of English grammarians, both traditional and modern.

phrase, as in the derivation of (29), will not be met. Consequently, the deep structure underlying (33*b*) is quite different from that underlying (33*a*). Not only is the embedded sentence passivized, but the object "the doctor" must be replaced in (31) by "John." The grammatical relations are, consequently, quite different, and the semantic interpretation differs correspondingly. It remains true, in both cases, that passivization does not affect meaning (in the sense of "meaning" relevant here). The change of meaning in (30*a*) when "the doctor to examine John" is replaced by "John to be examined by the doctor" is occasioned by the change of grammatical relations, "John" now being the direct object of the verb phrase in the underlying structure rather than "the doctor." There is no corresponding change in the case of (34*a*), so that the meaning remains unaltered when the embedded sentence is passivized.

The example (30*a*), (30*b*) illustrates, once again, the inadequacy (and, quite generally, irrelevance) of surface structure for the representation of semantically significant grammatical relations. The labeled bracketing that conveys the information required for phonetic interpretation is in general very different from the labeled bracketing that provides the information required for semantic interpretation. The examples (30*a*), (30*b*) also illustrate how difficult it may be to bring one's "linguistic intuition" to consciousness. As we have seen, the grammar of English, as a characterization of competence (see p. 108f), must, for descriptive adequacy, assign different deep structures to the sentences (30*a*) and (30*b*). The grammar that each speaker has internalized does distinguish these deep structures, as we can see from the fact that any speaker of English is capable of understanding the effect of replacing the embedded sentence by its passive in the two cases of (30). But this fact about his internalized grammatical competence may escape even the careful attention of the native speaker (see note 33).

Perhaps such examples as these suffice to give something of the flavor of the syntactic structure of a language. Summarizing our observations about the syntactic component, we conclude that it contains a base and a transformational part. The base generates deep structures, and the transformational rules convert them to surface structures. The categorial component of the base defines the significant grammatical relations of the language, assigns an ideal order to underlying phrases, and, in various ways, determines which transformations will apply.[34] The lexicon specifies idiosyncratic properties of individual lexical items. Together, these two components of the base seem to provide the information relevant for semantic interpretation in the sense in which we have been using this term, subject to the qualifications mentioned earlier. The transformational rules convert phrase-

---

[34] It is an open question whether this determination is unique.

markers to new phrase-markers, effecting various kinds of reordering and reorganization. The kinds of changes that can be effected are quite limited; we will, however, not go into this matter here. Applying in sequence, the transformations may affect the organization of a base-phrase-marker quite radically, however. Thus the transformations provide a wide variety of surface structures that have no direct or simple relation to the base structures from which they originate and which express their semantic content.

It is a fact of some significance that the mapping of deep to surface structures is not a matter of a single step but is, rather, analyzeable into a sequence of successive transformational steps. The transformations that contribute to this mapping of deep to surface structures can be combined in many different ways, depending on the form of the deep structure to which they apply. Since these transformations apply in sequence, each must produce a structure of the sort to which the next can apply. This condition is met in our formulation, since transformations apply to phrase-markers and convert them into new phrase-markers. But there is very good empirical evidence that the surface structures that determine phonetic form are, in fact, phrase-markers (that is, labeled bracketing of formatives). It follows, then, that the deep structures to which transformations originally apply should themselves be phrase-markers, as in our formulation.

In principle, there are many ways in which a network of grammatical relations might be represented. One of the major reasons for selecting the method of phrase-markers generated by base rules is precisely the fact that transformations must apply in sequence and therefore must apply to objects of the sort that they themselves produce, ultimately, to phrase-markers that have the same formal properties as surface structures.[35]

CONCLUDING OBSERVATIONS

The grammatical theory just presented calls for several comments. We pointed out earlier that the grammar of a language must, for empirical adequacy, allow for infinite use of finite means, and we assigned this recursive property to the syntactic component, which generates an infinite set of paired deep and surface structures. We have now further localized the recursive property of the grammar, assigning it to the categorial component of the base. Certain base rules introduce the initial symbol S that heads derivations, for example, the fourth rule of (19). It may be that introduction

---

[35] There are other supporting reasons. For one thing, grammatical relations are not among words or morphemes but among phrases, in general. For another, empirical investigation has uniformly shown that there is an optimal ideal order of phrases in underlying structures, consistent with the assumption that these are generated by a base system of the sort discussed above.

of "propositional content" in deep structures by this means is the only recursive device in the grammar apart from the rules involved in forming coordinated constructions, which raise various problems going beyond what we have been discussing here.

It is reasonable to ask why human languages should have a design of this sort—why, in particular, they should use grammatical transformations of the sort described to convert deep structures to surface form. Why should they not make use of deep structures in a more direct way?[36] Two reasons suggest themselves at once. We have already observed that the conditions of lexical insertion are essentially transformational rather than phrase-structural (see p. 138). More generally, we find many nonphrase-structural constraints (for example, those involved in deletion of identical items—see p. 140 and 143) when we study a language carefully. Thus transformations not only convert a deep structure to a surface structure, but they also have a "filtering effect," ruling out certain potential deep structures as not well-formed.[37] Apart from this, we would naturally be inclined to seek an explanation for the use of grammatical transformations in the empirical constraints that linguistic communication must meet. Even the simple fact that sound is unrecoverable imposes conditions on speech that need not, for example, be imposed on a linguistic system designed only for writing (for example, the artificial systems mentioned in note (36). A written system provides an "external memory" that changes the perceptual problem in quite a significant way. We would expect a system designed for the conditions of speech communication to be somehow adapted to the load on memory. In fact, grammatical transformations characteristically reduce the amount of grammatical structure in phrase-markers in a well-defined way, and it may be that one consequence of this is to facilitate the problem of speech perception by a short-term memory of a rather limited sort.[38] This observation suggests some promising directions for further research, but little of substance can be said with any confidence on the basis of what is understood today.

One further point requires some clarification. We noted at the outset that performance and competence must be sharply distinguished if either is to be studied successfully. We have now discussed a certain model of compe-

[36] It is interesting to observe, in this connection, that the theory of context-free phrase structure grammar (*see* p. 132) is very close to adequate for "artificial languages" invented for various purposes, for example, for mathematics or logic or as computer languages.

[37] And hence, in certain cases, as underlying "semigrammatical sentences" that deviate, in the indicated way, from grammatical rule. This suggests one approach to the problem touched on in Note 24.

[38] For some speculations about this matter and discussion of the general problem, see G. A. Miller and N. Chomsky, "Finitary models for the user," in R. D. Luce, E. Galanter, and R. Bush (eds.), *Handbook of Mathematical Psychology*, Vol. II, John Wiley, New York, 1963. The suggestion that transformations may facilitate performance is implicit in V. Yngve, A model and a hypothesis for language structure, *Proc. Am. Philosoph. Soc.*, 444–466 (1960).

tence. It would be tempting, but quite absurd, to regard it as a model of performance as well. Thus we might propose that to produce a sentence, the speaker goes through the successive steps of constructing a base-derivation, line by line from the initial symbol S, then inserting lexical items and applying grammatical transformations to form a surface structure, and finally applying the phonological rules in their given order, in accordance with the cyclic principle discussed earlier. There is not the slightest justification for any such assumption. In fact, in implying that the speaker selects the general properties of sentence structure before selecting lexical items (before deciding what he is going to talk about), such a proposal seems not only without justification but entirely counter to whatever vague intuitions one may have about the processes that underlie production. A theory of performance (production or perception) will have to incorporate the theory of competence—the generative grammar of a language—as an essential part. But models of performance can be constructed in many different ways, consistently with fixed assumptions about the competence on which they are based. There is much that can be said about this topic, but it goes beyond the bounds of this chapter.

Specifying the properties of the various components and subcomponents of a grammar precisely, along the lines outlined in this discussion, we formulate a highly restrictive hypothesis about the structure of any human language. As we have remarked several times, it is far from necessary, on any a priori grounds, that a language must have a structure of this sort. Furthermore, it seems quite likely that very heavy conditions can be placed on grammars beyond those outlined above. For example, it may be (as, in fact, was traditionally assumed) that base structures can vary only very slightly from language to language; and, by sufficiently restricting the possible range of base structures, it may be possible to arrive at quite general definitions for the categories that function as "nonterminal symbols" in the rules of the categorial component. As observed previously, this would provide language-independent definitions of grammatical relations, and would raise the possibility that there exist deep-seated universal principles of semantic interpretation.

In mentioning such possibilities, we must take note of the widespread view that modern investigations have not only conclusively refuted the principles of traditional universal grammar but have, moreover, shown that the search for such principles was ill-conceived from the start. But it seems to me that such conclusions are based on a serious misunderstanding of traditional universal grammar, and on an erroneous interpretation of the results of modern work. Traditional universal grammar tried to demonstrate, on the basis of what information was then available, that deep structures vary little from language to language. That surface structures might be highly diverse was never doubted. It was also assumed that the categories of syntax, semantics, and phonetics are universal and quite restricted in variety. Actually, modern "anthropological linguistics" has provided little evidence that bears on the assumption of uniformity of deep structures, and insofar as the universality of categories is concerned, conclusions rather like the traditional ones are commonly accepted in practice in descriptive work.[39]

Modern linguistics and anthropological linguistics have concerned themselves only marginally with deep structure, either in theory or practice. A great diversity of surface structures has been revealed in descriptive work, as anticipated in traditional universal grammar. Nevertheless, a good case can be made for the conclusion that the fundamental error of traditional universal grammar was that it was not sufficiently restrictive in the universal conditions it proposed for human languages—that much heavier constraints must be postulated to account for the empirical facts.

Our discussion of the structure of English in the illustrative examples given previously has necessarily been quite superficial and limited to very simple phenomena. But even a discussion of the topics we have touched on requires a fairly intimate knowledge of the language and a reasonably well-articulated theory of generative grammar. Correspondingly, it is only when problems of the sort illustrated are seriously studied that any contribution can be made to the theory of universal grammar. Under these circumstances, it is not too surprising that even today, the hypotheses of universal grammar that can be formulated with any conviction are supported by evidence from a fairly small number of studies of very few of the languages of the world, and that they must therefore be highly tentative. Still, the inadequacy of the evidence should not be overstated. Thus it is surely true—and there is nothing paradoxical in this—that a single language can provide strong evidence for conclusions regarding universal grammar. This becomes quite apparent when we consider again the problem of language acquisition (see p. 112). The child must acquire a generative grammar of his language on the basis of a fairly restricted amount of evidence.[40] To account for this achievement, we must postulate a sufficiently rich internal structure—a sufficiently restricted theory of universal grammar that constitutes his contribution to language acquisition.

---

[39] Traditional theories of universal phonetics have been largely accepted as a basis for modern work, and have been refined and amplified in quite important ways. See the references in Note 7.

[40] Furthermore, evidence of a highly degraded sort. For example, the child's conclusions about the rules of sentence formation must be based on evidence that consists, to a large extent, of utterances that break rules, since a good deal of normal speech consists of false starts, disconnected phrases, and other deviations from idealized competence.

The issue here is not one of "normative grammar." The point is that a person's normal speech departs from the rules of his own internalized grammar in innumerable ways, because of the many factors that interact with underlying competence to determine performance. Correspondingly, as a language learner, he acquires a grammar that characterizes much of the evidence on which it was based as deviant and anomalous.

For example, it was suggested earlier that in order to account for the perception of stress contours in English, we must suppose that the user of the language is making use of the principle of cyclic application. We also noted that he could hardly have sufficient evidence for this principle. Consequently, it seems reasonable to assume that this principle is simply part of the innate schematism that he uses to interpret the limited and fragmentary evidence available to him. It is, in other words, part of universal grammar. Similarly, it is difficult to imagine what "inductive principles" might lead the child unerringly to the assumptions about deep structure and about organization of grammar that seem to be necessary if we are to account for such facts as those we have mentioned. Nor is a search for such principles particularly well-motivated. It seems reasonable to assume that these properties of English are, in reality, facts of universal grammar. If such properties are available to the child, the task of language-acquisition becomes feasible. The problem for the child is not the apparently insuperable inductive feat of arriving at a transformational generative grammar from restricted data, but rather that of discovering which of the possible languages he is being exposed to. Arguing in this way, we can arrive at conclusions about universal grammar from study of even a single language.

The child is presented with data, and he must inspect hypotheses (grammars) of a fairly restricted class to determine compatibility with this data. Having selected a grammar of the predetermined class, he will then have command of the language generated by this grammar.[41] Thus he will know a great deal about phenomena to which he has never been exposed, and which are not "similar" or "analogous" in any well-defined sense to those to which he has been exposed.[42] He will, for example, know the relations among the sentences (33) and (34), despite their novelty; he will know what stress contours to assign to utterances, despite the novelty and lack of physical basis for these phonetic representations; and so on, for innumerable other similar cases. This disparity between knowledge and experience is perhaps the most striking fact about human language. To account for it is the central problem of linguistic theory.

The basic conclusion that seems to be emerging with increasing clarity from contemporary work in linguistics is that very restrictive initial assumptions about the form of generative grammar must be imposed if explana-

---

[41] We are presenting an "instantaneous model" of language acquisition which is surely false in detail, but can very well be accepted as a reasonable first approximation. This is not to deny that the fine structure of learning deserves study. The question, rather, is what the range of possibilities may be within which experience can cause knowledge and belief to vary. If the range is quite narrow (as, it seems to me, is suggested by considerations of the sort mentioned above), then a first approximation of the sort suggested will be a prerequisite to any fruitful investigation of learning. Given an instantaneous model that is empirically well-supported, as a first approximation, there are many questions that can immediately be raised: for example, what are the strategies by which hypotheses are sampled, how does the set of hypotheses available at one stage depend on those tested at earlier stages, etc.

[42] Except, tautologically, in the sense that they are accounted for by the same theory.

tions are to be forthcoming for the facts of language use and language acquisition. Furthermore, there is, so far, no evidence to suggest that the variety of generative grammars for human languages is very great. The theory of universal grammar suggested by the sketchy description that we have just given will no doubt be proven incorrect in various respects. But it is not unlikely that its fundamental defect will be that it permits far too much latitude for the construction of grammars, and that the kinds of languages that can be acquired by humans in the normal way are actually of a much more limited sort than this theory would suggest. Yet even as the theory of generative grammar stands today, it imposes fairly narrow conditions on the structure of human language. If this general conclusion can be firmly established—and, furthermore, significantly strengthened—this will be a highly suggestive contribution to theoretical psychology. It is hardly open to controversy that today, as in the seventeenth century, the central and critical problem for linguistics is to use empirical evidence from particular languages to refine the principles of universal grammar. I have tried, in this chapter, to suggest some of the principles that seem well-established and to illustrate some of the empirical considerations that bear on such principles.[43]

Study Questions

1. Distinguish as clearly as you can between competence and performance. With which did Jespersen seem most concerned? Could you relate the competence-performance distinction to the different treatments of English stress by Smith and Chomsky? Does the word *generate*, as Chomsky uses it, refer to an actual mental process?

2. "A sentence," Smith wrote, "can now be seen as one of several easily statable sequences of words, phrases, or clauses bounded by certain kinds of intonation patterns" (p. 102). Chomsky argues that in any

---

[43] In addition to works mentioned in earlier notes the following books can be consulted for further development of topics touched on in this chapter: Chomsky, *Syntactic Structures*, Mouton and Co., The Hague (1957); *Current Issues in Linguistic Theory*, Mouton and Co., The Hague (1964); *Aspects of the Theory of Syntax*, M.I.T. Press, Cambridge (1965); Halle, *Sound Pattern of Russian*, Mouton and Co., The Hague (1959); Katz and Postal, *An Integrated Theory of Linguistic Description*, M.I.T. Press, Cambridge (1964). See also many papers in Fodor and Katz (eds.), *Structure of Language: Readings in the Philosophy of Language*, Prentice-Hall, New Jersey (1964). For more information on aspects of English structure touched on here, see also Lees, *Grammar of English Nominalizations*, Mouton and Co., The Hague (1960), and P. Rosenbaum, *Grammar of English Predicate Complement Constructions*, M.I.T. Ph.D. dissertation (1965). For further material see the bibliographies of the works cited. [Rosenbaum's *Grammar* was published by the M.I.T. Press in 1967.—*Eds.*]

language "the set of paired phonetic and semantic representations" (the set of sentences) "will be infinite" (p. 110). Are these two statements necessarily conflicting? If they are, which one of them (if either) is correct?

3. Language is culture, says Smith (p. 91), and culture is learned. Can you reconcile this belief with Chomsky's idea of an "innate conception of 'human language' that makes language acquisition possible" (p. 112)? Is recognition of the diversity of languages and cultures compatible with the pursuit of a universal grammar?

4. According to Smith, "we can get at meaning *only through structure*, and we cannot get at structure through meaning" (p. 91). Did Goold Brown hold any such opinion? Did Jespersen? What contribution does Chomsky say semantic theory can make to syntax (p. 116)? Can you relate the difference on this point between him and Smith to the different roles they assign to phonology in their grammatical systems? Might the difference have any connection with the two men's theories of perception?

5. In what terms does Smith describe the "relatively small number of sound types" which each individual language "settles for" (p. 95)? What does Chomsky mean by "distinctive features"? What two functions do the features serve in Chomsky's grammar? In which of the two grammars, Smith's or Chomsky's, would the underlying forms of words, their phonemic representations, be more abstract, more remote from the concrete sounds of actual speech?

6. What is Chomsky's argument for the conclusion "that a principle like the principle of cyclic application in phonology should hold in the semantic component" (p. 128)? Why does he say that in general "we cannot expect deep structure to be very close to surface structure" (p. 128)? How would Chomsky use deep structures to define such notions as subject and object? Does the idea of deep structure enter into Smith's system? Is the syntax in a generative grammar a syntax in Jespersen's sense? Would you choose to defend a generative syntax against a possible charge (by a disciple of Smith's) that it is based on "the shifting sands of meaning," or against a possible charge (by a disciple of Jespersen) that it is a "squinting grammar" and confuses grammar with semantics?

7. Would Chomsky agree with Goold Brown that the "significations" of words "pertain to lexicography, and not to grammar, except in-

cidentally"? What kinds of information would Chomsky's lexicon provide? Would it be fair to say that the maker of such a lexicon must set out to catalogue the universe as knowable by man?

8. Explain Chomsky's terms *base, phrase-structure grammar, base phrase-marker, lexical category, terminal symbol, dummy symbol, derivation.*

9. Why does Chomsky say that it would be absurd to regard the "model of competence" which he has proposed "as a model of performance as well" (p. 147)?

10. How, in Chomsky's view, can a child "know a great deal about [linguistic] phenomena to which he has never been exposed" (p. 149)? If Chomsky is right about innate ideas and universal grammar, do different languages impose different ways of seeing the universe upon their speakers, or would the limitation be the nature of the human mind itself?

Part 2
Dialectology

When we look at its manifestation in speech, it is apparent that no language is ever completely uniform. It does not take a trained linguist to observe that no two individuals ever talk in identical ways or that there are differences in the talk of Northerners and Southerners, New Yorkers and Chicagoans. We amuse our friends with jokes told in bad imitations of Brooklynese or southern rural, and sometimes we puzzle them, as the native Californian wife of one of the editors did when she offered a midwestern neighbor a snail with her breakfast coffee. Around San Francisco, a snail is a sweet roll of a particular shape, not something restaurateurs call escargot and charge $5 the half dozen for. We all encounter similar localisms as we move busily about the country, and we also hear sounds different from the ones we utter coming out of other people's mouths. Unless we are linguistically sophisticated, we are probably less likely to notice differences in grammar among speakers of American English, or if we do notice them we may call them errors. But variation in language shows itself at all levels: in syntax, lexicon, phonology, and semantics.

Dialectology, the study of language variation, concerns itself with all four levels, seeking to identify groups of speakers by their possession of similar linguistic traits. It deals, in other words, with linguistic entities larger than an idiolect—the characteristic speech of a single speaker—but smaller than a language. As the following articles show, the study of dialects is beset with a number of difficulties, both theoretical and practical. A major theoretical problem is that the object of the study is hard to define. What is a dialect? How does it differ from an idiolect and from a language? Is it simply a linguist's abstraction inferred from a set of idiolects with the loose strings lopped off, or is it a norm which governs language behavior and has psychological reality? Is a dialect a discrete linguistic system, related by partial similarities to other dialects, and are they all incorporated by those similarities under another abstraction called a language? Or are dialects merely superficially different subsystems of another psychologically real norm called a language?

And how do we study dialects? To draw the line between dialect and language is it sufficient to rely on a test of mutual intelligibility, to say that dialects are mutually intelligible but that languages are not? If so, how do we define mutual intelligibility? Can we describe a dialect simply by displaying its differences from other dialects? If so, how do we then relate the dialects to the language of which they *are* dialects? Or, finally, can we describe dialects as subsystems of a language and account for their differences by different low-level grammatical rules, their similarities by the same high-level rules? These are the kinds of problems the dialectologist must think about before he gets around to the task itself of describing language variation. His methods and results, in other words, are dependent on a general theory of language and of linguistic description.

Dialectologists have made significant contributions to our knowledge of languages by giving the best answers they can to such perplexing questions and then getting on with it. But even when dealing with the "substance" of language variation—observable differences in speech—the dialectologist encounters difficulty because of the variety in the differences he finds. If we were to set out on a survey of dialectal variation, traveling north along the east coast of the United States from Miami Beach, Florida, to Bangor, Maine, and then west to Chicago, we would find a number of variables which distinguish one community from another. Language variation would seem to have some geographical correlation. Speakers in Charleston, South Carolina, talk more like other Charlestonians than like Philadelphians. If we prolonged our stay in Chicago long enough for an extensive tour of the city from the stockyards to the executive offices of Marshall Field and Company, talking to laborers, janitors, bank clerks, school teachers, and vice-presidents, we would observe other differences ranging along the ladder of social prestige, and we would conclude that language variation correlates with class. If we stayed long enough with our vice-president, we would note that he does not talk the same way to the office boy who has spilled coffee into his desk drawer as he does to the man in the office with the private washroom. The speech of a single individual, in other words, will vary to fit the circumstances of its use. Briefly, there are many kinds of variations which might be and have been studied: local and regional dialects; social dialects; functional varieties from formal to informal, literary to colloquial; occupational varieties; variations in style. Add to these the complications of bilingualism or of recent migration from one part of the country to another, and the ever present phenomena of linguistic change, and you have some sense of the confusing situation the dialectologist faces when he studies a complex linguistic community.

Is the dialectologist equally concerned with all possible variations? We will find various answers to this question, and various emphases on the "substance" of dialectal variation, in the following essays. It is important to emphasize again that these different answers and emphases grow out of differing linguistic interests and theoretical positions.

The serious study of dialects began as an adjunct to historical linguistics in a form better termed *dialect geography:* the study of local differentiation in a speech area. The comparative method of historical linguistics assumed that similarities among languages could be explained on the theory that the languages exhibiting them were descended from a common ancestor; thus, German, Dutch, Danish, English are differentiated offspring of a single parent language just as French, Spanish, Portuguese, Italian are offspring of another. The comparative method further assumed that the descendant languages split off from a parent stock which was itself completely uniform; thus the history of the Germanic family could be represented by a tree diagram:

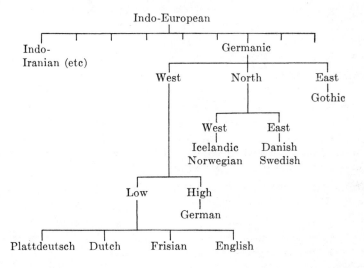

In the course of the nineteenth century, a number of historical linguists attacked the validity of the assumption of uniform splitting, pointing out that no one had ever observed a completely uniform language and questioning whether any had ever existed. In addition, these critics pointed out significant exceptions to the statements of the historical changes which had differentiated the offspring from the parent, exceptions which could only be explained on the assumption that the parent language was itself split up into dialects. These linguists proposed that linguistic differentiation in time could be better represented as waves spreading out from different dialect centers than as discrete splittings from a single branch, the typical representation in tree diagrams. A wave theory diagram would look something like Figure 3 on the following page.

Such a diagram emphasizes two things of importance to dialect geography: 1) that different changes spread over an area at different times and at different rates; and 2) that each change may be carried out only over a part of an area. It was taken to be the task of dialect geography to plot the spread of such changes as sets of isoglosses—lines drawn on maps to show the geographical distribution of distinct features.

Other influences, too, contributed to interest in the study of dialect, not all of them linguistic in the modern sense of the term, and some earlier in time than the development of linguistic history. The prescriptive

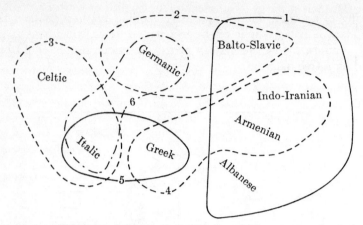

Figure 3 Some overlapping features of special resemblance among the Indo-European languages, conflicting with the family-tree diagram.*

1 Sibilants for velars in certain forms
2 Case-endings with [m] for [bh]
3 Passive-voice endings with [r]
4 Prefix ['e] in past tenses
5 Feminine nouns with masculine suffixes
6 Perfect tense used as general past tense

grammarians of the eighteenth century were aware of divergences from the standard literary languages in local speech forms. Earlier, the orthoepists and spelling reformers of the sixteenth and seventeenth centuries, who were interested in the "correct" spelling and pronunciation of English during the period when London dialect was establishing itself as a national standard, also had given some attention to local features. The prescriptive grammarians tended to view dialectal features as corruptions of the standard language, which they assumed to be the oldest form and the closest to right reason. Departures from the standard only convinced them of what they had suspected all along: that speakers of "dialect" were ignorant, lazy, and of questionable morality. However, the romantic movement of the late eighteenth and early nineteenth centuries suggested a different view of the folk and their ways. If the world was racing to hell in a handcart as the Dean Swifts were suggesting, maybe the corrupter was not man's nature but his civilization. Perhaps Wordsworth's leech-gatherer really was God's chosen and his language a more accurate reflection of Adam's natural name-giving ability. People began listening harder for those quaint terms of his.

When the people listening to the language of the folk were scholars who knew the ancient forms of languages like English or German, some surprising discoveries were made: many features in the "dialects" were more ancient than their corresponding features in the standard language. The local dialects, then, could not be corruptions of standard; in fact, perhaps it was the other way around. Perhaps in local dialects historians would find "unmixed" descendants of the antique tongues. Further study, of course, revealed that neither the standard nor the local dialects were unmixed; neither was closer to an original purity (which never existed) than the other. Rather, the conviction grew, the local dialects and standard were simply historical descendants of other dialects, and both were subject to similar if not identical historical forces. Most of the so-called standard languages of Europe were simply the descendants of local dialects made richer than their poor relations—ultimately because of the social, political, and economic prestige of their speakers.

The attention given to the relations between standard and divergent dialects led to further refinements in dialect study. In particular, dialectologists recognized the need to study the correlation of dialects with class as well as with geographical distribution. As we shall see, social dialectology has been and continues to be a central concern in American dialectology particularly. Hans Kurath led the way in the study of social dialects by having his field workers collect the speech of three classes, loosely identified by education and mobility. But during the decade when the methodology of the Linguistic Atlas of the United States was formulated—the 1930's—the question of the significance of social dialects was raised in another context. Linguists and English teachers engaged in a debate over the status of dialectal variations, a debate that has come to be known as the Usage Controversy.

The Usage Controversy was fought over the question of "correct" or "good" English. People interested in the teaching of English were asking for guidance in determining standards of correctness for language use. Should the basis of correctness be what educated speakers actually say and write, or is there some abstract set of rules by which usage should be governed? If the latter, on what are the rules founded? One party armed itself with the prescriptive grammars of Bishop Lowth, Lindley Murray, and their followers the handbook writers; the other with what facts they could gather about the actual usage of educated Americans. For the factually minded, the materials of the Linguistic Atlas—the first comprehensive and careful collection of actual usage made in this country—were to become a powerful arsenal. The controversy is far from dead, even though both sides have largely reformulated their positions, and its influence on recent dialect projects, particularly those being conducted in urban centers in the United States, is very noticeable.

At present, a number of major dialect surveys are being carried on in a variety of European countries and in major English-speaking areas: Canada, Great Britain, Ireland, Scotland, the United States, as well as some beginnings in Australia and New Zealand. Most of these projects continue to pursue older interests either in dialect geography or in social differentiation. The Survey of English Dialects, described below by Harold Orton, is a survey of folk dialects and their regional distributions in an attempt like Gilliéron's to provide detailed evidence for the study of linguistic change. American linguists like William Labov and Raven I. McDavid, Jr., in turning to the description of dialectal differentiation in large American cities, have extended Kurath's concern with correlations of dialect and class. This work, certainly the most interesting of that now being conducted by American dialectologists, has raised some old issues. Shades of the Usage Controversy lurk about the edges of the article by William Labov included here, as he explores the relations of standard and less prestigious dialects as well as attitudes toward the social status of each. Such work has attracted the attention and the support of the U. S. Office of Education since many linguists, joined by many educators, feel that some of the educational handicaps of the poor and ignorant can be overcome by the more effective teaching of Standard English.

But if the interests and lines of inquiry in current dialectology reflect older ones, they are indeed being pursued in many cases with new methodologies and in new theoretical frameworks. Atwood describes methodological advances in the Linguistic Atlas of the United States beyond the methods of earlier continental dialectologists, and Labov in turn reports advances in methods for describing social dialects beyond those employed in the Atlas. In addition, changes in theories of language and of linguistic description have necessitated changes in notions of what dialects are and how they might best be described.

Among the following selections, Sapir's essay is a general introduction to the range of linguistic variation and is suggestive of some of the problems involved in defining the term *dialect*. The article by Atwood is a discussion of the methods and findings of the Linguistic Atlas of the United States. Atwood surveys work accomplished on the American lexicon and on the regional atlases which together comprise the larger project; in the long note appended to his article we have presented a synopsis of the features which distinguish major dialects east of the Mississippi, drawing those features from an outline compiled by Atwood from Atlas materials. Supplementary details are from two similar lists by Raven I. McDavid, Jr. Harold Orton's article is a report on the aims, method, and progress of the Survey of English Dialects.

The final three articles point to methodological and theoretical advances. Uriel Weinreich discusses the gap between conventional dialectology and developments in descriptive linguistics as of 1954—that is, before Chomsky. The questions he asks raise doubts about the adequacy of the theoretical base for a dialectology which concentrates on differences in surface behavior without reference to the system underlying that behavior. In exploring the gap between theory and practice, Weinreich uncovers a paradox which needs resolution before conventional dialectology and structuralism can be reconciled. Structuralism views linguistic systems as unique and closed, discrete and homogeneous. If a dialect is such a linguistic system, how can it be compared to another dialect or related to the larger entity, the language? In other words, how can we describe what we know to be a fact—that some systems resemble one another closely enough for all to be regarded as divergent forms of a single entity—if we consider each of those systems unique? Weinreich makes suggestions for a structural dialectology which will permit the handling of partial similarities and partial differences within a general theory providing also for the handling of homogeneous systems. The real value of his article is less in his solution to the problem (a solution that has been pretty well overturned by recent developments in generative theory) than in the questions it raises about conventional dialectology. Weinreich was one of the first to carefully examine the inconsistencies between the methods of dialectology and the theory of structuralism.

James Sledd offers a different answer to some of the questions Weinreich asked, as he attempts a set of informal generative phonetic rules which will specify certain features of pronunciation in some superficially different dialects, while at the same time emphasizing their underlying similarity.

Sledd criticizes two much-followed phonemicizations of English vowels, those of Trager and Smith and of Kurath: the former for obscuring fundamental similarities by giving direct representation to the variations in vowels among dialects, consequently overemphasizing the dialectal differences; the latter for providing cover symbols for a variety of phonetic facts without an attendant theory for relating phonemes to phonetics. Sledd's orientation is MITesian, but he emphasizes the unofficial status of his effort.

William Labov, a student of Weinreich's who has been working on the dialects of New York City, is naturally most concerned with the complex problems of describing changing urban speech. The theoretical framework for his study is mainly derived from American structuralism, particularly in his treatment of phonology; yet he has made significant departures from the tenets of that school and has also attempted more sophisticated correlations between linguistic behavior and social class than those of the Linguistic Atlas. Labov believes that speakers' controlling attitudes toward linguistic variables, including their judgments of social and stylistic propriety, are as vital a part of the linguist's data as their overt behavior.

Though the materials he works with are hardly typical of the history of English, they are directly relevant to immediate social problems, and Labov has used them to support important suggestions about the social forces that may affect the spreading of linguistic innovations.

Taken together, the essays by Weinreich, Sledd, and Labov exemplify once more the continuance of productive controversy in all fields of linguistics, and remind the student that any account of language "facts" presupposes some general theory of language structure. Unfortunately, none of the essays says anything of the most interesting but least studied development in the recent history of English dialects: the spread of English, either as first or second language, throughout the world.

English spread first as the language of the explorers, pirates, transported convicts, merchants, and colonists who established the British Empire. When English-speaking colonists established themselves, in America, in Australia, in New Zealand, and when their colonies became new nations, a new kind of regional dialect arose: not the distinctive speech of a village, hamlet, or county, but a national norm, itself possessed of regional varieties.

This development has confronted dialectologists with a number of interesting problems. What, for example, is the status of major national varieties like Canadian English or Australian English? Should they be considered languages in their own right, or merely dialects? If they are merely dialects, are their relations to the over-arching language English the same as the relations—say—of the dialects of Atlanta and of New York City to the English of the United States? To what extent can we assume a unified entity called the English language, somehow including dialects which themselves are the norms for lesser regional dialects, and the vehicles of different political, economic, and cultural organizations? A student might learn a great deal about the relations between language and other human institutions simply by asking why the great national varieties of English have remained mutually intelligible, and easily so.

Linguistic historians must join the dialectologists to trace the processes by which these national varieties have arisen, to show the extent to which English has been modified through its use by speakers of widely divergent experience in environments as different as the African veldt, the Australian bush, the Malaysian rain forest, and the American Rockies. It is a commonplace that English has an extremely cosmopolitan vocabulary, largely because of the varied contacts and experiences of those who speak it; but much more work needs to be done on the less easily observed structural features of the language—on such questions as the influence which the languages of India have had on the phonology and syntax of Indian English.

Other questions arise from the fact that English has not been spread only by colonists from Britain and their offspring. Under the Empire, English became a second language for many imperial subjects of many races; and in spite of the independence of former colonies, it has continued to spread, maintained or adopted by citizens of the new nations who have wished to keep in contact with the industrial, scientific, economic, and cultural developments of the Western world. Often, the second language has become a first, and today English is either native or the language most often used among millions of people in what were once the far reaches of the earth—in India, Pakistan, Ceylon, Malaysia, Nepal, the Philippines, Nigeria, Rhodesia, Sierra Leone, in Ghana, Guiana, Hong Kong, Kenya, Liberia, Malawi, Singapore, Somalia, South Africa, Tanzania, Trinidad and Tobago, Uganda, the British West Indies, in Swaziland, Aden and South Arabia, Kuwait, Mauritius, and Fiji. Besides all this, English is the most commonly taught second language in Southeast Asia, in Japan, and in much of Europe, particularly in Germany, Holland, and Scandinavia.

The emergence of English among peoples of widely varied racial and linguistic stocks has interested scholars other than dialectologists and linguistic historians. Literary historians and literary critics are becoming increasingly aware of significant literatures in English, not just in nations like Canada and Australia, where the predominance of native speakers makes such writing as natural as it is in Britain itself, but also in nations where that predominance does not exist—in India, for example, and in Nigeria. Men of letters foresee the development of a truly *international* literature written in the first international language since Latin.

Sociolinguists, finally, are considering problems no more interesting but perhaps more vital to immediate political and economic concerns. The strength and prosperity of Britain and the United States, as well as their literature, will be affected by the decision whether or not English shall continue to be used in areas where free nations have replaced former colonies and dependencies. Will countries like India and Malaysia, now that they have established their independence, keep using English as they use it now? English today is an important vehicle of education there, a means of intellectual inquiry and of communication both among indigenous peoples of different racial and linguistic stocks and with the West; will it keep this status in the future?

The problem of what the national language should be is particularly acute for the citizens themselves of the newly born nations of Asia and Africa. In India, for example, there are over eight hundred languages spoken by the more than five hundred million inhabitants, many of the languages being mutually unintelligible. What language to choose for official government documents, or what language to use as the basis for instruction in reading and writing, is thus a question of unbelievable complexity. The government faces the problem of trying to urge unity on a vast population of widely varying cultures and religions spread over an immense country made even larger by poor communications: a common language would of course help. But what language will best serve?

The constitution of India, adopted in 1950, provided that each of the sixteen states which compose the Union of India could choose one of its regional languages as official in that state. The Union itself was to have two official languages at first: English, which was to serve as an auxiliary language from 1950 to 1965, and Hindi, which would eventually replace it. In 1965, bloody riots broke out over the language question. Some factions wanted to retain English, some wanted it replaced by Hindi as the constitution provided, others opposed Hindi altogether and fought for their own regional language. The government gave way to pressure and restored at least temporary calm by decreeing that English should be continued as a supplementary official language for as long as may be necessary, since English has the one advantage that, except among strong nationalists, it more nearly approaches social and religious neutrality than do indigenous languages which are the vehicles of major religions and which carry the overtones of race and caste. But final settlement of the question has only been delayed.

If English continues to be used in India, and in other young nations in Asia and Africa which face similar problems, both European and non-European stand to profit, for there will be one less obstacle to satisfactory international communication. The language was spread abroad by the colonial governments of England's Empire. The Empire is gone; but once planted, the language has continued to spread because of the remaining power and influence of the English-speaking nations, particularly the United States. Some things can be done to cultivate that growth. The British, more than the Americans, have been willing to commit money and manpower to the teaching of English to Asians and Africans, and as a consequence, they have maintained more influence in some areas than one would expect from their declining strength. At the moment, their language and ours is one of the four official languages of the United Nations, it is the most popular second language in the world, and it is second only to Chinese in the number of its speakers. But its continued enjoyment of such high favor is by no means a foregone conclusion.

SUGGESTED READINGS

Discussions of dialect and the study of dialects may be found in the general introductions to linguistics listed in the bibliographical notes to Parts One and Three. Students may find it interesting to compare the articles by

Sapir and Weinreich to André Martinet's "Dialect," *Romance Philology*, 8 (1954), 1–11. Raven I. McDavid's chapter "The Dialects of American English" in W. Nelson Francis' *The Structure of American English* (New York, 1958) is an excellent introduction to that subject. See also Jean Malmstrom's pamphlet *Dialects, USA* (Champaign, Ill., 1963), Roger W. Shuy's *Discovering American Dialects* (Champaign, 1967), and Carroll E. Reed's *Dialects of American English* (Cleveland, 1967). Further bibliography on American English dialects may be found in the notes to the article by Atwood. G. L. Brook's *English Dialects* (New York, 1963) is a popular and general overview of English dialects and their study. A discussion of dialect work in Scotland may be found in Angus McIntosh, *Introduction to a Survey of Scottish Dialects* (Edinburgh, 1961); for Ireland, see P. L. Henry, "A Linguistic Survey of Ireland: Preliminary Report," in *Lochlann, A Review of Celtic Studies*, 1 (1958), 49–208, and *Ulster Dialects: An Introductory Survey* (Cultra Manor, Holywood, Co. Down: for the Ulster Folk Museum, 1964). Information about dialect projects for Canada may be conveniently found in Walter S. Avis' *A Bibliography of Writings on Canadian English, 1857–1965* (Toronto, 1965), and in the *Journal of the Canadian Linguistic Society* (now called the *Journal of Canadian Linguistics*). In Australia, the Australian Language Research Centre publishes *Occasional Papers* of high quality and interest; the Linguistic Society of New Zealand publishes its *Proceedings*. A good survey of the achievements of (mainly) continental work appears in Gino Bottiglioni, "Linguistic Geography: Achievements, Methods and Orientations," *Word*, 10 (1954), 375–387. A comprehensive account of that work may be found in Sever Pop's *La dialectologie. Aperçu historique et méthodes d'enquêtes linguistiques* (Louvain, 1950).

The study of social dialects is one trend in the growing field of sociolinguistics, the study of relations between language and society. An introduction to some sociolinguistic interests can be gained from the following collections: Harry Hoijer, ed., *Language in Culture* (Chicago, 1954), also printed as Memoir No. 79 of the American Anthropological Association (1954); the Spring 1966 issue of *Sociological Inquiry;* W. Bright, ed., *Sociolinguistics: Proceedings of the UCLA Linguistics Conference* in 1964 (The Hague, 1966). Treatments of social dialects may be found in Raven I. McDavid, "Social Differences in Pronunciation: A Problem in Methodology," *General Linguistics*, 2 (1956), 15–21, "American Social Dialects," *College English*, 26 (1965–1966), 254–260, and "The Dialectology of an Urban Society," *Communications du Premier Congrès de Dialectologie*, 1 (Louvain, 1964), 68–80; John L. Fisher, "Social Influences in the Choice of a Linguistic Variant," *Word*, 14 (1958), 47–56; George N. Putnam and Edna M. O'Hern, *The Status Significance of an Isolated Urban Dialect*, Language Dissertation, No. 53; David W. Reed, "Establishing and Evaluating

Social Boundaries in English," in *Studies in Languages and Linguistics in Honor of Charles Carpenter Fries*, ed. A. H. Marckwardt (Ann Arbor, 1964); William Labov, "Phonological Correlates of Social Stratification" (in *The Ethnography of Communication*, ed. John J. Gumperz and Dell Hymes, appearing as the December 1964 issue of *American Anthropologist*) and *The Social Stratification of English in New York City* (Washington, D.C., 1966). Students interested in the pedagogical implications of recent research should consult: William A. Stewart, ed., *Non-Standard Speech and the Teaching of English* (Washington, D.C., 1964); *Language Programs for the Disadvantaged* (Champaign, Ill., 1965); Roger W. Shuy, ed., *Social Dialects and Language Learning* (Champaign, 1964).

For further discussion of structural dialectology, students should read: Edward Stankiewicz, "The Phonemic Patterns of the Polish Dialects," in Morris Halle and Horace Lunt, eds., *For Roman Jakobson* (The Hague, 1956), 518–531, and "On Discreteness and Continuity in Structural Dialectology," *Word*, 13 (1957), 44–59; William G. Moulton, "The Short Vowel Systems of Northern Switzerland, A Study in Structural Dialectology," *Word*, 16 (1960), 155–182, and "Dialect Geography and the Concept of Phonological Space," *Word*, 18 (1962), 23–33; Pavle Ivič, "On the Structure of Dialectal Differentiation," *Word*, 18 (1962), 33–53; Robert P. Stockwell, "Structural Dialectology: A Proposal," *American Speech*, 34 (1959), 258–268.

In the summer of 1968, there is little published material available on the specific application of generative theory to dialectology. Some general discussion may be found in Morris Halle's "Phonology in Generative Grammar," *Word*, 18 (1962), 54–72, reprinted in Fodor and Katz, *The Structure of Language*, and in the theoretical works on generative phonology mentioned elsewhere in the anthology. Some aging studies still of value are: Edward S. Klima, "Relatedness Between Grammatical Systems," *Language*, 40 (1964), 1–20; Sol Saporta, "Ordered Rules, Dialect Differences, and Historical Processes," *Language*, 41 (1965), 218–224; and Samuel Jay Keyser's review of *The Pronunciation of English in the Atlantic States*, *Language*, 39 (1963), 303–316.

Good general essays on the spread of English as a world language are hard to come by. The following, however, will provide an initial survey: the chapter "English Overseas" in Brook's *English Dialects;* Chap. XII, "The Future of the Language," in H. L. Mencken, *The American Language*, abridged ed. (New York, 1963); the short articles in *British and American English Since 1900* (London, 1951), by Eric Partridge and John W. Clark; and "A Language in Common," a special issue of the *Times Literary Supplement*, August 10, 1962, reprinted under the same title by the National Council of Teachers of English in 1963. Information about literature in the

Commonwealth may be found in A. L. McLeod, ed., *The Commonwealth Pen* (Ithaca, N.Y., 1961); the *Harvard Educational Review*, 34 (1964), contains a symposium on "The Use of English in World Literatures." A special group of the Modern Language Association (Group 12, World Literature Written in English) publishes a newsletter, the *WLWE Newsletter*, ed. J. J. Jones, Department of English, University of Texas, Austin; an "Annual Bibliography of Commonwealth Literature" may be found in *The Journal of Commonwealth Literature*. For interesting discussions of the use of English in new nations, see Robert B. LePage, *The National Language Question* (Oxford: Institute of Race Relations, 1964); and Punya Sloka Ray, *Language Standardization; Studies in Prescriptive Linguistics* (The Hague, 1963).

Some useful, if sometimes old, works on particular varieties of English are: IRELAND: P. W. Joyce, *English as We Speak It in Ireland* (London, 1910); Jeremiah J. Hogan, *The English Language in Ireland* (Dublin, 1927); J. M. Clark, *The Vocabulary of Anglo-Irish* (St. Gall, 1917); CANADA: Avis' bibliography mentioned above; *A Dictionary of Canadianisms on Historical Principles* (Toronto, 1967), the first large-scale study of the Canadian lexicon; SOUTH AFRICA: Charles Pettman, *Africanderisms* (London, 1913); L. W. Lanham, *English in South Africa* (Johannesburg, 1964); David Hopwood, *South African English Pronunciation* (Cape Town and Johannesburg, 1929); the journal *English Studies in Africa;* also John Spencer, ed., *Language in Africa* (London, 1963); AUSTRALIA AND NEW ZEALAND: W. S. Ramson, "A Critical Review of Writings on the Vocabulary of Australian English," *Australian Literary Studies*, 1 (1963), 89–103; E. E. Morris, *Austral English, A Dictionary of Australian Words, Phrases, etc.* (London, 1898), which has been supplemented by A. G. Mitchell and A. M. MacDonald, "Supplement of Australian and New Zealand Words," in *Chambers' Shorter English Dictionary* (Sydney, 1952); Sidney J. Baker, *The Australian Language*, 2nd ed. (Sydney, 1966); A. G. Mitchell, *The Pronunciation of English in Australia*, 2nd ed. (Sydney, 1965); W. S. Ramson, *Australian English: A Historical Study of the Vocabulary 1788–1898* (Canberra, 1966); G. W. Turner, *The English Language in Australia and New Zealand* (London, 1966); J. A. W. Bennett, "English as It Is Spoken in New Zealand," *American Speech*, 18 (1943), 81–95; Arnold Wall, *New Zealand English*, 3rd ed. (Christchurch, 1959); INDIA: R. C. Goffin, *Some Notes on Indian English*, Society for Pure English, Tract No. 41 (Oxford, 1934); Vinayak Krishna Gokak, *English in India, Its Present and Future* (New York, 1964); Henry Yule and A. C. Burnell, *Hobson-Jobson, A Glossary of Colloquial Anglo-Indian Words and Phrases*, 2nd ed. (London, 1903); G. Subba Rao, *Indian Words in English* (Oxford, 1954).

Edward Sapir

DIALECT

Starting from a historical orientation which recognizes a tendency of languages
to split into dialects which may in turn develop into mutually unintelligible
languages, Sapir searches for some means to identify dialects and minor local
varieties as distinguishable entities. Considering a group of dialects "merely
the socialized form of the universal tendency to individual variation"—a
partial definition which allows him to distinguish dialect from idiolect—he
makes suggestions about the psychological reality of dialectal norms and the
importance of attitudes toward local dialects and standard languages. Sapir
ends with an appraisal of the forces favoring linguistic standardization in the
modern world, raising problems which are now very much in the minds of
dialectologists and language teachers. Anyone interested in the "dialect
engineering" referred to by William Labov would do well to ponder the implications of Sapir's statement that "the modern problem is more complex than
the classical or medieval problem because the modern mind insists on having
the process of standardization take the form of a democratic rather than an
aristocratic process."

The term "dialect" has a connotation in technical linguistic usage which is
somewhat different from its ordinary meaning. To the linguist there is no
real difference between a dialect and a language which can be shown to be
related, however remotely, to another language. By preference the term is
restricted to a form of speech which does not differ sufficiently from another
form of speech to be unintelligible to the speakers of the latter. Thus,
Great Russian and White Russian are said to be dialects of the same
language. Similarly, Alsatian, Swabian, and Swiss German are dialects or
groups of dialects of a common folk speech. Literal mutual intelligibility,
however, is not a criterion of great interest to the technical linguist, who is
more concerned with the fact and order of historical relationships in speech.
To him Venetian and Sicilian are equally dialects of Italian, although as far
as mutual intelligibility is concerned these two might as well be called
independent languages. Russian, Polish, Czech, Bulgarian, and Serbian,
conventionally considered as independent languages because of their
national affiliations, are no less truly dialects of a common Slavic speech or
linguistic prototype than Venetian and Sicilian are dialects of a supposedly
common Italian language. If two obviously related forms of speech are

spoken at the same time, the linguist does not say that one of them is a dialect of the other but that both are sister dialects of some common prototype, known or inferred. When they diverge so far as not only to be mutually unintelligible but no longer to be too obviously related to each other, the term language is more freely used than dialect, but in principle there is no difference between the two. Thus in a sense all Romance languages, all Celtic languages, all Germanic languages, all Slavic languages and all Indo-Aryan vernaculars are merely dialect groups of a common Aryan or Indo-European language.

A group of dialects is merely the socialized form of the universal tendency to individual variation in speech. These variations affect the phonetic form of the language, its formal characteristics, its vocabulary and such prosodic features as intonation and stress. No known language, unless it be artificially preserved for liturgical or other nonpopular uses, has ever been known to resist the tendency to split up into dialects, any one of which may in the long run assume the status of an independent language. From dialects formed by inherent differentiation one may distinguish dialects which owe their origin to speech transfers. A community which takes on a language that is different from the one to which it has originally been accustomed will unconsciously carry over into the adopted language peculiarities of its own form of speech which are pronounced enough to give its use of the foreign language a dialectic tinge. Many linguists attach much importance to the influence of superseded languages in the formation of dialects. Thus some of the distinctive peculiarities of both Celtic and Germanic are supposed to be due to the retention of phonetic peculiarities of pre-Aryan languages.

In less technical or frankly popular usage the term dialect has somewhat different connotations. Human speech is supposed to be differentiated and standardized in a number of approved forms known as languages, and each of these in turn has a number of subvarieties of lesser value known as dialects. A dialect is looked upon as a departure from the standard norm, in many cases even as a corruption of it. Historically this view is unsound, because the vast majority of so-called dialects are merely the regular, differentiated development of earlier forms of speech which antedate the recognized languages. Popular confusion on the subject is chiefly due to the fact that the question of language has become secondarily identified with that of nationality in the larger cultural and ethnic group which in course of time absorbs the local tradition. The language of such a nationality is generally based on a local dialect and spreads at the expense of other dialects which were originally of as great prestige as the culturally more powerful one.

Of the large number of dialects spoken in Germany, German Switzerland

and Austria, for example, very few, if any, can be considered as modified forms of the culturally accepted *Hochdeutsch* of literature, the pulpit, the stage and cultural activity generally. The dialects of the German speaking folk go back unbrokenly to the Old High German of early mediaeval times, a German which was even then richly differentiated into dialects. The present standardized German of the schools arose comparatively late in the history of German speech as a result of the fixing of one of the Upper Saxon dialects as the recognized medium of official communication within the German speaking dominions. Luther's Bible helped considerably in the diffusion of this form of German as the recognized standard. It has taken a long time, however, for *Hochdeutsch* to take on a recognized phonetic form and to be looked upon as a well standardized form of oral communication, and to this day a large proportion of Germans, including the educated ranks, are bilingual in the sense that they use the standardized German for formal purposes but employ the local dialect for more familiar uses.

The history of German is paralleled more or less by the history of all the other national languages of Europe and of other parts of the world. As a result of cultural reasons of one kind or another a local dialect becomes accepted as the favored or desirable form of speech within a linguistic community that is cut up into a large number of dialects. This approved local dialect becomes the symbol of cultural values and spreads at the expense of other local forms of speech. The standardized form of speech becomes more and more set in its vocabulary, its form and eventually its pronunciation. The speakers of local dialects begin to be ashamed of their peculiar forms of speech because these have not the prestige value of the standardized language; and finally the illusion is created of a primary language, belonging to the large area which is the territory of a nation or nationality, and of the many local forms of speech as uncultured or degenerated variants of the primary norm. As is well known, these variations from the standard norm are sometimes much more archaic, historically speaking, than the norm from which they are supposed to depart.

Local dialects are in a sense minority languages, but the latter term should be reserved for a completely distinct form of speech that is used by a minority nationality living within the political framework of a nation. An example of such a minority language would be the Basque of southwestern France and northern Spain or the Breton of Brittany. These languages are not dialects of French and Spanish but historically distinct languages that have come to occupy culturally secondary positions.

There is naturally no hard and fast line between a dialect and a local variation of a minor nature, such as New England English or middle western English. In the case of the older dialects the connection with the standardized speech is quite secondary, while in the case of such local variations as New England and middle western American speech standard English, however loosely defined, is present in the minds of all as the natural background for these variations, which are thus psychologically, if not altogether historically, variations from the primary or standard norm. It would be possible for the speaker of a local Swiss dialect or of Yorkshire English to build up a nationalistic gospel around his local dialect in opposition to the accepted speech of the cultured group, but the attempt to do this for middle western English in America would have something intrinsically absurd about it because of the feeling that this form of English is at best but a belated departure from an earlier norm. As usual in social phenomena, however, it is the symbolism of attitude that counts in these matters rather than the objective facts of history.

Ever since the formation of the great national languages of Europe toward the end of the mediaeval period there have been many social and political influences at work to imperil the status of the local dialects. As the power of the sovereign grew, the language of the court gained in prestige and tended to diffuse through all the ramifications of the official world. Meanwhile, although the Roman Catholic and Greek churches with their sacred liturgical languages were little interested in the question of folk versus standardized speech, the Protestant sects with their concern for a more direct relation between God and His worshippers naturally emphasized the dignity of folk speech and lent their aid to the diffusion of a selected form of folk speech over a larger area. The influence of such documents as Luther's Bible and King James's Authorized Version in the standardization of English and German has often been referred to. In more recent days the increase of popular education and the growing demand for ready intelligibility in the business world have given a tremendous impetus to the spread of standardized forms of speech.

In spite of all these standardizing influences, however, local dialects, particularly in Europe, have persisted with a vitality that is little short of amazing. Obviously the question of the conservatism of dialect is not altogether a negative matter of the inertia of speech and of the failure of overriding cultural influences to permeate into all corners of a given territory. It is to a very significant degree a positive matter of the resistance of the local dialects to something which is vaguely felt as hostile. This is easily understood if we look upon languages and dialects not as intrinsically good or bad forms of speech but as symbols of social attitudes. Before the growth of modern industrialism culture tended to be intensely local in character in spite of the uniformizing influences of government, religion, education and business. The culture that gradually seeped in from the great urban centers was felt as something alien and superficial in spite of the prestige that unavoidably attached to it. The home speech was associated with kinship ties and with the earliest emotional experiences of the individual. Hence the learning of a standardized language could hardly seem natural except in the few centers in which the higher culture seemed properly at home, and even in these there generally developed a hiatus between the standardized language of the cultured classes and the folk speech of the local residents. Hence cockney is as far removed psychologically from standard British English as is a peasant dialect of Yorkshire or Devon. On the continent of Europe, particularly in Germany and Italy, the culture represented for example, by standardized German or standardized Italian was until very recent days an exceedingly thin psychological structure, and its official speech could hardly take on the task of adequately symbolizing the highly differentiated folk cultures of German speaking and Italian speaking regions.

The Age of Enlightenment in the eighteenth century was, on the whole, hostile to the persistence of dialects, but the romantic movement which followed it gave to folk speech a glamour which has probably had something to do with the idealization of localized languages as symbols of national solidarity and territorial integrity. Few writers of the seventeenth and eighteenth centuries would have taken seriously the use of dialect in literature. It was only later that Lowland Scotch could be romantically restored in the lyrics of Robert Burns, that Fritz Reuter could strive to establish a Low German (Plattdeutsch) literary language and that Mistral could attempt to revive the long lost glory of Provençal. One may suspect that this renewed emphasis on linguistic differences is but a passing phase in the history of modern man. Be that as it may, it has had much to do with the emergence of new nationalisms in recent times. It is doubtful if such countries as Lithuania, Esthonia, and Czechoslovakia could have so easily proved their right to exist if it had not come to be felt that just as every nationality needs its language, so every unattached language needs its nationality and territorial independence to fulfill its inherent mission. Perhaps the best example of what might be called linguistic romanticism is the attempt of the Irish nationalists to renew the vitality of Gaelic, a form of speech which has never been standardized for literary, let alone folk, purposes and which is profoundly alien to the majority of the more articulate of Irish nationalists.

No doubt the respect for local forms of speech has received assistance from scientific linguistics and its tendency to view all languages and dialects as of equal historical importance. It is very doubtful, however, if linguistic localism can win out in the long run. The modern mind is increasingly realistic and pragmatic in the world of action and conceptualistic or normative in the world of thought. Both of these attitudes are intrinsically hostile to linguistic localism of any sort and necessarily therefore to dialectic conservatism. Compulsory education, compulsory military service, modern means of communication and urbanization are some of the more obvious factors in the spread of these attitudes, which, so far as language is concerned, may be defined by the thesis that words should either lead to unambiguous action among the members of as large a group as is held together culturally or in the domain of thought should aim to attach themselves to concepts which are less and less purely local in their application. In the long run therefore it seems fairly safe to hazard the guess that such movements as the Gaelic revival in Ireland and the attempt to save as many minority languages and dialects from cultural extinction as possible will come to be looked upon as little more than eddies in the more powerful stream of standardization of speech that set in at the close of the mediaeval period. The modern problem is more complex than the classical or the mediaeval problem, because the modern mind insists on having the process of standardization take the form of a democratic rather than an aristocratic process.

A word may be added in regard to the social psychology of dialectic forms of speech. In the main, markedly dialectic peculiarities have been looked upon as symbols of inferiority of status, but if local sentiment is strongly marked and if the significance of the local group for the larger life of the nation as a whole allows, a local dialect may become the symbol of a kind of inverted pride. We thus have the singular spectacle of Lowland Scotch as an approved and beautiful linguistic instrument and of cockney as an undesirable and ugly one. These judgments are extrinsic to the facts of language themselves but they are none the less decisive in the world of cultural symbolisms.

If an individual is brought up in a community that has its characteristic dialect and if he becomes identified later in life with another community which has a second mode of speech, some very interesting personality problems arise which involve the status symbolism or affectional symbolism of these differing forms of speech. Individuals who vacillate somewhat in their conception of their own role in society may often be detected unconsciously betraying this feeling of insecurity in a vacillating pronunciation or intonation or choice of words. When under the influence of an emotional crisis such individuals are thrown back upon their earliest emotional experiences—"regress," in short—they are likely to relapse into early dialectic habits of speech. It is suggested that the question of the relation of the individual to the various dialects and languages to which he has been subjected from time to time is of far more than anecdotal interest, that it constitutes as a matter of fact a very important approach to the problem of personality subjected to the strains of cultural change.

Study Questions

1. How does Sapir define the term *dialect?* What distinctions does he make between *dialect* and *language, dialect* and *idiolect?* Is American English a dialect or a language? How would you support your answer? What does Sapir say about the causes of dialectal differentiation?

2. What is the difference between a standard language and a local dialect? What does Sapir say about the history of standard languages? Do they differ in origin from local dialects? Are local dialects debased forms of the standard language? Do the same historical forces operate on both the standard language and local dialects?

3. According to Sapir, strong social and psychological forces operate in advancing the standard language at the expense of local dialects. In particular, he suggests, speakers of local dialects feel ashamed of their native speech because of the prestige of the standard language. Do his remarks fit the dialect situation in the United States? Do you speak the prestige dialect of the area where you live? Are you aware of any prejudices in your area against divergences from the prestige dialect? How much of your schooling was devoted to learning the prestige dialect, or "Standard English"? Do you speak the same dialect you used as a child? What are some of the forces operating in contemporary America which might tend to level out differences between local dialects?

4. Sapir points to the persistence of local dialects in some parts of the world as evidence of hostility toward the standard language. Do similar social attitudes contribute to the preservation of local dialects in the United States? Do you know anyone who has retained his native speech even though it is not the prestige speech in the area in which he now lives? Why might a speaker who has lived in Chicago for ten or fifteen years, for example, retain his native Southern dialect? Would it be possible to make any correlations between his retention of his dialect and his attitudes toward the society in which he now lives, toward his native society, toward his parents? If you moved from Chicago to Atlanta, or from Atlanta to Chicago, would you be likely to try to change your speech if you knew that you would have an easier time making a living if you spoke like the people who would be

doing the employing? Is there a correlation between dialect and personality?

5. Have American writers participated in what Sapir calls the romantic use of folk speech in the production of literature? Can you think of any recent attempts to connect political nationalism with the revival of a local dialect or a minority language?

Elmer Bagby Atwood

THE METHODS OF AMERICAN DIALECTOLOGY

Elmer Bagby Atwood (1906–1963), although not one of the original planners and fieldworkers for the Linguistic Atlas of the United States and Canada, could be called one of the fathers of the project on the basis of his interpretive work, his teaching, and his original work on the dialects of the Southwest. His *Survey of Verb Forms in the Eastern United States* (1953) is an important contribution to our knowledge of morphological variants in American English and to our methodology for interpreting the Atlas records. *The Regional Vocabulary of Texas* (1962) contributes significant information about the spread of Southern features and presents new methodology for collecting and handling lexical materials which has been followed by some of Atwood's students and colleagues. His teaching inspired several workers to enter the field of dialectology. Atwood was also a medievalist of some distinction, co-editing the important *Excidium Troiae* with Virgil K. Whitaker for the Mediæval Academy of America.

Atwood's article is a comprehensive account of the development and progress of the large group of regional surveys loosely covered by the term the Linguistic Atlas of the United States and Canada, and of other work on regional American English. It is a particularly rich source of bibliographical information; and though we have not been able to reproduce Atwood's maps, we have retained the most useful of his footnotes, and have added a few more, for students who wish to read further in the field. We are indebted to Professor Atwood's widow, Mrs. Mary Atwood, for permission to reprint the article.

I. LEXICOGRAPHY

The earliest observations of what would nowadays be called "dialect" covered a variety of linguistic categories but tended to concentrate on lexical and grammatical peculiarities. They were, moreover, largely prescriptive, at least by implication, and observers usually regarded the collected material as something to be avoided. Probably the first collection that could be called in any sense systematic was that of the Rev. John Witherspoon, who published a series of papers on usage in the *Pennsylvania Journal and Weekly Advertiser* during the year 1781. He is credited with having coined the term *Americanism* to designate "ways of speaking peculiar to this country". Some of his examples, however, were neither American in origin nor "pecu-

"The Methods of American Dialectology" by E. Bagby Atwood. From pages 1–30 of *Zeitschrift für Mundart-forschung*, Vol. 30, 1963, by permission of Franz Steiner Verlag GmbH, Wiesbaden, Germany, and Mrs. Atwood.

liar" to the United States; for example, *fellow countrymen* for *countrymen* and *notify* with its modern meaning of 'inform'. Witherspoon also collected a number of "vulgarisms", which were undoubtedly genuine and which are common even today: *knowed* for *knew*, *this here* for *this*, *drownded* for *drowned*, *attacted* for *attacked*, and others.

The most famous of American lexicographers, Noah Webster, need not be treated in detail, since a vast body of material has been published concerning him. However, as far as I know, the effect of the regional American dialects, particularly those of New England, on his recording of words and meanings remains to be determined. Certainly his first dictionary, that of 1806,[1] was attacked for seeming to sanction "Americanisms and vulgarisms", and Webster felt need to defend himself for having included such terms as *docket, decedent, dutiable,* and even *lot* (of land)—as well as such "cant words" as *caucus*. In his *American Dictionary* of 1828[2] he recorded a considerable number of Americanisms, or at least new terms observable in America, including such controversial verb usages as *to notice, to advocate,* and *to progress,* all of which had been condemned by Benjamin Franklin. We can only wish that Webster had recorded more "cant" terms.

The numerous glossaries of Americanisms that appeared during the course of the nineteenth century are to a great extent the work of amateurs whose observation tended to be somewhat random and impressionistic. Among the compilers of such lists were David Humphries (1815), John Pickering (1816), Robley Dunglison (1829–30), John R. Bartlett (1848), and John S. Farmer (1889). None of these was primarily concerned with folk speech, yet occasionally items of considerable dialectal interest are entered and commented on; for example *be* (for *am, are*—Be you ready?), *clapboard* (siding), *poke* (bag), *run* (small stream), and *tote* (carry). All of these appear as early as Pickering, and most are recorded in Webster's first dictionary.

By far the greatest of the early collectors of American usages was Richard H. Thornton, an Englishman who migrated to the New World in the 1870's. Toward the end of the century he began to accumulate a carefully documented body of material, in which the source and the date of every usage were on record. His *American Glossary* was published in 1912 and later years[3]; although it is not primarily a dialect dictionary it still serves as a model of lexicographic procedure.

The idea that popular (in the sense of uneducated) speech is worthy of serious scholarly study arrived perhaps somewhat later in America than in

---

[1] Noah Webster, *Compendious Dictionary of the English Language* (Hartford and New Haven, Conn., 1806).
[2] *An American Dictionary of the English Language,* 2 vols. (New York, 1828).
[3] R. H. Thornton, *An American Glossary,* 2 vols. (London, 1912). The third volume was published piecemeal in *Dialect Notes (DN),* VI (1928–39). [All three volumes are now available in a single set, with an introduction by Margaret M. Bryant (New York, 1962).—*Eds.*]

Western Europe. The first public manifestation of interest on the part of scholars was the organization of the American Dialect Society (ADS), which took place at Harvard University in 1889. Evidently the idea was first suggested by Charles H. Grandgent, and the organization meeting was attended by twenty-eight persons, including Edward S. Sheldon, Francis J. Child, J. B. Greenough, George L. Kittredge, and others of their stature— men who were, or were to be, among the leading philological scholars of their time. The avowed object of the Society was "the investigation of the spoken English of the United States and Canada, and incidentally of other non-aboriginal dialects spoken in the same countries". By January of 1890 there were 158 members, and the official organ of the Society, *Dialect Notes*, began publication in that year.

As Louise Pound has pointed out, the early dialect scholars must have been strongly influenced by German thought and method. The first four presidents of the ADS had all studied in Germany, and George Hempl, the eighth, took his doctorate at Jena. The Wenker methodology,[4] however, seems not to have been adopted as a basis for dialect collection, except to a limited extent and in a modified form. Hempl prepared a standard question- naire of something over 90 items which he published in 1894, requesting the collaboration of his colleagues in its circulation. Hempl's questions were awkward and unwieldy, and it is difficult to see how most of them could have produced useful results. I believe that the only publication based on this material was Hempl's article on the pronunciation of *grease* (verb) and *greasy*, which appeared in 1896.[5]

From an early date, the ADS took the position that the great majority of members could make their most valuable contribution in the field of vo- cabulary. In various circulars, instructions were given as to the kinds of usages to be collected and the methods to be followed. It was the hope, obviously a rather naive one, that there might be assembled *"a complete record of American speechforms in our day,* say in 1900," and that in the fol- lowing years there might be published "an authoritative dictionary of American usage, which would supersede all other work in that line." In- deed, the idea of a dialect dictionary has always been prominent among the membership of the ADS; many have hoped that we might have a work com- parable to Joseph Wright's monumental *English Dialect Dictionary*.[6]

Unfortunately the contributions to *Dialect Notes* were extremely uneven, both in completeness and in reliability. Even after some forty years of col-

---

4 [From 1876 to 1881, Georg Wenker made a survey of dialects in the Rhine country near Düsseldorf. He had local schoolmasters translate forty test sentences into dialects they knew.—*Eds.*].

5 George Hempl, *"Grease* and *Greasy," DN*, I, Part IX (1896), 438–444.

6 Joseph Wright, *English Dialect Dictionary*, 6 vols. (London, 1898–1905). [Reprinted New York, 1962.—*Eds.*] The English Dialect Society, founded in 1873, regarded its work as complete when Wright's material was ready for publication; accordingly the Society disbanded toward the end of 1896.

lection, only a few names stood out for thoroughness of work—names such as L. W. Payne, H. Tallichet, Louise Pound, and Vance Randolph. Most reports were pitifully meager, and the total mass fell far short of original expectations.

During the period when Louise Pound was president of the ADS (1938–41) she arranged, "as a private person, not as president of the society", for the publication of the available dialect materials by the Crowell Company. On her recommendation, Harold Wentworth was chosen as editor. Within a relatively short time his *American Dialect Dictionary* had been prepared and published,[7] although without the official sanction of the ADS. In answer to criticisms of her arrangements, Miss Pound replied that "a standstill of more than half a century seemed long enough. When an opportunity offered, why not seize it?"

Wentworth's *Dictionary* must be regarded as an abridged one, whether so planned or not. It is very doubtful that all available material was included; and, in any case, the project was unfortunate in its timing. At least three important collections were being made during this period, of which publication was under way or would shortly begin. These were the materials of the *Dictionary of American English*,[8] the *Linguistic Atlas of New England*, and the Mencken Supplements to *The American Language*.[9] Moreover, the G. & C. Merriam Company must have had in its files a great deal of valuable dialectal material which would ultimately see publication.

In recent studies of the vocabulary of the Southwest and other areas I have had occasion to refer to Wentworth many times. Although I frequently find valuable material, I am often annoyed by the absence of terms that are of considerable dialectal significance. I cite forty such instances (out of a considerably larger number): *acequia* (irrigation ditch), *angledog* (earthworm), *banquette* (sidewalk), *belly band* (saddle girth), *(blue) norther* (sharp north wind), *burro* (donkey), *buttonwood* (sycamore tree), *Cajun* (Acadian), *chaparral* (bushy country), *charivari* (serenade), *clearseed peach* (freestone peach), *coon* (Negro), *cope!* (horse call), *corral* (horse pen), *devil's darning needle* (dragonfly), *dogie* (lone calf), *dog irons* (andirons), *eaves troughs* (gutters), *evener* (doubletree), *fatcake* (doughnut or cruller), *firedogs* (andirons), *hogshead cheese* (pork mixture), *hoosegow* (jail), *jackleg* (untrained person), *lead horse* (horse on the left), *llano* (prairie), *lumber room* (store room), *mesa* (plateau), *middling(s)* (salt pork), *milk gap* (cow pen), *mosquito hawk* (dragonfly), *nigger shooter* (boy's weapon), *olla* (water jar), *pilón* (something extra), *pirogue* (canoe), *rainworm* (earthworm), *redbug* (chigger), *snake*

[7] Harold Wentworth, *American Dialect Dictionary* (New York, 1944).

[8] William A. Craigie and James R. Hulbert, *A Dictionary of American English*, 4 vols. (Chicago, 1938–44).

[9] H. L. Mencken, *The American Language*, 4th ed. (New York, 1938); *Supplement I* (New York, 1945); *Supplement II* (New York, 1948); [one-volume ed., abridged and updated by Raven I. McDavid, Jr. (New York, 1963).—*Eds.*].

feeder (dragonfly), *toot* (paper bag), and *worm fence* (rail fence). That these
are common usages is attested by the fact that 31 of them are entered in the
Dictionary of American English, while no less than 38 of them are treated
in *Webster's Third New International Dictionary*, usually with some indication of their geographical distribution.

It is clear that there has never been assembled an American dialect lexicon
to compare with that of England. In fact, it is hardly possible that such a
collection can ever be made, since "dialect" in the European sense is much
less common in America than in England. The American population has
always been more fluid than that of Europe, both geographically and socially. Conditions were simply not right for the development of extensive
local patois. There is often little distinction between dialect and standard
speech; regional terms are frequently found in the usage of the educated,
and even "illiterate" features are common in the works of novelists who deal
with "local color". Most general dictionaries have taken cognizance of these
facts and have included a great many terms of regional and even local currency. The *Century Dictionary*, first published in 1889, in successive editions
entered and documented large numbers of American words of a "dialectal"
nature. The same may be said of the *Dictionary of American English* (as
exemplified on the preceding page), as well as of Mathews' *Dictionary of
Americanisms*.[10] *Webster's Third New International* includes most of the
words that are mapped in the *Linguistic Atlas of New England* and in Hans
Kurath's *Word Geography*—even down to such Northern localisms as *belly
bump(er)*, *belly bunt*, *belly bust(er)*, *belly flop(per)*, *belly gut(ter)*, and *belly
whop(per)*, all of which denote the act of coasting down a hill on one's belly.

In spite of the limitations that are apparent, and in spite of the overlapping that must of necessity take place, most members of the ADS, including myself, are hopeful that a truly systematic and comprehensive
dictionary of American dialect terms may be prepared. It is, however, only
realistic to recognize that such a project must have a single leading spirit as
director, who must have adequate time, adequate financing, and an adequate organization to carry the task to completion. No dictionary has ever
compiled itself.

Since 1944 the ADS has evidenced a considerable broadening of interests;
its new series of *Publications*[11] has by no means restricted itself to the amass-
ing of a dialect lexicon, but has on the other hand served as a medium for the
circulation of important monographs on many subjects.

As has been mentioned, new sources of lexical usage are now available.
Moreover, more systematic methods are being developed for the collection

---

[10] M. M. Mathews, *A Dictionary of Americanisms on Historical Principles* (Chicago, 1951).
[11] After a brief lapse during the Second World War, *Dialect Notes* was discontinued and the official series became *Publications of the American Dialect Society* (*PADS*) beginning in 1944.

of vocabulary. One such method, devised largely by Frederic G. Cassidy, involves the circulation of extensive questionnaires to individual informants so that at least a nucleus of items may be compared on a nationwide scale. The similarity of this procedure to that of many linguistic atlases is apparent, and other methods of the same sort will be discussed later.

In summary we may say that, although American words of a "dialectal" nature have been rather fully treated in separate studies and in general dictionaries, we still lack a comprehensive and fully documented dialect dictionary for the country as a whole.[12]

II. LINGUISTIC GEOGRAPHY

A. Atlases of the Atlantic States

The idea of preparing a linguistic atlas of the United States must have been current for a good many years before any actual work was undertaken. It was, however, in the years 1928 and 1929 that concrete proposals and plans were made. In December of 1928 the Present-Day English Group of the Modern Language Association approved the appointment of a committee to study the possibility of preparing an American atlas. At about the same time (independently, it seems), Edgar H. Sturtevant of Yale University, Director of the Linguistic Institute, had arranged for a conference of linguistic scholars to consider the same project. The two groups were very shortly acting jointly, and proposals were soon submitted to the American Council of Learned Societies with a view to financial support. In August of 1929 the Executive Committee of this body authorized the appointment of a committee, headed by Hans Kurath, to prepare a somewhat detailed plan and an estimated budget. In view of the magnitude of the project, it was agreed that a relatively small area should first be surveyed, and the choice of the New England states[13] seemed the most feasible one.

The methodology of the American *Atlas* has been essentially that of Gil-

---

[12] The Dictionary of American Regional English project directed by Professor F. G. Cassidy at the University of Wisconsin, Madison, is now (1967) in its third year of operation. Sponsored by the American Dialect Society and supported by a five year grant from the U.S. Office of Education and grants from the University of Wisconsin, DARE is well into the process of collecting and preparing data to be edited. Using a questionnaire of over 1300 items, field workers in camper trucks (Word Wagons) and local piece-workers have work underway in over forty states. A reading program of regional literature has readers in forty-eight states.

A computer program, written by Dr. Richard Venezky of the University of Wisconsin, which will allow rapid editing of large amounts of data, has been completed and storage of data in a central (computer) file has already begun.

With continued support, all the material should be assembled by 1970 with DARE itself possibly a reality by 1976.—James W. Hartman, Assistant Director, D.A.R.E.

[13] These states are Maine, New Hampshire, Vermont, Massachusetts, Rhode Island, and Connecticut.

liéron,[14] as refined and modified for Italy by Karl Jaberg and Jakob Jud.[15] During the summer of 1930, Kurath engaged in extended conferences with these scholars, as well as with Paul Scheuermeier, the leading fieldworker for the Italian *Atlas.*

The staff for the New England *Atlas* was shortly set up with Kurath as Director, Miles L. Hanley as Associate Director, and Marcus L. Hansen as Historian. Since it was desirable to complete the survey in a minimum of time, several fieldworkers were employed; the number was ultimately augmented to nine. Headquarters were established at Yale University, which also provided a Sterling Fellowship for one of the fieldworkers as well as half the salary of the Associate Director. Other universities and colleges likewise shared in financial support of the *Atlas;* these included Dartmouth, Brown, Mt. Holyoke, and the University of Vermont.

The staff of the *Atlas* underwent a short but concentrated training period during the summer of 1931, when Jakob Jud and Paul Scheuermeier were present as instructors and advisers. There followed the actual field work, which occupied a period of twenty-five months, ending in September of 1933.

The editing of the New England materials required several years, during which Kurath, with the able collaboration of Bernard and Julia Bloch, prepared 713 maps for publication. Between 1939 and 1943 the three volumes (bound in six parts)[16] were off the press, along with a *Handbook*[17] which explained the methodology, provided historical data, and summarized some of the most important dialectal features of the area.

Beginning in 1933, field work was continued in the Middle Atlantic and South Atlantic States.[18] Guy S. Lowman, the ablest of the New England fieldworkers, gathered material more or less continuously until his death in an automobile accident in 1941. By this time he had completed work in all of the Atlantic States[19] except South Carolina, Georgia, and New York. In the years following the Second World War, this work was brought to completion by Raven I. McDavid, Jr. As yet these raw materials have not been prepared for publication.[20]

---

[14] Jules Gilliéron and Edmond Edmont, *Atlas linguistique de la France* (Paris, 1902–12).

[15] Karl Jaberg and Jakob Jud, *Sprach- und Sachatlas Italiens und der Südschweiz,* 8 vols. (Zofingen, 1928–40).

[16] Hans Kurath, Miles L. Hanley, Bernard Bloch, and others, *Linguistic Atlas of New England,* 3 vols. in 6 parts (Providence, R. I., 1936–43).

[17] Hans Kurath and others, *Handbook of the Linguistic Geography of New England* (*Handbook*) (Providence, R. I., 1939).

[18] The Middle Atlantic States consist of New York, New Jersey, Pennsylvania, and West Virginia. The South Atlantic States are made up of Delaware, Maryland, Virginia, North Carolina, South Carolina, Georgia, and Florida.

[19] Only portions of Georgia and Florida were surveyed. In addition to the states mentioned above, several field records were made in the easternmost section of Ohio. A few were also made in parts of Canada that adjoin the United States—chiefly in New Brunswick and Ontario.

[20] [The materials have been used, however, in a good many publications since Atwood wrote—*e.g.,* by Kurath in *A Phonology and Prosody of Modern English* (Heidelberg, 1964) and by Carroll Reed in *Dialects of American English* (Cleveland and New York, 1967).—*Eds.*]

The procedures which were used in the New England survey, and which were essentially followed in the other Atlantic States, may be described under a number of headings.

Communities. Ultimately 213 New England communities were chosen for investigation. Of these a considerable majority were small towns or semi-rural communities; but the principal cities of the area were also included. The oldest settlements were given preference, and most of them were investigated; however, a fair selection was also made of secondary settlements and even of newer industrial areas. A brief history of each community was compiled, including its original settlement, subsequent changes in population, principal industries, and other pertinent characteristics. Communities tended to be more or less equidistant save in northern Maine, where population was sparse. In the Middle Atlantic and South Atlantic States the same principles were followed, with possibly greater attention given to the larger cities. There are, for example, twenty-two records from the adjoining boroughs of Manhattan and Brooklyn, and McDavid gathered at least ten in Charleston, South Carolina.

Informants. It is in the choice of informants that the American *Atlas* differs most strikingly from its European predecessors. Rather than restrict the investigation to rustic, or "folk", speech, Kurath required the inclusion of three principal types, which he describes as follows:

Type I: Little formal education, little reading and restricted social contacts.

Type II: Better formal education (usually high school) and/or wider reading and social contacts.

Type III: Superior education (usually college), cultured background, wide reading and/or extensive social contacts.

Each of these types is divided into two sub-classes: A, aged or old-fashioned, and B, middle-aged or younger, hence presumably more modern in usage. The idea of the divisions, of course, is to provide a means of determining the extent to which "dialect" characteristics appear in the speech of better-educated members of the various communities. Of the 413 informants actually represented in the New England *Atlas*, 148 fall in Type I, 214 in Type II, and 51 in Type III. In the remainder of the Atlantic States the proportions were about the same, except that in some areas Type I informants were proportionally more numerous than in New England. This would depend, of course, on the nature of the areas themselves. For example, during the 1930's in the Southern mountains it was not difficult to find illiterate or semi-literate informants of sufficient intelligence to answer the questions. In the whole of the Atlantic States there are 157 informants designated as "cultured." [21]

---

[21] Kurath and McDavid, *The Pronunciation of English in the Atlantic States*, pp. 23–27.

/

Actual choice of the informants was left to the individual fieldworkers, but certain general requirements were laid down. Every effort was made to secure truly native representatives, usually those born and reared in the area and descended from local families. No informant should have spent an extended period away from the area which he represented. Both men and women were accepted on equal terms and in about equal numbers. Fieldworkers were expected to provide material for a brief biography and character sketch of each informant.

Fieldworkers. The fieldworkers who did the interviewing in the Atlantic States are as follows: Hans Kurath, Bernard Bloch, Martin Joos, Guy S. Lowman, Miles L. Hanley, Lee S. Hulzén, Rachel S. Harris, Cassil Reynard, Marguerite Chapallaz, and Raven I. McDavid, Jr. All of these worked in New England except McDavid; in the other Atlantic States, as has been mentioned, Lowman and McDavid made all of the field records. All of the *Atlas* fieldworkers were highly trained. Several of them held the doctor's degree and were well grounded in the type of linguistic discipline that was current at that time. Moreover, they all underwent intensive training in phonetic transcription as part of their preparation for *Atlas* work. The idea of using several fieldworkers in New England has been justified by the relatively rapid completion of the *Atlas*. There are, however, certain unavoidable disadvantages. For one thing, most of the pronunciation features must be interpreted by someone who is thoroughly familiar with the materials. Moreover, some fieldworkers were more inclined than others to elicit archaisms in vocabulary and grammar. It is my opinion that where multiple fieldworkers are used their work should be spread over the same areas rather than confined to respective "territories". Otherwise there will appear what seem to be geographical cleavages in usage which must be discounted as merely fieldworker differences.

The Work Sheets. The actual questions that were posed to the informants were chosen after much research in previously published materials. Actually, the final form was not determined until after a certain amount of preliminary field work had been completed. In general, the items on the list represented everyday concepts, and sought to elicit usages that would ordinarily be transmitted orally within the family rather than in schools. Questions were arranged topically in order to avoid incoherence and to provide a more conversational atmosphere for the informant. Some of the topics were: the weather, the dwelling, utensils and implements, topography, domestic animals, and foods. The work sheets contained a sampling of pronunciation features, lexical peculiarities, morphological variants, and occasionally syntactic characteristics. Some pronunciation items sought to determine whether a phonemic distinction existed or not, or whether it existed in a certain environment (*mourning* as against *morning*); others were concerned with the incidence of a given phoneme (/s/ as against /z/ in *greasy*) or with the exact phonetic quality of a phoneme or sequence of phonemes (e.g., the vowel nucleus in *five*). Vocabulary items were concerned mainly with the currency of various synonyms for the same concept (*angleworm, angledog, eaceworm, mudworm, earthworm*). Very few, if any, were directly aimed at the recording of variant meanings, although most fieldworkers took note of deviant ideas or reactions on the part of the informants. The greater number of morphological items were concerned with verb forms, such as *clum* for *climbed, sot* for *sat*, or *hain't* for *haven't*. The total number of items (of all categories) used in New England was 711; this was augmented to 772 in the South Atlantic States. An interview was expected to occupy from eight hours to a good many more, depending on the personality of the informant.

Conducting the Interviews. Gilliéron's method of merely asking the informant to translate a term into his dialect would have little value in the United States, since no one wants to admit that he speaks a dialect. The desired response had to be elicited indirectly, if possible without using a word or phrase that might be part of the answer. No standard form was ever adopted for the questions themselves; each fieldworker was expected to use his ingenuity in producing a response. In the case of a concrete object, a brief description might be given. For example, Bloch would usually secure a term for *seesaw* by asking: "What do you call a plank laid across a trestle for children to play on"? McDavid's form for this question was somewhat fuller: ". . . you'd have a plank laying across—maybe a section of rail fence or a sawhorse or something like that, and a kid gets on one end and another gets on the other and they go up and down, what do you call that?" Sometimes, particularly in the case of a verb form or a phrase, a question might be of the completion type. McDavid builds up this imaginary situation in order to bring out *new suit:* "Say somebody's about to get married, and his mother or his sister will look him over and say, 'You can't get married in those old clothes—you better go round to the store and get you a . . .' ". Sometimes, in order to encourage the use of a synonym, a question might take the form: "Do you ever call it anything else?" Actual suggestion—that is, using what might be the response and asking the informant whether or not it is his usage—might be resorted to occasionally, but usually only if all other means of securing an answer had failed.

Fieldworkers were instructed to keep careful notations regarding the types of responses. Besides occurring normally in answer to a question, a word or phrase might come out in conversation without a question having been asked at all; or it might have been directly suggested; or it might have been "forced" by undue insistence on the part of the fieldworker. The informant might label the usage as old-fashioned or obsolescent; or he might obviously be using a term humorously; or he might (rightly or wrongly) state that a feature is often heard in the community but that he himself never employs it. It is doubtful that fieldworkers' practice in these matters was uniform, particularly with regard to old-fashioned usage. Indeed, McDavid often asked his original question in the form "What did you call so-and-so in the old days"?

Phonetic Transcription. The system of phonetic notation used in the American *Atlas* must be regarded as highly complicated by any standard. The editors take twenty pages in the *Handbook* to explain it, and it seems to me that the reader would need a rather good grounding in phonetics in order to understand the explanation. Thirty-two basic vowel symbols are provided, and each of these may be modified by "shift signs" to indicate intermediate vowel positions. Other diacritics may be used to indicate length or shortness, nasalization, labialization, retroflection, or devoicing. Over fifty consonant symbols are given, and many of these may also be marked so as to indicate special qualities such as aspiration, palatalization, velarization, dentalization, labialization, voicing, devoicing, retroflection, length, or syllabic quality. Stress marks were supposed to be used in polysyllabic words, and in some instances indications of intonation were required. The most skilled of the fieldworkers could manipulate the entire system accurately only in rather short utterances, and even then phonetic features were often overlooked or taken for granted. Different practices by the individual fieldworkers can frequently be detected; these are most noticeable in the case of the low back vowels. In view of the complexity of the system of transcription, we must say that the American *Atlas* is firmly committed to the idea of using "professional", or highly trained, fieldworkers; others can make little contribution, at least in the field of pronunciation.

Mechanical Recording. Although the desirability of a permanent aural record was recognized early, none of the actual *Atlas* interviews were mechanically recorded. In the early days this was partially attributable to the awkwardness of the mechanisms themselves. However, shortly after the completion of the New England field work, arrangements were made which permitted Miles L. Hanley to begin a collection of phonograph records in the area. In the years 1933 and 1934 he completed 657 double-faced twelve-inch records which contained natural conversation and narrative materials from a variety of informants and communities. Many of the speakers were the same informants that had previously been interviewed for the *Atlas*.

In the Middle and South Atlantic States no financial provision was made for the making of discs or tapes of informants' speech; hence mechanical recording in these areas has been very sporadic. I know of no comprehensive collection covering any large portion of the Atlantic States outside of New England.

Editing and Publication. The New England *Atlas* was prepared for publication according to Gilliéron's idea of entering each response in phonetic notation at its appropriate point on the face of a map. The mechanics of editing, important as they are, need be sketched only briefly. The first step was to stamp a positive identification on every page of every "work book" or field record. Then the books were disassembled so that all the page 1's, all the page 2's, and so on, might be placed together. After this all the responses to a single "item", or question, were copied in the form of a list, with each response given the number which had been assigned to the informant who uttered it and to his community. The entering of the data on the faces of the maps required a good deal of planning and experimentation. Kurath's original hope was that a font of phonetic type might be cast, but various practical difficulties led to the decision to have the transcriptions drafted by hand. The drafting was done (under the close supervision of Bernard Bloch) on a transparent overlay, and the base map was photographed through the overlay. The result was that the community numbers and the important geographical features (rivers, mountains, state boundaries, etc.) appeared in a light brown shade whereas the linguistic data came out in a clearcut black. . . .

The size chosen for the maps was 20 by 24 inches (about 51 by 62 centimeters). This permitted the entering of all actual responses at the proper point—even responses that were suggested, or heard from others, or regarded as obsolete, or used humorously, and so on. Entries of the latter types are preceded by an arbitrary symbol. However, a good deal of nonlinguistic or semi-linguistic material usually remained: deviant meanings, expressions of attitude toward a word and/or its referent, and similar data. The most important portion of this material was entered in the "commentaries" which appeared by the side of the maps. Some of these commentaries are very full, and contain observations of great interest to folklorists as well as to linguists.

The method used in publishing the New England records was obviously an expensive one and would be much more expensive at the present time. The published price of the New England *Atlas* was $180—a price which severely limited its circulation, yet one which today would cover only a fraction of the cost. We can hardly hope that the field records of the Middle and South Atlantic States will see publication in such a sumptuous format. If the complete raw materials of these areas are to appear, the most likely presentation seems to be in the form of lists or columns of responses, from which individual researchers may prepare maps to suit their purposes.

Interpretive Presentations. Both the published and the unpublished field records have been scanned by the *Atlas* staff and others, and various methods have been used for the cartographic presentation of linguistic

data in summary form. In the case of lexical variation, it is usually sufficient
to assign a symbol to each "word" and to enter this symbol at its appropriate point on a much reduced map. The New England *Handbook* (pp.
27 ff.) contains a number of such presentations, where the principal lexical
variants are entered on maps measuring only 3¾ by 4¾ inches (9½ by
12 centimeters). This type of cartography was used by Kurath in his *Word
Geography of the Eastern United States*,[22] which was based on the *Atlas* field
records of all of the Atlantic States. The maps on which the data is entered
measured about 7½ by 9 inches (19 by 22½ centimeters); the portion occupied by New England is only about 2¾ by 3 inches, a space only one-
eighth the diameter of the *Atlas* maps. In order to avoid overcrowding,
Kurath sometimes used more than one map to present all the responses to a
particular question. Another device which he developed was that of using
oversized symbols at intervals in order to indicate universality of usage
within a given area. . . .

The method of *isoglosses* has also been used for the cartographic presentation of lexical features. What must be realized is that an isogloss based on
the American materials can seldom, if ever, be more than approximate,
since usages do not as a rule terminate abruptly. Moreover, since responses
from more than one informant are normally entered at each "point", an
isogloss should never be regarded as a dividing line between two usages;
rather it is an indication of the approximate outer limit of a single feature.
Many usages are not amenable to presentation by this method, since they
appear in such scattered fashion that a large number of lines would have to
be drawn in order to encircle them accurately. No presentation by isoglosses
is very convincing unless these are drawn by a competent scholar, and even
then we need to know the individual distributions on which the lines are
based, so that we may judge the extent to which the materials have been
simplified.

The New England *Handbook* (p. 29) presents one map of lexical isoglosses,
but it contains so many lines that it has a maze-like and bewildering appearance. Kurath, in his *Word Geography*, gives no less than 119 isoglosses,
distributed over 41 maps. His use of these lines to determine the lexical
speech areas, as well as the focal areas, of the Atlantic States is one of the
major contributions of his book; his segmentation of the region into North,
Midland, and South (with various sub-areas) is now well known to scholars
and is finding its way into general use as well. His correlation of these areas
with the settlement and cultural history of the Atlantic Seaboard must be
regarded as a thorough and brilliant work of scholarship.

In my *Survey of Verb Forms in the Eastern United States*[23] I largely fol-

---

[22] Hans Kurath, *A Word Geography of the Eastern United States* (Ann Arbor, Michigan, 1949).
[23] E. Bagby Atwood, *A Survey of Verb Forms in the Eastern United States* (Ann Arbor, Michigan, 1953).

lowed Kurath's methods of cartographical representation. Ordinarily a separate symbol would be assigned to each verb form that was phonemically distinguishable from another. Problems of decision were relatively few, and pertained mainly to such matters as whether or not to group *taken* and *takened* together. I also experimented with the use of shading on some maps in order to indicate universality or near-universality of usage, particularly when interesting minority usages needed to be entered on the same map. I have never been very satisfied with this device, and feel that it should be used only sparingly.[24]

It is with regard to pronunciation features that interpretive presentations are most difficult. Kurath and McDavid, in their *Pronunciation of English in the Atlantic States*, have solved a great many of the problems in a logical way, although not within the framework used by many structural linguists. First of all, the idea (sometimes followed in Europe) of entering all variant pronunciations of the same "word" on the same map was rejected, if it was ever considered. To take an example, the word *father* in various dialects of England and America may show variation in the initial consonant ([f] as against [v]); it may also show a considerable number of vowel qualities for the *a*; the medial consonant may be [ð] or [d]; and the final syllable may show not only variant vowel qualities but also different types of /r/: retroflex, tongue-tap, tongue-trill, and even uvular. At least a hundred combinations of these features are possible, and the chances are that most of them would actually be used somewhere in the English-speaking world. The Kurath-McDavid principle, which is rigidly adhered to, is to observe one feature at a time, and to map only that feature on a particular map. Thus, in the case of *father*, the qualities of the first vowel are plotted on Map 32, those of the final syllable on Map 151. This method demands an early decision as to what features are to be observed. It also requires an understanding of what types of variation are possible; that is, whether we are dealing with a phonemic distinction (in certain environments), as in *four* and *forty* (Map 44), or with the incidence of a phoneme, as the /v/ in *nephew* (Map 169), or with the phonetic quality of a phoneme, as in the first vowel of *oxen* (Map 15). With regard to the last type of variation, Kurath has revived the term *diaphone*, but with a meaning somewhat different from that assigned to it by Daniel Jones.[25] As I understand Kurath's use of the term, it would denote the sort of variation that occurs in the word *nine* (Map 26), where most informants have the same phonemic arrangement, but where readily observable differences in quality exist. That is, *diaphones* are sub-

---

[24] Others, however, have used shading quite freely. See, for example, Raven I. McDavid, Jr., and Virginia G. McDavid, "Regional Linguistic Atlases in the United States," *Orbis*, V (1956), 349–386; and Sumner Ives, "Pronunciation of 'Can't' in the Eastern States," *American Speech*, XXVIII (1953), 149–157.

[25] Daniel Jones, *An Outline of English Phonetics*, 9th ed. (Cambridge, 1960), pp. 53–54.

phonemic differences that occur between one speaker and another, or between one area and another, as opposed to *allophones*, which occur in the speech of a single individual and which are determined by the environment of the phoneme. Kurath and McDavid have adopted the "unitary" system of interpreting English vowels; that is, for example, everything that comes between the /t/ and the /k/ in *take* is interpreted as a single entity /e/, as opposed to the two entities /ey/ required by the "binary" system of Trager and Smith.[26] Thus, maps in *The Pronunciation of English* present a great many vowel diaphones, since both monophthongal and diphthongal pronunciations may often be grouped together.

An interesting feature of Kurath and McDavid's presentation is the inclusion of a series of 70 vowel "synopses" (pp. 31–100) indicating the differences in vowel quality observed in the records of cultured informants. From these tabular chartings one can usually perceive at a glance the phonemic and sub-phonemic variations that occur in educated speech as one moves from region to region.

Obviously the Kurath-McDavid presentation could not be complete. Moreover, the huge mass and infinite variety of phonetic transcriptions had to be greatly simplified, so that sometimes a single symbol on a map covers a multitude of phonetic sins. Useful as the work is as a summary, it is not a substitute for the raw material itself, which we can only hope will soon be made available.[27]

It is not possible in the present paper to do justice to the numerous doctoral dissertations that have been based on the *Atlas* field records. One of the earliest of these was Bernard Bloch's study of the post-vocalic /r/. Others have been prepared by Rachel S. H. Kilpatrick, Yakira H. Frank, Sumner Ives,[28] T. H. Wetmore Jr.,[29] Walter S. Avis, and several others.[30] Most of these are detailed studies of individual problems of pronunciation or of small areas, and the methodology is too complex and varied for compact summary.

---

[26] George L. Trager and Henry L. Smith, Jr., *An Outline of English Structure* (Norman, Oklahoma, 1951).

[27] [Important recent publications by Kurath include "Area Linguistics in the U.S.A.," *Orbis*, XI (1962), 57–60; "Interrelation between Regional and Social Dialects," *Proceedings of the Ninth International Congress of Linguists* (The Hague, 1964), 135–144; "Some Aspects of Atlantic Seaboard English Considered in Their Connections with British English," *Communications du Premier Congrès de Dialectologie*, III (Louvain, 1965), 236–240. —*Eds.*]

[28] "The Negro Dialect of the Uncle Remus Stories" (University of Texas, 1950). Revised as "The Phonology of the Uncle Remus Stories," *PADS*, No. 22 (1954).

[29] "The Low-Central and Low-Back Vowels of the Eastern United States" (University of Michigan, 1957). *Diss. Abstracts*, XVIII, 1423. Revised as "The Low-Central and Low-Back Vowels in the English of the Eastern United States," *PADS*, No. 32 (1959).

[30] For a further listing see Raven I. McDavid, Jr., and Virginia G. McDavid, "Regional Linguistic Atlases in the United States," *Orbis*, V (1956), 353. [See also Amy E. Shaughnessy, *Dissertations in Linguistics: 1957–64* (Washington, 1965).—*Eds.*]

B. Extensions of Atlas Work

The originally planned "Linguistic Atlas of the United States and Canada", directed by Kurath and at least partially sponsored by the American Council of Learned Societies, will, it seems certain, be confined to the states of the Atlantic Seaboard. For some time, however, a framework has existed within which scholars in other areas could gather material comparable with that collected in the original *Atlas* survey, whether or not such material might result in a published atlas. An abridgement of the *Atlas* questionnaire consisting of about 500 items was prepared by Kurath in 1939; this has been the basis of most investigations to the westward. The "Short Work Sheets", as they are called, have usually been augmented by items which might elicit usages of a regional nature not current in the Atlantic States. A compilation of the regional work sheets was prepared by David W. Reed and David DeCamp.

The progress of linguistic geography in the United States as a whole since the Second World War has been slow and uneven.[31] This fact is usually attributable to lack of financial support rather than to lack of scholarly interest. Since the 1940's, particularly since the emergence of the "Cold War", both Federal and foundation support, as well as that of the American Council of Learned Societies, has gone chiefly to such "strategic" fields as the study of exotic languages and the teaching of English as a foreign language. Most dialect scholars have not been good beggars for private funds to carry on their research. Along with lack of money has gone lack of manpower, which, of course, is only another way of saying that times have changed. The field work for the Atlantic States was mostly done in a time of depression and unemployment, when the services of competent and even brilliant young scholars could be obtained for a bare living, if that. The stipend of Lowman's fellowship for the academic year 1935–1936 was $533. If he were available at the present time, there is not the slightest doubt that he would receive many offers of over ten times that amount to teach in one of our swollen colleges or universities.

In view of these difficulties, the use of multiple fieldworkers has become the rule rather than the exception. Most people engaged for this work can, or will, spend only a limited period of time at the task, usually as part of their work for an advanced degree. The use of tape recorders has varied from none at all to the taping of every interview complete. Publication of results will probably take many forms; and the various collections of data,

---

31 [See Raven I. McDavid, Jr., "The Second Round in Dialectology of North American English," *Journal of the Canadian Linguistic Association*, VI (1960), 108–115.—*Eds.*]

particularly in the field of pronunciation, are not likely to be fully comparable.

I believe that (aside from the Atlantic States) the regional atlas that has been longest in progress is that of the North Central States,[32] directed by Albert H. Marckwardt of the University of Michigan. Some records in this area were gathered as early as 1933, but it was in 1938 that the main body of the work was begun. The "Short Work Sheets", with a few modifications, were used, and interviewing practices were essentially the same as those used in the Atlantic States. Up to the present time, with the interviewing almost complete, work has been done by fifteen different fieldworkers, whose abilities have varied considerably. Among them they have gathered something like 460 field records. Tape recordings were sometimes made during the later years of the survey; in some cases the entire interview was recorded and transcribed later from the tapes. No concrete arrangements have been made for the publication of the raw materials themselves; and presentations of results have so far been of the interpretive sort. Toward the beginning of the survey, Marckwardt mapped a number of distributions by the use of symbols on maps[33]; more recently he has published some isoglosses (both lexical and phonological) based on a fuller coverage of the area.[34] These isoglosses are apparently only approximate, and are not accompanied by indications of exceptional usages. Nevertheless, Marckwardt's publications provide reasonably convincing evidence that Kurath's previously demonstrated cleavage between Northern and Midland continues through the North Central States.[35] Raven I. and Virginia G. McDavid have published grammatical materials from the same area.[36] Their maps provide both isoglosses and symbols for individual occurrences....

In the North Central States we were given our first convincing demonstration that lexical (as against phonological) features may be collected separately, by quicker and less costly methods than the employment of trained fieldworkers. Toward the end of the 1940's Alva L. Davis prepared a lexical questionnaire (now called a "checklist") of 100 items and sent copies of it by mail to various more-or-less academic people (usually teachers of history or some subject other than English) at many points in the area. These checklists were to be placed directly in the hands of suitable informants and ultimately mailed back. The items on the list were in the form of brief definitions followed by a number of synonyms; the informants were supposed to encircle the usage which they regarded as natural to them,

[32] These are the states of Ohio, Indiana, Illinois, Michigan, Wisconsin, and Kentucky.
[33] "Folk Speech in Indiana and Adjacent States," *Indiana History Bulletin*, XVII (1940), 120–140. [Department of Education, Indianapolis]
[34] "Principal and Subsidiary Dialect Areas in the North-Central States," *PADS*, No. 27 (1957), 3–15.
[35] [R. W. Shuy, "The Northern-Midland Dialect Boundary in Illinois," *PADS*, 38 (1962).—*Eds.*]
[36] "Grammatical Differences in the North Central States," *American Speech*, XXXV (1960), 5–19.

or to write it down if they did not find it listed. A typical example would be Item 45: "BEANS EATEN IN PODS: green beans, string beans, snap beans." The results of this survey were presented in Davis's doctoral dissertation.[37] The maps which Davis prepared indicated the actual incidence of the lexical variants in the different localities; but he was also able to draw isoglosses which corresponded remarkably well to those based on field work for the North Central Atlas. Other uses of checklists have been made in the area, but they are in the hands of different investigators, and I believe that they have not been incorporated into the atlas.

Another regional atlas in the northern part of the country is that of the Upper Midwest,[38] directed by Harold B. Allen of the University of Minnesota. Allen's basic procedure was very similar to Marckwardt's with regard to questionnaire, methods of interviewing, and so on; and he seems to have chosen about the same proportion of the different types of informants. Allen himself did a large part of the interviewing, working mainly in the summers with the support of the University of Minnesota. Six other field-workers contributed records from time to time. All together, 208 field records are on file, and I believe that the survey is regarded as complete. In addition to conventional field work, Allen made use of a checklist of 137 items; he was the first to definitely incorporate such materials into a regional atlas. Over a thousand of the checklists have been returned and are in the files. Since both field interviews and checklists were used through the same geographical areas, and since the latter were confined to vocabulary, there will be no possibility of methodological isoglosses to mislead a user of the atlas.

As in other areas, it is hoped that the raw materials from this region may be published, although no definite arrangements have been made. A presentation of the Gilliéron type (all transcriptions entered on maps) does not seem feasible, and Allen's present plan is the listing of responses in tables, with some of the distributions indicated by means of symbols on maps. Allen has already published some of his findings in the form of isoglosses of a simplified type.[39]

Students in the Midwestern states (North Central and Upper Midwest) have produced a number of doctoral dissertations dealing with a variety of topics. Two of these, by Virginia G. McDavid and Jean Malmstrom, have dealt with grammatical usage throughout the area. Dissertations by Edward E. Potter, Robert R. Howren, and several others have embodied complete studies of small areas or individual communities.

---

[37] A Word Atlas of the Great Lakes Region (University of Michigan, 1949).
[38] These are the states of Minnesota, Iowa, North Dakota, South Dakota, and Nebraska.
[39] "Minor Dialect Areas of the Upper Midwest," *PADS*, No. 30 (1958), 3–16. [See also "Aspects of the Linguistic Geography of the Upper Midwest," *Studies in Languages and Linguistics in Honor of Charles C. Fries* (Ann Arbor, 1964), 303–314.—*Eds.*]

Investigators in the westerly portions of the country are faced with extremely serious problems arising chiefly from settlement history. In many of
these areas, original settlement came relatively late, and population is still
very sparse in many places. Recent sizable increases in population have
come about largely through wholesale migration from many portions of the
country. The most striking illustration of this state of affairs is California,
which has been doubling its population about every twenty years. Between
1900 and 1960 the population of the United States as a whole increased by
a proportion of about 2.4 to 1. Not many Eastern states have exceeded that
rate, and the states of the Upper Midwest have fallen short of it. The population of California, however, has increased by a proportion of about 10.5 to
1, and the influx is continuing with phenomenal rapidity.

Fully aware of the difficulties, David W. Reed has nevertheless undertaken an atlas-type investigation of California and Nevada. Eleven fieldworkers have gathered some 300 records, and this phase of the work is regarded as complete. About 1500 checklists, of the type previously described,
have also been returned and are now in the files. All geographical areas have
been covered, but obviously many more records were collected in the centers
of population than in the mountainous and semi-desert areas. Tape recordings were not used as a regular feature of the survey.

Reed hopes ultimately to publish his raw materials in the form of lists.
However, as yet the only publications based on the California-Nevada survey have largely taken the form of statistical summaries. Reed's study of
Eastern dialect words in the region provides percentages of occurrence of
various lexical features characteristic of the North, the Midland, the South,
and various subdivisions and combinations of these areas.[40] In David
DeCamp's dissertation on the speech of San Francisco,[41] mathematical
methods were devised to compare usage with that of the Atlantic States in
matters of pronunciation as well. It seems to me that mathematical analysis
will be a highly important tool in the presentation of material from such
newly settled and linguistically mixed regions as the Pacific Coast. Moreover, although Reed's survey will determine some of the older and newer
layers of usage, it would be highly desirable that similar work should be repeated a generation later, in order to bring to light the processes of selection
and change that operate in such a situation.

Another atlas-type survey being conducted on the West Coast is that of
the Pacific Northwest,[42] directed by Carroll E. Reed of the University of
Washington. This project has made use of the "Short Work Sheets", with

[40] David W. Reed, "Eastern Dialect Words in California," *PADS*, No. 21 (1954), 3–15.
[41] The Pronunciation of English in San Francisco (University of California, Berkeley, 1954). Summarized
under the same title in *Orbis*, VII (1958), 372–391; VIII (1959), 54–77.
[42] This includes the states of Washington, Oregon, and Idaho.

a good many additions; six fieldworkers have collected something like 50 records. Over 1000 checklists are also on file. Both tape and disc recordings have been made in connection with many of the interviews. As in the case of California, a great deal of attention was paid to urban areas, and records from such communities outnumber those from rural districts.

It is the hope of Carroll Reed that his materials may be published in map form, although probably not in the large format of the New England *Atlas*. He has already published a short "Word Geography" based very largely on the lexical checklists.[43] In addition to tabulations of the relative frequency of Eastern usages, he includes a series of maps on which individual usages are entered by means of symbols. He has used the half-serious term "scattergram" to describe this type of presentation. Although no clearcut isoglosses are likely to emerge, he feels (rightly, I think) that individual usages should be presented cartographically, regardless of whether or not they show concentrations or cleavages.

Another westerly area for which atlas plans have been made is the Rocky Mountain region, in which two statewide surveys have so far been made. One of these, by T. M. Pearce, covers the state of New Mexico, in which 50 interviews have been conducted. In addition to Pearce himself, who did about half the interviews, some 19 graduate students contributed from one to seven field records each. Some use was made of disc recordings. Informants were more highly educated than in other areas; something over half of them are of Type III (with college education). About 500 lexical checklists are also on hand. Pearce's plan for publication envisages small maps with symbols for individual usages.

In the state of Colorado, a survey has been undertaken by Marjorie Kimmerle of the University of Colorado. Besides Miss Kimmerle, five fieldworkers were used, including McDavid, who conducted a summer course in field methods at the University of Colorado in 1950. Sixty-eight field records have been collected from 29 communities; the majority of these were made by Miss Kimmerle herself. The "Short Work Sheets" were used and it is clear that these had been augmented by items peculiarly adapted to the regional culture and topography.[44] Tape recordings were made of brief passages (five to twenty minutes) of connected material from about half the informants. Checklists were used in a preliminary survey, but it is my impression that these will not be incorporated into the atlas.

A survey of the Colorado lexical materials has been published by Clyde T.

---

[43] "Word Geography of the Pacific Northwest," *Orbis*, VI (1957), 86–93. See also, by the same author, "Washington Words," *PADS*, No. 25 (1956), 3–11. [More recently, "The Pronunciation of English in the Pacific Northwest," *Language*, XXXVII (1961), 559–564.—*Eds.*]

[44] See Marjorie M. Kimmerle, "The Influence of Locale and Human Activity on Some Words in Colorado," *American Speech*, XXV (1950), 161–167.

Hankey,[45] who used a variety of methods in presenting the results. Tables of relative frequencies of the Eastern words are, of course, indispensable. These indicate, for the state as a whole, a Northern-Midland mixture, with a rather low proportion of Southern usages. Clearcut isoglosses, as might be expected, are not numerous, and cannot be grouped in a convincing way. A more fruitful approach is the setting off of areas within which specific numbers of regional terms occur; from this presentation, for example, it can be observed that Southern usages as a group are largely limited to the eastern and southeastern extremities of the state, although any one individual usage might seem to show a scattered distribution. Another similar device is that of demarcating "participation areas"; that is, subdivisions of the state which share relatively high proportions of usages that are less frequent in other areas. It is unfortunate that individual word distributions are not given by the use of symbols on maps rather than by a presentation that involves somewhat wandering lines and shaded areas. Chaotic as they might seem on the surface, the "scattergrams" would have been welcome, if only as a means of judging the nature and validity of the isoglosses.

Another statewide survey which is well under way is that of Oklahoma, directed by W. R. Van Riper. Work sheets are rather full (over 900 questions) and include items of regional and local interest with regard to both pronunciation and vocabulary. Van Riper himself has done all the field work, and he has now completed about 40 records. His interviewing of informants has been largely by means of "directed conversation", with specific questions only if necessary. Every interview has been recorded in its entirety on magnetic tape. In addition to this type of field work, Van Riper has used special vocabulary questionnaires or checklists.

Undoubtedly a great deal of valuable material has been collected in other portions of the Western and Midwestern states, but, because of my lack of direct information on these projects, I am unable to describe them in any detail. McDavid[46] reports field work in progress in Utah, Wyoming, and Montana; and certainly there have been other dialect studies that have received little publicity or recognition.

In the states of the Gulf Coast and adjoining portions of the South,[47] the preparation of linguistic atlases in the traditional sense has not progressed rapidly, chiefly because of the lack of financial support. This is unfortunate, since these states offer an excellent field for investigation. With the exception of Texas, they have had a relatively slow population growth; and the

---

[45] "A Colorado Word Geography," *PADS*, No. 34 (1960). [See also "Semantic Features and Eastern Relics in Colorado Dialect," *American Speech*, XXXVI (1961), 266-270.—*Eds.*]

[46] "Regional Linguistic Atlases," pp. 377-378. [Cf. George B. Pace, "On the Eastern Affiliations of Missouri Speech," *American Speech*, XL (1965) 47-52.—*Eds.*]

[47] These are the states of Georgia, Alabama, Mississippi, Tennessee, Louisiana, Arkansas, and Texas.

lack of extensive industrialization has tended to preserve a greater stability of population and hence, presumably, of dialect features.

The oldest collection of atlas materials in the South Central part of the country is that of C. M. Wise of Louisiana State University. Between 1935 and 1945, Wise's advanced students gathered 68 field records from various parts of Louisiana,[48] and work of this sort has been continuing to the present time. The "Short Work Sheets" have been augmented by a rather large number of lexical items of regional interest. In recent years tape recordings of the interviews have been made. Under Wise's direction, a very considerable number of dissertations and theses have been prepared. Most of these pertain to pronunciation features, often those observed in a single community.

In other portions of the South and Southwest, there have developed certain departures from traditional atlas methodology. In my own investigations, which have centered in Texas, I have been able to assemble only a very limited number of satisfactory atlas field records of the conventional type; the best of these were collected by Arthur M. Z. Norman[49] and Janet B. Sawyer.[50] I came to the decision some time ago that field work in vocabulary and in pronunciation might well be conducted separately. This idea developed from a number of considerations. In the first place, I was highly dissatisfied with the practice of using considerable numbers of partially trained field workers for the making of phonetic transcriptions. I could hardly believe that in regions where this procedure was used the results would be satisfactory; yet there seemed to be no possibility of financing the work of a real expert for two or three years. On the other hand, experimental investigations had shown that it was relatively easy to teach advanced students to collect vocabulary features, especially if they worked in communities where they had friends or relatives. Accordingly I extracted from the *Atlas* work sheets those vocabulary items which had proved to be most productive in the Atlantic States, and added to them a fairly large number of items designed to elicit words of Southwestern origin or currency. The total number of vocabulary questions was about 270. Being addicted to the idea of field investigation *sur place*, I placed the vocabulary work sheets in the hands of fieldworkers rather than mail them out to be filled in by informants. Most of the interviewing was done by advanced students, orig-

---

[48] C. M. Wise, "The Dialect Atlas of Louisiana—A Report of Progress," *Studies in Linguistics*, III (1945), 37–42. [University of Buffalo, New York]

[49] A Southeast Texas Dialect Study (University of Texas, 1955). A summary, under the same title, is found in *Orbis*, V (1956), 61–79.

[50] A Dialect Study of San Antonio, Texas: A Bilingual Community (University of Texas, 1957). A partial summary is found in the article "Aloofness from Spanish Influence in Texas English," *Word*, XV (1959), 270–281.

inally those in my own classes, but later also students from other institutions under the direction of colleagues who were interested in linguistics. This type of work went on for several years; at the present time there are on hand about 470 vocabulary field records gathered in Texas and portions of adjoining states.

In order to expedite editing and publication of the vocabulary materials, I made use of mechanical sorting and listing processes. Every occurrence of every word was punched on a separate IBM card, together with coded data on the locality of its use and the characteristics of its user—age, education, sex, and so on. The tabulating machine was thus able to provide a running count not only of the total occurrences of a given usage, but also the occurrences in each geographical sub-area and each age and education group.

These lexical materials have recently been published in my volume entitled *The Regional Vocabulary of Texas.*[51] As might be supposed, I gave considerable attention to actual frequencies of occurrence, not only of individual words, but also of groups of words from the different dialect areas of the East, before ultimately concluding that the region is basically Southern. The editing methods also permitted a fairly precise examination of social distributions, as well as such matters as obsolescence and replacement. Geographical data was presented mainly in the form of individual "scattergrams"; but a fair number of isoglosses also emerged, notably a bundle separating Texas from southern Louisiana.

Other lexical studies based on similar methods have been made in both Texas and Louisiana. These include doctoral dissertations by Fred A. Tarpley and Lucille P. Folk, both of whom made use of mechanical processing methods under the direction of Nathan M. Caffee of Louisiana State University. Another lexical survey was that of the late Mima Babington, whose materials on southern Louisiana were to have been presented as a doctoral dissertation at The University of Texas.[52]

In other states of the Gulf Coast and interior South, a strictly lexical survey is being conducted by Gordon R. Wood of the University of Chattanooga (Tennessee). This is based on a postal checklist of 147 items, which is placed directly in the hands of informants. Out of a considerably larger number, Wood has selected about one thousand of the checklists for processing.[53] His methods of mechanical sorting and editing would seem to be similar to those used in Texas, although I am sure that he has made some significant advances. His reports have indicated an extensive use of arithmetical fre-

---

[51] University of Texas Press, 1962.

[52] For a summary of this work, see Mima Babington and E. Bagby Atwood, "Lexical Usage in Southern Louisiana," *PADS*, No. 36 (1961), 1–24.

[53] Gordon R. Wood, "Word Distribution in the Interior South," *PADS*, No. 35 (1961), 1–16. [See also "An Atlas Survey of the Interior South," *Orbis*, IX (1960), 7–12; "Dialect Contours in the Southern States," *American Speech*, XXXVIII (1963), 243–256.—*Eds.*]

quencies for terms used in the different portions of his territory. It seems that there will also emerge some very interesting concentrations and cleavages in lexical usage. It is to be strongly hoped that the cartographical presentation of these features will take some form other than the simplified lines and shaded areas that have appeared so far.

The concentration on vocabulary study in some of the major areas should not be interpreted to mean that the hope of recording pronunciation features has been abandoned. On the contrary, it is my own feeling that such work will be facilitated, in that the work sheets for pronunciation may be disencumbered of many items of purely lexical interest. Thus more samples may be taken in the same amount of time. Possibly in the future more attention may be paid to such features of suprasegmental structure as stress, intonation, and juncture. It seems clear that tape recording will be almost obligatory in future pronunciation surveys. Earlier difficulties, such as poor fidelity of the mechanisms and the lack of rural electrification, have been so nearly eliminated that there remain no reasons other than financial for neglecting the permanent preservation of speech itself. The newly developed science of sound spectrography will almost certainly prove to be of use in the examination of speech differences; for such an application to be made we will need high fidelity recordings of actual utterances.

The present paper has so far omitted mention of a great deal of important dialect work, particularly that which does not fit readily into the usual categories. For example, John S. Kenyon's observations of American pronunciation through the years have resulted in his very useful *Pronouncing Dictionary*,[54] which takes full account of differences in standards from one region to another. Charles K. Thomas has also assembled a great deal of recorded data on pronunciation, which forms the basis of several publications on regional and social variation.[55] His studies have been based to some extent on the reading and recording of standard texts by literate informants. Other investigators—for example Katherine E. Wheatley and Oma Stanley[56]—have applied this method in studies of particular areas.

In other English-speaking areas of the Western Hemisphere there has also been progress in dialectology. Field work in Canada, although not extensive, has been conducted by competent scholars.[57] In Jamaica, extremely sound work in lexicography has been accomplished by Frederick G. Cassidy; his

---

[54] John S. Kenyon and Thomas A. Knott, *A Pronouncing Dictionary of American English* (Springfield, Mass., 1944).

[55] A summary of Thomas's work is found in his *Introduction to the Phonetics of American English*, 2nd ed. (New York, 1958).

[56] The latest of their publications is "Three Generations of East Texas Speech," *American Speech*, XXXIV (1959), 83–94.

[57] For a summary of this work, see McDavid, "Regional Linguistic Atlases," pp. 380–381. [See also Walter S. Avis, "Problems in the Study of Canadian English," *Communications du Premier Congrès de Dialectologie*, III (Louvain, 1965), 183–191.—*Eds.*]

forthcoming dialect dictionary is a model of thoroughness. Robert B.
Le Page and David DeCamp have examined other aspects of usage by the use
of atlas methodology.[58] DeCamp's successful application of the word-and-
thing method[59] in his field work should result in important publications
concerning the relations of language and culture.

In summary we may say that dialect investigations of one sort or another
have been carried on in almost all parts of the United States. The multiplicity of fieldworkers, the unevenness of their training, and the variations
in their methodology will make much of their work very difficult to analyze
and evaluate. This is particularly true of the recording of pronunciation,
some of which in the long run may have to be done over again. We seem
closest to achieving an overall picture of dialect vocabulary, and indeed this
accomplishment will not be a trifling one. What is needed in all aspects of
the work is support, financial and moral; for a full measure of this we may
need to await a change in climate. The history of scholarship is to a considerable degree a history of patience, and of this quality the dialect scholar
has need of more than his share.

Austin (Texas)   E. Bagby Atwood

POSTSCRIPT: THE PRINCIPAL SPEECH AREAS OF
THE EASTERN UNITED STATES

As Atwood notes, the most extensive collections of materials for the
Linguistic Atlas were made for the Eastern United States, partly because
those states have been settled longest and consequently have the sharpest
dialectal divergences. By far the most extensive interpretive work is also of
Eastern materials. The purpose of the present note is not to review this
mass of scholarship but only to mention some notable features which are
said by Atlas workers to have characterized the Eastern dialect areas at
the time of the Atlas survey. Most of the material for the note is taken
(again by permission of Mrs. Atwood) from a summary which Atwood
compiled and published in mimeographed form for use by his students;
Atwood in turn had drawn "on the materials gathered for the *Linguistic
Atlas of the United States* and on some other works that were based on the
Atlas"—particularly Kurath's *Word Geography* "and his phonetic charts of

---

[58] See Le Page, "General Outlines of Creole English Dialects in the British Caribbean," *Orbis*, VI (1957), 373–
391, and VII (1958), 54–64; also Le Page and DeCamp, *Jamaican Creole* (London, 1960). [For Creoles in general,
see now Robert A. Hall, *Pidgin and Creole Languages* (Ithaca, N.Y., 1966). For Jamaican, see Cassidy, *Jamaica
Talk* (London and New York, 1961) and Cassidy and Le Page, *Dictionary of Jamaican English* (Cambridge,
1967). For another kind of island English, see Stanley M. Tsuzake and John E. Reinecke, *English in Hawaii:
An Annotated Bibliography* (Honolulu, 1966).—*Eds.*]
[59] For example, he gathered data on many styles of baskets, machetes, and other artifacts.

the *Atlas* data," Mrs. Y. H. Frank's Michigan dissertation (1948) on *The Speech of New York City*, A. L. Davis' *Word Atlas of the Great Lakes Area* (dissertation, Michigan, again 1948), and Atwood's own *Survey of Verb Forms*. Supplementary details for the note are from a summary by Raven I. McDavid, Jr., similar to Atwood's, in W. Nelson Francis' *The Structure of American English* (New York, 1958). The map showing major dialect areas is taken directly from Kurath's *Word Geography*, and, as Atwood acknowledges, the recognition of those areas—North, Midland, South, with various sub-areas—is also Kurath's contribution. Atwood would have been the first to remind readers of the dates and limitations of the Atlas interviews: since present tenses in the following statements may now be historical, the note should be taken, not as a contemporary review, but as a point of departure into more recent studies.

Atwood's summary follows Kurath, as we have said, in dividing the major areas of North, Midland, and South into a number of sub-areas. The North, in Atwood's account, includes Eastern New England, Inland Northern, and New York City; Kurath, McDavid, and others have recognized still more sub-areas within the North and have extended the line between North and Midland westward from the New Jersey coast below Sandy Hook through northern Pennsylvania, central to northern Ohio, Indiana, and Illinois, and beyond. Atwood's Midland includes Eastern Pennsylvania and Western Pennsylvania (which Kurath groups together within North Midland as the Philadelphia and Pittsburgh areas) and a large South Midland area, popularly thought of as hillbilly country, which would comprise parts of Virginia, West Virginia, Kentucky, Tennessee, North Carolina, South Carolina, Georgia, and Alabama. Within the South, Atwood attempted fewer sub-divisions. Acknowledging a particular debt to McDavid for data from South Carolina and Georgia, he distinguished only Eastern Virginia and the South Carolina–Georgia Low Country, leaving other areas as still unanalyzed. His divisions are comparable to Kurath and McDavid's Upper South, with the Virginia Piedmont as its center, and Lower South, notably including most of South Carolina and Georgia. Like the Midland and the North, the South undoubtedly extends westward from the Atlantic Seaboard for a considerable distance: in his *Regional Vocabulary of Texas*, Atwood later concluded "that, on the basis of actual proportion of occurrence, the regional vocabulary of Texas is basically Southern" (p. 84).

The details below are organized according to types of distinctions recognized by Atlas workers. As Atwood explains, fieldworkers in the Eastern States sampled "pronunciation features, lexical peculiarities, morphological variants, and occasionally syntactic characteristics." Though the distributions of different individual features, and the distributions of differing *types* of features, are not always the same, every type was ultimately considered in the designation of the major speech areas, and the evidence from pronunciation and grammar rather generally confirms the evidence from vocabulary. Readers may be trusted to remember, from their own experience, that the boundaries between dialects, which linguists attempt to approximate in drawing their maps, are not sharp and distinct, like the boundaries between political divisions.

The details which we have drawn from Atwood's summary have been left unmarked; the supplementary details from McDavid's chapter have been starred. No attempt has been made to give key-words showing the values of phonetic symbols (in square brackets) or phonemic symbols (between slant lines) since dialect differences among readers would make brief explanation futile. Students uninitiated into the mysteries will have to get help from their instructors. Large Roman numerals after dialect features indicate the types of informants represented, as those types are described by Atwood on p. 183 of his article. Parentheses around a numeral "indicate less currency in that group."

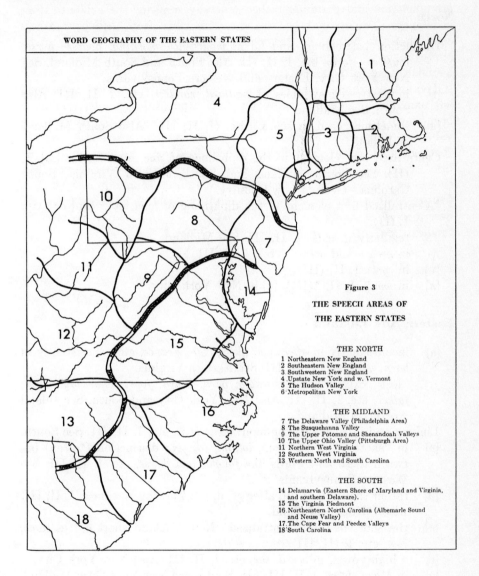

WORD GEOGRAPHY OF THE EASTERN STATES

Figure 3

THE SPEECH AREAS OF
THE EASTERN STATES

THE NORTH

1 Northeastern New England
2 Southeastern New England
3 Southwestern New England
4 Upstate New York and w. Vermont
5 The Hudson Valley
6 Metropolitan New York

THE MIDLAND

7 The Delaware Valley (Philadelphia Area)
8 The Susquehanna Valley
9 The Upper Potomac and Shenandoah Valleys
10 The Upper Ohio Valley (Pittsburgh Area)
11 Northern West Virginia
12 Southern West Virginia
13 Western North and South Carolina

THE SOUTH

14 Delamarvia (Eastern Shore of Maryland and Virginia,
   and southern Delaware).
15 The Virginia Piedmont
16 Northeastern North Carolina (Albemarle Sound
   and Neuse Valley)
17 The Cape Fear and Peedee Valleys
18 South Carolina

PRONUNCIATION DIFFERENCES

North

Distinction between [o] and [ɔ] in *mourning—morning, hoarse—horse, fourteen—forty*, etc. I, II, III. Also South and South Midland. See New York City, Eastern and Western Pennsylvania.

[ɪ]   in unstressed syllables of *haunted, careless*, etc. I, II, III. Also South. See Midland.

[æ]   sometimes used in *stairs, care*. (I, II; III.) Also South Midland and South.

Centralized first element in the diphthong of *fine*, etc.: [ɐɪ] or [ʌɪ]. I, (II). See South Midland and South, Eastern Virginia, South Carolina—Georgia Low Country.

* Centralized first element in the diphthong of *loud*, etc.: [ɐu] or [ʌu]. I, (II).

/ð/   regularly in *with*. I, II, III. See Midland.

/s/   in *greasy* and *grease* (vb.). I, II, III.

[ʊ]   in *roots*. I, II, (III).

[ʌ]   in *won't*. I, II, *(III). [u] in New York City.

Eastern New England

[a]   inconsistently in *afternoon, glass, bath, France*, etc.; consistently in *barn, yard*, etc. I, II, III. See Eastern Virginia.

/r/   "lost" except before vowels: *barn, beard, four, Thursday, horse, father*, etc. I, II, III. Also New York City and South. See Inland Northern, Midland.

Linking and intrusive [r] common: *idear of it*, etc. I, II, III. See South.

[ɒ]   in "short *o*" words: *crop, lot, on, fog*. No distinction (*often) between these and words like *fought, law, horse*, etc. I, II, III. See Western Pennsylvania.

[u]   rather than [ju] or [ɪu] after /t, d, n/: *Tuesday, due, new*. I, II, III. Also (*North) Midland.

[ɵ],   the shortened and centralized "New England short *o*," in *stone, coat*, etc. I, (II, III).

[i],   a high vowel, in *beard, ear*, etc. I, II, III. Also New York City.

[e]   in *Mary, dairy*. I, II, III. Also South. See New York City, Midland.

Inland Northern

/r/   "kept" after vowels in *horse, four, father*, etc. I, II, III. Also Midland.

[ɑ]   in *on, hog, frog, fog,* but not *dog, log.* I, II, III. Also Coastal South.
A fronted vowel, [ɑˑ], [a], often in "short *o*" words. I, II, III.

[ɪʊ]   sometimes after /t, d, n/: *Tuesday, due, new.* I, (II, III). See South
Midland and South.

New York City (mostly confined to the City's immediate vicinity)

/r/   "lost" except before vowels. I, II, III. Also Eastern New England
and South.

[o] and [ɔ] not distinguished before /r/ in *mourning—morning,* etc. I, II
III. Also (*North) Midland.

Adjourn—adjoin, etc. frequently not distinguished, [ɝ] or [ɚ] serving for
both. I, II.

*[ɛ°] in *Mary, dairy.* I, II, III. See Eastern New England, Midland,
South.

[ɑ]   in *foreign, borrow, orange;* also in *on, hog, frog, fog, log,* but not *dog.*
I, II, III.

[i],   a high vowel, in *beard, ear,* etc. I, II, III. Also Eastern New England.

Raised and lengthened [æ·^] and [ɔ·^] in *pan, lawn,* etc. *I, II, (III).

[u]   in *won't.* I, II, III. See South Carolina—Georgia Low Country.

/w/   regularly for /hw/ in *wheelbarrow,* etc. I, II, III. See Eastern
Pennsylvania, South Carolina—Georgia Low Country.

Glottal stop for /t/ in *bottle, mountain,* etc. I, II.

/d/   for /ð/ in *this,* etc., and [ŋg] for [ŋ] in *Long Island,* etc. I, II; but
chiefly in foreignized speech.

Note: The Atlas account of New York speech is in particular need of
extension and correction by more recent studies such as Labov's
Social Stratification of English in New York City.

Midland

/r/   "kept" after vowels. I, II, III. Also Inland Northern.

[ɔ]   in *on* (also South); in *wash, wasp;* in *log, hog, frog, fog.* I, II, III.

[ɛ]   in *Mary, dairy.* I, II, III. See Eastern New England, New York
City, South.

[ə]   in the unstressed syllables of *haunted, careless,* etc. I, II, III. See
North, South.

/θ/   regularly in *with.* I, II, III. See North.

/r/   frequently intrudes in *wash.* I, II.

Eastern Pennsylvania

[u]   after /t, d, n/: *Tuesday, due, new.* I, II, III. Also Western Pennsylvania, Eastern New England. See Inland Northern, South Midland and South.

[o]   and [ɔ] not distinguished before /r/ in *mourning—morning*, etc. I, II, III. Also Western Pennsylvania, New York City.

/w/   in *wheelbarrow*, etc. I, II, III. Also New York City.

[a]   in *frog, hog, fog.* (I), II, III. Also Inland Northern, New York City.

Western Pennsylvania

[u]   in *Tuesday, due, new.* I, II, III. Also Eastern Pennsylvania, Eastern New England.

[o]   and [ɔ] not distinguished before /r/ in *mourning—morning*, etc. I, II, III. Also Eastern Pennsylvania, New York City. See North, South and South Midland.

No distinction between [ɑ] and [ɔ] in *hot, crop, law, taught*, etc. I, II, III. Also (*often) Eastern New England.

*[ʊ]   in *food.* I, II.

[u]   in *drouth.* I, (II).

South Midland

*[a·], [a·ᵊ] for [aɪ] before both voiceless and voiced consonants, as in *nice time.* I, II. See North, South Midland and South, etc.

South Midland and South

[ju] or [ɪu] after /t, d, n/: *Tuesday, due, new.* I, II, III. See Inland Northern.

[aᵋ], [a·], etc. before voiced consonants and finally in *five, my*, etc. I, II, III. See South Midland, Eastern Virginia, South Carolina—Georgia Low Country.

[o] and [ɔ] distinguished before /r/ in *mourning—morning*, etc. I, II, III. Also North.

[æʊ] predominant in mountain, etc. *I, II, III.

[æ]   in *stairs, care, chair.* I, II, III. Also (sometimes) North.

[o]   in *poor, your*, etc. I, II.

* Centralized variants of [u] and [ʊ]. I, II, III.

*[ʊ]   in *bulk, bulge*, except on South Atlantic coast. I, II, (III).

*High central [ɨ] ("barred I") frequent in stressed syllable before [ə] in following unstressed syllable: *sister, dinner, scissors, mirror*, etc.

South

/r/ "lost" except before vowels; linking and intrusive /r/ usually do not occur. *(I, II), III. Also Eastern New England and New York City.

[e] in *Mary, dairy*. I, II, III. Also Eastern New England.

[ɨ] in unstressed syllables of *haunted, careless*, etc. I, II, III. Also North.

[ɑ] in *log, hog, frog, fog*, but not *dog*. (I), II, III. Also Inland Northern, New York City.

/z/ in *Mrs*. (I), II, III.

Eastern Virginia

[əu], [ʌu] before voiceless consonants: *house, out;* [æu] before voiced consonants: *down, loud*. I, II, III. Also in eastern South Carolina and in Canada. See North.

[əi], [ɐi] before voiceless consonants: *white, nice;* [aɨ], [aɛ], etc. before voiced consonants: *time*, etc. *I, II, III. Also in eastern South Carolina and in Canada. See North.

[a], [ɑ] in *pasture* and a few other words. I, (II). See Eastern New England.

[a], [ɑ] in *stairs*. I.

[ʊ] in *home*. I.

[ɛ] in *afraid*. I, II, III.

South Carolina—Georgia Low Country (information supplied to Atwood by McDavid)

Centralized first elements of diphthongs before voiceless consonants as in *house, night*. *I, II, III. *Tidewater only. Also Eastern Virginia and Canada.

Centering diphthongs in *road, post, eight, drain*. *I, II, III.

/w/ in *whip, wheelbarrow*, etc. (I, II, III.) Also New York City, Eastern Pennsylvania.

Rounded vowel in *pot, crop, oxen*. *I, II, III. Also Eastern New England.

[u, ʊ] in *won't*. (I, II, III.) See New York City.

Ear—air, fear—fair, etc. pronounced alike, with no contrasts among front vowels before /r/. I, II, III. Rare above tidewater.

DIFFERENCES IN VOCABULARY

North

angleworm "earthworm." I, II, III. See South Midland *redworm*.
brook "small stream." I, II, III. *Rare in Inland North. See Pennsylvania **run*, South Midland and South *branch*.
cherry pit "cherry seed." I, II, III.
clapboards. I, II, III. *Midland and Southern *weatherboards, weatherboarding*.
co-boss (call to cow). I, II, (III). See Midland *sook*, South *co-wench*.
eaves troughs "gutters." I, II, (III). Midland *spouting, spouts*.
fills, thills "shafts of a buggy." I, II.
johnnycake "cornbread." I, II, (III).
pail. I, II, III. *Midland and Southern *bucket*.
quite (*spry*). I, II, III. Midland and Southern *right*.
spider "frying pan." I, II. *Also South; receding in Inland Northern. See Midland *skillet*.
swill "garbage, food for pigs." *Midland and Southern *slop*.
whiffletree, whippletree "horizontal crossbar to which harness-traces are attached." I, II, III.

Eastern New England

apple dowdy "deep-dish pie." I, II, III.
bonnyclabber, bonnyclapper "curdled milk." I, II, III. See Inland Northern, Pennsylvania, South Midland, South Midland and South.
buttonwood "sycamore." I, II, III.
pig-sty "pig-pen." I, II, III.
sour-milk cheese "cottage cheese." I, II, III. See Inland Northern, New York City, Midland.

Inland Northern

Dutch cheese "cottage cheese." I, II.
lobbered milk, loppered milk "curdled milk." I, II, (III).
stone boat "wooden vehicle, without wheels, for moving stones." I, II, III.
stoop "porch." I, II, III. *Also New York City and Savannah Valley.
sugar bush "maple grove." I, II, (III).

New York City (usually with Hudson Valley)

barrack "haystack." I, II (rural only).
Dominie "preacher." I, II, III.
kill "brook" (only in proper names). I, II, III. See Northern *brook*, etc.
olicook "doughnut." I.
pot cheese "cottage cheese." I, II, III.
skimmerton, skimmilton "mock serenade." I, II (rural only).
suppawn "cornmeal mush." I, II (rural only).

Midland

a little piece * "short distance." I, II, III. Also South Carolina.
blinds "shades on rollers." I, II, III. *Also Canada.
green beans "string beans." I, II, III. Not in Eastern Pennsylvania. See
　　Southern *snap beans.*
to hull (beans) "to shell." I, II, (III).
poke "(*paper) sack." I, II, (III). Not in Eastern Pennsylvania.
skillet "frying pan." I, II, III. *Spreading. See Northern *spider.*
smearcase "cottage cheese." I, II, *(III). North Midland only.
snake feeder "dragon fly." I, II, (III). *In South Midland, also *snake
　　doctor.*
sook (call to cow). I, II, III. See Northern *co-boss,* Southern *co-wench.*
spouting, spouts "gutters." I, II, (III). See Northern *eaves troughs.*

Eastern Pennsylvania

baby coach. I, II, (III).
pavement "sidewalk." I, II, III.
run "small stream." I, II, III. See Northern *brook,* etc.
Germanisms, often occurring in other North Midland areas as well
　clook "setting hen." I.
　fatcakes "doughnuts." I, (II).
　ponhaws "scrapple." I, II. See South Carolina—Georgia Low Country
　　cripple.
　snits "dried fruit." I, II.
　spook "ghost." I, II, III. Also Hudson Valley.
　thick milk "curdled milk." I, II. See Eastern New England *bonnyclab-
　　ber,* etc.
　toot "paper bag." I, II.

Western Pennsylvania

carbon oil "kerosene." I, II.
crudded milk; cruds "curdled milk; cottage cheese." I, II. See Eastern
New England *bonnyclabber, sour-milk cheese,* etc.
doodle "haycock." I, II. See South Midland and South *hay shock.*
grinnie "chipmunk." I, II.
hap "comforter." I, (II).
mind "remember." I, II, (III).
*run "small stream." I, II, III. See Northern *brook,* etc.

South Midland

clabber milk "curdled milk." I, II, III.
fireboard "mantel, mantelpiece." I, II.
French harp "harmonica." I, II, (III). See Southern *harp.*
milk gap "cow pen." I, (II). See Eastern Virginia *cuppin.*
pack "carry, tote." I, II.
redworm "earthworm." I, II. See Northern *angleworm.*
sugar tree "sugar maple." I, II, (III).

South Midland and South

*branch "small stream." I, II, III. See Northern *brook,* etc.
clabber "curdled milk." I, II, III. See Eastern New England, etc.
corn shucks. I, II, III. Elsewhere *corn husks.*
disremember "forget." I, II.
ha'nts, haunts "ghosts." I, II, *(III).
*hay shock "haycock." I, II, III. See Western Pennsylvania *doodle.*
jackleg preacher *"unskilled preacher." I, II, (III). See South Carolina—
Georgia *yard-ax.*
light bread "wheat bread." I, II, III.
pallet "bed with bedding laid directly on the floor." I, II, III.
pully bone "wishbone." I, II, III. Some currency in North Midland.
snack "food eaten between regular meals." I, II, III. Also New York
City, Philadelphia.
snake doctor "dragon fly." I, II, (III). See Midland *snake feeder.*

South

carry "take, escort." I, II, (III).
chittlins "pig's intestines as food." I, II, III.
co-wench (call to cow). I, II, III. See Northern *co-boss,* etc.

harp, mouth harp "harmonica." I, II, III. See South Midland *French harp.*

hasslet "edible insides of home-butchered farm animal." I, II, III. Also parts of South Midland and North.

lightwood "resinous kindling." I, II, (III). See South Carolina—Georgia *fatwood.*

low "moo." I, II, III.

snap beans, snaps "string beans." I, II, III. See Midland *green beans.*

tote "carry." I, II.

turn of wood "armful of wood." I, II, (III).

Eastern Virginia

batter bread "spoon bread, egg bread." I, II, III.

corn house "corn crib." I, II.

croker sack (crocus sack) "burlap bag." I, II, III. Also Carolinas and Georgia.

cuppin "cow pen." I. See South Midland *milk gap.*

*goobers "peanuts." I, II, (III). Also Georgia, Alabama. See South Carolina—Georgia *groundnuts, pinders.*

hoppergrass "grasshopper." I.

lumber room "store room." I, II, III.

South Carolina—Georgia Low Country (information supplied to Atwood by McDavid)

bloody-noun "bullfrog." *I, II, III. From Georgetown to the St. Mary's River.

*buckra "white man." I, II, III. Also in Jamaica.

cooter "turtle" (with [ʊ] in the coastal plain, [u] inland). Known as far west as Texas.

cripple "scrapple." *(I, II, III.) See Eastern Pennsylvania *ponhaws.*

fatwood "resinous kindling." *I, II, (III). See Southern *lightwood.*

*groundnuts "peanuts." I, II, III. See Eastern Virginia *goobers.*

*joggling board "broad, strong, but flexible board, held loosely on supports at both ends, so that children can jump up and down on it." I, II, III.

*pinders "peanuts." I, II, (III). Also Alabama.

pinto "coffin" (chiefly among Negroes). *(I).

stoop "small porch." *(I, II, III.) Chiefly in the Savannah Valley; also Inland Northern, New York City.

yard-ax "jackleg preacher" (generally labeled a Negroism). (I.) See South Midland and South.

DIFFERENCES IN MORPHOLOGY AND SYNTAX

North

be in *How be you? Be I going to?* etc. I. *Rare in Inland Northern. See South *Is I?*
clim "climbed." I, (II). Also South. See Midland *clum,* Eastern Virginia *clome.*
dove "dived." I, II, III.
hadn't ought "oughtn't." I, II.
(It) wa'n't (me) "it wasn't me." I, (II). Also South.
see "saw." I, II. Midland *seen,* South Midland and South *seed,* etc.
sick to the stomach. I, II, (III).
**to home* "at home." I, II; receding in Inland Northern.

Eastern New England

div "dived," *driv* "drove," *gwine* "going," *riz* "rose." I. Northeastern New England; also South.
waked up. I, (II, III). Also South.

Inland Northern

No significant forms observed.

New York City

**(He lives) in* (King Street). I, II, (III). Also Charleston, S.C., and Canada.
**(We stood) on* (line). I, II, III.

Midland

all the further "as far as." I, II.
clum "climbed." I, (II). See Northern *clim.*
(I'll wait) on (you) "for you." I, II, (III).
I want off. I, II, (III).

(*quarter*) *till* (*eleven*). I, II, III. Northern *of, to;* Southern *to.*
seen "saw." I, II. See Northern *see.*
you-uns (plural). I, (II). Not in Eastern Pennsylvania. See South and
South Midland *you-all.*

Eastern Pennsylvania

Germanisms:
all "all gone" (as in * "The oranges are all"). I, II.
got awake "woke up." I, II. See Eastern New England *waked up.*

Western Pennsylvania

No significant forms observed.

South Midland

dogbit "bitten by a dog." I, II.
(*The sun*) *raised.* I, (II).

South Midland and South

a before nouns beginning with vowels, as in "Give me a apple." I, II.
**bought bread* (not home-made). I, II.
**done* in "perfective" use, as in "He done gone." I, II.
holp "helped." I, II.
(*I*) *might could.* I, II. Also Pennsylvania German area.
I'm not for sure. I, II.
mought "might." I.
riz "rose." Also Northeastern New England.
**seed* "saw." I. See Northern *see,* Midland *seen.*
(*I*) *taken* "took." (I), II.
**tuck* "took" (past tense and past participle). I, (II).
**used to didn't* (especially among Negroes). I, (II).
you-all (plural). I, II, III. See Midland *you-uns.*

South

**all two, all both.* I, (II).
(*He*) *belongs* (*to be careful*). I, II.
clim "climbed." I, (II). Also North.

div, driv, gwine, riz. I. Also Northeastern New England.

(He) do "does." I.

heern tell (heern = past participle). I.

Is I? I. See Northern *be.*

waked up. Also Eastern New England.

(It) wa'n't (me). I, II, (III). Also North.

(What) make (him do it?) "makes." I.

Eastern Virginia

clome "climbed." See Northern and Southern *clim,* Midland *clum.*

*(He did it) for purpose. I, (II).

*(I ran) up on (him). I, II.

see "saw." I, II. See Northern *see,* Midland *seen,* South Midland and
South *seed.*

South Carolina—Georgia Low Country

Forms cited by McDavid are mainly from Negro speech, which has not
been adequately investigated.

Study Questions

1. What is a *linguistic atlas?* What is an *isogloss?* What information does
    an isogloss convey? How does the information it provides differ from
    that provided by a symbol for an individual occurrence on a dialect
    map? Why are isoglosses more difficult to construct for American than
    for European materials?

2. What kinds of materials were collected for the New England *Atlas?*
    What kinds of informants were interviewed? What is meant by a *cul-
    tured* informant? How does the methodology of the Linguistic Atlas of
    the United States differ from that of most European atlases? What
    conditions peculiar to the United States led to the changes in method-
    ology? What might be the value of the Atlas materials for the deter-
    mination of "good" English? What limitations might they have for that
    use? Look up the word *ain't* in Webster's *Third.* What does the dic-
    tionary say about the use of that word by American speakers? Would

the Atlas materials, considering when they were collected, be useful to dictionary makers who wished to include usage labels for their entries?

3. What kind of a dialect dictionary of American English does Atwood wish for? Will *DARE* be such a dictionary? Why does Atwood feel that it will be more difficult to compile a dialect dictionary for the United States than for England?

4. What are the origins of local and regional variations in American English? Why is speech less diversified west of the original coastal settlements? Why might American dialectologists object, in spite of less diversification, to recognizing a "General American" speech for the Mid- and Far West? What is a localism? How does it differ from an Americanism? Hans Kurath has said elsewhere that "the vocabulary of the intimate life of the home will remain rich in local and regional expressions for generations to come." Does that statement fit your own experience? What has happened to the terms for the equipage of horses which your grandfathers used? If your parents or grandparents had a farm, but have now moved to the city, would you have a vocabulary similar to theirs? Do you talk about wringers, or washboards, or coal scuttles, or airtight stoves, or box stoves, or kerosene lamps, or lard lamps? Are changes in technology likely to affect home vocabulary? If everyone buys a rocking horse from Sears and Roebuck, is it likely to have one name or many?

5. What is the distinction between local speech, regional speech, and national speech? Are these in any way connected with the social scales? Would the division of informants into three classes—folk, common, and cultivated—be fine enough to cover class differences in the area in which you live? If you answered yes, do you live in the North or the South, in a rural or an urban area? What would folk speech be in Chicago? in the city or town in which you live?

6. What important systemic differences among American dialects emerge from the details in the sketch of the characteristics of Eastern areas? What might Kurath have meant when he said: "the system of grammatical forms and the system of consonants are nearly the same throughout the area, but differences in the incidence of certain forms and consonants do occur"? Using the features of the sketch, can you place your own dialect? Is it clearly Northern, Midland, or Southern? If you have a mixture of those features, can you explain why? For example, how far west do you live? Which of your usages are clearly

distinguished I, II, or III? What is meant by Kurath's term *transition belt?*

7. Why is Atwood generally pessimistic about the completion and publication of an Atlas for the whole of the United States? If surveys modeled on that of the New England States should be undertaken for the Western states, could the data be compared successfully? What factors might preclude such a comparison? What problems are the investigators of Western states likely to encounter that were not faced by the fieldworkers of the New England *Atlas?*

Harold Orton

AN ENGLISH DIALECT SURVEY:
LINGUISTIC ATLAS OF ENGLAND

Harold Orton (born 1898) brought to the *Survey of English Dialects* (described below) long interest and wide experience in dialectal studies. He was and is active in some of the numerous dialect societies in England, serving as joint editor of the *Transactions* of the Yorkshire Dialect Society from 1947 to 1961 and as president of the Yorkshire Society for Celtic Studies from 1951 to 1953. He has taught both abroad and in the United States, where he has also done field work, proving himself as capable as native Americans in drawing conversations from Kansas farmers and their wives. Before undertaking the *Survey* Orton had already published studies of local English speech, including one major work, *The Phonology of a South Durham Dialect* (1933).

Professor Orton is currently professor at the University of Leeds, where the *Survey* project resides and whence he departs for fairly frequent visiting positions in the United States. He is an honorary member of the Linguistic Society of America.

The following article, published in 1960, describes the inception of the *Survey*, the methods that were used in collecting the materials, and the very rapid completion of the field work. Since 1960 considerable progress has been made toward editing and publishing the results. The publication program, as announced in Orton's *Introduction* to the Survey, is as follows; the publisher for the survey is E. J. Arnold and Son, Leeds.

The material results of the Survey are to be published under the general title of *Survey of English Dialects* in the following series of books:

A. Introduction, by Harold Orton. [Published 1962.—*Eds.*]

B. Four volumes of Basic Material in tabular form, each in three parts, with the following titles:

1. *The Six Northern Counties and the Isle of Man*, edited by Harold Orton and Wilfrid J. Halliday [Part I published 1962, Parts II and III 1963.—*Eds.*]

2. *The West Midland Counties*, to be edited by Harold Orton and E. Kolb.

3. *The East Midland Counties*, to be edited by Harold Orton and Stanley Ellis.

4. *The Southern Counties*, edited by Harold Orton et al., in preparation. [Part I published 1967.—*Eds.*]

C. Four "Companion Volumes" of Selected Incidental Material, to correspond with the four volumes of Basic Material. These are designed to shed light upon the development, in each of the localities investigated, both of the chief Middle English sounds, isolatively and combinatively, and of certain morphological features and syntactical usages.

"An English Dialect Survey: Linguistic Atlas of England" by Harold Orton, from *Orbis*, Vol. 9, 1960, 331-348. Reprinted by permission of Centre International de Dialectologie Générale, Louvain, Belgium.

D. *Linguistic Atlas of England*, showing the distribution of various lexical, phonological, morphological and syntactic features over the whole network. [Orton notes that the late Eugen Dieth was engaged in preparing phonological maps for the six Northern Counties. Dieth's former research assistant, Dr. Eduard Kolb, has carried on Dieth's studies and has published the Atlas corresponding to the material in Vol. I: *Phonological Atlas of the Northern Region: The Six Northern Counties, North Lincolnshire, and the Isle of Man*. [Bern: Francke, 1966.—*Eds.*]

E. Phonetic transcriptions, in both broad and narrow systems, of the tape-recordings of the speech of selected informants.

The only part of the above program, however, that present circumstances permit us to undertake is the preparation of the Basic Volumes, and these we intend to produce as speedily as possible. Progress with the other parts is simply delayed by lack of the vitally necessary editorial and financial assistance.

Students should consult Orton's *Introduction* for a more detailed description of the *Survey* and a look at the questionnaire which field workers used. The complete publication of the materials is eagerly awaited by linguistic historians and by American dialectologists interested in the origins of dialect features in America.

The English Dialect Survey described below dates from 1946. And last year, 1959, the fieldwork in the entire network of 300 localities spread over the whole of England was completed. Further, preparations for the publication of the first volume containing the results of the Survey are well under way; it will contain in tabular form the material relating to the six Northern Counties and the Isle of Man. But first, a few words of a personal nature about the genesis of the Survey.

Early in 1946, after the European War was over, my old friend, Eugen Dieth, then Professor of English Language in the University of Zurich, resumed by letter our close relations of pre-war days. In it he suggested that we should collaborate on a linguistic atlas of English. We thereupon decided to go ahead together, at once, with a new survey of English dialects. It was no blind act of faith, but rather a perfectly rational step for us both to take together: for each of us had had over twenty years' activity in the practical study of English dialects, some of it, indeed, in collaboration.

That summer, still 1946, we started on our projected Linguistic Atlas during his brief stay in my home in Sheffield, where I was then on the staff of the University. We decided to undertake a systematic and comprehensive national investigation of the oldest existing forms of English used in this country and to collect enough representative and comparable material throughout a network of suitable localities to enable the production of a linguistic atlas of regional English spoken in England and elsewhere. However, when Professor Angus McIntosh's present Scottish Survey started from Edinburgh in 1949, our project became restricted to England. But many difficulties were expected to lie ahead; and not all of them would be financial and organisational. But the first question to be settled was the kind of dialect to be investigated.

Many grades of vernacular exist in England today. They vary from the oldest forms of regional dialect, localised in our rural communities, down through the numerous mixed dialects of our towns and cities, to the widely acceptable type of English often called Standard English: for example, that used by the B.B.C. news-reader on the General Home Service. All these diverse types have their special interest for phoneticians and philologists. Indeed, a historical analysis of their various elements would be a fascinating and worthwhile undertaking. Our target, however, was traditional vernacular, genuine and old; and we were fully determined to collect the essential material direct, and only through the medium of trained investigators working on the spot of each of the localities of a carefully chosen network. For this purpose we needed a special questionnaire. A postal questionnaire for indirect investigation, although it could provide certain advantages, attracted us but little. Already before the Second World War we had had some joint experience of this method, but without much success. Further, we knew that both A. J. Ellis and Joseph Wright had in their day utilised the postal questionnaire. But they had not, so it seemed to us, achieved the completely dependable results that we were anxious to secure from this new survey. So we agreed to spend the next Long Vacation—at Leeds University, whose staff I was soon to join—preparing the first version of our questionnaire, the fundamental instrument of our projected Atlas. This first version ultimately occupied almost ten weeks of our time in the wonderfully fine summer of 1947, most of which we spent in the sunless basement of the Brotherton Library at Leeds University. But by the beginning of the new University Session of 1947–48, our draft questionnaire was ready for testing in the field.

From 1946, and until his untimely death from a stroke on 24th May, 1956, Eugen Dieth and I collaborated very closely, especially at the beginning of our joint enterprise. During those ten years, he had come to work with me in Leeds at least once a year, and sometimes twice. A tremendous enthusiast for English philology, he was truly an inspiring colleague. His most fruitful work on the Survey undoubtedly went into the organisation and compilation of our questionnaire. It was for him a challenging, captivating task, one that he delighted in doing and into which he put all of his almost limitless physical and mental energy.

Our questionnaire was ultimately printed and published in January 1952 under the title of *A Questionnaire for a Linguistic Atlas of England*.[1] Between that date and the summer of 1955, when we agreed to work independently on the Northern material—he to construct and publish phonological maps, and I to prepare and publish the Basic Material in list form—he more or less restricted himself to his own private study of these Northern field-recordings. But he was destined never to realise his cherished ambition, namely the completion of the Atlas itself. He had only just started upon his Northern maps when he died. The loss to English Dialectology was a disaster; and my own debt to him is incalculable and permanent.

The goal that Dieth and I had before us was a linguistic atlas of England. Our task, as it presented itself to us in 1946, fell into several stages. First, there was the production of a comprehensive questionnaire, to reveal the distinctive lexical, phonological, morphological and syntactical features of all the main English dialects; second, the selection of an adequate network of rural localities with enough dialect-speaking informants of the right kind; third, the selection and training of competent fieldworkers to use the *Questionnaire* for securing the responses wanted from informants; fourth, the editing of all this material preparatory to publication; fifth, the publication of the results of the Survey in a suitable form, whether maps, or lists, or both; sixth, the provision of the necessary accommodation from which to carry on the Survey; lastly, the requisite money to finance the project had to be assured.

Our *Questionnaire* was printed in January 1952 after thorough testing in four separate versions in various parts of the country. By now it had been extensively revised. Version I had been purely notional. In essence it simply listed the notions for which equivalent dialectal expressions were wanted, for example, *fields, cowhouse, trough;* and the fieldworker was instructed to obtain them from chosen informants in his own way. The method was basically unsound. It was wrong not to prevent entirely the phrasing of the question as asked of the informant from suggesting the actual words of his response. The essential thing was to put the wanted notion clearly into his mind without even hinting at the wording of the desired response, and then let him give his answer absolutely in his own way, the local way. For example, our *Questionnaire* asks *Where do you keep the birds that lay eggs for you?*, I.1.6.[2] *What do you call the man who looks after the animals that give us wool?*, I.2.1. The informant then finds his own expression out of his own linguistic experience; he pronounces it entirely in his own way, the way he is accustomed to in his own locality.

---

[1] It was a reprint, with separate pagination, of Part IX of Vol. VI., *Literary and Historical Section, Proceedings of the Leeds Philosophical and Literary Society*, Leeds, 1952.

[2] The figures refer to question no. 6 on page 1 of Book I of the *Questionnaire*. We always refer to the questions in this manner.

We abandoned the method of Version I with its lists of wanted notions, and thereafter set out all the questions in full. Version II and all three later Versions are thus drawn up in this way: actual questions, expressed in full. We purposely excluded any words, phrases or sentences for translation by the informant into his own vernacular speech. Further, the fieldworker was regularly instructed to keep rigidly to the question as set out in the *Questionnaire*. In this way we expected to secure strictly comparable responses throughout the whole network of localities. And of course unless, as sometimes, the object varied according to region, we normally did so. Since publication, the *Questionnaire* has remained almost intact. One specimen page below exhibits its characteristic features.

Our *Questionnaire* contains 1095 numbered questions, though altogether there are some 1270. They are arranged in nine numbered Books, or sections, entitled respectively The Farmstead; Cultivation; Animals; Nature; The House and Housekeeping; The Human Body; Numbers, Time and Weather; Social Activities; and the ninth and last, States, Actions and Relations. In short, it concerns the farmer and his domestic and social life. Why the farmer? Because he and his family and the farming community in general, best preserve regional dialect in England today. We deliberately ignored all other industries, like mining, fishing, weaving. These are localised, whereas farming is universal. We also ignored the towns—though they should certainly be studied by somebody soon. In scope our *Questionnaire* is linguistically comprehensive. Of the questions, 365 are designed to throw light on any given dialect's sound system, 62 on its morphological features, 41 on its syntactical features, and at least 730 on its lexical features. Almost all the questions except the lexical ones are specially marked with signs, which are attached to the keywords, to show the fieldworker, and readers, at a glance why the questions have been included. Thus an asterisk marks a phonological question; a dagger, a morphological one, and a double dagger a syntactical question. Several examples occur on the specimen page [fig. 1]; and see particularly TEETH,* VI.5.6, included for both its phonological and its morphological importance.

Drawing up each question in full was a strenuous task. It meant learning a new technique; and there eventually emerged five types of questions. We called them naming, completing, talking, converting, and reverse questions. Most are naming, with completing questions good runners-up. All are expressed in simple, brief, direct and colloquial language. A few words about each in turn.

First, the naming question, the simplest type. Here we merely point to an object, describe it, show a picture or diagram of it; or else imitate an action or make an appropriate gesture; and then ask the informant to name it. For example:

VI.2.1.   *What do you call this?* HAIR.*
III.13.5.   *What do you call a dog with half a dozen breeds in it?* MONGREL.
I.1.1.[3]   *What do you call these?* FIELDS.
V.8.1.   *What am I doing now* [imitate]? DRINKING.

Second, the completing question. Here the question is set out in the form of a statement, which the fieldworker, by using a suitable intonation, invites his informant to complete with his own expression.

For example:

IX.3.5.   *Never drop a tumbler on the floor, because it's bound to* . . . BREAK.*
VI.3.4.   *A man who cannot see at all is* . . . BLIND.*

Third, the talking question—admittedly a poor name.

V.5.4.   *What can you make from milk?* BUTTER,* CHEESE.*
IV.10.1. *What trees have you round here?* BIRCH,* OAK,* ELM,* ELDER, WILLOW.

This type of question is very sparingly used; and we always go on to ask the appropriate specific question to ensure that the wanted response is secured.

The fourth kind is the conversion type. Two good examples occur on the specimen page.

VI.5.11.   *When I have an apple, I* [i.] . . . EAT* *it.*

Then to convert, as instructed, we ask

        Yesterday when I had an apple, I [i.] . . . ATE* *it.*
Whenever I've had an apple, I have always [i.] . . . EATEN* *it.*

See also VI.5.5. on the same page. We employ this type very infrequently, and only to obtain the forms of the irregular verbs.

Now the fifth and last type, the reverse question. Here we give the informant a particular word and ask him what he means by it. The question aims at ascertaining the range of meanings of a particular word—its local semantic variability. There are only ten of these special questions. For example:

I.1.11. Rev.   *What's the BARN for and where is it?*
II.5.1. Rev.   *What do you mean by CORN here in these parts?*

So much for the form of the questions. As for the kinds of notions involved, the questions mostly concern concrete ideas (nouns) and less fre-

---

[3] Denotes: "Show a picture"—an instruction to the fieldworker.

QUESTIONNAIRE

BOOK VI

4   THE EAR AND THE NOSE

1   ... these? **Ears.**
2   What do we do with them?   **To hear*.**
3   ... this, inside? **Ear-hole.**
4   And when someone does this [i. pulling a person's ear] to someone else, you say he is .... **pulling** his **ear.**
5   When a man is hard of hearing, we say he is .... **deaf*.**
6   What's your ordinary word for this? **Nose*.**
7   ... these? **Nostrils.**

5   THE MOUTH

1   ... this? **Mouth.**
2   ... these parts of the mouth?   **Mouth corners.**
3   When a child, while eating, gets all smeared with jam here [p. mouth], its mother will say [g.] .... **Wipe your mouth!**
4   What am I doing now [i. in derision]?   **Putting your tongue* out.**
5   My brother sometimes behaves as if he were dumb and never .... **speaks*.**
    Convert for p.t. and p.p.   **Spoke., spoken†.**
6   ... these? **Teeth*†.**
    And one of them?   **Tooth*.**
7   ... the teeth at the back?   **Molars.**
8   Seeing a boy sitting like this [put your hand to your jaw] might make you ask him: .... **Have you got toothache‡?**
9   Sometimes toothache may get so bad that you think you can hardly .... **bear it†.**
10   ... this, where the roots of the teeth are?   **Gums*.**
11   When I have an apple, I [i.] .... **eat*** it.
    Convert for p.t. and p.p.   **Ate†, eaten†.**
12   When, in eating, we crush applies or biscuits noisily with our teeth, we say we .... **crunch them†.**
13   If a man drinks noisily and greedily [i.], you say he .... **guzzles.**
    And if he eats the same way?   **To gobble.**
14   What am I doing now [i.]?   **Snoring.**
15   When a baby wakes up and starts making loud, shrill noises, you say the baby is .... **shrieking.**
16   When a man has a cold here [p. throat] and it affects his voice [i.], you say he is .... **hoarse.**

quently actions (verbs), qualities (adjectives) and grammar (morphology and syntax). They occur, when possible, consequentially, thereby avoiding any needless racing of the informant from one semantic area to another. When used by competent fieldworkers, who must of course be taught how to handle it properly, the *Questionnaire* has proved wholly successful. The informants really enjoy the interviews and often equate the procedure, and their performance, with programmes they can hear on the radio. Each of the nine books of the *Questionnaire* takes about two hours to answer; and the whole book, when progress is good, about a week of the fieldworker's time. But this includes everything, getting there, finding accommodation, making contacts, securing the best informants, making tape-recordings—the whole process from start to finish.

Our fieldworkers have all been specially trained for their task. We have had eight. . . . All but one had received special phonetic training prior to acceptance as fieldworkers, some of it in the University's Phonetics Department under Mr. P. A. D. McCarthy. Five of them had previously written, for their first degrees, short dissertations on the results of their independent investigations into the phonology of current dialectal English. And five subsequently submitted postgraduate theses[4] on the linguistic geography of counties they had recorded with the *Questionnaire*. A sixth is about to do so. . . . Fieldworkers need careful training. But academic competence in phonetics and English philology will alone not make a good fieldworker. He must, in addition, have physical and mental toughness, energy and drive, sociability, cheerfulness, tact in seeking out and handling informants, a certain histrionic ability and obvious sincerity. Nor need the fieldworker always be a male. . . .

Our informants were chosen by the fieldworkers themselves after direct inquiries on the spot. They (and preferably their parents too) had to be natives and natural dialect speakers; and small farmers, too, or else associated with the farming community. We never used professional dialect speakers, dialect reciters, or educated people, or people who practised cultivated vernacular for some private purpose. Informants had to be at least sixty years of age, and normally not above seventy-five, although some were actually eighty and over. Besides being knowledgeable, they had to have good heads, good mouths, good hearing, and good eyesight. Further, they had to be people who were willing to spare the necessary time for the

---

[4] S. Ellis, *A Study of the Living Dialects of Lincolnshire*, (1952); P. Gibson, *Studies in the Linguistic Geography of Staffordshire*, (1955); Averil H. Playford (now Mrs. G. Sanderson), *Studies in the Linguistic Geography of Leicestershire and Rutland*, (1957); D. R. Sykes, *The Linguistic Geography of Shropshire and Worcestershire* (1956); John T. Wright, *Studies in the Linguistic Geography of Somerset* (1957). These theses have all been deposited in the Brotherton Library of the University of Leeds; but all except the first mentioned are published on micro-cards and micro-films by Micro-Methods Ltd., East Ardsley, Wakefield, Yorks., to whom application for copies should be made.

interviews—and this often meant disrupting their normal daily life. We preferred to interview them in their own homes. Here they could be at their ease, and comfortable enough to cope with the unfamiliar, indeed unique situation that had so suddenly developed out of the fieldworker's intrusion into their privacy. Here, if anywhere, the fieldworker could most easily induce that satisfying and, to them very agreeable, relationship of master and pupil, which is always so favourable to effective recording. The informant plays the rôle of the teacher; he is the authority; the fieldworker is the pupil, university man though he is. Short as their stay was, our fieldworkers made friends with their informants; and never offered to pay a single penny for their services. Our informants gave their help voluntarily, and were almost always happy and proud to do so.

In each locality the whole *Questionnaire* was asked once only; but we did not rely upon only one informant. Few informants can reasonably be expected to spare the time required to answer some 1270 questions—unless of course they are house-fast and therefore, perhaps, anxious for unusual and interesting company. Yet the use of several informants did not, we think, prove a drawback; it was often very advantageous. So we usually took two or three informants. At first, inexperience sometimes forced the fieldworkers to employ as many as five. Very occasionally they were able to use only one.

The fieldworkers transcribed the informants' responses phonetically, and impressionistically, in the phonetic alphabet of the International Phonetic Association. They wrote them down on the left-hand side of specially prepared sheets (subsequently bound in one book); and on the right-hand side, they noted down any words and expressions from the informant's conversation during the interviews that had some bearing upon the problems implicit in the *Questionnaire*. This incidental information is truly invaluable, for it is quite unconditioned by the essentially artificial circumstances of the interview. Being wholly unprompted and spontaneous, it is used for confirming, correcting and amplifying the evidence that the responses themselves provide. Selections from this material will, when relevant, be included in the proposed four volumes of Basic Material; but most of it is more suitable for separate publication as "Companion Volumes of Incidental Material".

Besides these written recordings, our fieldworkers also made tape-recordings on portable recorders in most of the localities of the network. At the end of the week's interviews the fieldworker would invite his best informant to tell him about his daily life or work, about for example, ploughing, harvesting, stacking, hedging. This material was always informal, unscripted, unrehearsed, and unprepared, for example a topic that cropped up naturally in the conversation and seemed to merit discussion there and then. The fieldworker had his recorder ready, and switched it on at his discretion. The fieldworkers soon became expert in handling informants before the microphone and quickly got them to talk uninhibitedly. . . . These tape-recordings should, of course, have been preserved, but the cost was prohibitive. Instead, the best specimens of each dialect are being dubbed (in duplicate) onto double-sided 12″ gramophone records, one for preservation as a master record and the other for study. . . . These uninhibited, spontaneous records of dialectal English will be invaluable to future students of English Philology. When eventually published—and transcribed, I hope, in both phonetic and ordinary spelling—they should interest English scholars all over the world. Up to the present, tape-recordings have been made at 190 of the 300 localities in the network.

Our network of localities was provisionally decided at the beginning of the Survey by Mr. Peter Wright, my first Research Assistant, working under direction. In general geographical position and population figures determined the selection of the various places. They are mainly rural, with, preferably, some 400–500 inhabitants, and are suitably spaced, usually not more than about 15 miles apart. There has been no time, money, or enough trained fieldworkers to investigate more. Incidentally, the obligations of National (Military) Service took three of the fieldworkers away from the Survey just when they had reached the peak of their efficiency.

The cost of the Survey has been almost wholly covered by the University of Leeds. . . .

Study Questions

1. How do the *Survey of English Dialects* and the Linguistic Atlas of the United States differ in their choice of informants? What kind of dialect is Orton attempting to survey? What is Orton's reason for concentrating on this type of speech?

2. What range of linguistic features does the questionnaire cover? Why does the questionnaire specify the form of the question to be asked? How does this practice compare to that of American workers?

3. What was the reason for interviewing only farmers for the survey? Could a dialect dictionary be constructed from the results of such interviews? If so, what would be its limitations? Will the materials collected by Orton be useful in determining "correct" or "good" English? Is it Orton's aim that it should be useful for such a purpose?

4. Are Orton's materials more likely to provide a satisfactory framework for comparison among British dialects than the American materials provide for dialects in the United States? Why or why not? What will be the importance of the findings of the *Survey* for future study of American dialects? In what ways is surveying the dialects of England an easier task than surveying those of the United States?

Uriel Weinreich

IS A STRUCTURAL DIALECTOLOGY POSSIBLE?

Uriel Weinreich's distinguished career was tragically short. He was only forty-one at the time of his death in 1967. Born in Poland in 1926, Weinreich received his Ph.D. from Columbia University, where he was professor of linguistics and Yiddish studies and holder of the Atran Professorship of Yiddish from 1960 until his death. Weinreich published widely in his first field of interest, Yiddish language, linguistics, and folklore. In addition, he made significant contributions to the study of bilingualism, linguistic history, dialectology, and semantics. His most influential work has been *Languages in Contact* (1953), an important study of bilingualism and the relevance of contact phenomena in language history. Just before his death, Weinreich was engaged in work on semantic theory.

With William Moulton, Edward Stankiewicz, and others, Weinreich helped to develop *structural dialectology*, an attempt to bring traditional dialect study into conformity with developing linguistic theory, especially descriptive theory. In the following article, which was highly influential in that attempt, Weinreich asks whether dialectology as practiced in the linguistic atlases of the United States and Europe was based securely enough on adequate concepts of language and dialect. If a language system is unique and closed, and if its members are defined only by their oppositions within the system itself, how can dialects be compared, and how can they be related to the larger entity, a language? Weinreich's answer—the construction of a "diasystem"—must stand or fall with the structural notions of the nature of languages and linguistic descriptions that support it; but however his answer may be judged, Weinreich was among the first to see clear deficiencies in the dialectology of the fifties and before, and to recognize that those deficiencies were theoretical and not simply practical or terminological. In the work of his student William Labov, Weinreich's plea for "the use of the social-science tools of 'external dialectology' " to support structural dialect study has been fruitfully answered.

1. In linguistics today the abyss between structural and dialectological studies appears greater than it ever was. The state of disunity is not repaired if 'phoneme' and 'isogloss' occasionally do turn up in the same piece of research. Students continue to be trained in one domain at the expense of the other. Field work is inspired by one, and only rarely by both, interests. The stauncher adherents of each discipline claim priority for their own method and charge the others with 'impressionism' and 'metaphysics,'

"Is a Structural Dialectology Possible?" by Uriel Weinreich, from *Word*, Vol. 10 (1954), pp. 268–280. Reprinted by permission of The Linguistic Circle of New York, Inc.

as the case may be; the more pliant are prepared to concede that they are simply studying different aspects of the same reality.

This might seem like a welcome truce in an old controversy, but is it an honorable truce? A compromise induced by fatigue cannot in the long run be satisfactory to either party. The controversy could be resolved only if the structuralists as well as the dialectologists found a reasoned place for the other discipline in their theory of language. But for the disciplines to legitimate each other is tantamount to establishing a unified theory of language on which both of them could operate. This has not yet been done.

While the obstacles are formidable, the writer of this paper believes that they are far from insurmountable. The present article is designed to suggest a few of the difficulties which should be ironed out if the theories of two very much disunited varieties of linguistics, structural and dialectological, are to be brought closer together. A certain amount of oversimplification is inevitable, for the 'sides' in the controversy are populous and themselves far from unified. The author would not presume to function as an arbitrator. He simply hopes, without a needless multiplication of terms, to stimulate discussion with others who have also experienced the conflict of interests—within themselves.

If phonological problems dominate in this paper, this is the result of the fact that in the domain of sounds structural and non-structural approaches differ most;[1] semantic study has (so far, at least) not equalled sound study in precision, while in the domain of grammar, specifically structural points of view have had far less to contribute.

2. Regardless of all its heterogeneity, structural linguistics defines a language as an organized system. It was one of the liberating effects of structural linguistics that it made possible the treatment of a language as a unique and closed system whose members are defined by opposition to each other and by their functions with respect to each other, not by anything outside of the system. But since organization must have a finite scope, one of the major problems in a structural linguistic description is the delimitation of its object, the particular system described. Only in ideal cases can the linguist claim to be describing a whole 'language' in the non-technical sense of the word. In practice he must delimit his object to something less. One of the steps he takes is to classify certain items in his data as intercalations from other systems, i.e. as 'synchronically foreign' elements (e.g. *bon mot* in an otherwise English sentence). Another step is to make certain that only one variety of the aggregate of systems which the layman calls a

---

[1] Some of the phonological points made here were inspired by N. S. Troubetzkoy's article on linguistic geography, "Phonologie et géographie linguistique," *TCLP* 4.228–34 (1931); reprinted in his *Principes de phonologie*, Paris, 1949, pp. 343–50.

'language' is described. These steps are taken in order to insure that the material described is uniform. This seems to be a fundamental requirement of structural description.

To designate the object of the description which is in fact a subdivision of the aggregate of systems which laymen call a single language, the term 'dialect' is often used. But if 'dialect' is defined as the speech of a community, a region, a social class, etc., the concept does not seem to fit into narrowly structural linguistics because it is endowed with spatial or temporal attributes which do not properly belong to a linguistic system as such. 'Dialects' can be adjacent or distant, contemporary or non-contemporary, prestigious or lowly; linguistic systems in a strictly structural view can only be identical or different. It is proposed that the term 'dialect' be held in reserve for the time being and that, for purposes of structural analysis as set forth here, it be replaced by 'variety.'

In deference to the non-structural sense of 'dialect' as a type of speech which may itself be heterogeneous, some linguists have broken down the object of description even further to the 'idiolect' level. This term has been used in the United States to denote 'the total set of speech habits of a single individual at a given time.' The term has been seriously criticized on two grounds: (1) constancy of speech patterns may be more easily stated for two persons in a dialogic situation (a kind of *dialecte à deux*) than for a single individual; (2) there are differences even within an 'idiolect' which require that it be broken down further (e.g. into 'styles').

'Idiolect' is the homogeneous object of description reduced to its logical extreme, and, in a sense, to absurdity. If we agree with de Saussure that the task of general linguistics is to describe all the linguistic systems of the world,[2] and if description could proceed only one idiolect at a time, then the task of structural linguistics would not only be inexhaustible (which might be sad but true), but its results would be trivial and hardly worth the effort.

The restriction of descriptive work to homogeneous material has led to a paradox not quite unlike that proposed by Zeno about motion. A moving arrow is located at some point at every moment of time; at intermediate moments, it is at intermediate positions. Therefore it never moves. Rigidly applied, the typical elements of structural description—'opposition' and 'function of units with respect to other units of the same system'—have come close to incapacitating structural analysis for the consideration of several partly similar varieties at a time. Fortunately, the progress of research no longer requires absolute uniformity as a working hypothesis.[3]

Structural linguistic theory now needs procedures for constructing sys-

[2] Ferdinand de Saussure, *Cours de linguistique générale*, Paris, 1949, p. 20.
[3] André Martinet, in preface to Uriel Weinreich, *Languages in Contact*, Linguistic Circle of New York, Publication no. 1, 1953, xii + 148 pages, p. vii.

tems of a higher level out of the discrete and homogeneous systems that are derived from description and that represent each a unique formal organization of the substance of expression and content. Let us dub these constructions 'diasystems,' with the proviso that people allergic to such coinages might safely speak of supersystems or simply of systems of a higher level. A 'diasystem' can be constructed by the linguistic analyst out of any two systems which have partial similarities (it is these similarities which make it something different from the mere sum of two systems). But this does not mean that it is always a scientist's construction only: a 'diasystem' is experienced in a very real way by bilingual (including 'bidialectal') speakers and corresponds to what students of language contact have called 'merged system.' [4] Thus, we might construct a 'diasystem' out of several types of Yiddish in which a variety possessing the opposition /i $\sim$ ɪ/ is itself opposed to another variety with a single /i/ phoneme. Be it noted that a Yiddish speaker in a situation of dialect contact might find information in the confusion of /i/ and /ɪ/ of his interlocutor, which is opposed, on the diasystem level, to his own corresponding distinction. It might tell him (in a 'symptomatic' rather than a 'symbolic' way) where, approximately, his interlocutor is from.

It may be feasible, without defining 'dialect' for the time being, to set up 'dialectological' as the adjective corresponding to 'diasystem,' and to speak of dialectological research as the study of diasystems. Dialectology would be the investigation of problems arising when different systems are treated together because of their partial similarity. A specifically structural dialectology would look for the structural consequences of partial differences within a framework of partial similarity.

It is safe to say that a good deal of dialectology is actually of this type and contains no necessary references to geography, ethnography, political and cultural history, or other extra-structural factors. In Gilliéron's classic studies, the typical (if not exclusive) interest is structural rather than 'external.' In the diasystem 'French,' we may very well contrast the fate of *gallus* in one variety where *-ll-* $>$ *-d̦-* with its fate in another variety where this phonological change did not take place, without knowing anything about the absolute or even relative geography or chronology of these varieties. Non-geographic, structural dialectology does exist; it is legitimate and even promising. Its special concern is the study of partial similarities and differences between systems and of the structural consequences thereof. The preceding is not to say, of course, that 'external' dialectology has been surpassed; this subject will be referred to below (section 7).

Dialectological studies in the structural sense are, of course, nothing new.

---

[4] *Languages in Contact*, pp. 8f.

Binomial formulas like 'Yiddish *fus/fis* "foot",' which are often condensed to *fᵘᵢs* etc., have always been the mainstay of historical phonology. But it should be noted that structural dialectology need not be restricted to historical problems to the extent to which it has been in the past. Consequences of partial differences between varieties can be synchronic as well as diachronic. The following is an example of a 'synchronic consequence.' In one variety of Yiddish (we stick to Yiddish examples for the sake of consistency), the singular and plural of 'foot' are distinguished as (*der*) *fus* vs. (*di*) *fis*, while in another variety, both numbers are *fis*. Now, in the number-distinguishing variety, the singular, *fus*, occurs also as a feminine (with *di*); even so, the distinction between singular and plural can still be made in terms of the vowel: *di fus* 'sg.'—*di fis* 'pl.' In the other dialect, *fis* is invariably masculine, perhaps as a consequence of, or at least in relation to, the fact that there only a masculine could distinguish between sg. *der fis* and pl. *di fis.*[5]

If structuralism were carried to its logical extreme, it would not allow for the type of comparisons suggested here: it could only study relations within systems; and since in a perfect system all parts are interrelated ("tout se tient"), it is hard to see how systems could even be conceived of as partially similar or different; one would think that they could only be wholly identical or different. Considerations of this nature prevented orthodox Saussureanism of the Geneva school from undertaking the study of gradually changing systems, since it was felt that languages could only be compared, if at all, at discrete 'stages.'[6] But a more flexible structuralism has overcome this hurdle by abandoning the illusion of a perfect system, and is producing notable results in the diachronic field.[7] We should now take the further step of asserting the possibility of a synchronic or diachronic dialectology based on a combined study of several partially similar systems.

This step in structural linguistic theory would, it seems, do much to bring it closer to dialectology as it is actually carried on.

3. We come next to dialectology's share in the proposed rapprochement. The main objection raised by structuralists against dialectology as usually practiced might be formulated thus: in constructing 'diasystems' it ignores the structures of the constituent varieties. In other words, existing dialectology usually compares elements belonging to different systems without sufficiently stressing their intimate membership in those systems.

---

[5] For an example of synchronic consequences in phonemics, see Anton Pfalz, "Zur Phonologie der bairisch-österreichischen Mundart," *Lebendiges Erbe; Festschrift. Ernst Reclam*, Leipzig, 1936, pp. 1–19, which is at the same time one of the rare instances of German phonemics and of structural dialectology.

[6] Albert Sechehaye, "Les trois linguistiques saussuriennes," *Vox romanica* 5.1–48 (1940), pp. 30f.; H[enri] Frei, "Lois de passage," *Zeitschrift für romanische Philologie* 64.557–68 (1944).

[7] Cf. the bibliography of diachronic phonemics by Alphonse G. Juilland in *Word* 9.198–208 (1953).

In the domain of sounds, this amounts to a non-phonemic approach. A traditional dialectologist will have no scruples about listening to several dialect informants pronounce their equivalents of a certain word and proclaiming that these forms are 'the same' or 'different.' Let us assume four speakers of a language who, when asked for the word for 'man,' utter 1. [man], 2. [man], 3. [mån], and 4. [mån], respectively. On an impressionistic basis, we would adjudge 1 and 2 as 'the same,' 3 and 4 as 'the same,' but 1 and 2 as 'different' from 3 and 4. Yet suppose that informant 1 speaks a variety in which vowel length is significant; phonemically his form is ₁/mån/. Informant 2 does not distinguish vowel length, and has given us ₂/man/. We can further visualize a variety represented by informant 3 where a vowel with maximum degree of opening has the positional variant [å] between /m/ and /n/; phonemically, then, we have ₃/man/. In the fourth variety, no such positional variation exists; that form is perhaps ₄/mon/. The structural analysis is thus different from the non-structural one: 2 and 3 now turn out to be possibly 'the same' (but only, of course, if the systems are otherwise also identical), while 1 and 4 appear to be different. Structural linguistics requires that the forms of the constituent systems be understood first and foremost in terms of those systems, since the formal units of two non-identical systems are, strictly speaking, incommensurable.[8]

A similar requirement could be made about the units of content, or 'semantemes.' It would not do to say, for instance, that the word *taykh* in one variety of Yiddish is 'the same' as *taykh* in another if, in the one, it is opposed to *ózere* 'lake,' and hence means only 'river,' while in the other it is not so opposed and stands for any sizable 'body of water.' Similar structural cautions would be required with respect to 'synonyms' in the diasystem. In the diasystem 'Yiddish,' *baytn*, *shtékhɛvɛn*, and *toyshn* all signify approximately 'to exchange,' but they cannot be synonyms on the variety level if they do not all exist in any one variety.

A grammatical example might also be cited. In terms of function within the system, it would not be justified to identify the feminine *vaysl* 'Vistula River' of two Yiddish varieties if in the one it is opposed to a neuter *vaysl* 'eggwhite,' while in the other it is completely homonymous with the (also feminine) word for 'eggwhite.' It is even doubtful whether any two feminines in these two varieties could be legitimately identified in view of the fact that one of the varieties does not possess a neuter gender altogether.

The dialectologist is used to comparing directly the 'substance' of different varieties. The demand of the structural linguist that he consider the train of associations, oppositions, and functions that define linguistic forms seems

---

[8] *Languages in Contact*, pp. 7f.

to the dialectologist complicating, unreasonable, and unnecessary ('metaphysical'). To show up the disagreement most clearly, let us represent the phonic problem just discussed on a map and compare the traditional and the proposed structural treatments of it. Obviously the structural approach involves complications, but the dialectologist will become convinced of their necessity when he realizes that phonemics, like structural linguistics generally, represents not a special technique for studying certain problems, but a basic discovery about the way language functions to which structural linguists are completely committed.

Since, in the structural view, allophonic differences between sounds are in a sense less important than phonemic differences, the 'substantial' isogloss (Map 2) which separates [a] from [å] in the overall /a/ area is structurally somehow less important than the purely formal isogloss which separates pronunciations of [mån] = /man/ from those of [mån] = /mon/; the latter isogloss may not reflect any difference in 'substance' at all; it would not show up on the non-structural map (Map 1). The traditional dialectologist naturally wonders what he stands to gain by the drawing of such 'metaphysical' lines. But if dialectological maps are considered diachronically as snapshots of change, and if it can be shown that the difference between phonemes and allophones can be material in determining sound

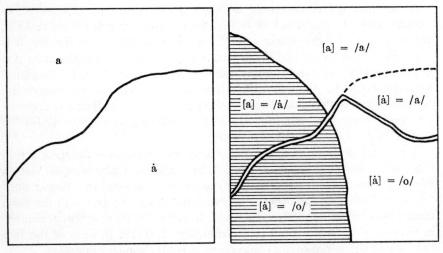

Map 1: Traditional   **Map 2:** Structural
The Vowel in 'Man' in Language X

On map 2, a continuous single line divides areas with different phonemic inventories (shaded area distinguishing vowel length, unshaded area not distinguishing it). The double line separates areas using different phonemes in this word (difference of distribution). The dotted line separates allophonic differences.

change, it may be possible to convince the dialectologist that the structural map is after all more true to the reality of functioning language. Similar arguments, perhaps, could also be persuasive insofar as they are pertinent to grammatical and lexical matters.

If dialectologists would consider the functions of the elements which they use in their comparisons, their conception of a 'diasystem' would come close to that proposed here for structural linguistics and might lead to the unified theory which is so badly needed.

4. The partial differences which are proposed as the specific subject matter of dialectologic study may be of two kinds: differences of inventory and differences of distribution. While the latter are the standard material of comparative study, the former have not received their due stress.

As an example of a difference in inventory, let us take a simple phonemic case first. In the following discussion, single slashes enclose sets of phonemes and single tildes designate phonemic oppositions in a variety identified by a preceding subscript number; oppositions in the constructed diasystem are characterized by double tildes, and the formulas for the diasystems are surrounded by double slashes. Given two varieties with identical five-vowel systems, we might construct the following diasystem: $_{1,2}//i \approx e \approx a \approx o \approx u//$. Now let us assume that in one of the varieties, the front vowel of the intermediate degree of openness is more open than in the other; choosing a phonemic transcription which would reflect this fact, we might indicate the difference in the diasystem thus:

$$_{1,2}\bigg/\bigg/ \; i \approx \frac{_1 e}{_2 \varepsilon} \approx a \approx o \approx u \; \bigg/\bigg/ \; .$$

Given two varieties, one of which (1) distinguishes three front vowels, the other (2) distinguishing four, we might formulate the corresponding part of the vowel diasystem thus:

$$_{1,2}\bigg/\bigg/ \; \frac{_1/i \sim e \sim \text{æ}/}{_2/i \sim e \sim \varepsilon \sim \text{æ}/} \approx a \approx o \cdots \; \bigg/\bigg/ \; .$$

Here is the actual vowel inventory of Yiddish considered as a diasystem of three dialects, 1. Central ("Polish"), 2. Southwestern ("Ukrainian"), and 3. Northwestern ("Lithuanian").

$$_{1,2,3}\bigg/\bigg/ \; \frac{\dfrac{_1/\text{i:} \sim \text{i}/}{_2/i \sim \text{I}/}}{_3 i} \approx e \approx \frac{_1/\text{a:} \sim \text{a}/}{_{2,3}\text{a}} \approx o \approx u \; \bigg/\bigg/ \; .$$

Similarly differences in inventory of irammatical categories might be stated, e.g. between varieties having two against three genders, three as against four conjugational types, and the like. All examples here are tentative and schematic; the possibilities of a more analytical statement of the diasystem, based e.g. on relevant features, remain to be investigated.

One thing is certain: In the study of language contact and interference (see section 5), a clear picture of differences in inventory is a prerequisite.[9]

Differences in distribution cannot be directly inferred from a comparison of the differences in inventory, although the two ordinarily stand in a definite historical relationship. For example, in the diasystem 'Yiddish' described above, the phoneme $_3$/i/ in variety 3 usually corresponds to either $_2$/i/ or $_2$/ɪ/ in cognates of variety 2, and to either $_1$/i:/ or $_1$/i/ in cognates of variety 1 ($_3$/sine/:$_2$/sɪne/:$_1$/sĭne/ 'enmity'). This is, as it were, a correspondence between the nearest equivalents. But many $_3$/o/'s correspond to /u/'s in variety 1 and 2, even though all three varieties today possess both /o/ and /u/ phonemes. Thus, /futer/ means 'father' in varieties 1 and 2, but 'fur' in variety 3; /meluxe/ means $_{1,2}$'craft' and $_3$'state'; /hun/ means $_{1,2}$'rooster' and $_3$'hen.' For the tens of thousands of speakers for whom the contact of these varieties is an everyday experience, these 'Yiddish' sound sequences are not fully identified until the particular variety of Yiddish to which they belong is itself determined. Now no one would deny that a form like Yiddish [fĭˇl] ($_{1,2}$'full,' $_3$'many') is identified fully only in conjunction with its meaning in one of the varieties, i.e. when account is taken of the differences in distribution of sounds in cognates occurring in the several varieties. The less obvious point made here is that the form is not fully identified, either, if relevant differences in *inventory* are not accounted for, i.e. if it is not rendered in terms of the phonemes of one of the concrete varieties: [fil] = $_1$/fĭl/, $_2$/fɪl/, $_3$/fil/.

Recent descriptive work on American English phonemics has come close to treating the language as a 'diasystem' without, however, satisfying the requirements set forth here. The widely adopted analysis of Trager and Smith[10] provides a set of symbols by which forms of all varieties of American English can be described. It makes it possible, for example, to transcribe Southeastern /pæys/ *pass* in terms of some of the same symbols used in /pæt/ *pat* of the same dialect or in /pæs/, /bəyd/ *bird*, etc., of other varieties. This violates the principle advocated here that the phonemic systems of the varieties should be fully established before the diasystem is constructed. We are not told whether in the phoneme inventory of Southeastern American English, the /æy/ of *pass* does or does not correspond as an inventory item to the /æ/ of other varieties. We cannot tell if the [o] of *home* of Coastal New England is the same phoneme, or a different pho-

[9] *Ibid.*, pp. 1f.
[10] George L. Trager and Henry Lee Smith, Jr., *An Outline of English Structure* (= *Studies in Linguistics, Occasional Papers* 3), Norman (Okla.), 1951, esp. pp. 27–9.

neme, from the [ow] in *go* in the same variety. For reasons of this type, the system has been criticized as providing not a phonemic description or a set of descriptions, but a "transcriptional arsenal." [11] Yet the remaining step toward the establishment of a phonemic diasystem is not difficult to visualize.

5. We might now restate and specify the suggested position of structural dialectology in linguistics as a whole. SYNCHRONIC DIALECTOLOGY compares systems that are partially different and analyzes the 'synchronic consequences' of these differences within the similarities. DIACHRONIC DIALECTOLOGY deals (a) with DIVERGENCE, i.e. it studies the growth of partial differences at the expense of similarities and possibly reconstructs earlier stages of greater similarity (traditionally, comparative linguistics); (b) with CONVERGENCE, i.e. it studies partial similarities increasing at the expense of differences (traditionally, substratum and adstratum studies, 'bilingual dialectology,' [12] and the like).

The opposite of dialectology, which hardly needs a special name, is the study of languages as discrete systems, one at a time. It involves straight description of uniform systems, typological comparisons of such systems, and diachronically, the study of change in systems considered one at a time.

6. It was stated previously that diasystems can be constructed *ad hoc* out of any number of varieties for a given analytic purpose. Constructing a diasystem means placing discrete varieties in a kind of continuum determined by their partial similarities. However, in passing from a traditional to a structural dialectology, the more pressing and more troublesome problem is the opposite one, viz. how to break down a continuum into discrete varieties. What criteria should be used for divisions of various kinds? Can non-technical divisions of a 'language' into 'dialects,' 'patois,' and the like be utilized for technical purposes? [13]

Before these questions can be answered, it is necessary to distinguish between standardized and non-standardized language. This set of terms is proposed to avoid the use of the ambiguous word, 'standard,' which among others has to serve for 'socially acceptable,' 'average,' 'typical,' and so on.

---

[11] Einar Haugen, "Problems of Bilingual Description," *Report of the Fifth Annual Round Table Meeting on Linguistics and Language Teaching* (= [Georgetown University] *Monograph Series on Languages and Linguistics* no. 7, 1954).

[12] For an essay in bilingual dialectology, see Uriel Weinreich, *"Sábesdiker losn* in Yiddish: a Problem of Linguistic Affinity," *Word* 8.360–77 (1952).

[13] The possibility of introducing some scientific rigor into existing loose terminology has been explored by André Martinet, "Dialect," *RomancePhilology* (1953/54). The article by Václav Polák, "Contributions à l'étude de la notion de langue et de dialecte," *Orbis* 3.89–98 (1954), which arrived too late to be utilized here as fully as it deserves, suggests that we call 'language' a diasystem whose partial similarities are grammatical while its partial differences are phonologic and lexical.

On the contrary, STANDARDIZATION could easily be used to denote a process of more or less conscious, planned, and centralized regulation of language.[14] Many European languages have had standardized varieties for centuries; a number of formerly 'colonial' tongues are undergoing the process only now. Not all leveling is equivalent to standardization. In the standardization process, there is a division of functions between regulators and followers, a constitution of more or less clear-cut authorities (academies, ministries of education, *Sprachvereine*, etc.) and of channels of control (schools, special publications, etc.). For example, some dialectal leveling and a good deal of Anglicization has taken place in the immigrant languages of the United States, and we might say that a word like *plenty* has become a part of the American Norwegian koinê.[15] But in the sense proposed here, there is no 'standardized' American Norwegian which is different from Old-World Norwegian, and from the point of view of the standardized language, *plenty* is nothing but a regional slang term.

Now it is part of the process of standardization itself to affirm the identity of a language, to set it off discretely from other languages and to strive continually for a reduction of differences within it. Informants of standardized languages react in a peculiar way; moreover, it is much easier to deal with samples of a standardized language, to make generalizations about it and to know the limits of their applicability. On the level of non-standardized or FOLK LANGUAGE,[16] a discrete difference between one variety and others is NOT a part of the experience of its speakers, and is much more difficult to supply. For example, it is easy to formulate where standardized Dutch ends and standardized German begins, but it is a completely different matter to utilize for technical purposes the transition between folk Dutch and folk German.

On the whole dialectologists have avoided dealing with standardized languages and have restricted themselves to folk language.[17] Consequently, in practice as well as in theory the problem of dividing and ordering the continuum of language is especially serious with respect to the folk level and not the standardized level. Time was when the continuum of folk language used to be divided on the basis of (usually diachronic) structural features, e.g. the geographic limits of a certain phonological development. Either one isogloss which the linguist considered important was selected

---

[14] Cf. *Languages in Contact*, pp. 99–103. An interesting book about standardization is Heinz Kloss, *Die Entwicklung neuer germanischer Kultursprachen von 1800 bis 1950*, Munich, 1952.

[15] Einar Haugen, *The Norwegian Language in America*, Philadelphia, 1953, p. 588.

[16] Interesting parallels could be developed between the sociolinguistic opposition 'standardized'—'folk' and the social anthropologist's opposition between the cultures of complex (industrialized) and folk societies or strata of society; cf. e.g. George M. Foster, "What Is Folk Culture?" *American Anthropologist* 55.159–73 (1953).

[17] Some people are not averse to calling modern standardized languages 'Indo-European dialects,' or speaking of 'literary dialects.' Dialectology in the sense proposed in this paper need not restrict itself to the folk level, but such usage is one more reason why the term 'dialect' ought to be held in abeyance.

(e.g. k/x as the line between Low and High German), or a bundle of isoglosses of sufficient thickness was used as a dividing line. In either case, the
resulting divisions were not, of course, all of the same degree; they were
major, minor, and intermediate, depending on the thickness of the bundle
or the relative importance of the key isogloss. It is evident that no unambiguous concept of dialect could emerge even from this optimistic
methodology any more than a society can be exhaustively and uniquely
divided into 'groups.'

Classificatory procedures of this type are today virtually passé. Dialectologists have generally switched to extra-structural criteria for dividing
the folk-language continuum. The concept of language area (*Sprachland-
schaft*) has practically replaced that of 'dialect' (*Mundart*) as the central
interest in most geographic work,[18] and ever more impressive results are
being obtained in correlating the borders, centers, and overall dynamics of
language areas with 'culture areas' in a broader sense. Instead of speaking,
for instance, of the *helpe/helfe* and *Lucht/Luft* isoglosses as the border between the Ripuraian and Moselle-Franconian 'dialects' of the German
Rhineland, linguistic geographers now speak of the Eifel Barrier between
the Cologne and Trier areas. This Eifel mountain range happens to be the
locus not only of those two random isoglosses, but, among others, also the
dividing line between *kend* and *keŋk* 'child,' *haus* and *hus* 'house,' *grumper*
and *erpel* 'potato,' *heis* and *gramm* 'hoarse'; between short-bladed and long-
bladed scythes, grey bread in oval loaves and black bread in rectangular
loaves, New Year's twists and New Year's pretzels, St. Quirin as the patron
saint of cattle and the same as the patron of horses, two different types of
ditty addressed to the ladybug, etc.[19] The line is meaningful as a reflex of a
medieval boundary which can in turn be accounted for by more permanent
climatic, orological, hydrographic, and other geographic factors.[20]

The search for ways to divide the folk-language continuum has also led
to statistical correlation methods.[21] Rather than plotting the border lines of
single selected structural features, which may be impossible in areas of
amorphous transition, the following procedure is used. Inquiries are made
at various points concerning the presence or absence of a whole list of test
features; then the correlation between the results at some reference point
and at all other points is computed, and may be represented cartographi-

---

[18] This is particularly evident in the methodologically most advanced German Swiss work; cf. the publications
series *Beiträge zur schweizerdeutschen Mundartforschung* edited by Rudolf Hotzenköcherle.

[19] Linguistic data from Adolf Bach, *Deutsche Mundartforschung*, Heidelberg, 1950, pp. 123ff.; ethnographic data
from Adolf Bach, *Deutsche Volkskunde*, Leipzig, 1937, p. 228.

[20] In the United States, Hans Kurath (*A Word Geography of the Eastern United States*, Ann Arbor, 1949), has
successfully combined strictly linguistic with 'external' criteria in breaking down the relatively undifferentiated American folk-language area.

[21] See David W. Reed and John L. Spicer, "Correlation Methods of Comparing Idiolects in a Transition Area,"
Language 28.348–60 (1952).

cally, points with similar correlation coefficients being surrounded by lines which have variously been called 'isopleths' or 'isogrades.' Theoretically related to this procedure are the tests of mutual intelligibility between dialects.[22] All these procedures must depend on an arbitrary critical constant (or constants) for the drawing of a dividing line (or lines, of various degrees of importance), but they do yield an insight into the makeup of a continuously varying language area which supplements, if it does not supersede, the results derived by other methods.

In the domain of dialect sociology, where transitions are perhaps even more continuous and fluid than in dialect geography, the use of extra-linguistic correlations and statistical sampling techniques offers promising possibilities of research in an almost untrodden field.[23]

The use of the social-science tools of 'external dialectology' can do much to supplement the procedures outlined for a structural dialectology. One problem for combined structural and 'external' linguistic investigation is to determine what structural and non-structural features of language have in fact helped to break up the folk-language continuum into the non-technical units of 'dialects,' 'patois,' etc. This combined research might get to the heart of the question of diasystems as empirical realities rather than as mere constructs. One of its by-products might be the formulation of a technical concept of 'dialect' as a variety or diasystem with certain explicit defining features.

7. Finally a word might be said about the interrelationship of structural and 'external' points of view applied to a specific dialectological problem. Given a map showing an isogloss, the 'external' dialectologist's curiosity is likely to concentrate on the locus of that isogloss. Why is it where it is? What determines the details of its course? What other isoglosses bundle with it? What communication obstacle does it reflect?

The structural dialectologist has another set of questions, stemming from his interest in partial differences within a framework of partial similarity. To take up the semasiological example of Map 3 (which is schematized but based on real data), if *shtul* means 'chair' in zone A, but 'easychair' in zone B, then what is the designation of 'easychair' in A and of 'chair' in B? Every semasiological map, due to the two-faceted nature of linguistic signs, gives rise to as many onomasiological questions as the number of zones it

---

[22] Cf. for example C. F. Voegelin and Zellig S. Harris, "Methods for Determining Intelligibility Among Dialects of Natural Languages," *Proceedings of the American Philosophical Society* 95.322–9 (1951).

[23] See the interesting paper by Stanley M. Sapon, "A Methodology for the Study of Socio-Economic Differentials in Linguistic Phenomena," *Studies in Linguistics* 11.57–68 (1953). A scheme for the classification of varieties of a language according to their function (ecclesiastic, poetic, scientific, etc.) to replace the unsatisfactory terminology of 'styles' has been proposed by Yury Šerech, "Toward a Historical Dialectology," *Orbis* 3.43–56 (1954), esp. pp. 47 ff.

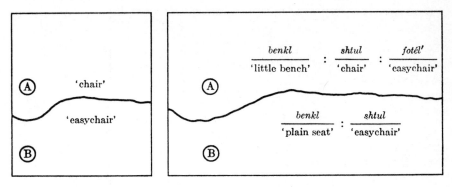

Map 3: Meaning of *shtul* in East European Yiddish (Schematized)
Map 4: Designations of Seats in East European Yiddish (Schematized)

contains, and vice versa. If we were to supply the information that in zone A, 'easychair' is *fotél'*, while in zone B 'chair' is *benkl*, a new set of questions would arise: what, then, does *fotél'* mean in B and *benkl* in A? [24] This implicational chain of questions could be continued further. The resulting answers, when entered on a map, would produce a picture of an isogloss dividing two lexical systems, rather than two isolated items (see Map 4). This would be the 'structural corrective' to a traditional dialect map.

It is easy to think of dialectological field problems for the solution of which 'external' and structural considerations must be combined in the most intimate manner. Such problems would arise particularly if the cartographic plotting of systems should produce a set of narrowly diverging isoglosses. Assume that an isogloss is drawn between a variety of a language which distinguishes short /u/ from long /u:/ and another variety which makes no such quantitative distinction. The structuralist's curiosity is immediately aroused about length distinctions in other vowels. Suppose now that the variety that distinguishes the length of /u/ does so also for /i/; but that the isoglosses, plotted independently, are not exactly congruent (Map 5). Some intriguing questions now arise concerning the dynamics of the vowel pattern of the discrepant zone. Nothing but an on-the-spot field study closely combining structural analysis and an examination of the 'external' communication conditions in the area could deal adequately with a problem of this kind.

8. In answer to the question posed in the title of this paper, it is submitted that a structural dialectology is possible. Its results promise to be most

---

[24] The actual answer is that *fotél'* is not current in zone B, while *benkl* means 'little bench' in zone A.

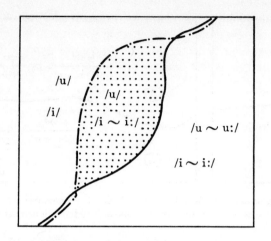

Map 5: Non-Congruent Vowel-Length
Isoglosses in Language *Y*

fruitful if it is combined with 'external' dialectology without its own conceptual framework being abandoned.

Study Questions

1. What two "varieties of linguistics" does Weinreich hope to bring "closer together" ? With what specific kinds of problems does he deal—phonological, semantic, or grammatical? Why?

2. How, according to Weinreich, does structural linguistics define a language? What adjectives does Weinreich apply, in his Section 2, to the systems which structuralists describe? How does he say the members of such a system are defined? What does each of these "discrete and homogeneous systems" represent? Do you find Weinreich's characterization of linguistic systems clear?

3. From what dilemma of logically "pure" structuralism does Weinreich use his diasystem to escape? Explain the two kinds of differences which, according to Weinreich, the structural dialectologist considers. How would you characterize the difference, in Sections 3 and 7, between the structural dialectologist's comparisons and the traditional dialectologist's comparisons? What is Weinreich's contrast between structural dialectology and external dialectology? Need structural dialectology be

restricted to problems of historical linguistics? From Yiddish, Weinreich gives an example of "synchronic consequences" of "partial differences" between dialects; how would you respond to the statement that the example is not really synchronic but a bit of causally interpreted history in disguise?

4. In Section 6, what meaning can you give to Weinreich's contrast between "a continuum" and "discrete varieties" ? Would you accept or reject the notion that a "standardized" language is not a real language at all but an artifact, an invention, a set of rules which some people think they ought to observe?

5. Does Weinreich say anything about the features which distinguish one item in a phonemic inventory from another—say the vowel of Yiddish *fus* from the vowel of Yiddish *fis?* Does he at any point relate his phonetic forms (in square brackets) to his phonemic forms (between slashes) by stated rules? When he sets up specific diasystems in Section 4, does Weinreich tell us anything about the distribution of the items in his inventories; that is, for example, do the words with /ɛ/ in the second dialect of the second diasystem have /e/ or /æ/ in the first dialect? Does Weinreich relate the phonology of Yiddish to any other part of the structure of that language? Does he give any characterization of "lexical systems" in Section 7?

6. Would a linguist continue to make the same kind of comparisons among linguistic systems if he changed his notion of the systems themselves? Suppose, for example, that a linguist thinks of the components of a linguistic description as integrated, so that the demands of one part, like the syntax, might shape another part, like the phonology, or the demands of the semantics might shape the syntax; would he then be optimistic about a "structural dialectology" while the semantics and the grammar remained relatively unexplored? Does Weinreich share the pessimism which the preceding question suggests? How in fact does he answer the question which is his title?

James Sledd

BREAKING, UMLAUT, AND THE
SOUTHERN DRAWL

James Sledd (born in Atlanta, Ga., 1914) is a professor at the University of
Texas and president of the Whole Child Foundation. Besides a few literary
essays, he has written on English grammar and English lexicography, on American dialects, and on the teaching of the English language in American schools.

In the following article, Sledd discusses some phonetic characteristics of
certain dialects in the southern United States. Like Weinreich, he criticizes
dialectologists for preoccupation with the physical details of dialectal divergence and unconcern for the system which underlies those facts; but whereas
Weinreich thought of that system in structural terms, Sledd borrows some
elementary notions from the transformationalists. He argues that the ordered
phonetic rules of a transformational grammar can accurately describe phonetic differences among the dialects without obscuring the underlying system
of the English language. Along the way, Sledd illustrates the familiar contention that the attempt to state descriptive rules for a dialect may lead to
discoveries about its history as well.

YET ONCE MORE, O YE VOWELS

In 1955, in a review of the Trager-Smith *Outline of English structure*,[1] I
made a first attempt at phonemicizing an old-fashioned dialect of Atlanta,
Georgia, which did not seem to fit the overall pattern of nine vowels and
three semivowels that Trager and Smith had proposed. Further discussion
followed at the First Texas Conference in 1956, where the arguments for a
tenth vowel were strengthened by Raven I. McDavid and Sumner Ives;
but even the rebellious, at that time, were still working within the Smith
and Trager framework, and when their arguments were published in the
proceedings of the Conference, they suffered because the secretary who
transcribed them had been unable to cope with so many different dialects
and because proof-reading had been peccable. A tentative report on the
Conference to the 1956 Linguistic Institute at Ann Arbor was received with
benevolent amusement, and ensuing debates with myself and Hans Kurath
appeared in later numbers of *Language*[2] and in my *Short introduction to*

"Breaking, Umlaut, and the Southern Drawl" by James Sledd, from *Language*, Vol. 42, 1966, pp. 18–41,
copyright 1966. Reprinted by permission of the Linguistic Society of America and the author.
[1] *Lg.* 31.312–45 (1955).
[2] 33.111–22 (1957), 34.252–60 (1958).

English grammar.[3] Kurath has maintained his outspoken skepticism of all Trageretic analyses in *The pronunciation of English in the Atlantic States*[4] and in *A phonology and prosody of modern English.*[5] Meanwhile Morris Halle and Noam Chomsky launched their attack on 'the taxonomic approach,' and Chomsky suggested, at the Fourth Texas Conference, that the phonetic features which seemed to set the Atlanta dialect so distinctively apart are really predictable by low-level rules in the morphophonemic component of a generative grammar, so that the dialect's phonemic system is actually the same or much the same as his, which in turn is much like the General American of Kenyon and Knott's *Pronouncing dictionary.*[6] If this is true, then the analysis in *A short introduction*, which seemed to me in 1959 a departure from the Trager-Smith system, was in fact an unintentional reduction to absurdity of their still dominant bad principles; and Kurath's analysis, though closer to The Truth, still recognizes unnecessary phonemes and is unsupported by adequate theory. Chomsky invited me to contemplate these unflattering conclusions at MIT in the summer of 1962. The result is the present paper, which owes a great deal to the continuing spiritual ministrations both of Chomsky and Halle and of my colleagues William B. Rood Jr. and Harold Hungerford.

No one, I hope, will suspect my mentors of the light-mindedness and informality which characterize the discussion: any guilt is mine. The intention is, however, that the earnest and competent inquirer should be able to translate my conclusions into the MItesian lingo of distinctive features and formally stated rules. The rules would appear in the third and last part of the morphophonemics, so that my transcriptions belong in the no-man's-land between systematic phonemics and systematic phonetics. Hence they are enclosed neither in phonetic brackets nor phonemic slants, but within vigilant exclamation points; and on the occasions when I do refer to distinctive features, the context must indicate whether they are the binary features of phonemics or the graded features of phonetics. Quotations and citations from other work naturally follow the authors' usage of slants or brackets.

More particularly, I assume seven pairs of vowels which I am rashly calling tense and lax. The seven tense vowels are the !i! of *meet*, the !e! of *mate*, the !æ! of *bare*, the !u! of *boot*, the !o! of *boat*, the !ɔ̄! of *bought*, and the !ā! of *bar*. The first five are matched by lax !ɪ! in *mitt*, !ɛ! in *met*, !æ! in *mat*, !ʊ! in *put*, and !ʌ! in *mutt*. Lax !ɑ! is in *pot* and lax !ɔ! is decorative and may be nice to keep in the house for British guests, though I have no im-

[3] Chicago, 1959.
[4] Ann Arbor, 1961 (with Raven I. McDavid).
[5] Ann Arbor, 1964.
[6] Springfield, 1944.

mediate use for it myself. I call the first elements of the four diphthongs lax: !ɑɪ! in *file,* !ɑʊ! in *foul,* !ɔɪ! in *foil,* and !ɪu! in *tune.* Only !ɑɪ! and !ɑʊ! are important to the argument.

Latent indignation unaroused by those assumptions may be visited on my nontechnical use of the term *glide,* which is prompted by the optimistic thought that the context should usually keep things fairly clear while I avoid hassles over consonantal and vocalic and pluses and minuses. Anyway, I recognize three glides, two that I call velar and one palatal. The velar glide !ʊ! is upward and backward toward high back round, as usual; the velar glide !ə! is centering; the palatal glide !ɪ! is upward and forward toward unround high front; but—again as usual—the areas represented by the chosen letters include a considerable range of ending-points. I suppose it is useless to remind the indignant that in the context of this discussion the choice of alphabetic symbols is ultimately of no importance; and if these explanations will not suffice, I can only predict that catharsis will be complete when I sometimes use *preconsonantal* in reference to positions before Jakobsonian consonants, glides, and liquids—all three. The symbol !⌗!, I should add, is Chomskyite, not Trageretic: not double cross, but the boundaries in *hear ⌗* and *hear ⌗ing.*

As for the argument itself, it begins with Kurath's free mid-central vowel /ɜ/ as in *word,* which I think is neither /ɜ/ nor the !ʌr! sequence. The set of informal rules which closes this first section is expanded, at the end of the second, to apply to other developments involving preconsonantal and final !r!; and after announcing a belated conversion to the doctrine that the *r*-less dialects are *r*-ful, I next attempt to apply much the same rules to words with final and preconsonantal !l!. The most hubristic section defends the Anglo-Saxon heritage of the South by discovering that breaking and umlaut are vigorously alive in Modern English—and governed by the same rules that handle !l! and !r!. A final section reviews and illustrates all the rules, restores the South to the Union by emphasizing that its differentness is only superficial, and repeats a number of exaggerated claims.

/ɛ/

In Modern British and American English, words like *bird, earth, err, first, fur, work,* and *word* itself are pronounced in a good many different ways, as everybody knows. In the Received Pronunciation of British English, they have a long, unrounded, mid-central vowel without *r*-color, which Jones writes as [ə:] in his *Pronouncing dictionary,*[7] Gimson as /ɜ:/ in

---

[7] 11th ed.; London, 1956.

his *Pronunciation of English*.[8] In the English of Scotland and in some dialects of the north of England, according to Gimson, a pronunciation with [ɪ], [ɛ], [ʌ], or [ʊ] plus /r/ is used instead of [ɜ:]; and in southwestern English dialects one hears either the obscure vowel [ə] followed by a usually retroflex /r/ or else the obscure vowel with simultaneous retroflexion of the tongue, the well-known *r*-colored vowel of much American English.[9] In the United States, the situation is just as complicated. Kurath describes the most common variant as 'a more or less "constricted" mid-central [ɜʳ] sound, in which the tongue is withdrawn, humped up in the back, and laterally constricted. Not infrequently, there is an upglide with progressive constriction of the tongue.'[10] Some American pronunciations, however, are phonetically *r*-less. In particular, they include various long mid-central vowels like that of RP, and a diphthong (Kurath's [ɜɪ]) which is popularly regarded as Brooklynese but has been reported from various other localities in the Atlantic States for three-quarters of a century. Though its origin is unexplained, it is so common in the up-country of the lower South that Kurath calls it dominant 'from South Carolina westward.' Despite such phonetic variety, he treats the mid-central vowel of RP and all the American variants as one and the same free vowel /ɜ/, whether the variants are retroflex or nonretroflex, constricted or unconstricted, monophthongal or diphthongal.

Not every linguist has been as willing as Kurath to accept the consequences of univocalic analyses like his (or as unwilling to supply an explanatory theory). The phonetic manifestations of his postulated vowel differ widely—but without explanation—both within and between dialects; its acceptance forces the recognition of surprising word-structures, like /hɜ-i/ (*hurry*) in some American English; a certain amount of morphophonemic alternation becomes necessary, as in *furry* with /r/ but *fur* without it; the postulated vowel itself adds one to the roster of phonemes; and if that addition is made, the force of system may compel the addition of still other units, like Kurath's vowel /ɑ/ as in *car* and his semivowel /ə̬/ in words like *dear*, both of which he assumes for dialects where post-vocalic /r/ has been 'lost as such.'[11] These last postulations are not only open to many of the same objections which can be made to Kurath's free mid-central vowel: they also create an appearance of greater structural difference between dialects than the fact of easy communication would suggest. Historians, finally, might think it significant that the free mid-central vowel, without an /r/, should appear only in words where /r/ historically did oc-

[8] London, 1962.
[9] Gimson 117.
[10] *Phonology* 120.
[11] Op. cit. 108, 81.

cur and where *r*-coloring is still heard in the speech of millions. The modern dialects show plainly that *r*-lessness in *bird*, etc. is a late phonetic development from an earlier sequence [ər], which itself had resulted from the merging of three lax vowels before /r/ plus a consonant or before /r/ final.

In these circumstances, the obvious proposal has repeatedly been made —namely, to replace Kurath's free mid-central vowel with the sequence /ər/ as the basis for the dialectal variants. But Kurath's is not the only way to construct an overall pattern. One may also reject altogether any single underlying representation, whether /ɜ/ or /ər/ or anything else, and propose instead a whole set to match the variants, as Trager and Smith have done: /ər/, /əhr/, /əh/, /əy/, etc. The three questions which thus emerge are (1) whether to represent the variants individually or by some underlying form or forms from which they can be derived, (2) what underlying form or forms to postulate if derivation is attempted, and (3) by what precise phonetic rules to describe that derivation. Trager and Smith have chosen individual representation; Kurath has postulated a dubious underlying form; and no one, so far as I know, has even attempted to formulate phonetic rules. That attempt should make the previous questions easier to talk about.

For the northern British dialects which Gimson mentions, there is apparently no problem. Since they preserve the historical three-way distinction, a single representation, like /ɜ/ or /ər/, would only force a second listing of most of the relevant words in the rules that would divide them into their three groups. Hence underlying forms with !er!, !ɪr!, and !ʊr! will have to be entered in the North Briton's lexicon and will emerge on the phonetic level generally unmodified by the operation of any rules. In a grammar of American English, on the other hand, three separate vowels in underlying forms cannot normally be assumed. In *work* (say), and *bird*, and *earth*, the vowels are alike, whatever they are, and the language affords the native speaker no cues for making a distinction, which would have no psychological reality even for the ingenious dialectologist. The familiar /ər/, in these circumstances, seems at first a plausible analysis. The difference between Scottish and American dialects, in the /ər/ words, would then be statable as the falling together of American lax vowels in the one lax vowel /ə/ before /r/ plus a consonant, liquid, glide, or major morpheme boundary.[12]

---

[12] It seems necessary here to say !r! plus major morpheme boundary instead of !r! final, for inflected and derived forms of words with final !r! have been reshaped by analogy with the simplices: *carry* and *hurry* show that *starry* and *stirring* are not regularly developed. The analogy belongs to history, not description, which it awkwardly complicates. For example, between a tense vowel and intervocalic !r! in *hairy*, *boring*, and the like, one hears the same glide as in *hair* and *bore;* but the glide of *feel* does not appear in *feeling*, though the two liquids are governed generally by the same rules.

To say 'word boundary' would confuse the absolute final of *star* with the medial !r! of *starry;* and to say 'major' is necessary because the boundary in *error* is not the same as the boundary in *erring*.

The statement would be purely historical and would not enter into the description of any dialect.

Unfortunately for the advocates of single representations, whether /ər/ or Kurath's /ɜ/, it turns out that that statement actually is necessary, as a descriptive phonetic rule, for all of Kurath's and Gimson's dialects except only the northern British. The evidence is clear, though limited to a rather small group of words of which the noun *error* and the verb *to err* provide a good example. In the noun, [ɛr] (with retracted vowel) before a vowel matches Kurath's free mid-central in word-final in the verb; and since *hear* and *heard* are comparable to *bleed* and *bled*, *err* is comparable to *heard* and !ɛ! underlies *heard*, *err*, and *error*—all three. Parallels to *hear* and *heard* include *dear*, *dearth*, *inferior*, *infernal*, *superior*, *superlative*, while *error* and *err* are related as *clerical* to *clerk*, *deterrent* (sometimes with retracted [ɛ]) to *deter*, and *experiment* to *expert*. (I will not risk *eremite* and *hermit*.) Such pairs demand the rule for collapsing the distinctions among the lax vowels in the stated environments before !r!.

And the rule does not complicate the grammar. On the contrary, its incorporation into American and southern British grammars may really simplify them, since the rule allows some hundreds of words to be represented, before it operates, with nothing more definite than lax vowels, instead of particular lax vowels fully specified. So, because *err* happens to be paired with *error*, the grammar of an American dialect will specify !ɛ! as the underlying vowel in both words; but in *work* and *bird* and *earth*, since no such cue as *error* is available, a correct specification, and one sufficient for the phonetic rules, will be lax vowel only, without the full range of distinctive features. In this connection, therefore, northern British will differ from American English in two ways: it will distinguish different lax vowels before !r!, whether or not the !r! is prevocalic; and a grammar for northern British will lack the suggested phonetic rule that lax vowels in the stated environments fall together as !ʌ!. The phonetic rules will operate quite satisfactorily without giving !ʌr! (more commonly taken as /ər/) a place in the American lexicon.

For some southwestern British as described by Gimson, !ʌ! would itself be phonetically adequate and no further rules of derivation would be necessary; but divergent rules would split the other dialects into at least two groups. The *r*-colored vowel of American English and of other southwestern British results from the application of a rule by which the articulation of !r! is anticipated in the sequences !ʌrC! and !ʌr ⚹ !, so that the entire syllabic assumes the *r*-coloring; in other dialects the articulation is not anticipated but perhaps delayed, for a glide develops between the !r! and the syllabic peak. Glides of at least two kinds must be assumed. The mid-central vowel of RP presupposes a schwa glide, which would be extended (as the articulation of the !r! failed altogether) and ultimately absorbed into the stressed vowel, which would thus become long; but in some kinds of southern American, though the long vowel of *fur* presupposes schwa as the glide, the diphthong of *word* requires that the glide be palatal, not velar. This bifurcation into syllabic !ʌ! plus velar glide and syllabic !ʌ! plus palatal glide may be accounted for by a rule which distinguishes two varieties of !r!, with the palatal variety between stressed !ʌ! and an immediately following consonant (and possibly elsewhere). In fact such varieties of !r! have already been distinguished by American phoneticians. Arthur J. Bronstein, for example, describes the palatal variety as follows: 'In another common formation of /r/, the tongue tip remains low, while the central part of the tongue bunches and is raised toward the posterior section of the hard palate.' [13] One might thus score a debating point by noting that the machinery which the present hypothesis demands is independently available.

The necessary sequence of descriptive phonetic rules may now be summarized more directly though still informally.

Rule A. In dialects other than northern British, lax vowels fall together as !ʌ! before !r! plus consonant, liquid, glide, or major morpheme boundary. (No other rule applies to some southwestern British speech as Gimson describes it.)

Rule B. In some southern American dialects, and in at least some others, !r! becomes palatal between stressed !ʌ! and an immediately following consonant, glide, or liquid. The !r! of !ʌr ⚹ ! remains velar.

Rule C. In dialects having the *r*-colored vowel, the articulation of the !r! before a consonant, glide, liquid, or major boundary is anticipated so that the entire syllabic assumes *r*-coloring; in RP, in some varieties of southern American, and in some other dialects the articulation is not anticipated but perhaps delayed, so that a glide develops after the syllabic peak—a palatal glide !ɪ! before the palatal variety of !r!, a velar glide !ə! elsewhere. (This rule accounts for Kurath's 'upglide with progressive constriction' in *r*-ful dialects and for the Trager-Smith sequence /əhr/.)

Rule D. For phonetic accuracy in describing some dialects, one might wish, at this point, to give a rule that the syllabic !ʌ! remains or is somewhat lowered and retracted before the velar glide, but is somewhat raised and fronted before the palatal glide. (These differences are clearly audible, in the old-fashioned Atlanta speech with which I am most familiar, in *cur, her, purr* as opposed to *curt, hurt, pert.*)

Rule E. In *r*-less dialects, the glides of Rule C are now extended in duration as the tongue fails to reach the position for *r*-coloring; that is, the *r*-less

---

[13] *The pronunciation of American English* 116 (New York, 1960).

dialects become so by the vocalization of the !r! in absolute final and before a consonant, glide, or !l!. (The Brooklynese pronunciation, Trager-Smith /əy/, is explained in this way.)

Rule F. The sequence !ʌə!, for the *r*-less, becomes Gimson's [ɜ:] and Jones's [ə:] as the vowel absorbs the matching glide. (Hence RP, and southern American *stir* and *stirred*, Trager-Smith /əh/, which does not rhyme with *bird* when *bird* has the palatal glide.)

The mere statement of these six descriptive rules may be the strongest argument against both Kurath's /ɜ/ and the Trageretic miscellany of /əhr/, /əh/, /əy/, and the like. While preserving the underlying unity of English, it might be said, the rules not only represent but explain its superficial phonetic diversity, to which the Trager-Smith analysis only points and for which Kurath's free mid-central vowel is only a cover symbol. And the rules may have other advantages. They make the distribution of !r! more similar to that of its companion liquid !l!; they suggest the possibility of further simplification by the elimination of Kurath's vowel /ɑ/ in *car* and his semivowel /ə̯/ in *dear;* they relate description to history without confusing the two; by suggesting an answer to a particular historical riddle, they may cast some light on the dark souls of Brooklyn and South Carolina; and they offer one practical suggestion for the making of textbooks and pronouncing dictionaries—such books may be most useful internationally if they write *word* at least as abstractly as *wʌrd* (or *wərd*)[14] and give the phonetic rules in their introductions, so that there will never be an embarrassing discrepancy between less abstract transcriptions and the individual teacher's pronunciations.

But exaggerated claims were to be saved for the conclusion. It is more prudent to say that at least the rules cannot be rejected as 'too complicated', for they add nothing to the complexity of the grammar. They all have independent motivations. All of them, or their analogues, would have to be stated even though English had no such word as *word*.

THE GHOSTLY SNARLS OF LITTERA CANINA

If *word* is usually !wV̆rd! and if *err* is !ɛr!, the *r*-ful consequences for the *r*-less dialects must be accepted: Kurath's /ɑ/ and /ə̯/ must be abandoned, and the liquid !r! will appear in the representations of such words as *beer, beard, hear, hair, laird, lure, bore, board, war, ward, bar, bard, fire,* and *our,*

---

14 The argument about identifying stressed [ʌ] with unstressed [ə] loses much of its interest when one characterizes the two by their distinctive features. The [ə] is simply the back reduction vowel as opposed to the front reduction vowel, but [ʌ] must be further specified as lax, noncompact, etc. The choice of an alphabetic writing is practical, not theoretical.

as well as *beery, hearing, boring,* and the like, where the intervocalic !r! is regularly preserved though the development of the vowels preceding it looks like analogy. Three principal phonetic rules will be necessary for the *r*-less !r!—the first analogous to Rule C above, by which the schwa glide develops between a vowel or diphthong, on the one hand, and !r! plus consonant or plus major morpheme boundary on the other; the second analogous to Rule E, by which preconsonantal and final !r! is fully vocalized; the third analogous to Rule F, by which the glide is optionally absorbed by back vowels except !ʊ!. These three rules alone will account for a good many of the phonetic facts in a number of dialects.

Some modifications and extensions, however, are obviously desirable before these rules and the previous set can be combined in a single sequence. Rule A above provides the first suggestion. When lax !ɪ!, !ɛ!, and !ʊ! fall together as !ʌ! before !rC! and !r ⚹ !, no contrast remains with tense !i!, !e!, and !u! in these environments; and in some dialects the three tense vowels become phonetically lax themselves. In some old-fashioned Georgia speech, for example, *err* is !ɛr! = [ʌ:]; the vowels of *hair, bore, war,* and *bar* are tense; but *beer* has lax !ɪ!, *here* lax !ɛ!, and *lure* lax !ʊ!. Both the !ʊ! and the !u! of this dialect, it should be observed, are noticeably fronted, so that clever people might make !i!, !e!, and fronted !u! a plausible set in at least this respect, that none of them is fully back (or grave). Their phonetic laxness, of course, does not determine their phonemic representation. Apparently they are phonemically tense, since they are tense phonetically in other dialects and since tenseness must be assumed for alternations like *sincere, sincerity.* At some point, therefore, a descriptive phonetic rule must specify the result of the historical phonetic change.

Another feature of some southern American dialects suggests that the scope of Rule B above should also be extended. Just as forms like *work* show a palatal glide (/y/ for /r/ in the Trager-Smith system), so the same glide may appear in *porch, scorch, gorge, march, large,* and *harsh.*[15] The explanations in the two cases are quite similar. For these dialects, that is, the palatal variety of !r! must be assumed not only between stressed !ʌ! and any following consonant but between tense !o!, !ɔ!, or !ɑ! and a following palatal. The palatal glide which accordingly develops is not absorbed by the preceding vowels. *Err* phonetically is long [ʌ:], and there may be no centering glide in words like *pork;* but *work* and *porch* keep their front glides after their back vowels.

Though this statement may later be made a little simpler, for the moment it may be allowed to stand while some of its consequences and relations

---

[15] For a few such forms, see James B. McMillan, *Phonology of the standard English of east central Alabama* 57, 62, 93 (University of Chicago dissertation, 1946).

are explored. In these southern American dialects for which the palatal !r! in certain environments has here been assumed, the *larger* words have made a difficulty for phonemicists, particularly for the followers of Trager and Smith. A palatal glide of course appears in *Elijah* as well as in *larger*, yet *larger* and *Elijah* do not rhyme. The Trager-Smith transcriptional arsenal would give /ay/ for *Elijah*, but then only /ar/, /ahr/, or /ahy/ remains for *larger*. Within the Trager-Smith system, none of these writings is satisfactory. If /ar/ or /ahr/ is chosen, the system does not allow the student to explain why he assigns an upward and forward glide now to /r/ in *larger* and now to /y/ in *Elijah*. If on the other hand the choice is /ahy/, clusters of semivowels must be accepted freely after vowels as well as before them, the already large number of possible syllabic nuclei is much increased, and the suspicion grows that the system does not provide phonemic analyses at all but only an odd phonetic alphabet.

The representation !lārǰ⧣ər! is descriptively and historically much more plausible. Descriptive phonetic rules then make the first !r! palatal but leave the second velar; the palatal and velar glides develop in their respective positions; in both positions the !r! is fully vocalized; after the back vowel !ā! the front glide remains; but the schwa glide in the second syllable is absorbed, and a final rule then shortens the resulting long schwa in unstressed position. The difficulty vanishes with the abandonment of the Trager-Smith alphabet.

The word *Elijah*, with its !aɪ!, suggests the controversy about the tenth or Confederate vowel, for whose addition to the nine vowels of Trager and Smith I share the guilt. The argument began when it was pointed out that with only nine vowels it is impossible to write such common words as *fire*, since all the plausible front and central slots are already filled by *fear*/ih/ or /ih/, *here*/eh/, *fair*/æh/, *far*/ah/, and *fur*/əh/. No symbol remains for writing the vowel of *fire* or *wire*, in which Kurath and McDavid's Atlanta synopsis shows a long, retracted, and raised [a] followed by [ə], as opposed to the [ɑ·ə] of *garden*,[16] and with more or less reluctance, the orthodox were thus obliged to shatter the symmetry of the nine-vowel square.

An argument can be made out, however, for the representation of *Elijah* simply with !aɪ! and of *fire* with !aɪr!, both of them contrasting with the !ār! of *larger*, which has already been justified, and with !aʊr! for *our*, which may conveniently be discussed in this connection. One relevant phonetic rule, though it would not apply directly to the three suggested underlying forms, is the familiar one for the difference in length of vowels and of diphthongs before following voiced and voiceless sounds. It may be phrased as the simple statement that vowels and diphthongs become somewhat shorter

---

[16] *PEAS* 100.

when they are followed by voiceless consonants. The diphthongs of *fire*, *our*, and *Elijah* are therefore longer than those of *fight* and *out*, to which the rule for shortening does apply.

Another of the relevant rules is also needed for more dialects than one and is necessary, in much southern American speech, to account for other pronunciations than those of *Elijah*, *fire*, and *our*. The lax vowel !ɑ!, this rule asserts, is considerably fronted wherever it occurs before a nonintrusive palatal or labiovelar glide—namely, before the !ɪ! and !ʊ! that appear in words with Middle English tense /i/ and tense /u/. Thus the same rule that fronts the first element of the Southerner's diphthong in words like *out*, where the fronting is extreme,[17] will in addition help to explain why *fire* and *far* do not rhyme 'in the piedmont of South Carolina and adjoining parts of Georgia';[18] nor will *Elijah* rhyme with *larger* in dialects where *larger* has its palatal glide, since in *larger* the glide intrudes after a tense !ā! when the rule which strongly fronts the *lax* vowel !ɑ! before NONintrusive glides has already operated. The !ɑ! in the diphthong !ɑɪ! in *fire* and *Elijah* is indeed the lax counterpart of the tense !ā! of *far* and *larger*, but phonetically it differs also by its fronting.

When the two rules which have just been stated have applied, together with the rules for final !r! in *r*-less dialects, the stressed syllabic of *Elijah* will be !ɑ·ɪ!, *fire* will be !fɑ·ɪə!, and *our* !ɑ·ʊə!, the first vowel fronted in each diphthong, and each of the last with two successive glides. For phonetic accuracy, another rule for length or tempo must next be invoked. As Kurath points out, diphthongs in words with Middle English tense /i/ and tense /u/ have fast and slow variants before following voiceless and voiced sounds respectively in both the upper and the lower South.[19] In some speech from the Georgia piedmont, the rule seems to be that diphthongs as in *wide* and *loud*, which are temporally long, are produced by physically short, slow movements of the tongue, while diphthongs as in *white* and *lout*, which have been temporally shortened before voiceless consonants, are made with physically long, fast glides. The stressed syllable of *Elijah*, then, as actually pronounced, is [ɑ·ɛ], and the first of the successive glides in *our* and *fire* must be regarded as similarly reduced in physical length. That fact helps to explain the last rule for words like *fire:* the nonintrusive palatal and velar glides disappear between the long, somewhat fronted !ɑ·! and a following glide or unstressed vowel (in *our* only in connected speech). The approximate end-products of the derivations are *fire* [fɑ·ə] and *our* [ɑ·ə] or [ɑ·oə], which are strikingly similar to the transcriptions in the Atlanta synopsis in Kurath-McDavid.

---

[17] Kurath, *Phonology* 106f.
[18] *PEAS* 122.
[19] *PEAS* 19, 22.

Though the Confederate vowel thus suffers filicide, the ridiculous suggestion should carefully be avoided that with more abstract underlying forms and ordered phonetic rules all phonological problems are now well along toward solution. On the contrary, the proposed rules have not been fitted into the total structure of the phonological component of a grammar; their extremely tentative ordering has been in part expository, not descriptive; and as yet they apply only to some more striking features of a few selected dialects, though their extension to related materials elsewhere (no doubt with modifications) is obviously necessary if the rules are to win any general acceptance. (So for at least twenty-five years in some advanced forms of RP, words like *tire, tower,* and *tar* have rhymed, plainly by the loss of the !ɪ! and !ʊ! from *tire* and *tower* and the subsequent absorption of the final !ə! into the stressed vowel; but the present rules do not exploit these parallels to developments in southern American speech.) The rules, moreover, must offend all readers who wrongly ask them to do what grammars never do and to predict the unpredictable variability of real talk in mixed dialects. To take only one instance, *r*-lessness seems to be losing its old status in some parts of the American South, so that the same speaker may have some words regularly *r*-less, others regularly *r*-ful, and still others flopping back and forth; yet this vacillation does not appear in the rules, a sort of ideal pattern from which raw speech nearly always deviates more or less. The answer may not commend itself even to other students who are willing to try all things: without the rules for the impossibly UNmixed dialect, the objection itself could not be stated, and the field notes of the dialectologist would remain what they have too often been, an unintelligible barrenness.

However that may be, the rules still have some advantages over competing analyses, of which none is beyond criticism. The abolition of the Confederate vowel is certainly an unmixed blessing; another stone on the grave of the post-vocalic semivowel /h/ will not strike everyone as desecration; and the given arguments against /ɜ/, /ɚ/, and /ǝ/ at least deserve discussion. Other benefits too are imaginable. The principles of Trager and Smith, and the ideal of total accountability, were rarely taken in all seriousness, and the few half-hearted attempts to take them seriously led to unpromising complexities like my long and short diphthongs, as in *veer* [vɪə] (with retracted [ɪ]) but *via* [vɪə]. This contrast is better explained by assuming that *veer* is !vir! and applying the relevant phonetic rules. Other ingenious inventions turn out to be as illusory as the long diphthongs. The stressed 'barred eye' for instance, with which Trager and Smith would have to corrupt good southern *beer*—[bɪə] (with retracted [ɪ]) = /bɨh/—is no real English phoneme, nor is the fourth semivowel which they should logically accept in contrasts between length and a centering glide: the *r*-less !r! is a good way to separate words like *bare*, with tense !æ! and a centering glide, from oddities like the sheep's cry, *baa*, or like *pa* and *ma* with the vowel of *bad* in low-country South Carolina.[20] Where no solution is perfect, a less imperfect one should still be welcome.

Exaggeration, however, has got ahead of itself again. The rules which have so far been proposed, combined now in a single set, must speak for themselves as a conceivable alternative to the treatments of final and preconsonantal !r! by Kurath and by Trager and Smith. For simplicity and a minimum of security, the rules are here limited to certain dialects of the American South, principally to my old-fashioned variety of Atlanta speech, though some of the rules are much more widely applicable. Emphatically, their now descriptive ordering is tentative at several points.

Rule i. Lax !ɑ! is strongly fronted before !r! and !ʊ! (the nonintrusive glides in words with ME tense /i/ and tense /u/).

Rule ii. Tense !u! and lax !ʊ! are fronted generally.

Rule iii. Lax vowels fall together as !ʌ! before !r! plus consonant, liquid, glide, or major morpheme boundary. (Cf. Rule A in the previous list.)

Rule iv. In the same environments, tense !i!, !e!, and fronted !u! become lax.

Rule v. Vowels and diphthongs are somewhat shortened before voiceless consonants.

Rule vi. !r! becomes palatal between stressed !ʌ! and an immediately following consonant, glide, or liquid and between !o!, !ɔ̄!, or !ɑ̄! and an immediately following palatal consonant. (Cf. Rule B in the previous list.)

Rule vii. Between any vowel or diphthong and a following !r! plus consonant, liquid, glide, or major boundary, a glide develops—a palatal glide before the palatal !r!, elsewhere a velar glide. (Cf. Rule C in the previous list.)

Rule viii. Lax vowels move slightly toward the end positions for following glides. (Cf. Rule D in the previous list.)

Rule ix. !r! vocalizes (optionally?) before a consonant, glide, or !l! and in absolute final. (Cf. Rule E in the previous list.)

Rule x. Back vowels except fronted !ʊ! absorb following velar glides, with accompanying lengthening if the absorbing vowel is short. The absorption is obligatory for !ʌ!, optional for other vowels. (Cf. Rule F in the previous list.)

Rule xi. Unstressed long vowels are shortened.

Rule xii. The second elements of diphthongs as in *wide*, *loud*, *buy*, and *bough*, though temporally long, become physically short. (That is, the tongue takes a long time to move a short distance.)

---

[20] *PEAS* 165.

Rule xiii. The second element is lost from triphthongs as in *fire* and *our* (only in connected speech in *our*).

Readers will hardly need the warning that these rules may be still further modified and rearranged as they are applied to more and more material.

!l!-*PLAYING*

One minimal defense of the rules for the *r*-less !r! is that they seem to escape some difficulties in which other analyses are trapped: the rules can hardly raise more doubts than Kurath's /ɜ/, /ɚ/, and /ə̣/ or the Trager-Smith maneuvering with the semivowels /y/, /h/, and /w/. A much stronger defense has of course been suggested in the remark that the rules which abolish the phoneme /ɜ/ would be necessary even if the phoneme /ɜ/ had never been invented. That defense may now be elaborated, and first with examples involving the other liquid, !l!.

Historians are of course familiar with the influence of !l! on preceding vowels and with the occasional vocalization of !l! itself, and scholars as different as Joseph Wright and Cabell Greet have independently described similar phenomena in living speech. In 1940, for example, N. M. Caffee reported both the development of glides and the subsequent vocalization of 'Southern "l" plus a consonant'.[21] In some sections of the United States, Caffee said, 'a glide is formed before *l* when it is preceded by any vowel'; and after the glide has intruded, *l* is optionally but frequently lost before *k*, occasionally lost before *m*, *b*, *f*, and *p*. 'When the *l* is lost, the glide vowel originally preceding the *l* is extended to a complete vowel sound and, as far as has been discovered, is invariably formed in the same manner. The back of the tongue is raised, no contact is made by the tip of the tongue, the sides of the tongue may or may not touch the upper teeth, and the back of the throat is constricted.' Though the articulation is vocoidal, 'the speakers themselves who have lost the *l* believe, however, that they form an *l;* and apparently the sound is heard as an *l*, even by those people who regularly have the normal lingual lateral continuant in all positions in their speech.' Citing Greet, Kurath, Stanley, and Wright, Caffee reported the glides and the vocalization from British dialects, from New England, and from Virginia, South Carolina, Georgia, Mississippi, and east Texas.

A number of the forms with vocalization or only glides are particularly troublesome in a Trager-Smith analysis. For example, a good deal of morphophonemic alternation has to be accepted (*fill* /fɪhl/: *filling* /fɪlɪŋ/ etc.), clusters of post-vocalic semivowels are again necessary (*feel* /fiyhl/ and

---

[1] 'Southern "L" plus a consonant,' *American Speech* 15.259–61.

the like), and at least one obvious contrast cannot be written at all, since *million* and *billion* keep their stressed vowels short after !l! has vocalized and so do not rhyme with *paeon* and *eon*: both pairs cannot be written with /iyə/. Such forms provide a test for the rules for *r*-less !r!, which might be expected to have their analogues for !l!.

It turns out that they do. Just as it is necessary to establish a palatal and a velar !r!, so clear !l! and dark !l! must be distinguished. Ideally the distinction should be made for all environments and made along a scale (distinctive features at the phonetic level need not be binary); but in some southern American speech !l! is obviously clear at least before and after palatal glides (*million, hellion, scallion; oil, vile*) and obviously dark at least before !r! (*Elroy*), before !w! (*Elwin*), and before any consonant (*silk, help, Alf, pelt, Elgin*). Final !l! is generally dark, though in the speech here described it is certainly clear after the palatal glide in the words like *oil* and *vile* (contrast the very dark !l! in *vial*).

These statements are sufficient for an admittedly tentative and incomplete account. After the rule that establishes the two !l!s, there must then follow the analogue to Rules vii and ix in the second list above: between any vowel or diphthong and a following dark !l! in the specified environments, a raised back glide develops; before clear !l! in the specified environments, the intrusive glide is palatal; and both !l!s next optionally vocalize in words like *million* and before labials and !k! (not !g!).[22] The products of these rules include a good many actually occurring forms. Front vowels before preconsonantal and final !l! are properly glided (*feel, field, fill, build,* etc.), while *feeling, failing* and the like are properly glideless (since analogy with the simplices did not operate as it did in *beery*); and !l! is sometimes vocalized in *billion, William, silk, milk, help, kelp, elm, helm, helve, Ralph, salve, valve, talcum, solve, revolve, bulb, gulf,* and *polka.*

Yet obvious inexactitudes remain, particularly after back vowels, where in actual speech no glides are heard, and in such words as *file, oil, owl,* and *billion,* where the rules seem wrong in predicting identical successive glides. Happily, the rules for *r*-less !r! again provide the needed analogies. The development of the schwa glide and the vocalization of !r! after the stressed lax vowel in *err* result in a single long vowel, [ʌː]; the similarly developed long vowel in *pattern* is shortened because unstressed. One would expect, therefore, that lax back vowels preceding the raised back glide before dark !l! would be pronounced quite long but without perceptible glide, which seems to be the case in *pull, gull, gulf,* and *doll,* and that the unstressed second syllables of *buckle, opal,* and the like would be the simple back

---

[22] There is no final -!lg!, and syllable-break hinders the vocalization. In a more precise statement, !g! might not need to be excepted. Cf. McMillan 18.

reduction vowel, which also seems correct. Finally, if the model of *pattern* and *buckle* may serve for the identical successive glides, one should hear only one glide in *file, oil, owl,* and *billion,* and the tense back vowels should be heard simply as tense back vowels, since the syllabics of *fraud, load,* and *rood* are commonly up-gliding even without the following ǃlǃ Observing the slight retraction of the vowels in *pill, bell,* and *pal,* one may conclude with some justice that Rules viii, x, and xi for ǃrǃ must be extended to apply to ǃlǃ and that the behavior of the two liquids and of vowels before them does indeed form a single pattern.

HUBRIS

If the defense of the rules for *r*-less ǃrǃ is strengthened by their applicability to ǃlǃ, the irresistible temptation is to push the rules as far as they will go. An enthusiastic yielder therefore suggests that the most striking phonetic peculiarities of his kind of Atlanta talk, which has baffled him and others by its apparent complexity, can actually be traced to two very simple causes: first, the dialect has two reduction vowels, not just one; and second, two corresponding kinds of glide appear between its consonants and liquids and the syllabics that precede them. The behavior of ǃrǃ and ǃlǃ is only a special case of very general tendencies, and those tendencies (to defy Nemesis utterly) may be given their proper names of umlaut and of breaking. Even in speech, the South is distinguished by its Anglo-Saxon heritage.

The existence of the two reduction vowels, ǃɪǃ and ǃəǃ, is obvious in a good many dialects of southern England and the United States. 'All dialects of American English,' according to Kurath and McDavid,[23] 'have a free vowel /ə/ that occurs only in unstressed syllables', and some also have /ɪ/, particularly 'before /s, z, t, d, ǧ, č/.' [24] Similar observations have been made from the very beginnings of American dialectology, professional and amateur. Among southern speakers, Grandgent reported 'unaccented *I*' as strongly dominant in words like *palace, courage, fountain, orange, senate, Monday, naked, college, fishes, goodness, finest,* and *sonnet,*[25] and the keen amateur Joel Chandler Harris indicated the two unstressed vowels in his Uncle Remus stories.[26] More recent observers tell the same story, sometimes with a good deal of vehemence. From east central Alabama, J. B. McMillan coolly reports 'two unstressed syllabic phonemes. . ., /i/ and /ə/';[27] and in

[23] *PEAS* 8f.
[24] Kurath, *Phonology* 123f.; *PEAS* 8f.
[25] *Dialect notes* 1.319–23 (1894).
[26] Sumner Ives, 'The phonology of the Uncle Remus stories,' *Publications of the American Dialect Society* 22.29 (1954).
[27] Op. cit. 26, 67f.

her spirited discussion of 'Southern standards',[28] Katherine E. Wheatley records [ɪ] in syllabic plurals and in such words as *pocket, palace, goodness, naked, sonnet, rabbit, prelate, minute, poem, college, courage, usage, damage, manage, darkness, bucket,* and *honest.* With schwa-users in these words, Miss Wheatley is righteously vexed. The schwa, she says, is 'vulgar,' 'unpleasant to the Southern ear', 'extremely offensive'; and though there may be a good deal of vacillation among Southerners, even in the same word as pronounced by the same speaker, still the extent of agreement among the Cultured is perhaps more significant (in the face of Yankee scepticism): my own lists for old-fashioned Atlanta speech would coincide with Miss Wheatley's lists nine times in ten. Contrasting pairs, for the sake of the sceptical, are not hard to find. A few hours with informants from Georgia, Alabama, and Mississippi will certainly turn up the opposition in pairs like *pagan:chicken, minus:promise, ballot:salad, mattock:rustic, ballot:palate, Stella:belly, Duncan:dunking, gallus:necklace, ballast:Dallas,*[29] or in *chorus: iris, crocus:heiress, robot:cubit, stomach:garlic, mammoth:stinketh, Philip: tulip, Aaron:Reuben, seraph:sheriff, forehead:torrid, sofa:Sophy, mister: misty, comma:Commie, Willa:Willy* (pairs which have been successful with informants from Atlanta to Lubbock, Texas). The contrast is structurally of great importance.

The palatal and velar glides to match the contrasting unstressed vowels have already been seen in the discussions of !r! and !l!, but they are not limited to position before the liquids. Rather generally in the drawling South, the !ɪ! and !ə! appear under changing pitch between lax stressed vowels and following consonants, with the nature of the glide apparently determined in part by the consonants and in part by the vowels themselves; and their common appearance clearly sets off southern speech from the speech (say) of New England. Kurath's synopses suggest the three possibilities. Throughout the Atlantic States, his fieldworkers report, the vowel of *six* is generally unglided; *crib* has either no glide, as in much of New England, or a schwa, with the schwa heavily predominant in most of the South; while *bag* and the dissyllabic *ashes,* which most commonly show no glide in Synopses 3–91, are usually glided in the South, where up-glides and centering glides compete. It is drawlers, then, who favor the glides; and the glides' appearance, and their nature when they do appear, depend both on the vowels and on the following consonants.

To make that statement usefully precise, however, is extremely difficult. There is a great deal of individual and dialectal variation, and even within relatively homogeneous areas not everything is always clear. In the first place, the distinctions that I have assumed between lax and tense vowels,

---

[28] *American Speech* 9.36–45 (1934).
[29] All taken from Oma Stanley, 'The speech of east Texas,' *American speech* 11.159–64 (1936).

short and long, are difficult to agree on. Is the checked vowel of words like *college*, which Kurath describes as 'rather short' above the fall line in the lower South,[30] really to be considered lax or tense? What shall be made of the low front vowel, which in the same area (Kurath says) is 'usually . . . upgliding'? Is it a single vowel or a tense-lax pair (with the tense vowel in words like *bare, half, glass,* and *aunt*); and if indeed it is sometimes tense, is the upglide that commonly accompanies it a manifestation of the tenseness, or is it a glide intruding before the following consonant? How, moreover, shall the consonants be grouped according to the glides which they determine? In particular, do the dentals and alveolars favor schwa glides or no glides at all? Or must one distinguish still more finely, as between !t! and !s! and !n!? A pretended final answer to these and similar questions would only provoke a justified disbelief.

In these circumstances, the answer which is here attempted for old-fashioned Atlanta speech must be plainly labeled tentative, schematic, and nonetheless quite venturesome. To avoid argument, Kurath's description of the correlation between checked vowels and the following preconsonantal glides will be repeated. 'In the Lower South', he says, 'the checked high and mid vowels . . . are normally ingliding'; above the fall line the low-front commonly has an upglide; and in the same area the vowel of *crop* and *college* (here taken as lax) is 'rather short.' Without too great inaccuracy, those values of the glide may be considered typical before dental and alveolar consonants, as in *pit, pet, put, putt, pot;* there no glide is very clearly audible, so that with respect to glide-conditioning, the dentals and alveolars as a group may be considered neutral. The labials, on the other hand, seem to belong with velar !r! and dark !l!. An obvious glide of the schwa variety may be heard between them and the front vowels, and the apparent exception of words like *half* may be disposed of by treating the vowel there as tense (and similarly with such words as *path, grass,* and *can't*). The remaining consonants are the palatals, which condition the palatal glide (like palatal !r! and clear !l!), as might be expected. The !n! in words like *lunch* and *lunge* must be included among them, and probably !k! and !g! after front vowels; but [ŋ] should perhaps be classed with the alveolars as a cluster !ng!, and !k! and !g! after back vowels with the schwa-conditioners.

That classification fits the more obvious facts rather well. Given the inherent tendency of lax vowels to trail off toward the Ruhelage, one would expect the very easily audible schwa glide between the lax fronts and the labials; that such forms do occur widely in the South is a commonplace observation.[31] After back vowels, one would expect the contrasting palatal

[30] *PEAS* 21.
[31] McMillan, op. cit.; Robert Howren, 'The speech of Ocracoke, North Carolina,' *American speech* 37.163-75 (1962); etc.

glide to be less obvious, though sometimes it does overcome both the inherent centralizing tendency in words like *bush, push, gush, hush, much, such* and the shortness of lax !ɑ! in *wash, bosh, watch, dodge.*[32] Finally, one might expect the general centralizing drift of lax front vowels to be simply blocked by the influence of a following palatal, though occasional reports of a very high vowel in such words as *itch* and *inch* may indicate a genuine palatal glide.[33] The most common exceptions to all this, though not the only ones, are the upglides before the voiced alveolar stop in words like *bad* and *bed* and the apparent tensing of lax !æ! (which has already been mentioned) before final and preconsonantal voiceless spirants as in *half, path,* and *grass* and sometimes before final and preconsonantal nasals as in *pan* and *aunt.* That tensing, or its consequences, are widely observable in both British and American dialects. Its phonetic manifestation, in a good deal of the lower South, is either length or an upward glide.

With so much by way of preparation, the phenomena of umlaut and breaking in some forms of Modern English may now be described in moderate detail. Both, it is here maintained, exist in modern dialects, and both should be investigated as possibilities (no more) in any dialect which has the two reduction vowels and the corresponding palatal and velar glides between stressed vowels and the following consonants or liquids. Surprisingly, though the glides which are part of breaking have been frequently observed, the full range of both developments has never been explored; and hence the essential unity of the two processes with one another, with the influence of !r! and !l!, and with parallel developments over the centuries from Old English to modern times—all these things have been missed as well. A venturesome attempt may have this merit: that it will either fail utterly or else brighten some dark corners of history and description.

It is fairly easy to extend the partial account of breaking which has already been given in the description of the glides before consonants and liquids. Principally, the account must be extended (for lax vowels only) to medial consonants and liquids as well as finals; and the point of departure may be a kind of kittenish, female southern speech in which pitch-changes often occur within the stressed syllable of plurisyllabic words and not between the syllables. Twenty years ago, Kenneth Pike remarked briefly on the speech of a female 'graduate student . . . from Houma, Louisiana'.[34] 'Instead of using steps of pitch, or delaying the glide', Pike wrote, 'she tended to give a glide to the stressed syllable at the beginning of the contour even when a stressed one appeared in the same contour with it.' Pike's

---

[32] George P. Wilson, 'Some unrecorded southern vowels,' *American speech* 9.212 (1934); Howren 167; McMillan 44.
[33] McMillan 49 n., citing Wilson 210.
[34] *The intonation of American English* 105f. (Ann Arbor, 1945).

example was the phrase *Northern part*, in which he marked his °3–2 pitch-change not on *part* but within the first syllable of *Northern*. He concluded by adopting the suggestion of C. M. Wise, that the southern drawl is not primarily a matter of intonation but 'rather a system of diphthongization, triphthongization and double diphthongization, affecting vowels. . . .'

Pike was both right and wrong about the drawl. Extensive off-gliding of the vowels is indeed an obvious characteristic of southern speech, but the placing of pitch changes within the stressed syllables of plurisyllabics makes the gliding of the vowels easier to hear. Close listening to the kittenish female turns up a glide not only in words like *rib* but also in words like *ribbon*, which she is likely to pronounce as something like [rɪəbən] (with retracted [ɪ]). The same sort of thing, presumably, is what Wilson describes[35] when he reports a schwa glide before the !l! in *balance, gallon*, and *valentine* and a palatal glide before !š! in *bushel* and *cushion*. In the description of less drawling kinds of southern American, therefore, one must first introduce the proper glides between lax vowels and medial as well as final consonants and liquids, but must then add rules by which these vowels absorb the medial glides but are somewhat assimilated to them. Hence the thoroughly centralized stressed vowel of the less drawling southern *ribbon*, which has often but wrongly been treated as a separate phoneme, /ɨ/ not /i/. The vowel is centralized by the glide which it absorbs, so that the !ɪ! of *ribbon* is further back than that of *richer*, where the consonant is palatal not labial. One may hear similar contrasts in pairs like *picking:pippin, picker:ripper, pitcher:piffle, fickle:Philip, pickle:pillar, heckle:heron*.

Umlaut sometimes enhances the effects of breaking and sometimes reduces them, but it too is immediately explicable as the influence of a consonant or a liquid on a lax preceding vowel. An easy example is the contrast between *ribbing*, with the front reduction vowel in the unstressed syllable, and *ribbon*, with the schwa. In this pair, the greater centralization of the stressed vowel of *ribbon* cannot be explained by breaking, the explanation which serves for the moderate centralization in *pippin* as opposed to *picking*. The vowel of *ribbon* is more fully central than that of *ribbing* or *pippin*, yet the medial consonants in all three words are labials. The immediate explanation must be that the !b! of *ribbon* is even more conducive to the development of a schwa glide than the !b! of *ribbing* or the !p! of *pippin*, and the remote cause must lie in the difference between the reduction vowels, the !ə! of *ribbon* and the !ɪ! of *ribbing*.

That these affect their preceding consonants differently is not only plausible, historically and phonetically; it is also definitely suggested by certain statements in the literature. Arthur Norman, for example, reports

---

[35] Op. cit. (fn. 32).

clear ‼! intervocalically before 'mid-high or high front and central vowels, . . . as in *Dallas*, . . . *jelly, Nelly, pallet.'* [36] In umlauting dialects, the stressed vowels of these words will be more advanced than the stressed vowels of *ballast, bellow, seller,* or *ballot,* where the ‼! is not so clear. Wheatley and Stanley[37] are even more revealing in their comment on the pronunciation of the name *Horace,* where the reduction vowel of their rebel informants was not !ə! but 'centralized [ɪ] or [ɛ].' With all but one of their nine victims, Wheatley and Stanley write, 'the stressed vowel was followed by a retroflex glide for which we use [letters with subscript circle] to show retroflexion, rather than [ɚ], because there is a distinct [ɪ] or [ɛ] quality to the glide which [ɚ] would not adequately represent. These pronunciations differ markedly from that heard in some Midwestern speech, where the word occurs as [hɔɚs]. The difference between the Southern and this Midwestern pronunciation is as marked in the glide as in the stressed vowel.'

To understand the precise mechanism of umlaut, one needs only to add that in umlauting dialects the vowel of *Horace* is distinctly less retracted than the vowel of *horror.* The inherent qualities of the medial consonants and liquids are modified, that is, by the following reduction vowels; the glides which must be postulated before the consonants and liquids differ accordingly; and the lax stressed vowels which absorb the glides are in turn retracted or advanced along a finely graded scale. Among the manifestations of the high front lax vowel !ɪ!, for example, one may find at least four degrees, and perhaps six, by combining the two series *picket, pick, picker* and *ripping, rip, ripper;* and along the low row a moderate ear can sometimes distinguish at least three degrees in *packet, parry, parrot.* An understanding of breaking and umlaut thus allows the prediction of finer phonetic detail than dialectologists have normally observed; for relevant data may escape the observer who has no hypothesis to guide his search through the brute mass of the merely given.

Historians will see immediately that the phonetic rules which are here postulated for some contemporary southern American speech are strikingly similar to the rules for breaking and the umlauts in Old English, and phonologists will recognize the consequences for descriptive analysis (if other investigations confirm my data). Those consequences involve a good deal more than the explanation of particular oddities, though such explanation is also provided. To dispose quickly of a few quaint specimens, one may cite the remark of Joseph Sargent Hall[38] to the effect that the vowel of *hollow* is likely to be somewhat rounded or at least very far back, while the vowel of *holly* is usually unround and less retracted, or the comment of Argus

[36] 'A southeast Texas dialect study,' *Orbis* 5.76 (1956).
[37] 'Three generations of east Texas speech,' *American speech* 34.91 (1959).
[38] *The phonetics of Great Smoky Mountain speech* 28 (New York, 1942).

Tresidder[39] that *'miracle* has a lowered vowel that often becomes [ɛ]', or the puzzlement of George P. Wilson[40] at the centralized vowels of *dinner, sinner, winner* and *better, letter, setter,* or the observation of Carroll Reed,[41] from a very different part of the country, that 'the nuclear [il] of *milk* (and similar words) is strongly velarized', or the eyebrow-raising of Charles K. Thomas[42] at the retracted varieties of !ɪ! and !ɛ! before !r!, !l!, and the labials. Breaking and umlaut undoubtedly operate, to some degree, in many dialects, both of the Confederacy and of less civilized areas.

But the time for quaintness in dialectology is long past, like the heyday of *lighthouse-keepers.* To observe the Alabaman's retracted vowels in words like *cripple, river, dinner, trestle, little, till, pillow,* and *children*[43] is useful indeed, but much more useful if such observation leads to consequences beyond itself. One consequence is that the refusal to accept two reduction vowels will merely lead, in some dialects, to a completely unacceptable multiplication of lax stressed vowels. In the second member of each of the following pairs, umlauters will have a more retracted vowel than in the first—*cereal, mirror; jelly, mellow; parry, parrot; hopping, hopper; putty, putter; bully, buller;* yet without the two reduction vowels the difference is unpredictable, and six vowels must become twelve. Conceivably, that is a structural reason for Confederate indignation at Midwesterners who cannot pronounce *Horace* to suit a southern lady.

A more devastating consequence is one more dilemma for users of the Trager-Smith phonemic system. They are committed to the recognition of a high central vowel, /ɨ/, which McDavid[44] quite accurately observed in transcribing his *ribbon* as /rɨbən/ and his *ribbing* as /ribɨn/, though the alleged contrast is a transparent result of umlaut. A number of unanswerable questions now arise. For one, where does /i/ end and /ɨ/ begin on the scale of four to six degrees provided by *picket, pick, picker,* and *ripping, rip, ripper?* The influence of the front reduction vowel keeps the !ɪ! of *picket* fronter than it is in *pick,* while in *picker* the other reduction vowel causes backing; similarly there are three degrees of frontness in *ripping, rip,* and *ripper;* and the vowel of *rip* is more centralized before the labial than the vowel of *pick* before the palatal. Again, if one phonemicizes the high central (whether or not he knows where he should write it), what defensible theory can save him from phonemicizing retracted /e/ in *heron* (vs. *herring*), retracted /æ/ in *parrot* (vs. *parry*), or fronted /u/, /a/, and /ə/ in *bushy, horrid,* and *hurry* (vs. *pusher, horror, furrow*)? To say that umlaut and

---

[39] 'The speech of the Shenandoah Valley,' *American speech* 12.284–88 (1937).
[40] Op. cit. (fn. 32) 211.
[41] 'The pronunciation of English in the state of Washington,' *American speech* 27.186–89 (1952).
[42] *An introduction to the phonetics of American English*[2] 63, 75 (New York, 1958).
[43] McMillan passim.
[44] *Lg.* 26.330 n.4 (1950).

breaking do not operate with perfect regularity only compounds the difficulty; for irregularity in the operation of the rules will only multiply the different shapes of taxonomic morphemes, which will already be distressingly numerous if *filling* (to repeat an instance) gives us /fil/, *fill* gives /fihl/ or /fihl/, and *filler* an indubitable /fil/. The seductive shapeliness of a system of nine vowels and three semivowels loses much of its attractiveness when once one faces the complications to which flirtation with the aging lady inevitably leads.

But hubris has gone far enough.

IN CALM OF MIND

Though it is not actually of the first importance that the bookkeeping should be correct in every detail, the argument of the preceding sections leads to the following combined set of partially ordered rules. The first seven are preliminary and need not be strictly ordered among themselves, though 3 must precede 4 and 4 precede 6, and though 1–7 must precede the rest. With one or two exceptions, the ordering of those that follow and do the most work is essential but obvious. Together the rules repeat the assertion that the superficial phonetic complexity of old-fashioned Atlanta speech results very largely from the development of characteristic glides before consonants and liquids.

Rule 1. By processes unstated here, some vowels reduce to !ɪ!, others to !ə!.

Rule 2. Lax !ɑ! is strongly fronted before a glide as in *bite* and *bout*.

Rule 3. The tense and lax vowels !u! and !ʊ! are fronted generally.

Rule 4. Lax vowels fall together as !ʌ! before !r! plus consonant, liquid, glide, or major morpheme boundary.

Rule 5. Lax !æ! becomes tense before final and preconsonantal voiceless spirants as in *half*, *path*, and *grass* and (with unspecified limitations) before final and preconsonantal nasals.

Rule 6. Tense !i!, !e!, and fronted !u! become lax before !r! plus consonant, liquid, glide, or major boundary.

Rule 7. Vowels and diphthongs are somewhat shortened before voiceless consonants. (In the following derivations, the operation of this rule is tacitly assumed unless there is some special reason to call attention to it.)

Rule 8. Consonants and liquids in various environments are placed along a scale with three main divisions (sharp, flat, plain?). Specifically:

   a. Normally retroflex or velar !r! becomes palatal between stressed !ʌ! and an immediately following consonant, glide, or liquid and between !o!, !ɔ!, or !ɑ̄! and a following palatal consonant. The !r! of !r ⚹ C! remains velar.

b. Normally dark or velar !l! becomes palatal or clear before and after palatal glides.

c. Normally velar !k! and !g! become palatal after front vowels.

d. Plain (?) !n! becomes palatal (sharp?) before a palatal consonant or palatal glide.

e. Medial consonants and liquids move toward the clear or dark ends of the scale according as they stand before the front or back reduction vowel (!ɪ! or !ə!). The rule does not apply to !r ⚡ V!.

Rule 9. Palatal or velar glides develop before consonants and liquids in certain positions. Specifically:

a. Between any vowel or diphthong, on the one hand, and, on the other, a liquid which is either final or itself followed by a consonant, glide, or liquid, there develops a glide which is palatal before palatal !r! and clear !l!, otherwise velar. The velar glide also develops before !r! plus major boundary.

b. Between any stressed lax vowel, and any prevocalic liquid (except !r ⚡ V!) or any consonant except a dental or alveolar whose neutrality has not been modified by Rule 8, there develops a glide which matches the position of the consonant or liquid on Rule 8's scale. The glides of 9b are distinct from those of 9a.

Rule 10. Stressed lax vowels move slightly toward the end positions for following glides of opposite quality—front toward back or back toward front.

Rule 11. The glides of 9a are extended in duration as the liquids vocalize in certain positions—!l! optionally, !r! perhaps optionally in today's changing social situation. Positions of vocalization for !r! are final and before consonants, glides, or !l! (not before ! ⚡ V!); !l! vocalizes before labials and velars (not !g!), and between a stressed lax front vowel plus a palatal glide, on the left, and a palatal glide plus an unstressed vowel on the right.

Rule 12. Some glides are now absorbed by preceding vowels and diphthongs. Specifically:

a. The glides of 9b are absorbed before a medial consonant or liquid in a plurisyllable.

b. With the exception of fronted !ʊ! before !ə!, lax back vowels and tense !ā! absorb the velar glides of 9a and are thus lengthened. For !ā! before !ə!, the absorption is optional. In unstressed position, long vowels are shortened.

c. The tense back vowels except !ā! absorb velar glides without change. The absorption is optional and sporadic for !o! and !ɔ! before !ə!.

d. Two successive identical glides are reduced to one.

(The basic principle of b, c, and d is apparently the coalescence of matching vocoidal segments—to use Pike's term again. Conceivably, a simpler statement would relate Rules 6, 10, 12, and 14 (below) in a broader generalization having something to do with the rarity of triphthongs and the frequent neutralization of the tense-lax opposition before !r!.)

Rule 13. Before voiced sounds and finally, the second elements of the diphthongs !aɪ! and !aʊ! (with first vowel fronted), though temporally long, become physically short.

Rule 14. From triphthongs as in *fire* and *our*, the second element is lost (only in connected speech in *our*).

Though many things must be wrong with this first effort to predict minute phonetic detail, yet a few examples will show that together the rules do account for a good many distinctive pronunciations in a believable way. The chosen examples are words that might all give some difficulty.

1. *bird* !bV̆rd!: lax vowel becomes !ʌ! (4); palatal !r! (8a); palatal glide (9a); vowel raised and fronted (10); !r! vocalizes (11): [bʌɪd] with raised and fronted [ʌ].

murder !mV̆rdər!: lax stressed vowel becomes !ʌ! (4); first !r! palatalized (8a); palatal glide before first !r!, velar glide before second (9a); stressed vowel raised and fronted (10); both !r!'s vocalize (11); unstressed vowel absorbs following glide, lengthens, then shortens (12b): [mʌɪdə] with raised and fronted [ʌ].

stirred !stV̆r⚹d!: lax vowel becomes !ʌ! (4); velar glide (9a); !r! vocalizes (11); vowel absorbs glide and lengthens (12b): [stʌːd].

2. *err* !er!: vowel becomes !ʌ! (4); velar glide (9a); !r! vocalizes (11); vowel absorbs glide and lengthens (12b): [ʌː].

erring !er⚹ɪn!: stressed vowel becomes !ʌ! (4); velar glide (9a); stressed vowel absorbs glide and lengthens (12b): [ʌːrɪn].

error !erər!: velarity of !r! reinforced (8e); strongly velar glide before first !r!, velar glide before second (9b, 9a); stressed vowel retracted (10); final !r! vocalizes (11); stressed vowel absorbs following glide (12a); unstressed vowel absorbs following glide, lengthens, then shortens (12b): [ɛrə] with retracted [ɛ].

3. *star* !stār!: velar glide (9a); !r! vocalizes (11); !ā! optionally absorbs glide and lengthens (12b): [stɑˑə], [stɑː].

starry !stār⚹ɪ!: velar glide (9a); !ā! optionally absorbs glide and lengthens (12b): [stɑˑərɪ], [stɑːrɪ].

4. *dear* !dir!: !i! becomes !ɪ! (6); velar glide (9a); !ɪ! lowered and retracted (10); !r! vocalizes (11): [dɪə] with lowered and retracted [ɪ].

dearest !dir⚹ɪst!: !i! becomes !ɪ! (6); velar glide (9a); !ɪ! lowered and retracted (10): [dɪərɪst] with lowered and retracted [ɪ].

5. *porch* !porč!: palatal !r! (8a); palatal glide (9a); !r! vocalizes (11): [poɪč].

larger !lārǰ ✳ər!: first !r! palatalized (8a); palatal glide before first !r!, velar glide before second (9a); stressed vowel unfronted because tense (10); both !r!s vocalize (11); unstressed vowel absorbs following glide, lengthens, then shortens (12b): [la·ɪǰə].

Elijah !əlaɪǰə!: lax !a! strongly fronted (2, 10); second element of diphthong physically shortened (13): [əla·ɛǰə] with fronted [a].

6. *fire* !faɪr!: lax !a! strongly fronted (2, 10); velar glide before !r! (9a); !r! vocalizes (11); !ɪ! becomes physically short (13), then disappears (14): [fa·ə] with fronted [a].

our !aʊr!: lax !a! strongly fronted (2); velar glide before !r! (9a); !r! vocalizes (11); !ʊ! becomes physically short (13), then disappears in connected speech: [a·oə], [a·ə] with fronted [a].

7. *million* !mɪljən!: clear !l! (8b); palatal glide before it (9a); !l! optionally vocalizes (11); identical glides reduced to one (12d): [mijən]. (The predicted form with unvocalized !l! is phonetically inaccurate in having a palatal glide before the liquid.)

oil !ɔɪl!: clear !l! (8b); palatal glide before it (9a); identical glides reduced to one (12d): [ɔɪl].

vile !vaɪl!: !a! strongly fronted (2, 10); clear !l! (8b); palatal glide before it (9a); identical glides reduced to one (12d); !ɪ! physically shortened (13): [va·ɛl] with fronted [a].

vial !vaɪəl!: !a! strongly fronted (2, 10); velar glide in unstressed syllable (9a); unstressed vowel absorbs glide, lengthens, then shortens (12b); !ɪ! physically shortened (13) and then lost (14): [va·əl] with fronted [a].

8. *help* !help!: velar glide (9a); stressed vowel retracted (10); !l! optionally vocalized (11): [heʊp], [heʊlp] with retracted [ɛ]. (Note that the glide before !l! ends higher than the schwa glide before !r!.)

bulb !bʌlb!: velar glide (9a); !l! optionally vocalizes (11); glide absorbed and vowel lengthened (12): [bʌ:b], [bʌ·lb].

polka !polkə!: velar glide (9a); !l! optionally vocalizes (11); glide absorbed (by 12c where !l! has vocalized, by 12d before retained !l! if tense !o! is upgliding): [pokə], [polkə].

talcum !tælkəm!: velar glide (9a); stressed vowel retracted (10); !l! optionally vocalizes (11): [tæʊkəm], [tæʊlkəm] with retracted [æ].

9. *picket* !pɪkɪt!: vowels very short (7); !k! palatal (8c, 8e); palatal glide before it (9b; but the effect is only to overcome the inherent centralizing of

the lax vowel); stressed vowel very front (10); any glide absorbed (12a): [pɪkɪt].

pick !pɪk!: like *picket* but without so front a vowel, since 8e does not apply.

picker !pɪkər!: stressed vowel very short (7); !k! weakly velar (8e opposes 8c); velar glide in both syllables (9a, 9b); stressed vowel slightly retracted (10); !r! vocalized (11); glide before !k! absorbed (12a); unstressed vowel absorbs following glide, lengthens, then shortens (12b): [pɪkə] with retracted [ɪ].

ripping !rɪpɪn!: stressed vowel very short (7); gravity of !p! somewhat reduced (8e); weakly velar offglide (9b); stressed vowel slightly retracted (10); glide absorbed (12a): [rɪpɪn] with first [ɪ] retracted. (The rules seem accurate in predicting that the vowel of *ripping* is further back than those of *picket* and *pick;* but the equation with the vowel of *picker* is uncertain.)

rip !rɪp!: short vowel (7); velar glide (9b); vowel definitely retracted (10): [rɪəp] with retracted [ɪ]. (The retraction is greater than in *picker*, where the gravity of the !k! is reduced by 8c.)

ripper !rɪpər!: 8e reinforces the gravity of the !p!, so that the stressed vowel is more completely centralized than in *picker*, *ripping*, or *rip*.

10. *heckle* !hɛkəl!: stressed vowel short (7); !k! weakly velar (8e opposes 8c); velar glide in both syllables (9a, 9b); stressed vowel slightly retracted (10); glide before !k! absorbed (12a); unstressed vowel absorbs glide, lengthens, shortens (12b): [hɛkəl] with retracted [ɛ].

heron !hɛrən!: !r! strongly velar (8e); velar glide before it (9b); stressed vowel definitely retracted (10); glide absorbed (12a): [hɛrən] with retracted [ɛ]. (The rules accurately predict a more retracted vowel than in *heckle*, where 8c reduces the gravity of !k!.)

The proposed rules and their applications should now be clear enough for judgment, one extreme of which will certainly be instant dismissal as irresponsible ingenuity. That extreme will certainly be wrong; but how far wrong is another question. The most hastily lenient judge is sure to observe both the rash ambition and yet the incompleteness of an argument which imposes a sometimes minutely detailed pattern on speech behavior that may seem chaotic. More vigorously condemnatory judges will find out more inaccuracies even than have been confessed—for example, the failure to provide for umlaut through consonant clusters as in *whiskey* and *whisker* or (perhaps) through !r ⚹ ! as in *hearing, hearer.* If amusement should be the majority response, in this case it will hardly be benevolent.

A good many stone-throwers, however, entertain improper guests in their own glass houses. If I am obliged to admit that the description in my *Short introduction* was misguided, I must also say that I see no reason for anyone to defend any longer a high-central vowel phoneme /ɨ/, or /h/ as a semivowel, or Kurath's /ɜ/, /ʊ/, and /ə/. In Kurath's terms, perhaps there is a better argument for a tense low front than for a free mid-central—at least it would help to make sense of the very rapid upglides that become obvious when some southern pronunciations of *bare* and *pass* are played backwards on a tape: they have three vocoidal segments, so that Smith[45] transcribed an Alabaman's *chair* as /čay(y)ə/. In such forms the upglide may represent tenseness. Anyway, there is some excuse for a rashly novel exercise when the established analyses themselves have so many faults.

And the exercise suggests that there is something to be said for MItesian vowel-breeding. An amateur linguist-watcher is much impressed by the attempt to discover more abstract underlying forms than Kurath or Trager and Smith provide, and the phonetic rules are an illuminating device for comparing dialects. As a discovery procedure if nothing else, the attempt to write them compels one to take a general view of facts which are meaningless in isolation.

Since self-education is no excuse for publishing, and a distant follower derives no credit from those he follows, it might finally be said that the present paper makes one or two specific observations of some importance. Two reduction vowels, it maintains, are structurally necessary for some southern American dialects, where umlaut is a live phenomenon, along with breaking; and breaking and umlaut in turn are closely related to the parallel developments before the liquids !r! and !l!. The southern drawl and Brooklyn *woik* are boids of a feather—which is about the right note for an inconclusive conclusion.

Study Questions

[Sledd presupposes familiarity with earlier analyses of American pronunciation, in particular with the Trager-Smith *Outline*, which assumes nine simple vowels, each of which may be followed by three semivowels. The nine vowels are high front /i/ (*pit*), mid front /e/ (*pet*), low front /ae/ (*pat*); high central /ɨ/ (some pronunciations of *dinner*), mid central /ə/ (*putt*), low central /a/ (*pot*); high back /u/ (*put*), mid back /o/ (some pronunciations of *gonna;* "New England short *o*" in *home*), low back /ɔ/ (Southern British *pot*). The three semivowels are /y/ (a glide to high front or mid front position, as in *night* /nayt/), /w/ (a glide to high back or mid back position, as in *out* /awt/), and /h/ (a glide to mid central position, as in *boa* /boh/).

[45] *Lg.* 28.147 (1952).

Nine vowels and twenty-seven combinations of vowel with semivowel add up to the large number of thirty-six, which is increased if vowels can be followed by more than one semivowel (as in /lahyǰ/, a proposed transcription for a Southern pronunciation of *large*.]

1. In the theory of grammar which Sledd assumes, are the phonemic shapes of words, their forms in the underlying system of the language, the same as their physical pronunciations, or are they different? Are Sledd's transcriptions between exclamation points phonemic, or do they represent the actual pronunciations, or do they lie between those two extremes? When Sledd writes *word* as !wʌrd!, does he want his transcription to apply to one dialect or to many? Are the phonetic differences among dialects which he discusses superficial only, or do they touch the common underlying phonemic system? How does Sledd move from his initial transcriptions, like !wʌrd!, toward transcriptions of real pronunciations? How can such rules as his be viewed as attempts to solve, within a different grammatical theory, the problem that Weinreich attempted to solve by his diasystems?

2. Is it an argument for Sledd's rules A–F that (in his view) they would all be necessary for other dialects even if his own dialect did not exist? If his rules for the loss of /r/ do not fit actual pronunciations in mixed dialects, does his idealized description lose its value? Which of Sledd's rules i–xiii apply to the word *beer* (!bir!)? If Rule iv applied before Rule iii, what would happen to the vowel !i! in that word, and what final pronunciation would the following rules predict? Does Sledd ever justify the vocabulary in which the rules are stated (*vowel, consonant, tense, lax, voiced, voiceless,* etc.)?

3. What does Sledd mean by a "reduction vowel"? How many reduction vowels does he assume for Southern speech? How do the reduction vowels affect the consonants which immediately precede them? What determines the glide that develops after a stressed vowel? Is it possible to find just one process in breaking (the development of this glide) and in umlaut, the mediated influence of an unstressed vowel on the stressed vowel of a preceding syllable? Would it be accurate to say that Sledd's whole paper deals with the influence of consonants on preceding vowels? How, in a specific instance, does he explain the differing stressed vowels in Southern pronunciations of *fill, filler, filling?* Why is it advantageous to be able to postulate just one underlying stressed vowel, and not three, in such sets of related words, or (more generally) to be able to explain a great many different pronunciations as the results of a single process?

4. How might sets of rules like Sledd's be used to explain why speakers of different dialects can understand one another quite readily? For the history of pronunciation in *r*-less dialects, what are the implications of the descriptively motivated statement that the *r*-less dialects are really *r*-ful?

5. Why does Sledd say that the rules he postulates can never "predict the unpredictable variability of real talk in mixed dialects"? Is this a recognition of the distinction between competence and performance drawn by Chomsky? Is it a limitation on the explanatory power of the rules? To what causes would Sledd attribute the re-emergence of *r* in Southern speech? Are they the same kinds of causes as those which presumably led to its loss?

William Labov

STAGES IN THE ACQUISITION OF STANDARD ENGLISH

William Labov has done original and valuable work on urban American dialects and on the processes of linguistic change. His Columbia University dissertation, directed by Uriel Weinreich, has been published by the Center for Applied Linguistics: *The Social Stratification of English in New York City* (Washington, D.C., 1966). In that book, Labov starts from suggestions about social dialects in the materials of the Linguistic Atlas of the United States and follows Weinreich's plea that structural dialectology be supplemented by methods of correlating language and culture which have been developed by sociolinguists and students of contact languages. His immediate aim is to identify the social dialects of New York City with greater precision than his predecessors did; his ultimate purpose is to shed light on the complex and little understood causes of linguistic change; and his work has had a strong impact both on the scientific study of urban dialects and on the practices of teachers in urban schools. He has written papers addressed to both interests.

In the following article, Labov draws on materials from his New York study in order to address a question which has puzzled both English teachers and linguists: Why is it that many people of certain social and ethnic groups in northern cities never learn those cities' prestige dialects, even though they and their parents may have been born there? Labov seeks an answer by exploring not just dialect differences themselves, but also attitudes toward them. His findings about the social dialects in one of the monster cities that characterize twentieth-century America are important in and for themselves, but they have been given a more urgent significance by the events of recent years. Riots in Watts, Newark, Cleveland, Detroit, Chicago, Washington, D.C.— in almost every American city which encloses a large Negro ghetto—have emphasized the fact of social cleavage in this country, as well as the fact that one line of cleavage is racial. Such events, and the anxious articulation of their causes, have destroyed the comfortable assumption that all Americans share the same ideal—an ideal based on the values of the middle class. In addition, the outcry for Black control of ghetto schools emphasizes that a system of education based on the inculcation of middle-class values ignores the desires and the needs of a large segment of our population.

Since dialects are so closely associated with class and race, attitudes toward them inevitably reflect other social attitudes toward the groups which speak them. As a consequence, many linguists have felt that one way to attack sharp cleavages among classes is to erase the socially significant dialect features. They have argued that educational disadvantage is a necessary consequence of nonstandard language, since the standard language is the vehicle of education, business, and government; the nonstandard speaker, they have said, can improve his competitive position in the marketplace only if he acquires the

"Stages in the Acquisition of Standard English" by William Labov from *Social Dialects and Language Learning*, 1964. Reprinted with the permission of the National Council of Teachers of English and William Labov.

prestige dialect of those who control it. Hence some "dialect engineers" have urged the abandonment of nonstandard dialects altogether, while others (who have been more influential, perhaps because their position conforms more closely to the democratic process of standardization that Sapir refers to) have urged the development of a kind of bi-dialectalism in which the speaker of nonstandard retains his native dialect but learns also to use standard well enough to operate comfortably with it. Still other linguists have questioned both the morality and the viability of either proposal.

Labov's article thus raises many extremely serious issues which today's student, teacher, and citizen must face up to. What are the class lines in American society? How inflexibly are they drawn? How deep are the correlations of class, race, and dialect? Is it practical to insist that we should all be able to speak middle-class English? Is the insistence moral or democratic? What is the role of the English teacher in a revolutionary situation?

1. INTRODUCTION: THE SIGNIFICANCE OF URBAN LANGUAGE PROBLEMS FOR LINGUISTS

It is frequently said that children learn to speak the English language long before they learn to read and write it, and in its most obvious sense this statement can hardly be disputed. It is evident that the six-year-old child has mastered the greatest part of the machinery of spoken English. Yet there are many stages in the learning of spoken English which cannot be reached until much later in life, and there are skills in the speaking of English which the grade school child knows nothing about. In the following discussion, I would like to present evidence for the existence of such stages in the acquisition of Standard English, and show how this is related to the educational process in the schoolroom. Most of the data will be drawn from a study of the New York City speech community, and primarily from a survey of the Lower East Side of New York completed this year.[1]

This work is part of a continuing interest on my own part, as a linguist, in the study of speech in its community context. One of the major questions that remain unsolved for linguists is the mechanism by which languages evolve and change, and the process that has led to the great diversity of languages in the world today. Part of the answer can be found by a close

---

[1] The most complete report of this work is given in "The Social Stratification of English in New York City," Columbia University dissertation, 1964. The use of quantitative indexes is discussed in some detail in "Phonological Correlates of Social Stratification," in Gumperz and Hymes (eds.), *The Ethnography of Communication*, appearing as the December 1964 issue of the *American Anthropologist*. One aspect of linguistic change of special interest for the problem of school dialects is presented in "Hypercorrection by the Lower Middle Class as a Factor in Linguistic Change," in the proceedings of the UCLA Conference on Sociolinguistics, Los Angeles, 1964.

examination of contemporary changes that are taking place in the speech community. The case of New York City has a special interest, because of the unusually high degree of fluctuation in speech forms that has been reported. Previous investigators had written of extensive variation that was "thoroughly haphazard," and "the product of pure chance." [2] Our studies of the variable elements in New York City speech have shown that this is far from the case: that the use of these language variants is determined by a pattern of social and stylistic norms. We find that there is a continuous and measurable influence of social factors upon language change. We also find, in the course of this work, a series of challenging questions which have immediate application to the problems of education: Why is it that young people, who are exposed to the Standard English of their teachers for ten or twelve years, still cannot use this form of speech no matter how badly they need it? Why is it, Negro parents ask me, that young Negro people who are raised in the North, of northern parents, speak like southerners?

The answers to these questions do not lie in the study of conscious choice. Most of the factors that influence speech performance lie well below the level of conscious awareness. It is therefore possible for us to use the evidence of speech variation in overt behavior to infer the deeper, underlying processes which must be understood if we are to solve the urgent problems of the urban schools. To present the evidence clearly, it will first be necessary to discuss the methods used to study the sociolinguistic structure of the New York City speech community.

2. METHODS FOR THE STUDY OF URBAN DIALECTS

a. Sampling the Population

In studying the urban dialects of the eastern United States, we are quite fortunate in being able to build upon the results of the Linguistic Atlas, which employed the highly systematic methods of dialect geography to study regional variation in the speech patterns of the most stable sections of the population. Kurath further refined and sharpened the methodology of European dialect geographers, and the American Atlas provides a reliable base for our present investigations of urban speech communities. It shows us the traditional regional pattern and allows us to recognize the intrusion of other regional features into the community.[3]

[2] Cf. A. F. Hubbell, *The Pronunciation of English in New York City* (New York: King's Crown Press, 1950), p. 48.

[3] H. Kurath, *Handbook of the Linguistic Geography of New England* (Providence: American Council of Learned Societies, 1939). In the study of New York City, various publications based on the Atlas materials were valu-

A simple approach to the study of urban speech communities would be to apply the methods of dialectology to social strata and attempt to isolate the characteristic speech forms of class groups, ethnic groups, and racial groups. Such an approach would not be adequate, for a number of reasons. Dialectology begins with the laying out of a geometric grid that divides the area to be investigated into sectors; the field worker finds one or more informants within each sector of the grid. An informant must have certain specific characteristics—his age, his education, and his history of residence are important—but within a particular subgroup he is only one of many. It is assumed, for example, that the subgroup of old, uneducated, local residents is reasonably homogeneous. The choice of this typical informant must be dictated partly by convenience, partly by the informant's working habits and his willingness to talk for several days.

The method works well, for several reasons: (1) the important variable is specified in advance as geographic location, and there is no doubt about that; (2) if any characteristics of the informant make him atypical, his eccentricity will show up clearly on the finished maps, for dialect maps are self-confirming; the important regional markers appear as areas of solid agreement, and atypical cases stand out as isolated dots in a large area of uniformity; (3) in dialect geography, we are usually investigating separate speech communities which have little contact with each other, and contamination by direct contact is low.

In studying a complex urban area, these favorable factors are not present. We do not know the significant variables in advance, and there is far more contact within the different segments of the population. We cannot pick out a typical informant by chance or convenience and *then* describe his social characteristics. Instead, we must plan in advance to describe a specific population and then select a representative group from that population. One of the basic approaches to this problem is that of survey methodology. A set of informants is randomly drawn from an exhaustively enumerated portion of the community, and then considerable effort is made to interview every one of these informants. The more inconvenient it is to speak to an informant, the more effort is made to contact him. At the end, there always remains a small group that has refused the interview or eluded the field workers. This group must be sampled in turn by a more intensive approach, to determine whether or not it differs in any important aspect of speech behavior from the main body of informants.[4]

able sources of background data, particularly Y. Frank, "The Speech of New York City" (University of Michigan dissertation, 1948), and H. Kurath, *A Word Geography of the Eastern United States* (Ann Arbor: University of Michigan Press, 1949).

[4] Methods for sampling refusals are discussed in "The Social Stratification of English in New York City," cited above, Appendix D. There are many ways of surveying a population, and the most accurate means are undoubtedly those based upon the procedures of survey methodology. Supplementary surveys of special cross sections, however, can be carried out much more quickly and can provide a great deal of useful informa-

In New York City, this method was carried out for the 100,000 residents of the Lower East Side by utilizing a sample already constructed for a sociological survey.[5] We thus gained all of the rigor of the survey approach, with the data on the social characteristics of the informants, so that we could concentrate entirely upon their linguistic behavior.

b. The Isolation of Contextual Styles

The dialect geographer attempts to isolate the regionally significant variables in the speech of his informants, and these are usually consistent for any one informant. The method of dialectology is therefore not overly concerned with the problem of style: the interviewer is usually quite skilled in putting the subject at ease, and he uses his own judgment in discarding replies that seem to be overly careful. But in urban studies, many of the significant variables are not constant in the speech of the informants; they vary continuously over the full range of possibilities. Furthermore, the informant is not necessarily an eager and congenial respondent: he may be pressed for time, suspicious, or only half willing in his response, and the field worker cannot expect complete success in creating the same informal atmosphere for each interview. Different class groups have different conceptions of the appropriate style of speech for an interview. In our interviews, we assumed that informants would normally use a style of speech that they, consciously or unconsciously, considered appropriate for the interview situation. We defined this style as careful speech. We made no attempt to judge from our own immediate impressions whether this was careful or casual: we assumed that the speaker had another style, a *more* casual style, that he used with his family or friends when the interviewer was not present.

The problems produced by wide changing variability and by the ap-

---

tion. A rapid survey of one characteristic of department store employees is discussed in Chapter III of the reference cited above, which tested the general hypothesis that any groups of New Yorkers who show socio-economic stratification will also be stratified by their use of (r).

[5] This sample was constructed by Mobilization for Youth's research staff after an exhaustive enumeration of all of the residents of the area. They selected 1,250 informants and completed interviews with 988. The linguistic survey, conducted two years later, was concerned with the 450 adult native speakers of English in the MFY sample. Thirty percent of these had moved from the area; of the remainder, 195 were randomly selected as the target sample for the linguistic survey. A total of 81 percent, or 157 informants were interviewed by the methods described. The data given here are based on 81 informants interviewed at length who were born and raised in New York City. [The comparable analysis for those who were raised outside of New York City allows us to distinguish those patterns which are peculiar to the city itself.] It should be noted that the pattern of social and stylistic stratification given here is so regular that it appears in subsections of the sample as small as 25 informants. Linguistic behavior, as measured here, is far more regular than most other forms of social behavior. It can be stated with considerable certainty that such relatively small samples are adequate for many forms of linguistic research if the informants are selected in a systematic manner and the biases of selection are minimized.

propriateness of careful speech in an interview were the problems that previous studies of New York City could not solve. We set about finding ways to isolate, elicit, and define the most casual style of the speaker, within the framework of the interview. The interview itself was constructed about several topics which were designed to elicit casual or spontaneous speech. One of these was a discussion of childhood rhymes and folklore. We found, for example, that careful speech could not be used by the informant when he repeated such rhymes as:

> Glory, glory, hallelujah
> The teacher hit me with a ruler,
> The ruler turned red
> And the teacher fell dead
> And that was the end of her.[6]

Another topic which was effective in overcoming the constraints of careful speech was the "danger of death." The informant was asked, at a particular point in the interview sequence, if he had ever been in a situation where he was in serious danger of being killed. If the informant had such an experience to retell, he usually became involved in the emotional tension of the situation as he recalled it, and he no longer concentrated on the task of maintaining careful speech patterns.

In these two situations and three others, we found that casual or spontaneous speech was likely to occur. The actual occurrence of this style was defined by the presence of at least one of five "channel cues": changes in tempo, volume, pitch, breathing, or laughter. If any one of these cues was present in one of the five situations designated, we measured the linguistic variables of that utterance under the heading of "casual speech." Then, in the more formal direction, we added a series of contexts in which more and more attention was paid to speech: the reading of a text, the pronunciation of isolated words, and the comparison of minimal pairs of words that differed only by the variable in question.

c. The Phonological Variables

Five chief phonological variables were measured throughout the various styles and various social groups in the New York City population. One of these was the form of the first consonant of *thing, three, thought,* etc.

---

[6] Note that *hallelujah* and *ruler* rhyme; this is perfectly regular in the [r]-less pattern of casual speech, but in the careful speech of many New Yorkers, *ruler* will be pronounced [rʊlə] and the two words will not rhyme at all. In casual speech, we also find that the final word *her* may be pronounced as [hʌ], with considerably greater effect than the careful style, [hə].

Sometimes New Yorkers say [θɪŋ], with a fricative consonant; sometimes they use a stop consonant [tɪŋ] and sometimes a combination of the two, an affricate as in [tθɪŋ]. The prestige form, as elsewhere in the United States, is the fricative form, [θɪŋ]. In our analysis of the tape recorded interviews, every single occurrence of this variable was counted—not only those in stressed, short replies—and from this count a quantitative index was constructed. If a person always said [θɪŋ], his index score would be (th)-00. If he always used stops, as in [tɪŋ], his score would be (th)-200. In practice, no native speaker uses only stops: scores varied from 00 to a high of 150. A typical performance for one informant, a white collar worker, would be:

Casual speech	*Careful speech*	*Reading style*	*Word lists*
(th)- 35	20	05	00

A working man, of Italian background would typically show the same pattern of declining index scores with increasing formality, but at a higher level:

105	75	35	25

A college educated professional might show only a trace of the nonstandard form and follow the same pattern at a lower level:

19	15	00	00

When the values for all of the informants in the survey are calculated and averaged, the regular pattern of Figure 1 is obtained. Here the horizontal axis represents the range of contextual styles, and the vertical axis the range of (th) index scores. The immediate interest here is in the relation between socioeconomic stratification and the use of (th), so the average index scores for a number of socioeconomic subdivisions of the population are plotted and connected along straight lines. The socioeconomic ratings are based upon an objective index which is the combination of three indicators: the occupation of the informant, his education, and the income of his family in relation to its size.[7] The ten point scale for this index is broken up into subgroups which are named informally in Figure 1. The result is a regular pattern of stylistic and social stratification, in which the two lower groups, "working class" and "lower class" informants, show a much higher degree of nonstandard forms than the "middle class" groups.

There are two aspects to this regular pattern. On the one hand, we see regular social stratification at every level of stylistic performance. From the middle class standpoint, the stigmatized form [tɪŋ] is a marker of lower

[7] For details on this index, see "The Social Stratification of English in New York City," Ch. VII.

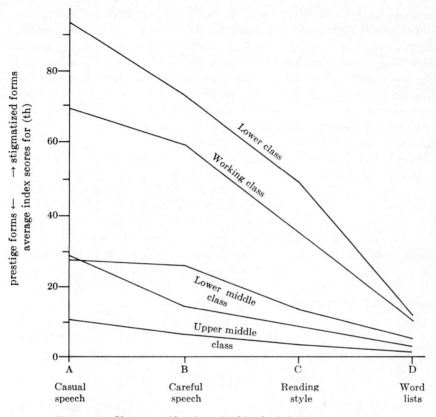

Figure 1 Class stratification of (th): the initial consonant of
thing, through, three, etc.

class and working class speech. Although the middle class speaker uses a small percentage of stigmatized forms himself, he is not aware of this fact. From his point of view, socioeconomic differentiation is the most obvious kind of regularity. Yet the opposing aspect is equally striking in an examination of Figure 1. Almost all New Yorkers behave in the same way in their regular transition from a greater to a lesser use of stigmatized forms with increasing formality of context. The other variables studied reveal this same duality of stratification in the speech community.

d. The Subjective Evaluation of Linguistic Variables

The preceding discussion has shown that New Yorkers generally agree in their social evaluation of (th), if we are to judge by their regular shift of style towards the standard fricative form. A few individuals, mostly from the lower class, do not show this shift: they are "outside" the pattern, and they will be a group of particular interest to us in studying the problems of teaching Standard English. But first we would like to penetrate more deeply into the question of subjective evaluation. Is there any connection between the pattern of performance and the attitudes and value judgments of the speakers? The problem is complicated because people react to speech as a whole, and they seldom are aware of what they like or dislike in the speech pattern of others. There is no socially regulated vocabulary that can be used to communicate this information.

In the study of New York City, a test was developed which successfully isolated and measured the unconscious subjective reactions of the informant to individual variables in the speech of others.[8] The uniform nature of these reactions was surprising. Although New Yorkers vary widely in their use of (th), most of them can detect low prestige variants of this feature in the speech of others and downgrade the speaker who uses the nonstandard forms. For example, the proportion of informants who showed the ability to detect and stigmatize nonstandard (th) forms in the subjective response test was 82 percent. The greatest concentration of those who were insensitive to (th) was among lower class speakers.

	% of (th)-insensitive subjects
Lower class	42
Working class	24
Lower middle class	19
Upper middle class	8

Furthermore, it was surprising to learn that those who showed the highest use of the nonstandard forms in their own speech were often among the most sensitive in detecting and stigmatizing these forms in the speech of others.[9] Although the informants of Italian background showed many more [t] and [tθ] forms in speech than those of Jewish background, they showed only half as many who were insensitive to (th): 14 percent for the Italians as against 27 percent for the Jewish group. An even more striking

---

[8] The details of this test are given in the reference cited above, Ch. XI, and in "Subjective Dimensions of a Linguistic Change in Progress," a paper given before the Linguistic Society of America, Chicago, December 1963. Further discussion of subjective reactions is given below.

[9] It should be noted that this test does not attempt to measure the entire range of subjective evaluations possible, but only those which reflect the suitability of a speech form for various levels in the occupational hierarchy. The subject marked each of the samples of speech that he heard according to the highest of seven job classifications which the speaker could hold, "speaking as she does." These ratings show the subject's recognition of the value system overtly endorsed by the schools and other social institutions: it is essentially a middle class value system. Other value systems exist, and their analysis is important for an understanding of the speech community.

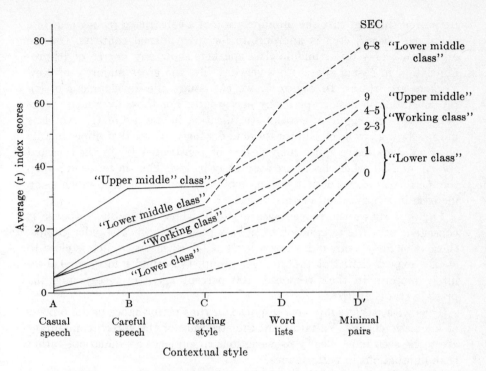

SEC

6–8 "Lower middle class"

9 "Upper middle"
4–5 } "Working class"
2–3 }

1 } "Lower class"
0 }

"Upper middle" class"

"Lower middle class"

"Working class"

"Lower class"

A	B	C	D	D'
Casual speech	Careful speech	Reading style	Word lists	Minimal pairs

Contextual style

Figure 2 Class stratification of (r) in *guard, car, beer, beard,* etc.

comparison can be made between men and women. Men showed much higher index scores for (th) than women: in fact, they used on the average more than twice as many nonstandard forms. But only 9 percent of the male informants were insensitive to (th) in the subjective reaction test, and 30 percent of the women were insensitive to this variable.

On the whole, it appears that the subjective responses of speakers are more uniform than performance. When a new prestige pattern enters the language, it is accepted on the level of unconscious subjective response before it achieves uniformity in actual usage. The case of final and preconsonantal (r) in New York City illustrates the dramatic character of such a shift in response. Figure 2 shows the pattern of social and stylistic variation in the use of (r); again, the horizontal axis shows the range of stylistic contexts, and the vertical axis shows the average index scores for the new prestige feature (r).[10] It is evident that all classes agree, from their

[10] In the notation used here, parentheses enclose a *linguistic variable,* while brackets indicate, as usual, a phonetic transcription. The variable (r) is the percentage of plainly constricted phones in all of the words where historical [and orthographic] *r* appears in final and preconsonantal position. The word classes in which *r* follows a mid central vowel—*her, were, bird, work,* etc.—are not included, as these form separate indexes. Where the following word begins with a vowel, as in *four o'clock,* the occurrence of *r* is noted as an example of intervocalic, not final position.

pattern of shifting, that the pronunciation of a constricted [r] in words like *guard, car, board,* etc., is appropriate for more formal contexts. On the other hand, only upper middle class speakers show any degree of [r]-pronunciation in casual speech; in everyday life, the great majority of New Yorkers are [r]-less. In Figure 3, we can study the development of [r]-pronunciation in casual speech by age groups. For those over forty years old, there is no significant social stratification in the use of (r). All class groups show a low level. But for those under forty, we see that upper middle class speakers use a quite high degree of constricted (r) in their casual speech, and all other classes are absolutely [r]-less. Thus in terms of objective performance, we do not see an increase in the use of [r] so much as an increase in stratification of this variable.[11]

Figure 4 shows the percentages of those whose subjective response is consistent with the recognition of [r] as a prestige form. The older groups, those over forty years old, show a level of (r)-sensitivity which is close to chance expectation. But the younger group, those under forty, are absolutely uniform in their response: 100 percent agree in recognizing the prestige status of [r].

Thus we see that subjective response outruns performance in the process of linguistic change. Variations in the structure of the speech community are to be seen most clearly as variations in subjective evaluation, rather than fluctuations in performance.

In addition to the subjective response test, a *self-evaluation test* was used in which the informant was asked to choose one of several pronunciations as the form that he actually employed most often. The answers to these questions had no relation to performance, but they did reflect the pattern of evaluative norms that the informants had already given us in their shifts of style and in their subjective response tests. At least as far as sound patterns are concerned, the speaker hears himself as speaking the norm that he considers correct.

We were interested in exploring further the speakers' feelings of security or insecurity about their own speech: that is their anxiety or motivation for improving their speech in terms of middle class values. For this purpose, we turned to words which had socially significant variants and which had received a great deal of public attention. Alternate pronunciations were given for eighteen such words, such as [ant, ænt], [lɛnθ, lɛŋθ], [ɛskələtə, ɛskjʊletə]. The informant was asked to circle the number of the variant that he considered correct. He was then

---

[11] The evidence of the department store survey, noted above, confirmed the findings of the survey of the Lower East Side in this respect. The distribution of (r) among department store employees by age levels showed no overall increase if the three stores were taken together; we did find an increase in stratification, for the differences between the stores were by far the greatest for the youngest employees.

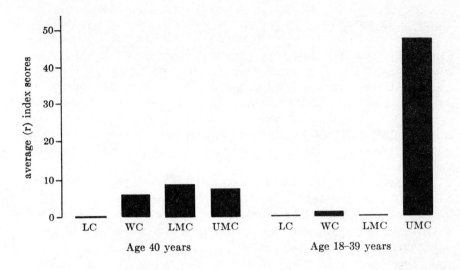

LC: "Lower class," SEC groups 0–1   LMC: "Lower middle class," SEC groups 6–8
WC: "Working class," SEC groups 2–5   UMC: "Upper middle class," SEC group 9

Figure 3 Class stratification of (r) by age in casual speech

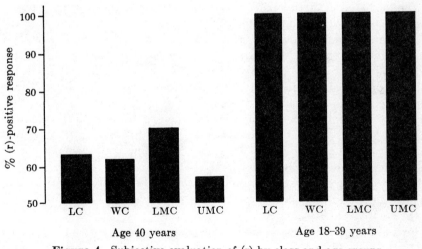

Figure 4 Subjective evaluation of (r) by class and age groups

asked to check the form that he usually used. The number of items in which the choices were different formed the "index of linguistic insecurity." This index represented the willingness of the speaker to recognize an exterior standard of correctness. For upper middle class speakers, the index was low: one or two out of a possible eighteen. For lower class speakers, it was often zero: as one person said, "How could I speak any other way than I do?" Working class speakers showed higher indexes, but by far the greatest amount of such insecurity was shown by lower middle class speakers: white collar workers, substitute teachers, and the higher ranks of skilled workers. The term *insecurity* expresses only one aspect of the situation; one can look at the matter the other way around and say that this recognition of an external standard of correctness is an inevitable accompaniment of upward social aspirations and upward social mobility.

Through the various means described here, we succeeded in penetrating deeper into the structure of linguistic behavior than earlier studies of urban speech had done. We would now be inclined to define a speech community as a group of people who share a set of common norms in regard to language, rather than as a group of people who speak in the same way.

3. THE ACQUISITION OF STANDARD ENGLISH BY CHILDREN

a. The Gradual Development of Adult Norms

The first section of this paper was concerned with the various types of linguistic behavior shown by adults. We can now turn to the question of the acquisition of these norms and levels of behavior by children. The sample of informants under twenty years old was not as systematic as the sample of adults in the study of New York City; we depended primarily upon the children of our adult informants, and it was not possible to obtain a high percentage of the total sample population. Fifty-eight children of the New York City informants were interviewed, ranging from eight to nineteen years of age. The evidence brought forward in this section is consistent with that of the preceding, but the type of sampling used does not permit the same high level of confidence in the conclusions. We may consider the following outline of the acquisition of the levels of competence in Standard English as a series of tentative statements to be confirmed by further study in the New York City area.[12]

First of all, we may look at the overall performance of young people in all

---

[12] The data given in this paper as a whole apply primarily to New York City. There is reason to think that the behavior of the Lower East Side informants is characteristic of linguistic behavior within the city as a whole, and that regional differences within New York are minor. Several supplementary studies have given essentially the same results as the survey of the Lower East Side. On the other hand, it has been possible to show in great detail how New York City informants differ from those who were raised outside of the city. The two variables discussed here, (th) and (r), are the ones which are most general in their application, and which are essentially the same for the New York and non-New York informants. The principles of sociolinguistic organization illustrated here are therefore more general than the limitation to New York City would imply.

of the measures outlined above: their use of the linguistic variables in the various contextual styles, their subjective response tests, and their self-evaluation tests. The overall percentage of cases in which they follow the predominating pattern of the adult community climbs gradually as they approach adult status:

Age	% Conformity with Adult Norms
8–11	52
12–13	50
14–15	57
16–17	62
18–19	64
(20–39	84)

We can view this process of acculturation most clearly if we examine families with more than one informant below the age of twenty. The table given above reflects a rather uneven distribution of informants in the various age groups; but if we take brothers and sisters within the same family, we can minimize fluctuations due to factors other than age. Figure 5 shows the percentage of agreement with adult norms shown by members of twenty-eight families. Here the horizontal axis represents the age of the informants, and the vertical axis the percentage of agreement. Points representing members of the same family are connected along straight lines.

Figure 5 shows graphically the process of acculturation which is often described in less specific terms. The linguistic indicators give us a precise measure of the extent to which the young person has grasped the norms of behavior which govern the adult community. It can be seen that some families begin this process relatively high in the continuum: middle class families are to be found near the top of the diagram, together with a few working class families. Some working class families, and all of the lower class families, are to be seen operating at a much lower level of conformity to adult norms. Despite this great variation in relative position, we see that the slope of most of the lines is similar. Some working class and most lower class families are apparently too far removed from the middle class norms to assimilate them efficiently, and we can see that those youngsters who are below 50 percent at eighteen or nineteen years old will probably not reach any significant degree of conformity while they still have the learning ability to match performance to evaluation. At the ages of thirty-five or forty, these individuals may be able to evaluate the social significance of their own and other speech forms, without being able to shift their own performance. At the same time, there is also a correlation between those

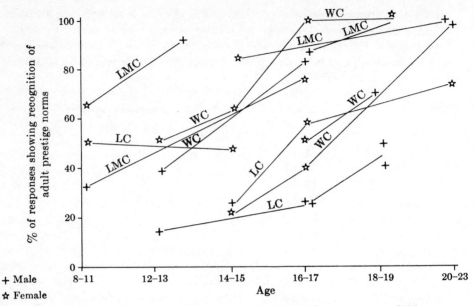

Figure 5   Acquisition of prestige norms in families with two or more children

families that expressed the most hostility to middle class norms of social behavior, and those who appeared low on Figure 5. We can infer that there are other values operating to produce the differential of Figure 5, beyond mere differences in familiarity with middle class patterns.

b. Levels in the Acquisition of Spoken English

From some of the evidence discussed above, and from other details obtained in the interviews with young people, we can construct a model of six stages of the acquisition of the full range of spoken English.

(1) **The Basic Grammar.** The first level is the mastery of the main body of grammatical rules and the lexicon of spoken English, in such a form that the child can communicate his basic needs and experiences to his parents. This stage is normally achieved under the linguistic influence of the parents— that is the case with all of our younger informants, who are at least third generation New Yorkers.

(2) **The Vernacular.** The second stage is the most important one from the point of view of the evolution of the language. In the preadolescent years, roughly ages five to twelve, the child learns the use of the local dialect in a form consistent with that of his immediate group of friends and associates. At this stage, neighborhood dialect characteristics become automatically established responses in the pattern of everyday speech, and the influence of

the parents is submerged under the influence of the peer group. It is during this period that the child begins to learn to read in school.

(3) Social Perception. The third stage begins with early adolescence, as the child begins to come into wider contact with the adult world. The social significance of the dialect characteristics of his friends becomes gradually apparent to him as he becomes exposed to other speech forms, even while he himself is still confined to the single style of his own vernacular. At the age of fourteen or fifteen children begin to respond to the subjective reaction test with patterns that resemble the adult pattern.

(4) Stylistic Variation. In the next stage, the child begins to learn how to modify his speech in the direction of the prestige standard, in formal situations, or even to some extent in casual speech. The great turning point seems to be exposure to a group larger than the neighborhood group in the first year of high school. In our sample, for instance, we find that the number of stops and affricates used for (th) differs greatly between those speakers who have never been to high school and those who have had at least one year.

(5) The Consistent Standard. It is not enough to be able to use standard speech forms sporadically. The ability to maintain standard styles of speech for any length of time is often not acquired at all. At best, some New Yorkers may be able to add a few corrected forms to their speech patterns. The ability to switch to a consistent style of speech and maintain that style with reasonable consistency is acquired primarily by the middle class groups. In Figure 2, such consistency can be seen as a goal of the lower middle class group. The lower middle class line for (r) ranges from a very low position to the highest position, crossing over the upper middle class line in the two most formal styles of speech. This mobility of the lower middle class is apparently an important factor in the evolution of new and consistent styles of speech.[13]

(6) The Full Range. Some speakers attain complete consistency, or something close to it, in a range of styles appropriate for a wide range of occasions. Comparatively few New Yorkers attain this level of skill in speaking, and those who do are mostly college educated persons with special interest in speech. In the case of (th), quite a few of our subjects did use the fricative form all of the time. We also found that there were many subjects who did not depart at all from standard syntax and word morphology. This mastery of the prestige forms seemed to accompany a certain rigidity of linguistic style: few of these speakers seem to have retained the ability to switch "downwards" to their original vernacular. On the other hand, there was a continual shift in the percentage of (r) used, but not one of our in-

---

[13] See "Hypercorrection by the Lower Middle Class . . ." cited above.

formants who was raised in New York City had achieved complete consistency in the use of the prestige form.[14]

From this outline, it is plain that the relations between learning to speak and learning to read are not as simple as they have been sometimes said to be. The pattern of the vernacular is not fully formed when the child first learns to read, and there are many further steps in the mastery of spoken English which are still beyond his horizon. And success or failure in learning to read may have a strong effect upon the development of these other verbal skills.

By examining linguistic changes in progress, we have seen that the ability to perceive the social significance of dialect differences precedes the acquisition of consistent prestige styles in Standard English. For example, in the subjective evaluation of (r), we find that there is a sudden increase in the recognition of the prestige status of (r) for the group of sixteen–seventeen year olds. For eighteen–nineteen year olds, there is almost the same total agreement in the recognition of (r) as for the young adults, the twenty to thirty-nine year olds. At the same time, only the upper middle class speakers show any ability to use (r) in their everyday speech. Since the great majority of the members of the adult community agree in the evaluation of speech forms, why then do most New Yorkers fail to acquire levels (5) and (6) in the series sketched above?

c. Obstacles to the Acquisition of Standard English

The regular patterns of social stratification in the use of linguistic variables reflect a balance of forces, rather than a simple, overall trend. On the one hand, the vernacular of the New York City speech community evolves in its own consistent pattern, following a mechanism that is not yet wholly understood. On the other hand, the New York City speech community has also maintained prestige patterns borrowed from other communities: from England, New England, or most recently, from (r)-pronouncing areas outside of the city. While almost everyone recognizes the middle class values inherent in this borrowed prestige pattern, there is a wide range of differences in the actualization of this pattern. We can consider the following bases for such a range of performance.

(1) Isolation. It is possible that working class and lower class speakers are

---

[14] Throughout this paper, I have used the conception of stylistic levels which is most commonly employed in the discussion of social variation. However, this approach in the New York City speech community leads to a multiplication of structural devices that seems increasingly unrealistic as we gather more data. It is possible to view the sociolinguistic structure as a single complex, within which continuous variation occurs along the social and the stylistic dimension. Cf. "The Linguistic Variable as a Structural Unit," paper given before the Washington Linguistics Club, Washington, D.C., November 1964.

simply not as familiar with the prestige norms as middle class speakers—
that they have less opportunity to hear the prestige dialect. At one time,
this may have been an important factor, but it is clearly becoming less
important with the development of the mass media. The great majority of
prestige figures on radio and television in the New York City area use the
prestige dialect consistently. Furthermore, the conditions of daily life in a
large city permit a considerable amount of interaction between speakers of
various levels.

(2) **Structural Interference.** It is also possible that there are mechanical
constraints upon the linguistic performance of some speakers, proceeding
from differences in the structure of their vernacular and the structure of the
prestige pattern.

We can see such interference in the case of a young New Yorker who
enters the sixth grade speaking a vernacular in which *bad, bared*, and *beard*
are completely homonymous, together with thousands of other words in
these classes. If we add to this list the homonymy of *laud, lord*, and *lured;
god* and *guard; dot* and *dart; pin* and *pen;* it is apparent that a great many
new distinctions must be learned if the child is to master the Standard
English spoken by the teacher.

In the case of the new population of in-migrants from the South who
speak a nonstandard dialect, or in the case of the Puerto Rican group, such
interference may be important. It is not as likely to be a strong factor in
the speech of the main body of New Yorkers, who began to acquire early
in life the pattern of stylistic shifting which carries them from their basic
vernacular to the prestige forms.

Nevertheless, an important step in the study of any such system of social
stratification is to attempt an analysis of the vernacular of each social
group, showing the internal relations of the elements within each system.
(See footnote 14.) This analysis will be essential for the understanding of
linguistic change, and it will isolate the differences between systems which
must be adjusted in the mastery of Standard English.

(3) **Conflict of Value Systems.** It can easily be seen that any systematic
differences between dialects of English in New York City are small in
comparison with the similarities. One can hardly imagine a theory of
mechanical constraints which could account for the dilemma proposed at
the beginning of this paper: How is it that young people who are exposed
to the Standard English of their teachers for twelve years cannot reproduce
this style for twelve minutes in a job interview? The problem is parallel to
the more serious question as to how a student can sit through eight to ten
years of school without learning to read more than a few words. Those who
feel that they can solve this problem by experimenting with the machinery
of the learning process are measuring small causes against large effects.

My own feeling is that the primary interference with the acquisition of Standard English stems from a conflict of value systems.

Language may be looked upon as a system for integrating values. Linguistics has made the most progress in analyzing the cognitive component; but many elements of language (certainly not all) are imbued with non-cognitive values as well, and the total information conveyed in these non-cognitive functions may outweigh the cognitive information. In our subjective reaction tests we have studied only those values which follow the middle class patterns: the suitability of a speech form for various occupations. But there are other values, values which support the use of the vernacular style of the working class, and the social stratification of language seen in Figures 1–5. There are many New Yorkers, for example, who feel no desire to be identified with middle class, white collar workers. They deliberately turn aside from white collar jobs in seeking lower skilled, lower paid manual work. Identification with the class of people that includes one's friends and family is a powerful factor in explaining linguistic behavior. Furthermore, I believe that we can establish that the working class style of casual speech has values strongly associated with masculinity. In the work now being carried on in Harlem and other parts of New York City, we plan to explore these value systems.

There are also negative factors in the conflict of value systems. The adolescent peer group exerts strong pressure against any deviation in the direction of middle class standards. This is a type of behavior that we would like to investigate in more detail; there is a great deal of anecdotal evidence of such pressure, but it consists mostly of recollections of striking incidents in the past. Evidence to the contrary—group approval of the verbal proficiency of a member—might not be so striking and therefore would not appear in anecdotal evidence. Therefore we need observations of group pressures upon language behavior as these pressures operate. If it is true that adolescent groups do not permit free experimentation with middle class language styles, and that they penalize members who try to put into practice the teaching of the schools,[15] then the practical problem of urban dialect engineering will have such group constraints as a major focus. It will be necessary to build into the community a tolerance for style shifting which is helpful in educational and occupational advancement.

Another negative factor undoubtedly exists in the conflict of values symbolized by the difference between the teachers' speech and the students'.

---

[15] The current program for research in Harlem among teenage speakers is designed to obtain further evidence on this point. No one would deny that such tendencies exist; the question is, to what extent do they influence behavior? Only quantitative methods can answer such questions; after a certain point, anecdotal evidence only confuses the issue.

Although English teachers have been urged for many years to treat the nonstandard vernaculars as simply "different" from Standard English, it is clear that the prevailing attitude is that the students' vernacular is "bad English," "incorrect," and "sloppy" speech. It would be surprising if this were not so. The survey of New York City shows that such opinions of the teacher reflect an almost universal sentiment of the speech community.[16] The conflict is a covert one: both teacher and student may be only partly aware of the value systems which bring them into unyielding opposition.

Most teachers in the New York City system probably follow the pattern of group 6–8 in Figure 2 for a great many features of speech. In casual speech, they unconsciously use forms which they themselves stigmatize in the speech of others. When they pronounce words in isolation, they use an even higher percentage of prestige forms than those who use these forms naturally in casual speech. Their performance is governed by certain norms, and these norms are the sounds or images that they hear themselves use. Thus the teacher will frequently condemn students in strong, moralistic terms for the use of speech forms that she frequently uses herself without being aware of them. There are undoubtedly many nonstandard forms used by the students that the teacher does not use, but the essential fact is that the teacher has no more tolerance for style shift than the adolescent groups mentioned above. Neither teacher nor student is aware of the fact that they both follow the same pattern of style shifting in their language, though at different levels. The teacher struggles to impose a fixed standard, which she mistakenly believes she follows herself, upon youngsters who mistakenly believe that they also make no concession to the other side in daily life. In the data from the New York City survey, we see some evidence for the view that teachers may be transferring to the students their own inner conflicts; they recoil from a kind of behavior that is still very much a part of their own personalities. On the other hand, the student may rightfully feel that the teacher threatens him in trying to abolish completely the speech pattern that identifies him as a member of his own group: this is the group that he respects, that awards him prestige, that establishes his masculinity.

These comments suggest that the conflict of values should be investigated in the classroom itself. The foregoing remarks are merely extrapolations from observations made in a community study, and they are based on the least favorable case, in which a male student faces a female teacher. But the view given here becomes somewhat more plausible when we consider the even more serious problem produced by the new polarization within the New York speech community.

---

[16] Again, one should note that this agreement extends only to those attitudes which reflect the middle class value system.

4. OPPOSING VALUE SYSTEMS WITHIN THE NEW YORK CITY SPEECH COMMUNITY

The view of the speech community given so far is not complete. There are signs of a developing lower class group which is breaking away from the pattern shown in Figures 1 through 5, a group which has adopted other reference points and other values, and is drifting in a different direction from the main group.

Evidence for such a trend can be seen in some of the details of the phonological system. Whereas the traditional New York City system is continuing to evolve towards higher and higher in-gliding vowels in word groups such as *bad, ask, dance, where*, etc., and *off, talk, law*, etc., there is an opposing trend towards lower in-gliding vowels in these groups. Similarly, we find that the traditional New York City system shows a systematic backing of the first element in the diphthong of *my, side, why*, etc., while a separate trend exists towards the fronting of this element and the loss of the up-glide. These contrary directions are all the more striking when they are seen against a view of the overall structure of New York City speech.[17] The great majority of working class and middle class speakers follow the first direction mentioned, which continues the evolution which began in the nineteenth century. The second direction is characteristic of a sizeable group of Negro speakers, Puerto Ricans, and lower class white speakers who live in close contact with these other groups.

The differences in speech performance are matched by a new polarization of values developing in New York City. The old polarization of ethnic groups showed a number of equally balanced interest groups: Italians, Jews, Negroes, Irish, who determined the political character of the city as well as its informal social structure.[18] The newer pattern shows that a growing minority of Negroes, Puerto Ricans, and lower class whites reject the value system implied by the dominant speech pattern and adopt a new reference point in which southern Negro speech is central.

This new development is best illustrated by considering the overt attitudes expressed by New Yorkers about speech itself. Most white New Yorkers do not like the sound of New York City speech. Almost all of our informants agree that they would be complimented if they were told that they did *not* sound like New Yorkers. As far back as we can go, the city's prestige patterns have always been borrowed from other regions. On the other hand, many white New Yorkers like the sound of white southern

[17] See "The Social Stratification of English in New York City," cited above, Ch. XII.
[18] The ethnic composition of New York City is described in N. Glazer and D. Moynihan, *Beyond the Melting Pot: The Negroes, Puerto Ricans, Jews, Italians and Irish of New York City* (Cambridge: M.I.T. and Harvard University Press, 1963).

speech. The attitudes of most Negro informants are quite the reverse. They like almost any type of northern speech, and dislike southern speech intensely. Southern speech is considered "rough," "uneducated," "bad" speech. One excerpt from an interview with an older Negro informant in New York City will illustrate this value pattern vividly. Mr. Joseph McSorley was born and raised in New York City sixty years ago. He works as a guard at a YMCA building, and although he has had little formal education, he is a well-read, well-spoken man. In answer to the question on the danger of death, he told of an incident in which he was asked to investigate a report that someone had a gun in his room and had threatened some other tenant with it. In this narrative, Mr. McSorley used two very different voices: his own quiet, pleasant, and cultivated northern manner, and a rough, rapid style with many strongly southern characteristics and a tone of voice that was rasping and whining. The first style is indicated in regular type below— the second in capitals.

> I go up whistlin', let him know I'm comin', shakin' my keys, you know. "Hey, Bill! What are you doin'?"
> "WHADA YOU WANT?"
> I said, "What are you doin'?"
> "I AIN'T DOIN' NUTTIN', JOE."
> I said, "Well, they claim a little disturbance up here, somebody says you chased them with something. What did you chase them with?"
> "OH JOE, I AIN'T GOIN' BOTHER 'EM. I WASN'T DOIN' NOTHIN'."
> I said, "Open the door, Bill. Let me look." So he opened the door and I went in there. He did have a gun. So I said, "You better get rid of that because down at the desk, they're calling for the police department."
> "I GOT A P'MIT FO' IT."
> I said, "You better show it to the cops when they come."
> "O.K. JOE, O.K."

The voice that Mr. McSorley usually used is not easily identified as that of a Negro by most listeners, but the second voice was plainly that of a southern Negro. At the end of the interview, I complimented Mr. McSorley on his ability to sound like two different people. He was quite mystified by my remark. He had no idea that he had used any voice other than his usual one; yet his niece, who had been listening, agreed that he had done so, and she told him that he had sounded "just like a southern Negro." Finally I asked Mr. McSorley what sort of a man Bill was—what was his background. "I don't know," said Mr. McSorley, "some kind of a Hungarian, I think."

In this incident we see a process of unconscious substitution taking place in accordance with the value system of the speaker. The man Mr. McSorley was imitating used a speech pattern that was evidently rough and uneducated, but unfamiliar in detail to him. In representing this style, he automatically and unconsciously substituted the only rough uneducated low prestige dialect with which he was intimately familiar—that of non-standard southern Negro English.

Mr. McSorley is typical of the many Negro New Yorkers who are puzzled by the recent trend towards southern speech among the young people he knows. He finds it hard to understand why people would go out of their way to talk in a rough, uneducated way. In actual fact, this polarization of linguistic values about a new norm is a sign of a cultural split in New York City which goes beyond language. We find that even lower class whites who live in apparent hostility with Negroes have unconsciously adopted the Negro delinquent youth as a reference group for their own behavior.[19] This trend is dramatically evident in a section of another interview from the Lower East Side survey. The subjects were six brothers, from thirteen to nineteen years old, from an Irish-Italian family that would be rated on most indicators near the lower end of the socioeconomic scale. In their social attitudes and aspirations most of the Riley brothers show overt hostility to middle class values. The most vocal is the second oldest, Jimmy Riley, the natural joker and storyteller of the group. At eighteen, he had resisted all of the schools' efforts to teach him white collar skills, and more or less decided to become a longshoreman, like his father. In his account of a situation in which he was in danger of being killed, he told of being attacked by a group of Negroes. In the course of the narrative, he drifted into a style of speech which is remarkably like that of the Negro boys who are his immediate enemies:

> I went ice skatin' in Jersey—Hoboken. Came back two o'clock in the mornin'. Whole bunch of guys went—I come back, everybody says, "I'm hongry, I'm hongry." I say, "I'll be right back."
>
> I go next door for a pizza. I come out, and there's five big niggers standin' there. They say, "Gimme that!" I say, "Give you *wot*." Yerrr whop! I went down. They kicked me, everything. Boom!
>
> I got up, 'n' ran in the house, 'n' grabbed a steak knife and chased them. A guy jumped into his car and chased them. Spanish guy named Rickey, he took out a bread knife, ran down the subway, and scared an old lady silly. Thought he was gonna kill her.
>
> Bright cop comes over—cullud ['kʌlʌd] cop. "Wha' happened?" I say, "Five of your bright people jumped me." He says, "What were dey?" I say, "Yeah, they were colored." He says, "Den they—they ain't my people." I said, "You cullud." He says, "They ain't my people." I say, "O.K., g'bye, f'get everyt'ing. Went t'the hospital."

Again, this stylistic behavior proved to be quite unconscious. When one of

[19] "Reference group" is used here in the technical sense introduced by Herbert Hyman in *The Psychology of Status*, 1942, and utilized by Robert Merton in *Social Theory and Social Structure* in 1949. When an individual or a group adopts the values of some other group outside of their own network of social contacts, that other group is said to serve as a reference group for them.

Jimmy Riley's own brothers told him that he sounded like a nigger himself when he was telling the story, he was quite surprised. Yet he had quoted himself saying "You cullud," a form of predication without the copula which is highly characteristic of Negro speech as opposed to other vernacular speech forms.

In the case of Jimmy Riley, we see a constellation of factors that seems to lead to low educational achievement, lack of occupational skills, and un-employment. His speech patterns are sensitive indicators of these trends. It is not likely that any change in the methods of teaching English will be powerful enough to cope with problems such as these. I think, however, that we must be aware of these problems, because they reflect social processes that will continue to operate to produce similar results in the future. No amount of research into the mechanism of language learning will remove these larger social forces from the scene. The polarization of linguistic be-havior serves as an excellent indicator of the social processes that are occur-ring, but these indicators do not give us any immediate program for cor-rective action, or even for amelioration. The linguist is essentially an analyst, not an educator; it would seem that his goal in attacking the problems of the urban schools is to give the educators information with which they can build programs and check the results of their efforts.

5. SOME DIRECTIONS FOR RESEARCH ON URBAN SCHOOL PROBLEMS

a. Describing the Structure of Nonstandard English

The first task of the linguist in any community is a descriptive one. There is little to say about educational problems, or motivation, or interference, until one can give an account of the linguistic behavior of the native speakers of the particular speech community in question. From the evidence brought forward in the present conference, we know that there are striking similarities in the linguistic problems that have arisen in many different cities across the United States. Nevertheless, we can take nothing for granted in approaching the language of Detroit, or Wilmington, or Newark: the following suggestions will outline several lines of research which will give us the data we need on actual linguistic behavior.

(1) **Isolating the Chief Variables.** It is necessary to have a clear idea of what features are constant in the speech of a given area and which tend to fluctuate. Wherever social forces interact with linguistic behavior, we find variation, and this variation is usually the focal point of social values. The traditional method has been to record the mistakes that children make in the classroom; certainly this is important, and it should be done. The

teachers in any and all parts of the school system can help the linguist by giving him a quantitative tabulation of the grammatical and lexical errors that children make in their written and oral work. To interpret these errors, it is of course necessary to give an exact account of the form of Standard English from which they deviate and also to show which deviations are not considered errors but are tolerated as acceptable variation. For this latter task, the educator may need direct help from the linguist in the classroom, as he observes the type of Standard English used by the teacher and administrators of the school.

A more systematic approach to the isolation of the variables can be followed by the linguist in his exploratory interviews and observations in the community. From this work, he can begin to divide variables into two types: those which show *social variation*, but are essentially constant in the speech of any one person, and those which also show *stylistic variation*, shifting in occurrence or frequency from one style or context to another.

(2) **Structural Descriptions.** The next step is undertaken by the linguist. He must attempt to organize the constant and variable factors in the speech of the community, or any subsection of the community, into a structural description. As we know, a complete structural description is hardly possible, since it has never been accomplished for any variety of English. The linguist therefore concentrates upon certain areas of language which he knows are most tightly organized, such as the phonological system, or the system of verbal auxiliaries, and pays particular attention to those areas that are marked by the greatest variation.

A structural description of this type serves three chief purposes: (a) It enables the linguist to locate other variables in the system which have not been noticed before. At alternate and opposite points in the structure, it is not uncommon to find parallel variation; furthermore, pressure from variation at one point frequently produces shifts or mergers with neighboring elements; (b) The structural analysis frequently explains one form of linguistic behavior as a structural consequence of other forms. Several isolated examples of differences between Standard and nonstandard English may actually be instances of a single difference in the operation of a more general rule; (c) The structural description may show that forms which are superficially identical with Standard English (or with other forms within the same system) are actually different in syntactic or semantic value. In a highly organized system, the value of each term is based upon its relation with all other terms, so that a different organization or inventory of terms will affect the meaning of all the terms. We find such underlying differences frequently in pronoun systems, or in the tense and modal systems of the verb.

(3) **Social and Stylistic Distribution.** The distribution of the variables throughout the speech community must be studied in order to assess the

social significance of the different forms and systems that have been isolated. Some of the methods used and the purposes of such a description are
outlined in this paper. It is not always necessary to construct a random
sample of all of the individuals in the speech community. More rapid
samples can be made by various methods, in the school system and through
other institutions.[20] The greater the degree of social and stylistic variation,
the more necessary to avoid the bias of *convenience* in selecting informants,
and to avoid the bias produced by approaching informants through formal
institutions such as the school. For this work, the linguist can draw upon
other social scientists for assistance, and whenever possible, he should
couple his study with other social surveys so as to devote the maximum
energy to the study of language itself. One of the great advantages of a
representative survey of linguistic behavior is that it allows us to study
change. Through the distribution of linguistic forms through various age
levels in the population, we can infer the existence of linguistic and social
change; even more valuable information eventually can be derived by
repeating the study at a later time. If, on the other hand, we remain content with an impressionistic account of a particular dialect derived from
the study of a few "typical" informants, we will have no means of measuring
these observations against any later research.

(4) **The Influence of Other Languages.** In many areas of the United
States, we must consider the effect of languages other than English upon
the linguistic behavior of particular ethnic groups and perhaps upon the
entire population. For this purpose, it is necessary to provide formal descriptions of the particular dialect of the foreign language which is used, and
of the English used by the second and third generation members of that
ethnic group, and then to chart the possible relations between these.[21]
While the main task of this description falls upon the linguist, the teacher
can help greatly by making separate reports of the errors made by students
with the foreign language background in question and giving some estimate
of the relative difficulty encountered in changing these patterns.

b. The Social Significance of Nonstandard English

Information on the social distribution of speech forms tells us a great
deal about social significance, but it is possible to make a more direct attack
upon this question. In order to make intelligent decisions about which forms

[20] In a recent study in the Phoenix Union Central High School of Phoenix, Arizona, it was possible to obtain
a great deal of information about the sociolinguistic structures of Phoenix in a few days, by interviewing classes
of students as a whole. Of the many favorable circumstances, not least was the cooperative and helpful attitude of the school administration.
[21] The lines of research to be followed here have been laid out in some detail by Uriel Weinreich in *Languages
in Contact* (New York: Linguistic Circle of New York, 1953).

of language require correction or suppletion with alternate forms, we have to know which markers of linguistic behavior have serious effects upon the life chances of the individual. In different areas, we might find the same nonstandard forms, but with radically different social significance. For example, one can hear stops and affricates used for /θ/ and /ð/ in the Southwest, but there this feature does not seem to have the same strong social impact as in Chicago or New York.

The methods required to measure subjective evaluation are complex, and they are not generally available to linguists or educators. The school system can, however, provide information on the ability of students to perceive the differences between standard and nonstandard variants. The ability of the student to hear the difference between two forms consistently is closely correlated with their social significance.[22]

The information on subjective evaluation can be used to classify linguistic variables into three basic categories:

indicators, which show social variation but usually not stylistic variation, and have little effect upon the listener's judgment of the social status of the speaker

markers, which show both social and stylistic variation, and have consistent effects upon the conscious or unconscious judgment of the speaker's status by the listener

stereotypes, which are the overt topics of social comment in the speech community, and may or may not correspond to actual linguistic behavior.

It is evident that most of the attention of the educators will be concentrated upon the markers and upon systems which contain a great many markers. Thus we may find that there are regular characteristics of Negro speakers which are indicators, but do not function as markers, and there would be little justification for including these elements as "errors," "mistakes," or deviations from Standard English.

The study of subjective evaluation must be carried out in many different communities if we are to resolve questions raised concerning the cultivated regional varieties used in the South. If indeed there are many students who enter northern school systems using such varieties, it is important to discover how the northern speech community evaluates them. As far as the children's vernacular is concerned, we have every reason to think that pressure from their friends and associates will lead to the adoption of the local forms. Whether or not the school should take any position at all on the

---

[22] In a study of 53 delinquent youths at New York City's Youth House, carried out in the summer of 1964, we obtained information on the speaker's ability to perceive a series of phonological contrasts. The contention that native speakers can hear phonemic distinctions much better than nonphonemic distinctions was not borne out by the evidence. Instead, one might say that the ability to perceive distinctions is determined largely by the social significance of the distinction to the listener.

status of cultivated southern speech probably depends more upon the frequency of such cases than any other factor.

c. The Acquisition of Standard English

This topic has been the principal concern of the present paper, and some of the tentative findings have been outlined on the basis of the New York City study. Future research programs would necessarily be concerned with testing preliminary notions on all of the aspects of language acquisition for many communities. One important focus of such research would be this question: given a regular pattern of social and stylistic stratification, how can one give lower class children the same wide range of stylistic variation that is open to middle class children? It would seem that there are two main types of solutions: early training which permits lower class children to enter the acquisition route (Figure 5) at a higher point than they normally would, or special training which increases the normal rate of acquisition of Standard English.

d. Resistance to the Acquisition of Standard English

The three areas of research outlined above are only preliminary to the major question of analyzing the reasons why those who are exposed to Standard English, and who need the ability to use Standard English, do not learn this form of the language. We can point to four major aspects of this question, recapitulating in part the discussion of **2c** above.

(1) Structural Interference. The results of research under section **5a** above can be applied to the analysis of interference between the underlying vernacular and the standard language as it is taught in the schools. Teaching methods which focus upon the contrastive points of interference can then be formulated.

(2) Opposing Motivations. Although it has been shown that most New Yorkers endorse the value of Standard English, we have also seen that there must exist opposing motivations which must be made explicit in further research. Furthermore, it is necessary to find the particular variables upon which these opposing value systems are focused. All variables may not bear equal weight in this respect.

(3) Resistance in the Peer Group. Small group studies are required to show in detail the means by which the adolescent and preadolescent group behavior interferes with the acquisition of second dialects.

(4) Teacher-Student Interaction. Studies in the classroom are needed to investigate the type of adjustment in language behavior which the teacher makes to the vernacular of the students and which the students make to the normal style of the teacher. It is possible that teachers who show a wider range of stylistic performance in their own speech have greater (or lesser) effectiveness in persuading students to accept a form of Standard English. Research of this type would require close cooperation between educators and linguists. While linguists may provide indexes for measuring linguistic interaction in the classroom, they have no means of measuring teacher effectiveness. . . .

Study Questions

1. What, in Labov's opinion, is the value of the Atlas materials for future studies of urban speech? What are some of the limitations of its methodology for the handling of urban speech? How would Labov's methods overcome these limitations? Labov says that linguists have reported a "high degree of fluctuation in speech forms" in New York City and suggests that New York presents the dialectologist with some unique problems. If the dialectal situation in New York is unique, or highly unusual, is it possible to draw useful generalizations from the New York situation which might be applied to dialect situations in other cities, or to linguistic change in general? Is the linguist examining urban speech in Boston, Chicago, or Los Angeles likely to find the same social and psychological forces at work?

2. What does Labov mean by "social and stylistic norms"? How does he attempt to correlate phonological features with these norms? How would he distinguish "careful speech" from "casual speech"? Did the Atlas make any attempt to correlate specific linguistic features with social class? Why does Labov feel that it is important to measure the subjective reactions of his informants to individual variables in speech as well as to observe their overt behavior in speaking? Do such measurements violate the tenets of American structuralism?

3. How does Labov identify and define prestige features in the variables? What is the function of the "self-evaluation" tests? Does the "subjective response" test evaluate how the speaker himself feels about the linguistic variables, or how the schools and other institutions of the power structure in the community tell him he should feel about them? Labov reports that "those who showed the highest use of the non-standard forms in their own speech were often among the most sensitive in detecting and stigmatizing these forms in the speech of others." Does he offer any explanation for this? What is the significance, for example, of the "index of linguistic insecurity"?

Does a high index indicate acceptance or rejection of the middle class value system? Does a zero score indicate acceptance, rejection, apathy, or rebelliousness? What are the implications for teachers of English in ghetto schools of Labov's statement that a "recognition of an external standard of correctness is an inevitable accompaniment of upward social aspirations and upward social mobility"? On what sort of scale would we measure *upward?*

4.   Labov constructs what he calls a tentative model "of the acquisition of the full range of spoken English." What does he mean by "the full range of spoken English"? Labov asks: "Since the great majority of the members of the adult community agree in the evaluation of speech forms, why then do most New Yorkers fail to acquire levels (5) and (6) in the series [i.e., the stages in acquisition listed on pp. 288–290] . . . ?" What answers does he give? How important is "conflict of value systems"? If there is a serious conflict of value systems, what kind of "agreement" about speech forms is there likely to be? Do the Black Power movements and the riots suffered by many American cities suggest that the conflicts are more basic than Labov seems to indicate in this article? What is likely to be a Black Power advocate's reaction to an attempt "to build into the community a tolerance for style shifting which is helpful in educational and occupational advancement"? Labov says that "the ability to perceive the social significance of dialect differences precedes the acquisition of consistent prestige styles in Standard English," but also that an awareness of the social significance of dialect begins only at adolescence (stage 3). Many psychologists say that adolescence is about the time when children lose their facility in mastering another language. Would this late awareness of the social significance of dialect suggest another reason why New Yorkers do not acquire levels (5) and (6)?

5.   What is Labov's attitude toward "urban dialect engineering"? Does he feel that it is the function of the schools to promote the use of prestige forms? If the stigmatizing of certain linguistic variables is, as Labov asserts, connected with middle class values, does the school which accepts the task of promoting prestige forms also accept the value system?

6.   Labov says that a "structural analysis frequently explains one form of linguistic behavior as a structural consequence of other forms." If this is true, what are the dangers of drawing conclusions from the study of a limited number of dialect features? Does Labov agree or disagree with the structuralist contention that the phoneme, as structuralists define it, is psychologically real, and that speakers do not hear allophonic variations?

Part 3
Historical Linguistics

Dialectology and linguistic history are both concerned with diversity in language: the dialectologist with variations from place to place and along scales of social class, language function, and style; the historical linguist with changes in unity or variety through time. Often the two students consider the same facts, and often their two studies overlap, as when the dialectologist tries to tell how the differences he observes have come to be; and while each study must meet its own theoretical demands, both depend for their success on an adequate general theory of language and of linguistic description. Perhaps the difficulties of the historical linguist are the more complex, since his work presupposes descriptions of existing structures and variations, whose development he must then explain.

A history must be much more than a list of superficial differences between earlier and later stages of a language. If we take a passage of Middle English, for example, and set it beside a modern translation, many changes catch our eyes at once:

> Þa þe king Stephne to Englaland com, þa macod he his gadering æt Oxeneford; and þar he nam þe biscop Roger of Serebyri and Alexander biscop of Lincol and te canceler Roger, hise neues, and dide ælle in prisun til hi iafen up here castles.
>
> When King Stephen came to England, he held his council at Oxford; and there he seized Roger, the Bishop of Salisbury, and Alexander, the Bishop of Lincoln, and the Chancellor Roger—his nephews—and put them all in prison until they had given up their castles.

The merest glance will tell us that since the days of the Peterborough chronicler, some words have disappeared from the language (*nam* is obsolete for "seized" or "took"), that others—still current—are used in different oral or written forms (*com* but *came*, *macod* but *made*, *gadering* but *gathering*, *æt* but *at*), and that not just words have changed but the ways of putting them together in sentences (for example, the different positions of the verbs *came* and *com*).

But such differences are only the materials for history, not history itself: they raise many questions, but answer none. Is the difference between *æt* and *at* a difference in spelling only, or in pronunciation too? What sound does the letter *thorn* represent in *þe* "the," and why is the same word spelled with a *t* between *and* and *canceler?* Does the final *-e* of *hise* have any grammatical function, or would *his* do just as well? Why does *he* follow *macod* after *þa* but precede *nam* after *þar?* Why has *gadering* been translated *council*, though *gathering* remains in the language? How can we generalize about the innumerable brute facts of difference, how did the changes that explain them come about, and why? To answer questions like these, the historian needs his general theory. He needs to know what languages are, and how and why they change. Without such a theory, he can point to differences between Middle and Modern English, but he can never explain them—or even be sure that the differences he points to are the ones that matter most: *data* means "things given," but the right data are not given to the man who asks the wrong questions.

Though everyone knows, then, that languages do change, linguistic historians are a long way from satisfactory answers to their *how*'s and *why*'s. The reason is plain. Theories of language, and theoretically based descriptive grammars, are both essential to histories of languages; and as anyone who has struggled with the first section of this anthology will know, there is very basic disagreement among linguists about what language is and how it is best described.

But if we still have no adequate theory of language and its changes, and if we must consider as tentative any theories already formulated, we do have great stores of information about the histories of individual languages, and consequently some knowledge of what an adequate theory must account for. The great historical linguists of the nineteenth century built a foundation for the study of language history which supported work of the first importance, not just on single languages but on groups whose members were historically related though mutually unintelligible. Those great men, and their successors, have put some kind of history for many languages at the disposal of the modern student and have made it commonplace to talk about language *families* (Indo-European, for example). The articles in the following section all testify to the significance of these historians' accomplishments: without traditional theory and method in historical linguistics, no one would know enough to be critical of the tradition.

One of the most fruitful analogies for nineteenth-century work is old and simple: family resemblances among languages suggest a common ancestor. The standard regional and national varieties of Modern English are so much alike that speakers of one can easily understand the speakers of the others; but if Canada and Australia understand one another amiably, and Boston and Austin unamiably, the obvious reason is that all four varieties are ultimately derived from the English of earlier times in England. Old English, in turn, resembles Old Saxon, and Gothic, and Old Norse, because all of these Germanic dialects are descended from a still older parent language. That was the conclusion which scholars in the nineteenth century finally established, though scholars earlier had observed resemblances among European and Asiatic languages, and had even suggested family relationships, though without defining the resemblances or explaining them in convincing ways. Sir William Jones, a servant of expanding empire in India, saw that Sanskrit clearly resembled both Greek and Latin, was attested in records older than any then known for Europe's classical languages, yet could not be the original of either. He proposed in 1786 that all three must have "sprung from some common source, which, perhaps, no longer exists."

If Jones was not the first to suggest the possibility of genealogical relatedness among languages, his statement was more provocative than earlier ones for at least two reasons. First, the languages he talked about were very old, in the sense that written records of Latin were older than those of any Western language except Greek, and Sanskrit records were older still. If these three ancient languages themselves had a common source, man must have talked for a very long time indeed; and if the history of man's languages stretched into the darkness beyond the oldest records, there was little reason to suppose, with earlier linguistic genealogists, that any existing or recorded language was the parent of all others. Jones' suggestion put the origin of human speech beyond antiquity. Second, the languages Jones was comparing had been spoken in very different cultures in widely separated areas: Greek and Latin in the Mediterranean, Sanskrit in ancient India. Geographical contiguity and similarity of cultural content could no longer be taken as necessary conditions for linguistic kinship. The sounds and forms of languages themselves were the best evidence that languages were related, and comparison of those sounds and forms might lead to no extant language as a common ancestor, but to the systematic reconstruction, bit by bit, of a language older than any records of its descendants. The oldest languages of the Old World had shown linguists a new world to explore.

If some likenesses among languages are best explained by derivation from a common origin, then differences among those same languages must also be historically explicable: where related languages differ, some or all of them have changed. Linguists compare languages which they suspect are genealogically related, and reconstruct some fragments of the parent language and parts of the subsequent history by means of their comparisons. It is easy to go wrong in the process. French *rat* is not derived from Latin *mūs*, though their meanings are similar and a great French scholar did once perpetrate the derivation; but English *goose* and Latin *ānser* have the same Indo-European source, though they look less alike than Latin *montem* (the accusative of the word for "mountain") and French *mouton* "a sheep," whose lack of relationship did not prevent the same scholar from equating them because the words do look alike and because the sheep feeds on the mountain.

Besides wide factual knowledge of the languages concerned, or at least a keen awareness that one lacks it, two main defenses against such blunders are the distinction between borrowing and historical descent and the recognition that neither likeness in meaning nor chance resemblances in phonetic shape are solid evidence that words are cognate: rats and mice are both rodents, and *mouton* and *montem* look alike; but the real cognates include *goose* and *ānser*, though they look so different, and (shockingly) *charity*, from Latin *cāritās*, and *whore*, though the semantic connection is not obvious. *Charity*, we know, was borrowed into English from central Old French *charité*, the historical descendant of *cāritātem*, the accusative of *cāritās*, the noun derived from the Latin adjective *cārus*, meaning "dear"; and we relate *cārus* to Old English *hōre* because Latin *ā* matches Old English *ō*, and Latin *c* /k/ matches Old English *h*, in whole sets of words: *māter*, *mōdor* "mother"; *frāter*, *brōþor* "brother"; *fāgus*, *bōc(trēōw)* "beech-tree"; *canis*, *hund* "dog"; *cor*, *heorte* "heart"; *centum*, *hund* "hundred." Where borrowing can be ruled out, such sets of phonetic correspondences are the surest evidence that individual words are cognate elements of languages which have evolved from the same original: mere chance is no explanation of so systematic a relationship.

Likenesses due to borrowing are easily illustrated in English, and the mistakes they might induce are easily avoided, because we have an ample supply of English documents from the last thousand or twelve hundred years and because the political and social history of England is familiar. Thus there are clear connections, in form and in meaning, among sets of words like these:

Latin	English	
pater	paternal	father
pēs	pedal	foot
piscis	piscine	fish
tenuis	tenuity	thin
trēs	trinal	three
frāter	fraternal	brother
canis	canine	hound
caput	capital	head
cor	cordial	heart

If we were trying to state correspondences between Latin *p, t, k* and corresponding English sounds, we might at first conclude that the correspondences are unpredictable, since each one of the Latin sounds seems to be matched by two in English: *p* by *p* and *f*, *t* by *t* and *th*[θ], *k* (spelled *c*) by *k* and *h*. A somewhat more ingenious guess might be that in adjectives the English sounds match the Latin ones, but that the English sounds differ in the English nouns; but *tenuity* and *three* would then be unexplained. In fact, however, such guesses are unnecessary. All the words in the right-hand column, we know from our documents, were current already in Old English and in other Germanic languages; but the words in the center column, all of them bookish, are first recorded from Middle English or Early Modern English. *Pēs* and *foot* (Greek *pous* and German *Fuss*) are true cognates, related by descent from a common ancestor and differentiated by sound-changes in the descendant languages. *Pedal* and the other bookish words were simply transferred bodily from Latin into English, directly or through French; and a word like *tenuity* begins with *t* and not *th* because the first Englishmen who used it pronounced it with *t* as they heard it pronounced in French and Latin.

Words borrowed from one of two related languages into another are not, of course, independent evidence of the shape of those words in the common ancestral language: English *paternal* tells us nothing that Latin *pater* does not tell us about the initial consonant in the Indo-European etymon of *pater* and *father*. Not all the Indo-European languages use this word for the male parent. Welsh, for example, has *tad*, and Gothic regularly *atta*—perhaps historically children's words (like English *dad*) which replaced the original term. The surviving cognates of *pater* and *father*, moreover, do not all begin with a consonant: Irish, in earlier and later times, has *athir* and *athair*. But the independent agreement of Sanskrit, Greek, and Latin (all with *p-*) with the Germanic languages (*f-*) proves that some initial consonant was original and that its absence in Irish is due to a later change; and the majority vote for *p-* against Germanic *f-* is confirmed by the whole series of sound-changes which we saw in *father*, *thin*, and *hound*—Indo-European voiceless stops became voiceless spirants in Germanic. Thus it is possible to say with some confidence that the Indo-European word from which Latin *pater* and English *father* are independently descended began with a consonant, and that that consonant was *p*. By multiplying such comparisons many times over, and by extending them to other aspects of the languages involved, the comparative grammarians of the last two centuries have gained considerable knowledge of the structure of Indo-European and of the history of its descendants. Similar results have been achieved for other language families.

Textbooks based on nineteenth-century historical studies often present a simple typology of linguistic change:

I. Internal change

   A. Sound change
   B. Analogy

II. External change: borrowing

A. From another dialect
B. From another language

The classification is easy to criticize, but its headings *have* served as useful reminders to beginning students. Borrowing from one dialect of English to another, for example, explains why Old English *fyxen* begins with *f* while Modern English *vixen* begins with *v;* the differences between the poetic vocabularies of *Beowulf* (say) and the *Canterbury Tales* are partly explicable in terms of obsolescence and of borrowing from another language; and *analogy* is something more than a mere label for the distinctive kind of change that allowed the Peterborough chronicler to use both analogical *bokes* and older *bec*, which in Modern English would be *books* and *beech,* for the plural of *book*. Both convention and convenience, then, have led us to organize this third and last part of our anthology in the familiar terms. After still another general discussion by Sapir, the two essays by W. P. Lehmann and Paul Kiparsky deal mainly with sound change; the selections from Leonard Bloomfield and Einar Haugen treat analogy and borrowing and the spread of such innovations; and the concluding selection, from Stephen Ullmann, goes on from changes in form to changes in meaning. Prudently followed, this organization will do no harm.

Of all the headings in the outline, sound change was most discussed in the nineteenth century (with the result that generations of English majors have dutifully parroted OE *hūs*, MnE *house;* OE *wīf*, MnE *wife;* OE *mōd*, MnE *mood;* OE *fēt*, MnE *feet*). Perhaps the most famous of all sound changes are those summarized by what is called Grimm's Law, after the great German grammarian and lexicographer, Jacob Grimm. The sounds involved are the Indo-European stops, which underwent a series of striking changes in the Germanic languages, though often the original sounds remained unchanged in other members of the family, including Greek and Latin. The changes in the voiceless stops, *p, t,* and *k,* have already been illustrated; in Germanic, they became the voiceless spirants *f,* [θ] as in *thin,* and *h.* The voiced stops of Indo-European, on the other hand, remained stops in Germanic but became voiceless: *b* became *p; d, t; g, k.* That change is reflected in the following pairs of Latin and Old English words (where the Latin words, of course, are not the ancestors of the English, but are cited because they keep the Indo-European voiced stops unchanged):

ager "field"	æcer (Gothic: akrs)
egō "I"	ic (Gothic: ik)
genu "knee"	cnēo (Gothic: kniu)

decem "ten"   tīen
dēns "tooth"   tōþ
edō "eat"   etan

Since Indo-European *b* was rare, other languages must sometimes be cited to illustrate its change to *p:*

Latin: cannabis "hemp"   hænep (MnE: hemp)
Lithuanian: dubùs "deep"   dēop
Latin: scabō "scratch"   scieppan "shape"

The statement of such regular phonetic correspondences between the sounds of different languages or of earlier and later stages of a single language was a great advance over previous methods of cataloguing haphazard "permutations of the letters"; and as the firm distinction between letters and sounds became commonplace, and knowledge of articulatory phonetics both deeper and more accessible, scholars saw regularity emerging where earlier they had seen chaos. In the earlier decades of the nineteenth century they were still willing, in many instances, to admit unexplained deviations from their patterns of change and correspondence. The correspondence, for example, between voiceless stops in Latin and Greek and voiceless fricatives in Germanic was observed in many words, but in others Germanic languages had other sounds—a *d* for an expected [*θ*] or [ð], as in Old English *weorþan* "to become" but *wurdon* "they became," or a *g* for an *h*, as in Old Saxon *tiohan* "to draw" but past participle *gitogan*. Scholars worried this problem for a long time, but in the 1870's it became apparent that the exceptions were not exceptions after all. The unexpected sounds, it turned out, appeared in voiced surroundings if the preceding syllable had been unstressed in Indo-European; and the irregularities too were regular, provided due attention was paid to their phonetic environment. By at least some linguists, the tempting conclusion was duly drawn. As the Dane Karl Verner phrased it, "There must be a rule for irregularity; the problem is to find it." [1] In a given position in words (it came to be held), at a given time and in a given dialect, every instance of the same sound changes in the same way; or, to put the principle bluntly, sound laws admit of no exceptions.

The methods and theories of late nineteenth-century comparative grammarians were carried into the first three decades of the twentieth century with relatively little change. American scholars in particular agreed broadly on the basic assumptions which they had inherited, and lavishly praised

---

[1] Holger Pedersen, trans. J. W. Spargo, *The Discovery of Language* (Bloomington, 1962), p. 292n.

their nineteenth-century predecessors. Sapir, for example, wrote:

> In the course of their detailed researches Indo-European linguists
> have gradually developed a technique which is more nearly perfect
> than that of any other science dealing with man's institutions.[2]

And Bloomfield:

> The method of [historical linguistics] may fairly be called one of the
> triumphs of nineteenth century science. In a survey of scientific
> method it should serve as a model of one type of investigation, since
> no other historical discipline has equalled it.[3]

Like the *Junggrammatiker* or Neo-grammarians of the 1870's, Bloomfield
accepted the hypothesis of regular sound change, and the historical chapters in his great book *Language* (which became a manual for revolution in
American descriptive studies) may be viewed at least in part as a synthesis
and summation of nineteenth-century developments in theory and method.

But the notion of exceptionless sound laws was never unopposed; and a
century after the Neo-grammarians, the whole question of the nature of
sound-systems and their actual and possible changes is energetically con-
troverted. Among linguists whose work has been thought to weaken the
Neo-grammarian position, one of the most formidable was the French dialectologist Jules Gilliéron. In his work on the French linguistic atlas, Gilliéron turned up numerous words whose histories were so complicated that
he could not explain them in purely phonological terms, by exceptionless
sound laws, without appeal to syntax or semantics. Instead, Gilliéron insisted on the pervasiveness of the exception and on the necessity for considering a whole complex of historical processes, grammatical and semantic
as well as purely phonological. His famous pronouncement that "every
word has its own history" has been taken to heart by generations of dialect
geographers, lexicographers, and semanticists. It is echoed most clearly in
Stephen Ullmann's careful detailing of evidence in the final selection of this
section, but is also heard in Weinreich's and Labov's arguments for a combination of external and internal dialectology and for the relevance of
sociological as well as more narrowly linguistic evidence in studying dialectal differentiation and linguistic change.

Besides Gilliéron, many other Romance scholars, in both the nineteenth
and the twentieth centuries, objected to the confident typology which we

---

[2] "The Status of Linguistics as a Science," *Language*, 5 (1929), p. 207.
[3] "Linguistic Aspects of Science," p. 2.

have quoted (sound change, analogy, borrowing) and to naturalistic conceptions of regular sound laws, which suggested that sound laws operate like the exceptionless laws of physical science, mechanically, through minute but gradually cumulative modifications in habits of articulation. Now, in the United States, the generative grammarians have brought new vigor and acuteness to the attack on the established notions of sound change and analogy which American structuralists in general have accepted. The very sharp differences between the two schools that the reader has encountered in the first two sections of this anthology may also be found in such structural and generative statements about language history as those by Lehmann and Kiparsky.

That generative grammarians are more willing than structuralists have usually been to admit exceptions to their rules is today a relatively minor difference: both groups would agree that the linguist should try to find and state every significant generalization that his material allows, and when this obvious point of method has been safely put beyond dispute, only a very stiff-necked theorist with a taste for specious argument is likely to deny that in every language there are forms whose pronunciation remains exceptional to any general rules that have been proposed. It is much more important that the generalizations themselves which men like Lehmann and men like Kiparsky are seeking are of different kinds. These men have different ideas about the nature of changes in pronunciation, their processes, their kinds and causes; and the reason for the disagreement lies in different theories of what a language is.

Lehmann attempts a typology of pronunciation-changes which is generally consistent with the structuralist view of phonology outlined in the essay by Henry Lee Smith, Jr., in Part One. In this view, the design of languages is such that phonology is a separate and autonomous layer of linguistic structure, an independent system, which can and must be described without reference to morphology, syntax, or semantics. The units of sound that distinguish one word from another are phonemes, like the vowels that keep *pit* apart from *pet* or the consonants that distinguish *pit* from *sit;* and each phoneme, in turn, is represented by one or more subvarieties of sound, one or more allophones, as they are called. Both allophones and phonemes are characterized by distinctive features of articulation. The phoneme /p/, for example, is a voiceless bilabial stop consonant, and each of its allophones has those same articulatory features, plus others (like aspiration) which can be predicted by rule from the phonetic environment, as when one observes that the initial [p] of *pep* is aspirated between the word-boundary and the following stressed vowel, while the final [p] is unaspirated and perhaps even unexploded. It is only the differences between phonemes, however, which keep words apart and which therefore enter the consciousness of native speakers in normal situations.

The distinction between phonemes and allophones gives Lehmann his first distinction between different kinds of changes in pronunciation. Since both phonemes and allophones are distinguished by articulations, since native speakers are said to be normally unconscious of differences among allophones, and since a good deal of regularity is directly observable in the differences between cognate words in different languages and in different stages of the same language, it seems plausible to maintain that change by allophone is gradual, regular, unconscious—a slow accumulation of minute changes in articulation which for some reason happen to move in the same direction until at last they may eventuate in a change in phonemes. Change by phonemes, on the other hand, since native speakers are said to be conscious of phonemic differences, is sporadic, not regular, and instantaneous, not gradual: the change from *perspire* to substandard "prespire," it is assumed, did not take long years of articulatory drifting, as the change from Middle English /e:/ to Modern English /iy/ as in *see* is said to have done.

The question why articulations should drift in this mysterious way leads to another distinction among pronunciation-changes, this one in terms of cause and effect. Either regular or sporadic changes which make neighboring sounds more similar are called assimilations. They are said to promote "ease of articulation," as changes with the opposite effect, dissimilations, allegedly promote neural ease (however neural ease may be defined). Ease, then, whether muscular or neural, is suggested as a principal cause of pronunciation-changes in Lehmann's account. Other suggested causes include a tendency toward symmetry in phonemic systems, the conflict of homonyms, taboo, the inventions of individuals, and the influence of other languages, as presumably when a whole population abandons one language for another which it learns imperfectly.

Kiparsky's flat rejection of such ideas, and his emphasis on the need for refinement in generative theories, are a salutary reminder both that much progress has been made in linguistic history—and that much remains to be done. Most modern linguists have accepted the notion that the abstract underlying forms of words are related to their concrete realizations by phonological rules: if the first consonant in *pep* is aspirated and the second unexploded, there must be rules to relate the two consonants to the single phoneme /p/ which underlies them both. Generative grammarians take the idea of phonological rules in full seriousness, develop it carefully, and draw its logical consequences. The ordered rules of the phonological components of their grammars are more numerous and more complex than the phonological rules of structuralists have been, and in a generative grammar the rules of the phonology are not independent of the syntax. Instead, the superficial syntactic structure of sentences is essentially involved in the rules which turn the highly abstract underlying forms into phonetic transcriptions, into instructions for articulation. The rules, for example, which predict the position of stress in English sentences cannot be stated just in terms of phonetic environments, like the number of consonants that follow a vowel; the rules also have to refer to syntax, to word-classes, parts of speech like nouns and verbs and adjectives.

The consequences for history which follow from this descriptive theory are revolutionary (just as history has its consequences for description in the continuing interplay between the two). For one thing, the descriptive theory immediately limits the kinds of changes which a compatible history can allow. The changes must be changes either in the underlying forms or in the phonological rules, and if that is true, then the changes cannot be gradual. The rules and the underlying forms exist in the minds of native speakers; and though changes in them may sometimes be minute, inconsistently observed even by their makers, and slowly adopted by the speech community, still the changes must be discrete and instantaneous in the grammars of the innovating individuals. The opposition on this point may not be so sharp as the distinction between the two words *gradual* and *discrete* may make it appear, but the believers in gradual change will certainly have to clarify their ideas—perhaps by extending their notion of innovation and by refining their distinctions among different kinds of innovations and between innovations and their spreading through the community.

Other reinterpretations, it is argued, will also be necessary. Traditional sound laws (change by allophones) will be commonly interpreted, in generative histories, as added rules, especially as rules added so late in the ordered series that they do not affect the underlying forms, which will be seen as remaining constant through long periods; and, obviously, only such rules can be historically added as linguistic theory allows in descriptive grammars. New emphasis will also be placed on the discontinuity of the generations as a condition of linguistic change. Knowledge of a language is never directly given to young children. They must invent the language freshly, discover it anew, find its rules for themselves in a relatively short time and by using quite limited and imperfect evidence. It is altogether likely, the generativists maintain, that children will sometimes construct a simpler grammar than the grammar of their elders (even if those elders are only older children) by a kind of imperfect learning which simplifies some rules or sets them in a different order. Such simplification would be a generative parallel to traditional proportional analogy, by which, for example, a child may come to say *foots* instead of *feet:* incorrect *foots* is to *foot* as correct *books* is to *book*, and so the normal rule for forming plurals is extended to another noun, and an exception is removed. Generative grammarians are unhappy with this usual account of analogy, just as they are with the very name of "sound change" (it is grammars that change in the first instance, they say, and sounds only as a consequence). If analogy is to remain a useful means of historical explanation, they contend, some limits must be placed on the forms it can affect and the results it can produce, while at the same time its operations must be studied in phonology and syntax, not just in morphology.

Something more will also be done, both linguist and layman will hope wistfully, to answer the great question *why* (which Sapir introduces in the first of the following selections). Traditional sound laws match the forms of words before and after changes and assure us, for example, that Indo-European /p/ became Germanic /f/ or that Old English *hē* came pretty close to rhyming with Modern English *day* but now rhymes with *sea* instead. But such changes (the generative group are saying now) are not just changes in brute noise. They are changes inside of people, changes in the form and content of the knowledge which lets people talk; and it is painfully unsatisfying, to the average mind, to be told that maybe the explanation is "drift," or maybe some undefined "ease of articulation" or some still more mysterious "neural ease"—but maybe that the explanation is something else again, like the natural instability of man or his capability of purposefully changing his styles of life and speech. It is a little more helpful to say that one change may precipitate others, since no rule is isolated but all are parts of a single system, which may somehow become asymmetric or unstable (observe what Sapir says when he *exemplifies* drift); and certainly one cause of linguistic change is imitation of the speech of people whom we want to be like, since we all use our speech to announce our real or desired identity. One must eventually admit, however, that the hope for causal explanations, in the present state of knowledge, is often disappointed. It will never be richly satisfied if linguists content themselves with bilingual puns, like saying that sound change is regular because it is change in rules.

Readers familiar with traditional histories of the English language will be aware of two other defects in present knowledge: linguistic historians have neglected syntax, at least in comparison with phonology and morphology and especially the vocabulary, whose superficial aspects are most accessible to popular discussion; yet the extended discussions of the vocabulary, for all the great accomplishments of historical lexicographers since the Brothers Grimm, remain semantically naïve, as if the makers and users of dictionaries and the framers of philosophic theories had determined never to speak to one another. Bloomfield commented long ago on both deficiencies, yet to some extent it was the assumptions of Bloomfield himself that prevented American structuralists from taking meaning as a central object of their investigations. Men who thought of meaning as the speaker's total situation and the hearer's full response were naturally reluctant to seek knowledge of what their assumption made apparently unknowable, to bring within the purview of their discipline the entire universe as known to man. "Fluctuation [of competing forms]," Bloomfield observed, "does not depend upon formal features, but upon meaning, and accordingly escapes a purely linguistic investigation." The crippling implication seemed to be that the linguistic historian is at once obliged to study meaning—and unable to.

Making a dictionary, a lexicon, is indeed a frightening task, to some extent a delimiting of the possibilities of human thought and knowledge; yet dictionary-makers went placidly on with their lives' works, despite Bloomfield's doubts; and today the theories of the generative grammarians compel a new age to lexicography and semantics. Within the syntax of a classical generative grammar there must be a lexicon, which must tell, among other things, what words and idioms mean; and the semantic component of the description must in turn give rules for determining the meanings of sentences from their elements and from the ways in which those elements are combined. Some first steps have already been taken to construct a theory of the lexicon and a theory of semantic interpretation, so that the most alert of popularizers are talking now of generative semantics as well as—or even instead of—generative grammar. Though the results are still limited, still mainly theoretical, still savagely debated, the new interest is a welcome sign of life and growth, and if scholars can become theorists, and theorists scholars, today's intellectual daydreams may be tomorrow's solid accomplishments. Meanwhile it has seemed best, in this introductory book, to represent the past few decades of good work on historical semantics by the chapter from Stephen Ullmann, so that the reader may see what traditional scholarship offers for reinterpretation and possible new synthesis: a rich detailing of the histories of individual words, some efforts at typologies of semantic change, and some understanding of processes by which such change may come about.

The situation in historical syntax is much the same. The structuralists, in their thirty years' domination of the linguistic scene in the United States, had a good deal to say about the inadequacy of traditional syntax, both historical and descriptive, which was founded, they thought, on irrelevant philosophical prepossessions; yet the structuralists produced at most one major English grammar and no serious history of the English language. The great individualist Otto Jespersen (whom structuralist and generativist alike have called traditional) had perhaps a more subtle instrument for describing syntax than Bloomfield and his followers; but though Jespersen's seven volumes on modern English grammar say a good deal about history, still he had no *explicit* means for stating syntactic relations between successive stages of a language. More recent Continental scholars like Brunner, Mustanoja, and most lately Visser have also gathered great masses of syntactic data, but again without the clear analysis which contemporary linguists properly demand.

Generative historians, on the other hand, have been handicapped by the fact that almost none of them have the detailed factual knowledge of earlier stages of English which the writer of a good history must possess. Their principal accomplishment so far has been the sharpening of theoretical discussion, the raising of intellectual standards, the framing of new and more subtle questions. No one who talks today about Old or Middle English can be content with the kind of statement which he might happily have made or tolerated ten or twenty years ago, but similarly no one can be content with the kinds of answers to the new questions that have so far been proposed.

Yet if it is impossible to anthologize a new order of questions or a new level of acuity and awareness, it is equally impossible not to sense the high hopes they have bred in a time of general desperation. Readers will not forget that our brief remarks and even our selections from famous scholars are the merest introduction to some main lines of development in historical linguistics, especially English linguistics. Those who take the bibliography's suggestions for further reading may share the excitement of an enterprise which seems constantly to renew itself.

It would almost be a pity for speech to destroy the speaking animal.

BIBLIOGRAPHY OF HISTORICAL LINGUISTICS

The development of traditional historical linguistics is most clearly traced in Holger Pedersen, *Linguistic Science in the Nineteenth Century*, tr. by J. W. Spargo (Cambridge, Mass., 1931); reprinted as *The Discovery of Language* (Bloomington, Indiana, 1962). Weaknesses in Pedersen's account are, first, an overconcentration on Indo-European work and, second, a tendency to treat the development of theory and technique as rather too neat and straightforward. A limited but useful corrective is Hans Aarsleff, *The Study of Language in England, 1780–1860* (Princeton, 1967), which sets forth the conflicting traditions from which "modern linguistics" emerged in England. The synthesis of nineteenth-century labors can best be seen in

Sapir's *Language* (New York, 1921) and Bloomfield's *Language* (New York, 1933). Other valuable studies, presenting somewhat different theories to varied audiences, include Charles Hockett, *A Course in Modern Linguistics* (New York, 1958), Chaps. 41–61; Henry M. Hoenigswald, *Language Change and Linguistic Reconstruction* (Chicago, 1960); Winfred P. Lehmann, *Historical Linguistics: An Introduction* (New York, 1962); Antoine Meillet, *Linguistique historique et linguistique générale* (2nd ed.; Paris, 1938); Hermann Paul, *Prinzipien der Sprachgeschichte* (5th ed.; Halle, 1920), translated as *Principles of the History of Language* by H. A. Strong (revised ed.; London, 1891); E. H. Sturtevant, *An Introduction to Linguistic Science* (New Haven, 1947), Chaps. VIII–XV, and *Linguistic Change: An Introduction to the Historical Study of Languages* (Chicago, 1917), reprinted as a Phoenix paperback (Chicago, 1961). Two recent statements which do not depart from Bloomfield or Sapir in principle but take note of current objections are Mary R. Haas, "Historical Linguistics and the Genetic Relationship of Languages," in *Current Trends in Linguistics* 3 (The Hague, 1966), 113–153, and Charles Hockett, "Sound Change," *Language* 41 (1965), 185–205. A more challenging essay is Uriel Weinreich, William Labov, and Marvin I. Herzog, "Empirical Foundations for a Theory of Language Change," in W. P. Lehmann and Yakov Malkiel, eds., *Directions for Historical Linguistics* (Austin, Texas, 1968).

Some lines in the European tradition of dissent, with its insistence that "every word has its own history," are conveniently traced in the aging account by Iorgu Iordan (translated by John Orr), *An Introduction to Romance Linguistics* (London, 1937). For a discussion of the importance of contact phenomena in linguistic change, see Uriel Weinreich, *Languages in Contact* (New York, 1953). For social factors, see William Labov, "The Social Motivation of a Sound Change," *Word* 19 (1963), 273–310, and "On the Mechanism of Linguistic Change," *Georgetown University Monographs in Languages and Linguistics*, 18 (1966), 91–114.

For transformational discussions of historical phonology, see Paul M. Postal, *Aspects of Phonological Theory* (New York, 1968), Part II, and Noam Chomsky and Morris Halle, *The Sound Pattern of English* (New York, 1968), Part III. An earlier attempt is Halle's "Phonology in Generative Grammar," reprinted in Fodor and Katz, *The Structure of Language* (Englewood Cliffs, N.J., 1964). A number of unpublished papers and dissertations have been done, among them Paul Kiparsky's MIT dissertation "Phonological Change" (Cambridge, 1965). A large-scale historical treatment is promised in Morris Halle and Samuel Jay Keyser, *The Evolution of English Stress*.

Transformational discussions of syntactic change are harder to come by. They include Elizabeth Closs (Traugott), "Diachronic Syntax and Generative Grammar," *Language* 41 (1965), 402–415, and Edward S. Klima, "Relatedness between Grammatical Systems," *Language* 40 (1964), 1–20. Unpublished work (some of it widely available on microfilm or in mechanically duplicated versions) includes Klima's Harvard dissertation, *Studies in Diachronic Transformational Syntax* (1965); Rudolfo Jacobson, *The London Dialect of the Late Fourteenth Century: A Transformational Analysis in Historical Linguistics* (Michigan dissertation, to appear); and Mrs. Traugott's essays, "Deep and Surface Structure in Alfredian Prose" (August, 1967) and "Toward a Grammar of Syntactic Change" (April, 1968).

Useful older textbooks for the history of English include A. C. Baugh, *A History of the English Language* (2nd ed.; New York, 1957); Thomas Pyles, *The Origins and Development of the English Language* (New York, 1964), with an accompanying workbook by Pyles and John Algeo; Stuart Robertson and Frederic G. Cassidy, *The Development of Modern English* (revised ed.; Englewood Cliffs, N.J., 1954); Margaret Schlauch, *The English Language in Modern Times* (Warsaw and London, 1959); and H. C. Wyld, *A History of Modern Colloquial English* (3rd ed.; Oxford, 1956), notable for its special concentration on the spoken language. Among more recent textbooks are Robert A. Peters, *A Linguistic History of English* (New York, 1968); Robert D. Stevick, *English and Its History* (Boston, 1968); and Charles T. Scott and Jon L. Erickson, *Readings for the History of the English Language* (Boston, 1968).

There are no larger-scale histories of English *in* English; but a valuable one in German is Karl Brunner, *Die englische Sprache* (2nd ed.; Tübingen, 1960, 1962), and large partial histories have been published by Tauno F. Mustanoja (*A Middle English Syntax*, Part I; Helsinki, 1960) and F. Th. Visser (*An Historical Syntax of the English Language*, Parts I and II; Leiden, 1963, 1966). Of particular value are the big historically oriented grammars like Otto Jespersen's *A Modern English Grammar on Historical Principles* (7 vols.; reprinted London, 1961). *The Oxford English Dictionary*, of course, is a rich source of information on morphological and syntactic change as well as historical semantics. For more specialized studies, the student should consult Harold B. Allen's bibliography *Linguistics and English Linguistics* (New York, 1966), the bibliographies in the texts listed above, and the annual bibliography in the journal *PMLA*.

Edward Sapir

LANGUAGE AS A HISTORICAL PRODUCT: DRIFT

Sapir's earliest graduate work, undertaken in the first decade of the twentieth century, was in historical linguistics, Indo-European, particularly Germanic. Although he was to go on to work in other fields—anthropology and psychology —as well as linguistics, and to emphasize the study of American Indian languages, he never lost interest in the Indo-European family or in the phenomena of linguistic change. Working from the classical assumptions of the historians, he attempted to postulate genetic relationships among the numerous and widely divergent languages of the Americas (for a sampling of this work see the section "Studies of American Indian Languages" in *Selected Writings of Edward Sapir*, edited by David G. Mandelbaum, Berkeley, 1951). In his monograph *Time Perspective* he sought to apply methods derived from historical linguistics to other cultural data.

The following chapter from Sapir's important but only book for a general audience reflects both his indebtedness to established historical theory and his most important and characteristic contribution to the study of language: an interdisciplinary approach and an eagerness to go beyond data to explanation.

Everyone knows that language is variable. Two individuals of the same generation and locality, speaking precisely the same dialect and moving in the same social circles, are never absolutely at one in their speech habits. A minute investigation of the speech of each individual would reveal countless differences of detail—in choice of words, in sentence structure, in the relative frequency with which particular forms or combinations of words are used, in the pronunciation of particular vowels and consonants and of combinations of vowels and consonants, in all those features, such as speed, stress, and tone, that give life to spoken language. In a sense they speak slightly divergent dialects of the same language rather than identically the same language.

There is an important difference, however, between individual and dialectic variations. If we take two closely related dialects, say English as spoken by the "middle classes" of London and English as spoken by the average New Yorker, we observe that, however much the individual speakers in each city differ from each other, the body of Londoners forms a compact, relatively unified group in contrast to the body of New Yorkers. The individual variations are swamped in or absorbed by certain major agreements—say of pronunciation and vocabulary—which stand out very strongly when the language of the group as a whole is contrasted with that of the other group. This means that there is something like an ideal linguistic entity dominating the speech habits of the members of each group, that the sense of almost unlimited freedom which each individual feels in the use of his language is held in leash by a tacitly directing norm. One individual plays on the norm in a way peculiar to himself, the next individual is nearer the dead average in that particular respect in which the first speaker most characteristically departs from it but in turn diverges from the average in a way peculiar to himself, and so on. What keeps the individual's variations from rising to dialectic importance is not merely the fact that they are in any event of small moment—there are well-marked dialectic variations that are of no greater magnitude than individual variations within a dialect—it is chiefly that they are silently "corrected" or canceled by the consensus of usage. If all the speakers of a given dialect were arranged in order in accordance with the degree of their conformity to average usage, there is little doubt that they would constitute a very finely intergrading series clustered about a well-defined center or norm. The differences between any two neighboring speakers of the series[1] would be negligible for any but the most microscopic linguistic research. The differences between the outermost members of the series are sure to be considerable, in all likelihood considerable enough to measure up to a true dialectic variation. What prevents us from saying that these untypical individuals speak distinct dialects is that their peculiarities, as a unified whole, are not referable to another norm than the norm of their own series.

If the speech of any member of the series could actually be made to fit into another dialect series,[2] we should have no true barriers between dialects (and languages) at all. We should merely have a continuous series of individual variations extending over the whole range of a historically unified linguistic area, and the cutting up of this large area (in some cases embracing parts of several continents) into distinct dialects and languages would be an essentially arbitrary proceeding with no warrant save that of practical convenience. But such a conception of the nature of dialectic variation does not correspond to the facts as we know them. Isolated individuals may be found who speak a compromise between two dialects of a language, and if their number and importance increases they may even end by creating a new dialectic norm of their own, a dialect in which the

---

[1] In so far as they do not fall out of the normal speech group by reason of a marked speech defect or because they are isolated foreigners that have acquired the language late in life.

[2] Observe that we are speaking of an individual's speech as a whole. It is not a question of isolating some particular peculiarity of pronunciation or usage and noting its resemblance to or identity with a feature in another dialect.

extreme peculiarities of the parent dialects are ironed out. In course of time the compromise dialect may absorb the parents, though more frequently these will tend to linger indefinitely as marginal forms of the enlarged dialect area. But such phenomena—and they are common enough in the history of language—are evidently quite secondary. They are closely linked with such social developments as the rise of nationality, the formation of literatures that aim to have more than a local appeal, the movement of rural populations into the cities, and all those other tendencies that break up the intense localism that unsophisticated man has always found natural.

The explanation of primary dialectic differences is still to seek. It is evidently not enough to say that if a dialect or language is spoken in two distinct localities or by two distinct social strata it naturally takes on distinctive forms, which in time come to be divergent enough to deserve the name of dialects. This is certainly true as far as it goes. Dialects do belong, in the first instance, to very definitely circumscribed social groups, homogeneous enough to secure the common feeling and purpose needed to create a norm. But the embarrassing question immediately arises: If all the individual variations within a dialect are being constantly leveled out to the dialectic norm, if there is no appreciable tendency for the individual's peculiarities to initiate a dialectic schism, why should we have dialectic variations at all? Ought not the norm, wherever and whenever threatened, automatically to reassert itself? Ought not the individual variations of each locality, even in the absence of intercourse between them, to cancel out to the same accepted speech average?

If individual variations "on a flat" were the only kind of variability in language, I believe we should be at a loss to explain why and how dialects arise, why it is that a linguistic prototype gradually breaks up into a number of mutually unintelligible languages. But language is not merely something that is spread out in space, as it were—a series of reflections in individual minds of one and the same timeless picture. Language moves down time in a current of its own making. It has a drift. If there were no breaking up of a language into dialects, if each language continued as a firm, self-contained unity, it would still be constantly moving away from any assignable norm, developing new features unceasingly and gradually transforming itself into a language so different from its starting point as to be in effect a new language. New dialects arise not because of the mere fact of individual variation but because two or more groups of individuals have become sufficiently disconnected to drift apart, or independently, instead of together. So long as they keep strictly together, no amount of individual variation would lead to the formation of dialects. In practice, of course, no language can be spread over a vast territory or even over a considerable area without showing dialectic variations, for it is impossible to keep a large population from segregating itself into local groups, the language of each of which tends to drift independently. Under cultural conditions such as apparently prevail to-day, conditions that fight localism at every turn, the tendency to dialectic cleavage is being constantly counteracted and in part "corrected" by the uniformizing factors already referred to. Yet even in so young a country as America the dialectic differences are not inconsiderable.

Under primitive conditions the political groups are small, the tendency to localism exceedingly strong. It is natural, therefore, that the languages of primitive folk or of non-urban populations in general are differentiated into a great number of dialects. There are parts of the globe where almost every village has its own dialect. The life of the geographically limited community is narrow and intense: its speech is correspondingly peculiar to itself. It is exceedingly doubtful if a language will ever be spoken over a wide area without multiplying itself dialectically. No sooner are the old dialects ironed out by compromises or ousted by the spread and influence of the one dialect which is culturally predominant when a new crop of dialects arises to undo the leveling work of the past. This is precisely what happened in Greece, for instance. In classical antiquity there were spoken a large number of local dialects, several of which are represented in the literature. As the cultural supremacy of Athens grew, its dialect, the Attic, spread at the expense of the rest, until, in the so-called Hellenistic period following the Macedonian conquest, the Attic dialect, in the vulgarized form known as the "Koine," became the standard speech of all Greece. But this linguistic uniformity[3] did not long continue. During the two millennia that separate the Greek of to-day from its classical prototype the Koine gradually split up into a number of dialects. Now Greece is as richly diversified in speech as in the time of Homer, though the present local dialects, aside from those of Attica itself, are not the lineal descendants of the old dialects of pre-Alexandrian days.[4] The experience of Greece is not exceptional. Old dialects are being continually wiped out only to make room for new ones. Languages can change at so many points of phonetics, morphology, and vocabulary that it is not surprising that once the linguistic community is broken it should slip off in different directions. It would be too much to expect a locally diversified language to develop along strictly parallel lines. If once the speech of a locality has begun to drift on its own account, it is practically certain to move further and further away from its linguistic fellows. Failing the retarding effect of dialectic interinfluences, which I have already

---

[3] It is doubtful if we have the right to speak of linguistic uniformity even during the predominance of the Koine. It is hardly conceivable that when the various groups of non-Attic Greeks took on the Koine they did not at once tinge it with dialectic peculiarities induced by their previous speech habits.
[4] The Zaconic dialect of Lacedaemon is the sole exception. It is not derived from the Koine, but stems directly from the Doric dialect of Sparta.

touched upon, a group of dialects is bound to diverge on the whole, each from all of the others.

In course of time each dialect itself splits up into subdialects, which gradually take on the dignity of dialects proper while the primary dialects develop into mutually unintelligible languages. And so the budding process continues, until the divergences become so great that none but a linguistic student, armed with his documentary evidence and with his comparative or reconstructive method, would infer that the languages in question were genealogically related, represented independent lines of development, in other words, from a remote and common starting point. Yet it is as certain as any historical fact can be that languages so little resembling each other as Modern Irish, English, Italian, Greek, Russian, Armenian, Persian, and Bengali are but end-points in the present of drifts that converge to a meeting-point in the dim past. There is naturally no reason to believe that this earliest "Indo-European" (or "Aryan") prototype which we can in part reconstruct, in part but dimly guess at, is itself other than a single "dialect" of a group that has either become largely extinct or is now further represented by languages too divergent for us, with our limited means, to recognize as clear kin.[5]

All languages that are known to be genetically related, i.e., to be divergent forms of a single prototype, may be considered as constituting a "linguistic stock." There is nothing final about a linguistic stock. When we set it up, we merely say, in effect, that thus far we can go and no farther. At any point in the progress of our researches an unexpected ray of light may reveal the "stock" as but a "dialect" of a larger group. The terms dialect, language, branch, stock—it goes without saying—are purely relative terms. They are convertible as our perspective widens or contracts.[6] It would be vain to speculate as to whether or not we shall ever be able to demonstrate that all languages stem from a common source. Of late years linguists have been able to make larger historical syntheses than were at one time deemed feasible, just as students of culture have been able to show historical connections between culture areas or institutions that were at one time believed to be totally isolated from each other. The human world is contracting not only prospectively but to the backward-probing eye of culture-history. Nevertheless we are as yet far from able to reduce the riot of spoken languages to a small number of "stocks." We must still operate with a quite considerable number of these stocks. Some of them, like Indo-European or Indo-Chinese, are spoken over tremendous reaches; others, like

---

[5] Though indications are not lacking of what these remoter kin of the Indo-European languages may be. This is disputed ground, however, and hardly fit subject for a purely general study of speech.

[6] "Dialect" in contrast to an accepted literary norm is a use of the term that we are not considering.

Basque,[7] have a curiously restricted range and are in all likelihood but dwindling remnants of groups that were at one time more widely distributed. As for the single or multiple origin of speech, it is likely enough that language as a human institution (or, if one prefers, as a human "faculty") developed but once in the history of the race, that all the complex history of language is a unique cultural event. Such a theory constructed "on general principles" is of no real interest, however, to linguistic science. What lies beyond the demonstrable must be left to the philosopher or the romancer.

We must return to the conception of "drift" in language. If the historical changes that take place in a language, if the vast accumulation of minute modifications which in time results in the complete remodeling of the language, are not in essence identical with the individual variations that we note on every hand about us, if these variations are born only to die without a trace, while the equally minute, or even minuter, changes that make up the drift are forever imprinted on the history of the language, are we not imputing to this history a certain mystical quality? Are we not giving language a power to change of its own accord over and above the involuntary tendency of individuals to vary the norm? And if this drift of language is not merely the familiar set of individual variations seen in vertical perspective, that is historically, instead of horizontally, that is in daily experience, what is it? Language exists only in so far as it is actually used—spoken and heard, written and read. What significant changes take place in it must exist, to begin with, as individual variations. This is perfectly true, and yet it by no means follows that the general drift of language can be understood[8] from an exhaustive descriptive study of these variations alone. They themselves are random phenomena,[9] like the waves of the sea, moving backward and forward in purposeless flux. The linguistic drift has direction. In other words, only those individual variations embody it or carry it which move in a certain direction, just as only certain wave movements in the bay outline the tide. The drift of a language is constituted by the unconscious selection on the part of its speakers of those individual variations that are cumulative in some special direction. This direction may be inferred, in the main, from the past history of the language. In the long run any new feature of the drift becomes part and parcel of the common accepted speech, but for a long time it may exist as a mere tendency in the speech of a few, perhaps of a despised few. As we look about us and observe current usage, it is not likely to occur to us that our language has a "slope," that the changes of the next few centuries are in a sense prefigured in certain obscure tendencies of the present and that these changes, when consummated, will be seen to be but

---

[7] Spoken in France and Spain in the region of the Pyrenees.
[8] Or rather apprehended, for we do not, in sober fact, entirely understand it as yet.
[9] Not ultimately random, of course, only relatively so.

continuations of changes that have been already effected. We feel rather that our language is practically a fixed system and that what slight changes are destined to take place in it are as likely to move in one direction as another. The feeling is fallacious. Our very uncertainty as to the impending details of change makes the eventual consistency of their direction all the more impressive.

Sometimes we can feel where the drift is taking us even while we struggle against it. Probably the majority of those who read these words feel that it is quite "incorrect" to say "Who did you see?" We readers of many books are still very careful to say "Whom did you see?" but we feel a little uncomfortable (uncomfortably proud, it may be) in the process. We are likely to avoid the locution altogether and to say "Who was it you saw?" conserving literary tradition (the "whom") with the dignity of silence.[10] The folk makes no apology. "Whom did you see?" might do for an epitaph, but "Who did you see?" is the natural form for an eager inquiry. It is of course the uncontrolled speech of the folk to which we must look for advance information as to the general linguistic movement. It is safe to prophesy that within a couple of hundred years from to-day not even the most learned jurist will be saying "Whom did you see?" By that time the "whom" will be as delightfully archaic as the Elizabethan "his" for "its."[11] No logical or historical argument will avail to save this hapless "whom." The demonstration "I:me = he:him = who:whom" will be convincing in theory and will go unheeded in practice.

Even now we may go so far as to say that the majority of us are secretly wishing they could say "Who did you see?" It would be a weight off their unconscious minds if some divine authority, overruling the lifted finger of the pedagogue, gave them *carte blanche*. But we cannot too frankly anticipate the drift and maintain caste. We must affect ignorance of whither we are going and rest content with our mental conflict—uncomfortable conscious acceptance of the "whom," unconscious desire for the "who."[12] Meanwhile we indulge our sneaking desire for the forbidden locution by the use of the "who" in certain twilight cases in which we can cover up our fault by a bit of unconscious special pleading. Imagine that some one drops

[10] In relative clauses too we tend to avoid the objective form of "who." Instead of "The man whom I saw" we are likely to say "The man that I saw" or "The man I saw."

[11] "Its" was at one time as impertinent a departure as the "who" of "Who did you see?" It forced itself into English because the old cleavage between masculine, feminine, and neuter was being slowly and powerfully supplemented by a new one between thing-class and animate-class. The latter classification proved too vital to allow usage to couple males and things ("his") as against females ("her"). The form "its" had to be created on the analogy of words like "man's," to satisfy the growing form feeling. The drift was strong enough to sanction a grammatical blunder.

[12] Psychoanalysts will recognize the mechanism. The mechanisms of "repression of impulse" and of its symptomatic symbolization can be illustrated in the most unexpected corners of individual and group psychology. A more general psychology than Freud's will eventually prove them to be as applicable to the groping for abstract form, the logical or esthetic ordering of experience, as to the life of the fundamental instincts.

the remark when you are not listening attentively, "John Smith is coming to-night." You have not caught the name and ask, not "Whom did you say?" but "Who did you say?" There is likely to be a little hesitation in the choice of the form, but the precedent of usages like "Whom did you see?" will probably not seem quite strong enough to induce a "Whom did you say?" Not quite relevant enough, the grammarian may remark, for a sentence like "Who did you say?" is not strictly analogous to "Whom did you see?" or "Whom did you mean?" It is rather an abbreviated form of some such sentence as "Who, did you say, is coming to-night?" This is the special pleading that I have referred to, and it has a certain logic on its side. Yet the case is more hollow than the grammarian thinks it to be, for in reply to such a query as "You're a good hand at bridge, John, aren't you?" John, a little taken aback, might mutter "Did you say me?" hardly "Did you say I?" Yet the logic for the latter ("Did you say I was a good hand at bridge?") is evident. The real point is that there is not enough vitality in the "whom" to carry it over such little difficulties as a "me" can compass without a thought. The proportion "I:me = he:him = who:whom" is logically and historically sound, but psychologically shaky. "Whom did you see?" is correct, but there is something false about its correctness.

It is worth looking into the reason for our curious reluctance to use locutions involving the word "whom," particularly in its interrogative sense. The only distinctively objective forms which we still possess in English are *me*, *him*, *her* (a little blurred because of its identity with the possessive *her*), *us*, *them*, and *whom*. In all other cases the objective has come to be identical with the subjective—that is, in outer form, for we are not now taking account of position in the sentence. We observe immediately in looking through the list of objective forms that *whom* is psychologically isolated. *Me*, *him*, *her*, *us*, and *them* form a solid, well-integrated group of objective personal pronouns parallel to the subjective series *I*, *he*, *she*, *we*, *they*. The forms *who* and *whom* are technically "pronouns" but they are not felt to be in the same box as the personal pronouns. *Whom* has clearly a weak position, an exposed flank, for words of a feather tend to flock together, and if one strays behind, it is likely to incur danger of life. Now the other interrogative and relative pronouns (*which*, *what*, *that*), with which *whom* should properly flock, do not distinguish the subjective and objective forms. It is psychologically unsound to draw the line of form cleavage between *whom* and the personal pronouns on the one side, the remaining interrogative and relative pronouns on the other. The form groups should be symmetrically related to, if not identical with, the function groups. Had *which*, *what*, and *that* objective forms parallel to *whom*, the position of this last would be more secure. As it is, there is something unesthetic about the word. It suggests a form pattern which is not filled out by its fellows. The only way to remedy the irregularity of form distribution is to abandon the *whom* altogether, for we have lost the power to create new objective forms and cannot remodel our *which-what-that* group so as to make it parallel with the smaller group *who-whom*. Once this is done, *who* joins its flock and our unconscious desire for form symmetry is satisfied. We do not secretly chafe at "Whom did you see?" without reason.[13]

But the drift away from *whom* has still other determinants. The words *who* and *whom* in their interrogative sense are psychologically related not merely to the pronouns *which* and *what*, but to a group of interrogative adverbs— *where, when, how*—all of which are invariable and generally emphatic. I believe it is safe to infer that there is a rather strong feeling in English that the interrogative pronoun or adverb, typically an emphatic element in the sentence, should be invariable. The inflective-*m* of *whom* is felt as a drag upon the rhetorical effectiveness of the word. It needs to be eliminated if the interrogative pronoun is to receive all its latent power. There is still a third, and a very powerful, reason for the avoidance of *whom*. The contrast between the subjective and objective series of personal pronouns (*I, he, she, we, they: me, him, her, us, them*) is in English associated with a difference of position. We say *I see the man* but *the man sees me; he told him*, never *him he told* or *him told he*. Such usages as the last two are distinctly poetic and archaic; they are opposed to the present drift of the language. Even in the interrogative one does not say *Him did you see?* It is only in sentences of the type *Whom did you see?* that an inflected objective before the verb is now used at all. On the other hand, the order in *Whom did you see?* is imperative because of its interrogative form; the interrogative pronoun or adverb normally comes first in the sentence (*What are you doing? When did he go? Where are you from?*). In the "whom" of *Whom did you see?* there is concealed, therefore, a conflict between the order proper to a sentence containing an inflected objective and the order natural to a sentence with an interrogative pronoun or adverb. The solution *Did you see whom?* or *You saw whom?*[14] is too contrary to the idiomatic drift of our language to receive acceptance. The more radical solution *Who did you see?* is the one the language is gradually making for.

These three conflicts—on the score of form grouping, of rhetorical emphasis, and of order—are supplemented by a fourth difficulty. The emphatic *whom*, with its heavy build (half-long vowel followed by labial con-

[13] Note that it is different with *whose*. This has not the support of analogous possessive forms in its own functional group, but the analogical power of the great body of possessives of nouns (*man's, boy's*) as well as of certain personal pronouns (*his, its;* as predicated possessive also *hers, yours, theirs*) is sufficient to give it vitality.

[14] Aside from certain idiomatic usages, as when *You saw whom?* is equivalent to *You saw so and so and that so and so is who?* In such sentences *whom* is pronounced high and lingeringly to emphasize the fact that the person just referred to by the listener is not known or recognized.

sonant), should contrast with a lightly tripping syllable immediately following. In *whom did*, however, we have an involuntary retardation that
makes the locution sound "clumsy." This clumsiness is a phonetic verdict,
quite apart from the dissatisfaction due to the grammatical factors which
we have analyzed. The same prosodic objection does not apply to such
parallel locutions as *what did* and *when did*. The vowels of *what* and *when*
are shorter and their final consonants melt easily into the following *d*,
which is pronounced in the same tongue position as *t* and *n*. Our instinct for
appropriate rhythms makes it as difficult for us to feel content with *whom
did* as for a poet to use words like *dreamed* and *hummed* in a rapid line.
Neither common feeling nor the poet's choice need be at all conscious. It
may be that not all are equally sensitive to the rhythmic flow of speech,
but it is probable that rhythm is an unconscious linguistic determinant even
with those who set little store by its artistic use. In any event the poet's
rhythms can only be a more sensitive and stylized application of rhythmic
tendencies that are characteristic of the daily speech of his people.

We have discovered no less than four factors which enter into our subtle
disinclination to say "Whom did you see?" The uneducated folk that says
"Who did you see?" with no twinge of conscience has a more acute flair for
the genuine drift of the language than its students. Naturally the four re-
straining factors do not operate independently. Their separate energies, if
we may make bold to use a mechanical concept, are "canalized" into a
single force. This force or minute embodiment of the general drift of the
language is psychologically registered as a slight hesitation in using the word
whom. The hesitation is likely to be quite unconscious, though it may be
readily acknowledged when attention is called to it. The analysis is certain
to be unconscious, or rather unknown, to the normal speaker.[15] How, then,
can we be certain in such an analysis as we have undertaken that all of the
assigned determinants are really operative and not merely some one of
them? Certainly they are not equally powerful in all cases. Their values
are variable, rising and falling according to the individual and the locution.[16]
But that they really exist, each in its own right, may sometimes be tested
by the method of elimination. If one or other of the factors is missing and
we observe a slight diminution in the corresponding psychological reaction
("hesitation" in our case), we may conclude that the factor is in other uses
genuinely positive. The second of our four factors applies only to the interrogative use of *whom*, the fourth factor applies with more force to the inter-

---

[15] Students of language cannot be entirely normal in their attitude towards their own speech. Perhaps it would
be better to say "naïve" than "normal."
[16] It is probably this *variability of value* in the significant compounds of a general linguistic drift that is responsible for the rise of dialectic variations. Each dialect continues the general drift of the common parent,
but has not been able to hold fast to constant values for each component of the drift. Deviations as to the
drift itself, at first slight, later cumulative, are therefore unavoidable.

rogative than to the relative. We can therefore understand why a sentence like *Is he the man whom you referred to?* though not as idiomatic as *Is he the man (that) you referred to?* (remember that it sins against counts one and three), is still not as difficult to reconcile with our innate feeling for English expression as *Whom did you see?* If we eliminate the fourth factor from the interrogative usage,[17] say in *Whom are you looking at?* where the vowel following *whom* relieves this word of its phonetic weight, we can observe, if I am not mistaken, a lesser reluctance to use the *whom. Who are you looking at?* might even sound slightly offensive to ears that welcome *Who did you see?*

We may set up a scale of "hesitation values" somewhat after this fashion:

Value 1: factors 1, 3.   "The man whom I referred to."
Value 2: factors 1, 3, 4.   "The man whom they referred to."
Value 3: factors 1, 2, 3.   "Whom are you looking at?"
Value 4: factors 1, 2, 3, 4. "Whom did you see?"

We may venture to surmise that while *whom* will ultimately disappear from English speech, locutions of the type *Whom did you see?* will be obsolete when phrases like *The man whom I referred to* are still in lingering use. It is impossible to be certain, however, for we can never tell if we have isolated all the determinants of a drift. In our particular case we have ignored what may well prove to be a controlling factor in the history of *who* and *whom* in the relative sense. This is the unconscious desire to leave these words to their interrogative function and to concentrate on *that* or mere word order as expressions of the relative (e.g., *The man that I referred to* or *The man I referred to*). This drift, which does not directly concern the use of *whom* as such (merely of *whom* as a form of *who*), may have made the relative *who* obsolete before the other factors affecting relative *whom* have run their course. A consideration like this is instructive because it indicates that knowledge of the general drift of a language is insufficient to enable us to see clearly what the drift is heading for. We need to know something of the relative potencies and speeds of the components of the drift.

It is hardly necessary to say that the particular drifts involved in the use of *whom* are of interest to us not for their own sake but as symptoms of larger tendencies at work in the language. At least three drifts of major importance are discernible. Each of these has operated for centuries, each is at work in other parts of our linguistic mechanism, each is almost certain to continue for centuries, possibly millennia. The first is the familiar tendency to level the distinction between the subjective and the objective, itself but a late chapter in the steady reduction of the old Indo-European

---

[17] Most sentences beginning with interrogative *whom* are likely to be followed by *did* or *does, do.* Yet not all.

system of syntactic cases. This system, which is at present best preserved in Lithuanian,[18] was already considerably reduced in the old Germanic language of which English, Dutch, German, Danish, and Swedish are modern dialectic forms. The seven Indo-European cases (nominative, genitive, dative, accusative, ablative, locative, instrumental) had been already reduced to four (nominative, genitive, dative, accusative). We know this from a careful comparison of and reconstruction based on the oldest Germanic dialects of which we still have records (Gothic, Old Icelandic, Old High German, Anglo-Saxon). In the group of West Germanic dialects, for the study of which Old High German, Anglo-Saxon, Old Frisian, and Old Saxon are our oldest and most valuable sources, we still have these four cases, but the phonetic form of the case syllables is already greatly reduced and in certain paradigms particular cases have coalesced. The case system is practically intact but it is evidently moving towards further disintegration. Within the Anglo-Saxon and early Middle English period there took place further changes in the same direction. The phonetic form of the case syllables became still further reduced and the distinction between the accusative and the dative finally disappeared. The new "objective" is really an amalgam of old accusative and dative forms; thus *him*, the old dative (we still say *I give him the book*, not "abbreviated" from *I give to him;* compare Gothic *imma*, Modern German *ihm*), took over the functions of the old accusative (Anglo-Saxon *hine;* compare Gothic *ina*, Modern German *ihn*) and dative. The distinction between the nominative and accusative was nibbled away by phonetic processes and morphological levelings until only certain pronouns retained distinctive subjective and objective forms.

In later medieval and in modern times there have been comparatively few apparent changes in our case system apart from the gradual replacement of *thou—thee* (singular) and subjective *ye—*objective *you* (plural) by a single undifferentiated form *you*. All the while, however, the case system, such as it is (subjective-objective, really absolutive, and possessive in nouns; subjective, objective, and possessive in certain pronouns) has been steadily weakening in psychological respects. At present it is more seriously undermined than most of us realize. The possessive has little vitality except in the pronoun and in animate nouns. Theoretically we can still say *the moon's phases* or *a newspaper's vogue;* practically we limit ourselves pretty much to analytic locutions like *the phases of the moon* and *the vogue of a newspaper.* The drift is clearly toward the limitation of possessive forms to animate nouns. All the possessive pronominal forms except *its* and, in part, *their* and *theirs*, are also animate. It is significant that *theirs* is hardly ever used in

---

[18] Better, indeed, than in our oldest Latin and Greek records. The old Indo-Iranian languages alone (Sanskrit, Avestan) show an equally or more archaic status of the Indo-European parent tongue as regards case forms.

reference to inanimate nouns, that there is some reluctance to so use *their*, and that *its* also is beginning to give way to *of it*. *The appearance of it* or *the looks of it* is more in the current of the language than *its appearance*. It is curiously significant that *its young* (referring to an animal's cubs) is idiomatically preferable to *the young of it*. The form is only ostensibly neuter, in feeling it is animate; psychologically it belongs with *his children*, not with *the pieces of it*. Can it be that so common a word as *its* is actually beginning to be difficult? Is it too doomed to disappear? It would be rash to say that it shows signs of approaching obsolescence, but that it is steadily weakening is fairly clear.[19] In any event, it is not too much to say that there is a strong drift towards the restriction of the inflected possessive forms to animate nouns and pronouns.

How is it with the alternation of subjective and objective in the pronoun? Granted that *whom* is a weak sister, that the two cases have been leveled in *you* (in *it, that,* and *what* they were never distinct, so far as we can tell[20]), and that *her* as an objective is a trifle weak because of its formal identity with the possessive *her*, is there any reason to doubt the vitality of such alternations as *I see the man* and *the man sees me?* Surely the distinction between subjective *I* and objective *me*, between subjective *he* and objective *him*, and correspondingly for other personal pronouns, belongs to the very core of the language. We can throw *whom* to the dogs, somehow make shift to do without an *its*, but to level *I* and *me* to a single case—would that not be to un-English our language beyond recognition? There is no drift toward such horrors as *Me see him* or *I see he*. True, the phonetic disparity between *I* and *me, he* and *him, we* and *us,* has been too great for any serious possibility of form leveling. It does not follow that the case distinction as such is still vital. One of the most insidious peculiarities of a linguistic drift is that where it cannot destroy what lies in its way it renders it innocuous by washing the old significance out of it. It turns its very enemies to its own uses. This brings us to the second of the major drifts, the tendency to fixed position in the sentence, determined by the syntactic relation of the word.

We need not go into the history of this all-important drift. It is enough to know that as the inflected forms of English became scantier, as the syntactic relations were more and more inadequately expressed by the forms of the words themselves, position in the sentence gradually took over functions originally foreign to it. *The man* in *the man sees the dog* is subjective; in *the dog sees the man*, objective. Strictly parallel to these sentences are *he sees the dog* and *the dog sees him*. Are the subjective value of *he* and the objective

[19] Should *its* eventually drop out, it will have had a curious history. It will have played the rôle of a stop-gap between *his* in its non-personal use (see footnote 11, page 327) and the later analytic *of it*.
[20] Except in so far as *that* has absorbed other functions than such as originally belonged to it. It was only a nominative-accusative neuter to begin with.

value of *him* entirely, or even mainly, dependent on the difference of form? I doubt it. We could hold to such a view if it were possible to say *the dog sees he* or *him sees the dog*. It was once possible to say such things, but we have lost the power. In other words, at least part of the case feeling in *he* and *him* is to be credited to their position before or after the verb. May it not be, then, that *he* and *him*, *we* and *us*, are not so much subjective and objective forms as pre-verbal and post-verbal[21] forms, very much as *my* and *mine* are now pre-nominal and post-nominal forms of the possessive (*my father* but *father mine; it is my book* but *the book is mine*)? That this interpretation corresponds to the actual drift of the English language is again indicated by the language of the folk. The folk says *it is me*, not *it is I*, which is "correct" but just as falsely so as the *whom did you see?* that we have analyzed. *I'm the one, it's me; we're the ones, it's us that will win out*—such are the live parallelisms in English to-day. There is little doubt that *it is I* will one day be as impossible in English as *c'est je*, for *c'est moi*, is now in French.

How differently our *I:me* feels than in Chaucer's day is shown by the Chaucerian *it am I*. Here the distinctively subjective aspect of the *I* was enough to influence the form of the preceding verb in spite of the introductory *it;* Chaucer's locution clearly felt more like a Latin *sum ego* than a modern *it is I* or colloquial *it is me*. We have a curious bit of further evidence to prove that the English personal pronouns have lost some share of their original syntactic force. Were *he* and *she* subjective forms pure and simple, were they not striving, so to speak, to become caseless absolutives, like *man* or any other noun, we should not have been able to coin such compounds as *he-goat* and *she-goat*, words that are psychologically analogous to *bull-moose* and *mother-bear*. Again, in inquiring about a new-born baby, we ask *Is it a he or a she?* quite as though *he* and *she* were the equivalents of *male* and *female* or *boy* and *girl*. All in all, we may conclude that our English case system is weaker than it looks and that, in one way or another, it is destined to get itself reduced to an absolutive (caseless) form for all nouns and pronouns but those that are animate. Animate nouns and pronouns are sure to have distinctive possessive forms for an indefinitely long period.

Meanwhile observe that the old alignment of case forms is being invaded by two new categories—a positional category (pre-verbal, post-verbal) and a classificatory category (animate, inanimate). The facts that in the possessive animate nouns and pronouns are destined to be more and more sharply distinguished from inanimate nouns and pronouns (*the man's*, but *of the house; his*, but *of it*) and that, on the whole, it is only animate pro-

---

[21] Aside from the interrogative: *am I? is he?* Emphasis counts for something. There is a strong tendency for the old "objective" forms to bear a stronger stress than the "subjective" forms. This is why the stress in locutions like *He didn't go, did he?* and *isn't he?* is thrown back on the verb; it is not a matter of logical emphasis.

nouns that distinguish pre-verbal and post-verbal forms[22] are of the greatest theoretical interest. They show that, however the language strive for a more and more analytic form, it is by no means manifesting a drift toward the expression of "pure" relational concepts in the Indo-Chinese manner.[23] The insistence on the concreteness of the relational concepts is clearly stronger than the destructive power of the most sweeping and persistent drifts that we know of in the history and prehistory of our language.

The drift toward the abolition of most case distinctions and the correlative drift toward position as an all-important grammatical method are accompanied, in a sense dominated, by the last of the three major drifts that I have referred to. This is the drift toward the invariable word. In analyzing the "whom" sentence I pointed out that the rhetorical emphasis natural to an interrogative pronoun lost something by its form variability (*who, whose, whom*). This striving for a simple, unnuanced correspondence between idea and word, as invariable as may be, is very strong in English. It accounts for a number of tendencies which at first sight seem unconnected. Certain well-established forms, like the present third person singular -*s* of *works* or the plural -*s* of *books*, have resisted the drift to invariable words, possibly because they symbolize certain stronger form cravings that we do not yet fully understand. It is interesting to note that derivations that get away sufficiently from the concrete notion of the radical word to exist as independent conceptual centers are not affected by this elusive drift. As soon as the derivation runs danger of being felt as a mere nuancing of, a finicky play on, the primary concept, it tends to be absorbed by the radical word, to disappear as such. English words crave spaces between them, they do not like to huddle in clusters of slightly divergent centers of meaning, each edging a little away from the rest. *Goodness*, a noun of quality, almost a noun of relation, that takes its cue from the concrete idea of "good" without necessarily predicating that quality (e.g., *I do not think much of his goodness*) is sufficiently spaced from *good* itself not to need fear absorption. Similarly, *unable* can hold its own against *able* because it destroys the latter's sphere of influence; *unable* is psychologically as distinct from *able* as is *blundering* or *stupid*. It is different with adverbs in -*ly*. These lean too heavily on their adjectives to have the kind of vitality that English demands of its words. *Do it quickly!* drags psychologically. The nuance expressed by *quickly* is too close to that of *quick*, their circles of concreteness are too nearly the same, for the two words to feel comfortable together. The adverbs in -*ly* are likely to go to the wall in the not too distant future for this very reason and in

---

[22] *They: them* as an inanimate group may be looked upon as a kind of borrowing from the animate, to which, in feeling, it more properly belongs.

[23] [According to Sapir, the Indo-Chinese languages "keep the syntactic relations pure and . . . do not possess the power to modify the significance of their radical elements by means of affixes or internal changes."—*Eds.*]

face of their obvious usefulness. Another instance of the sacrifice of highly useful forms to this impatience of nuancing is the group *whence, whither, hence, hither, thence, thither*. They could not persist in live usage because they impinged too solidly upon the circles of meaning represented by the words *where, here* and *there*. In saying *whither* we feel too keenly that we repeat all of *where*. That we add to *where* an important nuance of direction irritates rather than satisfies. We prefer to merge the static and the directive (*Where do you live?* like *Where are you going?*) or, if need be, to overdo a little the concept of direction (*Where are you running to?*).

Now it is highly symptomatic of the nature of the drift away from word clusters that we do not object to nuances as such, we object to having the nuances formally earmarked for us. As a matter of fact our vocabulary is rich in near-synonyms and in groups of words that are psychologically near relatives, but these near-synonyms and these groups do not hang together by reason of etymology. We are satisfied with *believe* and *credible* just because they keep aloof from each other. *Good* and *well* go better together than *quick* and *quickly*. The English vocabulary is a rich medley because each English word wants its own castle. Has English long been peculiarly receptive to foreign words because it craves the staking out of as many word areas as possible, or, conversely, has the mechanical imposition of a flood of French and Latin loan-words, unrooted in our earlier tradition, so dulled our feeling for the possibilities of our native resources that we are allowing these to shrink by default? I suspect that both propositions are true. Each feeds on the other. I do not think it likely, however, that the borrowings in English have been as mechanical and external a process as they are generally represented to have been. There was something about the English drift as early as the period following the Norman Conquest that welcomed the new words. They were a compensation for something that was weakening within.

Study Questions

1. Explain Sapir's distinction between dialectal variations and individual variations within a dialect—that is, between dialect and idiolect. Why does he feel it essential that the historical linguist make the distinction? What does Sapir seem to mean by a dialectal *norm?* Does he suggest that the norm has psychological reality, or that it is a quantitative average of usage within a given speech area?

2. Sapir asserts that it is impossible to account significantly for linguistic

change simply by pointing out constant variation in speech. Why? What other factors must be recognized? Why is linguistic change more than the arithmetical accumulation of minute variations?

3. What is drift? If we do not identify it with individual variation in speech, where does it arise and where does it exist? Is it a tendency inherent in the language itself? Is it social, and related to the leveling effects of the dialectal norm? Would Labov's notion that a speech community might be better recognized "as a group of people who share a set of common norms in regard to language, rather than as a group of people who speak in the same way" help explain drift? Is drift psychological? What have repressed wishes and hesitation got to do with it? Where would the wishes come from?

4. Sapir recognizes three drifts of major significance operative in English. What are they? How do they reveal themselves? How do many drifts add up to one big drift? Could the idea of drift be reformulated within a theory of a language as a system of rules? For example, how does the *who-whom* example define *drift?* Is the implied definition compatible with a notion of linguistic change as rule-change—as regularization or simplification of a system of rules?

5. If Sapir's notion of drift is at all accurate, what are its implications for anyone trying to determine standards of correctness in language use? Can you think of any other examples of divided usage similar to *who-whom* which might be a result of "our unconscious desire for form symmetry"? Should teachers of English attempt to prescribe usage in such cases? What criteria other than historical ones might be relevant to determining what prescriptive statements to make? What assumptions about historical change and its relation to bases of usage underlie Sapir's statement: "It is of course the uncontrolled speech of the folk to which we must look for advance information as to the general linguistic movement"? Who are the folk?

Winfred Phillip Lehmann

CHANGE IN PHONOLOGICAL SYSTEMS

Winfred Phillip Lehmann (born 1916) is Ashbel Smith professor of linguistics and director of the Linguistics Research Center at the University of Texas. Although his major interest has been Indo-European linguistics with an emphasis on Germanic, his studies have ranged over a much wider area: Germanic verse forms, the teaching of second languages (English and Japanese as well as German), machine translation, and historical theory. His major books are *Proto-Indo-European Phonology* (1952), *The Development of Germanic Verse Form* (1956), and *Historical Linguistics*, from which the following selection is taken. He has recently edited and translated a collection of major documents in nineteenth-century historical linguistics (*A Reader in Nineteenth-Century Historical Indo-European Linguistics*, 1967) and with Yakov Malkiel has edited the symposium, *Directions for Historical Linguistics* (1968).

In this selection, Lehmann presents a typology and terminology of sound change consistent with American structuralist phonemics. He attempts to reinterpret the major types of sound change recognized in traditional theory—changes both isolative and contextually determined—by employing the structuralist concepts of *phoneme* and *allophone*. Lehmann criticizes traditional accounts of sound change for their failure to place individual changes within the sound systems which they affect, and suggests ways in which the view provided by structural phonemics might overcome this deficiency. As Lehmann acknowledges in bibliographical notes not reprinted here, his introductory treatment draws on the discussion of sound change in Bloomfield's *Language* (Chapters 20–22) and in Henry M. Hoenigswald's advanced text *Language Change and Linguistic Reconstruction*.

10.1   When languages are compared at various periods, we find correspondences between their entities. In comparing Middle English with Modern English, for example, we observe obvious correspondences between ME *set*, NE *set*, somewhat less obvious between ME *wīf*, NE *wife*, ME *hūs*, NE *house*. We conclude that NE *set, wife, house* are the contemporary forms of ME *set, wīf, hūs*, and we label these Modern English forms replacements for the Middle English. The investigation of such replacements between successive stages of a language is one of the chief concerns of historical linguistics. In this chapter we will deal with the patterns of replacement in sound systems and with phonological correspondences between entities at two or more stages of a language.

10.2   Between the English of Chaucer (†1400) and that spoken today probably all entities in the phonological system have changed. Some of the changes were very minor; Chaucer's pronunciation of ME *set* would probably be understood by us today, though in details it might seem odd. Other pronunciations of his we might not understand at all, such as his ME *see* /sē:/ versus our NE *see* /síy/, ME *tōth* /to:θ/versus our NE *tooth* /túwθ/. Historical grammars concern themselves largely with such striking changes. Yet to understand the process of change in language we must also deal with replacements which do not modify the system, and which therefore seem minor or not worth notice in general surveys dealing with the history of a language.

One feature of Chaucer's pronunciation of *set* which may seem odd to us is his articulation of /t/; it would probably remind us of the *t* used by a Spanish speaker. For at one time English /t d n/ were dentals. Over the past centuries their articulation has been progressively retracted, so that they are now alveolars. As this retraction took place, it caused no changes in the morphological system of the language. Nor was the system of phonemic contrasts affected. NE /t/ contrasts with NE /p k/ etc. just as did ME /t/ with ME /p k/ etc.

While such modifications are apparently going on constantly in language, we have little information about them. For only when phonological systems are altered, do speakers, including scribes, take account of changes. Since we have very few detailed descriptions of past languages, we will be able fully to understand sound changes only after linguists have compiled numerous statements on gradual modifications as well as phonemic changes in language. Such information has been assembled only recently, as for the voicing of American intervocalic /t/, as in *bottle, latter*. It must be gathered from all languages in which changes are observable.

10.3   For languages of the past we hypothecate modifications in pronunciation chiefly on the basis of subsequent changes in the system. In Middle English we do not posit a phoneme /ŋ/. We assume that /n/ had an [ŋ] allophone before velars. For when final /g/ was lost in forms like early NE *sing, sing* did not fall together with *sin*. Moreover, in his partial rimes, Layamon paired *stronge* and *londe* (see H. Pilch, *Layamons "Brut"* [Heidelberg, 1960], page 150). We assume therefore that ME /n/ before /k g/ was pronounced [ŋ], as in NE *stronger, finger*. In some stage of the language before Middle English, possibly very much earlier, [n] before /k g/ had undergone a subphonemic change to [ŋ].

The constant changes taking place in language may in this way lead to modifications in sound.[1] These modifications have no effect on the system

---

[1] [Lehmann appears to mean here that the constant nondistinctive or subphonemic changes lead to modifica-

until some further disruption occurs; by one such the conditioning element for a specific allophone may be lost, as in early NE *sing*. The appearance of new phonemes on such occasions informs us of previous allophonic changes in the language.

As a further example we may note pre-OE [y]. With [u] this must have been an allophone of pre-OE /u/; [y] occurred before /i iː j/, [u] elsewhere. Since the interchange was automatic, no new allophones of /u/ would have been apparent to the speakers. Only when in late pre-Old English the conditioning elements were modified was [y] distinguished from [u]. At that time [y] became a separate phoneme, as in OE *fyllan* 'fill' < **fulljan* versus OE *full*.

Scribes generally indicate contrasts which distinguish meaning, or betray them by inconsistencies or errors of spelling. With a long series of texts, we therefore are usually aware of any changes in the phonological system which have taken place over periods of a language.

10.4   In dealing with changes affecting a phonemic system we now require grammars to note not only individual changes but also that they present them within the systems of the two stages. In comparing Middle English and Modern English, for example, we expect that the Middle English and Modern English consonants as well as the vowel systems be provided us. Since grammars of the past dealt largely with individual phonological entities, they have rarely provided phonological systems of the languages under discussion. With our present awareness of the importance of structures and substructures in language, we find such historical grammars inadequate and look forward to improved presentations.

Comparing the Middle and Modern English consonant systems, we find little difference between them in number of phonemes.

Middle English						Modern English				
p	t	č	k			p	t	č	k	
b	d	ǰ	g			b	d	ǰ	g	
f	ϑ	s	š	x	h	f	ϑ	s	š		h
v	ð	z				v	ð	z	ž	
m	n					m	n	ŋ		
w	l	r	y			w	l	r	y	

One Middle English consonant phoneme /x/ has been lost, as in *thought*. Two new consonant phonemes have been added: /ŋ/ as noted above, and /ž/, which developed from clusters of /z/ and /y/, as in *vision*, and in

---

tions in the sound *system*, not just in sounds, since the constant changes he mentions *are* modifications in sound.—*Eds.*]

French loanwords, such as *rouge*. In structure, and number of members, the consonant systems of the two successive stages are markedly alike.

10.5   The vowel systems, however, are strikingly different. We give first the Middle English system, using a notation similar to Middle English orthography.

Short vowels		Long vowels		Diphthongs				
i	u	i:	u:					
e	o	e:	o:	ei	eu		oi	ou
a		æ:	a:			ai	au	

Apart from rearrangements, vowels of the Middle English short-vowel system underwent few modifications, as we may illustrate:

> ME ship   NE ship   ME busch   NE bush
> ME set   NE set   ME lock   NE (Brit.) lock
> ME bak (OE bæk)   NE back

In the environments given here, the allophones of the Middle English short vowels agree with those of Modern English, though ME /a/ was probably articulated farther back than is NE /æ/. Simply listing these correspondences, however, gives a completely inadequate view of the relationships between the two systems. For between Middle English and Modern English, additional vowel phonemes were added to the system, and the characterization of vowels by quantity was abandoned. Further, ME [ə], an allophone of ME /e/, has become a Modern English phoneme, with many additions from ME /u/, which in general became NE /ə/ except after labials, where it may have been restored, as in *put, bush, full, wolf*. The number of Modern English vowels was expanded by reduced long vowels which lost their quantity before two or more consonants. Before reviewing examples, we may compare correspondences between the Middle English long vowels and their Modern English counterparts.

Between Middle English and the present, the long vowels have changed markedly, undergoing a series of changes known as the Great English Vowel Shift. This shift is remarkable, for all the Middle English long vowels are modified similarly, by raising; /i: u:/, however, were already high vowels and could be raised no further. Their counterparts in Modern English are diphthongs, with first element at the lowest position of simple vowels, resulting in /ay/ and /aw/. ME /e:/ and /æ:/ have fallen together to NE /iy/; ME /a:/ was fronted and raised to the approximate position of the vowel in ME *seen;* ME /o:/ was raised to NE /uw/. Examples are:

ME	NE	ME	NE
wīf /wi:f/	wife /wáyf/	hous /hu:s/	house /háws/
seen /se:n/	seen /síyn/	spon /spo:n/	spoon /spúwn/
see /sæ:/	sea /síy/	name /na:me/	name /néym/

These remarkable changes alone would have resulted in a totally different vowel system, but the Middle English symmetrical system of diphthongs (the three low short vowels followed by the two high) was also markedly changed, especially those ending in *u*.

Middle English /ei ai/, which had probably fallen together by the time of Chaucer, coalesced with ME /a:/, e.g., ME *vein*, NE *vein* /véyn/, ME *day, dai* /dai/ > NE *day* /déy/.

ME /oi/ remained unchanged, e.g., ME *boi, boy* /boi/ > NE *boy* /bɔy/.

ME /eu/ coalesced with /uw/ from ME /o:/, e.g., ME *fruit* /freut/, NE *fruit* /frúwt/ (also /yuw/, e.g., *pure*).

ME /ou/ remained unchanged, e.g., ME *boue* /boue/ > NE *bow* /bów/.

ME /au/ became a low, back vowel, e.g., ME *cause* /kauze/ > NE *cause* /kɔz/.

It is clear from these examples that the Middle English vowel system was modified so markedly that it is difficult to plot the Modern English system beside it, as we have done for the consonants. Following the diphthongal analysis, proposed by Sweet, Wyld, Bloomfield, Bloch, Trager and others, we may present the Modern English vowel system of one idiolect as follows:

i ship		u bush	iy see		uw spoon
e set	ə some		ey say		ow bow
æ back	a lock	ɔ cause	ay wife		aw house
			ɔy boy		

Some sources, by no means all, for the fourteen entities listed here have been given above to furnish patterns of replacement. Further Middle English sources will be listed below, though for a complete account one must consult an English historical grammar.

10.6 From the changes between the Middle English and the Modern English phonological systems we may illustrate the essentials necessary for general understanding of sound change. Since sound changes of the types we have observed take place with modifications of sounds to sounds with similar articulation (for example, ME [e:] became NE [i:] rather than the totally different [u:] or [s]), thorough knowledge of articulatory phonetics is essential for understanding the mechanism of changes or shifts. By shifts we mean any modifications in sounds, whether or not they lead to changes in the phonological system. When they do lead to changes in the phonological system, for example when PGmc -[v]'- from PIE /p/ merged with PGmc [v] from PIE /bh/, or when ME /n/ split into NE /n/ and/ŋ/, the rearrangements follow certain patterns, mergers, and splits. To understand sound change we must accordingly observe both the mechanism and the patterns which may be involved.

10.7   Understanding the mechanism of sound change involves a knowledge of the types of modification that sounds have undergone, as well as an understanding of articulations themselves. In setting up correspondences between Middle and Modern English we have provided only the simplest, and proceeded as if all Middle English phonemes had merely one reflex in Modern English, for example, as if all ME /u/ had become NE /u/. Such a highly simple treatment is unrealistic. For sound changes of the type we have been considering take place by allophones. ME /u/, for instance, is reflected as NE /u/ only after labials (see page 341); elsewhere it became /ə/. The differing developments correlate with differing allophones in Middle English. The changes we have been discussing we therefore label change by allophones.

Allophones of phonemes are generally restricted to certain environments; here they are conditioned by their surroundings. When such allophones undergo a change, we speak of a conditioned or a combinatory change. Examples are: ME /u/ to NE /u/ after labials; PGmc /f ϑ s χ/ to /v ð z g/ when not preceded by the chief stress; some American English intervocalic /t/ to /d/, through [ṱ]. Much more rarely all phones of a phoneme change, and we speak of an unconditioned change. Examples are: PIE /o/ to PGmc /a/, as in Goth. *asts* 'branch' < PIE /ósdos/, with loss in Germanic of the second vowel; PGmc /z/ to OE /r/.

Whether conditioned or unconditioned changes take place, when a shift occurs it generally involves modification of a distinctive feature of articulation. NE /t/, for example, is a stop, produced by alveolar closure while the velum is raised and the glottis is open.[2] Some of its allophones may be further modified by aspiration. Its allophone before stressed vowel is aspirated, as in *top;* that after /s/ as in *stop* is unaspirated. Similarly /t/ in American English (*butter, bottom*, etc.) was unaspirated and very short; articulated in this way it became voiced between voiced sounds, with some restrictions. In accounts of shifts we accordingly identify the distinctive features of allophones, for through their modification sound changes take place.

---

[2] [The last part of this statement needs qualification. A glottalized stop is common at the ends of words like *pot*, and in the middle of words like *button* and *bottle.—Eds.*]

10.8   A shift may take place because of a change in place of articulation: labials may become labiodentals, dentals may become alveolars, velars may become palatals, and so on. A shift of labial to labiodental occurred when PIE /p/ became PGmc /f/; cf. Gk. *patér* = Goth. *fadar*. A shift from dental to alveolar, when PGmc /t/ became OHG /s/; cf. Eng. *hate* = Germ. *hassen*. A shift of velar to palatal, when early PIE /k/ under certain conditions became [š]; cf. Lat. *centum* = Skt. *śatam*.

A shift may take place in manner of articulation; stops may become fricatives or affricates, aspirates may become unaspirated or vice versa, and so on. A shift from stop to fricative occurred when PIE /p/ became PGmc /f/; cf. Lat. *pater* = Goth. *fadar*. A shift from stop to affricate, when PGmc /p/ became OHG /pf/; cf. Eng. *pool* = Germ. *Pfuhl*. A shift from aspirate to lack of aspirate, when PIE /bh/ became PGmc /v/; cf. Skt. *bharati* 'he bears' = Goth. *bairiþ*.

A shift may take place in the position of the velum; nasal sounds may become denasalized, non-nasals may become nasals. OIcel. *ellefo* 'eleven' corresponds to Goth. *ainlif;* OIcel. *annar* 'other' on the other hand corresponds to Goth. *anþar*. Nasal consonants were lost in Old English, with lengthening of the preceding vowel, when they occurred before voiceless fricatives; cf. Eng. *five* = Germ. *fünf*, Eng. *goose* = Germ. *Gans*. Nasal articulation may not be lost completely, but may affect neighboring vowels, as in Fr. *vin* [vẽ] < Lat. *vinum* 'wine.'

A shift may take place in the position of the glottis; voiced sounds may be devoiced, voiceless sounds voiced. An example of voiced sounds becoming devoiced is PIE /b d g/ becoming PGmc /p t k/; cf. Lat. *duo* = Eng. *two*. An example of voiceless sounds becoming voiced, PGmc /f θ s χ/ without chief stress on the preceding syllable becoming /PGmc /v đ z g/. As a remainder of this shift we may cite Eng. *r* < PGmc /z/ varying morphophonemically with *s* in *frore* versus *frost*.

In discussing shifts we may deal separately with those affecting vowels, though the modifications may be similar to those for consonants.

Shifts may take place in the degree of vowel opening. Open vowels may become more closed, closed vowels more open. In Middle English, /æ:/ as in *sea*, became more closed, so that we now rime its vowel with that of *see*. The closed vowels /i:/ and /u:/ of *wife* and *house* on the other hand came to be more open.

Shifts may take place in the degree of fronting. Back vowels may become front vowels, and vice versa. When the umlaut was carried through in pre-Old English, when for example /u:/ became /y:/ as in /my:s/ the plural of /mu:s/ 'mouse,' a back vowel was fronted.

Shifts may take place in labial articulation. The /y:/ of /my:s/ which was fronted in pre-Old English times later lost its lip rounding and coalesced with /i:/, so that in Middle English the vowel of *mice* fell together with that of *wife*.

A knowledge of articulatory phonetics is accordingly essential for the understanding and the interpretation of shifts. For the allophones of phonemes are determined by their phonetic environment; when sound changes take place, the direction may be a result of the earlier phonetic surroundings of the sounds concerned. Since phonemes are used to mark meaning in a language, however, they and their allophones generally are maintained without change. For if they, or allophones of the phonemes which comprise their environment, change, distinctions in the language are lost. When the allophones of English *t d n* became alveolar rather than dental, the number of distinctions in the language remained unchanged. When on the other hand /y y:/ became unrounded and merged with /i i:/, the possible distinctions for English were reduced. When the allophones of PGmc /f/ after vowels which did not have the chief accent split from the phoneme and fell together with allophones of PGmc /v/ < PIE /bh/, there were in this environment only voiced fricatives; accordingly the number of contrasts was reduced. Allophonic shifts may in this way lead to rearrangements in the morphological and semantic structure of a language; for when contrasts are eliminated, the number of potential morphological and semantic markers is reduced. Such rearrangements follow general patterns. Besides a knowledge of articulation, which permits us to understand the mechanism of sound changes, we must therefore know the patterns according to which phonological structures are rearranged.

10.9   There are two such patterns, mergers and splits. By mergers we refer to coalescences of phonemes. ME /e:/ and /æ:/ coalesced in NE /iy/; ME /a:/, /ai/ and /ei/ coalesced in NE /ey/.

By splits we refer to bifurcation of phonemes. ME /n/ developed to NE /ŋ/ and /n/; ME /u/ to NE /ə/ as in *run* and to NE /u/ as in *put*.

Merger is the more important of these patterns; for often when a sound change results from a split, the rearrangement has taken place in such a way that one of the split allophones has merged with allophones from another source. The [v] which split off from PGmc /f/, for example, merged with [v] which resulted from PIE /bh/. Moreover, allophones may become phonemes when their conditioning entities merge with others; pre-OE [y] and other rounded allophones became phonemes when following *i j* merged with reflexes of other weakly stressed vowels or were lost. Merger may therefore be considered the central process in sound change.

Merger may be conditioned or unconditioned. Unconditioned merger, when a phoneme merges completely with another phoneme, is relatively infrequent. An example is PGmc /z/, which merged in pre-Old English and other Germanic dialects with PGmc /r/. When such mergers take place, we cannot determine the earlier forms solely from one language. Using English alone we cannot distinguish the source of the *r* in *were* (PIE *s*) from that of the *r* in *four* (PIE *r*). Examples of other unconditioned mergers are: that of PIE /o/ with PIE /a/ to PGmc /a/; those of PIE /bh dh gh/ with /b d g/ in Iranian, Baltic, Slavic, Celtic.

Much more frequent is conditioned merger, with primary split. PGmc [v], an allophone of PGmc /f/ after weakly stressed vowels, merged with /v/ from PIE /bh/, leaving [f] as the sole allophone of the /f/ phoneme. Numerous instances of such merger can be cited: NE /u/ from /u:/ in closed syllables merged with earlier ME /u/, both becoming NE /ə/ except after labials (see page 341), as in *blood*, cf. Germ. *Blut*, and *nut*, cf. Germ. *Nuss;* NE /ž/ from [zy] merged with /ž/ in borrowings from French, like *rouge*. Often after such mergers we find alternations which reflect the earlier situation such as the /ž/ in *vision* which alternates with the /z/ in *visible*. As noted in Chapter 6, these are useful in applying the method of internal reconstruction.

Besides merger, the examples in the preceding paragraph illustrate primary split. When primary split occurs, some allophones continue the original phoneme, others merge with a different phoneme. PGmc /f/, ME /u:/ and NE /z/ were all maintained after the allophones discussed above had been regrouped. Primary split generally leads to an expansion of the members of one phoneme, with reduction in the members of another, but not to a new phoneme in the system.

New phonemes may be introduced by a split if the conditioning features for one set of allophones are modified or lost. Such a phenomenon we refer to as secondary split. The pre-Old English front rounded allophones of /o o:/ and /u u:/ became phonemes when the conditioning /i i: j/ were modified. Pre-OE /o o: u u:/ were continued, but from some of their allophones four new phonemes /φ φ: y y:/ were added to the system. On the other hand, no new phonemes were produced when at the same time the fronted allophones of /a a:/ fell together with /e e:/ by secondary split. The essential difference between primary split and secondary split, therefore, is not the result but rather the process by which the sound change takes place.

Many sound changes involve loss. OE /h/ before /l n r/ was lost, as in *loud* < OE /hlu:d/, *nut* < OE /hnut/, *ring* < OE /hring/; ME [g] was lost after [ŋ], as in *long*. It may simplify presentation of such sound changes to consider loss a merger with zero. Moreover, as in ME *rime* 'hoar-frost' < OE *hrīm* and *rime* 'rhyme' < OE *rīm*, the loss of sound may result in a homophone with a word in which there was no sound, so that a loss literally results in merger with zero. We may then account for the origin of NE

/ŋ/ in secondary split, for the previous conditioning element *-g* was modified by merger with zero.

10.10   In the paragraphs above we have dealt with sound changes that arise from the rearrangements of allophones. Some allophones of one phoneme in the course of time come to resemble allophones of another phoneme and may merge completely or in part with them. In sound changes of this type all allophones which are similar in articulation undergo the change. Moreover, when the change has taken place, the new alignment is maintained, until another shift occurs. NE /ŋ/, for example, has remained distinct from /n/ since the loss of a following /g/. Besides such change we find in language sporadic changes which affect sounds only in some of their occurrences, and may not be permanent. Since these changes involve a direct change from one phoneme to another, with no gradual modification of allophones, we refer to them as changes by phonemes.

As an example we may cite the pronunciation of NE *seven* [sévm̩]. There has been no long gradual development of a final alveolar nasal to a labiodental or bilabial nasal. Speakers use either one of the two phonemes. We find such changes especially in rapid, informal speech, although their results may often be maintained in a language. They are especially common in everyday words. Though a similar change is often to be observed for NE *eleven* [əlévm̩], it would be rare, or nonexistent, in *leaven*, which has the same phonetic environment for *n*, but a different environment in the social strata of the language.

Speakers are often conscious of changes by phonemes, though they are unaware of the changes by allophones, as in the gradual voicing of [the /t/ in] NE *water, bottle,* and so on. Except for self-conscious speakers, who in this period of general advanced education flourish more widely than at any previous time, changes by allophone are carried through in all morphs in which the allophone occurs; the *t* in Modern English forms like *better, bottom,* for example, is consistently modified. The different attitude of speakers to change by phonemes on the other hand probably results from an awareness that such phenomena are associated with movement from one social dialect to another.

Changes by phoneme like changes by allophone, are governed by articulatory possibilities and can best be understood by observing the underlying changes in articulation.

10.11   The most frequent such changes are assimilatory. Assimilation is a change in the articulation of a sound to one more like that of neighboring sounds. To illustrate we may note changes of the consonant of Latin *ad* 'to' when it was prefixed to morphs beginning with consonants. (For the sake of simplicity, examples are given from contemporary English, even though the assimilatory changes took place in Latin and their results were borrowed into English. The varying forms of the English morpheme *ad*, as in *adjourn*, illustrate morphophonemic interchanges; I rely here on morphophonemic variation to provide a compact series of examples because it is difficult to illustrate sound changes without citing a huge amount of material.) *Apparatus*, from *ad* + *pārāre* 'make ready,' illustrates assimilation in place of articulation; the dental *d* was changed to a labial. *Assimilation*, from *ad* + *similāre* 'resemble,' illustrates assimilation in manner of articulation; the stop *d* was changed to a fricative. *Annex*, from *ad* + *nectere* 'bind,' illustrates assimilation in position of the velum; the oral *d* was changed to a nasal. *Attempt*, from *ad* + *temptāre* 'try,' illustrates assimilation in position of the glottis; the voiced *d* has become unvoiced.

As in these four examples, the preceding element is most commonly assimilated, and the articulation of the second element is anticipated. This type of assimilation is referred to as regressive.

The articulation of the prior element may also be maintained, as in [sévm̩]; in this pronunciation the labial articulation is maintained for the nasal from the preceding fricative. This type of articulation is referred to as progressive.

The articulation of both elements may be modified, by reciprocal assimilation, as in [sébm̩]; in this pronunciation the closure of the second element is anticipated in the *b*, and the position of the *b* is maintained for the nasal.

The assimilated sound may not always be contiguous with the sound to which it is changed. An example is Eng. *orangutang*, which was taken over from Malay *orang* 'man' + *ūtan* 'forest; wild.' The nasal of *ūtan* was modified to the velar position of the nasal in *utang* by assimilation at a distance.

Assimilation may be complete, as in *annex*, or partial as in [sévm̩]. Partial assimilation is common in inflection, as in the German weak verb. The past of *lieben* [lí:bən] 'love' is *liebte* [lí:ptə], of *sagen* [zá:gən], 'say' *sagte* [zá:ktə], of *reisen* [ráyzən] 'travel' *reiste* [ráystə], in all of which the final consonant of the stem was once voiced. The past of Eng. *live* is [livd] but that of *lick* [likt].

Word boundaries often fall before junctures, and accordingly the final sounds of words may be assimilated, especially to voicelessness. In German, for example, voiced stops become voiceless when final: *lieb* [lí:p] 'dear' but *liebe* [lí:bə], *Hund* [húnt] 'dog' but *Hunde* [húndə], *trag* [trá:k] 'carry' but *trage* [trá:gə].

10.12   Assimilation in word-ending position may lead to development of an additional consonant, as in the pronunciation [sinst] for *since*. In this pronunciation the tongue makes a closure against the alveolar ridge before articulation of the word is completed. The closure is heard as a stop. Such additional consonants are referred to as excrescent. Further examples may be taken from English, e.g. *varmint* < *vermin,* or from German; compare Germ. *Axt,* Eng. *ax;* Germ. *Sekt* 'champagne,' Eng. *sack* 'dry sherry'; Germ. *Habicht,* Eng. *hawk.*

We may also view apocope, the loss of final vowels, as assimilation to post-word juncture. In Old English, the first singular present ended in *-e,* for example, *helpe.* Such final vowels were lost in the late Middle English period. Apocope and syncope, the loss of medial vowels, are prominent in languages with a strong stress accent on initial syllables. In the Germanic languages there has been continuous loss of vowels, until in present-day English many of the native words have become monosyllabic. The Old English first singular preterite of *temman* 'tame' was *temede;* both weakly stressed vowels have been lost, to yield NE *tamed* [teymd].

Final assimilatory changes we associate with delimitation of words by some type of juncture. We may find other indications of junctures in erroneous word division. NE *newt* is from *an ewt/eft,* wrongly divided; since the forms *a/an,* like *my/mine,* etc., were interchanged in accordance with the following sound, speakers not completely conversant with a word might not know where to make the division. *Newt* has remained in English beside *eft.* The reverse type of erroneous division was made in *adder,* cf. Germ. *Natter,* and *apron,* cf. OFr. *naperon.* Such forms, plus assimilation of final elements, enable us to draw inferences about juncture phenomena in the past.

10.13　We have been viewing assimilation as a sporadic sound change, involving change by phonemes. Yet we can also understand as assimilatory many changes by allophone that have taken place. We cannot therefore associate assimilation solely with sporadic changes, but must expect it in any articulatory changes. In the history of English we may observe many instances of assimilation of dentals and alveolars, some of which are sporadic; others are allophonic changes leading to modifications of the system. The following assimilatory changes occur sporadically in Modern English:

won't you	did you	miss you	raise you
[wównčə]	[díǰə]	[míšə]	[réyžə]

These forms may be used in rapid speech, are considered informal by some speakers, substandard by others, and have by no means replaced the more careful [wównt yùw] and so on.

Similar changes took place in early Modern English, and many of the changed forms have remained in the language. From the eighteenth century

[ty] is attested with the pronunciation [š], as in *nation;* similarly [sy] as in *issue*, and especially before [yu:] as in *sugar, sure, assure*. (This change also took place in such words as *assume, consume, suet*, but subsequently [s] was reintroduced in these words as a spelling pronunciation.) Similarly [zy] became [ž] as in *measure, pleasure, treasure;* [dy] became [ǰ], as in *soldier, grandeur, Indian, educate, hideous;* here too all words but *soldier* and *grandeur* were remodeled by spelling pronunciation. *Injun* has survived only as a pejorative term; many *educators* consider the regular pronunciation of this word undignified and insist on the spelling pronunciation.[3]

In pronunciations like [dídʒə díǰə] of *did you*, which has not universally replaced the nonassimilated form, and [sówlǰər] of *soldier*, which has, we observe the same articulatory phenomenon: the neighboring sounds have been assimilated to one another. In [dídʒə díǰə], the [ʒ] is closer in articulation to [d] than is [y]. Generally in speech, allophones result which accord with neighboring sounds.

10.14   Native speakers are not aware of allophonic modification. Foreign speakers, however, hear languages other than their own with their native allophonic and phonemic system, and they distinguish between allophones in a foreign language if these are similar to phonemes in their own language. As example we may note the Japanese form of English *cap*. In English a front variant of /k/ is used before front vowels, as in

$$\text{keep} \qquad \text{cape} \qquad \text{cap}$$

a back variant before back vowels, as in

$$\text{coop} \qquad \text{cope} \qquad \text{cop}$$

The five vowels of Japanese /i e a o u/ are equated by native speakers to the vowels in these words, with /a/ corresponding to the vowels of both *cap* and *cop*. Yet when *cap* was taken into Japanese, speakers observed the front [k] and reproduced it as *ky*, to yield *kyappu* [kyap:ɯ].

We may use the Japanese development to speculate on possible future changes of English /k/. As long as the present articulation of English /k/ with that of following vowels is maintained, there will be no sound change. If however [k] before [æ], as in *cap*, should become sufficiently like the allophones of /š/ to be interchangeable with them, a primary split would occur, and all /k/ before /æ/ would merge with the /š/ phoneme. If on the other hand the conditioning vowels should merge, e.g. /æ/ and /a/, a

---

[3] [To be completely accurate, these statements about the occurrences of [dy] and of [ǰ] would have to be considerably qualified. Pronunciations of *educate* with [ǰ] and of *grandeur* with [dy] do occur in the speech of educated Americans.—*Eds.*]

secondary split would occur; all /k/ before former/æ/ might then merge with the /š/ phoneme, or they might become a separate phoneme.

10.15 Changes of this type, in which consonants have been assimilated to a neighboring [j] or to front vowels, have taken place at various times in the history of English, and even more widely in Baltic, Slavic and other Indo-European languages. Such assimilation of consonants to front vowels and [j] is referred to as palatalization.

In early Old English, allophones of /k/ and /g/ were palatalized in the neighborhood of front vowels, so that modifications arose as follows:

cīdan 'chide'	cū 'cow'	geard 'yard'	gold 'gold'
[k'i:dan]	[ku:]	[g'ɛard]	[gold]
pic 'pitch'	bōc 'book'	dæg 'day'	longra 'longer'
[pik']	[bo:k]	[dæg']	[loŋgra]

Gradually the palatalized allophones, as in *chide, pitch, yard, day,* came to be further differentiated from the velar allophones, as in *cow, book, gold, longer.* Eventually by primary split the palatalized allophones of /k/ fell together with reflexes of [tj] as in *feccan* [fetjan] 'fetch' and the new phoneme /č/ arose; the palatalized allophone of /g/ fell together with the earlier phoneme /j/ as in OE *gear* 'year' and split from the /g/ phoneme. For some time after this split and this merger /k g/ occurred only before consonants and back vowels in English. . . .

10.16 Assimilation may also take place in the articulation of vowels. When clusters of vowels or vowels plus certain consonants, such as [j], occur in a language, neighboring vowels may become more alike in articulation. PIE /e/ before [j] became raised in Germanic, so that PIE /ey/ > PGmc. /i:/, as in OE *stīgan,* OHG *stīgan* 'climb,' compare Gk. *steíkhō* 'come.' Modern English cognates are *sty* and *stile.*

PGmc. /e/ was also assimilated to an *i* in the following syllable, as in Goth. *midjis,* OE *midd* 'mid' = Lat. *medius.*

The most far-reaching of these assimilations in the Germanic languages took place in the early period of the individual dialects, and is generally known by the term umlaut or mutation. Pre-OE short and long *a o u* standing before *j* or short or long *i* of the following syllable became fronted; *a > e, o > φ,* later *e, u > y,* later *i.*

Germanic umlaut provides excellent examples of split. By secondary split the fronted allophones of *o u* became phonemes when the conditioning *j* was lost or the conditioning vowels merged to a central vowel. By primary split the fronted allophones of *a* merged with the earlier *e.* Compare the Proto-Germanic or Gothic and the Old English cognates:

PGmc. mūsiz > OE mȳs 'mice'
PGmc. dōmjan 'judge' > OE døman > dēman > NE deem
Goth. satjan = OE settan 'set'

Since umlaut is an instance of split, we expect to find morphophonemic variants in the later language. These exist abundantly in English and in German, as in *mouse:mice, louse:lice, goose:geese, doom:deem, man:men.*

Umlaut is an example of regressive assimilation at a distance.

Vowels may also be modified by progressive assimilation, as in the vowel harmony of various languages. Examples below illustrate how the vowel of Turkish *-dir* 'is, are, am' varies from *i* to *ü* to *ı* to *u*, depending on the vowel of the final syllable of the base; since the *d* is also assimilated to *t* when following a voiceless consonant, *-dir* may occur in eight forms, of which four are given here.

iyidir 'it is good'   süttür 'it is milk'
kızdır 'it's a girl'   kuştur 'it's a bird'

As illustrated here, vowels may be assimilated to back as well as front articulation. . . .

10.18   Assimilation may also lead to weakening in articulation, and even to loss. Intervocalic NE *t*, for example, has been voiced, like neighboring sounds, as in *bottle, butter, bottom.* That this is assimilation may be demonstrated by absence of voicing before *n*, as in *button;* here the articulation of the following alveolar has apparently served to check the assimilatory voicing of *t*.[4]

Assimilation of *w* to following back vowels in early Modern English, evident in NE *sword*, has led to its complete loss in some environments.

10.19   Losses may be complete, with an effect on a neighboring element, often lengthening it. When for example [χ] was lost in *night, height, fight* and so on in early Modern English, the preceding vowel was lengthened. This phenomenon is known as compensatory lengthening. Other examples are OE *gōs* < pre-OE **gans*, cf. Germ. *Gans* 'goose,' OE *ūs* < pre-OE **uns*, cf. Germ. *uns* 'us,' in which nasals were lost before voiceless fricatives, with compensatory lengthening of the preceding vowel. The same change occurred earlier in OE *brōhte* < PGmc. /branχta/ 'brought,' OE *þōhte* 'thought.'

Weakening of articulation may also lead to the introduction of vowels or consonants, so-called epenthesis. We find epenthetic vowels for example

---

[4] [Since /n/ is a voiced sound, it is not clear how it would serve to check assimilation to a voiced allophone of /t/. However, glottalization would check it. See note 2.—*Eds.*]

in OE *æcer*, cf. OIcel. *akr* 'acre,' OE *ofen*, cf. OIcel. *ofn* 'oven,' and in many other words before *r l m n;* we find epenthetic consonants in OE *bræmbel* beside *brēmel* 'bramble,' OE *gandra* beside *ganra* 'gander,' and so on. Prothetic vowels were introduced in French and Spanish before *s* plus consonant, as in Fr. *école* < OFr. *escole*, Span. *escuela*, Port. *escola* from Lat. *schola, scola* 'school.'

10.20   A much more subtle change occurred in Middle English, when syllables were balanced. At this time short vowels in open syllables came to be lengthened, as in ME *māken* 'make,' cf. OE *macian*, ME *stēlan* 'steal,' cf. OE *stelan*, ME *wēvel* 'weevil,' cf. OE *wifel*, ME *hōpe* 'hope,' cf. OE *hopa*, ME *wōde* 'wood,' cf. OE *wudu*. Conversely long vowels in closed syllables—before long consonants or some consonant clusters—came to be shortened, as in ME *ledde* 'led,' cf. OE *lǣdde*, ME *kepte* 'kept,' cf. OE *cēpte*, ME *wimman* 'woman,' cf. OE *wīfman*, ME *softe* 'soft,' cf. OE *sōfte*, ME *huswif* 'hussy (housewife),' cf. OE *hūswīf*. Similar balancing of syllables took place in German, and other languages. In Modern English, Modern German, and other such languages there is then no phonological differentiation between light and heavy syllables, as there was in Old English, Greek, or Latin. In spite of attempts to the contrary, poets accordingly cannot reproduce the rhythm of Old English, Greek or Latin verse in Modern English. For the regularization of syllabic quantity has brought about a completely different rhythm.

Balancing, like assimilatory changes can be viewed as resulting from a tendency of languages to develop towards ease in articulation. For when two sounds are produced more like each other, the effort involved in their production is obviously lessened. Accordingly assimilation seems to function in keeping with the "principle of least effort"; since we can find instances of assimilation in virtually any language, the conclusion may seem justified that languages are evolving towards simpler forms. Not enough evidence has been assembled to argue with assurance for or against this conclusion.

One may point to facets of a language which seem comparable to those in another language, yet the two languages are going different ways rather than moving in parallel fashion to forms which require least effort. The weakening and voicing of intervocalic *t*, for example, is occurring only in American English, not in British, Australian or other English dialects. The velar fricative [χ] was lost before consonants in English, see *light*, but not in German, note *Licht*. Languages are so complex in structure— they contain so many substructures that are themselves in some kind of balance and at the same time in balance with other substructures—that we cannot select a random change as evidence of development towards simplicity. Moreover, simplicity in the muscular activity involved in the articulation of speech may differ from simplicity in the neural activity underlying that articulation.

10.21   It is apparently to a tendency towards simplification of neural activity that we can ascribe dissimilation, the production of sounds so that they will be more unlike one another. For we find dissimilation particularly among the more complex sounds, such as *l* and *r*, as in NE *turtle* < Lat. *turtur*, NE *pilgrim* < Lat. *peregrinus*, NE *marble* < Lat. *marmor*. It is less commonly attested for stops, as in Germ. *Kartoffel* 'potato,' in which the initial *k* was dissimilated from *t* in the seventeenth century; the earlier term was *Tartuffeln*, which was borrowed from Ital. *tartuffeli*. (When in the sixteenth century the plant was imported to Italy from Peru, it was named after the truffle.) As in all these examples, it is usually the sound of the unaccented syllable which is modified. Dissimilation is much less prominent in linguistic change than is assimilation.

Dissimilation may also involve the loss of a form segment; this is called haplology. As examples we may cite the Modern English adverbs in *-ly* made from adjectives ending in *-le*. In these, one syllable has been lost, as in *gently* rather than **gentlely*, *simply* rather than **simplely*. Another example is *England* < *Engla lond* 'land of the Angles.' As a phenomenon of change, haplology is relatively infrequent.

Another type of change which apparently results from neural rearrangements rather than muscular is metathesis. By metathesis we mean interchange of phonemes. Metathesis was remarkably frequent in late West Saxon, where we find *āxian* 'ask,' *dox* 'dusk,' *flaxe* 'flask,' *waxan* 'wash' and many others. Metathesis of consonant and vowel (to which some scholars restrict the term metathesis) is also frequently attested more generally in Old English, as in *hors* < *hros*, cf. NG *Ross* 'horse,' *ðirda* < *ðridda* 'third,' cf. NG *dritte* and NE *three*. Again complex sounds are most commonly involved, as in the substandard NE *irrevelant*. Moreover, metathesis, like dissimilatory change, is apparently attested only as a sporadic change.

10.22   When we investigate change by allophones we find it carried out gradually and over a long period of time. Instances of ME *e*² (*ǣ*), which now rime with *ē*¹,[5] were for example treated differently in the sixteenth and seventeenth centuries. Dryden rimed *dream* with *shame*, *sea* and *obey*. Pope rimed *weak* with *take*, *eat* with *state;* Swift rimed *seat* with *weight*,

---

[5] [e¹ and e² are reflexes of two distinct OE vowels, [e:] and [æ:], which have merged in MnE [i:] after, as Lehmann shows, remaining distinct in Early Modern English.—*Eds.*]

meat with *say't,* and so on. Much earlier the pronunciation [i:] for $\bar{e}^2$ is attested by grammarians, but not favored by them. We assume it was used by Queen Elizabeth I, for she wrote 'biquived' for *bequeathed*. Although this pronunciation is attested in the sixteenth century, still in 1747 Johnson was troubled about riming *great*, whether with *seat* [i:] or with *state* [e:].

We may ascribe Johnson's perplexity in part to the variation of usage, in part to the gradual and slow carrying out of the shift. For the shift of ME $\bar{e}^2$ and other long vowels must have been similar to the shift of intervocalic *t* in contemporary American English, in which some speakers pronounce *butter* [bədər], others [bəţər], still others [bətər]. As allophones are modified, their articulation is changed gradually until they reach a new stabilized position in the phonological system, as has *dream* today.

Eventually the higher vowel [i:] for $\bar{e}^2$ was generalized in standard English. Though we have extensive evidence on very few such changes, we can assume that those we have furnish us with a typical picture of sound change by allophones. Further such changes occurring in contemporary languages must now be studied and thoroughly documented.

10.23   For the understanding of sound change attempts have been made to determine its causes and to predict the possible development of given entities. As we have noted above, assumption of change towards ease in articulation is based on a very simple view of language. For what seems easy in one language is difficult in another. German still maintains initial [kn], which has been lost in English; compare *Knie* 'knee,' *Knecht* 'knight,' *Knoten* 'knot,' and so on. Though in Latin there was relative freedom of occurrence of final consonants, in Classical Greek the only final consonants to occur are *n r s*. PIE *-m* in the accusative singular, e.g. Lat. *lupum* 'wolf' shows up as Gk. *-n, lúkon*. Other final consonants were lost, as illustrated by the vocative singular *paî* of *paîs,* gen. *paidós* 'boy'; Lat. *quid* 'what' corresponds to Gk. *tí.*

It is obvious from differences like these in various languages that we can only provide very general statements about sound changes tending towards simplicity.

10.24   We can state somewhat less tentatively that sound systems tend to maintain or develop towards symmetry. When PIE /p/ > PGmc /f/, a similar change to voiceless fricatives affected PIE /t/ and /k/; subsequently the other orders were affected, the Proto-Indo-European voiced aspirates and voiced stops. When ME $\bar{e}$ was raised, to yield NE /iy/, the other long vowels also were affected, as we have noted above. As in these changes, we can understand the tendency towards maintenance of symmetry by observing that contrasts must be maintained unless the sound system is to become impoverished; moreover, a balance of like sounds assists in controlling the language.

Yet phonological systems are modified toward imbalance adequately often so that we reject overenthusiastic endorsement of development towards symmetry—of therapeutic sound changes which heal holes in the system. Under-exploited contrasts, such as those of PIE *b*, may indeed come to be more fully utilized. In Germanic, many borrowings increased the number of *p*, originally a reflex of PIE *b*. In Slavic, however, *bh* fell together with *b* and one potentially important contrast was lost entirely. When we will have materials available on sound changes in a great variety of languages, we may deal more assuredly with change towards symmetry.

10.25   Gilliéron's view, that one homonym tends to force out another, has also been demonstrated to be exaggerated. English maintains *pair, pear; bear, bare,* (polar) *bear,* etc., though the early NE *let* 'hinder' has survived the competition of *let* 'permit' only in *let ball,* now commonly *net ball.* If on the other hand homonyms are of the same set, morphological or semantic, one of them may be lost. Such modifications are however very minor in a language.

10.26   Somewhat more far-reaching, possibly, is the effect of taboo, of avoidance of the unspeakable. Topics which may not be discussed vary from language to language, from clothing, in Japanese, to animal names for hunters, names of excretory functions, death, and divinity for us.

Taboos affect the use of words rather than sounds, though it is strange that among the possible monosyllables **pes, *shet* and **fət* do not exist in English. Similarly in Thai there are sanctions against phonological patterns which may suggest tabooed words.

Although the study of taboo is highly interesting, in linguistic change its effect is limited.

10.27   The influence of individuals on phonological change is also limited. Van Helmont indeed added the word *gas* to his and other languages, yet his proposed *blas* 'emanation from stars' was a failure. George Eastman introduced *Kodak* as a deliberate creation, after he noted the restrictions on the letter *k* in the English writing system; other merchants have followed him in introducing names such as *Kix* for breakfast cereals, *Krax* for crackers, *Klenso* for soaps, yet these have had an effect on external elements rather than on the phonological system. They may have an effect through changing the frequency and distribution of phonological entities, as may any new words, such as names for newly discovered elements: *Curium*, *Californium*.

Vigorous personalities may exert some effect on the language—poets may look to Latin for models, as did Milton, or to the rustic, as did Wordsworth. The net effect of such innovations is difficult to assess. A poet who has had an extraordinary influence is the Norwegian Ivar Aasen, who in the nineteenth century created a new language, *landsmaal*, from western Norwegian dialects and Old Norse. His creation, adopted as a second standard language by short-sighted politicians, has plagued his countrymen to the present, and will for some time to come, until the two Norwegian languages *nynorsk* and *bokmål* are merged. In spite of Ivar Aasen's success, chiefly with vocabulary but also with the structure of Norwegian, the effect of most would-be linguistic innovators is very minor.

10.28   Nor has it been adequately substantiated whether the interaction of two or more dialects or languages brings about sound changes. Romance historical linguists especially have attempted to account for the separate developments of Spanish, French and other dialects by assuming articulatory modifications carried over by speakers who adopted Latin as their second language. Such supposed underlying influences are referred to as substrata, superstrata or adstrata. The French front rounded vowels are, for example, ascribed to a Celtic substratum. The effects of language interaction are determined largely by social conditions. When in some areas non-native speakers acquire a new language, the second generation masters it with rather general adequacy, if the linguistic tradition is well-established. In the United States grandsons of Italians, Germans, Spaniards, Negroes, Irish, Danes speak the English used by their associates without notable differences in linguistic structure.

When substrata have led to modifications of a language, as of English in India, the linguistic tradition has been less powerful; native speakers may have been outnumbered, or open to modification of their speech. In India relatively few native speakers were available to teach English to speakers who constantly used their native languages.

There is now considerable interest in multilingual communities such as those in India, Africa, and other areas of the world which are predominantly multilingual. The effects on languages involved may be ascertainable after further study, which may permit generalizations about sound changes. If then the linguistic situations of previous times can ever be adequately determined—the proportion of speakers of Latin to speakers of Gaulish, closeness of contact between Gaul and Rome, complete descriptions of the Gaulish and Latin dialects involved—we may also be able to apply the findings from contemporary sociolinguistic study in attempts to describe the development of languages in the past. Until we have such material, we must be cautious in ascribing the development of phonological entities of a language, for example, those of French, to substrata.

10.29   With our present knowledge of sound change, based largely on that in Indo-European dialects, we can make assured statements about its mechanism and processes; about its direction or causes we can only propose hypotheses. Further study is essential to provide information in these spheres comparable to that gathered over the past century and a half on the mechanism and processes of sound change.

Study Questions

1.   Lehmann states: "In dealing with changes affecting a phonemic system we now require grammars to note not only individual changes but also that they present them within the system of the two stages." After a careful reading of the article, try to state as precisely as you can how Lehmann conceives of a phonological system. For example, is phonology a level of analysis separate from morphology, syntax, and lexicon, or one part of an integrated set of rules describing sentences and the pronunciation of sentences? How would Lehmann define the terms *phoneme* and *allophone?* What effect would the voicing of /t/ in words like *butter* have on the phonemic system of American English? Would it affect the inventory of phonemes, the membership of phonemes, the distribution of phonemes? How would Lehmann describe phonemic contrasts? Would his description be similar to Sledd's in "Breaking, Umlaut, and the Southern Drawl"?

2.   What evidence does Lehmann give for his statement that /t d n/ were dentals in Chaucer's English? Does he suggest what kind of evidence might be found, and where? Would scribes using conventional writing systems be likely to record the "gradual modifications" Lehmann considers necessary for adequate accounts of sound change? If not, where might relevant evidence be found?

3.   If you are studying the history of English sounds, compare the treatments you have read with Lehmann's comparison of the phonemes of ME and MnE. Would all phonologists agree that /x/ and /h/ were

distinct phonemes in ME? Was there no *long* open *o* /ɔ:/ in addition to /ɔ/ and /o:/? If not, how would we account for the different vowel sounds in MnE *thought* and *grow* if the vowel sounds did not differ in ME? What justification is there for considering [ə] in unaccented syllables an allophone of /e/ when [ə] reflects earlier unaccented vowels like *a, o, u* in inflectional syllables? Does Sledd suggest a similar treatment?

4. Define and give examples of the following terms: *conditioned change, unconditioned change, merger, split, primary* and *secondary split, loss.* What is the distinction Lehmann makes between the "mechanism of sound change" and the "patterns according to which phonological systems are rearranged"? Which of the above terms refer to mechanisms and which to patterns?

5. Lehmann follows other structuralists in asserting that "native speakers are not aware of allophonic modification." What does this statement imply about the psychological reality of phonemes? If it is true, how do we explain our ability to identify non-native speakers of English or immediately recognize a dialect as different from our own? If a Chicagoan can tell an Atlantan from a San Franciscan, would we have to conclude that the phonemic structures of the dialects differ? If such dialects differ in phonemic structure, how do we explain mutual intelligibility?

6. Labov describes fluctuations in New York City speech such as the presence or absence of post-vocalic /r/ and the use of either [θ], [tθ] or [t] for the initial sound of *think.* Would Lehmann classify these two changes as change by allophone or as change by phoneme? Where might the change to the presence of post-vocalic /r/ have come from? Does Labov suggest any causes for the change? Would Labov's evidence support or contradict Lehmann's statement that speakers (unless they are self-conscious) are unaware of change by allophone, but conscious of change by phoneme since the latter phenomenon is "associated with movement from one social dialect to another"? Is change by phoneme, then, an example of dialect borrowing? Would Lehmann seem to agree with Labov that social consciousness is a powerful force in sound change, or with Labov's finding that a speaker's awareness of prestige forms outstrips his ability to use them?

7. Does Lehmann's distinction between change by allophone and change by phoneme suggest agreement or disagreement with the neo-gram-

marian hypothesis that phonetic laws admit no exceptions? Does the evidence in 10.22 about fluctuations between [e:] and [i:], or between [d], [ṭ], and [t] support the argument that some changes are gradual? What are the implications of Lehmann's suggestion that some changes involve neural activity while others involve only muscular activity? Is it possible to have muscular activity without neural activity? What might Chomsky say about a statement that some changes in sounds reflect gradual changes in habits of articulation?

8.   If there is wide disagreement about the nature of sound systems and how to describe them, is it accurate to assert that "we can make assured statements about the mechanism and processes" of sound change?

Paul Kiparsky

LINGUISTIC UNIVERSALS AND
LINGUISTIC CHANGE*

Paul Kiparsky was born in Helsinki, Finland in 1941, received his undergraduate education at the University of Helsinki, and took his doctorate at MIT in 1965. Like most transformationalists, his primary interest is in general linguistic theory; his special interest has been historical and comparative studies. His dissertation was a study of sound change, and he has published articles on phonology and syntax in a number of journals. Kiparsky is assistant professor of linguistics at MIT.

The following paper, given at the Texas Conference on Language Universals in 1967, is in part a justification of certain notational conventions in generative rules, in part an argument that linguistic history be given more serious attention in general linguistic theory than has been customary in twentieth-century work. In the course of developing these two points, Kiparsky discusses the nature of sound change in general and describes a number of particular sound changes from a variety of languages. The conception of language on which Kiparsky bases his discussion differs sharply from that underlying Lehmann's chapter, so it is not surprising that there should be broad and irreconcilable differences in the two men's conceptions of phonological development. For Kiparsky, a language is best described as a set or system of rules: linguistic change, then, involves the alterations that the rules undergo—addition, deletion, reordering. Like language itself, change in language is thus a mental phenomenon. If the grammarian is obliged to go beneath the observable facts of speech to the description and explanation of the knowledge a speaker has that enables him to speak, the historical linguist is obliged to trace changes in the content and form of that knowledge which cause speech to change through time.

1. THE PSYCHOLOGICAL REALITY PROBLEM

Suppose that someone succeeds in writing a grammar which correctly enumerates the sentences of a language and assigns them the right structural descriptions. Such a grammar would ipso facto correctly represent the substance of a fluent speaker's knowledge of this language. But it would not necessarily represent the form of this knowledge in the sense of

From *Universals in Linguistic Theory* edited by Emmon Bach and Robert Harms. Copyright © 1968 by Holt, Rinehart and Winston, Inc. Reprinted by permission of Holt, Rinehart and Winston, Inc.
* This work was supported in part by the National Institutes of Health (Grant 1 PO1 MH 13390-02).
I would like to thank J. R. Ross and W. G. Moulton for suggesting to me many improvements in this paper. But they do not necessarily agree with me, and the responsibility is mine alone.

actually corresponding to the system of rules which is internalized by the speaker and constitutes part of what enables him to produce and understand arbitrary utterances in the language. Similarly, the knowledge of someone who has learned arithmetic, that is, the infinite set of correct arithmetical computations, could be defined by many different systems of rules, including both psychologically incorrect ones, such as certain axioms of set theory, computer programs, and so on, and the psychologically correct one, namely whatever knowledge is actually used in arithmetical performance, such as the rules of school arithmetic and the multiplication table. How do we know that generative grammar is not psychologically as wrong a model of linguistic competence as set theory is of arithmetical competence?

The linguistic universals which linguistic theory specifies include fixed notations in which grammars are written and an evaluation measure, which together establish a hypothesis about which of the innumerable grammars that might characterize the sentences of a language possesses psychological reality in the sense of representing the form rather than just the substance of a fluent speaker's competence. From among the pile of generalizations that might be made about the sentences of a language they select certain ones as being linguistically significant and corresponding to the generalizations that a child hearing such utterances would actually arrive at in constructing his grammar. The question, then, is how the various aspects of this hypothesis are justified.

For many features of universal grammar there is justification enough in the fact that without them it would simply not be possible to write grammars that account for the sentences of a language. Particularly in syntax, as Chomsky has pointed out, the typical problem is not choosing the right one among various theories that work but finding even one that will work at all. But with conventions which are essentially abbreviatory in nature, such as braces and parentheses, among others, real problems of empirical justification can arise. A grammar can always be replaced by another, descriptively equivalent one, in which any one of these abbreviatory notations is not made use of. There could not be a language whose sentences could be enumerated one way but not the other. Then what is the empirical force, if any, of such notational conventions?

For example, most linguists would agree that two rules of the form

$$X \to Y$$

$$Z \to Y$$

if not separated in the ordering by any other rule, should be combined by factoring out their common right hand side as follows:

$$\begin{Bmatrix} X \\ Z \end{Bmatrix} \rightarrow Y$$

We would say that the braces represent a linguistically significant generalization about these two rules. But how do we know that they do? How would we justify this convention to some linguist A who maintained that it was wrong and that the two rules should be kept separate? Or, to take a more likely contingency, how would we justify it to another linguist B who maintained that neither theory makes any verifiable truth claim as against the other, that since they are mutually convertible notational variants of each other, they represent equivalent hypotheses about the speaker's internalized grammar?

There are no conscious a priori ideas of generality that we can appeal to here in the way that we can appeal to intuitions that reflect features of structural descriptions, such as ambiguity and synonymy. The processes of normal language learning being unconscious, we have absolutely no ideas about the form of grammars, though we have clear ideas about the forms of sentences which grammars account for. It is true that the practicing linguist soon acquires ideas about the form of grammars and such concepts as generality. But these ideas are somehow the result of his work on languages, and we would like to know what the ideas are based on.

Nor is the fact that a generalization can be stated enough to show that it is real. All sorts of absurd notational conventions can easily be dreamed up which would express the kinds of spurious generalizations that we would want to exclude from grammars. It is necessary to justify conventions by showing that the generalizations they allow one to express do not hold accidentally. One might try to do this by arguing that a convention which can be used frequently in grammars cannot represent an accidental fact about language. But many presumably spurious conventions would come in handy very often in linguistic descriptions. For example, what about a linguist C who says that the brace notation should be extended to collapse rules of the form

$$X \rightarrow Y$$
$$Z \rightarrow X$$

into the form

$$Z \rightarrow \begin{Bmatrix} X \\ \end{Bmatrix} \rightarrow Y$$

He will be able to show us just as many cases where such braces could be used in grammars to group rules together. Or, to cite an actual linguist, Pāṇini often makes use of an abbreviatory convention which corresponds to the following kind of use of braces, ruled out in generative grammar:[1]

$$
\begin{array}{l}
A \rightarrow \left. B \right\} \Big/ \_C \\
D \rightarrow \left\{ \begin{array}{l} E \\ F \ / \ \_G \end{array} \right.
\end{array}
$$

What seems wrong about this is that it allows collapsing rules which represent heterogeneous processes. Of the three rules combined here, two have absolutely nothing in common with each other: the top rule

$$A \rightarrow B \ / \ \_C$$

and the bottom rule

$$D \rightarrow F \ / \ \_G$$

But we would like the rules in a grammar to form blocks whose parts are related in some sense that goes beyond just partial identity. Ideally, the rules should be grouped into natural blocks whose parts represent different aspects of the same basic process.

Can psycholinguistics provide experimental evidence on the form of grammars? Recent psycholinguistic experiments designed to test the psychological reality of generative grammar have been concerned mainly with two questions. One group of experiments has sought behavioral correlates to the structural descriptions postulated by generative grammar. Bever, Fodor and Garrett have, for example, carried out a series of experiments in which they found that the location at which a burst of sound is perceived in a synchronously presented sentence differs from its objective location in a way that can be predicted from the surface constituent structure of the sentence. The goal of another group of experiments was to find evidence bearing on the claim that a system of rules such as that postulated by generative grammar is involved in producing and understanding utterances. In contrast with the successful experiments concerned with the psychological reality of structural descriptions, those concerned with the psychological reality of grammars have on the whole been a failure (Fodor and Garrett 1967). It is true that there was an initial spate of successes in which a clear relationship seemed to emerge between the grammatical complexity of a sentence, as measured by the number of rules that con-

---

[1] The reason is that abbreviatory conventions, in the Indian grammatical tradition, originally an oral one, were not graphic devices such as braces, parentheses, or anything directly equivalent to them, but rather resembled the conjunction-reduction processes of natural language.

tribute to its formation, and its perceptual complexity, as measured by various experimentally obtained performance parameters. But in recent experiments with more complex linguistic material this relationship has all but disappeared. It stands to reason that the utilization of the speaker's internalized grammatical rules is a highly complex process involving elaborate ways of tracking down the relevant rules and processing sentences in such a way that parameters which tap performance directly are not going to be related at all directly to such crude grammatical properties of sentences as the number of rules involved in their derivation. The fact that grammars are not performance models presumably means that the answer to the question of whether they are correct competence models is not likely to be forthcoming by any currently known experimental techniques until the contributions of competence can be separated out from the facts about performance.

What we really need is a window on the form of linguistic competence that is not obscured by factors like performance, about which next to nothing is known. In linguistic change we have precisely such a window.

2. THE FORM OF LINGUISTIC CHANGE [2]

We can think of linguistic change in roughly the following terms. Grammars are subject to changes of two kinds: the addition of new rules to them

---

[2]
[Although students should by now have some general understanding of the status and shape of the phonological component of a generative grammar from their reading of Chomsky, Sledd, and the introduction to this section, some few words of explanation may help them follow Kiparsky's discussion more easily. The theory of generative phonology includes a universal or general phonetics which provides a set of distinctive features for the description of sounds. Individual segments of sound are conceived of not as indivisible units (which can be represented with single letters in a phonetic alphabet) but as bundles of these features. The distinctive features are determined on the basis of acoustic and articulatory properties of the sounds produced by humans and constitute a theory of the phonetic materials available to a speaker of a language from which that speaker constructs the sounds he utters (for example, he has available a certain number of positions of jaw height, degrees of tenseness or laxness of the musculature of the vocal tract, etc.). In early statements (see Roman Jakobson, Morris Halle, C. G. M. Fant, *Preliminaries to Speech Analysis*) some 15 or 16 features were recognized. Although Kiparsky states most of his rules in generally familiar terms, it may be useful to identify less familiar features with articulatory correlates: (1) *consonantal*—sounds produced with extreme degrees of narrowing in the vocal tract so that friction or complete stoppage of breath occurs; (2) *vocalic*— sounds produced without such a degree of narrowing; (3) *grave*—sounds produced with narrowing at the periphery of the vocal tract, at the lips or in the velar region; (4) *diffuse*—high vowels, labial and alveolar consonants; (5) *strident*—noisy consonants like /s/, where the air stream is directed under pressure against an obstruction at right angles to it; (6) *voiced*—sounds produced with vibration of the vocal cords. Each feature is either present or absent in a given segment; thus we have sounds consonantal or nonconsonantal, vocalic or nonvocalic, grave or nongrave, etc. One difference between distinctive feature notation and traditional articulatory description is that in the former, all sound types are identified by use of the same set of features.

In a generative grammar (to summarize an early version of generative phonology which Kiparsky uses here as his basis), lexical entries are representations of the unpredictable syntactic, semantic, and phonological properties of the morphemes in the language. The phonological properties are represented by matrices with columns standing for individual segments (the vowels and consonants, e.g.), rows for distinctive features (vocalic, consonantal, etc.). In such a matrix, each feature is specified as either +, −, or 0 (i.e., the cell in the matrix is left blank). *Zero* indicates that a given feature is predictable by general rule; *plus* and *minus* indicate that a feature is not so predictable and consequently must be specified in the representation. The specified and simplification of them. In phonology, the addition of rules corresponds roughly to the concept of "sound change" (Halle 1962, Postal 1968). For example, the sound change whereby word-final obstruents[3] became voiceless in German and many other Germanic languages is the addition of the rule

$$(1) \qquad [+ \text{ obstruent}] \rightarrow [- \text{ voiced}] / \underline{\qquad} \#$$

Through alternations such as [bunt]:[bunde] (versus [bunt]:[bunte]), in which this rule is reflected, it is learned anew as part of the language by each generation of speakers, and even in Modern German the underlying representations of most words retain the medially pronounced voiced segment. Yet the addition of Rule (1) does not leave the lexicon entirely unaffected. Words like *ab*, *ob*, and *weg*, which never came to stand before an inflectional ending that would cause the reappearance of an underlying voiced obstruent, are never heard after the sound change with anything but a voiceless final obstruent; in these isolated forms, succeeding generations of speakers therefore have no reason to set up underlying forms with

---

features thus serve to contrast individual entries. For example, in the entry for *spin*, if the second segment is marked + consonantal and − vocalic (indicating a true consonant), the first segment need be marked *only* for the features + consonantal and − vocalic, since in English only *s* can precede true consonants in initial consonant clusters. Since only *s* can appear in that environment, it need not be marked for those features which would distinguish *s* from other consonants like *t* or *k*. A consonant appearing in initial position before a vowel, however, would have to be specified to show its distinctness from other consonants which can also appear freely in that position. Thus, the lexical entry is quite abstract, serving as a categorial input for the phonological component of the grammar.

The phonological component contains rules which interpret that input in terms of sounds; that is, the rules convert the underlying abstract representations in the lexicon (which are binary, expressed either by + or −) into representations of actual pronunciation (where features are no longer binary, but expressible as degrees along scales such as frontness or backness, high or low). The rules in the phonological component are ordered, and take into account grammatical as well as phonological environments. Thus a rule such as:

$$[+ \text{ obstruent}] \rightarrow [- \text{ voiced}] / \underline{\qquad} \#$$

says that obstruents become voiceless when they immediately precede a word boundary. The square brackets enclose features, the arrow means "is realized as," the slash means "in the following environment," the line indicates the slot where the feature in question appears, # is a boundary mark. Note that such a conception of lexicon and phonology provides a number of distinctions in the kinds of linguistic changes that may occur: there may be a change in the underlying representation provided in the lexicon; rules may be added to the phonological component or deleted from it; the order of rules in the phonological component may change.

The version of the theory of generative phonology which Kiparsky uses as the basis of this paper is an early one similar to that summarized by Morris Halle in two articles reprinted in Fodor and Katz, *The Structure of Language:* "On the Bases of Phology," 324–333, and "Phonology in Generative Grammar," 334–352. However, Kiparsky suggests that a number of revisions should be made in that theory, and readers are cautioned that many changes from the version of generative phonology sketched in this note have been made in recent works—changes both in the list of features which phonetic theory provides and in the form of lexical representations and of phonological rules. Later theory is detailed in two important recent works: Paul Postal, *Aspects of Phonological Theory* (New York, 1968) and Noam Chomsky and Morris Halle, *The Sound Pattern of English* (New York, 1968).—*Eds.*]

3 [Stops, fricatives, and affricates are *obstruents:* a sound type distinguished primarily on the basis of place of closure in the vocal tract and the effects of that closure on air pressure above or below the glottis. See *Sound Pattern*, pp. 300–03.—*Eds.*]

voiced obstruents. The change thus brings about a restructuring in a tiny corner of the vocabulary.

I hope that this use of the term *generation* will not convey the absurd picture of a society horizontally segmented into a number of discrete age groups, each with its own grammar. The point is simply that a language is not some gradually and imperceptibly changing object which smoothly floats through time and space, as historical linguistics based on philological material all too easily suggests. Rather, the transmission of language is discontinuous, and a language is recreated by each child on the basis of the speech data it hears. Nor should the term *restructuring* be understood as denoting a change of some speaker's grammar into another grammar, for it refers just to a discontinuous linguistic change arising from the difference between the grammar constructed by a child and the grammar of those whose speech constituted his linguistic experience. In discussing linguistic change in these elementary terms we are, of course, missing a number of important factors which cannot in the long run be ignored. For example, as Jakobson has pointed out, metalinguistic information concerning such things as the social value of different speech forms is an important part of what a speaker knows, and Labov's recent studies (1963, 1965) show its diachronic relevance very clearly. A conception of grammar in which these broader aspects of competence are explicitly accounted for will hopefully provide a general basis for the study of their role in linguistic change.

A sound change that I will frequently refer to is umlaut in Germanic. By this rule, vowels were fronted before i (for example, Old High German *wurmi* > *würmi* 'worms', *tāti* > *tǣti* 'deeds', *nōti* > *nöti* 'needs'). Short *a* was not only fronted but also raised to *e* (for example, *slagi* > *slegi* 'strokes', *gasti* > *gesti* 'guests'). The original umlaut rule, then, was the following:[4]

$$(2) \quad \begin{bmatrix} \text{V} \\ \langle-\text{long}\rangle \end{bmatrix} \rightarrow \begin{bmatrix} -\text{back} \\ \langle-\text{low}\rangle \end{bmatrix} \Big/ \underline{\quad} C_o i$$

In modern German we encounter this rule in a somewhat different form. In the majority of dialects what we find as the productive umlaut of *a* is not *e*, as originally, but *æ*. For example, in the Low German dialect of Prignitz (Mackel 1905–7) we have *gast:gæst*, *kraft:kræftig* with a low front vowel in the umlauted forms, rather than the expected *gast:gest*, *kraft:-kreftig*. But the only *e*'s that have thus gone to *æ* are those that were productively umlauted from *a*. Phonemic *e*'s have remained unchanged. These include not only original Germanic *e* in words like *nest* but also *e* from historically umlauted *a* in words like *bet* 'bed', *net* 'net' where *e* has become phonemic since there was no reason to derive it synchronically from an

---

[4] The rule must be complicated somewhat to include secondary umlaut.

underlying *a*. Analogous facts hold true in Old English as well. In terms of the grammar, this widespread change is a simplification of the umlaut rule from its original form of (2) to the form in (3):

$$(3) \qquad V \rightarrow [- \text{ back}] \; / \; \ldots$$

(I leave open here the question of what exactly the environment of umlauting in Modern German is, which is irrelevant for present purposes.)

The change from (2) to (3) is an instance of the second basic type of linguistic change, simplification.[5] I shall merely illustrate this type for the moment but hope to justify it in more detail later. Simplification is a generalized and reinterpreted version of the traditional concept of analogy (Matthews, forthcoming; Kiparsky 1965, 1967). This is particularly evident in its simplest form, namely morphological regularization as in changes of the type *brought* > *bringed*, which amount to loss of the special mark associated with lexical entries like *bring* that singles them out as morphological exceptions and specifies the nature of their exceptional behavior. Much more interesting in many respects are cases in which the simplification affects the rules of the grammar rather than the lexicon. Quite commonly, such simplification leads to the loss of parts of rules from the grammar, as in the change of the umlaut rule just cited, where what is lost is the part of the rule which raises *a*. The process may even lead to the loss of entire rules. For example, Rule (1), which devoices word-final obstruents and once was common to all dialects of German, has been lost in some dialects of Northern Switzerland as well as in some varieties of Yiddish. In place of *bunt:bundes* they have *bund:bundes*, with the morphophonemic distinction of voicing now again appearing phonetically in word-final position. We know that these languages once possessed Rule (1), as it has permanently affected the handful of isolated words like *(a)vek* 'away', *ap* (Yiddish *op*) 'away', which had a voiced final obstruent but lost it even morphophonemically after the phonetic devoicing took place because retention was not motivated by any inflected forms. Hence there was also no basis for reintroducing the voicing in these words once Rule (1) had dropped out of the language by simplification.

It is also evident that the *order* of rules in a grammar is subject to historical change. Later, I will try to show that this is a special case of simplification; right now a few examples will do. By a historically fairly old rule of Finnish, underlying long mid vowels are diphthongized, for example, *vee* > *vie*. Subsequently, the loss of certain medial voiced continuants

---

[5] The term *generalization* is sometimes confusing, and I will not use it here. It is applicable in the natural sense of the word only to simplification in the structural analysis of a rule; simplification in the structural change is hardly generalization in this same sense. Even regarding the structural analysis, it is hard for some people to get used to the idea that a rule applying to stops and to *f* is less general than one applying just to stops.

introduces new long mid vowels, for example, *teɣe* > *tee*. In standard Finnish, these new long mid vowels stay, and the rule introducing them must therefore follow the diphthongization. That is, the order is

    a. diphthongization
    b. loss of medial voiced continuants

Yet in many dialects of Finnish the new long mid vowels have subsequently come to join in the diphthongization, for example, *teɣe* > *tee* > *tie*. What this means is that the order of the rules has changed to

    a. loss of medial voiced continuants
    b. diphthongization

Notice also what it does *not* mean. It does not mean what anyone coming from traditional historical linguistics automatically tends to think it means, namely that in standard Finnish, where *tee* from *teɣe* does not diphthongize, the diphthongization rule is not "productive". On the contrary, it is perfectly productive since it must apply to underlying forms like *vee*, in which the underlying long mid vowel must be assumed because of morphophonemic rules such as those for past formation, for example, *vee + i* > *vei* like *saa + i* > *sai*, as McCawley (forthcoming *a*) has shown. The difference between the two kinds of dialects has nothing to do with the productivity of the diphthongization rule but simply with its order with respect to the loss of medial voiced continuants.

An example of reordering which once again involves the umlaut is the following. In the dialects of Northeastern Switzerland the back mid vowel *o* becomes lowered to *ɔ* if it immediately precedes a dental or palatal (non-grave, or what Halle now calls a coronal)[6] true consonant or *r*. Compare, in the Kanton of Schaffhausen (Wanner 1941):

Retention of *o*:
    before *l*: *foll, holts, gold*
    before labials: *grob, ops, hobəl, xnopf, dobə, ofə, xopf*
    before velars: *xoxxə, xnoxxə, rokx, kflogə, bogə.*

Lowering to *ɔ*:
    before *r*: *hɔrn, tɔrn, šɔrə*
    before dentals and palatals: *rɔss, xrɔttə, lɔsə, ksɔttə, bɔdə, pɔšt.*

The distribution of allophones is given by the rule

$$(4) \qquad \begin{bmatrix} V \\ -\text{ high} \\ +\text{ back} \end{bmatrix} \rightarrow [+\text{ low}] \Big/ \underline{\hspace{2cm}} \begin{bmatrix} +\text{ consonantal} \\ -\text{ grave} \\ -\text{ lateral} \end{bmatrix}$$

It is necessary to restrict (4) to the back vowels. The umlauted variant *ö*

---

[6] [For the term *coronal*, see *Sound Pattern*, p. 304.—*Eds*.]

of the vowel *o* is not lowered. The plurals of *bogə* and *bɔdə* are *bögə* and *bödə*, both with a mid *ö*. Hence the synchronic relative order of (4) and umlaut must be

   a. Rule (3) (umlaut)

   b. Rule (4) (lowering)

This is the situation in some dialects on the northern fringe of Switzerland. Elsewhere a different state of affairs obtains.

I will take a dialect which in all other relevant respects is identical to that of the Schaffhausen area, namely that of Kesswil, in neighboring Oberthurgau (Enderlin 1911). Rule (4) operates in unmodified form here too. All the vocabulary items cited above for the Schaffhausen dialects are found, with the same distribution of *o* and *ɔ*, in Kesswil. But the difference is that Kesswil, along with most of Northeastern Switzerland, has *ö* as the umlauted form of *o*, but *ɔ̈* as the umlauted form of *ɔ*. In these dialects the plural of *bogə* is *bögə*, but the plural of *bɔdə* is *bɔ̈də*.

The solution which first might come to mind is that the lowering rule in (4) was simplified to apply to rounded vowels regardless of whether they are front or back. But this fails since phonemic *ö* does not lower to *ɔ̈* in the environment of (4). The crucial cases are such forms as *plötsli* and *fröšš* 'frog' (originally a plural form). The behavior of these isolated forms, whose vowels are not lowered, shows conclusively that we are in reality not dealing with a lowering of *ö* to *ɔ̈* at all, but rather with the umlauting of *ɔ* as well as *o*. That is, the order of the rules has now become

   a. Rule (4) (lowering)

   b. Rule (3) (umlaut)

Applying to the same underlying forms as before, these rules now produce the segment *ɔ̈*, which did not arise under the old ordering.

3. *A CRITERION FOR PSYCHOLOGICAL REALITY*

Returning after this brief survey of some main types of phonological change to the initial question about the justification for assuming the psychological reality of generative grammar, suppose that we now raise this question about some aspect of generative grammar, such as the requirement that grammars contain a certain level of representation, or that they be written using certain notational conventions. The conception of linguistic change sketched out above, in which linguistic structure crucially figures at several points, suggests as one test for determining the answer that we ask the following question: Do the levels, the kinds of rules, and so on, which are required by this theory ever play a role in linguistic change? Taking as our example again the simple case of the brace notation, we can ask: Do blocks of rules collapsed by braces form units of a kind which can undergo systematic change? If they do, this will be a powerful argument for this notation, and if not, we will have prima facie evidence that it is linguistically irrelevant. On such questions, evidence of the following kind can be found.

In English, underlying long vowels, which are otherwise‑realized as diphthongs, are shortened in two main phonological environments: before two or more consonants (for example, *keep*:*kept*) and in the third syllable from the end of the word (for example, *vain*:*vanity*, *severe*:*severity*). The rules which bring these shortenings about are the following:

$$(5') \qquad V \rightarrow [- \text{ long}] \; / \; \underline{\quad} CC$$

$$(5'') \qquad V \rightarrow [- \text{ long}] \; / \; \underline{\quad} C \ldots V \ldots V$$

The theory of generative grammar requires that (5') and (5'') be collapsed into a single rule as follows:

$$(5) \qquad V \rightarrow [- \text{ long}] \; / \; \underline{\quad} C \begin{cases} C \\ \ldots V \ldots V \end{cases}$$

It asserts that of the two descriptively equivalent grammars, one of which contains the two rules (5') and (5'') as separate processes and the other as a single process combined into (5) by factoring out their common part and enclosing the remainder in braces, it is the latter which is the psychologically correct one.

Rule (5) arose in Early Middle English as a generalization of a much more restricted process of shortening. In Old English, vowels were shortened before *three* or *more* consonants (for example, *gōdspell* > *godspell*, *brǣmblas* > *brǣmblas*) and in the third syllable from the end provided they were followed by *two* consonants (for example, *blēdsian* > *bledsian*).[7] The corresponding rules were:

$$(6') \qquad V \rightarrow [- \text{ long}] \; / \; \underline{\quad} CCC$$

$$(6'') \qquad V \rightarrow [- \text{ long}] \; / \; \underline{\quad} CC \ldots V \ldots V$$

Again, these rules must be collapsed as before:

$$(6) \qquad V \rightarrow [- \text{ long}] \; / \; \underline{\quad} CC \begin{cases} C \\ \ldots V \ldots V \end{cases}$$

On comparing the Old English rule in (6) and the Early Middle English (and indeed Modern English) rule in (5) we see that the only difference

---

[7] Luick (1921, pp. 204, 352–3). In isolated words the Old English shortening also applied before geminates. But in these isolated words it led to restructuring, and since there was no shortening before *derived* geminates (geminates arising in combinations of morphemes) the (synchronic) phonological rule of Old English was as stated here (Rule (6)). This rule covers all cases where there was actual alternation between long and short vowels in Old English.

between them is that the later rule (5) has lost one of the required consonants in its environment. It represents a simpler, more general form of the Old English vowel-shortening process. It will apply in all cases where (6) applied but also in cases where (6) would not have applied. Evidently the change from (6) to (5) is an instance of simplification, which we have seen to be one of the basic mechanisms of linguistic change. But in a linguistic theory in which the brace notation plays no role, the relation between the Old English and the Early Middle English shortening processes is a different one. If the brace notation were not part of linguistic theory we would have two separate changes—namely $(6') > (5')$ and $(6'') > (5'')$—on our hands and we would be faced with the very peculiar fact that two separate, unrelated rules have undergone an identical modification at the same point in the history of English. The linguistic theory on which traditional historical grammar was based is an instance of such a theory, and traditional historical grammar has in fact failed to see the regularity here and has treated the change as two separate processes.

In the same way, we can go on to ask whether rules of the form

$$\begin{Bmatrix} X \\ Y \end{Bmatrix} \to Z$$

can be added to grammars. On the assumption that sound changes are natural processes, and that the brace notation groups rules into natural blocks, we should predict that rules collapsed by braces should be capable of being added to grammars. There are of course numerous instances of this type of change. In fact, the addition of rule (6) to the grammar of Old English is probably just such an instance. Similarly we should predict that rules collapsed by braces should participate in reordering as blocks.

The proposed test also has the virtue of rendering such notations eminently vulnerable to potential counterevidence from historical change. The counterclaim which would be made by the theory which excludes braces is that rules like $(5')$ and $(5'')$, or $(6')$ and $(6'')$, when found together in a grammar with no necessarily intervening rules forcing them apart, should be able to undergo simplification individually, in such a way that the resulting pair of rules could not subsequently be collapsed by braces. Such a change, which in this theory would be a legitimate simplification, would be neither a possible sound change nor a simplification in a theory which allows collapsing by braces, and it would therefore be excluded in the latter. If such changes could be found, they would be clear counterevidence against the brace notation and would suggest that the generalizations effected by means of braces are spurious ones. The position which excludes braces would also entail that a rule could be inserted between two rules collapsed by braces in such a way that they subsequently could no longer be so collapsed. And finally, it would also entail that the parts of rules collapsed in this way should be individually capable of reordering with other rules of the grammar. The fact that no such changes appear to exist is strong negative evidence which adds to the historical support for the essential correctness of this abbreviatory convention of generative grammar.

The aforementioned linguist C, who wanted to introduce abbreviations like

$$Z \to \left. \begin{cases} X \end{cases} \right\} \to Y$$

and Pāṇini, who supported other conventions which generative grammar does not countenance, now both get a real opportunity to prove their points by showing that the blocks of rules resulting from such conventions act as units in simplification (for example, by showing cases in which the joint environment X is simplified) or by showing that they are added as units to grammars, or reordered as units with respect to other rules. There is no evidence in sight that I know of to encourage them in this search.

One answer, then, to the question concerning the empirical basis for the notational conventions of linguistic theory is that these conventions are an essential part of any attempt to characterize what is a possible linguistic change and what is not a possible linguistic change. It involves in a sense only systematically drawing the conclusions from Halle's idea (1962) that the class of possible sound changes (qua added rules) is the same as the class of possible phonological rules and bringing in the additional evidence of simplification, whose role in linguistic change Halle did not consider.

In many crucial respects this criterion for rule naturalness lends support to the assumptions which are currently made in the theory of generative grammar. But accepting the equivalence of possible sound change and possible rule commits one to placing many restrictions on the notations of grammatical descriptions which are not at present acknowledged, and on the other hand, it suggests the need for many new conventions and new extensions of notations which should be incorporated into linguistic theory. For example, by saying that braces are needed we have only told half the story. We would like to limit the use of braces in such a way as to combine only processes which are indeed in some sense related and can jointly produce a sound change. Suppose, for example, that we found a language with three phonological processes that all applied before vowels and that did not have to be separated by other rules:

  a. voiced stops become continuants
  b. *s* becomes *h*
  c. vowels drop.

For all three processes to take place before vowels is quite natural, and examples for each of them could be cited from dozens of languages. Yet there would be something wrong about combining all three by virtue of their shared environment. It is evident that *a* and *b* are more closely related than either of them is to *c*, and that an adequate theory should require the combining of *a* and *b* but not *c*. The basis for this feeling is, I think, nothing but the fact that *a* and *b* characteristically occur together in linguistic change and thus form a natural block of phonological processes. In fact, their relatedness has really nothing to do with the fact that they share a common environment but follows from an essential kinship of the phonetic processes involved. Thus they should be grouped together in a grammar even if they both were context free. To determine the natural groupings of rules was a goal of traditional historical linguistics which has been abandoned to a large extent in structuralism, at least in America. For example, *a* and *b* would have been considered *weakenings*. Probably phonology would profit by attempting to develop further and to make precise such concepts, which traditional grammars use to introduce an organization into their treatments of diachronic phonology.

4. DIACHRONIC EVIDENCE CONCERNING PHONOLOGICAL LEVELS

The psychological reality of levels of representation which emerge in different linguistic theories is subject to verification and falsification by diachronic evidence along the same lines. A question to be asked whenever some level of representation is proposed as linguistically relevant is whether this level functions in linguistic change. For example, it would be a striking and to my mind conclusive piece of evidence for the reality of autonomous ('taxonomic') phonemics if it could be shown that there were sound changes whose conditioning environment could be stated naturally only at precisely this level. It should be made clear just what such a demonstration would involve. It would involve showing both that the environments of this sound change were not morphophonemic and (the crucial part) that they could not be reformulated in terms of the phonetic level without restating exactly the rules that relate the phonetic and phonemic level. Of course, it is always by definition possible to reformulate a phonemic environment in terms of phonetic representations, and what would have to be shown is therefore that such a restatement of the conditioning environment of a sound change would lose a significant generalization. A hypothetical example of what to look for would be a change in some Russian dialect which affected all voiced obstruents except for [ž̌] and [ɜ], the two voiced obstruents in Russian which are not phonemic but always come about only by automatic voicing assimilation of /č/ and /c/. As far as I know, no one has ever presented any instance of this kind, and there is therefore no basis for the claim that the facts of sound change somehow support a level of autonomous phonemics. And as has been repeatedly argued (Halle 1962, Chomsky and Halle 1968, Postal 1968, Kiparsky 1965, 1967), the facts of sound change do provide clear evidence for a deeper level of representation in phonology.

The contention has often been made that the level of autonomous phonemics is relevant to sound change in a somewhat different way. The suggestion is that the direction of sound change is determined by tendencies towards a symmetry of phonological units. What is important for our present discussion is that these units are often held to be specifically autonomous phonemes. Much the same comments again apply: if the level in question were demonstrably the relevant one here, and the tendencies in question could really be shown to exist, then this would decisively refute those who deny its existence. But once again, the necessary proof has, to my knowledge, never been provided.

Moulton had studied the vowel systems of Swiss dialects with the purpose of testing these concepts of "phonological space". He maintained (1961) that Rule (4)—the lowering of o to $\mathfrak{o}$ before dentals, palatals and r, whose relation to umlauting we discussed as an example of reordering— was caused by a drive towards symmetry through "filling" the "empty slot" in the systems which Moulton supposes that these dialects possessed before the lowering took place:

	i	ü	u		i	ü	u
(A)	e	ö	o	(B)	e	ö	o
	ɛ				ɛ		
	æ		a				a

But what is the justification for assuming that System (B) had this asymmetrical structure rather than the symmetrical structure (C) which one would have normally supposed it to have?

	i	ü	u
(C)	e	ö	o
	ɛ		a

Why did Moulton not assign a to the back vowels in these dialects as he did in the (A) dialects? Moulton has discussed the reason for his choice in another article (Moulton 1960, p. 174), where the justification given for the asymmetrical System (B) is that these dialects underwent the lowering by Rule (4): "The fact that the subsequent development of the vowel system of the North was parallel not to that of the West and Center but to that of the East confirms the belief that arrangement [(B) above] represents linguistic reality more faithfully, and suggests that arrangement [(C) above] would indeed be only a playful manipulation of symbols on paper." In other words, these dialects had an asymmetrical system because they underwent lowering of *o* to *ɔ*, and they underwent lowering of *o* to *ɔ* because they had an asymmetrical system!

In sum, one prediction to which such theories lead is that certain phonological changes should be determined by whether or not pairs of certain sounds are contrastive in some phonetic environment and hence that isoglosses formed by phonological changes should characteristically be coextensive with boundaries between different autonomous phonemic systems. Other predictions are certainly also entailed, and the cases I have mentioned by no means constitute a full or even representative illustration of the range of predictions made, nor of the kind of evidence that is available to test them. But they nevertheless show how this theory and related ones do have very specific consequences which can be tested fully on historical material. I would guess that when this is done it will turn out that real enough tendencies towards phonological symmetry exist, but that they have nothing to do with the autonomous phonemic level for which they are often claimed. Rather they are probably brought about by simplificatory phonological changes such as rule simplification and rule reordering, and the symmetry they result in is phonetic rather than phonemic symmetry. This at any rate is what the Swiss German dialect material recently investigated by Moulton clearly suggests.

5. DIACHRONIC EVIDENCE CONCERNING FEATURES AND UNDERLYING REPRESENTATIONS

The particular Swiss German example that I have talked about also raises a nest of further problems unrelated to that of the reality of the autonomous phonemic level, but highly relevant to the general topic of the relevance of linguistic change to linguistic universals. It will have been noticed that phonemic System (A) above, with four distinctive vowel heights, is a clear counterexample to Jakobson's distinctive feature system,[8] which allows only three phonemic degrees of vowel height to exist in a language. First of all, the four degrees clearly contrast in simple, underived words and cannot be predicted by any general rules from some system with only three heights in any way that would not be ad hoc. For example,

ælf 'eleven'	*gɛld* 'money'	*šelm* 'rogue'	*bild* 'picture'
sæməl 'stool'	*swɛbəl* 'sulphur'	*šnebəl* 'sty (in the eye)'	*šwibəl* 'grip'
hæks 'witch'	*xrɛps* 'crayfish'	*nets* 'net'	*blits* 'lightning'
hællər 'small coin'	*šɛllə* 'bell'	*xellə* 'scoop'	*willə* 'will'

---

8 [See n. 2 for a description of the features presented here.—*Eds.*]

In addition these dialects have a phonemic *a* which is quite distinct from all of these front vowels. Evidently, then, Jakobson's features compact and diffuse (low and high) should be replaced by two other features which allow four distinctive degrees of vowel height. A natural one would be the following:

	æ	ɛ	e	i
High	−	−	+	+
Mid	−	+	+	−

Yet if we shift our point of view somewhat and regard impossible systems simply as the end points of increasing scales of markedness, the proposed change to allow four heights is a relatively minor one. In a sense, these dialects, particularly if the historical evidence is brought in, support Jakobson's thesis in the modified form that vowel systems with four heights are complex, that is, highly marked systems, in the technical sense.[9] For historically, a four-height system of this kind had to arise in all High German dialects. However, everywhere, with the exception of some tiny Swiss areas in Appenzell and Toggenburg, the four heights have been reduced to three by mergers either of the two mid vowels or of the two low vowels. These mergers have taken place quite independently in numerous dialects and thus have the character of drift or simplification rather than of normal sound changes. What this seems to indicate is that systems of four vowel heights are unstable because of their complexity, a conclusion which is indicated in any case by the rarity of such systems in the languages of the world.

The particular way in which these four-height systems have merged to three in the various dialects is itself a small piece of historical support for the feature system which I have proposed. The other possible alternative of characterizing four vowel heights by two features would be this:

	æ	ɛ	e	i
High	−	−	+	+
Raised	−	+	−	+

---

[9] [Kiparsky alludes here to the most recent revisions in the theory of generative phonology. The theory of markedness is a proposal for changing the representation of phonological properties of items in the lexicon. Although the theory is too complex to summarize briefly, the suggestion is that a deeper level of representation be provided than the matrix which specifies features in terms of + or −. Instead, entries would be represented as either Marked or Unmarked, *M* or *U*, where *U* would designate features, whether + or −, which are predictable, in some sense "normal" or "natural," and *M* marks properties not thus predictable. Both M and U markings would then be translated by general rules into + or − designations for features. A "highly marked system" would thus be one which requires a high number of M markings, and would be, consequently, a system of more than "normal" or "natural" complexity. For discussion of the theory, see *Sound Pattern*, Chapter 9, and Paul Postal, *Aspects of Phonological Theory*, Chapter 8.—*Eds.*]

There would be no natural way of formulating the merger of mid vowels here since mid vowels do not make up a natural class under these features. On the other hand, this alternative suggests mergers such as *æ* and *e* or *ε* and *i* which certainly do not occur. Vowel shifts of the type *ī* > *æi*, which are common in many languages, would also be expressed more simply in the system I have proposed. However, an alternative which may be even preferable and should in any case not be counted out yet is that vowel height is not broken down into two binary dimensions at all but forms a single dimension expressed by a feature which in underlying representations can assume at most four values (and must assume at least two).

Against the analysis which posits four heights of vowels in these dialects one might try to carry the argument that this analysis is implausible because closely related dialects have only three heights, and one would expect closely related dialects to differ not in their underlying phonemic system, but only in the rules which relate phonemic representations to phonetic representations. This would be a complete non sequitur. It is an empirical observation that related dialects often have the same phonemic system, but it is not a theoretical condition on related dialects that this should be the case. To say otherwise would be to credit children with historical or dialectological knowledge which they cannot possibly possess. The fact that the children of each generation in learning their language take a fresh look at the facts means that there is reason for underlying representations to be transmitted only when the synchronic facts of the language warrant it. The argument is just as irrelevant, and for just the same reason, as it would be to maintain that language *L* must have rule *R* in its grammar because *R* was a sound change in *L*.

A more difficult objection is based on the fact that *æ* in these dialects is the productive umlaut of *a*. To account for morphological umlaut in a language like German it is necessary to set up some abstract conditioning environment which will be a property of certain endings, such as plural *-er*. Whether this is a feature [± umlaut] as proposed by Zwicky (1967) or some phonological property of underlying representations will not matter here. Whatever this abstract environment is, generative phonology at present allows—and indeed probably requires—the trick of making it an obligatory part of isolated words like *schön*, *plötzlich*, *Tür*, which have umlaut vowels that correspond to no back vowels in any related forms. These words are then entered with underlying back vowels which undergo obligatory umlauting by virtue of this property of their underlying representations. The effect is to do away altogether with umlaut vowels in the phonemic system. In our case, then, *æ* would never be treated as phonemic and there would be only three phonemic vowel heights to worry about.

It is again the historical evidence which shows that this trick is wrong and that words like *schön, plötzlich, Tür* must have phonemic umlaut vowels. To see this let us go back to the example of reordering involving Rules (3) and (4) in Northeastern Switzerland. It will be recalled that as a result of the reordering, derived *ö* as in plural *böda* became *ɔ̈* but phonemic *ö* as in *plötsli* was not changed. There would be no way of accounting for a change like this (by no means an atypical case) in a theory which asserted that *all* umlaut vowels are underlying back vowels, for then we would have no natural way of telling apart those that are really so derived and do undergo lowering from those which are only fictitiously so derived and do not undergo lowering. This linguistic change cannot be accounted for unless phonological theory is tightened up in some way to exclude tricks of such a kind. It is interesting to note that whatever exactly the right way to do this turns out to be, it will bring the underlying representations of generative phonology a step closer to Sapir's descriptive practice (McCawley 1967).[10] And once this necessary move is made, the existence of systems with four vowel heights cannot be argued away.[11]

This last conclusion has the peculiar status of at present resting entirely on historical evidence, and of a fairly indirect kind at that. Whether or not we draw it depends on what we consider the subject matter of linguistics to be. We could not draw it if we regarded a grammar simply as a theory of the sentences of a language, and a linguistic theory as a theory of grammars. For this position would entail that linguistic change is no concern of linguistic theory, although it might of course be a pleasant bonus if linguistic theory could be usefully "applied" to questions of linguistic change. But it would not cause us to demand of a linguistic theory that it must (in conjunction with a theory of linguistic change) provide an explanation of the linguistic regularities of diachrony. It is a very different matter if we regard a grammar as a theory of linguistic competence, and the field of linguistics as the study of universal grammar. On this view, which forms the topic of this conference and which I share, the facts of linguistic change assume a new relevance as empirical evidence on the nature of language. We must be prepared to allow them to bear on even purely synchronic questions and, for example, to let the fact that some phonological change is explainable by one linguistic theory but not by another carry weight in the choice between

---

[10] [For additional discussion of Sapir's practice and its affinity to generative phonology, see *Sound Pattern*, pp. 344-50. Essentially, the similarity stressed here is Sapir's employment of two orthographies in phonological representations: a "phonological orthography" and a "phonetic orthography." The former is an abstract representation of morphemes, the latter a record of speech sounds. Of the relation between the two Sapir says: "the phonetic forms result from the phonologic only by the application of absolutely mechanical phonetic laws of spirantizing, alternating stress, and unvoicing." See Sapir's "The Psychological Reality of Phonemes," in D. G. Mandelbaum, ed., *Selected Writings of Edward Sapir in Language, Culture, and Personality* (Berkeley, 1949), pp. 46-60.—*Eds.*]

[11] [David Stampe points out to me that the naturalness condition he proposes (at this same conference) requires exactly the underlying representations which we have seen to be justified on historical grounds.—*Eds.*]

these two theories. The application of linguistic change to linguistic theory now becomes at least as important as the converse process.

The above rather scattered observations illustrate various types of inferences that can be made about grammatical form from the ways in which it shapes linguistic change. The reason I have dealt with phonological changes and not syntactic ones is partly that I know more about phonology, but also that the historical facts are here much easier to come by and the evidence they give is more needed in phonology than in syntax. I have been concerned not so much with establishing the virtues and faults of specific notations, levels, and so forth—much more evidence would be needed for that in almost every kind of problem dealt with above—as with making a case for the legitimacy and potential fruitfulness of certain general patterns of inference from linguistic change to the nature of grammar. In no case have the conclusions depended on very specific or controversial assumptions about linguistic change. The basic assumption from which these conclusions follow has been the very tame one that where grammar is involved in linguistic change it is involved in terms of its natural components and rules.

It is not so with another kind of inference from linguistic change to grammatical form to which I should now like to turn. This inference is based so heavily on the existence of grammatical simplification as a form of linguistic change that before proceeding to it I should like to outline the justification for assuming the existence of such a form of linguistic change.

6. FORMAL JUSTIFICATION FOR SIMPLIFICATION

The conclusion that such changes as simplification and reordering must exist does not and could not rest just on the fact that we observe related dialects to differ in the ordering of their rules, or to show minor differences in the details of essentially shared rules. That such differences are typical isoglosses is true but compatible with the position that addition of rules is the only form of phonological change. For as long as we look at dialects without knowledge of their historical origin we could explain any rule-ordering difference between them in a wave-theory fashion. For example, a spreading rule might be adopted at one position in the sequence of rules in one dialect and at some other position in another. There is another wave-theory effect which can cause pairs of rules to be differently ordered in different dialects. If Rule A spreads from West to East and Rule B spreads from East to West across some dialect area, then, if the two rules are critically ordered with respect to each other, the Western area will end up with the order (A, B) and the Eastern area with the order (B, A). Undoubtedly these are both, in fact, quite common causes of ordering differences between dialects. Small differences in the form of rules can well occur in the course of their diffusion from one dialect to another. It has been observed that in such borrowing a narrowing down in the scope of rules often takes place. Thus the diphthongization of the long high vowels of Middle High German during its spread southward in Swiss territory was restricted to word-final position at a certain point before it stopped spreading altogether. Compare also the gradual curtailment of the High German consonant shift in the so-called Rhenish Fan.[12]

However, we find just the same types of minor differences in the form of rules and in their ordering when we compare successive stages of the same dialect rather than geographically adjacent dialects, and here the wave-theory and imperfect borrowing explanations are excluded. Furthermore, in such cases the form of rules almost always changes in the direction of greater simplicity. Can such changes be accounted for on the assumption that addition of rules is the only form of phonological change?

Consider the Finnish example cited in Section 2, in which the diphthongization rule was dialectally shifted down to follow loss of medial voiced continuants so as to apply to the long vowels which arose by this historically later rule (for example, *teγe* > *tee* > *tie*). Technically, it is not impossible to account for this change by means of added rules. There are even two ways of doing it. One is to assume that a rule of loss of medial voiced continuants, identical with the original one, was entered before diphthongization, causing the original one to become vacuous and to be dropped. The other is to assume that a diphthongization rule, identical with the original diphthongization rule, was entered *after* loss of medial voiced continuants. The optimal grammar for the resulting output would once again be the desired one. The unfortunate aspect of this is the arbitrariness of the choice between the two descriptions. It is hard to see how the distinction between them could correspond to any linguistic difference. The two distinct grammars containing an identical rule at two different points which are required as virtual intermediaries seem to be mere artifacts of a theory which excludes reordering as a mechanism of change and therefore must make an inappropriate extension of rule adding to account for a quite different kind of process.

---

[12] [The High German Consonant Shift was a set of sound changes which differentiate certain stops and spirants in the High and Low Germanic dialects. The individual shifts spread over most High German dialects, but in certain dialects of the lower Rhine region they were restricted in their operation. The term *Rhenish fan* refers to the resulting configuration of isoglosses, which spread out in a fan shape as they cross the Rhine. For details of the Consonant Shift and its curtailment see Eduard Prokosch, *A Comparative Germanic Grammar* (Philadelphia, 1939), and Wilhelm Braune and Walther Mitzka, *Althochdeutsche Grammatik*, 11th ed. (Tübingen, 1963), pp. 80–88. For a discussion of the Rhenish fan see Bloomfield, *Language*, 343–345. Kiparsky's own note on this passage follows immediately.

E. Bach has pointed out to me that these examples are not certain. If, as he suggests, rules are never narrowed down in borrowing, the case for simplification becomes even stronger.—*Eds.*]

The difficulties become considerable in such a case as the loss of word-final devoicing in Swiss German and Yiddish. We cannot, clearly, simply suppose that a late rule which made final obstruents voiced was added. Such a rule could not distinguish between morphophonemically voiced and voiceless stops and would wrongly turn into *bund* not only the *bunt* that is related to *bunde* but also the *bunt* that is related to *bunte*. In desperation we would take recourse to an ad hoc rule which somehow would provide morphophonemically voiced stops with a diacritic feature[13] before they got devoiced and later would use this diacritic feature as an environment for revoicing, after which the diacritic feature could be deleted again. Obviously this bears not the faintest resemblance to what actually happened, and no one would want to salvage a theory at the price of such an absurd analysis.

Chomsky and Halle (1968) discuss a convention for handling exceptions to rules which might be used in this particular example.[14] The idea is that grammars can contain rules of the form

$$X \rightarrow [- \text{ next rule}]$$

where X is a specification of the special cases in which some rule must not apply. Then it would be possible to say that a rule

$$[\quad] \rightarrow [- \text{ next rule}]$$

was placed directly before the devoicing of word-final obstruents, thus preventing everything from undergoing it. The inoperative devoicing rule would then simply not be incorporated into the grammars of the next generation.

The difference here is not merely notational. The exception-rule solution generalizes neither to the reordering example that was just cited nor to cases like the simplification of the umlaut rule from (2) to (3) which was mentioned earlier. Since what was deleted here was *part* of a rule and the Chomsky-Halle convention for handling exceptions does not allow items to be exceptions to parts of rules, the solution which the convention made possible in the previous case is not available here. The best we can do is to say that the change consists of two separate but simultaneous events: first, the rendering inapplicable of the old umlaut rule (2) by the placement of a Chomsky-Halle exception rule before it, and second, the entering of the new umlaut rule (3) in its stead. That is, we are forced to treat this event as a composite product of two simultaneous changes, one of which alone would have far more spectacular consequences than the two have

---

[13] [Diacritic features are notations in lexical entries indicating that particular rules apply or do not apply to the individual lexical items so marked. They are thus a means of handling exceptions to more general rules—for example, the special pronunciation of certain foreign loans in the lexicon of English.—*Eds.*]

[14] [See *Sound Pattern*, pp. 373-80.—*Eds.*]

together. This leaves us completely in the dark as to why so many dialects (quite independently of each other, as is clear from the geographical distribution) should have undergone such a complicated pair of changes.

We see that to account for such examples by added rules, we would be forced to relax the proposed restriction that a sound change is the addition of a rule to the grammar to the extent of allowing a single historical change to involve the addition of *two* rules. In that case all arguments like those in Section 3 about sound change as a criterion for rule naturalness at once go out the window. And if this is done we also prepare a welcome for innumerable absurd descriptions of other changes. For example, in the case of the Finnish reordering of diphthongization and loss of medial voiced continuants (see Section 2 above) there are now two further alternatives which add to the general arbitrariness: the change might consist of simultaneously making diphthongization inapplicable and adding an exact replica of it after the loss of medial voiced continuants, or of simultaneously making loss of medial voiced continuants inapplicable and adding an exact replica of it before diphthongization.

Also, it is now just as easy to express the reverse change, that is, a change as a result of which the order

a. loss of medial voiced continuants

b. diphthongization

changes into

a. diphthongization

b. loss of medial voiced continuants

The effect of this would be that all *ie* diphthongs derived by way of *ee* from *eγe* would revert to their intermediate representation *ee*, while the *ie* diphthongs derived from basic *ee* would stay unchanged. There is no doubt that a theory of linguistic change should either completely exclude the possibility of such a change or at least reflect the obvious fact that it would be a far more complex and unlikely historical event than what actually happened. But the version to which the theory that rule addition is the only form of linguistic change has been driven at this point is completely incapable of doing so. As the brute necessity of somehow accommodating one set of data has forced it to be relaxed and extended more and more, it has lost the capacity of expressing the facts about sound change that originally motivated it.

7. SIMPLIFICATION AND LANGUAGE ACQUISITION

To avoid this hopeless mess, the concept of simplification would be necessary even if we were concerned merely with characterizing the possible ways in which successive stages of a language could differ (which would be enough for purposes of linguistic reconstruction). But we also would like to find an explanation for why languages can change in the ways that they do. In that case, the reasons for assuming that simplification is a form of linguistic change become more compelling still. We cannot, then, close our eyes to the fact that the kind of driftlike changes which rule addition fails to handle without the special acrobatics of which samples were performed in Section 6 result in just the kind of grammars that appear spontaneously as intermediate stages in the course of the child's language-learning process.

I am not thinking just of the fact that instances of morphological analogy (*oxes, bringed*) are as characteristic of child language as they are of historical change, although this is perhaps the most evident instance of the correspondence. The parallelism goes deeper than that. For example, there is in many languages a drift towards multiple negation, as in substandard English "I don't see nothing nowhere." Such multiple negation has developed in the Romance languages and elsewhere in Europe too. Jespersen tried to attribute this drift to some vague tendency towards redundancy which he thought governed the direction of linguistic change. But this can hardly be true, for in other languages, such as Finnish, no comparable drift towards multiple negation is observed. Then it cannot be true that multiple negation is simply a general target in the direction of which all languages develop. In fact, I think it is true that multiple negation appears only in those languages that have the equivalent of Klima's *neg*-incorporation rule which produces negative quantifiers such as in English *nobody, nothing* and French *rien*.[15] Surely this is related to the facts about the development of negation in child language found by Bellugi (cited from McNeill 1966). She discovered that at the point at which the child's sentences like

> I didn't see something.
> You don't want some supper.

give way to sentences with negative quantifiers like *nobody, nothing, no supper*, a period of multiple negation at first sets in. As the child first formulates his *neg*-incorporation rule, it has not the form of standard English but of substandard English (which he very well may never have heard); and instead of producing the "normal" sentences like

> I saw nothing.
> Nobody likes me.

he at first comes out with

---

[15] [Finnish has indefinite pronouns such as *kukaan, mikään*, corresponding to English *anybody, anything*, but a negative cannot be incorporated into them to form any equivalents of *nobody, nothing.—Eds.*]

> I didn't see nothing
> Nobody don't like me.

Thus some relationship between "substandard" *neg*-incorporation and "standard" *neg*-incorporation may be responsible for the fact that the former is the natural predecessor of the latter in the development of a child's linguistic system and also the natural result of the latter by linguistic change.

These facts begin to add up when we think of language acquisition as a process in which the child arrives at adult grammar gradually by attempting to match to the speech it hears a succession of hypotheses of an increasing order of complexity (in the linguistic sense of complexity) as these increasingly complex hypotheses become available to the child through maturational change. For phonology this was clearly shown by Jakobson's spectacular discovery that the child learns phonemes in a largely fixed order, which is determined not externally by the order or frequency with which they are heard, but internally by their relative linguistic complexity, as reflected also in the rules governing the possible phonemic systems of the languages of the world (Jakobson 1942). Thus the child first produces the maximally unmarked, unvoiced, unaspirated stops, even if these, as in English, happen not to occur (except in some special environments) and only then splits up this first stop series into two series. In phonology, then, the order in which a child incorporates a particular piece of data into his internalized grammar is determined not by frequency or order of presentation, but by the readiness of the child to assimilate the kind of structure that underlies it. If we assume that the order in which the syntactic rules of the child unfold is internally determined in the same way, we can think of the child's multiple negation as analogous to his unvoiced, unaspirated stop in the sense that both are necessary prior structures which can be discarded only after the full structure develops. This is reasonable in view of the fact that multiple negation is produced by a version of *neg*-incorporation which is in two respects simpler than the adult version of this transformation. In the first place, the adult rule not only adds a *neg* to the quantifier, but it also deletes the original *neg* after the tense; this additional operation of deletion is absent from the child's first version of the rule. Secondly, the adult rule adds a *neg* to just one single quantifier in the sentence, whereas the child spreads the *neg* over all quantifiers that appear in the sentence, producing such specimens as the following:

> I can't do nothing with no string.

Normally these oversimplified intermediate grammars which the child constructs on its way to adult language eventually give way to the full complexity of the adult system. The linguistic change of simplification takes place on those relatively rare occasions when some feature of these intermediate grammars survives into adulthood and becomes adopted by the speech community as a new linguistic norm. See Jakobson's remark (p. 332 of the 1962 reprinting): "Die Sprachveränderung ist kein äusserer Beitrag, den die Kinder dem Sprachgebilde aufzwingen, sondern sie antizipieren dessen innerlich vorherbestimmte, sozusagen in der Luft schwebende Umwandlungen."[16] That such survival is possible is not quite so surprising when we consider the extreme imperviousness of children to adult correction of their speech, as illustrated for multiple negation by the following dialogue (McNeill 1966, p. 69):

Child: Nobody don't like me.
Mother: No, say "nobody likes me."
Child: Nobody don't like me.

⋮

(eight repetitions of this dialogue)

⋮

Mother: No, now listen carefully; say *"nobody likes me."*
Child: Oh! Nobody don't likes me.

Thus we can relate the concepts of rule addition and simplification to adult and child language, respectively. The typical form of rule addition is the borrowing of rules among adults; simplification typically occurs in the learning of language by children. An interesting consequence of this is that isoglosses formed by the spread of rules over a speech territory should form large, coherent dialect areas, whereas those formed by simplification should be characteristically discontinuous because of independent development of the same change in several speech communities. The historically interesting isoglosses, therefore, should be based on the presence versus absence of rules, and not on differences in the form and order of shared rules. Indeed, this is what dialectologists have always implicitly assumed. The boundaries between the major dialect areas of Germany are drawn according to the rules they have, such as the consonant shifts. The isogloss between the two forms of the umlaut rule, (2) and (3) (that is, between *e* and *æ* as the productive umlaut of *a*), would form a useless patchwork of no historical significance. Nor would anyone suppose a historical relationship between Yiddish and Swiss German on the grounds that they share the loss of the word-final devoicing rule. Very schematically, the two types of isoglosses would look like this (shaded areas are the innovating ones):

---

[16] ["Children do not impose change externally on language structure, but rather they anticipate internally pre-determined shifts as if these were, so to speak, floating in the atmosphere."—*Eds.*]

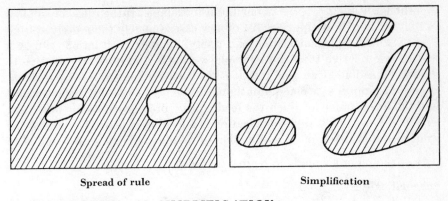

Spread of rule   Simplification

8. REORDERING AS SIMPLIFICATION

Reordering resembles simplification both in the negative property that rule addition miserably fails to do justice to it and in the positive property of its driftlike character. I shall now claim that reordering is in fact a special case of simplification, and that the direction of reordering is predicted by general principles which assign certain types of order a higher value than others. If this can be established, then current phonological theory, which does not distinguish different kinds of linear order, is wrong and must be revised to account for this asymmetry.

To be convinced that reordering is a one-way affair, much as other simplification is, it is enough to examine the individual examples. For instance, many Swiss dialects have put the umlaut rule (3) after $o > ɔ$ (Rule (4)), but none of these have made the reverse switch, and we could not easily imagine it taking place. And a dialect of Finnish in which *tie* from *teγe* > *tee* becomes *tee* again but *vie* from *vee* retains the diphthong, that is, a dialect in which diphthongization reverts to its original position before the loss of medial voiced continuants (which I will now call $γ > ø$ for short) is inconceivable. The question is how this asymmetry, intuitively evident enough in each particular case, can be given a general characterization.

Of the various functional relationships that can hold between rules, two are of relevance here. One way in which two rules A and B can be functionally related is that the application of A creates representations to which B is applicable. That is, the application of A converts forms to which B cannot apply into forms to which B can apply; schematically:

A. [ ] > [φ]
B. [φ] > [ ]

Such a relationship holds for example between $γ > ø$ (*teγe* > *tee*) and diphthongization (*tee* > *tie*) in our Finnish example. If the rules are applied in that order, $\gamma > \phi$ supplies a set of new cases (namely those derived from *eye*) to which diphthongization can apply. In such a situation, call A a *feeding rule* relative to B (for example, $\gamma > \phi$ is a feeding rule relative to diphthongization). Call this relationship between rules a *feeding relationship* (for example, $\gamma > \phi$ and diphthongization are in a feeding relationship) and the linear order in which the feeding rule precedes a *feeding order* (for example, 1. $\gamma > \phi$, 2. diphthongization is a feeding order). Then one of the principles that determine the direction of reordering is

(I) Feeding order tends to be maximized.

Schematically:

$$A. [\varphi] > [\ ] \atop B. [\ ] > [\varphi] \quad > \quad B. [\ ] > [\varphi] \atop A. [\varphi] > [\ ]$$

A further example of (I) involves the several palatalizations in Slavic. By the so-called first palatalization, k and g became $\check{c}$ and $\check{\jmath}$, respectively, before front vowels and y, for example, *kĭto* > *čĭto* 'what', *givŭ* *žĭvŭ* 'alive'.[17]

$$(7) \quad \begin{bmatrix} + \text{ consonantal} \\ - \text{ diffuse} \end{bmatrix} \rightarrow \begin{bmatrix} - \text{ grave} \\ + \text{ strident} \end{bmatrix} / \underline{\hspace{2em}} \begin{bmatrix} - \text{ consonantal} \\ - \text{ back} \end{bmatrix}^{[18]}$$

But the resulting voiced affricate $\check{\jmath}$ has become a continuant $\check{z}$ in all Slavic languages by the rule

$$(8) \quad \begin{bmatrix} + \text{ voiced} \\ - \text{ grave} \\ + \text{ strident} \end{bmatrix} \rightarrow [+ \text{ continuant}]$$

For example, *žĭvŭ* > *živŭ*.

Subsequently new front vowels came to stand after velars by the rule

$$(9) \quad \text{ai} \rightarrow \check{e}$$

By the so-called second palatalization k_1 and g_1 (derived from k and g by an earlier rule) became c and $\jmath$ before these new front vowels, for example, *k₁ěna* > *cěna* 'price', *g₁ělo* > *ʒělo* 'very':

$$(10) \quad \begin{bmatrix} + \text{ obstruent} \\ - \text{ grave} \\ - \text{ strident} \\ - \text{ diffuse} \end{bmatrix} \rightarrow \begin{bmatrix} + \text{ strident} \\ + \text{ diffuse} \end{bmatrix}$$

---

[17] [Other aspects of the Slavic palatalizations are dealt with by Halle and Lightner in a forthcoming study. My knowledge of the rules is based entirely on their work. I state the rules here with the Jakobsonian features rather than with any of the recent alternative proposals which have greatly improved the system.
[18] [See n. 2.—*Eds.*]

The resulting affricate $\mathfrak{z}$, unlike the earlier $\check{z}$, is retained in Old Church Slavic and in modern Polish. The grammars of these languages have Rules (7–10) as phonological rules in an order that matches their relative chronology. But elsewhere in Slavic, $\mathfrak{z}$ also has been replaced by its corresponding continuant, namely z, for example, $\mathfrak{z}\check{e}lo > z\check{e}lo$. These languages have the same four rules, but (8) must here follow (10), in order to apply to the affricate produced by the second palatalization as well. It is these two rules between which the feeding relationship obtains. Rule (10) is the feeding rule and the reordering establishes a feeding order between (10) and (8).

It should be noted that this relationship is a matter of the function and not of the form of the rules. In the Slavic example there is, as is often the case elsewhere too, a formal similarity between the related rules in that they mention some of the same features. But it would not be possible to define the correct relationship on the basis of the form of the rules. The two Finnish rules previously cited have very little in common, and the relationship is simply based on properties of the derivations the language has.

Another possible functional relationship between two rules is that A removes representations to which B would otherwise apply:

$A.$ [ ] $>$ [$\sim\!\varphi$]
$B.$ [φ] $>$ [   ]

Such a relationship holds for example between umlaut (A) and $o > \mathfrak{o}$ (B) in the example of Section 2. Thus the application of umlaut turns o into $\ddot{o}$, a front vowel to which the lowering rule is no longer applicable. If the lowering rule comes first in the ordering, it applies, turning o to $\mathfrak{o}$, and umlaut can then still apply. In the terms of the Indian grammatical tradition, umlaut is here the *nitya* or 'constant' rule. Call A a *bleeding rule* relative to B, the relationship between A and B a *bleeding relationship*, and the ordering in which A precedes B a *bleeding order*. The principle which underlies the asymmetry of order in this case is the following:

(II) Bleeding order tends to be minimized.

$A.$ [ ] $>$ [$\sim\!\varphi$] $\quad$ $B.$ [φ] $>$ [   ]
$B.$ [φ] $>$ [   ] $\quad > \quad$ $A.$ [ ] $>$ [$\sim\!\varphi$]

In this way the original order, in which umlaut preceded lowering, became switched around into the new order, in which the bleeding did not take place.

As another illustration of the effect of (II), consider the relation of two rules pertaining to voiced obstruents in German. One of them, which is historically the older, is the devoicing of obstruents in word-final position (for example, $bund > bunt$, $t\bar{a}g > t\bar{a}k$). This is Rule (1), which has come up in the discussion several times already. The other, found only in a certain group of dialects (Schirmunski 1962, p. 302) is the spirantization of post-vocalic voiced stops, for example, *tāgə* > *tāɣə*, *sāgt* > *sāɣt* (> *sāxt*). Originally, devoicing preceded postvocalic spirantization. Since, with this order, morphophonemic final voiced stops lost their voicing before spirantization applied, they remained stops and the contrast of *tāk*:*tāɣə* resulted. This bleeding order, in which word-final devoicing deprives spirantization of some of the voiced stops to which it would otherwise apply, is still retained in some Alsatian, Bavarian, and Middle German dialects. More frequently the reverse ordering is found, with final voiced stops undergoing first spirantization (*tāg* > *tāɣ*) and then devoicing (*tāɣ* > *tāx*). This order is widespread and especially common in the Low German dialects. We know that this order is a secondary development because some words like (*a*)*wek* (Standard German *weg*)¸ where the voicing of the stop had no morphophonemic support, failed to spirantize even in the reordering dialects. This would be inexplicable unless we suppose that the devoicing was historically earlier even in these dialects in spite of the fact that it is synchronically later.

Another example can be cited from this same familiar area. A very widespread sound change in German dialects (Schirmunski 1962, p. 212) is the rounding of *ā* to *ɔ̄*. As *ǣ*, the umlaut of *ā*, is unaffected by this change, it brings about alternations between *ɔ̄* and *ǣ* such as *šwɔ̄n* 'swan':*swǣn* 'Pl.', *špɔ̄t* 'late':*špǣtər* 'later'. Hence there is a bleeding order between the rules

    a. umlaut

    b. *ā* > *ɔ̄*

Many modern German dialects have just this system (see Rabeler 1911, Hotzenköcherle 1934, for a Low German and Swiss German dialect, respectively). In others (for example, Wanner 1941) the system has changed in that the umlauted form of *ɔ̄* is *ɔ̄̈*, for example, *šwɔ̄n*, *špɔ̄̈tər*. The grammatical difference is that umlaut now applies after rather than before the rounding of *ā*. As phonemic *ǣ* in words like *tsǣ* 'tough', *lǣr* 'empty' stays unrounded (more proof of the correctness of the argument is in Section 5) it is clear that the possibility of a simplification of the rounding rule to all long compact vowels is excluded and we are again faced with a case of reordering, which conforms perfectly to Principle (II).

There is a more general principle underlying the two reordering tendencies (I) and (II), which combines them under a single wider concept of fuller utilization, and makes their nature intuitively much clearer:

    (III) Rules tend to shift into the order which allows their fullest utilization in the grammar.

If I am right that such a principle determines the direction in which reordering proceeds, then it follows that the order towards which rules gravitate in this way is linguistically simpler than its opposite. It is hard to see what other explanation there could be for such a consistent tendency towards a specific kind of order in linguistic change. As a convenient designation for the order types which are shunned and preferred according to Principles (I–III), I suggest *marked* and *unmarked* order, respectively. It may well be that marking conventions analogous to those which assign the unmarked feature values in segmental phonology are the appropriate device for reflecting the asymmetry of ordering relations as well.

9. LEVELING AND EXTENSION

As further justification for my assertion that unidirectional reordering tendencies exist and that they obey Principles (I–III), I want to adduce an unexpected parallelism which obtains between reordering, if so constrained, and rule simplification. We can begin with a distinction drawn in traditional and structural historical grammar between two types of analogy, one called *leveling* and the other called *polarization* or *extension*. By leveling was meant roughly that existing alternations are either curtailed or eliminated altogether, with the result that allomorphs of some morphemes become more similar to each other or merge completely. Thus the change of *bunt: bunde* to *bund:bunde* would have been regarded as a leveling of the alternation of voiced and voiceless stops in word-final position. The simplification of the umlaut rule (2) to its other version (3), which replaced *kraft:kreftig* by *kraft:kræftig* would have been regarded as a leveling of the height alternation in favor of the low vowel throughout the paradigm.

Polarization, or extension, on the other hand, refers to a type of analogical change in which existing alternations spread to new instances. Here linguistic contrasts come to be more fully implemented than before, whereas leveling has precisely the opposite effect. We would presumably be dealing with extension if, for example, the alternation of medial voicing and final voicelessness in obstruents as in *tāge:tāk, bunde:bunt,* instead of being eliminated altogether, had become extended beyond its original domain to the sonorants, as has in fact happened in Icelandic. The change of the limited Old English vowel shortening rule (6) to its present more general form (5) is another instance of extension.

This distinction, implicit in traditional historical studies, though rarely drawn systematically (but see Hoenigswald 1960, pp. 63, 108), is a useful one, partly for reasons that have to do with linguistic reconstruction. Leveling will often be recoverable by historical reconstruction, because of the relic forms which reflect older linguistic stages that leveling leaves behind. Extension, however, will in general not be so recoverable because, with certain very interesting exceptions, it cannot leave relic forms behind.

The difference between these two types of analogy can be defined in terms of the formal differences of two kinds of rule simplification in a very straightforward manner. Rules consist of two parts, a structural analysis, which specifies to what forms the rule applies, and a structural change, which says what happens to these forms. In the customary notation for phonological rules, the structural change is the part between the arrow and the slash and the structural analysis is everything else. Then any rule simplification which modifies the structural change of a rule (whether or not it also modifies the structural analysis) is a *leveling*, and any rule simplification which does not modify the structural change of a rule is an *extension*. Thus the loss of final devoicing (Rule (1)) and the simplification of Rule (2) to Rule (3) affect the structural change of the rule and are hence levelings, but the change of the shortening rule in English did not affect its structural change and is hence an extension.

It is a fairly surprising fact that the two kinds of reorderings we have found, namely those governed by (I) and (II), correspond pairwise to these two kinds of rule simplifications and in turn to the traditional distinction between extension and leveling. Reordering by (II) results in leveling and thus corresponds to simplification in the structural change of a rule. For example, the effect of placing umlaut after *o > ɔ* is that the height alternation in *bɔdǝ:bödǝ* and innumerable similar cases is leveled and the resulting forms, *bɔdǝ:bɔ̈dǝ*, retain the low vowel throughout the paradigm. So, too, the reordering of spirantization and word-final devoicing results in the dropping of a two-feature alternation *tak:taɣǝ* (with change of both voicing and continuance), in favor of a simpler one-feature alternation *tax:taɣǝ* (with a continuant throughout the paradigm), that is, again in leveling. In their effect on surface forms and on the relation of surface forms, leveling by simplification in the structural change of rules and leveling by reordering in accordance with Principle (II) have similar effects in that they make more alike the different shapes in which morphemes appear. But they bring this effect about in different ways because leveling by rule simplification brings the forms closer to the base forms, whereas leveling by reordering takes forms farther away from their base forms. But both types share the property that they can leave behind relic forms which make the recovery of these processes by linguistic reconstruction a possibility. What guarantees us the earlier grammar in each of these cases are the forms like *weg* (in the case where the devoicing rule is lost and in the case in which it is reordered with spirantization), *plötsli* (in reordering of umlaut and *o > ɔ*), and so on.

On the other hand, reordering by (I) results in extension (polarization) and so corresponds to simplification which affects only the structural analysis of rules. In the case of the Slavic palatalizations (see Section 8), for example, the voiced stop:voiced affricate alternation is polarized into a voiced stop:voiced continuant alternation. It is clear that in this case any forms which undergo the old form of the rules are also going to undergo them after the reordering, so that relic forms which would allow reconstruction of the change could not be created.

These relationships are summarized in the following table.

Reordering	Corresponds to simplification of	Reconstructible by relic forms?	Surface effect
by (I)	Structural analysis only	No	Extension (polarization)
by (II)	Structural change	Yes	Leveling

SELECTED BIBLIOGRAPHY

Chomsky, N., and M. Halle, *The Sound Pattern of English*. New York, Harper and Row (1968).

Enderlin, F., *Die Mundart von Kesswil*. A. Bachmann (ed.), *Beiträge zur Schweizerdeutschen Grammatik*, Vol. 5 (1913).

Fodor, J., and M. Garrett, 'Some Reflections on Competence and Performance'. In J. Lyons and R. J. Wales (eds.), *Psycholinguistics Papers*. Chicago, Aldine (1967).

Halle, M., 'Phonology in Generative Grammar', *Word* 18.54–72 (1962).

Hoenigswald, H. M., *Language Change and Linguistic Reconstruction*. Chicago, University of Chicago Press (1960).

Hotzenköcherle, R., *Die Mundart von Mutten*. A. Bachmann (ed.), *Beiträge zur Schweizerdeutschen Grammatik*, Vol. 19 (1934).

Jakobson, R., *Kindersprache, Aphasie, und allgemeine Lautgesetze. Språk- vetenskapliga Sällskapets i Uppsala Förhandlingar* (1942). Reprinted in *Selected Writings*, Vol. I (1962).

Kiparsky, P., *Phonological Change*. M.I.T. dissertation, unpublished (1965).

Kiparsky, P., 'A propos de l'histoire de l'accentuation grecque', *Langages* 8.73–93 (1967).

Luick, K., *Historische Grammatik der englischen Sprache* (1921). Reprinted from the first edition: Oxford/Stuttgart (1964).

Mackel, E., *Die Mundart der Prignitz. Niederdeutsches Jahrbuch*, 31, 33 (1905–1907).

McCawley, J., 'Sapir's Phonologic Representation'. IJAL 33.106–11 (1967).

McCawley, J., *Finnish Phonology* (forthcoming).

McNeill, D., 'Developmental Psycholinguistics'. In F. Smith and G. Miller (eds.), *The Genesis of Language*. Cambridge, Mass., M.I.T. Press (1966).

Matthews, G. H., 'Proto-Siouan Obstruents' (forthcoming).

Moulton, W., "The Short Vowel Systems of Northern Switzerland," *Word* 16.155–82 (1960).

Moulton, W., 'Lautwandel durch innere Kausalität: die ostschweizerische Vokalspaltung,' *Zeitschrift für Mundartforschung* 28.227–51 (1961).

Postal, P., *Aspects of Phonological Theory*. New York, Harper & Row (1968).

Rabeler, T., 'Niederdeutscher Lautstand im Kreise Bleckede,' *Zeitschrift für deutsche Philologie*, 43: 141–202, 320–77 (1911).

Schirmunski, V., *Deutsche Mundartkunde. Deutsche Akademie der Wissenschaften zu Berlin, Veröffentlichungen des Instituts für deutsche Sprache und Literatur*, Band 25. Berlin (1962).

Wanner, G., *Die Mundarten des Kantons Schaffhausen*. A. Bachmann (ed.), *Beiträge zur Schweizerdeutschen Grammatik*, Vol. 20 (1941).

Zwicky, A., 'Umlaut and Noun Plurals in German.' *Studia Grammatica*, 6: 35–45 (1967).

Study Questions

1. What conception of grammar supports Kiparsky's statement that "Grammars are subject to changes of two kinds: the addition of new rules and simplification?" Is change in the order of rules a third kind of change? Could these two kinds of changes incorporate the traditional triad of sound change, analogy, and borrowing? Why does Kiparsky feel that linguistic change provides a "window on the form of linguistic competence that is not obscured by factors like performance"? Is his proposal in violation of the widely held tenet that synchronic and diachronic studies must be kept strictly separate?

2. What is "simplification"? How does Kiparsky use the concept of simplification to explain a change from *brought* to *bringed*? How is that kind of change different from the kind of change that affects "the rules of the grammar"? On what notions of the structure of a grammar does the distinction depend?

3. Kiparsky speaks of "driftlike" changes, and distinguishes these from

others which appear sporadic. Does he mean the same thing by "drift" as Sapir does? Does he apply the term to one language or to many? Does Sapir's term have meaning when applied to more than one language or one group of languages? Could Kiparsky's treatment of changes be used to give an explicit specification to Sapir's term "drift"?

4. Traditional historical theory, and revisions of that theory made by structuralists, claimed that sound changes like the Great Vowel Shift were gradual, coming about through minute adjustments in the manner of articulating sounds. Would Kiparsky agree? If we conceive of sound change as involving a change in rules, will that change be gradual or instantaneous? Do we have to distinguish between the origin of a change and its spread in order to answer the preceding question? Will origin and spread be governed by the same forces? What support for his argument does Kiparsky find in the work of William Labov?

5. Kiparsky speaks of the necessity of specifying the concept "possible sound change" for human language. What would be the value of such a concept to a linguist working on the history of a single language or language group? Did traditional theory as outlined in the introduction concern itself with such concepts? Does Lehmann?

6. What objections does Kiparsky raise to assuming an autonomous level of phonemics for describing the history of sounds? Does Lehmann assume such a level? Does Kiparsky use the terms *phoneme, phonemic,* and *contrastive* in the same way Lehmann does?

7. In Section 6, Kiparsky argues that sound change does not always involve the addition of rules. What are his objections to that view? What criteria of judgment is he using when he says: "There is no doubt that a theory of linguistic change should completely exclude the possibility [of such changes as he describes on p. 383] or at least reflect the obvious fact that it would be a far more complex and unlikely historical event than what actually happened"? How would we know that a given formulation of a linguistic change is more complex than the actual historical event it attempts to explain?

8. Why might the study of child language provide the theorist of language with valuable evidence concerning the nature of linguistic change?

Leonard Bloomfield

FLUCTUATION IN THE FREQUENCY OF FORMS

The name of Leonard Bloomfield (1887–1949) is familiar to everyone who has paid the slightest attention to recent developments in the study of language. His influence has been so extensive that many of the best-known developments in linguistic study in the United States, at least during the period from 1933 (the year *Language* was published) to 1957 (the year Chomsky's *Syntactic Structures* appeared), can be called Bloomfieldian. Although Bloomfield was not without predecessors, particularly among structuralists in Europe and anthropological linguists in this country, he was the major prophet of structuralism for at least two generations of American scholars who took as their central tasks the exploration of his ideas and the refinement of his methods and terminologies. Nor has his work been without influence on the development of generative theory. Although Chomsky has been vigorous in pointing out deficiencies in Bloomfieldian structural analysis and the theory of language which supports it, he has praised the rigor introduced in such analysis, and generative phonologists have found much to please them in Bloomfield's work on Menomini phonology.

It is perhaps ironic that Bloomfield, who founded a school of descriptive study, should be represented in this anthology only by writings on the history of languages. But Bloomfield was a master of historical linguistics, called by Mary Haas perhaps the greatest historical linguist of the twentieth century, and credited by Charles F. Hockett with a part in one of the few major advances in historical theory: the reinterpretation of phonetic "laws" in phonemic terms, answering the objections of nineteenth-century phoneticians. The historical chapters in *Language* are a brilliant synthesis of nineteenth-century theory and burgeoning developments of the twentieth.

Bloomfield began his career with studies of Indo-European and particularly Germanic linguistics, and did post-doctoral work under the neo-grammarians August Leskien and Karl Brugmann. Like Sapir, he was a pioneer in applying the methods of historical linguistics to non-Indo-European languages, in particular the Indian languages of America. In the following two chapters from *Language*, Bloomfield considers innovative changes, those changes which are not brought about by gradual sound change. In the first chapter he discusses the fluctuations which arise when innovations enter the language as competitors to established forms. In the second, he treats the operation of analogic change, a historical mechanism which he considers to be widely operative in reshaping languages.

22.1 The assumption of phonetic change divides linguistic changes into two principal types. Phonetic change affects only the phonemes, and alters linguistic forms only by altering their phonetic shape. The English form *wolf* is the modern pronunciation of Primitive Germanic nominative *['wolfaz], accusative *['wolfan], and several other case-forms, and the merging of these (syncretism) is merely the result of the phonetic change. English [mijd] *meed, mead* is the modern pronunciation of Old English [mɛːd] 'meadow,' [meːd] 'reward,' and ['medu] 'honey-drink'; the homonymy results simply from the change in habits of articulation. When we have listed the phonetic correlations, there remain a great many discrepancies. Thus, having found that Old English [aː] appears in modern standard English as [ow], as in [baːt] > *boat*, and so on, we see a discrepancy in the parallelism of Old English [baːt] 'bait' with the modern *bait*. Seeing Old English initial [f] preserved in *father, five, foot,* and so on, we find a discrepancy in the sets Old English [fɛt]:modern *vat* and Old English ['fyksen]: modern *vixen*. While the modern form *cow* stands in a normal phonetic correlation with Old English [kuː], just as *house, mouse, out* correspond to Old English [huːs, muːs, uːt], the plural *cows* cannot be the modern form of the Old English plural [kyː] 'cows,' in view of cases like Old English [hwyː] > *why*, [fyːr] > *fire*, [myːs] > *mice*. If we adhere to the assumption of regular phonetic change, we cannot class forms like *bait, vat, vixen, cows* as modern pronunciations of Old English forms, but must view them as the products of factors other than simple tradition. Our problem, therefore, is to find among these residual forms some uniformity or correlation; to the extent that we succeed in this, we shall have confirmed the value of the assumption of phonetic change and of the particular phonetic correspondences we have set up. The neo-grammarians claim that the assumption of phonetic change leaves residues which show striking correlations and allow us to understand the factors of linguistic change other than sound-change. The opponents of the neo-grammarian hypothesis imply that a different assumption concerning sound-change will leave a more intelligible residue, but they have never tested this by re-classifying the data.

If the residual forms are not continuants of ancient forms with only the alterations of sound-change, then they must have come into the language as innovations. We shall see that two kinds of innovation account for the residual forms—namely, the adoption of forms from other languages (*bait* from Old Norse) or other dialects (*vat, vixen* from southern-English local dialects) and the combining of new complex forms (*cow-s* on the pattern "singular noun plus plural-suffix gives plural noun"). These two kinds of innovation, *borrowing* and *analogic change*, will occupy us in the following chapters; now we are concerned merely with the claim that the forms which are not accounted for by phonetic correlation, got into the language at various points in time.

22.2 If a form which has been introduced into a language prevails in general usage—as, for instance, *cows* prevails as the ordinary plural of *cow*—we have to suppose that it has gained in popularity since its first introduction. Conversely, if an old form—such as the Old English plural [ky:], which, by phonetic development, would today be pronounced *[kaj]—has disappeared, we must suppose that it went through a period of decline, during which it was used less and less as the years went by. *Fluctuation in the frequency of speech-forms* is a factor in all non-phonetic changes. This fluctuation can be observed, to some extent, both at first hand and in our written records. For instance, since the introduction of the automobile, the word *garage*, borrowed from French, has become very common. We can actually name the speakers who first used the words *chortle, kodak*, and *blurb;* since the moment of that first use, each of these words has become common. The disappearance of a form cannot be observed at first hand, since we can have no assurance that it will not be used again, but in older written records we find many speech-forms that are no longer in use. In Old English, ['weorθan] 'to become' was one of the commonest words: [he: 'wearθ 'torn] 'he got angry,' [he: je'wearθ 'mɛ:re] 'he became famous,' [he: 'wearθ of'slɛjen] 'he got killed,' [heo 'wearθ 'widuwe] 'she became a widow.' In the Dutch-German area this verb, Dutch *worden* ['wurde], German *werden* ['verden], is still so used. The ordinary Old English word for 'large,' *mycel*, survives in Scotch *mickle*, but has disappeared from standard English. In our fragments of the Gothic Bible-translation, the word *mother* is entirely replaced by a term ['ajθi:], and the word *father* occurs only once (*Galatians* 4, 6) and is in all other passages replaced by ['atta], a word familiar to us from the Gothic nickname of the king of the Huns, *Attila* 'little father.' This, apparently in its original connotation a nursery-word, is perhaps somehow connected with the Slavic term for 'father,' Primitive Slavic *[otɪ'tsɪ], Russian [o'tets], which in pre-Slavic must have crowded out the reflex of Primitive Indo-European *[pə'te:r].

Most frequently we observe the complementary fluctuation of two forms; thus, *it's I* and *it's me* or *rather* with [ɛ] and with [a], are evidently *rival forms* in present-day American English. The plural-form *kine* beside *cows* is still very rarely used as a poetic archaism. In Elizabethan writings we still find the spelling *fat* for *vat*, evidencing a survival of Old English [fɛt], which has since been crowded out by *vat*. Where a speaker knows two rival forms, they differ in connotation, since he has heard them from different persons and under different circumstances.

Fluctuations in the frequency of forms could be accurately observed if we had a record of every utterance that was made in a speech-community during whatever period of time we wanted to study. We could then keep a tally-sheet for every form (including grammatical forms, such as the type *he ran away; he fell down* in contrast with *away he ran; down he fell*); whenever an utterance was made, we could score a point on the tally-sheet of every form in this utterance. In this way we should obtain tables or graphs which showed the ups and downs in frequency of every form during the time covered by our records. Such a system of scoring will doubtless remain beyond our powers, but this imaginary system gives us a picture of what is actually going on at all times in every speech-community. We can observe the fluctuation with the naked eye when it is especially rapid, as in the sudden rise and equally sudden disuse of popular slangy witticisms. On a smaller scale, but contributing to the total fluctuations in the community, small groups and individuals indulge in similar whims; everyone can recall old favorite words and phrases which he and perhaps his associates once used at every turn. Most fluctuation is less rapid and escapes direct observation, but reveals itself in its results—in the differences of vocabulary and grammar which appear when we compare different historical stages of a language, or dialects of an area, or related languages.

Leaving aside the origination of new forms, which will concern us in the following chapters, we must now consider the factors which lead to the rise or to the decline in frequency of speech-forms. Until recently this topic was neglected, and our knowledge is still far from satisfactory.

22.3 We naturally ask at once whether any linguistically definable characteristics of a form may favor or disfavor its use. The stylist and the rhetorician tell us that some speech-forms sound better than others. The only criterion of a phonetic sort seems to be this, that repetition of phonemes or sequences is often avoided: a phrase like *the observation of the systematization of education* is disfavored. In ordinary speech, however, euphony seems to play no part; the stock examples of troublesome phonetics are far-fetched combinations like *Peter Piper picked a peck of pickled peppers* or *she sells seashells*. On the other hand, various patterings of recurrent phonemes, such as alliteration (*hearth and home, cabbages and kings*), assonance (*a stitch in time saves nine*), and rime, and rhythmic repetitions (*first come, first served*), seem to favor many a speech-form.

In all ordinary cases, semantic rather than formal factors contribute to the favor or disfavor of a form. It is natural to suppose, however, that a form which differs strikingly from the other forms of comparable meaning, will be disfavored. Several students have conjectured that certain speech-forms fell into disuse because they were shorter than ordinary speech-forms of similar meaning. Gilliéron believed that Latin *apis* 'bee' has died out in nearly all dialects of the French area because its modern pronunciation would consist of only a single phoneme [e]. It would be no counter-argument to say that French has grammatical and relational words of this pattern, such as *et* [e] 'and,' but a case like *eau* [o] 'water' (< *aquam*) does militate against the theory. It seems that some verb-forms in the older stages of the Indo-European languages fell into disuse because they were shorter than ordinary forms of the same kind. The Menomini language, like French and English, seems to tolerate words of all sizes. Menomini [oːs] 'canoe' is shorter than ordinary nouns, and [uah] 'he uses it' shorter than ordinary verb-forms. These forms, which are ancient inheritances, have been largely replaced in the sister languages: Primitive Central Algonquian *[oːši] 'canoe' by longer derivative nouns, such as Fox [anakɛːweni], Cree and Ojibwa [čiːmaːn],—though Cree has also [oːsi]—and Primitive Central Algonquian *[oːwa] 'he uses it' by a reduplicated form, Fox [ajoːwa] or by other words, such as Cree [aːpačihtaːw]. All this, however, is doubtful.

The semantic factor is more apparent in the disfavoring of speech-forms that are homonymous with tabu-forms. The reader will have no difficulty in finding speech-forms that he avoids for this reason. In America, *knocked up* is a tabu-form for 'rendered pregnant'; for this reason, the phrase is not used in the British sense 'tired, exhausted.' In older French and English there was a word, French *connil*, *connin*, English *coney*, for 'rabbit'; in both languages this word died out because it resembled a word that was under a tabu of indecency. For the same reason, *rooster* and *donkey* are replacing *cock* and *ass* in American English. In such cases there is little real ambiguity, but some hearers react nevertheless to the powerful stimulus of the tabu-word; having called forth ridicule or embarrassment, the speaker avoids the innocent homonym. It is a remarkable fact that the tabu-word itself has a much tougher life than the harmless homonym.

22.4   These cases suggest that homonymy in general may injure the frequency of a form. Many homonyms are distinguished by differences of grammatical function, as are *leader* (noun) and *lead'er* (infinitive phrase) or *bear* (noun), *bear* (verb), and *bare* (adjective); in French, [saⁿ] is *sang* 'blood,' *cent* 'hundred,' *sans* 'without,' *sent* 'feels, smells,' and *s'en* 'oneself of it,' as in *s'en aller* 'to go away.' Even with largely similar grammatical functions, homonymies like *pear*, *pair* or *piece*, *peace* or *mead*, *meed* do not seem to lessen the frequency of forms.

Nevertheless, there is some evidence that homonymy may lead to troubles of communication which result in disuse of a form. The classical instance is Gilliéron's explanation of the disappearance of Latin *gallus* 'cock' in southwestern France (Figure 14). In southern France generally this word is still in use in its modern forms, such as [gal] or [žal]. A fair-sized area in the extreme south, however, uses for 'cock' another Latin word, *pullus*, modern [pul], which originally meant 'chick.' Now, the southwestern corner of the French area has made a sound-change by which Latin [ll] at the end of a

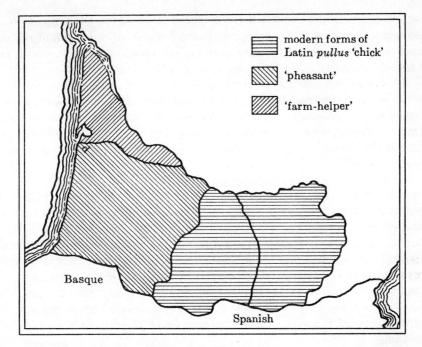

modern forms of
Latin *pullus* 'chick'

'pheasant'

'farm-helper'

Figure 14. The southwestern part of the French dialect-area.—Southwest of the heavy line ———— Latin [ll] appears in final position as [t]. The unshaded part of the area uses modern forms of Latin *gallus* "cock." The shaded areas use other words for "cock."—After Dauzat.

word has become [t]; thus, Latin *bellus* 'pretty,' modern [bɛl],[1] appears in the southwestern corner as [bɛt]. The isogloss of this sound-change cuts the *pullus*-district into an eastern part, where one says [pul] and a western part where one says [put]. Outside the *pullus*-district we should accordingly expect to find a form *[gat] 'cock,' corresponding to the [gal] of ordinary southern French, but actually this form nowhere appears: the entire [-t]-area, in so far as it does not say [put], calls the cock by queer and apparently slangy names, either by local forms of the word *pheasant*, such as [azaⁿ], from Latin *phāsiānus*, or by a word [begej] which means 'farm-helper, handyman' and is thought to represent Latin *vicārius* 'deputy, proxy, vicar.'

Now, Gilliéron points out, the form *[gat] 'cock' in this district would be homonymous with the word 'cat,' namely [gat] from Latin *gattus*. This homonymy must have caused trouble in practical life; therefore *[gat] 'cock' was avoided and replaced by makeshift words.

What lends weight to this theory is the remarkable fact that the isogloss

---

[1] Standard French *bel* [bɛl] before vowels, *beau* [bo] before consonants.

which separates the queer words [azaⁿ] and [begej] from the ordinary [gal], coincides exactly with the isogloss between [-t] and [-l]; this is highly significant, because isoglosses—even isoglosses representing closely related features—very rarely coincide for any considerable distance.

Adjoining this stretch, the isogloss between [-t] and [-l] coincides for a ways with the isogloss between [put] and [gal]. This too is striking and seems to be explicable only if we suppose that this part of the [-t]-region formerly used *gallus* and, when the change of [-ll] to [-t] had occurred, replaced the troublesome *[gat] by borrowing [put] from the neighboring *pullus*-district.

On the rest of its course, the isogloss between [-t] and [-l] cuts through the *pullus*-district, and merely separates western [put] from eastern [pul]; in the *pullus*-district the sound-change caused no homonymy and left the lexicon undisturbed.

One may ask why *[gat] 'cock' rather than [gat] 'cat' was affected by the homonymy. Dauzat points out that the morpheme *[gat] 'cock' occurred only in this one word, since the derived form, Latin *gallīna* 'hen' was subject to a different change, giving [garina], while [gat] 'cat,' on the other hand, was backed by a number of unambiguous derivatives, such as the equivalents of standard French *chatte* 'she-cat,' *chaton* 'kitten,' *chatière* 'cathole.'

While few instances are as cogent as this, it is likely that homonymy plays more than an occasional part in the obsolescence of forms. A few centuries ago, English had not only our present-day verb *let* (which represents the paradigm of Old English ['lɛːtan]), but also a homonymous verb which meant 'to hinder' (representing Old English ['lettan]); we still have the phrases *without let or hindrance* and *a let ball*, at tennis. When Shakspere has Hamlet say *I'll make a ghost of him that lets me*, he means 'of him that hinders me.' After it had become homonymous with *let* 'permit,' this word must have been singularly ineffective. A speaker who wanted his hearers to stop someone—say, a child that was running into danger, or a thief—and cried *Let him!* might find his hearers standing aside to make way. Then he would have to add *Stop him!* or *Hold him!* After a few such experiences he would use one of the effective forms at the first trial.

22.5 We frequently find regular, or at least more regular, combinations by the side of irregular complex forms, as, *roofs*, *hoofs*, *dwarfs* by the side of *rooves*, *hooves*, *dwarves*, or *dreamed*, *learned* by the side of *dreamt*, *learnt*, or *you ought to* by the side of *you had better*. In some cases the irregular form is decidedly infrequent, as in *cows*, *eyes*, *shoes*, *brothers* versus *kine*, *eyne*, *shoon*, *brethren*. Other examples are, regular *forehead* ['fowr-ˌhed], *gooseberry* ['guws-ˌberij], *seamstress* ['sijmstres] against irregular ['fared, 'guwzbrij, 'semstres]. History shows us that in such cases the irregular form frequently dies out, or survives only in special senses, as when *sodden*, the old participle of *seethe*, survives only in a transferred meaning. The plurals of *goat*, *book*, *cow*, if we continued using the Old English forms [gɛ:t, be:k, ky:] would be today *[gijt, bijč, kaj]. Whenever we know the history of a language through any considerable period, we find many cases of this kind, but the operation of this factor is obscure, because in many cases the regular form makes no headway at all. The utterance of a regular *foots* instead of *feet*, or *bringed* instead of *brought* is so rare as to be classed as a childish "mistake" or, in older people, as a "slip of the tongue." Languages seem to differ in toleration of irregular forms, but in general it would seem that a regular rival, given a good start, has much the better chance. Very common forms, such as in English the paradigm of the verb *be* and the pronouns *I, we, he, she, they*, with their over-differentiation, persist in spite of great irregularity.

22.6 For the most part, fluctuation does not depend upon formal features, but upon meaning, and accordingly escapes a purely linguistic investigation. The changes which are always going on in the practical life of a community, are bound to affect the relative frequencies of speech-forms. The introduction of railways, street-cars, and motor-cars has lessened the frequency of many terms relating to horses, wagons, and harness, and increased that of terms relating to machinery. Even in the most remote and conservative community there is a constant displacement of things talked about; if nothing else should alter, there is at least the change of birth and death.

A new object or practice which gains in vogue, carries a speech-form, old or new, into increased frequency; examples are many in modern life, such as the terms of motoring, flying, and wireless. If the practical situation ceases to exist, the forms which are used in this situation are bound to become less common and may die out. The terms of falconry, for instance, have suffered this fate. Though we still hear beauty in Othello's words, we do not understand them:

> If I do prove her haggard,
> Though that her jesses were my dear heart-strings,
> I'd whistle her off, and let her down the wind,
> To prey at fortune.

The word *haggard* was used of a wild-caught, unreclaimed mature hawk; *jesses* were leather straps fastened to the legs of a hawk, and were not removed when the hawk was unleashed; if a hawk flew with the wind behind her, she seldom returned.

In the early centuries of our era, some of the Germanic tribes contained a class of people called [la:t], South-German [la:ts], who were intermediate in rank between freemen and serfs. The English form of this word, [lɛːt], occurs only once in our records, in the oldest English law-code, and even here the word is explained—incorrectly, at that—by the word [θeːow] 'serf' written above the line. The new social organization of the English-speaking tribes in Britain contained no such class of people, and the word went out of use along with the institution.

22.7   Words that are under a ritual or ill-omened tabu, are likely to disappear. The Indo-European languages use the most varied words for 'moon'; it is notable that Russian has borrowed Latin ['luːna] as [lu'na], though otherwise it makes scarcely any but highly learned borrowings from Latin. It may be due to a ritual or hunters' tabu that the Primitive Indo-European word for 'bear,' surviving in Sanskrit ['r̥kšah], Greek ['arktos], Latin *ursus*, has disappeared in Germanic and in Balto-Slavic. In Slavic it has been replaced by the type of Russian [med'vet], originally a transparent compound meaning 'honey-eater.' The like of this seems to have happened in Menomini, where the old word for 'bear,' preserved in Fox [mahkwa], Cree [maskwa], has been replaced by [awɛːhsɛh], a diminutive formation that seems to have meant originally 'little what-you-may-call-him.' Cree ['maː–čiːw] 'he goes hunting' originally meant simply 'he goes away'—presumably there was danger of being overheard by the game or by its spiritual representatives. The term for the 'left' side appears to have been replaced in various languages; the Indo-European languages use many words, among which Ancient Greek [ew-'oː-numos], literally 'of good name,' is evidently euphemistic. One can often observe people avoiding unpleasant words, such as *die, death*—these words in pre-Germanic replaced the Primitive Indo-European term represented by Latin *morī* 'to die'—or names of serious diseases. The term *undertaker* was, to begin with, vaguely evasive, but the undertakers are now trying to replace it by *mortician*. In cases like these, where the unpleasantness inheres in the practical situation, the speech-form becomes undesirable as soon as it is too specifically tied up with the painful meaning.

Tabus of indecency do not seem to lead to obsolescence; the tabu-forms are excluded in many or most social situations, but by no means avoided in others. The substitutes may in time become too closely associated with the meaning and in turn become tabu. Our word *whore*, cognate with Latin *cārus* 'dear,' must have been at one time a polite substitute for some word now lost to us. On the whole, however, words of this type do not seem especially given to obsolescence.

The practical situation works in favor of words that call forth a good response. In commerce, the seller finds advantage in labeling his goods attractively. This is probably why terms for the young of animals sometimes replace the more general name of the species, as when we say *chicken* for 'hen.' French *poule* [pul] 'hen' and dialectal [pul] 'cock' continue a Latin word for 'chick.' The word *home* for 'house' has doubtless been favored by speculative builders. In Germany, an *express* train has come to mean a slow train, as has *Schnellzug* ['šnel-ˌtsuːk], literally 'fast-train'; a really fast train is *Blitzzug* ['blits-ˌtsuːk], literally 'lightning-train'—just as in the United States *first class* on a railroad means the ordinary day-coach accommodation.

There is an advantage, often, in applying well-favored terms to one's hearer. The habit of using the plural pronoun 'ye' instead of the singular 'thou,' spread over Europe during the Middle Ages. In English, *you* (the old dative-accusative case-form of *ye*) has crowded *thou* into archaic use; in Dutch, *jij* [jej] has led to the entire obsolescence of *thou*, and has in turn become the intimate form, under the encroachment of an originally still more honorific *u* [yː], representing *Uwe Edelheid* ['yːwe 'eːdelhejt] 'Your Nobility.' Honorifics of this sort often replace the ordinary second-person substitutes. Similarly, one speaks in honorific terms of what pertains to the hearer. In Italian, 'my wife' is *mia moglie* [mia 'moʎe], but for 'your wife' one says rather *la sua signora* [la sua si'ɲora] 'your lady.' In French and in German one prefixes 'Mr., Mrs., Miss' to the mention of the hearer's relatives, as, *madame votre mère* [madam vɔtr mɛːr] 'your mother'; in German, moreover, one likes to use for the hearer's husband or wife archaic terms of distinguished flavor: *meine Frau* [majne 'fraw] 'my wife,' but *Ihre Frau Gemahlin* ['iːre fraw ge'maːlin] 'your Mrs. consort,' and *mein Mann* [majn 'man] 'my husband', but *Ihr Herr Gemahl* [iːr her ge'maːl] 'your Mr. consort.' In the Central Algonquian languages the literal terms for both 'my wife' and 'thy wife' are tabu—ogres use them in fairy-tales—and one says rather 'the old woman' or 'the one I live with' or even 'my cook.'

In general, honorific terms for persons spread at the cost of plain ones; *gentleman* and *lady* are more genteel than *man* and *woman*.

22.8 General effectiveness, in the shape of violence or wit, is a powerful factor in fluctuation, which unfortunately quite escapes the linguist's control. It leads, for instance, to the sudden rise and fall of slang expressions. Round 1896 or so, a transferred use of the word *rubber* in the sense of 'stare, pry' played a great part in slang; ten years later it was obsolescent, and only *rubberneck-wagon* 'sight-seeing omnibus' has now any great frequency. Then, round 1905, an interjection *skidoo* 'be off' and, in the same meaning, an interjectional use of *twenty-three*, came into fashion and as suddenly died out. The rise of such forms is due, apparently, to their effectiveness in producing a response from the hearer. At first they owe this to their novelty and apt yet violent transference of meaning; later, the hearer responds well because he has heard them in favorable situations and from attractive people. All these favorable factors disappear from sheer repetition; the novelty wears off, the violent metaphor lapses when the transferred meaning becomes more familiar than the central meaning; the average of situations and speakers associated with the form becomes indifferent. Thereupon the slang form dies out. In some cases, however, the older form has meanwhile gone out of use or become archaic or specialized; the witticism, having lost its point, remains in use as a normal form. Thus, Latin *caput* 'head' survives in Italian and French in specialized and transferred senses, but in the central meaning has been displaced by reflexes of Latin *testa* 'potsherd, pot,' Italian *testa* ['tɛsta], French *tête* [tɛ:t]. Similarly, in German, the cognate of our *head*, namely *Haupt* [hawpt], survives in transferred uses and as a poetic archaism, but has been replaced, in the sense of 'head' by *Kopf*, cognate with English *cup*. The forceful or witty term, weakened through frequency, may suffer encroachment by new rivals, as in the countless slang words for 'head' or 'man' or 'girl' or 'kill,' or in a set like *awfully, terribly, frightfully (glad to see you)*.

This factor is easily recognized in extreme cases, but figures doubtless in many more which elude our grasp, especially when the fluctuation is observable only from far-off time.

22.9   The most powerful force of all in fluctuation works quite outside the linguist's reach: the speaker favors the forms which he has heard from certain other speakers who, for some reason of prestige, influence his habits of speech. This is what decides, in countless instances, whether one says *it's me* or *it's I*, *rather* with [ɛ] or with [a], *either* and *neither* with [ij] or with [aj], *roofs* or *rooves*, *you ought to* or *you'd better*, and so on, through an endless list of variants and nearly synonymous forms. Dialect geography and the history of standard languages show us how the speech of important communities is constantly imitated, now in one feature and now in another, by groups and persons of less prestige. The more striking phases of this leveling process will concern us in connection with linguistic borrowing. We may suppose that many features of lexicon and grammar, and some features of phonetics, have a social connotation, different for different groups and even for individual speakers. In the ideal diagram of density of communication,[2] we should have to distinguish the arrows that lead from each speaker to his

<hr/>

[2] [Bloomfield's term *density of communication* refers to the frequency with which any given member of a linguistic group communicates with other members of that group. The diagram he speaks of would be constructed theoretically, by drawing arrows from a dot representing a single speaker to other dots representing his hearers, one arrow for each sentence. Bloomfield says: "At the end of a given period of time . . . this chart would show us the density of communication within the community." Bloomfield's point is that differences in speech within the community are dependent on density of communication: people tend to conform in speech to the speech of those they talk to most often. See *Language*, Chapter 3, pp. 46–47.—*Eds.*]

hearers by gradations representing the prestige of the speaker with reference to each hearer. If we had a diagram with the arrows thus weighted, we could doubtless predict, to a large extent, the future frequencies of linguistic forms. It is in childhood, of course, that the speaker is most affected by the authority of older speakers, but all through life he goes on adapting his speech to the speech of the persons whom he strives to resemble or to please.

Study Questions

1. Of the competition among differing usages, Bloomfield says that "semantic rather than formal factors contribute to the favor or disfavor of a form." How would Bloomfield distinguish between formal factors and semantic factors? What assumptions about the nature of linguistic investigation underlie his statement, "For the most part, fluctuation does not depend upon formal features, but upon meaning, and accordingly escapes a purely linguistic investigation"?

2. What fluctuations such as Bloomfield discusses for English are you aware of in your own speech? Where you have alternate forms, can you identify situations in which you would avoid using one of the alternatives? Can you generalize about the factors involved in those situations? Bloomfield and Labov seem to agree that a powerful force in fluctuation is the influence of prestige speakers. However, would Labov agree that "it is in childhood . . . that the speaker is most affected by the authority of older speakers"? To what extent are Labov's methods for examining the social status of linguistic variants an attempt to provide the kind of information Bloomfield would like in his diagram of density of communication? How would Labov define prestige? Would Labov have to conclude from his evidence that Inland Northern and Middle Western now have prestige for New York City?

3. Which of the kinds of innovations pointed out by Bloomfield seem to you most amenable to description as changes in rules? For example, in 22.5 Bloomfield says "we frequently find regular, or at least more regular, combinations by the side of irregular complex forms. . . ." Might rule change be involved in the origination of the forms he mentions? Would describing such forms as having originated through rule change tell us anything about factors favoring or disfavoring their frequency of use?

4.   What kinds of activity familiar to you from your childhood either have suffered or are likely to suffer obsolescence? What areas of activity are most likely to contribute new forms in the future? What effects might such cultural trends have on your vocabulary? Are such trends likely to affect anything other than vocabulary?

5.   What topics seem to be most subject to tabu in American society? Make a collection of words associated with one of these topics. How many of the words you have collected were originally euphemistic? How many have bad connotations for you and cannot be used comfortably in all types of company?

6.   Bloomfield speaks of effectiveness of wit as one of the factors favoring slang expressions. Can you think of any other reasons why speakers might favor slang over standard equivalents? For example, is there any reason why the following groups should be fertile producers of slang: teen-agers; gamblers; criminals; sailors; jazz musicians; members of minority groups?

Leonard Bloomfield

ANALOGIC CHANGE

23.1 Many speech-forms are not continuants of forms that existed in an older stage of the same language. This is obvious in the case of borrowings: a word like *toboggan*, taken over from an American Indian language, cannot have been used in English before the colonization of America, and, of course, we do not find it in documents of the English language which date from before that time. In very many instances, however, the new form is not borrowed from a foreign language. Thus, the plural-form *cows* does not appear in Old and Middle English. The Old English plural of *cu* [ku:] (whence modern *cow*) is *cy* [ky:], which survives, as [kaj], in a number of modern English dialects. Round the year 1300 there appears in our records a form *kyn*, which survives in the modern archaic-poetic form *kine*. Only some centuries later do we meet the form *cows;* the *New English Dictionary's* first reference, from the year 1607, has it as an alternative of the older form: *Kine or Cows*. Evidently *cows* is not the continuant, with only phonetic change, of *kine*, any more than *kine* bears this relation to *kye:* in both cases a new speech-form has come into the language.

The fact that the form *cows* is not the continuant, with only alterations of sound-change, of the older forms, is self-evident. Strictly speaking, however, this is only an inference which we make from the primary fact of phonetic discrepancy. We know that Old English [y:] appears in modern standard English as [aj], e.g. in *why, mice, bride* from Old English [hwy:, my:s, bry:d], and that modern [aw], as in *cows*, represents an Old English [u:], as in *cow, how, mouse, out* from Old English [ku:, hu:, mu:s, u:t]. Further, we know that modern [z], as in *cows*, is not added by any sound-change, but represents Old English [s], as in *stones* from Old English ['sta:nas]. In many cases, however, the novelty of a speech-form is not so apparent and is revealed only by a systematic comparison of sounds. The form *days* superficially resembles the Old English plural-form *dagas*, which we interpret as ['dagas], presumably with a spirant [g], but the phonetic development of the Old English sound-group [ag] appears rather in forms like ['sage] > *saw* (implement), ['sagu] > *saw* 'saying,' ['hagu-'θorn] > *hawthorn*, ['dragan] > *draw*. This is confirmed by the fact that in earlier Middle English we find spellings like *daues, dawes* for the plural of *dei* 'day,' and that spellings which agree with the modern form *days* appear only round the year 1200.

If our statements of phonetic correspondence are correct, the residues will contain the new forms. One of the strongest reasons for adopting the assumption of regular phonetic change is the fact that the constitution of the residues (aside from linguistic borrowings), throws a great deal of light upon the origin of new forms. Most of the word-forms which arise in the course of time and reveal themselves by their deviation from normal phonetic correspondence, belong to a single well-defined type. This cannot be due to accident: it confirms the assumption of phonetic change, and, on the other hand allows us to study the process of new-formation.

The great mass of word-forms that arise in the course of history consists in new combinations of complex forms. The form *cows*, arising by the side of *kye*, *kine*, consists of the singular *cow* (< Old English [kuː]) plus the plural-suffix [-z] (<Old English [-as]); similarly, *days*, arising by the side of older *daws*, consists of the singular *day* (<Old English [dɛj]) plus the same suffix. A vast number of such instances, from the history of the most diverse languages, leads us to believe that the analogic habits[1] are subject to displacement—that at a time when the plural of *cow* was the irregular form *kine*, the speakers might create a regular form *cows*, which then entered into rivalry with the old form. Accordingly, this type of innovation is called *analogic change*. Ordinarily, linguists use this term to include both the original creation of the new form and its subsequent rivalry with the old form. Strictly speaking, we should distinguish between these two events. After a speaker has heard or uttered the new form (say, *cows*), his subsequent utterance of this form or of the older form (*kine*) is a matter of fluctuation, such as we considered in the last chapter; what we did not there consider and what concerns us now, is the utterance, by someone who has never heard it, of a new combination, such as *cow-s* instead of *kine*.

23.2   In most cases—and these are the ones we come nearest to understanding—the process of uttering a new form is quite like that of ordinary grammatical analogy. The speaker who, without having heard it, produced the form *cows*, uttered this form just as he uttered any other regular plural noun, on the scheme

$$sow:sows = cow:x.$$

---

[1] [Bloomfield uses the term *analogy* here and on the following page for the morphological and syntactic patterns of a language which permit a native speaker to construct words, phrases, and sentences that he has never heard before by substituting within those patterns. Thus, by *ordinary grammatical analogy* he means those patterns that constitute linguistic creativity. Analogic habits, which Bloomfield takes to be essentially habits of substitution, are speaker's responses conditioned by his language learning, which he employs in constructing grammatical forms. Thus the native speaker can substitute within the regular pattern of the sentence "The boy kicked the dog" to form the new sentence "The astronaut reached the moon." A change in analogic habits such as Bloomfield refers to here would be a shift from one pattern to another, as if we were, for example, to construct a form *foots* according to the pattern for *cat-cats*, rather than the pattern for *man-men* or *goose-geese*. For further discussion, see *Language*, Chapter 16, pp. 275-277.—*Eds.*]

The model set (*sow:sows*) in this diagram represents a series of models (e.g. *bough:boughs, heifer:heifers, stone:stones*, etc., etc.), which, in our instance, includes all the regular noun-paradigms in the language. Moreover, the sets at either side of the sign of equality are not limited to two members. The independent utterance of a form like *dreamed* instead of *dreamt* [dremt], could be depicted by the diagram:

$$scream:screams:screaming:screamer:screamed$$
$$= dream \ :dreams \ :dreaming \ :dreamer \ :x$$

Psychologists sometimes object to this formula, on the ground that the speaker is not capable of the reasoning which the proportional pattern implies. If this objection held good, linguists would be debarred from making almost any grammatical statement, since the normal speaker, who is not a linguist, does not describe his speech-habits, and, if we are foolish enough to ask him, fails utterly to make a correct formulation. Educated persons, who have had training in school grammar, overestimate their own ability in the way of formulating speech-habits, and, what is worse, forget that they owe this ability to a sophisticated philosophical tradition. They view it, instead, as a natural gift which they expect to find in all people, and feel free to deny the truth of any linguistic statement which the normal speaker is incapable of making. We have to remember at all times that the speaker, short of a highly specialized training, is incapable of describing his speech-habits. Our proportional formula of analogy and analogic change, like all other statements in linguistics, describes the action of the speaker and does not imply that the speaker himself could give a similar description.

In studying the records of past speech or in comparing related languages and dialects, the linguist will recognize many differences of word-form, such as the emergence of *cows* beside older *kine*. The habits of morphology are fairly rigid; word-lists and tables of inflection are relatively easy to prepare and help us to detect innovations. It is otherwise with phrasal forms. Aside from the imperfection of our descriptive technique in syntax, retarded, as it has been, by philosophic habits of approach, the syntactic positions of a language can be filled by so many different forms that a survey is hard to make. The linguist who suspects that a certain phrase departs from the older syntactic habits of its language, may yet find it difficult or impossible to make sure that this older usage really excluded the phrase, or to determine the exact boundary between the older and the newer usage. Nevertheless, we can sometimes recognize syntactic innovations on the proportional pattern. From the sixteenth century on, we find English subordinate clauses introduced by the word *like*. We can picture the innovation in this way:

> *to do better than Judith : to do better than Judith did*
> = *to do like Judith   : x,*

where the outcome is the construction *to do like Judith did*.

A phrasal innovation which does not disturb the syntactic habit may involve a new lexical use. In this case, our lack of control over meanings, especially, of course, where the speech of past times is concerned, acts as an almost insuperable hindrance. The practical situations which make up the meaning of a speech-form are not strictly definable: one could say that every utterance of a speech-form involves a minute semantic innovation. In older English, as in some modern dialects, the word *meat* had a meaning close to that of *food*, and the word *flesh* was used freely in connection with eating, as in this passage (from the year 1693): *who flesh of animals refused to eat, nor held all sorts of pulse for lawful meat.* A compound *flesh-meat* served, for a while, as a compromise. The prevalence of *food* and *fodder* where at an earlier time the word *meat* was common, and the prevalence of *flesh-meat* and *meat* where at an earlier time *flesh* would have been the normal term, must be attributed to a gradual shifting of usage. The difficulty of tracing this has led linguists to view the process as a kind of whimsical misapplication of speech-forms. If we remember that the meaning of a speech-form for any speaker is a product of the situations and contexts in which he has heard this form, we can see that here too a displacement must be merely an extension of some pattern:

> *leave the bones and bring the flesh : leave the bones and bring the meat*
> = *give us bread and flesh   : x,*

resulting in *give us bread and meat.* Doubtless we have to do, in both grammatical and lexical displacements, with one general type of innovation; we may call it *analogic-semantic change.*

23.3   We can distinguish only in theory between the actual innovation, in which a speaker uses a form he has not heard, and the subsequent rivalry between this new form and some older form. An observer who, a few years ago, heard the form *radios*, might suspect that the speaker had never heard it and was creating it on the analogy of ordinary noun-plurals; the observer could have no assurance of this, however, since the form could be equally well uttered by speakers who had and by those who had not heard it before. Both kinds of speakers, knowing the singular *radio*, would be capable of uttering the plural in the appropriate situation.

It may be worth noticing that in a case like this, which involves clear-cut grammatical categories, our inability to define meanings need give us no pause. A formula like

Singular Plural
piano:pianos
= *radio :x*

will hold good even if our definitions of the meanings of these categories (e.g. 'one' and 'more than one') should turn out to be inexact.

The form *radios* did not conflict with any older form. The difficulty about most cases of analogic change is the existence of an older form. An observer round the year 1600 who heard, let us suppose, the earliest utterances of the form *cows*, could probably have made the same observations as we, a few years ago, could make about the form *radios:* doubtless many speakers uttered it independently, and could not be distinguished from speakers who had already heard it. However, the utterances of the form *cows* must have been more thinly sown, since there was also the traditional form *kine.* In the ensuing rivalry, the new form had the advantage of regular formation. It is safe to say that the factors which lead to the origination of a form are the same as those which favor the frequency of an existing form.

We do not know why speakers sometimes utter new combinations instead of traditional forms, and why the new combinations sometimes rise in frequency. A form like *foots*, instead of *feet*, is occasionally uttered by children; we call it a "childish error" and expect the child soon to acquire the traditional habit. A grown person may say *foots* when he is tired or flustered, but he does not repeat the form and no one adopts it; we call it a "slip of the tongue."

It seems that at any one stage of a language, certain features are relatively stable and others relatively unstable. We must suppose that in the sixteenth century, owing to antecedent developments, there were enough alternative plural-forms (say, *eyen:eyes, shoon:shoes, brethren:brothers*) to make an innovation like *cows* relatively inconspicuous and acceptable. At present, an innovation like *foots* seems to have no chance of survival when it is produced from time to time; we may suppose that innovation and fluctuation are at work rather in the sphere of plurals with spirant-voicing: *hooves:hoofs, laths* [leðz:leθs], and so on.

The creation of a form like *cow-s* is only an episode in the rise in frequency of the regular plural-suffix [-ez, -z, -s]. Analogic-semantic change is merely fluctuation in frequency, in so far as it displaces grammatical and lexical types. The extension of a form into a new combination with a new accompanying form is probably favored by its earlier occurrence with phonetically or semantically related forms. Thus, the use of [-z] with *cow* was probably favored by the existence of other plurals in [-aw-z], such as *sows, brows.* Similarity of meaning plays a part: *sows, heifers, ewes* will attract *cows.* Frequent occurrence in context probably increases the attraction of a

model. The Latin noun *senatus* [se'na:tus] 'senate' had an irregular inflection, including a genitive *senatus* [se'na:tu:s]; by the side of this there arose
a new genitive on the regular model, *senati* [se'na:ti:]. It has been suggested
that the chief model for this innovation was the regular noun *populus*
['populus] 'people,' genitive *populi* ['populi:], for the two words were
habitually used together in the phrase *senatus populusque* [se'na:tus
popu'lus kwe] 'the Senate and People.' The most powerful factor is surely
that of numbers and frequency. On the one hand, regular form-classes increase at the cost of smaller groups, and, on the other hand, irregular forms
of very high frequency resist innovation. Irregular forms appear chiefly
among the commonest words and phrases of a language.

23.4   The regularizing trend of analogic change appears plainly in inflectional paradigms. The history of the regular plural-formation of English is
a long series of extensions. The suffix [-ez, -z, -s] is the modern form of an
Old English suffix [-as], as in *stan* [sta:n] 'stone,' plural *stanas* ['sta:nas]
'stones.' This suffix in Old English belonged only to the nominative and accusative cases of the plural; the genitive plural *stana* ['sta:na] and the dative
plural *stanum* ['sta:num] would both be represented today by the form
stone. The replacement of this form by the nominative-accusative form
stones, which is now used for the whole plural, regardless of syntactic position, is part of a larger process, the loss of case-inflection in the noun, which
involved both phonetic and analogic changes.

The Old English nominative-accusative plural in *-as* occurred with only
one type (the largest, to be sure) of masculine nouns. There were some
classes of masculine nouns which formed the plural differently, as, ['sunu]
'son,' plural ['suna]; among these was a large class of *n*-plurals, such as
['steorra] 'star,' plural ['steorran]. Some nouns fluctuated: [feld] 'field,'
plural ['felda] or ['feldas]. We do not know the origin of this fluctuation, but,
once granted its existence, we can see in it a favoring condition for the
spread of the [-as]-plural. A neologism like ['sunas] instead of older ['suna]
'sons' would perhaps have had no better chance of success than a modern
foots, had it not been for the familiar fluctuation in cases like the word
'field.'

Neuter and feminine nouns in Old English had not the *s*-plural. Examples
of neuter types are [word] 'word,' with homonymous plural, ['spere] 'spear,'
plural ['speru], ['e:aje] 'eye,' plural ['e:agan]; feminine types, ['karu] 'care,'
plural ['kara], ['tunge] 'tongue,' plural ['tungan], [bo:k] 'book,' plural
[be:*k*].

Even where the *s*-plural was traditional, sound-change led to divergent
forms. Thus an early voicing of spirants between vowels led to the type
knife:knives. Other irregularities of this sort have been overlaid by new-

formations. In pre-English, [a] became [ɛ] in monosyllables and before [e] of a following syllable; after this change, [g] became [j] before a front vowel and in final position after a front vowel. The result was a set of alternations, as in the paradigm of 'day':

	Singular	Plural
nom.-acc.	[dɛj]	['dagas]
dat.	['dɛje]	['dagum]
gen.	['dɛjes]	['daga]

Later, there came a change of [g] to [w], whence the Middle English irregularity of *dei*, plural *dawes;* the latter form, as we have seen, was superseded by the regular new combination of *day* plus [-z].

The early Old English loss of [h] between vowels with contraction, led to paradigms like that of 'shoe,' which were regular in Old English, but by subsequent phonetic change, would have led to highly irregular modern sets:

	Old English	Modern Phonetic Result
singular		
nom.-acc.	[sko:h]	*[šof]
dat.	[sko:]	[šuw]
gen.	[sko:s]	*[šos]
plural		
nom.-acc.	[sko:s]	*[šos]
dat.	[sko:m]	*[šuwm, šum]
gen.	[sko:]	[šuw]

Among the Old English paradigms of other types, that of 'foot' shows us an interesting redistribution of forms:

	Singular	Plural
nom.-acc.	[fo:t]	[fe:t]
dat.	[fe:t]	['fo:tum]
gen.	['fo:tes]	['fo:ta]

Here the form with [o:], modern *foot*, has been generalized in the singular, crowding out the old dative, and the form with [e:], modern *feet*, in the plural, crowding out the old dative and genitive forms.

In a few cases, two forms have survived with a lexical difference. Our words *shade* and *shadow* are reflexes of different forms of a single Old English paradigm:

	Old English	Modern Phonetic Equivalent	
singular			
nominative	['sḱadu]	[šejd]	*shade*
other cases	['sḱadwe]	['šɛdow]	*shadow*
plural			
dative	['sḱadwum]	['šɛdow]	*shadow*
other cases	['sḱadwa]	['šɛdow]	*shadow*

Both forms, *shade* and *shadow*, have been generalized for the whole singular, and have served as underlying forms for new regular plurals, *shades, shadows;* the rivalry of the two resulting paradigms has ended in a lexical differentiation. The words *mead* and *meadow* arose in the same way, but in this case the fluctuation seems to be ending in the obsolescence of the form *mead*.

The word 'gate' had in Old English the nominative-accusative singular *geat* [jat], plural *gatu* ['gatu]. The old singular, which would give a modern **yat*, has died out; the modern form *gate* represents the old plural, and the new plural *gates* has been formed on the regular model.

Analogic creation is not limited to complex forms. A simple form may be created on the analogy of cases where a complex form and a simple form exist side by side. The Middle English noun *redels* 'riddle,' with homonymous plural, was subjected to analogic change of the pattern

$$
\begin{array}{ccc}
\text{Plural} & & \text{Singular} \\
\textit{stones} & : & \textit{stone} \\
= \textit{redels} & : & x,
\end{array}
$$

whence the modern singular form *riddle*. This creation of shorter or underlying forms is called *back-formation*. Another example is Old English ['pise] 'pea,' plural ['pisan]; all the forms of the paradigm lead to modern *pease, peas* [pijz], and the singular *pea* is a back-formation. Similarly, Old French *cherise* 'cherry' was borrowed in Middle English as *cheris*, whence modern *cherries;* the singular *cherry* is an analogic creation.

23.5   In word-formation, the most favorable ground for analogic forms is a derivative type which bears some clear-cut meaning. Thus, we form all manner of new agent-nouns in *-er*, on what is at present a normal grammatical analogy. This suffix was borrowed in pre-English time from Latin, and has replaced a number of native types. In Old English, the agent of ['huntian] 'to hunt' was ['hunta], which has been replaced by *hunter*. At a later time, *webster* was replaced by *weaver*, and survives only as a family-name. In *boot-black*, *chimney-sweep* old forms survive as compound-members. We not only form new agent-nouns, such as *camouflager, debunker, charlestoner,* but also make back-formations, such as the verb *chauffe* [šowf] 'drive (someone) about in a motorcar' from *chauffeur* ['šowfr̥]. An analogy that permits of new formations is said to be "living."

The old suffix *-ster* in *webster* is an example of a type which perhaps never could have been described as "regular" or "living" and yet had its period of expansion. It seems to have denoted (as is still the case in Dutch) a female agent. The female meaning survives in *spinster,* originally 'spinneress.' Apparently, the female meaning was not obvious in all the words: the suffix became indifferent as to sex and appears in *tapster, huckster, teamster, maltster, webster* 'weaver,' *dunster* 'dunner, bailiff.' The action was not necessarily useful, witness *songster, rimester, trickster, gamester, punster.* A non-human agent appears in *lobster,* which probably represents Old English *loppestre,* originally 'jumper.' An inanimate object is *roadster.* An adjective, instead of verb or noun, underlies *youngster.* After the restriction to females was lost, words in *-ster* combined with *-ess: huckstress, songstress, seamstress.* This last, by the shortening of vowels before clusters, became ['semstres]; the more regular rival form ['sijmstres] is analogic, with the vowel of the underlying *seam.* In cases like *-ster* we see a formation spreading from form to form without ever attaining to the free expansion of "living" types.

Some formations become widely usable without pre-empting a domain of meaning. In English, the suffixes *-y, -ish, -ly,* which derive adjectives, have all remained quite "alive" through the historical period, spreading from word to word, and settling in various semantic patches. Thus, with the suffix *-y* (from Old English *-ig*), some words appear in our Old English records (e.g. *mighty, misty, moody, bloody, speedy*), while others appear only later (e.g. *earthy, wealthy, hasty, hearty, fiery*). When the suffix is added to words of foreign origin, the date of the borrowing gives us a limit of age ("terminus post quem") for the new combination: *sugary, flowery, creamy.* At present, this suffix is expanding in certain zones of meaning, such as 'arch, affected': *summery* (e.g. of clothes), *sporty, swanky, arty* ('pretendedly artistic'), *booky* ('pretendedly bookish'). In the same way, *-ish,* in some combinations a mere adjective-former (*boyish, girlish*), has staked a claim in the zone of 'undesirably, inappropriately resembling,' as in *mannish, womanish* (contrast *manly, womanly*), *childish* (contrast *childlike*). The starting-point of semantic specialization is to be sought in forms where the underlying word has the special value; thus, the unpleasant flavor of *-ish* comes from words like *loutish, boorish, swinish, hoggish.*

The shape of morphologic constituents is subject to analogic change, especially in the way of enlargement. In Latin, the set *argentum* [ar'gentum] 'silver': *argentarius* [argen'ta:rius] 'silversmith' represents a regular type of derivation. In the history of French there was repeated losses of final phonemes; the modern forms are *argent* [arža^n]: *argentier* [arža^{n}tje]. The formula of derivation has become: add the suffix [-tje]. This suffix, accordingly, appears in words which (as the historian, quite irrelevantly, remarks) never contained a [t] in the critical position: French *ferblanc* [fɛrbla^n] 'tin' (Latin type **ferrum blankum* 'white iron,' with the Germanic adjective *blank*) underlies *ferblantier* [fɛrbla^{n}tje] 'tinsmith'; *bijou* [bižu] 'jewel' (from Breton *bizun*) underlies *bijoutier* [bižutje] 'jeweler,' and so on.

In time, an affix may consist entirely of accretive elements, with no trace of its original shape. In Old English, verb-paradigms were derived from nouns on the pattern [wund] 'a wound':['wundian] 'to wound,' and this is still the living type, as in *wound:to wound, radio:to radio*. In a few instances, however, the underlying noun was itself derived, by means of a suffix [-en-], from an adjective, as in the set [fɛst] 'firm, strong':['fɛsten] 'strong place, fortress':['fɛstenian] 'to make firm, to fortify.' Thanks to some fluctuation in frequency or meaning—such, perhaps, as a decline or specialization of the noun ['fɛsten]—the pair [fɛst] 'firm':['fɛstenian] 'to make firm' served as a model for new-formations on the scheme

$$fast:fasten = hard:x,$$

with the result of forms like *harden, sharpen, sweeten, fatten, gladden* in which a suffix *-en* derives verbs from adjectives.

Less often, a relatively independent form is reduced to affixal status. Compound-members are occasionally reduced, by sound-change, to suffixes; thus, the suffix *-ly* (*manly*) is a weakened form of *like*, and the suffix *-dom* (*kingdom*) of the word *doom*. This happens especially when the independent word goes out of use, as in the case of *-hood* (*childhood*), which is a relic of an Old English word [ha:d] 'person, rank.' German *Messer* ['meser] 'knife' is the modern form, with analogic as well as phonetic shortening, of Old High German ['messi-rahs] originally 'food-knife,' in which the second member, [sahs] 'knife,' had been disfigured by Verner's change and the subsequent change of [z] to [r]. In German *Schuster* ['šu:ster] 'shoemaker' the unique suffix [-ster] reflects an old compound-member [su'tɛ:re] 'cobbler.' Merging of two words into one is excessively rare; the best-known instance is the origin of the future tense-forms in the Romance languages from phrases of infinitive plus 'have':Latin *amare habeo* [a'ma:re 'habeo:] 'I have to, am to love' > French *aimerai* [ɛmre] '(I) shall love'; Latin *amare habet* [a'ma:re 'habet] 'he has to, is to love' > French *aimera* [ɛmra] '(he) will love,' and so on. This development must have taken place under very unusual conditions; above all, we must remember that Latin and Romance have a complicated set of verb-inflections which served as a model for one-word tense-forms.

Back-formations in word-structure are by no means uncommon, though often hard to recognize. Many verbs in the foreign-learned vocabulary of English resemble Latin past participles; this is all the more striking since English has borrowed these words from French, and in French the Latin past participles have been obscured by sound-change or replaced by new-formations: Latin *agere* ['agere] 'to lead, carry on, do,' past participle *actus* ['aktus] 'led, done':French *agir* [aži:r] 'to act,' participle (new-formation) *agi* [aži] 'acted':English *to act;* Latin *affligere* [af'fli:gere] 'to strike down, afflict,' participle *afflictus* [af'fliktus] 'stricken, afflicted': French *affliger* [afliže], participle *affligé* [afliže]:English *to afflict;* Latin *separare* [se:pa'ra:re] 'to separate,' participle *separatus* [se:pa'ra:tus]: French *séparer* [separe], participle *séparé* [separe]:English *to separate.* The starting-point for this habit of English seems to have been back-formation from nouns in *-tion:* English verbs like *act, afflict, separate* are based on nouns like *action, affliction, separation,* from Latin *actionem, afflictionem, separationem* [akti'o:nem, afflikti'o:nem, se:para:ti'o:nem] via French *action, affliction, séparation,* in modern pronunciation [aksjo^n, afliksjo^n, separasjo^n]. The immediate models must have been cases like *communion:to commune* (Old French *communion:comuner*); the general background was the English homonymy of adjective and verb in cases like *warm:to warm = separate:to separate.* This supposition is confirmed by the fact that the nouns in *-tion* appear in our records at an earlier time, on the whole, than the verbs in *-t.* Of the 108 pairs with initial A in the *New English Dictionary,* the noun appears earlier than the verb in 74 cases, as, *action* in 1330, but *to act* in 1384; *affliction,* in 1303, but *to afflict* in 1393. Moreover, we sometimes see the late rise of the verb with *-t:* in the case of *aspiration:to aspire* we have stuck to the Latin-French scheme, but round 1700 there appears the new-formation *to aspirate.* Modern formations of this sort are *evolute,* based on *evolution,* as a rival of the older *evolve,* and *elocute* based on *elocution.*

23.6 The task of tracing analogy in word-composition has scarcely been undertaken. The present-day habits of word-composition in English produce the illusion that compounds arise by a simple juxtaposition of words. The reader need scarcely be told that the modern English pattern, in which the compound word equals the independent forms of the members, with modification only of word-stress, is the product of a long series of regularizing analogic changes. Thus, ['fowr-,hed] *forehead,* as a rival of ['fared], which has been irregularized by sound-change, is due to analogic re-formation:

> *fore, arm :fore-arm* ['fowr-,arm]
> = *fore, head:x.*

The relation of the compound to independent words often suffers displacement. Primitive Indo-European did not use verb-stems as compound-members; to this day, English lacks a verbal type, **to meat-eat*, which would match the noun and adjective types *meat-eater* and *meat-eating*. Several Indo-European languages, however, have developed compounds with verbal members. In English we have a few irregular forms like *house-keep, dressmake, backbite*. From a compound noun like *whitewash* we derive, with a zero-element, a verb to *whitewash*, and from this an agent-noun *whitewasher*. The irregular type to *housekeep* is probably a back-formation on this model:

whitewasher : to whitewash
= *housekeeper : x.*

In a now classical investigation, Hermann Osthoff showed how forms of this kind arose in several of the Indo-European languages. In Old High German, abstract nouns like ['beta] 'prayer' were used, in the normal inherited fashion, as prior members of compounds: ['beta-ˌhuːs] 'prayer-house, house for prayer.' The morphologically connected verb ['betoːn] 'to pray' had a different suffixal vowel and did not interfere with the compound. During the Middle Ages, however, unstressed vowels were weakened to a uniform [e] and in part lost; hence in Middle High German (round the year 1200), in a set like ['beten] 'to pray': ['bete] 'prayer': ['bete-ˌhuːs] 'house for prayer,' the compound-member resembled the verb as much as it resembled the noun. If the noun lost in frequency or was specialized in meaning, the compound-member became equivalent to the verb-stem. Thus ['bete] 'prayer' lost in frequency—the modern language uses a different derivative, *Gebet* [geˈbeːt] 'prayer'—and, for the rest, was specialized in a meaning of 'contribution, tax.' As a result of this, compounds like *Bethaus* ['beːt-ˌhaws] 'house for praying,' *Bettag* ['beːt-ˌtaːk] 'day of prayer,' *Betschwester*, ['beːt-ˌšvester] 'praying-sister,' that is 'nun' or 'over-pious woman,' can be described only as containing the verb-stem [beːt-] of *beten* [beːten] 'to pray.' Accordingly, ever since the Middle Ages, new compounds of this sort have been formed with verbal prior members, as *Schreib-tisch* ['šrajp-ˌtiš] 'writing-table,' from *schreiben* 'to write,' or *Lesebuch* ['leːze-ˌbuːx] 'reading-book' from *lesen* 'to read.'

The fluctuation between irregular compounds, such as ['fared] *forehead*, and analogically formed regular variants, such as ['fowr-ˌhed], serves as a model for new-formations which replace an obscure form by a compound-member. Thus, *inmost, northmost, utmost* (and, with regularization of the first member, *outmost*), with the word *most* as second member, are analogic formations which replace the Old English type ['innemest, 'norθmest, 'uːtemest]; the [-mest] in these words was a special form (with accretion) of the superlative suffix [-est]. Regularizing new-formations like this, which (as the historian finds) disagree with the earlier structure of the form, are sometimes called *popular etymologies*.

23.7 Analogic innovation in the phrase is most easily seen when it affects the shape of single words. Conditioned sound-changes may produce different forms of a word according to its phonetic positions in the phrase. In the types of English which lost [r] in final position and before consonants, but kept it before vowels, there resulted sandhi-alternants of words like *water:* in final position and before consonants this became ['wɔtə], but before a vowel in a close-knit phrase it kept its [r]: *the water is* ['wɔtər iz], *the water of* ['wɔtər ov]. The final vowel of *water* was now like that of a word like *idea* [aj'dijə], which had never had final [r]. This led to a new-formation:

> *water* ['wɔtə]:*the water is* ['wɔtər iz]
> = *idea* [aj'dijə]:*x*,

which resulted in the sandhi-form *the idea-r is* [aj'dijər iz].

In a language like modern English, which gives special phonetic treatment to the beginning and end of a word, the phonemes in these positions rarely fulfil the terms of an ordinary conditioned sound-change, but are subject rather to conditioned changes of their own. Only phrases with atonic words parallel the conditions which exist within a word. Hence English sandhi-alternation is limited largely to cases like the above (. . . *of*, . . . *is*) or to such as *don't, at you* ['ɛčuw], *did you* ['dijuw]. Moreover, the plain phonetic marking of most words, and in some positions even of ordinarily atonic words, favors the survival or new-formation of variants that agree with the absolute form: *do not, at you* ['ɛt juw], *did you* ['did juw].

In languages which give a less specialized treatment to word-boundaries, sandhi-alternants arise in great numbers and give rise to irregularities which are in turn leveled out by new-formations. In French, the noun is on the whole free from sandhi-alternation:words like *pot* [po] 'pot' or *pied* [pje] 'foot' are invariable in the phrase. However, we need only look to phrase-like compounds, such as *pot-au-feu* [pɔt o fø] 'pot-on-the-fire,' that is 'broth', or *pied-à-terre* [pjet a tɛ:r] 'foot-on-ground,' that is 'lodgings,' to see that the apparent stability is due to analogic regularization. Third-person singular verbs which were monosyllabic in the early Middle Ages, have, by regular phonetic development, a final [t] in sandhi before a vowel: Latin *est* > French *est* [ɛ] 'is,' but Latin *est ille* > French *est-il* [ɛt i] 'is he?' On the other hand, verb-forms of more than one syllable had not this [t]; Latin *amat* 'he loves' gives French *aime* [ɛm] 'loves' even before a vowel. However, the pattern

$$[\varepsilon]{:}[\varepsilon t\ i] = [\varepsilon m]{:}x$$

resulted in a modern sandhi-form *aime-t-il* [ɛmt i] 'does he love?'

In the later Old English period, final [n] after an unstressed vowel was lost, except in sandhi before a vowel. Thus, *eten* 'to eat' became *ete, an hand* became *a hand*, but *an arm* remained. In the case of the article *a:an* the resulting alternation has survived; in early modern English one still said *my friend:mine enemy*. One must suppose that at the time of the loss of *-n*, the language did not distinguish word-boundaries in the manner of present-day English. The sandhi [n] was generalized in a few cases as a word-initial. Old English *efeta* ['eveta] 'lizard' appears in Middle English as *ewte* and *newte*, whence modern *newt*. A phrase like *an ewte* must have been pronounced [a'newte] and (doubtless under some special conditions of frequency or meaning) subjected to the new-formation

$$[\text{a'na:me}] \text{ 'a name'}{:}[\text{'na:me}] \text{ 'name'}$$
$$= [\text{a'newte}] \text{ 'a lizard'}{:}x,$$

with the result that one said *newte*.[2] Similarly, *eke-name* 'supplementary name' gave rise to a by-form with *n-*, modern *nickname; for then anes* is now *for the nonce*. On the other hand, an initial [n] was in some forms treated as a sandhi [n]. Thus, Old English *nafogar* ['navo-ˌga:r], literally 'nave-lance,' Middle English *navegar*, has been replaced by *auger;* Old English ['nɛ:dre] gives Middle English *naddere* and *addere*, whence modern *adder;* Old French *naperon*, borrowed as *napron*, has been replaced by *apron*.

After this loss of final [n], another sound-change led to the loss of certain final vowels, through which many hitherto medial [n]'s got into final position, as in *oxena > oxen*. These new final [n]'s came into final position too late to suffer the dropping; hence the language had now, beside the sandhi [n], which appeared only before vowels, also a stable final [n]. This led to some complicated relations:

| | Old English > | Early Middle English | |
		before vowel	otherwise
singular			
nominative	*oxa*	*ox*	*oxe*
other cases	*oxan*	*oxen*	*oxe*
plural			
nom.-acc.	*oxan*	*oxen*	*oxe*
dat.	*oxum*	*oxen*	*oxe*
gen.	*oxena*	*oxen*	*oxen*

[2] [Compare Bloomfield's treatment of these changes with Lehmann's. Bloomfield assumes that there was no audible juncture between *an* and *ewte*, Lehmann that there was one, and that it shifted. Which is the more likely explanation?—*Eds.*]

This complicated habit was re-shaped into our present distribution of singular *ox*, plural *oxen*.

In most cases, a phrasal innovation results not in a new word-form, but in a new syntactic or lexical usage, such as the use of *like* as a conjunction (§ 23.2). In German we find such appositional groups as *ein Trunk Wasser* [ajn 'truŋk 'vaser] 'a drink of water,' where the related languages would lead us to expect the second noun in genitive case-form, *Wassers* 'of water.' The genitive case-ending in feminine and plural nouns has been reduced to zero by phonetic change: the genitive of *Milch* [milx] 'milk' (feminine noun) is homonymous with the nominative and accusative. The old locution *ein Trunk Wassers* has been replaced by the present one, which arose on the scheme

> *Milch trinken* 'to drink milk': *ein Trunk Milch* 'a drink
> of milk'
> = *Wasser trinken* 'to drink water': *x*.

This was favored, no doubt, by the existence of nouns whose genitive wavered between zero and *-es*, and by the circumstance that the genitive case was declining in frequency. It seems likely, in spite of the obvious difficulties, that further research will find many examples of analogic innovation in the phrase, both syntactic and lexical. Our philosophic pre-possessions have led us too often to seek the motives of change in the individual word and in the meaning of the individual word.

23.8 For many new-formations we are not able to give a proportional model. We believe that this is not always due to our inability to find the model sets, and that there is really a type of linguistic-change which resembles analogic change, but goes on without model sets. These *adaptive* new-formations resemble an old form with some change in the direction of semantically related forms. For instance, of the two slang forms *actorine* 'actress' and *chorine* 'chorus-girl,' only the former can be described as the the result of a proportional analogy (*Paul:Pauline = actor:x*). Now, *chorine* seems to be based in some way on *actorine*, but the set *chorus: chorine* is not parallel with *actor:actorine* either in form or in meaning. The set *Josephus:Josephine* [jow'sijfos, 'jowzefijn] is uncommon, remote in meaning, and phonetically irregular. We can say only that many nouns have a suffix [-ijn], e.g. *chlorine, colleen;* that this suffix derives some women's names and especially the noun *actorine;* and that the *-us* of *chorus* is plainly suffixal, in view of the adjective *choral*. This general background must have sufficed to make someone utter the form *chorine*, even though there was no exact analogy for this form.

A new form (such as *chorine*), which is based on a traditional form (*chorus*,

chorus-girl), but departs from it in the direction of a series of semantically related forms (*chlorine, colleen, Pauline*, etc., including especially *actorine*), is said to originate by *adaptation*. Adaptation seems to be favored by more than one factor, but all the factors taken together would not allow us to predict the new form. Often, as in our example, the new form has a facetious connotation; this connotation is probably connected with the unpredictable, far-fetched shape of the new word. This is true of mock-learned words, like *scrumptious, rambunctious, absquatulate*. It seems unlikely that more than one speaker hit upon these forms: we suspect them of being individual creations, determined by the linguistic and practical peculiarities of some one speaker. They must have agreed to some extent, however, with the general habits of the community, since they were taken up by other speakers.

Some adaptations are less far-fetched and merely produce a new form which agrees better with semantically related forms. English has borrowed many French words with a suffix *-ure*, such as *measure, censure, fracture*. The Old French words *plaisir, loisir, tresor*, which contain other suffixes, have in English been adapted to the *-ure* type, for the [-žr̩] of *pleasure, leisure, treasure* reflects an old [-zju:r]. Among our foreign-learned words, *egoism* follows the French model, but *egotism* is an adaptive formation in the direction of *despotism, nepotism*.

In the Romance languages, Latin *reddere* ['reddere] 'to give back' has been largely replaced by a type **rendere*, as in Italian *rendere* ['rɛndere], French *rendre* [raⁿdr], whence English *render*. This **rendere* is an adaptation of *reddere* in the direction of the series Latin *prehendere* [pre'hendere, 'prendere] 'to take' > Italian *prendere* ['prɛndere], French *prendre* [praⁿdr]; Latin *attendere* [at'tendere] 'to pay attention' > Italian *attendere* [at'tɛndere] 'to wait,' French *attendre* [ataⁿdr] (and other compounds of Latin *tendere*); Latin *vendere* ['we:ndere] 'to sell' > Italian *vendere* ['vendere], French *vendre* [vaⁿdr]; here the word for 'take,' with its close kinship of meaning, was doubtless the main factor.

Sometimes it is a single form which exercises the attraction. Beside the old word *gravis* 'heavy,' later Latin has also a form *grevis*, whose vowel seems to be due to the influence of *levis* 'light (in weight).' Formations of this sort are known as *blendings* or *contaminations*. We cannot always be sure that the attraction was exercised by only a single form; in our example, the word *brevis* 'short' may have helped toward the formation of *grevis*.

The paradigm of the word for 'foot,' Primitive Indo-European **[po'ds], genitive **[po'dos], Sanskrit [pa:t], genitive [pa'dah], appears in one ancient Greek dialect in the expected shape, [ˇpo:s], genitive [po'dos], but in the Attic dialect has the unexpected nominative form ['pows]; this has been explained as a contamination with the word for 'tooth,' [o'dows], genitive [o'dontos], which is a phonetically normal reflex of a Primitive Indo-European type *[o'donts].

In the earlier stages of the Germanic languages, the personal pronouns must have been in a state of instability. The old form for 'ye' seems to have been a Primitive Germanic type *[ju:z, juz], which appears in Gothic as *jus* [ju:s] or [jus]. The other Germanic dialects reflect a Primitive Germanic type *[jiz]: Old Norse [e:r], Old English [je:], Old High German [ir]. This form has been explained as a contamination of *[juz] 'ye' with the word for 'we,' Primitive Germanic *[wi:z, wiz], reflected in Gothic [wi:s], Old Norse [ve:r], Old English [we:], Old High German [wir].

Similarly, in Gothic the accusative case of 'thou' is [θuk] and the dative case [θus]. These forms disagree with the other dialects, which reflect the Primitive Germanic types accusative *['θiki], Old Norse [θik], Old English [θek], Old High German [dih], and dative *[θiz], Old Norse [θe:r], Old English [θe:], Old High German [dir]. The Gothic forms have been explained as contaminations with the nominative *[θu:], Gothic, Old Norse, Old English [θu:], Old High German [du:]. For this, the word 'I', which had the same vowel in all three forms, Gothic [ik, mik, mis], may have served as a kind of model, but there is no exact analogy covering the two paradigms, and we might equally well expect [mik, mis] to work in favor of *[θik, θis].

Numerals seem to have been contaminated in the history of various languages. In Primitive Indo-European, 'four' was *[kʷe'two:res], and 'five' *['penkʷe]; witness Sanskrit [ča'tva:rah, 'panča] or Lithuanian [ketu'ri, pen'ki]. In the Germanic languages both words begin with [f], which reflects a Primitive Indo-European [p], as in English *four, five;* and *five,* moreover, has an [f] for the [kʷ] of the second syllable, as in Gothic [fimf]. In Latin, on the other hand, both words begin with [kw]: *quattuor, quinque* ['kwattuor, 'kwi:nkwe]. All of these deviant forms could be explained as due to "distant assimilation"; it seems more probable, however, that the changes described under this and similar terms are in reality contaminative or adaptive. Ancient Greek [hep'ta] 'seven' and [ok'to:] 'eight' led in one dialect to a contaminative [op'to:] 'eight,' and in others to [hok'to:]. The words 'nine' and 'ten,' Primitive Indo-European *['newn̥, 'dekm̥], as in Sanskrit ['nava, 'daça], Latin *novem, decem,* both have initial [d] in Slavic and Baltic, as in Old Bulgarian [deveⁿtɪ, deseⁿtɪ].

Psychologists have ascertained that under laboratory conditions, the stimulus of hearing a word like 'four' often leads to the utterance of a word like 'five'—but this, after all, does not account for contamination. There is perhaps more relevance in the fact that contaminative "slips of the tongue" are not infrequent, e.g. "I'll just *grun* (*go* plus *run*) over and get it."

Innovations in syntax sometimes have a contaminative aspect. The

type *I am friends with him* has been explained as due to contamination of
I am friendly with him and *we are friends.* Irregularities such as the "attraction" of relative pronouns[3] seem to be of this nature.

So-called popular etymologies (§ 23.6) are largely adaptive and contaminative. An irregular or semantically obscure form is replaced by a new form
of more normal structure and some semantic content—though the latter
is often far-fetched. Thus, an old *sham-fast* 'shame-fast,' that is, 'modest',
has given way to the regular, but semantically queer compound *shame-
faced.* Old English *sam-blind,* containing an otherwise obsolete first member
which meant 'half,' was replaced by the Elizabethan *sand-blind.* Old English
bryd-guma ['bry:d-ˌguma] 'bride-man' was replaced by *bride-groom,* thanks
to the obsolescence of *guma* 'man.' Foreign words are especially subject to
this kind of adaptation. Old French *crevisse,* Middle English *crevise* has
been replaced by *cray-fish, craw-fish; mandragora* by *man-drake; asparagus*
in older substandard speech by *sparrow-grass.* Our *gooseberry* seems to be a
replacement of an older **groze-berry,* to judge by dialect forms such as
grozet, groser; these forms reflect a borrowed French form akin to modern
French *groseille* [grɔzɛ:j] 'currant; gooseberry.'

Probably forms like our symbolic words, nursery words, and short-
names are created on general formal patterns, rather than on exact analogic
models. It seems, however, that forms like *Bob, Dick* existed as common
nouns, perhaps with symbolic connotation, before they were specialized as
hypochoristic forms of *Robert, Richard.* It is a great mistake to think that
one can account for the origin of forms like these by merely stating their
connotation.

In some instances we know that a certain person invented a form. The
most famous instance is *gas,* invented in the seventeenth century by the
Dutch chemist van Helmont. In the passage where he introduces the word,
van Helmont points out its resemblance to the word *chaos,* which, in Dutch
pronunciation, is not far removed (though phonemically quite distinct)
from *gas.* Moreover, van Helmont used also a technical term *blas,* a regular
derivative, in Dutch, of the verb *blazen* 'to blow.'

It is evident that in such cases we cannot reconstruct the inventor's
private and personal world of connotations; we can only guess at the
general linguistic background. Charles Dodgson ("Lewis Carroll") in his
famous poem, "The Jabberwocky" (in *Through the Looking-Glass*), uses a
number of new-formations of this sort and, later in the book, explains the

---

[3] [By "attraction of relative pronouns," Bloomfield means the phenomenon in languages with elaborate case
forms by which pronouns take the case of the antecedent rather than as usual the case demanded by the function of the pronoun in the clause in which it appears. Bloomfield's example is the Latin phrase "in hāc vītā
quā nunc ego dēgo" (in this life which now I lead), where the relative *quā* has been attracted into ablative
case by its antecedent *vītā,* rather than appearing as *quam,* accusative case, as the object of *dēgo* in the relative clause.—*Eds.*]

connotative significance they had for him. At least one of them, *chortle*, has come into wide use. More recent examples are the mercantile term *kodak*, invented by George Eastman, and *blurb*, a creation of Gelett Burgess.

Study Questions

1. Why is the assumption that phonetic change is regular important to an understanding of historical processes like analogy? How, in turn, does the discovery of analogic forms help confirm that assumption?

2. Can you construct analogic explanations for the following forms? *ain't* in *ain't I; you-all; brang, brung;* Winston tastes good *like* a cigarette should?

3. When Bloomfield constructs an analogy like:

    $$boot:boots = foot:(foots)$$

    what do the symbols (:) and (=) mean? In constructing an analogical formula, are we making claims about the psychological processes involved in the change? What does analogic change have to do with everyday use of language in which we make up new sentences as we have need of them? What would be the difference between a form like *foots* and the form *coots* if we had heard only the singular *coot*? Would there be any difference in the way the forms were created?

4. Compare Bloomfield's description of analogic change with Kiparsky's. In what ways do they differ? Bloomfield says: "We do not know why speakers sometimes utter new combinations instead of traditional forms. . . ." Does Kiparsky offer an explanation? If a linguist finds forms that appear to reflect analogic change, how does he go about setting up the left-hand side of the analogy? What might lead him to suspect that *walk:walked = talk:(talked)* is a possible analogy, but that *walk:wander = talk:(tonder)* is not? Does Bloomfield's discussion exclude the latter possibility? Does Kiparsky's? What does Kiparsky mean when he states that the basic assumption of his study is "the very tame one that where grammar is involved in linguistic change it is involved in terms of its natural components and rules"?

5. What does Bloomfield mean by the term "the syntactic habit" (p.

411)? Particularly, what does the word *habit* mean here? If a speaker's knowledge of the syntax of his language permits him to make up new sentences—to use his language to express his thoughts and wants—can we equate that knowledge with what is customarily meant by *habit?* What does use of the term tell us of Bloomfield's assumptions about the nature of language?

6. Bloomfield says: "the meaning of a speech form for any speaker is a product of the situations and contexts in which he has heard this form." Do "practical situations" constitute the meaning of speech forms? What role does the quotation assign to the human mind? If situations and contexts produce meanings, how do we explain the native speaker's ability to use his language to talk about new experiences? Would such a definition of meaning allow us to talk about the meanings of linguistic forms with any precision?

7. Define the following terms: *analogic-semantic change, back-formation, popular etymology, contamination.* How does analogic innovation in the phrase differ from analogic change in inflectional paradigms? What is the distinction between proportional analogy and adaptation? Which of the types of analogy require semantic analysis for support?

8. How would a generative grammarian classify Bloomfield's adaptive formations? For example, when *reddere* is made to rhyme with *prehendere,* or *gravis* changed to *grevis* (presumably because of the influence of *levis*), do these changes reflect changes in the rule system or changes in the shape of single lexical items? Bloomfield says of *chorine* and words like *scrumptious,* "we suspect them of being individual creations, determined by the linguistic and practical peculiarities of some one speaker. They must have agreed to some extent, however, with the general habits of the community, since they were taken up by other speakers." How might one account for such individual contributions either as analogy or as change in rule? Was Gilliéron's suggestion that each word has its own history right? Will we have good histories—or good grammars—without good dictionaries?

Einar Haugen

THE ANALYSIS OF LINGUISTIC BORROWING

Einar Haugen (b. 1906) has won many honors for his writings on the Scandinavian languages and on bilingualism, among them several honorary degrees, Fulbright and Guggenheim Fellowships, and Sweden's Order of the North Star. He has served as president of the Linguistic Society of America (1950) and of the International Congress of Linguists (1962). He is currently professor of Scandinavian languages and linguistics at Harvard.

Haugen's work with bilingualism and with the mutual influences of English and Norwegian in the United States gives particular authority to his remarks on borrowing. His *Norwegian Language in America* (1953) is a classic study of the effects of a majority language and culture on the way a minority behaves linguistically. His other contributions to the understanding of bilingualism include *Bilingualism in the Americas* (1956), a bibliographical and research guide, and *Language Conflict and Language Planning: The Case of Modern Norwegian* (1966). Professor Haugen has also made translations from Norwegian, and has written introductions to the study of that language. His article is a lucid examination of the processes of borrowing based on observation and analysis of the behavior of bilingual speakers, mainly speakers of Norwegian in the United States. The article is particularly valuable because it treats the process of borrowing as well as the results, and draws its documentation from real speech as well as written records. In doing so, it reminds us that the borrowing process is not restricted to scholars and scientists who seek new words for their findings, but also goes on in the everyday use of everyday language whenever the proper conditions of bilingualism exist. Haugen's treatment should be of particular interest to students who wish to understand what happened during the Middle English period when English speakers borrowed widely from the French-speaking Normans and from Scandinavians.

1. BILINGUALISM AND BORROWING

As early as 1886, Hermann Paul pointed out that all borrowing by one language from another is predicated on some minimum of bilingual mastery of the two languages.[1] For any large-scale borrowing a considerable group of bilinguals has to be assumed. The analysis of borrowing must therefore begin with an analysis of the behavior of bilingual speakers. A vast literature has come into being on the subject of borrowing, particularly in the historical studies of individual languages; but there is still room for discussion

From *Language*, Vol. 26 (1950), pp. 210–231. Reprinted by permission of the Linguistic Society of America and the author.
[1] Prinzipien der Sprachgeschichte,[2] Chap. 22 (Halle a. S., 1886).

of the relationship between the observed behavior of bilingual speakers and the results of borrowing as detected by linguists. Any light that can be thrown on the question by a study of bilingual speakers should be welcome to all students interested in borrowing and in the general linguistic problems associated with this process.[2] In the present article an effort will be made to define more precisely the terminology used in the linguistic analysis of borrowing, and to set up certain hypotheses concerning the process of borrowing. It should then be possible to test these by their usefulness of application to particular studies of bilingualism and borrowing.[3]

2. MIXING THE LANGUAGES

Perhaps the most widely understood term for the phenomena we are here considering is based on the metaphor of 'mixture.' Among speakers of immigrant languages in America it is indeed a popular term; cf. the practice of AmN speakers when they say *han mikser* 'he mixes' or the AmG book title *Gemixte Pickles*, in which the loanword *mix* is at once a description and an example of the process. From popular speech it has passed into the usage of linguists, especially of the older generations; Hermann Paul headed his chapter in the Prinzipien 'Sprachmischung,' and the term was regularly used by men like Whitney and Schuchardt. As a description of the process it might seem to have a certain vividness that justifies its use, but on closer inspection it shows disadvantages which have apparently led later linguists, such as Sapir and Bloomfield, to abandon it. Even Paul had to warn against the misunderstanding that it was possible to mix languages 'ungefähr in gleicher menge,' as if they could be poured together into a cocktail shaker and result in an entirely new concoction. Except in abnormal cases speakers have not been observed to draw freely from two languages at once. They may switch rapidly from one to the other, but at any given moment they are speaking only one, even when they resort to the other for assistance.[4] The introduction of elements from one language into the other means merely an alteration of the second language, not a mixture of the two. Mixture implies the creation of an entirely new entity

---

[2] See the writer's árticle, Problems of bilingualism (Lingua 2.271–90, 1950), for a discussion of the social pressures that lead to bilingualism, and for some recent studies of the problem.

[3] Languages frequently referred to are abbreviated as follows: E English; N Norwegian; PaG Pennsylvania German; AmG American German; AmN American Norwegian; AmPort. American Portuguese. Other abbreviations are standard or obvious.

Examples from AmN are taken from the writer's own materials, collected chiefly in Wisconsin. . . .

The examples from AmPort. are taken from Leo Pap, Portuguese-American speech (New York, 1949).

[4] Paul, Prinzipien 338; Meillet, La méthode comparative 82 (Oslo, 1925); Meillet, Linguistique historique et linguistique générale 76 (Paris, 1921).

and the disappearance of both constituents; it also suggests a jumbling of a more or less haphazard nature. But speakers of e.g. AmN continue to speak a recognizably Norwegian language distinct from their English down to the time when they switch to the latter for good.

So much for the process itself. A further inaccuracy is introduced if the resulting language is called 'mixed' or 'hybrid.' It implies that there are other languages which are 'pure,' but these are scarcely any more observable than a 'pure race' in ethnology. The term is ambiguous because it can mean either that the language has adopted elements of foreign origin at some time in the past, or that it shows mutually inconsistent elements in its present-day structure as a result of such adoption. Yet we know that great numbers of words in English which once were adopted are now quite indistinguishable from native words by any synchronic test. Schuchardt insisted that all languages were mixed, but in saying this he gave the word so wide an application that its value for characterizing individual languages would seem to be greatly reduced. In some circles the term 'mixed' or 'hybrid' has actually acquired a pejorative sense, so that reformers have set to work 'purifying' the language without seeing clearly what they were about. For the reasons here given, the term 'mixture' is not used in the present discussion. It may have its place in a popularized presentation of the problem, but in technical discussion it is more usefully replaced by the term 'borrowing,' which we shall now proceed to define.

3. A DEFINITION OF BORROWING

At first blush the term 'borrowing' might seem to be almost as inept for the process we wish to analyze as 'mixture.' The metaphor implied is certainly absurd, since the borrowing takes place without the lender's consent or even awareness, and the borrower is under no obligation to repay the loan. One might as well call it stealing, were it not that the owner is deprived of nothing and feels no urge to recover his goods. The process might be called an adoption, for the speaker does adopt elements from a second language into his own. But what would one call a word that had been adopted—an adoptee? Anthropologists speak of 'diffusion' in connection with a similar process in the spread of non-linguistic cultural items. We might well speak of linguistic diffusion, though this would suggest the spread of the language itself rather than of elements from it. The real advantage of the term 'borrowing' is the fact that it is not applied to language by laymen. It has therefore remained comparatively unambiguous in linguistic discussion, and no apter term has yet been invented. Once we have decided to retain this well-established linguistic term, we shall simply have to disregard its popular associations, and give it as precise a significance as we can.

(1) We shall assume it as axiomatic that EVERY SPEAKER ATTEMPTS TO REPRODUCE PREVIOUSLY LEARNED LINGUISTIC PATTERNS in an effort to cope with new linguistic situations. (2) AMONG THE NEW PATTERNS WHICH HE MAY LEARN ARE THOSE OF A LANGUAGE DIFFERENT FROM HIS OWN, and these too he may attempt to reproduce. (3) If he reproduces the new linguistic patterns, NOT IN THE CONTEXT OF THE LANGUAGE IN WHICH HE LEARNED THEM, but in the context of another, he may be said to have 'borrowed' them from one language into another. The heart of our definition of borrowing is then THE ATTEMPTED REPRODUCTION IN ONE LANGUAGE OF PATTERNS PREVIOUSLY FOUND IN ANOTHER. We shall not here take up the question of what is meant by 'another language'; Bloomfield has adequately pointed out the difficulties involved.[5] The term reproduction does not imply that a mechanical imitation has taken place; on the contrary, the nature of the reproduction may differ very widely from the original, as we shall see.

For our definition it does not matter why the speaker does it, nor whether he is conscious of what he is doing. We shall proceed to analyze what he does by comparing the pattern that he is reproducing with the results that he succeeds in turning out. While it is true that we shall rarely if ever be able to catch a speaker in the actual process of making an original borrowing, it is clear that every loan now current must at some time have appeared as an innovation. Only by isolating this initial leap of the pattern from one language to another can we clarify the process of borrowing.

4. TYPES OF BORROWING

Since borrowing has been defined as a process involving reproduction, any attempt to analyze its course must involve a comparison of the original pattern with its imitation. We shall call the original pattern the MODEL, and recognize that the loan may be more or less similar to it. It may vary all the way from an imitation satisfactory to a native speaker to one that the native speaker would not recognize at all. Where the loan is (to a native speaker) noticeably different from the model, we are faced with a case of partial learning due to the interference of other factors, as yet unnamed. If we assume, on the basis of common observation, that these factors are the previously established patterns of the speaker's language, we shall be able to separate out two distinct kinds of reproduction. If the loan is

[5] Language 445 (New York, 1933).

similar enough to the model so that a native speaker would accept it as his own, the borrowing speaker may be said to have IMPORTED the model into his language, provided it is an innovation in that language. But insofar as he has reproduced the model inadequately, he has normally SUBSTITUTED a similar pattern from his own language. This distinction between IMPORTATION and SUBSTITUTION applies not only to a given loan as a whole but to its constituent patterns as well, since different parts of the pattern may be treated differently. An AmN speaker who tries to reproduce AmE *whip* [hwɪp] will often come out with [hypp-]; he has imported the whole form itself with its meaning, but he has substituted his own high-front-round vowel for the E rounded glide plus lowered-front vowel. If the loan contains patterns that are not innovations in the borrowing language, it becomes impossible to distinguish the two kinds of reproduction. Thus importation and substitution fall together in the initial consonant [h], which are not distinguishable in N and E.

A study of the way these two kinds of reproduction operate in speech suggests that whenever the patterns of the model are new to the borrowing language, a compromise is likely to take place between the two sets of patterns. Some kind of adjustment of habits occurs, whereby the speaker chooses one of his own patterns to stand for a similar one in the model. A study of the results of this normally unconscious procedure indicates that while there are many apparently capricious choices, the overall pattern is not unreasonable. The bilingual speakers who make the first substitutions are in a rough way carrying on an operation of comparative linguistics. That substitution is a common phenomenon under such circumstances has been recognized for phonetics, where the term is well established. That it also applies to elements of inflection, word formation, and syntax has not been so clearly recognized. Yet when an AmPort. speaker substitutes the agent suffix *-o* for English *-er* in *boarder*, producing *bordo*, he is giving evidence that he recognizes the equivalence between the two suffixes. He would not be able to formulate it, but his behavior is evidence of some kind of complex reaction which for brevity's sake we may as well call 'mental,' though it can hardly have been conscious. It is the linguist's task to make the speaker's procedures explicit, a task for which he has the advantage of a sophistication that comes from having a vocabulary with which to talk about linguistic behavior. Whether the distinction between importation and substitution can be shown to correspond to mental procedures is uncertain. But it is clear that it is useful in describing the course of borrowing over a period of time, when there is a growing tendency to import rather than substitute as the bilingual command of the languages grows more adequate.

5. THE TERMINOLOGY OF BORROWING

Borrowing as here defined is strictly a process and not a state, yet most of the terms used in discussing it are ordinarily descriptive of its results rather than of the process itself. We shall discuss later the question of the role which loans play within the structure of a language and the extent to which they can be identified without resort to comparative studies. We are here concerned with the fact that the classifications of borrowed patterns implied in such terms as 'loanword,' 'hybrid,' 'loan translation,' or 'semantic loan' are not organically related to the borrowing process itself. They are merely tags which various writers have applied to the observed results of borrowing. We shall illustrate their usual meanings with examples and then try to relate them to the terminology so far proposed and defined.

LOANWORD is the vaguest of the group, since it may include practically any of the others. But it is ordinarily limited to such terms as AmE *shivaree* 'an uninvited serenade of newlyweds' from Fr. *charivari*, in which speakers have imported not only the meaning of the form but also its phonemic shape, though with more or less complete substitution of native phonemes.[6] HYBRID is sometimes used to distinguish loanwords in which only a part of the phonemic shape of the word has been imported, while a native portion has been substituted for the rest. Thus PaG has adopted AmE *plum pie* as [blaʊməpaɪ], in which the morpheme [paɪ] has been imported, but the native [blaʊmə] has been substituted for *plum*.[7] In this case the borrowing speakers must have analyzed the compound into its component morphemes while they were borrowing it, or else they could not have made this partial substitution. This distinction puts the process on a different level from the merely phonemic substitution of the preceding type, so that we are required by the evidence to postulate a MORPHEMIC SUBSTITUTION which operates independently of the phonemic.

If we turn now to the LOAN TRANSLATION (known in French as a CALQUE), we encounter such examples as the French *presqu'île*, German *Halbinsel*, modeled on Latin *paeninsula;* or German *Wolkenkratzer*, Fr. *gratte-ciel*, Sp. *rascacielos*, modeled on E *skyscraper*.[8] But are these anything more than an extension of the process observed in the preceding 'hybrid' examples? Instead of substituting only one half of the word, the borrowers have here analyzed and substituted both halves. They have imported a particular structural pattern, viz. the combination of the two constituents into a compound expression with a new meaning of its own not derivable

---

[6] On *shivaree* see Alva L. Davis and Raven I. McDavid Jr. in American Speech 24.249–55 (1949).
[7] Paul Schach, Hybrid compounds in Pennsylvania German, American Speech 23.121–34 (1948).
[8] Kr. Sandfeld-Jensen, Die Sprachwissenschaft 69 (Leipzig and Berlin, 1915).

by a simple addition of the two parts.[9] Closely related to this is the SE-MANTIC LOAN, which is exemplified by the AmPort. use of *humoroso* with the meaning of the AmE *humorous*, though it meant only 'capricious' in Portugal.[10] Here no formal structural element whatever has been imported, only a meaning, and the substitution of phonemic shape is complete. To call this a 'semantic loan' overlooks the fact that all the loans described above are semantic; it is merely that in this case the new meaning is the only visible evidence of the borrowing. The morphemic substitution is complete. This is true also of phrasal loans, in which syntactic patterns are involved, such as AmN *leggja av* 'discharge,' modeled on AmE *lay off*.

If we now try to sum up this discussion, we see that we have succeeded in establishing a division of loans according to their extent of morphemic substitution: none, partial, or complete. Complete morphemic substitution precludes phonemic substitution, but within the morphemic importation there may be a division into more or less phonemic substitution. We thus arrive at the following groupings, based primarily on the relationship between morphemic and phonemic substitution; the terms used to describe them are makeshift expressions, in lieu of an established terminology or better inventions:

(1) LOANWORDS show morphemic importation without substitution. Any morphemic importation can be further classified according to the degree of its phonemic substitution: none, partial, or complete.

(2) LOANBLENDS show morphemic substitution as well as importation. All substitution involves a certain degree of analysis by the speaker of the model that he is imitating; only such 'hybrids' as involve a discoverable foreign model are included here.

(3) LOANSHIFTS show morphemic substitution without importation. These include what are usually called 'loan translations' and 'semantic loans'; the term 'shift' is suggested because they appear in the borrowing language only as functional shifts of native morphemes.

Separate sections will be devoted to the study of each of these types. For all of them it is taken for granted that semantic importation has taken place. It should be noted that the term 'morpheme' does not here include inflectional modifications; when these are applied, they do not affect the grammatical function of the word, but are necessary and therefore non-distinctive accompaniments of its use in the sentence.

---

[9] Cf. the apt criticism of the term in Pap 176–7, note 58.
[10] Pap 87–8.

6. LOANWORD PHONOLOGY

The simplest and most common substitution is that which takes place when a native sound sequence is used to imitate a foreign one. Complete substitution is characteristic of naive language learners and is heard as a 'foreign accent' by native speakers. However undesirable this may be when one is speaking a foreign language, it is normal when reproducing foreign materials in one's own. The results may be almost completely unrecognizable to the speakers of the model language, as when Spanish *virgen* is reproduced in the language of the Taos Indians as [m'ilxina] or English *spade* is introduced into AmPort. as [ʃi'peiro].[11] In many cases the speakers are completely unaware that they have changed the foreign word, as in the story told by Polivanov of the Japanese student who asked his teacher whether *dzurama* or *dorama* was the correct pronunciation of the European word *drama*. When the teacher answered that it was neither one, but *drama*, he nodded and said, 'Ah yes, then it's *dorama*.' [12] Hermann Paul and many writers after him have described this process as one in which the speaker substitutes 'the most nearly related sounds' of his native tongue for those of the other language.[13] But neither the speaker himself nor the linguist who studies his behavior is always certain as to just what sound in his native tongue is most nearly related to the model. Only a complete analysis of the sound system and the sequences in which sounds appear could give us grounds for predicting which sounds a speaker would be likely to substitute in each given case. When the Yaqui Indians reproduce Sp. *estufa* as [ehtúpa], the [h] for [s] is a substitution that occurs only before [t] and [k], where [s] does not occur in their native language; elsewhere they have no trouble with [s]. Polivanov expressed it as follows:[14] 'En entendant un mot inconnu étranger . . . nous tâchons d'y retrouver un complexe de *nos* représentations phonologiques, de les décomposer en des phonèmes propres à *notre* langue maternelle, et même en conformité à *nos* lois de groupement des phonèmes.' Speakers have been trained to react to certain features in the stream of speech and to reproduce these in their own; but they are also trained to reproduce them only in a limited number of combinations and sequences. Loanword phonology is the attempt to recapture the process of analysis that results in phonemic substitution.

---

[11] George L. Trager, IJAL 10.146 (1944); Pap 94.
[12] TCLP 4.79–96 (1931).
[13] Paul, Prinzipien 340–1; George Hempl, TAPA 29.37; Bloomfield, Language 446.
[14] TCLP 4.80 (1931). "When we hear an unknown foreign word, we try to find in it a complex of our own sounds, to analyze it into the phonemes of our own native tongue in conformity with our laws for the grouping of phonemes."

7. *PHONOLOGICAL IMPORTATION*

The problem of description is greatly complicated by the fact that the process of learning changes the learner's view of the language. The more he acquires of the new language the less necessary it is for him to interpret its habits in terms of the old language. So he gradually begins to import into his own language those habits of the other which he has mastered and which are not too incompatible with his previously established habits. Linguists have generally assumed that a scale for the time of borrowing can be set up on the basis of phonological form. Early loans are assumed to be the more distorted words, while the late are more similar to their models. Thus Trager in his list of Spanish loans in Taos distinguishes between the 'oldest,' the 'more recent,' and the 'most recent' largely on the basis of differences in loanword phonology.[15] In general the principle is sound, but we need to make certain reservations. First, there are some words that offer us no criteria, since they do not happen to contain the critical sounds. Second, the difference between the most and the least distorted depends not so much on time as on the degree of bilingualism. Bilingualism may come suddenly or slowly; it may persist over many generations, as among the PaG, and words may come in through various members of the community in several different forms. In AmN communities most loanwords may appear in various forms, with more or with less phonemic substitution; but some substitutions are so widespread that they can hardly have been borrowed recently. It is also possible for bilinguals to touch up the form of an older word and introduce a more 'correct' form if they happen to know it.

Since we cannot follow the fate of individual words and expressions from their earliest introduction, we can only guess at the factors that have influenced the form of any given word. We are entitled, however, to make certain assumptions. First, that A BILINGUAL SPEAKER INTRODUCES A NEW LOANWORD IN A PHONETIC FORM AS NEAR THAT OF THE MODEL LANGUAGE AS HE CAN. Secondly, that IF HE HAS OCCASION TO REPEAT IT, OR IF OTHER SPEAKERS ALSO TAKE TO USING IT, A FURTHER SUBSTITUTION OF NATIVE ELEMENTS WILL TAKE PLACE. Thirdly, that IF MONOLINGUALS LEARN IT, A TOTAL OR PRACTICALLY TOTAL SUBSTITUTION WILL BE MADE.

In the case of AmN we are dealing very largely with bilinguals, most of whom learned E in childhood, so that many words may vary from a wholly adapted form to one that is almost wholly unadapted. We shall here reckon with certain characteristic stages, while realizing that these are not always chronological:

[15] IJAL 10.145 (1944).

(1) A PRE-BILINGUAL period, in which the loans are made by a relatively small group of bilinguals and spread widely among the monolingual majority; the words show (almost) complete native substitution, with great irregularity in the phonetic results. Some phonemes and phoneme sequences will cause the speakers to vacillate, so that they choose now one, now another of their own as substitutes. In AmN the rhyming words *road* and *load* are reproduced with different N phonemes as /råd/ and /lod/. Such behavior may be called ERRATIC SUBSTITUTION, and is comparable to the scattering of shots over the target of a novice marksman.

(2) A period of ADULT BILINGUALISM, when growing knowledge of E leads to a more SYSTEMATIC SUBSTITUTION, in which the same N phoneme is consistently employed for new E loans. This may often be accompanied by the use of familiar sounds in new positions where they were not found in the native tongue. Thus the initial *v* in E *very*, *vicious*, and other words of French origin must once have seemed strange to Englishmen who were used to pronouncing it only between vowels. In modern Czech *g* is found initially only in loanwords; elsewhere it is only an allophone of *k*.[16] We shall call this process PHONEMIC REDISTRIBUTION, since it affects the distribution of the phonemes.

(3) A period of CHILDHOOD BILINGUALISM, in which the characteristic process is one of PHONEMIC IMPORTATION, i.e. completely new sound types are introduced. The Yaqui whose first-generation speakers had to substitute *p* for *f* in Spanish *estufa* 'stove,' saying [ehtúpa], are by now sufficiently bilingual to produce [fonografo] 'phonograph' without difficulty. AmN speakers acquired E *whip* as /ˈhyppa/ in the first generation, but as /ˈwippa/ in the second.

8. THE GRAMMAR OF LOANWORDS

If loanwords are to be incorporated into the utterances of a new language, they must be fitted into its grammatical structure. This means that they must be assigned by the borrower to the various grammatical classes which are distinguished by his own language. Insofar as these are different from those of the model language, an analysis and adjustment will be necessary here as in the case of phonology, and we observe the same predominance of substitution in the early phases, which later yields to a certain degree of importation. The broadest kind of form classes are those that are traditionally known as the 'parts of speech.' In the case of E and N there is no problem at this level, since their structures are closely parallel: E nouns are adopted as AmN nouns, and so forth. It is reported from Chiricahua, an Athabaskan language, that the Spanish adjectives *loco* 'crazy' and *rico*

---

[16] V. Mathesius, Englische Studien 70.23 (1935–6).

'rich' are borrowed as verbs.[17] But within the form classes (at least those that have inflections), there are problems for AmN also. N nouns belong to one of three classes known traditionally as masculine, feminine, and neuter, which differ from each other in inflection and syntactical environment. Since E has no corresponding division, an E noun must be assigned to one of these classes on the basis of analogies which are often difficult to discover both for the speakers and for the analyst. In most languages for which the phenomenon has been studied a clear tendency is seen to assign loanwords to one particular gender unless specific analogies intervene to draw them into other classes. This is even more marked in AmN verbs, where practically every loanword falls into the first class of weak verbs. Such grammatical categories as definiteness, possession, and plurality correspond with sufficient closeness so that little more is involved than a substitution of N forms for E. Again, this would not be true in languages less closely related; the Yaqui have given many loanwords a suffix *-um* with a singular sense though the suffix is plural in Yaqui.[18]

But even in the relation of E and N there are many cases of erroneous analysis, based on special situations, so that e.g. E *-s* (plural) may be borrowed with its stem and treated as if it were part of a singular noun. An example is *kars* 'car,' plural *karser;* similarly in AmItalian *pinozzi* 'peanuts.' But the next step, correlated to a bilingual stage of learning, is to import the plural suffix for E loanwords. This becomes such a common thing that the N suffixed article may be added to it, producing a hybrid inflection *-s-* + *-a* 'the,' e.g. *kisa* 'the keys.' Adjectives and adverbs may also receive N suffixes, but to a much lesser extent. Here the E influence has frequently led to an importation of zero suffixes, i.e. the abandonment of inflection. Aasta Stene has pointed out that this is promoted by the fact that N also has zero suffixes in some positions.[19] The verbs, on the other hand, have invariably a complete N inflection, with practically no substitution from E. This phenomenon has been noted for several languages, and is sufficiently striking to merit some consideration.[20] Miss Stene stresses the opportunity available to nouns and adjectives of appearing in positions where inflection can be avoided, which is not possible for verbs. While this is true, it should not be overlooked that the function of verb inflections is somewhat different from that of the rest. Tense is a necessary feature of every N (and E) sentence in a way that plurality is not; verbs have no inflectional form with the kind of generalized function that the noun singular has. The noun singular not only refers to individuals of the species, but also to the species itself, and in many cases this is quite sufficient

[17] Harry Hoijer, *Lg.* 15.110-5 (1939).
[18] Spicer, Am. Anthr. 45.410-26 (1943).
[19] English loan-words in Modern Norwegian 164 (London and Oslo, 1945).
[20] Stene 163 (her opinion that borrowed verbs are for this reason fewer than nouns seems insufficiently founded); Pap 106.

(e.g. *rabbit* as a loanword may refer either to a single rabbit or to rabbits in general). The adjective inflections are even more secondary, since they have no independent meaning but are dependent on the nouns which they modify. Thus the importation of the E lack of inflection is facilitated by the relative unimportance of the corresponding N inflections and we need not assume any deliberate 'avoidance of inflection,' at least by the unsophisticated speakers dealt with in this study.

9. LOANBLENDS

In reproducing the forms of another language speakers will frequently go farther in their adaptation than merely to substitute native sounds and inflections for the foreign ones. They may actually slip in part or all of a native morpheme for some part of the foreign, as in AmPort. *alvachus* 'overshoes,' *alvarozes* 'overalls,' where the native prefix *al-* has been substituted for the E *o-*.[21] Such substitutions are only discernible when the phonetic results differ from those that derive from phonological substitution. Thus E *-er* is reproduced as AmN /-ər/; only when it is not, can one be sure of a suffix substitution, as in /'kårrna/ 'corner' (by blending with N *hyrrna* 'corner'). The same would not be true in AmPort., where Eastern AmE *-er* [-ə] is normally reproduced as /-a/. Suffix substitution is obvious in such a word as /'bordo/ 'boarder,' since /-o/ is a regular agent suffix.[22] The /-a/ is actually ambiguous, since it not only reproduces E *-er*, but is added as a regular suffix to many words which in E end in consonants.[23] In cases like AmN /'kårrna/, where the suffix is itself meaningless, hardly more than a gender marker, we are dealing with a BLENDED STEM. Nearest to this is the BLENDED DERIVATIVE, in which native suffixes are substituted for the foreign. Thus in PaG *-ig* is often substituted for E *-y*, e.g. *bassig* 'bossy,' *fonnig* 'funny,' *tricksig* 'tricky.'[24] In AmN it is often hard to distinguish E from N suffixes, since many of them are phonologically equivalent; e.g. E *-y* [-i] is homophonous to N /-i/. BLENDED COMPOUNDS constitute the largest class of blends in AmN. Compounds may be borrowed about as freely as simple stems, since the two languages have parallel structures in compounding. But about half of the compounds show substitution of one or both parts. It is conspicuous that in practically every case the substitute closely resembles the foreign term in sound and has a meaning not too remote from it. An example from PaG is *bockabuch* 'pocketbook,' where *buch* was substituted for E *book*. The force of the compounding

---

[21] Pap 96.
[22] Pap 97.
[23] Pap 101.
[24] Paul Schach, Symposium 3.120 (1949).

pattern was such that even some phrases which were not compounds in E became so in AmN, e.g. *black walnut* > /'blakkval,not/. Only such terms as had direct E models have here been considered loanblends. Independent AmN formations involving E morphemes are here regarded as creations which fall outside the process of borrowing.

10. LOANSHIFTS

Some foreign loans appear in the language only as changes in the usage of native words. Such changes will here be classed as 'shifts,' which will be made to include all changes that are not strictly phonological and grammatical. Complete substitution of native morphemes has taken place. When this occurs in simple stems, two possibilities result according to the degree of similarity between the new and the old meanings of the word. If the new meaning has nothing in common with the old, it may be described as a LOAN HOMONYM. This is the situation when AmPort. has substituted its word *grosseria* 'a rude remark' for E *grocery;* the result is that the word *grosseria* has two homonymous meanings. In a dictionary they would presumably be listed as two distinct words. When there is a certain amount of semantic overlapping between the new and old meanings, one may speak of a LOAN SYNONYM, which only adds a new shade of meaning to the native morpheme. These can in turn be distinguished into SEMANTIC DISPLACE-MENTS, in which native terms are applied to novel cultural phenomena that are roughly similar to something in the old culture, and SEMANTIC CONFU-SIONS, in which native distinctions are obliterated through the influence of partial interlingual synonymity. It is a semantic displacement when AmPort. uses *pêso* 'weight' (from Span. *peso*) to mean 'dollar'; but it is a semantic confusion when they substitute the native *livraria* 'bookstore, home library' for E *library* instead of using the Port. *biblioteca.*[25] This process may be symbolized as follows: if language A has two words a_1 and a_2 which both overlap some meanings of word b in language B, pressure of B on A will often lead to confusion of a_1 and a_2; if a_1 resembles b phonetically, it may even displace a_2 entirely.

The lack of any satisfactory method of classifying degrees of semantic similarity means that it is not always possible to make the distinctions here suggested. Thus it would be possible to disagree on the classification of AmPort. *crismas* 'Christmas.' It is similar enough to the AmE model so that one might at first imagine it to be a loanword with phonemic substitution; only the fact that a word with exactly this phonemic form already exists in Port. requires us to class it as a loanshift. But is it a loan homonym

[25] Pap 79, 88.

or a loan synonym? Pap regards its native meaning, 'oil of sacrament,' as sufficiently similar to the new meaning to call it the latter ('semantic loan' in his terminology); but one might well feel that there is no common 'area of synonymity' between them, so that it should rather be called a loan homonym.[26] Compounds may also show complete native substitution, as when N *korn* 'grain' + *krubba* 'fodder-rack' are substituted for *corncrib* in the sense of a building for storing unshelled maize. These are the so-called LOAN TRANSLATIONS, which have played a great role in the development of many languages. Thus Gk. *sympátheia*, which was reproduced in E by importation, was reproduced by morpheme substitution in Lat. *compassiō*, G *Mitleid*, Dan. *Medlidenhed*, and Russ. *sobolĕžnovanie*.[27] Substitution may equally well extend to complete phrases, whose parts are reproduced as native words; we may call these SYNTACTIC SUBSTITUTIONS, and include such expressions as AmPort. *responder para tras* 'to talk back.' [28]

Loanshifts in general occur most readily when there is both phonetic and semantic resemblance between foreign and native terms. Terms that are interlingually similar will be called ANALOGUES; if the similarity is purely phonetic, they will be called HOMOPHONES, and if it is purely semantic, HOMOLOGUES. All three kinds can become starting-points for a morphemic substitution; in the case of AmN it is noteworthy how strong the force of pure homophony is. The similarity of E and N makes it easy to pour new wine into old bottles—for the old bottles are scarcely distinguishable from the new.

11. CREATION

Loanword lists are often made to include a number of terms whose existence may ultimately be due to contact with a second culture and its language, but which are not strictly loans at all. These did not come into being as direct imitations of a foreign model, but were secondarily created within the borrowing language. An example is the Yaqui term *liósnóoka* 'pray,' composed of the loanword *liós* 'God' (from Sp. *dios*) and the native *nóoka* 'speak.' [29] Such formations are sometimes confused with loanblends, since they resemble these in being 'hybrid.' But seen in the light of the borrowing process as here defined, they cannot have come into being as imitations of a foreign model, for there is no Spanish word of the shape *god-speak* meaning 'pray.' A parallel from AmN is *sjærbrukar* 'one who operates a farm for a share of the profits,' a technical term much used in

[26] Pap 87.
[27] Sandfeld-Jensen 69.
[28] Pap 89.
[29] Spicer, Am. Anthr. 45.410–26.

the tobacco-raising districts of Wisconsin. The first part is a loanword *sjær* (from AmE *share*), the second is a N *brukar* 'farmer, tenant.' The AmE *sharecropper* is not in use in these districts; a word *shareman* is sometimes heard in English. But neither of these can have suggested the AmN word; its origin must be sought in the N word *gardbrukar* 'farmer (lit. farm-user),' in which the loanword *sjær* was substituted for the native *gard*. This kind of REVERSE SUBSTITUTION, in which loan morphemes are filled into native models, is clearly different from the borrowings previously described and should be distinguished from them. PaG has an interesting series of terms of the type *Gekick* 'habitual kicking or objecting' (e.g. *Gekooks* 'coaxing,' *Gepeddel* 'peddling,' *Getschäbber* 'jabbering').[30] When classified without regard to the borrowing process, they appear as 'hybrids'; but their starting point is different from such loanblends as *blaumepai* 'plum pie' previously cited. These do not have a specific E model, for English has no words of this type, implying a habitual or even annoying activity. They appear to be secondary derivatives from the borrowed verbs (e.g. *kicken*), and are filled into the pattern of the native words of the type *Gejämmer* 'incessant moaning or lamenting.' The only criterion available for deciding whether a term belongs to this class of native creation is that no model exists in the other language. This may be difficult to ascertain without a rather complete knowledge of the language in question. A doubtful case is raised in the AmIt. word *sciainatore* 'boot-black,' apparently formed by substituting the loanword *sciainare* 'shine (shoes)' in a native pattern of the type represented by *trovatore* 'troubadour.' But if, as the Italian scholar A. Menarini supposes, there is an AmE word *shiner* meaning 'boot-black,' it could be a loanblend, in which the native *-tore* was simply substituted for AmE *-er*.[31] This writer has never heard or seen such a word (except in the sense of a black eye), the usual word being *boot-black*, but he recognizes that it does exist in the compound *shoe-shiner* (also and more commonly *shoe-shine*).

Since the type of creation here discussed needs a name to distinguish it from the kind of creation that consists entirely of native material, we might dub it HYBRID CREATION, thus emphasizing its bilingual nature. But it must be recognized that it is not a part of the borrowing process; rather does it give evidence of an intimate fusion into the language of the borrowed material, since it has become productive in the new language. The number of hybrid creations seems to vary markedly according to circumstances. PaG appears to have great numbers of them, involving such highly productive suffixes as *-erei*, *-es*, *-sel*, *-keet*, *-meesig*, *-voll*, *-weis* and the verbal

---

[30] Schach, Symposium 3.115.
[31] A. Menarini, Ai margini della lingua 145-208 (Firenze, 1947); reviewed by Robert A. Hall Jr. in Lg. 24.239-41 (1948).

prefix *var-*.[32] AmN, on the other hand, has relatively few, which may be due to the comparative lack of productive affixes in Norwegian, but also to the briefer period of residence in America. Most hybrid creations are of the type in which loan morphemes have been substituted in the nucleus, while the marginal parts (the affixes) are native. The opposite kind, showing marginal substitution (exemplified by E *talkative*), is not found at all in the AmN materials.

Occasionally one finds reference in loanword studies to a completely native kind of creation, when this has occurred in response to stimuli from another culture. Examples from the Pima Indians have been presented by George Herzog of such newly created descriptive terms as 'having downward tassels' (oats), 'wrinkled buttocks' (elephants), 'dry grapes' (raisins), 'lightning box' (battery), etc.[33] A solitary example from AmN is the word *kubberulla* 'oxcart,' from N *kubbe* 'chunk of wood' and *rulla* 'cart' (the wheels were made of slabs of wood).

12. *CROSS-CURRENTS OF BORROWING*

We may assume that unless a number of individuals borrow a word, it is not likely to attain great currency. If they learn it from the same source, and speak the same dialect and have the same degree of bilingualism, the effect will merely be one of reinforcement of the original form. But the situation is rarely, if ever, as simple as this. The speaker of AmPort. in New Bedford, Mass., is not exposed to the same English as the speaker of the same language in California. More important within any one community is the fact that in a bilingual group the same word is liable to variations in reproduction because of the varying degree of bilingualism. The loan is subject to continual interference from the model in the other language, a process which will here be called REBORROWING. It is a commonplace among immigrant groups in America that younger and older speakers will use different forms of the same loanwords. The difference usually consists in the extent of phonological and morphological importation. Some examples from AmN are the following:

Model:	whip	tavern	surveyor	Trempealeau	crackers	mocassin	lake
Older:	hyppa	tavan	saver	tromlo	krækkis	maggis	lek
Younger:	wippa	tævərn	sørveiər	trempəlo	krækərs	magəsin	leik

The forms acquired will also be differently reproduced when speakers of different dialects attempt them. This follows from our previous definition of

[32] Schach, Symposium 3.115.
[33] Language, culture, and personality (Essays in memory of Edward Sapir) 66–74 (Menasha, Wis., 1941).

borrowing; but the situation becomes almost hopelessly confused when speakers of different dialects live together in the same community, as is the case among immigrants, and the form is passed from speaker to speaker, many of whom may be monolingual at the beginning. It has been possible in the case of AmN dialects to isolate a few instances that seem reasonably certain evidence for the transmission of loanwords within the dialects. At least it is simpler to account for them as INTERDIALECTAL loans than as directly derived from E models. They are listed in the following tabulation:

	Original Borrowing	Interdialectally Transmitted Form
English Model		
(1) E [dl] > WN [dl] > EN [ll]		
cradle (grain harvester)	krıdl	krill
middling (coarse flour)	mıddlıng	milling
peddler	peddlar	pellar (1 inf.)
(2) E [eɪ] > EN [ei] > WN [ai]		
lake	leik	laik
pail	peil	pail
jail	jeil	jail
frame	freim	fraim
(3) E [ɔʊ] > EN [å] > WN [ao]		
hoe	hå	hao
(4) E [aʊ] > EN [æu] > Solør [əy] > Røros [ö]		
flour	flæur	fləyr, flör
(5) E [ɔ] > EN [å] > Gbr. [öu]		
log	lågg	löugg

In each of these cases the variations within the loanword forms correspond to different reflexes from the same Old Norw. originals, found in a considerable number of native words also. But other loanwords with the same E phonemes have different forms, e.g. *mail* has not become [mail] in the dialects referred to above, but [meil].

A further source of interference with the process of borrowing is the influence of SPELLING. Spelling pronunciations may be suspected wherever the reproduction varies from normal in the direction of a pronunciation traditionally given to a letter in the borrowing language. In any literate community such influence is likely to be present in a number of words which have been brought to the community in writing. Among immigrants this is not true to any considerable extent, but at least in AmN there is a marked tendency to pronounce AmE [æ] as /a/ and [a] as /å/, spelled respectively *a* and *o*.

	bran	*alfalfa*	*saloon*	*tavern*	*lot*	*gallon*	*battery*
Eng. model	[bræn]	[æl'fælfə]	[sə'lun]	['tævərn]	[lat]	['gælən]	['bæt(ə)ri]
Oral reprod.	*bræn	*æl'fælfa	*sa'lun	'tævərn	latt	*gælən	'bætri

Spelling pron. brann ''alfalfa ''salon ''tavan lått ''gallan ''battəri
                                                              ''gallon

Such words as *lot* probably come from official documents, *bran* and *alfalfa* from sacks, *saloon* and *tavern* from signs, *gallon* and *battery* from advertisements. The striking part of it is that the spelling pronunciation does not usually affect the entire word, where a choice is possible, so that e.g. *gallon* may have an /a/ in the second syllable, corresponding to the [ə] of the original. A comparison with the E loanwords adopted in N, as reported by Aasta Stene, shows a much higher proportion of spelling pronunciations in the latter, e.g. *buss* 'bus' for AmN *båss*, *kutte* 'cut' for AmN *katta*, *hikkori* 'hickory' for AmN *hekkri* (or even *hikkrill*). As one AmN informant commented, when asked for the word for 'battery': 'They just give Norwegian sounds to the English letters.'

13. STRUCTURAL RESISTANCE TO BORROWING

It has long been known that some kinds of linguistic patterns are more likely to be borrowed than others. As long ago as 1881 William Dwight Whitney set up a scale in which he ranged the various patterns according to the freedom with which they are borrowed.[34] Nouns are most easily borrowed, then the various other parts of speech, then suffixes, then inflections, then sounds. He did not deny the possibility of borrowing even members of the last two classes, but contended that they are unusual and generally secondary to the borrowing of vocabulary items. 'The exemption of "grammar" from mixture is no isolated fact; the grammatical apparatus merely resists intrusion most successfully, in virtue of its being the least material and the most formal part of language. In a scale of constantly increasing difficulty it occupies the extreme place.'[35] Emphasis should be laid on Whitney's explanation, viz. that 'whatever is more formal or structural in character remains in that degree free from the intrusion of foreign material.' The same view is expressed by Lucien Tesnière in 1939, apparently without awareness of Whitney's earlier formulation: 'La miscibilité d'une langue est fonction inverse de sa systematisation.'[36]

Whatever the explanation, the facts are abundantly supported by the available lists of loanwords, e.g. for AmN and American Swedish. The following figures show the percentage of each of the traditional parts of

3
4

[3] W. D. Whitney, On mixture in language, TAPA 12.5–26 (1881).
[5] Whitney's statement in Language and the study of language 199 (New York, 1867) to the effect that 'a mixed grammatical apparatus' is a 'monstrosity' and an 'impossibility' has often been quoted, while his later, more considered statement has been overlooked, e.g. by Otto Jespersen in Language 213 (New York, 1922) and by Alf Sommerfelt, Un cas de mélange de grammaires 5 (Oslo, 1926).
[36] TCLP 8.85 (1939).

speech in the total number of loanwords listed:

	Nouns	Verbs	Adj's	Adv.- Prep.	Interj.
AmN (author's word list)	75.5	18.4	3.4	1.2	1.4
AmN (Flom, Koshkonong Sogning)	71.7	23.0	4.2	0.8	0.5
AmSw. (Johnson, Chisago Lake Småland)	72.2	23.2	3.3	0.4	0.8

It is conspicuous that articles and pronouns do not appear in the lists, though again it would be foolish to deny that they can be borrowed (e.g. English *they* from Scandinavian). All linguistic features can be borrowed, but they are distributed along a SCALE OF ADOPTABILITY which somehow is correlated to the structural organization. This is most easily understood in the light of the distinction made earlier between importation and substitution. Importation is a process affecting the individual item needed at a given moment; its effects are partly neutralized by the opposing force of entrenched habits, which substitute themselves for whatever can be replaced in the imported item. Structural features are correspondences which are frequently repeated. Furthermore, they are established in early childhood, whereas the items of vocabulary are gradually added to in later years. This is a matter of the fundamental patterning of language: the more habitual and subconscious a feature of language is, the harder it will be to change.

This discussion raises the further question whether there is a corresponding difference between languages with respect to borrowing. It would seem that if internal differences exist within a language, similar differences might exist between languages, insofar as these are structurally different. This has frequently been asserted, on the basis of the greater homogeneity of vocabulary in some languages than in others. Typical is the treatment by Otakar Vočadlo, who set up what might be called a SCALE OF RECEPTIVITY among languages, dividing them into the major groups of homogeneous, amalgamate, and heterogeneous.[37] Unfortunately Vočadlo excludes in his definition of 'receptivity' the words borrowed from other languages of the same stock, so that he regards e.g. Danish as a 'homogeneous' language. He is also more concerned with practical problems of linguistic purification, so that the basic question of whether structural or social forces are more important does not emerge too clearly. Kiparsky, in commenting on Vočadlo's paper, declared flatly, 'die Fähigkeit der sog. "homogenen" Sprachen, Entlehnungen aufzunehmen, hängt *nicht* von der linguistischen Struktur der Sprache, sondern von der politisch-sozialen Einstellung der Sprecher ab.'[38]

[37] Otakar Vočadlo, Some observations on mixed languages, Actes du IVe congrès internationale de linguistes 169-76 (Copenhagen, 1938).

[38] Op. cit. 176. "The capacity of a so-called 'homogeneous' language to admit borrowings depends not on the linguistic structure of the language but rather on the political and social attitudes of its speakers."

Perhaps one of the most hopeful fields for finding an answer to this question is the situation in the United States. Here a relatively uniform language and culture has exerted a similar pressure on a large number of different languages; much could be learned by comparing the borrowings of immigrant languages of different structures, and by then comparing these with the borrowings of Indian languages, whose structures are even more different than the immigrant languages among themselves. Most of the differences brought out by Vočadlo are not differences in actual borrowing, but in the relationship between importation and substitution, as here defined. Some languages import the whole morpheme, others substitute their own morphemes; but all borrow if there is any social reason for doing so, such as the existence of a group of bilinguals with linguistic prestige.

14. STRUCTURAL EFFECTS OF BORROWING

Closely related to the preceding is the problem of what borrowing does to a language. The classic instance of English (with which may also be compared Danish) leads one to believe that borrowing is at least a contributory cause of structural reorientation (we avoid as scientifically questionable the term 'simplification'). But if it is true, as pointed out earlier, that the more structural a feature is, the less likely it is to be borrowed, it will be evident that a corollary is that the effects of borrowing on structure are likely to be small. The instances of new inflections actually introduced into wide use in the language are few, cf. the uncertain fate of classical plurals in E words like *phenomena*, *indices*, etc. In the lexicon the foreign patterns may actually predominate over the native, but the structural elements tend to persist. The chief danger represented by loanwords is the instability of classification which they bring in. They have been shown to vacillate to a statistically higher degree than native words, since they often fail to show criteria that make it possible to classify them immediately in one or another category of gender, number, or the like.[39] The fact that they tend to fall into only one class where there is a choice of several, will strengthen that class at the expense of others. They will often introduce affixes or other bound morphemes that stand in a different relation to their stems from that of affixes in native words. While some of these will not be discovered by the borrowing speakers, others will, and may even, as we have seen, become productive.

In phonology the effects may consist exclusively of the filling up of gaps in the native utilization of possible phoneme sequences. Thus when AmN acquires E *street* in the form /strit/, no new phoneme sequence is added:

[39] Cf. Stene 5.

words like *stri* 'stubborn' and *krit* 'chalk' exhibit the same types. But sooner or later loanwords introduce sequences not previously utilized, as when AmFinnish adopted the word *skeptikko* 'sceptic,' which then became the only word with *s* before a stop; words like *stove* were reproduced as *touvi*.[40] This type of change has here been called PHONEMIC REDISTRIBUTION, since it will require a different statement concerning the distribution of phonemes and their allophones. There is also the possibility of PHONEMIC IMPORTATION, though the usual rule is that this does not extend beyond bilingual speakers. In English the last sound of *rouge* is limited to words of French origin, but its importation is hardly thinkable if English had not already had it as a 'bound' phoneme occurring after *d* in words like *edge*.

Very little thoroughgoing study has been given so far to the structural effects of borrowing on the phonemic systems, so that we are still uncertain just how to evaluate contentions like those of Pike and Fries concerning the existence of 'conflicting coexistent systems.' [41] Pike's studies of Mazateco have shown that in this language [d] occurs only after nasals and may there be regarded as an allophone of *t*. But the Spanish loanword *siento* 'hundred' is one of a small number of loans in which [t] occurs after nasals, thus setting up a constrast of *t* and *d* not found elsewhere in the language. Yet, as Pike has shown, it contradicts the 'sprachgefühl' of the natives to recognize [d] after nasals as a separate phoneme for this reason. It seems probable, however, that this is a temporary and marginal situation in the language; for according to his own evidence, monolingual speakers tend to nasalize the preceding vowel and drop the *n*, thus restoring the more common native situation. Meanwhile, it is hardly more than a phonemic redistribution which permits voiceless *t* to occur in a position that is otherwise not known in the language, parallel in effect to that which occurred in English when medial *v* was introduced in initial position by the entry of French loanwords. As pointed out by Paul Garvin in commenting on a similar situation in Zoque, no new features of articulation are introduced; but it may happen that they are combined in a new way.[42]

15. THE IDENTIFICATION OF LOANS

So far the identification of loans has been taken for granted, but it must not be inferred from the confidence with which such lists are put forward that it is always possible to isolate loan material in each given case. The

---

[40] J. I. Kolehmainen, Am. Soc. Rev. 2.62–6 (1907).

[41] Fries and Pike, Lg. 25.29–50 (1949).

[42] Paul Garvin, Distinctive features in Zoque phonemic acculturation, SIL 5.13–20 (1947); cf. William Wonderly, IJAL 12.92–5 (1947).

difficulty, as elsewhere, is that the historical and the synchronic problem have not been clearly distinguished by those who have written about it. Non-scientific writers or speakers show an interesting tendency: if they are monolinguals, they are quite unaware of loans; if they are polylinguals, they suspect them everywhere.

(1) The Historical Problem

As here defined, borrowing is a historical process and therefore to be identified only by historical methods. This means a comparison between earlier and later states of a given language, to detect possible innovations; and thereupon a comparison of the innovations discovered with possible models in other languages. This double comparison is a corollary of our definition of borrowing; its application requires a knowledge of earlier states of the language, as well as of whatever languages may conceivably have exerted the influences in question. As applied specifically to immigrant speech in America, this means a comparison of present-day speech with the speech brought to these shores, and then a comparison of the innovations with AmE as spoken within the areas inhabited by the immigrants. The complete success of this venture depends on a number of factors which will be obvious to the reader, such as the existence of studies of the language in its homeland describing it at the time of immigration. Certain more special problems which the writer has encountered in treating AmN may be less obvious.

(a) **Pre-immigration Loans.** Some E loanwords penetrated into N speech, even the more remote rural dialects, before immigration. Trade, shipping, and the tourist traffic had led to contacts with the English-speaking world even in those classes that lacked the educational opportunities of acquiring the English language. Some immigrants may even have picked up their first E loanwords from N sailors on board the immigrant ships, not to mention the fact that there were many sailors among the immigrants themselves.[43] An example of a preimmigration loan is the word *træn* 'train,' apparently introduced by the English builders of Norway's first railroad in 1855. In cultivated N usage it was soon replaced by *tog* (a loanshift modeled on G *Zug*), but it is still widely known among dialect speakers.[44] A further com-

---

[43] Unfortunately no study has been made of E words in the N dialects, parallel to Aasta Stene's for the standard language; anyone who has heard Norwegian sailors speak is aware that they have borrowed heavily from English. Cf. Ivar Alnæs, Bidrag til en ordsamling over sjømandssproget (Christiania, 1902); R. Iversen, Lånord og lønnord hos folk og fant (Trondheim, 1939); A. Larsen and G. Stoltz, Bergens bymål (Christiania, 1912).

[44] Evidence on this point was gathered for the writer from the N dialect archives in Oslo by Magne Oftedal and in Bergen by Olai Skulerud. The related term *rells* 'rails,' on the other hand, does not seem to have been known in Norway, though it took root in Sweden; cf. G. Langenfeldt, Språk och Stil 15.88–110 (1915).

plication is introduced by the fact that returning immigrants brought English words back to the homeland.[45]

(b) **International Words.** A special category of words is made up of those that are sufficiently common to most west European languages to have a similar spelling and meaning, in spite of widely differing pronunciations. Cultivated people in Norway certainly knew such words as *cigar, district, section* at the time of emigration, so that it becomes uncertain whether they should be regarded as loans even in the rural dialects when they turn up in forms not markedly different from that of the spelling. It is not always possible to say whether given words were current in the dialects; and the spelling pronunciations which they have in AmN might as well have arisen in America as in Norway. This was certainly true of *alfalfa* and *timothy*, which must have been learned in this country since they were the names of American products first met with over here. On the other hand, such words as *music, museum*, and *university* reveal by a highly Americanized pronunciation that the words were not in common use among the immigrants in their Norwegian forms at the time of immigration; yet they can hardly have failed to have heard them in Norway.

(c) **Interlingual Coincidences.** Where semantic-phonetic similarities exist between two words in different languages, it may be quite impossible to be certain whether borrowing has taken place. Such similarities are of unquestionable importance in causing confusion between two languages spoken by bilinguals. Typical AmN wordshifts are the substitutions of the N *korn* 'grain' for E *corn* 'maize,' *grøn* 'food prepared from grain' for E *grain* 'grain other than maize,' *brusk* 'tuft of straw' for E *brush* 'thicket.' In each of these cases the fact that we are dealing with the N word in question is confirmed by the variation in phonetic form from dialect to dialect, even though the limited distribution might speak against it in some cases. But when E *crew* is reproduced as N *kru*, we have very little to help us decide whether this is a loanword or a loanshift. The N form is identical with a dialect word *kru* 'crowd, household, multitude.' The AmN word has been identified with this by an AmN writer, Jon Norstog, who asserted that *kru* was not an English word at all, but a Telemark word which he had known from his childhood. The claim must be disallowed, however; for the N word is highly limited in its occurrence and is always neuter in gender, while the AmN word is widespread in all dialects, is mostly feminine, and has nowhere been recorded over here in its N meaning. Similarly with the AmN *travla* 'walk,' a widely used word. There is a N dialect term *travla* 'struggle, labor,

---

[45] The words *river, ticket, coat, surveyor, courthouse*, and *table knife* are reported from Tinn, Norway, as characteristic of returned emigrants by Skulerud, Telemaalet 73 (Christiania, 1918) and Tinnsmaalet (Halle a. S., 1922); cf. similar reports from Sweden and Swedish Finland in Folkmålsstudier 2.137–40 (1934) and Svenskbygden 1932.3–5.

slave,' found only in remote sections of the country; nowhere does it have the meaning of the AmN word. Yet since its meaning is not identical with that of AmE *travel*, one might be in doubt whether it is a loan at all, were it not for the existence of an English dialect meaning of *travel* 'to walk' (very widespread according to Wright's EDD). Even though this is not at present recorded from Wisconsin, it seems most probable that it was used there and acquired by the N settlers in that state. The E word *cold* with the double meaning of 'a cold spell' and 'an infection' has influenced the meaning of the corresponding N words, which usually meant only 'a cold spell'; yet we find that in some N dialects the N word already had the double meaning.[46] In such cases it has been necessary to weigh the probabilities in the light of our knowledge of the state of the dialects at the time of immigration.

(2) The Synchronic Problem

It appears to be taken for granted, even by some linguists, that a borrowed word somehow occupies a special status within a language. The acute consciousness of the loanword as a 'problem' in certain modern cultures has led to some confusion in the question of what the loanword is and how it is to be regarded in a description of a language at a given time. The rise of synchronic linguistic studies (also called 'descriptive') has led to a renewed consideration of the question whether loanwords can be identified without the kind of double comparison described in the preceding section. Can loanwords be identified by a student who knows nothing of the previous stages of a language?[47] Such a technique, if there is one, would seem to be most useful in dealing with previously unwritten languages; indeed it would be the only one available.

The analyses made so far, however, have applied to languages where the historical facts were at least partially known, and the lists of loanwords to be analyzed have first been determined by historical means. This is true even of Miss Stene's list of E loanwords in modern Norwegian, though she has included in her final list only those words that could be identified by some synchronic criterion as 'not in complete agreement with the linguistic system of Norwegian.' These represent, she believes, the words that 'are felt by the language-conscious speaker to be "foreign." ' [48] She sets up a series of formal characteristics 'by which they reveal the fact that they are aliens in the system.' These are: non-Norwegian orthography,

---

[46] Cf. Aasen NO² s.v. *kjøld* 'Sogn og fler,' but not under *kulde* and the other words.
[47] Cf. V. Mathesius, Zur synchronischen analyse fremden sprachguts, Englische Studien 70 .21–35 (1935–6); B. Trnka, Phonological analysis of present-day standard English 49–53 (Prague, 1935); Stene, op. cit.
[48] Stene 5.

pronunciation, correspondence between spelling and pronunciation, musical accent, dynamic accent, morphology, word-formation, and meaning. Unfortunately no one of these is absolutely decisive (except perhaps the foreign spelling, which is not strictly a linguistic matter), since many of them occur also in words of native origin; and some are so common that it seems very doubtful if they are felt as 'foreign' by anyone except the professional linguist.[49] Furthermore, the criteria fail to include some quite obvious loans, such as *drible* 'dribble,' *start* 'start,' and *streik* 'strike': these have in every respect been assimilated to a common pattern.

Now it would be impossible to deny that, as we have shown in a preceding section, many loanwords have introduced features of arrangement which are numerically less common than certain other features and which sometimes stand in other relationships to the rest of the language than the previously existent patterns. But to identify the results of a historical process like borrowing is simply not possible by a purely synchronic study. What we find when we study a structure without reference to its history is not borrowing or loans, but something that might rather be described as 'structural irregularity.' This is not an absolute thing: word counts have shown that patterns vary in frequency from the extremely common to the extremely rare, with no absolute boundary between the two. Patterns of high frequency are certain not to sound 'queer' to native speakers; just how infrequent must a pattern be before it begins to 'feel foreign'? Very few studies have so far been made in which structural analysis is combined with frequency determinations.[50] Until a language is thus analyzed, any statement about the 'aberrations' of loanwords must remain open to question. Even so it is evident that no synchronic analysis can discover such loanwords as *priest*, *due*, *law*, or *skirt* in English. If other words contain sequences that are less common and are found by synchronic analysis to have a different status, they will not thereby be revealed as loanwords, but as something else to which a different name should be given. If confusion is not to be further confounded, the term 'borrowing' and its kinsmen should be limited to the uses of historical linguistics.

This is apparently the conclusion also of Pike and Fries when they state that 'in a purely descriptive analysis of the dialect of a monolingual speaker there are no loans discoverable or describable.'[51] The Germans here make a distinction between the Lehnwort, a historical fact, and the Fremdwort,

---

[49] Cf. the writer's review, Lg. 25.63–8 (1949).
[50] Cf. W. F. Twaddell, A phonological analysis of intervocalic consonant clusters in German, Actes du IVe congrès internationale de linguistes 218–25 (Copenhagen, 1938); Hans Vogt, Structure of Norwegian monosyllables, NTS 12.5–29 (1940).
[51] Lg. 25.31 (1949).

a contemporary fact.[52] But it does not appear just how the line is to be drawn. None of the languages of modern civilization are so simple in their structure that a single set of categories will exhaustively describe them. Along with their high-frequency habits they exhibit a great number of 'marginal' habits which come into play in given circumstances, perhaps only in given words. Current phonemic theory seems to assume that the only description of distribution that is relevant in phonology is the phonetic environment. But it seems impossible to get away from the fact that individual words and word groups may have habits of their own, which can only be described in terms of lexical distribution. This does not surprise anyone when speaking of morphological characteristics: thus the first person singular of the verb occurs only in one word in English, viz. *am*. The problem in phonology is not different in kind, only in extent. Rather than to regard such complications as 'coexistent systems,' it will probably be best to treat them as systemic fragments occurring under given circumstances—items of LIMITED LEXICAL DISTRIBUTION.

Summary. An attempt has been made in this article to establish a precise definition for the term 'borrowing' by describing it as the process that takes place when bilinguals reproduce a pattern from one language in another. Two kinds of activity which enter into borrowing are distinguished, viz. substitution and importation, which are defined in terms of a comparison between the model and the reproduction. By distinguishing morphemic and phonemic substitution it becomes possible to set up classes of loans: (1) loanwords, without morphemic substitution; (2) loanblends, with partial morphemic substitution; and (3) loanshifts, with complete morphemic substitution. The second of these includes what are more commonly known as 'hybrids,' the third the 'loan translations' and 'semantic loans.' Various periods of bilingualism are described, involving erratic and systematic substitution, or importation of phonemes. Loanblends are classified into blended stems, derivatives, and compounds, while loanshifts are divided into loan homonyms and loan synonyms. The process of hybrid creation is so defined as to distinguish it from borrowing, being a reverse substitution, in which the model is to be found in the borrowing language. Among the cross-currents of borrowing, which sometimes confuse the picture, are the procedures called reborrowing, interdialectal loans, and the influence of spelling. The question of structural resistance to borrowing is discussed, and a scale of adoptability is set up, which is shown to have a correlation to the structural organization of the borrowing language. It is shown that the

---

[52] Cf. Eugen Kaufman, Der Fragenkreis ums Fremdwort, JEGP 38.42–63 (1939). Kaufman wishes to eliminate Fremdwörter from German, but not Lehnwörter.

scale of receptivity assumed by some writers is really a difference in the relationship between importation and substitution. The structural effect of borrowing is found to be largely a certain instability in the categories; in phonology it may produce extensive phonemic redistribution, but little phonemic importation. The question of identification of loans is shown to be primarily a historical question, not susceptible to the methods of synchronic analysis. So far as loans are discovered by the latter method, it is not as loans, but as residual structural irregularities, which might rather be called 'systemic fragments' than 'coexistent systems.' The historical problem is difficult enough, fraught as it is with the problems of distinguishing loans made before immigration, international words, and interlingual coincidences from bona-fide loans made during the period of inter-language contact. But the synchronic problem is insoluble without complete analyses of structure which also take into account the relative frequencies of the elements analyzed.

Study Questions

1. What factors favor the borrowing of words from one language into another? Why did speakers of Norwegian in the United States borrow more actively from English than speakers of English did from Norwegian? Are speakers of the majority language, when they do borrow, likely to borrow the same kinds of words as speakers of the minority language do? How important is "structural resistance to borrowing" as a factor influencing the borrowing process? Can you think of any reason why nouns might be the most frequently borrowed words, as Haugen's evidence suggests?

2. Define the following terms: *importation, substitution, phonemic substitution, morphemic substitution.* How does Haugen use the latter two terms as a basis for a division of types of loans? What does Haugen's choice of the terms *importation* and *substitution* imply about his conception of the borrowing process? For example, does he conceive of the process as essentially imitative or as essentially creative in Chomsky's sense of the term? Does his choice of terms follow logically from his statement: "We shall assume it as axiomatic that every speaker attempts to reproduce previously learned linguistic patterns in an effort

to cope with new linguistic situations"? How might a transformation-alist criticize that axiom?

3. If a monolingual or partially bilingual speaker borrows a word, how might it differ in form from the same word borrowed by an accomplished bilingual? Which of the two speakers would be more likely to interpret the foreign word according to the rules for his native language? Is a form like [ʃi 'peiro] bad imitation or a creation based on the rules for Portuguese? Why does Haugen consider hybrid creation, productive of words like AmN *sjærbrukar*, not part of the borrowing process? Is such a term any more a "creation" than [ʃi 'peiro]? Is it a different kind of creation?

4. What does Haugen mean by the *habits* of a language? Does he use the term *habit* in ways similar to Bloomfield's use? Does he share Bloomfield's uneasiness with talking about linguistic events as mental? How important is the analysis of meaning to his classification of types of loans? Is his discussion limited in any way by a lack of such analysis?

5. Why does Haugen reject the term *mixture* for the process of linguistic borrowing? Why does linguistic borrowing not result in a language which can meaningfully be called mixed or hybrid? How would you argue against classifying English as a Romance language on the basis of its large numbers of French and Latin loans? Why does Haugen feel that in general "the effects of borrowing on structure are likely to be small"? Would all the linguists represented in Part One of this anthology accept his contrast of *lexicon* and *structural elements*? If "foreign patterns" find a place in the lexicon, are they unlikely to have effects on the other parts of the system?

6. On the basis of the evidence presented by Haugen, is it likely that learned borrowings and the borrowings of everyday words will have separate histories in the borrowing language? Are words borrowed from written sources likely to differ in any important ways from words borrowed from oral sources?

7. Concerning the identification of loans, Haugen speaks of a historical problem and a synchronic problem. How do these differ? Why does Haugen feel that borrowing can be identified only by historical methods? What historical problems might you encounter in trying to identify: 1) Latin loan words of the Old English period; 2) Scandinavian loan words of the Middle English period?

Stephen Ullmann

CHANGE OF MEANING

Stephen Ullmann (b. 1914) received his Ph.D. from the University of Budapest in 1936 but soon had to interrupt his academic career to flee Nazi tyranny. After working with the British Broadcasting Corporation during the war, Ullmann taught at the University of Glasgow from 1946 to 1953 and then became professor of Romance philology at the University of Leeds. His principal interests are best indicated by the titles of his books: *The Principles of Semantics* (1951); *Semantics: An Introduction to the Science of Meaning* (1962), from which the following chapter is taken; *Language and Style* (1963); *Style in the French Novel* (1957); and *The Image in the Modern French Novel* (1960).

Like many of his colleagues at Glasgow and at Leeds, particularly the late John Orr, Ullmann rejects many of the tenets of the approach to language typified in this book by Lehmann and Bloomfield. Although in *Semantics* he praises the accomplishments of Bloomfield and particularly of the Swiss structuralist de Saussure, he insists that language cannot be studied without a central concern with meaning, and that "language ought to be viewed against the background of a general theory of signs." For Ullmann, the study of language is a study of mental reality, and he feels that any approach which ignores the relationship of language to thought or refuses to go beyond external forms to a consideration of the mental processes of the speaker is doomed to superficiality.

In the following selection, Ullmann provides a broad survey of types of semantic change and their causes, drawing those types mainly from what might be termed "classic" studies of semantic change by scholars like Bréal and Stern. In his insistence on the multiplicity of the causes and mechanisms of change of meaning, and in his careful detailing of the histories of individual words, he shows his affinity for the tradition of the great Romance philologists Hugo Schuchardt and Jules Gilliéron. Although Ullmann sees the need for the clarification and unity that a general theory of semantics and of semantic change might provide for particular studies of changes in meaning in English, French, German, he also insists that such a theory be founded on sufficient empirical grounds and that it recognize that change of meaning is intimately tied to social and cultural change.

To conserve space, Ullmann's very full bibliographical notes have been severely curtailed.

Over forty years ago, Edward Sapir introduced a valuable new concept into linguistics. 'Language,' he wrote, 'moves down time in a current of its own making. It has a *drift*. . . . Nothing is perfectly static. Every word, every grammatical element, every locution, every sound and accent is a slowly changing configuration, moulded by the invisible and impersonal *drift* that is the life of language.' This Heraclitean conception of a perpetual and all-pervasive drift in language is of particular interest to the student of semantics. Of all linguistic elements caught up in this drift, meaning is probably the least resistant to change. This is due to the interplay of several forces some of which were identified by Antoine Meillet at the turn of the century, whereas others have been noticed only in recent years. Among the factors which facilitate semantic changes, the following seem to be of decisive importance:

(1) Language is handed down, as Meillet put it, in a *'discontinuous'* way from one generation to another: every child has to learn it afresh. It is common knowledge that children will often misunderstand the meaning of words. In most cases, such misconceptions will be corrected before they can go very far; but if, for some reason or another, this does not happen, a semantic change will take place in the usage of the new generation. Most linguists would probably agree that this is a factor of some importance; yet, by the very nature of things, it is difficult to prove that any particular change could have arisen only in child language. Meillet gives a plausible, but not entirely convincing example: the history of the French adjective *saoul* or *soûl*. This comes from the popular Latin *satullus* 'filled with food, satiated,' and preserved this meaning until the seventeenth century; the original sense still survives in locutions like *manger tout son soûl* 'to eat one's fill.' Since the sixteenth century, however, the adjective acquired the new meaning of 'drunk, tipsy,' which is its main sense today. Meillet argues that this shift is due to a misunderstanding which must have originated in the minds of children: adults would ironically refer to a drunk person as being 'replete,' and the child, missing these delicate undertones, would apply the word to the crude fact itself. This may well have been the case, but it is obviously impossible to prove it. The same may be said of other changes which have been attributed to this agency, such as the passage of the word *bead* from the sense of 'prayer' to that of 'small perforated ball':

The phrase *to count your beads* originally meant 'to count your prayers,' but because the prayers were reckoned by little balls, the word *beads* came to be transferred to these objects, and lost its original sense. It seems clear that this misapprehension could not take place in the brains of those who had already associated the word with the original signification, while it was quite natural on the part of children who heard and understood the phrase as a whole, but unconsciously analysed it differently from the previous generation (Jespersen, *Language*, p. 175).

(2) *Vagueness* in meaning is another source of semantic changes. The various forms of vagueness . . .—the generic nature of our words, the multiplicity of their aspects, lack of familiarity, absence of clear-cut boundaries—all conspire to facilitate shifts in usage. In this respect, there is a fundamental difference between the meaning of words and their phonetic shape, morphological structure or syntactical use, which are far more strictly defined and delimited and therefore less liable to change.

(3) A further factor which may lead to changes in meaning is *loss of motivation*.[1] As long as a word remains firmly attached to its root and to other members of the same family, this will keep its meaning within certain limits. Once these links are severed, . . . the sense may develop untrammelled and may move far away from its origins. In Old English, the words *lord* and *lady* were transparent compounds based on the noun *hlāf* 'loaf': *lord* had the form *hlāford* or *hlāfweard*, 'loaf-ward,' and *lady* the form *hlǣfdīge*, from *hlāf* + the root *dīg-* 'to knead,' connected with *dough*. When the connexion with *loaf* was obscured by phonetic development, the two words could evolve unhampered by etymological associations.

To these general factors identified by Meillet, at least another three may be added which are all conducive to mobility of meaning:

(4) The existence of *polysemy* introduces, as we have seen, an element of flexibility into language. There is nothing final about a semantic change: a word may acquire a new sense, or scores of new senses, without losing its original meaning. Some of these innovations are accidental and short-lived, confined to a single author or perhaps even to a single context; others will pass from speech into language and harden into permanent changes, giving rise to one of the forms of polysemy . . .: shifts in application, specialization in a social milieu, figurative expressions, etc.

(5) Many semantic changes arise in the first instance in *ambiguous contexts* where a particular word may be taken in two different senses while the meaning of the utterance as a whole remains unaffected. The phrase to *count one's beads*, which has just been mentioned, is an example in point. Whether *beads* is taken here to refer to prayers, or to the rosary balls used for counting one's prayers, will make no real difference to the total meaning of the phrase. Similarly, the word *boon* originally meant 'prayer, petition, request'; at quite an early date, however, it came to denote the thing prayed

---

[1] [*Motivation* is a term referring to some connection between the form of a word and its meaning that causes the word to be analyzable. In an earlier chapter, Ullmann distinguishes three types of motivation: 1) phonetic motivation, where there is an onomatopoeic relation between a word and what it means; 2) morphological motivation, where a word is analyzable into parts which have meaning, as *preacher* is analyzable into constituent morphemes, *preach* and *-er*, with a meaning specified for each; and 3) semantic motivation, where a meaning relation is transparent, as when we speak of the *hood* of a car or a *coat* of paint. A change of motivation, then, is a loss of connection between form and meaning caused usually by alteration of word form through sound change.—*Eds.*]

or asked for. Here again the change must have been facilitated by ambiguous contexts such as 'he gave her freely all her *boon*' (1300), where the word may be taken either in the first or in the second sense and yet the meaning of the sentence will be practically the same. Ambiguous constructions of this type are fairly common, and the lexicographer will often find it difficult to establish the precise date at which a new meaning emerged.

(6) Perhaps the most important of the general factors governing semantic change is the *structure of the vocabulary*. The phonological and grammatical system of a language is made up of a limited number of closely organized elements. The vocabulary, on the other hand, is a loose aggregate of an infinitely larger number of units; it is therefore far more fluid and mobile, and new elements, words as well as meanings, can be added more freely while existing ones will drop just as easily out of use. . . .

Change of meaning virtually monopolized the attention of all early semanticists. It will be remembered that the founder of modern semantics, Bréal, . . . had set the new science the task of exploring the laws which govern the development of meanings. Until the early 1930s, work in this field centred almost exclusively on two problems: the classification of changes of meaning, and the discovery of semantic laws. The quest for 'laws' met with very limited success, and the classificatory zeal resulted in a number of ambitious schemes built on slender empirical data—it was, as one linguist acidly remarked, as if someone tried to devise a comprehensive classification of plants while his own knowledge was confined to the poplar, the daisy and the toadstool. It must, however, be conceded that these early classifications often showed remarkable ingenuity, and that they made a substantial contribution to our better understanding of semantic processes. . . .

During the last thirty years, there has been a significant shift of emphasis in research: the interest of most semanticists has turned to descriptive and structural problems, and change of meaning has been relegated to the background. This does not mean, of course, that work in this field has come to a standstill. Monographs on specific problems continue to be published; there have been some valuable theoretical contributions, and changes of meaning occupy a prominent place in most of the latest manuals. Some of the structuralist experiments . . . are likely to rejuvenate the study of semantic change rather than superseding the solid achievements of the past, which are sometimes contemptuously dismissed as 'atomistic' or 'anecdotal' semantics.

To survey all the overlapping schemes of classification, based on a variety of different criteria, would be a Herculean as well as a thankless task. I shall therefore confine myself to a few selected problems grouped around three themes: the causes of semantic change, its nature and conditions, and its effects.

I. THE CAUSES OF SEMANTIC CHANGE

Changes of meaning can be brought about by an infinite multiplicity of causes. One early semanticist distinguished no less than thirty-one possibilities, but no matter how fine a mesh of distinctions one may devise, there will always be some cases which will slip through it. Many changes, including some which look deceptively simple, are due to unique causes which can be established only by reconstructing the whole historical background. A classic example of such an unique change is the origin of Latin *monēta* which has given the English words *mint* and *money*, the latter via French *monnaie*. *Monēta* comes from the verb *moneo* 'to admonish, to warn,' but at first sight it is difficult to imagine any connexion between the two ideas. The connexion, in fact, was purely fortuitous: *Monēta* was a surname of the goddess Juno in whose temple in Rome money was coined. To take a rather different example, it seems obvious that the French milk-roll known as *croissant* owes its name to the fact that it is crescent-shaped. This is of course true, but it is not the whole story. The French word is a translation of German *Hörnchen*, and the first rolls of this shape were made in Vienna in the late seventeenth century to commemorate a decisive victory over the Turks whose national emblem is the Crescent. Such cases contain a salutary warning to the etymologist and lend fresh force to the old slogan: 'words and things' (*Wörter und Sachen*); without close liaison between linguistics and the history of civilization, the origin of *money* would have remained an unsolved mystery and that of *croissant* would have been grossly oversimplified.

Yet, in spite of the complexity of these processes, it is possible to discern several major causes which account between them for a large proportion of semantic changes. Three of these were clearly identified in Antoine Meillet's fundamental article on the subject:[2]

(1) Linguistic Causes

Some semantic changes are due to the associations which words contract in speech. Habitual collocations may permanently affect the meaning of the terms involved; by a process known since Bréal as 'contagion,' the sense of one word may be transferred to another simply because they occur together in many contexts. Perhaps the most remarkable example of this tendency is the history of negation in French. A number of words which originally had a positive sense have acquired a negative value because they were often used in conjunction with the negative particle *ne*:

[2] In *Linguistique historique et linguistique générale*, I, 230–71.

Latin *passus* 'step'	*ne . . . pas* 'not'
" *punctum* 'point'	*ne . . . point* 'not, not at all'
" *persona* 'person'	*ne . . . personne* 'nobody'
" *rem*, accusative of *res* 'thing'	*ne . . . rien* 'nothing'
" *jam* 'now, already' + *magis* 'more'	*ne . . . jamais* 'never'

The contagion has been so effective that these terms now have a negative sense even when they stand by themselves, unsupported by *ne*. This has led to the paradoxical situation that the word *personne* has two diametrically opposite uses: as a noun it still means 'person'; used as a particle, as for instance in reply to a question, it means 'nobody':

J'ai vu une *personne*. 'I saw one person.'
Qui a dit cela?—*Personne*. 'Who said that?—Nobody.'

(2) Historical Causes

It often happens that language is more conservative than civilization, material as well as moral. Objects, institutions, ideas, scientific concepts change in the course of time; yet in many cases the name is retained and thus helps to ensure a sense of tradition and continuity. The process is too well known to require detailed discussion; one example for each of the main categories will be sufficient to show how it works:

(a) **Objects.** The English word *car* ultimately goes back to Latin *carrus*, a word of Celtic origin which meant a 'four-wheeled wagon' and was repeatedly mentioned in Caesar's commentaries on the Gallic war. Our modern cars bear little resemblance to the Celtic wagons of the first century B.C.; yet the technological development was so continuous that there was no need for the label to be replaced at any point, and the word has remained phonetically almost unaltered since Roman times (cf. also French *char*, Italian, Spanish and Portuguese *carro*, Rumanian *car*).

(b) **Institutions.** The meaning of the word *parliament*, borrowed from Old French *parlement*, has changed beyond recognition since the councils of the early Plantagenet Kings, but the development was gradual, the continuity of tradition was never interrupted, and the term survives to bear witness to this tradition; it will no doubt continue to do so whatever constitutional reforms the future may bring.

(c) **Ideas.** The term *humour*, which English took over from Old French, is based on totally antiquated physiological conceptions: the theory of the 'four chief fluids (*cardinal humours*) of the body (blood, phlegm, choler, and melancholy or black choler), by the relative proportions of which a person's physical and mental qualities and disposition were formerly held to be determined' (*NED*). Subsequently these notions were forgotten and *humour* gradually developed into one of the key-terms of the British way of life; yet once again the word has been retained since there has been no break in continuity. A number of other modern terms—*choleric, melancholy, phlegmatic, sanguine, temperament*—have their roots in the same physiological theory.

(d) Scientific Concepts. While *humour* and its group were at one time scientific, or pseudo-scientific, terms they have long since ceased to be regarded as such and have passed into the category of general ideas. There are, however, many scientific concepts proper which have preserved their traditional names in spite of all the changes they have undergone. A glance at the etymology of some of these terms will show how completely they have outgrown their original meanings. . . . *Geometry* once meant 'the art of measuring ground'; more recently even the word *atom* has . . . become etymologically inappropriate since it meant 'indivisible' in Greek.

(3) Social Causes

When a word passes from ordinary language into a specialized nomenclature—the terminology of a trade, a craft, a profession or some other limited group—it tends to acquire a more restricted sense. Conversely, words borrowed from a group-language into common use are apt to widen their meaning. There are thus two socially conditioned tendencies working in opposite directions: specialization and generalization.

Specialization of meaning in a restricted social group is an extremely common process, . . . one of the main sources of polysemy. In some cases, the specialized sense has completely superseded the more general one, and the range of the word has been considerably narrowed. This has happened in French to a number of ordinary verbs when they passed into the language of the farm-yard:

Latin *cubare* 'to recline, to lie down'	>	French *couver* 'to hatch'
" *mutare* 'to change'	>	" *muer* 'to moult'
" *ponere* 'to place'	>	" *pondre* 'to lay eggs'
" *trahere* 'to draw'	>	" *traire* 'to milk'

The converse process, *generalization*, is also very common. A number of terms from hunting and falconry, for example, have passed into ordinary language and have correspondingly widened their meaning. *Haggard* originally referred to a hawk which was 'caught after having assumed the adult plumage' and was therefore wild and untamed (*NED*). *Lure*, and the verb *to allure*, are also derived from falconry: a *lure* was 'an apparatus used by falconers to recall their hawks, being a bunch of feathers attached to a cord, within which, during its training, the hawk finds its food' (*Shorter*

OED). French *niais* 'foolish' comes from Vulgar Latin *nidax, *nidacem, a derivative of *nidus* 'nest'; it originally denoted a 'nestling', a young falcon taken from the nest. Many idiomatic expressions—'to be at bay,' 'to beat about the bush,' 'to be caught in the toils,' and others—can also be traced back to various aspects of the chase.

To these three major factors established by Meillet one may add at least another three which are responsible for many changes of meaning.

(4) Psychological Causes

Semantic changes often have their roots in the speaker's state of mind or in some more permanent feature of his mental make-up. Some of the psychological factors involved are superficial or even trivial. A chance similarity which catches the eye, a humorous association which comes to the mind, may produce an image which, because of its appropriateness or its expressive quality, will pass from individual style into common usage. The idea that something has a vague resemblance to a horse—in shape, situation or character—has inspired many graphic or jocular metaphors and idioms: *clothes-horse, horse-fish, horse-tail, horse-play, horse-sense,* 'to flog a dead *horse*,' 'to mount the high *horse*,' 'to look a gift *horse* in the mouth,' etc. Such metaphors will sometimes result in a permanent change of meaning: the painter's *easel*, for example, comes from the Dutch word *ezel* which means an 'ass' (cf. German *Esel*).

Psychologically more interesting are those changes of meaning which spring from some deep-seated feature or tendency in the speaker's mind. Two such causes in particular have been strongly emphasized in semantic studies: emotive factors and taboo.

(a) **Emotive Factors.** The part played by feeling in semantic change was explored in great detail by Professor H. Sperber in a book published in 1923,[3] which tried to apply a Freudian approach to these problems. Sperber argued that if we are intensely interested in a subject, we tend to talk frequently about it; we shall even refer to it when speaking of totally different matters. Such subjects are ever present to our minds and will therefore suggest similes and metaphors for the description of other experiences. In Sperber's terminology, they will become 'centres of *expansion*.' At the same time, these important spheres will also form 'centres of *attraction*': we shall enlist analogies from other fields in order to describe them with the maximum of precision, freshness and variety. There will thus be a twofold movement of metaphors from and towards these emotional centres.

---

[3] *Einführung in die Bedeutungslehre.*

Sperber cites some striking examples to show the impact of certain awe-inspiring weapons during the First World War. In the slang of the *poilus*, people and objects were sometimes nicknamed after these weapons: thus beans were called 'shrapnels,' and a woman with many children was referred to as a 'machine-gun' (mitrailleuse à gosses). Conversely, all kinds of picturesque and humorous metaphors were applied to the weapons themselves; in an attempt to rob them of some of their terror they were compared to familiar objects: a machine-gun became a 'coffee-mill' or a 'sewing-machine,' and a tank was nicknamed 'rolling kitchen.'

Of the two emotional forces posited by Sperber, 'attraction' certainly plays an important role, even though it will not always carry the far-reaching implications suggested by the theory. . . . Subjects in which a community is interested, which epitomize its fears, its aspirations or its ideals, will tend to attract synonyms from all directions, and many of these will be metaphorical since metaphor is the supreme source of expressiveness in language. The role of 'expansion' is less obvious and more problematical. There is certainly nothing like an automatic connexion between the interest which a subject commands and the number of metaphors inspired by it. If such a correlation did exist one would expect countless images from aviation in our air-minded age, whereas the actual number of such figures in ordinary language is quite small. On the other hand there are undoubtedly cases where the interests of a generation are reflected in its choice of metaphors. In sixteenth-century France, where religion was the most important of all public issues, a number of figurative expressions were derived from that field: *vray comme la messe* 'as true as mass'; *vray comme le patenôtre* 'as true as the Lord's prayer'; *se rendre au premier coup de matines* 'to go at the first stroke of the matins bell' (= as soon as one is summoned); *il faut laisser le moustier où il est* 'one should leave the monastery where it is' (= respect tradition), and many more. At the time of the French Revolution, there was a plethora of metaphors from science and medicine, reflecting public interest in recent advances in these fields: people spoke of the 'centrifugal force' of the revolutionary spirit and of the 'refrangibility of its regenerative rays,' of the 'electrifying' effect of public meetings, of the 'phosphorous globules' which Pitt was blowing in the eyes of the public, and of the need to 'phlebotomize' journalists. In the nineteenth century the introduction of railways into France was followed by the appearance of all kinds of metaphors from that sphere. . . .

(b) **Taboo.** *Taboo* is a Polynesian word which Captain Cook introduced into English whence it passed into other European languages. According to Captain Cook himself, the term 'has a very comprehensive meaning; but, in general, signifies that a thing is forbidden.' In his book *Totem and Taboo*, Freud has given an interesting analysis of the meaning and implications of the word:

> For us the meaning of taboo branches off into two opposite direc-
> tions. On the one hand it means to us sacred, consecrated: but on the
> other hand it means uncanny, dangerous, forbidden, and unclean. The
> opposite for taboo is designated in Polynesian by the word *noa* and
> signifies something ordinary and generally accessible. Thus something
> like the concept of reserve inheres in taboo; taboo expresses itself
> essentially in prohibitions and restrictions. Our combination of 'holy
> dread' would often express the meaning of taboo.

Taboo is of vital importance to the linguist because it imposes a ban
not only on certain persons, animals and things, but also on their names.
In most cases, though not in all, the tabooed word will be abandoned and
a harmless substitute, a *euphemism*, will be introduced to fill the gap.
This will often involve an adjustment in the meaning of the substitute,
and in this way taboo is an important cause of semantic changes.

Language taboos fall into three more or less distinct groups according
to the psychological motivation behind them: some are due to fear, others
to a feeling of delicacy, others again to a sense of decency and propriety.

(i) *Taboo of fear.* The awe in which supernatural beings are held has often
imposed taboo bans on their names. The Jews . . . were not allowed to
refer directly to God; they used their word for 'master' instead, and this
circumlocution still survives in English *the Lord*, French *Seigneur* and
other modern forms. The name of the devil has given rise to countless
euphemisms, including the curious expression *l'Autre*, 'the Other One,'
in French. In his *Address to the Deil* Burns has collected a whole series of
friendly nicknames designed to propitiate the devil and to show that one
is on familiar terms with him:

> O thou! whatever title suit thee—
> Auld 'Hornie,' 'Satan,' 'Nick,' or 'Clootie' . . .
> Hear me, auld 'Hangie,' for a wee . . .
> But fare-you-weel, auld 'Nickie-ben' !

Names of evil spirits are tabooed in the same way. The attempt to
propitiate them can go to remarkable lengths: witness Greek *Eumenides*,
one of the names given to the Furies, which literally means 'well-disposed,
gracious.'

Ordinary creatures and things endowed with supernatural qualities can
also become objects of fear and taboo. Particularly widespread are bans
on the names of animals. A recent book on the subject cites no less than
twenty-four animals whose names are tabooed in different languages; they

range from ants, bees and worms to bears, tigers and lions; even butterflies, rabbits and squirrels are included in the list. One of the most intriguing cases is the well-known series of euphemistic names for the weasel. In the Romance languages there are only isolated survivals of *mustela*, the Latin name of the animal. In French it has been replaced by *belette*, a diminutive of *beau, belle*, which literally means 'beautiful little woman.' Elsewhere, the euphemism has worked mainly by change of meaning: the Italians and the Portuguese call the weasel 'little lady' (*donnola, doninha*), the Spaniards 'gossip' (*comadreja*), whereas in Denmark it is known as 'beautiful' and 'bride,' in Sweden as 'pretty little girl' or 'young lady,' in Greece and Albania as 'sister-in-law,' etc. In English, the weasel once had the by-name *fairy*, and Erasmus has recorded that it was considered unlucky in England to mention the animal when one went hunting.

Names of inanimate objects can also be struck by a taboo ban. Superstitions connected with the left hand have led to the creation of many euphemisms in various languages. Latin *laevus* and *scaevus* have disappeared in Romance; *sinister* in the literal sense has survived in Italian *sinistro* but has fallen elsewhere into disuse. Spanish has turned to Basque for a replacement (*izquierdo*), whereas French uses a Germanic term, *gauche*, which originally meant 'the wrong way, clumsy.' English *left* had the primary sense of 'weak, worthless,' and one of the Greek words for 'left,' *euonymos*, is clearly a euphemism: its original sense was 'of good name, honoured; of good omen, prosperous, fortunate.'

(ii) *Taboo of delicacy.* It is a general human tendency to avoid direct reference to unpleasant subjects. We have already seen some of the numerous euphemisms connected with illness and death. The history of words like *disease* and *undertaker* shows that such substitutes can become so closely associated with the tabooed idea that they lose all euphemistic value, and fresh replacements have to be found to mitigate the unpleasantness.

Another group of words affected by this form of taboo are names of physical and mental defects. *Imbecile* comes via French from Latin *imbecillus*, or *imbecillis*, 'weak, feeble.' In the seventeenth century, Corneille could still refer to the 'gentle sex' as 'le sexe *imbécille*'; a century later, this usage had become so antiquated that Voltaire described it as a 'coarse and misplaced affront.' Other words in the same sphere have developed on similar lines. French *crétin* is a dialectal form of *chrétien* 'Christian,' borrowed in the eighteenth century from a Swiss French patois. *Benêt* 'silly, stupid, simple-minded' comes from *benedictus* 'blessed' and is an obvious echo of the first beatitude: '*Blessed* are the poor in spirit: for theirs is the kingdom of heaven.' It is quite probable that these uses were originally 'pseudo-euphemisms' rather than euphemisms proper: they were prompted by irony rather than by taboo. The same may be said of *idiot*, which goes back to a Greek word meaning 'private person, layman,' and of *silly*, earlier *seely*, which once meant 'happy' and 'blessed' (cf. German *selig*).

Yet another class of words which are often avoided for reasons of delicacy, or mock delicacy, are names of criminal actions such as cheating, stealing and killing. For 'cheating' there is in French a traditional periphrasis, *corriger la fortune*, which was made famous by a passage in Lessing's comedy, *Minna von Barnhelm* (Act IV, scene 2). 'Stealing' has given rise to numerous euphemisms in different languages; some of these have been noted in the chapter on synonymy. An amusing example occurs in *The Merry Wives of Windsor*, Act I, scene 3:

NYM: The good humour is to steal at a minute's rest.
PISTOL: 'Convey' the wise it call. 'Steal' foh! A fico for the phrase!

In Nazi concentration camps, the verb *to organize* came to be used in many languages as a euphemism for 'procuring by illicit means' and thus for 'stealing.' This produced some curious combinations: 'Les magasins du camp sont pleins de tout ce que les S.S. ont *organisé* en France.' [4]

An example of a radical change of meaning due to this type of taboo is the French verb *tuer* 'to kill,' which is derived from the Latin *tutari* 'to watch, to guard, to protect.' According to a recent inquiry, this usage seems to have 'originated as an ironic euphemism due ultimately to thieves' or soldiers' slang.'

(iii) *Taboo of propriety*. The three great spheres most directly affected by this form of taboo are sex, certain parts and functions of the body, and swearing. There are extremely wide variations between the standards of decency obtaining in different periods: the bawdy of a Rabelais and the prudery of the Précieuses, the forthrightness with which Madame de Ramboubliet in Sterne's *Sentimental Journey* refers to human physiology, and the hypersensitivity of nineteenth-century American ladies who would speak of the *limbs* of a piano and of their own *benders* rather than mention *legs*, and would say *waist* rather than utter the word *body*. Yet the sense of decency and propriety has been throughout the ages a rich source of taboos and euphemisms. A few expressions from the sphere of sexual relations will serve to illustrate this tendency.

The history of the French word *fille* shows that even one of the commonest words of a language can become tainted through euphemistic use. In the sense of 'daughter,' *fille* is still perfectly respectable, but in the sense of 'girl, young woman' it is now necessary to say *jeune fille*, since *fille* by itself was so frequently used as a euphemism for 'prostitute' that this eventually became its ordinary meaning. A sentence like the following, which occurs

---

[4] 'The camp stores are full of all the things the S.S. have *organized* in France.'

in the eighteenth-century writer Marivaux, would be impossible today: 'Tu me dégoûtes de toutes les *filles* qu'on pourrait m'offrir pour mon fils.' [5] Other words in this sphere have had a similar fate: *garce*, the feminine form of *garçon*, has become a term of abuse, and the German *Dirne*, which was once applied to the Virgin Mary as the handmaid of God, has come to mean a 'drab' except in the South German dialects.

Various terms connected with illicit love have deteriorated in meaning as a result of euphemistic use. When Alceste says to Célimène, in Molière's *Misanthrope:* 'Vous avez trop d'*amants* qu'on voit vous obséder' (Act II, scene 1),[6] this is far less insulting than it sounds to modern ears, for at that time *amant* merely meant 'someone in love with a woman'; it is only by euphemism that it gradually acquired the sense of 'lover,' which is its sole meaning today. Similarly, there was nothing very shocking in Pauline's words in Corneille's *Polyeucte:* 'Mon père fut ravi qu'il me prît pour *maîtresse*' (Act I, scene 3); in the seventeenth century, *maîtresse* simply meant 'bride.' [7]

Even the French word for 'kissing,' *baiser*, has fallen victim to a taboo ban. Since it came to be used as a euphemism with obscene connotations it has been largely replaced in its original sense by *embrasser* 'to embrace,' a derivative of *bras* 'arm'; hence such bizarre combinations as '*embrasser* quelqu'un sur la joue' 'to kiss someone on the cheek.'

This small selection of examples will have shown that taboo and euphemism are important causes of semantic change. It should be noted, however, that this is only one of the ways in which a gap created by taboo can be filled. As we have seen, a tainted word is sometimes replaced by a new formation (*belette*) or by a term taken over from a foreign language (Spanish *izquierdo*). Bloomfield has drawn attention to the curious fact that the Russians took their word for 'moon,' *luná*, from Latin whereas they have otherwise borrowed very little from that source, except some highly learned terms. Since every language is likely to have its own word for the moon, such a term would be imported from abroad only if the native name had been struck by a taboo ban. It can also happen that a tabooed word is not dropped altogether but is retained in a modified form. Archaic English *zounds* is a euphemistic variant of the oath *by God's wounds*, *drat* stands for *God rot!* and French *bougre*, though not as offensive as its English counterpart, becomes more respectable when it is changed to *bigre*. A number of French oaths ending in *-bleu*—*corbleu, morbleu, parbleu, ventrebleu*, etc.— have nothing to do with the adjective *bleu* 'blue'; *bleu* is merely a modified form of *Dieu*. The swearing *palsambleu*, which belongs to the same family,

---

[5] 'You make me feel disgusted with all the *girls* who might be offered to me for my son.'
[6] 'You have too many *admirers* whom one sees besieging you.'
[7] 'My father was delighted that he should have chosen me as his *bride*.'

is a well-camouflaged variant of the phrase *par le sang de Dieu* 'by God's blood'; cf. English *'sblood* and *'Od's blood*.

(5) Foreign Influence as a Cause of Semantic Change

Many changes of meaning are due to the influence of some foreign model. To take an obvious example, the use of the word *bear* to denote two constellations, the *Great* and the *Lesser Bear*, is paralleled in many languages: French *Ourse*, Italian *Orsa*, Spanish *Osa*, German *Bär*, Hungarian *Medve*, etc. None of these is a spontaneous metaphor: they are all based on Latin *Ursa* and, beyond that, on Greek *Arktos* 'she-bear,' both of which were already used in Classical Antiquity to denote the constellations. . . .

(6) The Need for a New Name as a Cause of Semantic Change

Whenever a new name is required to denote a new object or idea, we can do one of three things: form a new word from existing elements; borrow a term from a foreign language or some other source; lastly, alter the meaning of an old word. The need to find a new name is thus an extremely important cause of semantic changes.

The history of scientific and technological discoveries affords ample evidence of how such changes work. An interesting example is the use of the term *tank* to denote the armoured vehicle invented in the First World War. The new sense was added somewhat arbitrarily to the existing word in order to ensure secrecy during manufacture. The name of an earlier weapon, the *torpedo*, also had an unusual origin. In Latin *torpedo*, which comes from the same root as *torpor*, meant 'stiffness, numbness' and, by transfer, the 'cramp-fish' or 'electric ray.' When, in the latter half of the eighteenth century, a new under-water weapon was invented, it was called, first in English and later in other languages, by the Latin name of the fish. Another Latin word, *satelles*, *satellitis* 'attendant, life-guard,' had a more complicated history. When Kepler needed a name to describe a smaller planet revolving round a larger one, he used the word *satellite* in this sense rather than coining a new term. In the course of time, *satellite* acquired several technical meanings in anatomy, zoology and town-planning; in the political sense it was first used by Frederick Naumann in his book *Mitteleuropa* (1915). During the last few years, the launching of the first *earthsatellites* has widened further the semantic range of the word. In all these cases, scientific discoveries and other developments made it necessary to find a new name, and the need was met by adding fresh meanings to the Latin term.

The speed of scientific and technological progress in our time is making increasingly heavy demands on linguistic resources, and the possibilities of metaphor and other types of semantic change are being fully exploited. This can be seen, for example, in the rapidly changing nomenclature of the aircraft industry. First we had *flying-boats*, then *flying fortresses;* now we have *flying saucers* and even *flying bedsteads*. Many types of aircraft have expressive metaphorical names: *Hurricane, Spitfire, Comet, Constellation, Vampire*, and others. Among all the linguistic devices available, change of meaning is the simplest, the most discreet and perhaps the most elegant way of keeping pace with the progress of civilization.

II. THE NATURE OF SEMANTIC CHANGE

Leibniz's axiom: 'Natura non facit saltus' ('Nature makes no leaps'), is entirely applicable to semantic change. No matter what causes bring about the change, there must always be some connexion, some *association*, between the old meaning and the new. In some cases the association may be powerful enough to alter the meaning by itself; in others it will merely provide a vehicle for a change determined by other causes; but in one form or another, some kind of association will always underlie the process. In this sense association may be regarded as a necessary condition, a *sine qua non* of semantic change.

In the history of semantics, the associationist theory has appeared in two different forms. Some of the early semanticists professed a naïve associationism: they tried to explain changes of meaning as the products of associations between isolated words. In recent decades, a more sophisticated view, based on structural principles, has come to prevail; attention has shifted from single words to the wider units, the so-called 'associative fields,' to which they belong. . . .

Several attempts have been made to classify semantic changes according to the associations underlying them. By an ingenious combination of Saussure's structural approach with some of the principles of Bergson's philosophy, the French linguist Léonce Roudet outlined, forty years ago, the first comprehensive classification of this kind, which was developed further by subsequent research. Roudet's scheme has the immediate advantage of linking up with one of the basic definitions of meaning . . . One school of thought regards meaning as a 'reciprocal and reversible relation between name and sense.' [8] If this formula is accepted as a working hypoth-

---

[8] [In defining word meaning, Ullmann recognizes three components: *name, sense,* and *thing. Name* is "the phonetic shape of the word, the sounds which make it up and also other acoustic features such as accent." *Thing* is "the non-linguistic feature or event we are talking about." *Sense* is "the information which the name conveys to the hearer." Since the relation between name and thing is arbitrary—a product of convention and

esis, then semantic changes will fall naturally into two categories: those based on an association between the senses and those involving an association between the names. Each of these two categories can be further subdivided if we accept the customary distinction between two kinds of association: similarity and contiguity. These two pairs of criteria yield four cardinal types of semantic change, some of which can be broken down into further subdivisions.

1. Similarity of Senses (Metaphor)

The paramount significance of metaphor as a creative force in language has always been recognized, and many extravagant claims have been made on its behalf. According to Aristotle, 'the greatest thing by far is to have a command of metaphor. This alone cannot be imparted by another; it is the mark of genius.' In our own time Chesterton went so far as to assert that 'all metaphor is poetry,' while Sir Herbert Read has argued that 'we should always be prepared to judge a poet . . . by the force and originality of his metaphors.' Even more sweepingly, Proust declared in his article on the style of Flaubert: 'Je crois que la métaphore seule peut donner une sorte d'éternité au style.' [9] Even if one discounts some of these inflated claims, there can be no doubt about the crucial importance of metaphor in language and literature. . . .

The basic structure of metaphor is very simple. There are always two terms present: the thing we are talking about and that to which we are comparing it. In Dr. Richards's terminology, the former is the *tenor*, the latter the *vehicle*, whereas the feature or features they have in common form the *ground* of the metaphor. To take a concrete case, the Latin word *musculus* 'little mouse,' a diminutive of *mus* 'mouse,' was also used figuratively in the sense of 'muscle'; hence English *muscle* and other modern forms. In this metaphor 'muscle' is the tenor, 'little mouse' is the vehicle, and the fancied similarity between the two forms the ground of the image, the common element underlying the transfer. Instead of explicitly stating, in the form of a comparison, that a muscle *looks like* a little mouse, the tenor is identified with the vehicle by a kind of verbal shorthand. In this

---

acculturation—the linguist is concerned primarily with the relation between name and sense. Ullmann calls this relation "reciprocal and reversible" to have it refer to both speaker and hearer. From the hearer's point of view, the sequence of events in discourse is as follows: "hearing the word, say, *door*, he will think of a door and thus understand what the speaker was saying. For the speaker, the sequence will be just the reverse: he will, for some reason or another, think of a door, and this will make him pronounce the word. There is therefore a reciprocal and reversible relationship between name and sense: if one hears the word one will think of the thing, and if one thinks of the thing one will say the word. It is this reciprocal and reversible relationship between sound and sense which I propose to call the 'meaning' of the word." See *Semantics*, Chapter 3, pp. 54–64.—*Eds.*]

[9] 'I believe that metaphor alone can give style a kind of eternity.'

sense it is true to say that a metaphor is a 'condensed comparison positing an intuitive and concrete identity.'

It should be noted that the similarity between tenor and vehicle may be of two kinds: objective and emotive. It is objective in the example just quoted or, for instance, when the ridge of a mountain is called a *crest* because it resembles the crest on an animal's head. It is emotive when we talk of a *bitter* disappointment because its effect is similar to that of a bitter taste. This is how the French word *déboire*, a derivative of *boire* 'to drink,' which originally referred to the disagreeable after-taste of a drink, came to mean 'disappointment, blighted hope.' . . .

Among the innumerable metaphors in which the image-making faculty of man has expressed itself, there are four major groups which recur in the most diverse languages and literary styles.

(i) Anthropomorphic Metaphors. One of the first thinkers who noticed the extraordinary frequency of this type of transfer was the eighteenth-century Italian philosopher Giambattista Vico. 'In all languages,' he wrote in his *Scienza nuova*, 'the greater part of expressions referring to inanimate objects are taken by transfer from the human body and its parts, from human senses and human passions. . . . Ignorant man makes himself into the yardstick of the universe.' This tendency is attested in the most different languages and civilizations, and lies at the root of countless expressions in current usage. . . . We talk of the *brow* of a hill, the *ribs* of a vault, the *mouth* of a river, the *lungs* of a town, the *heart* of the matter, the *sinews* of war, the *hands* of a clock, and many more, whereas the metaphorical uses of other organs, such as the *foot* and the *leg*, are virtually unlimited.

Naturally there are also many transfers in the opposite direction, where parts of the body are named after animals or inanimate objects: *muscle*, *polypus*, *spine*, *Adam's apple*, *apple* of the eye, ear-*drum*, and various others. In Sperber's terminology, the human body is a powerful centre of metaphorical expansion as well as attraction; on the whole, however, metaphors *from* this sphere seem to be far more common than those directed *towards* it.

(ii) Animal Metaphors. Another perennial source of imagery is the animal kingdom. These metaphors . . . move in two main directions. Some of them are applied to plants or insentient objects. Many plants owe their name to some vague resemblance, often fanciful or jocular, to an animal: *goat's-beard*, *cock's-foot*, *dog's-tail*, etc. *Dandelion* comes from the French *dent de lion* 'lion's tooth.' There are even combinations of animal metaphors, as in the French *chiendent queue-de-renard* 'hunger-grass,' which literally means 'dog's tooth foxtail.' A great many inanimate objects, including various instruments, machines and parts of machines, are also called after an animal: *cat*, *cat-head*, *cat-o'nine-tails*, *crab*, *crane*, *cock* of a gun, *cock* in the sense of 'tap,' and countless others.

Another large group of animal images are transferred into the human sphere where they often acquire humorous, ironical, pejorative or even grotesque connotations. A human being can be likened to an inexhaustible variety of animals: a *dog*, a *cat*, a *pig*, an *ass*, a *mouse*, a *rat*, a *goose*, a *lion*, a *jackal*, etc.; he can look or behave in a *catty*, *dogged*, *sheepish*, *owlish*, *fishy* or *mulish* way; he can *dog* a criminal, *ape* or *lionize* those he admires, and even *parrot* their words. This abundant imagery springs from the same attitude as the numerous literary works, from Aesop to La Fontaine and from the Greek *Batrachomyomachia* (War of the Frogs and Mice) to Orwell's *Animal Farm*, where beasts are made to talk and act as human beings. Although animal images are among the oldest devices of literary style—Homer already calls the goddess Hera 'ox-eyed'—they have lost none of their expressive and evocative force: all readers of Proust will remember the terse and vivid caricature of M. de Palancy 'qui, avec sa grosse tête de carpe aux yeux ronds, se déplaçait lentement au milieu des fêtes en desserrant d'instant en instant ses mandibules comme pour chercher son orientation.' [10]

(iii) From Concrete to Abstract. One of the basic tendencies in metaphor is to translate abstract experiences into concrete terms. In many cases, the transfer is still transparent, but in others some etymological probing will be necessary to recapture the concrete image underlying an abstract word: to discover the Latin *finis* 'limit, end' behind *define* and *finance*, *limen* 'threshold' behind *eliminate*, *sidus* 'star' behind *desire*, *velum* 'veil' behind *reveal*, or *volvere* 'roll' behind *involve*. Such transfers are going on all the time; in fact it would be impossible to discuss any abstract subject without them. Take for example the innumerable metaphors connected with *light:* to throw *light* on, to put in a favourable *light*, leading *lights*, to *enlighten*, *illuminating*, *brilliant*, *beaming*, *radiant*, *coruscating*, *dazzling*, etc. That this metaphorical vein is far from exhausted can be seen from such comparatively recent expressions as *in the limelight, to hold the spotlight*, or *high-lights* in the sense of 'a moment or detail of vivid interest.'

Even such a highly abstract and elusive experience as time can be made concrete and tangible by the creative writer. The age-old cliché of the 'flow' of time is rejuvenated in the hands of Sartre when, evoking the languid atmosphere of a hot summer day, he speaks of 'time flowing softly, like an infusion warmed up by the sun.' Elsewhere time is visualized in novel and arresting images. To Shakespeare it appears as 'Old Time the clock-setter, that bald sexton Time' (*King John*, Act III, scene 1). Tennyson pictures it as a 'maniac scattering dust' (*In Memoriam*, L). In Proust,

[10] 'who, with his large carp's head and round eyes, moved about slowly in the midst of the party, opening and closing his mandibles as if to find his bearings' (*Du Côté de chez Swann*, vol. II, p. 143).

whose whole work is centred on the problem of time, there are endless variations on this theme, culminating, at the very end of the cycle, in the nightmarish vision of men mounted on the ever-growing stilts of time until finally they topple over.

(iv) 'Synaesthetic' Metaphors. A very common type of metaphor is based on transpositions from one sense to another: from sound to sight, from touch to sound, etc. When we speak of a *warm* or a *cold* voice, we do so because we perceive some kind of similarity between warm or cold temperature and the quality of certain voices. In the same way we talk of *piercing* sounds, *loud* colours, *sweet* voices and odours, and many more. . . .

2. Contiguity of Senses (Metonymy)

Metonymy is intrinsically less interesting than metaphor since it does not discover new relations but arises between words already related to each other. The difference between the two processes has been aptly summarized by M. Esnault: 'La métonymie n'ouvre pas de chemins comme l'intuition métaphorique; mais brûlant les étapes de chemins trop connus, elle raccourcit des distances pour faciliter la rapide intuition de choses déjà connues.' [11] But if metonymy is of limited interest to the student of style, it is an important factor in semantic change. . . .

Metonymies can best be classified according to the associations underlying them. Some metonymic transfers are based on *spatial* relations. The shift of meaning from Latin *coxa* 'hip' to French *cuisse* 'thigh' is explained by the fact that the hip and the thigh are two contiguous parts of our body, without any sharp boundaries between them. . . . This was not the ultimate cause of the change; it was merely the condition which made such a transfer possible. A similar metonymy lies at the root of the French word for 'strike,' *grève*, which derives its name from the *Place de Grève*, now called *Place de l'Hôtel de Ville*, where Parisian labourers used to assemble when they were out of work.

Another group of metonymies are based on *temporal* relations. . . . Association between successive events accounts in all probability for the sense-development of English *mass*, French *messe* and related terms which denote the Roman Catholic service in many languages. All these go back to Ecclesiastical Latin *missa*, feminine past participle of Latin *mittere* 'to send, to dismiss.' Since the service ended with the formula: 'Ite, *missa* est (contio)' 'Go now, the meeting is *dismissed*,' the word *missa* eventually came to stand

---

[11] 'Metonymy does not open new paths like metaphorical intuition; but, taking too familiar paths in its stride, it shortens distances so as to facilitate the swift intuition of things already known' (*Imagination populaire*, p. 31).

for the service itself. A closely similar case is that of the French word *veille* 'vigil,' which now chiefly means 'eve, preceding day.'

Among other relations which can result in a metonymic change, one type is so important that it is sometimes treated as a separate category: *pars pro toto* or 'part for the whole.' A simple example is the use of *redbreast* for 'robin,' naming the bird after the most conspicuous detail in its appearance. Similarly, human types and social classes are often called after some characteristic garment: *redcoat, redcap, blue-stocking, Blackshirt;* French *la blouse* 'workman; working class, proletariat,' and more recently *blouson noir*, the French equivalent of a 'teddy boy,' nicknamed after the black jacket worn by these youths. The connexion has ceased to be transparent in French *grisette*, a derivative of *gris* 'grey,' which originally meant a cheap grey dress-material and then came to designate, with pejorative overtones, the young working girls wearing this kind of dress.

Other types of metonymy are so simple and so well known that they require no detailed discussion. . . . Inventions and discoveries are often named after the person responsible for them; when a physicist says that one *ampère* is the current that one *volt* can send through one *ohm*, he is commemorating three great pioneers of his science: the Frenchman André Ampère, the Italian Count Alessandro Volta, and the German Georg Simon Ohm. Similarly, foods and drinks are called after their place of origin (*gruyère, champagne*), the content after the container ('to drink a *glass*, a *bottle* of wine'), and many more.

An interesting feature of metonymy is that, unlike metaphor, it tends to give abstract words a concrete meaning: the name of an action will stand for its result, the name of a quality for a person or object exhibiting it, etc. Bréal has graphically described these changes as 'thickening of meaning' (épaississement de sens). There are countless examples of this tendency in various languages: the act of *binding* and the *binding* of a book; the *performance* of one's duty and an operatic *performance;* to keep *guard* and the *Horse Guards*, etc. Qualities are treated in the same way: a thing whose *beauty* we admire is called a *beauty;* a person of whom his relations are proud is the *pride* of his family; *falsehood* means falsity in the abstract and also a particular falsehood, a lie. In some words this usage has led to a radical shift of meaning. French *addition* means not only the act of adding and its result, but also a bill in a restaurant. French *témoin*, which comes from Latin *testimonium* 'evidence, testimony,' now signifies almost exclusively 'a person who testifies, a witness'; the abstract meaning still survives in the legal phrase *en témoin de quoi* 'in witness whereof.' The English word *witness* has had a closely parallel development. In other cases the abstract sense has been completely eclipsed. French *ivrogne* 'drunkard' is derived from Vulgar Latin *ebrionia* 'drunkenness,' and *élite*, an old past participle of the verb *élire* 'to elect, to choose,' still meant 'choice, choosing' in the sixteenth century when Montaigne spoke of *'eslite* entre le bien et le mal,' [12] whereas now it refers only to the 'choice part' of a society.

3. Similarity of Names (Popular Etymology)

Popular etymology . . . can change both the form and the meaning of a word by wrongly connecting it with another term to which it is similar in sound. The investigations of Gilliéron and other linguistic geographers have shown that this is a more common process than one might have thought; nevertheless, it is obviously not on a par with metaphor or metonymy as a factor in semantic change. It does, however, contain an important warning to the etymologist: before trying to reconstruct the semantic history of a word, he must first satisfy himself that the development has been spontaneous and not induced by a phonetically similar term. Without this precautionary measure, some of our most plausible reconstructions may be purely gratuitous: we may be setting up what Professor Orr has called a 'pseudo-semantic development.' . . . Changes of meaning due to this factor fall into two groups. In the more deceptive of the two, the old sense and the new are fairly close to each other, so that the latter *could* have developed spontaneously from the former though in actual fact it did not. The French word *forain*, which has given the English *foreign*, is a clear example of this type. It comes from Low Latin *foranus*, a derivative of Latin *foris* 'abroad, without'; its original meaning was 'foreign,' as it still is in English. In the phrase *marchand forain* 'itinerant merchant,' the term became wrongly associated with *foire* 'fair' (from Latin *feria(e)* 'holiday(s)'), which is the same word as English *fair*, and this association has affected the whole meaning of *forain*. The semantic link between the ideas of 'itinerant merchant' and 'fair' no doubt facilitated the change, but the phonetic similarity with *foire* must have been the decisive factor. In some dialects there is a collateral form *foirain* where the connexion with *foire* is even more marked.

Another example of this type is the English noun *boon*. . . . This noun first meant 'prayer, request,' then 'the matter prayed for or asked'; its current sense is 'a blessing, an advantage, a thing to be thankful for.' The semantic development could again have been spontaneous, but it was probably influenced by the homonymous adjective *boon*, an Anglicized form of French *bon*.

The situation is rather different in the second type where the two mean-

---

[12] 'Choice between good and evil.'

ings are so diverse that there seems to be no connexion between them. Rather than positing a purely imaginary line of development, the trained semanticist will look for the influence of some phonetically similar word which may supply the missing link. Thus the French *gazouiller* 'to twitter, to warble, to babble' can mean in popular speech 'to have an unpleasant smell.' It would of course be naïve to try to derive this new meaning from the old, since it is obviously a vulgar witticism suggested by the assonance of the initial syllable with the word *gaz*. Far more complicated is the double meaning of French *essuyer:* 'to wipe, to dry' and 'to suffer, to endure.' Professor Orr has demonstrated that this is another case of 'pseudo-semantic development': the second sense did not grow organically out of the first but was due to confusion with *essayer* which now means 'to try' but which, as recently as the sixteenth century, could also mean 'to experience, to endure.' . . .

4. Contiguity of Names (Ellipsis)

Words which often occur side by side are apt to have a semantic influence on each other. We have already seen an example of this in the history of negation in French. The commonest form which this influence takes is *ellipsis:* in a set phrase made up of two words, one of these is omitted and its meaning is transferred to its partner. This may have grammatical consequences: an adjective may be turned into a noun (*the main* for *the main sea*, *a daily* for *a daily paper*), and in some languages there may be anomalies of number or gender, as in French *le cinquième hussards*, where *régiment* is left out, or in *un première Lyon* which is a double ellipsis for 'un (billet de) première (classe).'

In a number of cases, ellipses of this kind have led to drastic changes in meaning. Omission of the French word *carrosse* 'coach' explains two old terms of transport which have also passed into English: *diligence* is short for *carrosse de diligence*, and *coupé*, which is really the past participle of the verb *couper* 'to cut,' stands for *carrosse coupé*, a carriage one of whose two compartments has been cut off. In the same way, a *drawing-room* is really a *withdrawing-room;* French *bouclier* 'buckler, shield' was originally *escu boucler* 'a shield with a buckle,' *piano*, from an Italian adjective and adverb meaning 'soft, softly,' is a shortened form of *pianoforte* 'soft and strong,' so called by Cristofori, its inventor, to express the gradation of tone of which it is capable. A curious example is *porter*, which is short for *porter's ale*, *porter's beer*, apparently because this drink was originally made for porters and other labourers.

English compounds and phrases adopted into French have often been curtailed by ellipsis. This has produced some usages which sound curious to native ears. Thus 'smoking-jacket' has been reduced to *smoking*, which now means a 'dinner-jacket' in French and other Continental languages. Similarly, a 'cargo-boat' becomes *un cargo*, a 'midshipman' *un midship*, a 'sidecar' *un side*, and a 'pin-up girl' *une pin-up*. Such shortenings are common in sport where *un goal* can mean a 'goal-keeper,' *le catch* stands for 'catch-as-catch-can,' *le cross* for 'cross-country running,' while even 'football' and 'basket-ball' can be mutilated: 'des joueurs de *foot*, de *basket*.'

The above classification of semantic changes calls for the following general comments:

(1) The four cardinal types are very different in scope. Metaphor is by far the most important of the four, but metonymy too is an extremely common process. Ellipsis, though by no means infrequent, is on the whole of limited importance, whereas popular etymology, despite its great interest, is a marginal phenomenon. It would seem, then, that associations between senses are of incomparably greater significance than those between names. A language without ellipsis and popular etymology would be a perfectly adequate medium of communication, whereas a language without metaphor and metonymy is inconceivable: these two forces are inherent in the basic structure of human speech.

(2) There are many semantic changes which seem to fit into more than one category. One may wonder, for example, whether expressions like *a Picasso* for 'a painting by Picasso,' or *burgundy* for 'wine from Burgundy,' are metonymic or elliptical. Perhaps it might be simplest to regard them as '*composite*' changes due to the interplay of two different types of association.

(3) The semantic development of many words consists of a series of successive changes which may sometimes take them very far from their original sense. Darmesteter coined the term '*concatenation*' (enchaînement) to describe these complex processes. A good example is French *cadeau* which was borrowed from Provençal in the early fifteenth century in the sense of 'capital letter,' and did not reach its modern meaning of 'present, gift' until three and a half centuries later. The following were the main stages in the semantic history of the word: 1. 'capital letter'; 2. 'strokes of calligraphy'; 3. 'superfluous words used as mere ornaments'; 4. 'entertainment, amusement, especially when offered to a lady'; 5. 'present, gift.' The student of meaning will of course have to examine each change separately and try to reconstruct its background. An etymologist who gave only the starting-point and the terminal point of such a chain of events would be, according to Gilliéron's amusing simile, comparable to a literary critic who summarized the life of Balzac in these two sentences: 'Balzac, sitting in the lap of his nurse, wore a blue dress with red stripes. He wrote the *Comédie humaine*.'

(4) The question has often been asked whether semantic changes are entirely haphazard, or whether there is some kind of regularity or pattern behind them. Ever since Bréal suggested that the new science of semantics should try to establish the 'laws governing changes in meaning,' the search for *'laws'* has been one of the main preoccupations of workers in this field. Some linguists were sceptical about the prospects of this quest. Commenting on the sense-change of French *poutre*, which originally meant a 'filly' and now denotes a 'beam' or 'girder,' Saussure wrote: 'cela est dû à des causes particulières et ne dépend pas des autres changements qui ont pu se produire dans le même temps: ce n'est qu'un accident parmi tous ceux qu'enregistre l'histoire d'une langue.' [13] Nyrop was even more categorical: 'ici les conditions qui déterminent les changements sont tellement multiples et tellement complexes, que les résultats défient constamment toute prévision et offrent les plus grandes surprises.' [14] Yet, despite these and many other warnings, the quest went on and was not altogether barren of results. Even today there are linguists who firmly believe that the principal task of semantics is to study the 'specific laws of the development of language.'

Perhaps the most ambitious attempt to formulate such a 'specific law' was the late Gustaf Stern's monograph on Middle English terms for 'swift' and 'swiftly.' A thorough examination of chronological data led Stern to the following, remarkably precise conclusion:

> English adverbs which have acquired the sense 'rapidly' before 1300, always develop the sense 'immediately.' This happens when the adverb is used to qualify a verb, the action of which may be apprehended as either imperfective or perfective, and when the meaning of the adverb consequently is equivocal: 'rapidly/immediately.' Exceptions are due to the influence of special factors. But when the sense 'rapidly' is acquired later than 1300, no such development takes place. There is no exception to this rule (*Meaning and Change of Meaning*, p. 190).

If Professor Stern's formula is really valid, then he was right in claiming that it is on all fours with the phonetic laws of which nineteenth-century linguists were so proud: 'This "law" has the form of a sound-law: it gives the circumstances of the change and a chronological limit.' One may wonder, however, whether this can be accepted as a genuine semantic law. The parallel sense-developments did not arise spontaneously: the various words must have influenced each other by a process of analogy or 'synonymic radiation.' . . .

---

[13] 'This is due to particular causes and does not depend on other changes which may have taken place at the same time; it is a mere accident among all those recorded in the history of a language.'

[14] 'Here the conditions which determine the changes are so numerous and so complex that the results constantly defy any prediction and present the greatest surprises.'

It is in a different direction that most linguists have looked for regular patterns in semantic change. They tried to collect instances of similar changes which had occurred, independently of each other, in different languages and periods, and which could therefore be regarded as symptoms of a common tendency, of a widespread and abiding feature of the human mind. Some linguists confined themselves to specific developments whereas others tried to formulate more general laws. Among the specific tendencies examined, parallel metaphors have yielded some remarkable results. In many languages, for example, verbs meaning 'to catch' or 'to grasp' are used figuratively in the sense of 'to understand': English *catch, grasp;* French *comprendre* (from *prendre* 'to take'), *saisir;* Italian *capire,* from Latin *capere* 'to catch'; German *begreifen,* from *greifen* 'to grasp'; and there are similar formations in Russian, Finnish, Hungarian and Turkish. The difficulty is of course to determine how far these various languages may have influenced each other. This difficulty can be eliminated if the examples are taken from widely different idioms and civilizations which have had little or no contact with one another. Thus it is interesting to learn that the English expression *eye of a needle* has exact parallels in Eskimo and in Chuvash, a Turkish language spoken in Russia, and that the 'eyelid' is called 'skin' or 'rind' of the eye in Hungary and in the Marquesas Islands of Oceania as well as in some other areas. Even more surprising is the case of *pupil* 'apple of the eye,' which . . . is the same word as the other *pupil.* The Latin *pupilla* 'orphan girl, ward, minor' could also denote the apple of the eye, because of some vague similarity between a small girl and the minute figure reflected in the pupil. Now it has been found that in more than thirty languages belonging to the most different groups, the apple of the eye is called metaphorically 'little girl' or, more rarely, 'little boy.' Nor are such parallel developments confined to metaphor: metonymies can be just as widespread. The use of the word for 'tongue,' organ of speech, in the sense of 'language' occurs not only in many European idioms which may have influenced each other, but is also found in various non-European languages.

Some linguists have aimed even higher and have tried to identify certain broad tendencies governing semantic change. One of the first experiments of this kind was Bréal's 'law of differentiation between synonyms.' [15] . . . Most of the later attempts have centred on metaphor, though metonymy has also received some attention. G. Esnault threw out some brief and provocative hints on the nature of both processes, such as, for example, that we tend to describe time by means of metaphors from space, but not space by means of metaphors from time. Sperber has developed his theory

[15] [Bréal's law is: "words which should be synonymous, and which were so in the past, have acquired different meanings and are no longer interchangeable." *Essai de sémantique,* p. 26. See *Semantics,* Chapter 6, pp. 141 f. —*Eds.*]

of 'expansion' into a semantic 'law': 'If at a certain time a complex of ideas is so strongly charged with feeling that it causes *one* word to extend its sphere and change its meaning, we may confidently expect that other words belonging to the same emotional complex will also shift their meaning.' [16] Close study of anthropomorphic metaphors has convinced De Witte that transfers *from* the human body are more frequent than those directed *towards* that sphere. Bloomfield has plausibly suggested that 'refined and abstract meanings largely grow out of more concrete meanings.' I myself have found certain common features in the synaesthetic images of various English, French and Hungarian writers; it seems, for example, that transfers from the lower and less differentiated senses to the higher and more differentiated ones are more common than those in the opposite direction: acoustic and visual impressions are more often transcribed in terms of touch or heat than vice versa. Some of these 'laws' may well be confirmed, others contradicted by further research; what is needed for all of them is a far broader empirical basis, including statistical data from many different languages. In this sense Professor Spitzer was perfectly right when he declared in 1943 that 'no one has ever thought of offering a "semantic law".' In view of the scale of the investigations involved, these problems could best be tackled in the form of a series of international research projects. The results of such inquiries would be of great importance not only to linguistics, but also to psychology, to cultural anthropology and various other disciplines.

III. THE CONSEQUENCES OF SEMANTIC CHANGE

Among the innumerable consequences which may result from semantic changes, two problems have received particular attention: the range and the emotive overtones of the new meaning as compared to the old.

1. Changes in Range: Extension and Restriction of Meaning

Many early writers on semantics divided changes of meaning into three categories: extension, restriction, and a miscellaneous third group which showed neither widening nor narrowing of range. This so-called 'logical classification,' though simple and easy to handle, had some serious weaknesses. It rested on purely formal criteria and threw no light either on the ultimate causes of a change or on its psychological background. Another disadvantage was that all three categories were heterogeneous: under the

[16] Op. cit., p. 67; English translation by Professor W. E. Collinson, *Modern Language Review*, xx (1925), p. 106.

headings 'extension' and 'restriction' there appeared a wide variety of changes which had nothing in common beyond the superficial fact that the new sense was wider or narrower than the old; everything that was not amenable to this criterion was consigned indiscriminately to the miscellaneous group.

The fact remains that many words have, for a variety of reasons, widened or narrowed their meaning and continue to do so all the time. Some terms have almost exactly doubled or halved their range. Our word *uncle*, for example, comes via French from the Latin *avunculus* which meant only one kind of uncle, namely, the mother's brother, whereas the father's brother was called *patruus*. Since the latter word fell into disuse, the descendants of *avunculus* have come to stand for both kinds of uncle, so that the range of the Latin term has been doubled. In most cases, however, extension and restriction have altered far more drastically the field of application of the words involved.

(1) **Restriction of Meaning.** The mechanism at work can be demonstrated on a simple example. The English word *voyage* originally meant a 'journey,' as the corresponding French term still does. In the course of time, its range was narrowed and it came to refer more specifically to a 'journey by sea or water.' The net result of the change was that the word is now applicable to fewer things but tells us more about them; its scope has been restricted but its meaning has been enriched with an additional feature: that of travel by *water*. As a logician would put it, its 'extension' has been reduced while its 'intension' has been correspondingly increased. A similar change has overtaken the French *viande*, from Vulgar Latin *vivenda*, a derivative of *vivere* 'to live.' Until the seventeenth century, *viande* meant 'food' in general; since then it has become specialized in the sense of 'meat.' Corresponding words in other languages—Italian *vivanda*, Spanish *vianda*, English *viand(s)*—have preserved the wider sense.

The most frequent cause of restriction is specialization of meaning in a particular social group. More often than not this will merely give rise to polysemy, but it can also permanently reduce the range of the word as a whole. . . . Another cause of restriction is euphemism, including the variety which is prompted by irony rather than by taboo. A famous case in point is *poison* which is historically the same word as *potion*. The most unpleasant aspect of the sense, the fact that the potion is a 'poisonous' one, was left unsaid, but when the word became closely associated with the tabooed meaning, it was gradually limited to denote this particular kind of potion and no other. The German word for 'poison,' *Gift*, underwent an even more radical reduction: among all the possible 'gifts' one can bestow, it came to be applied to this single variety. Restriction of meaning can also result from ellipsis (*canine* for 'canine tooth'), from the need to fill a gap in vocabulary (*traire* 'to draw' replacing *moudre* in the sense of 'to milk'), and from various other causes.

Several names of animals have been restricted from genus to species or have suffered a more drastic reduction. *Deer* once meant a 'beast,' *hound* a 'dog,' and *fowl* a 'bird' in general: 'Behold the *fowls* of the air: for they sow not, neither do they reap, nor gather into barns' (*St. Matthew*, vi, 25). It is interesting to note that in all three cases the corresponding German word—*das Tier, der Hund, der Vogel*—has retained the wider sense. In the same way, French *oie*, Italian and Spanish *oca* 'goose,' come from Vulgar Latin *avica, derived from *avis* 'bird,' as if the goose were regarded as the domestic bird *par excellence*. By a different route, French *sanglier* 'wild boar' has evolved, through ellipsis, from Latin *singularis* 'single, solitary,' in the phrase *singularis porcus* 'solitary pig.' Some verbs have developed on similar lines: *to starve* once meant 'to die,' as it still does in German *sterben*, and French *nover* 'to drown' goes back to Latin *necare* 'to kill.'

An interesting example of restriction is the English word *corn* which, in addition to its general meaning of 'seed of cereal plants,' has come to denote the most important cereal crop produced in a particular area: wheat in England, oats in Scotland, maize in America.

(2) **Extension of Meaning.** Several linguists have suggested that extension is a less common process than restriction, and this has recently been borne out by experiments conducted by the psychologist Heinz Werner. According to Professor Werner himself, there are two main reasons for this tendency:

> One is that the predominant developmental trend is in the direction of differentiation rather than of synthesis. A second reason, related to the first, is that the formation of general concepts from specific terms is of lesser importance in non-scientific communication though it is rather a characteristic of scientific endeavour. In other words, language in everyday life is directed toward the concrete and specific rather than toward the abstract and general.[17]

Nevertheless, cases of semantic widening are fairly frequent in various languages. From a purely logical point of view, they are the exact opposite of restriction: here we have an increase in 'extension,' the word being applied to a wider variety of things; at the same time its 'intension' will decrease, it will tell us less about the things referred to. Thus the French *panier* 'basket' comes from the Latin *panarium* 'bread-basket,' derived from *panis* 'bread.' When the connexion with 'bread' disappeared, the word could be applied to more objects than before, but its meaning had been impoverished as it had lost one distinctive trait. *Target*, a diminutive

[17] 'Change of Meaning,' *Language*, xxviii (1952), p. 203.

of *targe* 'shield,' originally meant a 'light round shield or buckler,' as well as a 'shield-like structure, marked with concentric circles, set up to be aimed at in shooting practice'; now it has a far wider and therefore less specific range of meaning.

Extension, like restriction, is often due to social factors. As we have seen, a word passing from a limited milieu into common use will sometimes widen its meaning and lose some of its distinctive features in the process. An often quoted example is French *arriver*, English *arrive*, both of which once meant 'come to shore,' as did their Vulgar Latin ancestor **arripare*, a derivative of *ripa* 'bank, shore.' From a related sphere we have our modern word *rival*, due to an extension of meaning which goes back to Roman times: the Latin *rivales*, from *rivus* 'brook, small stream,' literally meant 'those who have or use the same brook, neighbours'; later on the 'rivalry' spread to love and other matters.

Another cause of extension is the need for 'omnibus words' with an extremely hazy and general meaning. Latin *causa* was a precise and well-defined term, whereas its Romance descendants, French *chose*, Italian and Spanish *cosa* 'thing,' are now among the vaguest words in those languages; in French the combination *quelque chose* has actually become an indefinite pronoun meaning 'something' or 'anything.' Meanwhile French *cause*, Italian and Spanish *causa*, which were borrowed directly from Latin, retain their pristine precision. The word *machine* has also become an omnibus word in French, in the sense of 'thing, gadget, contraption'; it has even given birth to a jocular masculine form *machin*.

Among words which have widened their meaning there are several names of animals and plants. A curious case is that of the word for 'rose' in some Southern Slav languages which use it in the generic sense of 'flower.' This usage has even affected some neighbouring German and Italian dialects. In several cases a term which once meant a young animal or plant has come to stand for the whole species: French *pigeon*, *dindon* 'turkey-cock,' and *hêtre* 'beech' acquired their present meanings in this way. At a more general level, *bird* comes from Old English *brid* 'young bird,' and *plant*, French *plante*, from Latin *planta* 'sprout, slip, cutting.'

2. Changes in Evaluation: Pejorative and Ameliorative Developments

Pejorative developments are so common in language that some early semanticists regarded them as a fundamental tendency, a symptom of a 'pessimistic streak' in the human mind. Bréal protested vigorously against this assumption. 'La prétendue tendance péjorative,' he wrote, 'est l'effet d'une disposition très humaine qui nous porte à voiler, à déguiser les idées fâcheuses, blessantes ou repoussantes. . . . Il n'y a pas là autre chose qu'un besoin de ménagement, une précaution pour ne pas choquer,—précaution sincère ou feinte, et qui ne sert pas longtemps, car l'auditeur va chercher la chose derrière le mot et ne tarde pas à les mettre de niveau.' [18]

As Bréal rightly saw it, *euphemism*, or pseudo-euphemism, is the motive force behind many pejorative developments. If a euphemistic substitute ceases to be felt as such, if it becomes directly associated with the idea it was designed to veil, this will result in a permanent depreciation of its meaning. It is this factor which accounts for the deterioration of many of the words examined in the section on taboo: *disease, undertaker, tuer, fille, amant, maîtresse, imbecile, crétin, silly* and others.

A second factor leading to pejorative sense-change is the influence of certain *associations*. The semantic ramifications of Latin *captivus* may serve to illustrate this. Starting from the idea of captivity, this word has acquired unfavourable meanings in various languages though not in all: Spanish *cautivo* still means 'prisoner.' In French it has become *chétif* 'weak, sickly, poor, miserable'; the connecting link was the idea of a man dominated and weakened by his passions. The same associations led to a different result in Italian where *cattivo* means 'bad.' Yet another line of development is found in English *caitiff*, of Anglo-Norman origin, which is now archaic and poetical. This has evolved through three stages: 1. 'a captive, a prisoner'; 2. 'one in a piteous case'; 3. 'a base, mean, despicable wretch, a villain.' In Shakespeare's phrase: 'the wicked'st *caitiff* on the ground' (*Measure for Measure*, Act V, scene 1), the word has travelled very far from its origins. A similar fate has befallen some other terms in the same sphere. English *wretch* once meant 'exile'; while its meaning has strongly deteriorated, the corresponding German word, *Recke*, has risen in estimation and now means 'warrior, hero.' The German adjective *schlecht*, related to English *slight*, has had a similar history: it meant first 'straight,' then 'smooth' (now *schlicht*), 'simple,' 'plain,' 'poor,' and finally 'bad, wicked.'

A third source of pejorative developments is human *prejudice* in its various forms. Xenophobia has . . . filled some foreign words with a derogatory sense: German *Ross* 'charger, steed' has given the French *rosse* 'sorry steed, crock,' and mediaeval Dutch *boeckin* 'little book' the French *bouquin* 'old book, book of no value,' though in familiar speech this term is now free from any unfavourable connotations. Portuguese *palavra* 'word' has become *palaver* in English. The same anti-foreign bias is reflected in the strange vicissitudes of some ethnic names. English *slave*, French *esclave*, etc., are the

---

[18] 'The alleged pejorative tendency is the result of a very human attitude which leads us to veil and disguise awkward, offensive or repulsive ideas. . . . It is no more than an effort to be tactful, to avoid shocking people—an effort which may be genuine or feigned and whose effects are short-lived since the hearer will look for the thing behind the word and will soon connect them with each other' (*Essai de sémantique*, pp. 100 f.).

same word as *Slav*, and *Bulgarus* 'Bulgarian' is the origin of French *bougre*, which has already been mentioned, and its more disreputable English counterpart. *Bougre* was used in the Middle Ages in the sense of 'heretic' because the Bulgarians were members of the Eastern Church; it then came to mean 'sodomite' and eventually developed into a term of abuse which gave Sterne the idea for a coarse but amusing incident in *Tristram Shandy* (Book VII, chs. 20–5).

Social prejudice against certain classes and occupations has also deformed the meaning of many words. Terms like English *boor* and French *rustre* 'boor, churl, lout,' from Latin *rusticus*, show the contempt in which peasants used to be held. Low Latin *villanus*, 'inhabitant of a farm *(villa)*,' has given in English the historical term *villein* 'serf' and also the pejorative *villain*, while Modern French *vilain* means 'ugly' and 'nasty.' Other social groups have been the victims of similar prejudices. A *brigand* was originally a 'light-armed, irregular foot-soldier,' and *knave* once meant a 'boy' (cf. German *Knabe*), and especially a boy employed as a servant. French *coquin* 'rogue, rascal' had the earlier meaning of 'beggar,' and *faquin* 'cad' that of 'porter.' Nor have the higher reaches of the social hierarchy been spared by prejudice. A *pedant* was once a 'pedagogue' or 'schoolmaster,' and the ups and downs of the word *bourgeois* would form an interesting chapter of social history. This class has been the target of attacks not only by its superiors and inferiors, but also by artists and intellectuals. Théophile Gautier defined a *bourgeois* as a man who 'has no understanding for any of the arts, no sense of form or style, who is without enthusiasm and passion, and does not admire nature,' and Flaubert put the same views more tersely and cuttingly in his famous dictum: 'J'appelle *bourgeois* quiconque pense bassement.' [19]

While there are thus many words which have deteriorated in meaning, others have changed in the opposite direction. These so-called *'ameliorative'* developments have received less attention than pejorative ones, and on the whole they seem to be less frequent. They fall into two categories. The first includes those cases where the improvement is purely *negative:* by a process of gradual weakening, a term with an unpleasant sense will lose much of its stigma and become only mildly unfavourable. Thus *to blame* is historically the same word as to *blaspheme*, and to *annoy*, French *ennuyer*, originated in the Latin phrase *in odio esse* 'to be the object of hatred.' French *regretter* once signified 'to lament over the dead,' and *gêne* meant 'physical or moral torture' until the end of the seventeenth century whereas now it has the much weaker sense of 'discomfort, embarrassment.' An extreme example of weakening is the English *pest* which once meant

'I call *bourgeois* whoever thinks meanly.'

pestilence and in particular the bubonic plague. The word *plague* has had a similar development.

In hyperbolical expressions, such weakening can completely cancel out the unpleasant meaning of a word. This has happened . . . with a number of English adjectives: *awful, dreadful, frightful* and others. A more advanced stage of this development can be seen in German *sehr* 'very' which is etymologically the same word as English *sore*.

There are also various cases of *positive* improvement of meaning. These may come about by a simple association of ideas. The adjective *nice* is derived, via Old French, from Latin *nescius* 'ignorant,' and in Shakespeare's time it had several unfavourable senses: it could mean 'wanton, lascivious':

'These are complements, these are humours; these betray *nice* wenches, that would be betrayed without these' (*Love's Labour's Lost*, Act III, scene 1),

and 'thin, unimportant, trivial':

> . . . feed upon such *nice* and waterish diet.
>
> *Othello*, Act III, scene 3.

> In such a time as this it is not meet
> That every *nice* offence should bear his comment.
>
> *Julius Caesar*, Act IV, scene 3.

Gradually the word developed, through meanings like 'fastidious' and 'delicate,' in an ameliorative direction; since the second half of the eighteenth century, it has had the sense of 'agreeable, delightful,' and since the early nineteenth, that of 'kind, considerate, pleasant to others.'

Other ameliorative developments are due to *social* factors. A modest or even a menial office may gradually rise in prestige and may even end up at the top of the hierarchy. *Chancellor*, French *chancelier*, is derived from Late Latin *cancellarius*, an 'usher who was stationed *ad cancellos* at the *bar* of a basilica or other law court. In the Eastern Empire this officer had risen to be a secretary or notary, and, later, had judicial functions. Edward the Confessor introduced the office into England, and its importance increased under the Norman Kings' (*Shorter OED*). *Ministers* too have risen to their present eminence from modest beginnings: the Latin *minister*, derived from *minus* 'less,' meant 'attendant, servant.'

As a result of movements up and down the social scale, the same word may appear at two widely different points in a particular hierarchy. *Marshal*, an old Germanic term compounded of the words for 'horse' (cf. *mare*) and 'servant,' is now the title of several high-ranking officers and functionaries in England, but in the French army there are two kinds of 'marshals': *maréchal* (*de France*) 'field-marshal,' and *maréchal des logis* 'sergeant';

there is also the *maréchal ferrant* 'farrier, shoeing-smith,' who has remained nearest to the etymological sense of the term. A similar ambivalence is sometimes found in meanings of the same word in different languages, as for instance in English *knight* compared with German *Knecht* 'servant.'

A special group of ameliorative and pejorative developments are those which affect the meaning of so-called *'middle terms'* (voces mediae): words which are intrinsically neutral and which will take on a favourable or unfavourable significance according to their context. It sometimes happens that such words, or their derivatives, become fixed either in the positive or in the negative meaning. *Fortune* is such a middle term since it may be either good or bad; but it has an exclusively positive value in the adjective *fortunate* and also when used metonymically in the sense of 'wealth.' *Luck*, though ambivalent, tends to imply 'good luck' when there is no counter-indication, and the adjective *lucky* has only the latter meaning. Similarly the old French word *heur*, from Latin *augurium* 'augury,' meant 'good or bad luck,' *bonheur* or *malheur*, whereas the adjective *heureux* means only 'happy, lucky.' *Chance*, from Vulgar Latin **cadentia* 'falling,' originally referred to the way the dice fell; it then widened its meaning and, in phrases like 'to give, to stand a *chance*,' it has come down on the favourable side. While all these words have evolved in an optimistic sense, others have moved in the opposite direction. *Hazard*, an Arabic term which also referred to the game of dice, has come to mean 'risk of loss or harm, peril, jeopardy.' *Accident* in some of its uses shows the same tendency, though the adjective *accidental* is immune from it. From *fate*, a middle term leaning towards the pessimistic side, two adjectives are derived: *fatal*, which is almost entirely unfavourable, and *fateful*, which is more noncommittal. A comparative study of the development of such expressions in various languages might throw an interesting sidelight on human psychology.

Study Questions

1. Why is meaning, of all linguistic elements, "probably the least resistant to change"? Why would meaning reflect cultural change more rapidly than other linguistic elements would? What causes of semantic change does Ullmann describe? Does Ullmann always limit his discussion to linguistic causes—causes within the linguistic system—or does he also recognize causes external to the linguistic system? Does he feel that it is possible to distinguish between the two? Does Ullmann distinguish clearly between causes and effects, causes and conditions which favor

change, causes and mechanisms? For example, is polysemy a cause of semantic change or an effect? Is "the structure of the vocabulary" cause or condition?

2. Ullmann mentions the learning of language by children as a factor of some importance in semantic change, but says "it is difficult to prove that any particular change could have arisen only in child language." What might constitute proof? Could we explain how "the generic nature of our words, the multiplicity of their aspects, lack of familiarity, absence of clear cut boundaries—all conspire to facilitate shifts in usage" if we did not assume that usage shifts as speakers learn words that they didn't know before?

3. Ullmann says: "Perhaps the most important of the general factors governing semantic change is the structure of the vocabulary." What does he mean by "the structure of the vocabulary"? What characteristics of vocabulary structure different from the structure of phonology or of morphology seem to him to account for the greater frequency of semantic change? Which of the changes he describes are influenced by the structure of the vocabulary?

4. What does Ullmann mean by *association* when he says that "association may be regarded as a necessary condition" of semantic change? What kinds of association does he find operative? Compare the treatments of popular etymology by Ullmann and Bloomfield: how do they differ? When Ullmann calls popular etymology "similarity of names" how does that differ from Bloomfield's classification of the phenomenon as a kind of analogy? Does the difference tell us anything about contrasts in their basic assumptions about language and how it is described?

5. In discussing several of his examples, Ullmann stresses that the history of a given word might not be recoverable without placing it in the context of the history of the thing that it signifies. If we were to characterize changes in meaning such as generalization or specialization as changes in the semantic markers of words in the lexicon, would such a characterization explain *how* or *why* the changes had come about?

6. Ullmann emphasizes the importance of metaphor both in language use and language change: "a language without metaphor is inconceivable." How does he define metaphor? Is his definition based on form (that is, statable in syntactic terms) or on meaning? Does he consider metaphor a function of language use or of language system, or does he not dis-

tinguish between the two? How might a generative grammarian define metaphor?

7. Ullmann says that "Changes of meaning can be brought about by an infinite multiplicity of causes" and (in discussing the history of the word *cadeau*) that "the student of meaning will . . . have to examine each change separately and try to reconstruct its background." Would he seem to agree or disagree with Gilliéron's motto, "chaque mot a son histoire"? What is Ullmann's attitude toward the possibility of successfully stating "laws governing change of meaning"? If the causes of semantic change are indeed infinite, would it be possible to state laws of semantic change, or to construct a theory of it? Ullmann says that what is needed to resolve such questions is "a far broader empirical base." Would Chomsky agree?